The Pentateuch as Torah

The Pentateuch as Torah

*New Models for Understanding Its
Promulgation and Acceptance*

Edited by

GARY N. KNOPPERS and BERNARD M. LEVINSON

Winona Lake, Indiana
EISENBRAUNS
2007

www.eisenbrauns.com

Cataloging in Publication Data

The Pentateuch as Torah : new models for understanding its promulgation and
    acceptance / Edited by Gary N. Knoppers and Bernard M. Levinson
        p.   cm.
        "The origins of this volume lie in the four special panels on Biblical and
    Ancient Near Eastern Law that convened at the 2006 International Meeting
    of the Society of Biblical Literature in Edinburgh . . ." — Introd.
        Includes bibliographical references and index.
        ISBN-13: 978-1-57506-140-5 (hardback : alk. paper)
        1. Bible. O.T. Pentateuch—History—Congresses.   2. Bible. O.T.
    Pentateuch—Canonical criticism—Congresses.   3. Bible. O.T.
    Pentateuch—Criticism, interpretation, etc.—Congresses.   4. Judaism—
    History—Post-exilic period, 586 B.C.–210 A.D.—Congresses.   I. Knoppers,
    Gary N., 1956–   II. Levinson, Bernard M. (Bernard Malcolm)
        BS1225.52.P46 2007
        222′.1066—dc22

                                                                    2007037247

In Memoriam

NATHAN MAX BERMAN
December 1, 1907–October 5, 2005

and

REV. NICOLAAS BASTIAAN KNOPPERS
March 3, 1917–October 28, 2006

Contents

PART 1
Ratifying Local Law Codes
in an International Age

PART 2
Prophets, Polemics, and Publishers:
The Growing Importance of Writing
in Persian Period Judah

Abbreviations

General Abbreviations

*	An asterisk following a chapter or verse reference (i.e., Exod 14:21*) indicates that the intent is not to refer to the entire verse or chapter but to an original layer that has been reconstructed in the given unit
//	parallel(s) *or* is parallel to (e.g., 2 Samuel 22 // Psalm 18)
CD	Cairo Genizah copy of the *Damascus Document*
D	Deuteronomy (pentateuchal source)
Dt *or* Dtn	The original "Deuteronomic" literary layer of Deuterononomy (generally connected with the reform of Josiah, ca. 622 B.C.E.); or the "Deuteronomist" as the author responsible for that work
Dtr	"Deuteronomistic," in contrast to Deuteronomic: designates secondary layers in Deuteronomy that represent the work of later editors (usually dated to the Babylonian Exile or later); alternatively, may designate the author of these layers. Dtr may also designate secondary layers elsewhere in the Bible (especially in the Deuteronomistic History or in the prophetic corpus) composed by or under the influence of the Deuteronomistic Historian
DtrH	The Deuteronomistic History (Joshua through 2 Kings); or the Deuteronomistic Historian, as the author of this material
DSS	Dead Sea Scrolls
E	Elohist source (of the Pentateuch)
ET	English translation
fr.	*fragmentum, fragmenta* (fragment, fragments)
frg.	fragment
H	Holiness Code (Leviticus 17–26; from German *Heiligkeitsgesetz*)
J	Yahwist source/writer of one portion of the Pentateuch ("J" from German *Jahwist*)
KJV	King James Version
LXX	Greek translation of the Hebrew Bible (Alexandria, Egypt, ca. 250–150 B.C.E.)
MT	Masoretic Text
(N)JPSV	*The Holy Scriptures: The New JPS Translation according to the Traditional Hebrew Text*
NKJV	New King James Version
NRSV	New Revised Standard Version
P	Priestly source/writer of one portion of the Pentateuch
pl.	plural
PN	Personal Name
RSV	Revised Standard Version
sg. *or* sing.	singular
SP	Samaritan Pentateuch
Vg.	Vulgate

Primary Sources: Ancient Texts

Hebrew Bible / Old Testament

Gen	Genesis	Eccl (*or* Qoh)	Ecclesiastes (*or* Qoheleth)
Exod	Exodus	Song (*or* Cant)	Song of Songs (*or* Canticles)
Lev	Leviticus	Isa	Isaiah
Num	Numbers	Jer	Jeremiah
Deut	Deuteronomy	Lam	Lamentations
Josh	Joshua	Ezek	Ezekiel
Judg	Judges	Dan	Daniel
Ruth	Ruth	Hos	Hosea
1–2 Sam	1–2 Samuel	Joel	Joel
1–2 Kgs	1–2 Kings	Obad	Obadiah
1–2 Chr	1–2 Chronicles	Mic	Micah
Ezra	Ezra	Nah	Nahum
Neh	Nehemiah	Hab	Habakkuk
Esth	Esther	Zeph	Zephaniah
Job	Job	Hag	Haggai
Ps	Psalms	Zech	Zechariah
Prov	Proverbs	Mal	Malachi

Apocrypha and Septuagint

Bar	Baruch	Sir	Sirach/Ben Sira
1–2 Esd	1–2 Esdras	Wis	Wisdom of Solomon
1–2 Macc	1–2 Maccabees		

Abbreviations of the Dead Sea Scrolls

The simplified abbreviation key provided here attempts to take into account the various systems that have emerged to refer to the Dead Sea Scrolls. One system classifies scrolls by cave number and an abbreviation for the text, so that, for example, 1QS refers to a document from Qumran Cave 1 that is also known as *Serekh ha-Yaḥad*, or "Rule of the Community." Abbreviations beginning with 4Q indicate documents from Qumran Cave 4, and so on. Another system uses the cave number followed by a manuscript number, as with, for example, 4Q364. Where multiple manuscripts of the same text are attested, they are designated with superscripted letters (a, b, c, etc.) following the document's name or siglum, as with Reworked Pentateuch[b] and Reworked Pentateuch[c]. Additional systems of naming and classification exist as well.[1]

---

1. For more detailed information, see Emanuel Tov, "Appendix F: Texts from the Judean Desert," in *The SBL Handbook of Style for Ancient Near Eastern, Biblical, and Early Christian Studies* (Peabody, MA: Hendrickson Publishers, 1999) 176–233 (see also 75–77); idem, "The Discoveries in the Judaean Desert Series: History and System of Presentation," in *The Texts from the Judaean Desert: Indices and an Introduction to the Discoveries in the Judaean Desert Series* (ed. Emanuel Tov, with contributions by Martin Abegg Jr. et al.; DJD 39; Oxford: Clarendon, 2002) 1–25; idem, "Provisional List of Documents from the Judean Desert," in *Encyclopedia of the Dead Sea Scrolls* (ed. Lawrence H. Schiffman and James C. VanderKam; 2 vols.; New York: Oxford University Press, 2000) 2.1013–49.

Dead Sea Scrolls

Abbreviation	Official Siglum or Title	Name of Text
1QDeut[b] (1Q5)	Deut[b]	Deuteronomy[b]
1QS (1Q28)	S (= Serekh ha-Yahad)	Rule of the Community *or* Manual of Discipline
4QpaleoExod[m] (4Q22)	paleoExod[m]	Paleo-Exodus[m]
4QNum[b] (4Q27)	Num[b]	Numbers[b]
4QJosh[a] *or* 4QJoshua[a] (4Q47)	Josh[a]	Joshua[a]
4Q158	RP[a]	Reworked Pentateuch[a]
4Q175	Test	Testimonia
4Q256	S[b] (= Serekh ha-Yahad[b])	Rule of the Community[b]
4Q258	S[d] (= Serekh ha-Yahad[d])	Rule of the Community[d]
4Q266	D[a]	Damascus Document[a]
4Q364	RP[b]	Reworked Pentateuch[b]
4Q365	RP[c]	Reworked Pentateuch[c]
4Q366	RP[d]	Reworked Pentateuch[d]
4Q367	RP[e]	Reworked Pentateuch[e]
4QMMT *See* 4Q394–4Q399 for the individual manuscripts	Miqṣat Maʿaśê ha-Torah Halakhic Letter *or* Some of the Torah Observations	A composite text reconstructed by Elisha Qimron and John Strugnell, *Qumran Cave 4, V: Miqṣat Maʿaśê ha-Torah* (DJD 10; Oxford: Clarendon, 1994) 43–63
4Q394	MMT[a]	MMT[a] (Miqṣat Maʿaśê ha-Torah[a])
4Q395	MMT[b]	MMT[b] (Miqṣat Maʿaśê ha-Torah[b])
4Q396	MMT[c]	MMT[c] (Miqṣat Maʿaśê ha-Torah[c])
4Q397	MMT[d]	MMT[d] (Miqṣat Maʿaśê ha-Torah[d])
4Q398	papMMT[e]	MMT[e] (Miqṣat Maʿaśê ha-Torah[e])
4Q399	MMT[f]	MMT[f] (Miqṣat Maʿaśê ha-Torah[f])
4Q448	Apocr. Psalm and Prayer	Apocryphal Psalm and Prayer
4Q524	halakhic text *or* T[b]	halakhic text *Sometimes regarded as an additional fragment of the* Temple Scroll
11QTemple[a] (11Q19)	T[a]	Temple Scroll[a]

Classical Authors and Their Works

Ag. Ap.	Josephus, *Against Apion*
Anab.	Xenophon, *Anabasis*
Ant.	Josephus, *Jewish Antiquities*
Ant. rom.	Dionysius of Halicarnassus, *Antiquitates romanae*
Ath. pol.	*Athenaion politeia* (*Constitution of Athens*): traditionally attributed to Aristotle, but authorship disputed
Comm. Jo.	Origen, *Commentarii in evangelium Joannis*
Hist.	Herodotus, *Historiae* (*Histories*)
Op.	Hesiod, *Opera et dies* (*Works and Days*)
Plut.	Plutarch
Vita Solon.	Plutarch, *Vita Solonis* (*Life of Solon*)

Secondary Sources
Journals, Series, and Major Reference Works

AASOR	Annual of the American Schools of Oriental Research
AB	Anchor Bible
ABD	*Anchor Bible Dictionary*. Edited by D. N. Freedman. 6 vols. Garden City, New York, 1992
ABRL	Anchor Bible Reference Library
AcT	*Acta theologica*
AGJU	Arbeiten zur Geschichte des antiken Judentums und des Urchristentums
AHw	*Akkadisches Handwörterbuch*. Wolfram von Soden. 3 vols. 2nd ed. Wiesbaden: Otto Harrassowitz, 1972–85
AJA	*American Journal of Archaeology*
AJBI	*Annual of the Japanese Biblical Institute*
AJSL	*American Journal of Semitic Languages and Literature*
AnBib	Analecta biblica
AOAT	Alter Orient und Altes Testament: Veröffentlichungen zur Kultur und Geschichte des Alten Orients und des Alten Testaments
AOS	American Oriental Series
AP	*Aramaic Papyri of the Fifth Century* B.C. Edited by A. E. Cowley. Oxford: Clarendon, 1923; repr., Osnabrück: Zeller, 1967; reprinted with new foreword and bibliography by K. C. Hanson. Ancient Texts and Translations. Eugene, OR: Wipf & Stock, 2005
ATANT	Abhandlungen zur Theologie des Alten und Neuen Testaments
ATD	Das Alte Testament Deutsch
ATLA	American Theological Library Association
BAIAS	*Bulletin of the Anglo-Israel Archeological Society*
BAR	*Biblical Archaeology Review*
BAR International Series	British Archaeological Reports, International Series. Oxford: Archaeopress
BASOR	*Bulletin of the American Schools of Oriental Research*
BBB	Bonner biblische Beiträge
BBET	Beiträge zur biblischen Exegese und Theologie
BEATAJ	Beiträge zur Erforschung des Alten Testaments und des antiken Judentum

BETL	Bibliotheca ephemeridum theologicarum lovaniensium
BetM	*Beit Mikra / Beth Mikra: Bulletin of the Israel Society for Biblical Research*
BHS	*Biblia Hebraica Stuttgartensia.* Edited by Karl Elliger and Wilhelm Rudolph. Stuttgart: Deutsche Bibelgesellschaft, 1983
BHT	Beiträge zur historischen Theologie
Bib	*Biblica*
BibOr	Biblica et Orientalia
BibS(N)	Biblische Studien. Neukirchen-Vluyn: Neukirchener Verlag, 1951–
BiSe	The Biblical Seminar
BJRL	*Bulletin of the John Rylands University Library of Manchester*
BJS	Brown Judaic Studies
BKAT	Biblischer Kommentar: Altes Testament
BWA(N)T	Beiträge zur Wissenschaft vom Alten (und Neuen) Testament
BZ	*Biblische Zeitschrift*
BZAW	Beihefte zur Zeitschrift für die alttestamentliche Wissenschaft
CAD	*The Assyrian Dictionary of the Oriental Institute of the University of Chicago.* Edited by A. Leo Oppenheim et al. Chicago: Oriental Institute, 1956–
CahRB	Cahiers de la Revue biblique
CANE	*Civilizations of the Ancient Near East.* Edited by Jack Sasson. 4 vols. New York: Scribners, 1995
CBET	Contributions to Biblical Exegesis and Theology
CBQ	*Catholic Biblical Quarterly*
CIL I² 3	*Corpus Inscriptionum Latinarum, volumen primus, editio altera, addenda tertia.* Edited by Attilio Degrassi and Joannes Krummrey. Berlin: de Gruyter, 1986
CML²	*Canaanite Myths and Legends.* Edited by G. R. Driver. Edinburgh, 1956. Revised by J. C. L. Gibson. 2nd ed, 1978
ConBOT	Coniectanea Biblica: Old Testament
CRAIBL	*Comptes rendus de l'Académie des inscriptions et belles-lettres*
CRINT	Compendia rerum iudaicarum ad Novum Testamentum
CSCO	Corpus scriptorum christianorum orientalium. Edited by I. B. Chabot et al. Paris, 1903–
CT	Cuneiform Texts from Babylonian Tablets in the British Museum
CurBR	*Currents in Biblical Research* (formerly, *Currents in Research: Biblical Studies*)
DBAT	*Dielheimer Blätter zum Alten Testament und seiner Rezeption in der Alten Kirche*
DBSup	*Dictionnaire de la Bible, Supplément.* Edited by L. Pirot and A. Robert. Paris: Letouzey & Anée, 1928–
DJD	Discoveries in the Judaean Desert
DMOA	Documenta et Monumenta Orientis Antiqui
DSD	*Dead Sea Discoveries: A Journal of Current Research on the Scrolls and Related Literature*
EdF	Erträge der Forschung
ErIsr	*Eretz-Israel: Archaeological, Historical, and Geographical Studies*
EvT	*Evangelische Theologie*
FAT	Forschungen zum Alten Testament
FB	Forschung zur Bibel
FRLANT	Forschungen zur Religion und Literatur des Alten und Neuen Testaments
GAT	Grundrisse zum Alten Testament

HALOT	*The Hebrew and Aramaic Lexicon of the Old Testament.* Ludwig Koehler, Walter Baumgartner, M. E. J. Richardson, and Johann Jakob Stamm. Translated and edited under the supervision of M. E. J. Richardson. 5 vols. Leiden: Brill, 1994–2000
HAT	Handbuch zum Alten Testament
HKAT	Handkommentar zum Alten Testament
HSM	Harvard Semitic Monographs
HSS	Harvard Semitic Studies
HTKAT	Herders theologischer Kommentar zum Alten Testament
HTR	*Harvard Theological Review*
HTS	Harvard Theological Studies
HUCA	*Hebrew Union College Annual*
IC IV	*Inscriptiones Creticae, IV: Tituli Gortynii.* Edited by Margarita Guarducci. Rome: Libreria dello Stato, 1950
IEJ	*Israel Exploration Journal*
ITC	International Theological Commentary
JANESCU	*Journal of the Ancient Near Eastern Society of Columbia University*
JAOS	*Journal of the American Oriental Society*
JBL	*Journal of Biblical Literature*
JCS	*Journal of Cuneiform Studies*
JNES	*Journal of Near Eastern Studies*
JNSL	*Journal of Northwest Semitic Languages*
JQR	*Jewish Quarterly Review*
JSHRZ	*Jüdische Schriften aus hellenistisch-römischer Zeit*
JSJ	*Journal for the Study of Judaism in the Persian, Hellenistic, and Roman Periods*
JSOT	*Journal for the Study of the Old Testament*
JSOTSup	Journal for the Study of the Old Testament Supplement Series
JSPSup	Journal for the Study of the Pseudepigrapha Supplements
JSS	*Journal of Semitic Studies*
JTS	*Journal of Theological Studies*
KAT	Kommentar zum Alten Testament
KNAW	Koninklijke Nederlandse Akademie van Wetenschappen
LAPO	Littératures anciennes du Proche-Orient
LCL	Loeb Classical Library
LD	Lectio divina
ML	Meiggs, Russell, and David Lewis. *A Selection of Greek Historical Inscriptions to the End of the Fifth Century* B.C. Rev. ed. Oxford: Clarendon, 1988
NCB	New Century Bible
NEAEHL	*The New Encyclopedia of Archaeological Excavations in the Holy Land.* Edited by Ephraim Stern, Ayelet Lewinson-Gilboa, and Joseph Aviram. 4 vols. Jerusalem: Israel Exploration Society and Carta / New York: Simon & Schuster, 1993
NEchtB	Neue Echter Bibel
NRTh	*La nouvelle revue théologique*
NTL	New Testament Library
NTOA	Novum Testamentum et Orbis Antiquus
OBO	Orbis biblicus et orientalis
ÖBS	Österreichische biblische Studien
OLZ	*Orientalistische Literaturzeitung*

OTL	Old Testament Library
OTP	*Old Testament Pseudepigrapha.* Edited by James H. Charlesworth. 2 vols. Garden City, NY: Doubleday, 1983–85
OTS	Old Testament Studies
OtSt	*Oudtestamentische Studiën*
PAAJR	*Proceedings of the American Academy of Jewish Research*
PEQ	*Palestine Exploration Quarterly*
PJ	*Palästina-Jahrbuch*
PVTG	Pseudepigrapha Veteris Testamenti Graece
QD	Quaestiones disputatae
RB	*Revue biblique*
RBL	*Review of Biblical Literature,* http://www.bookreviews.org/
REJ	*Revue des études juives*
RevQ	*Revue de Qumran*
RGG	*Religion in Geschichte und Gegenwart.* 3rd ed. Edited by Kurt Galling. 7 vols. Tübingen: Mohr, 1957–65. 4th ed. Edited by Hans Dieter Betz et al. 9 vols. Tübingen: Mohr Siebeck, 1998–2007
RIDA	*Revue internationale des droits de l'antiquité*
RSR	*Recherches de science religieuse*
RTL	*Revue théologique de Louvain*
SAA	State Archives of Assyria
SAOC	Studies in Ancient Oriental Civilizations
SBAB	Stuttgarter biblische Aufsatzbände
SBLDS	Society of Biblical Literature Dissertation Series
SBLSCS	Society of Biblical Literature Septuagint and Cognate Studies
SBLSymS	Society of Biblical Literature Symposium Series
SBLWAW	Society of Biblical Literature Writings from the Ancient World
SBS	Stuttgarter Bibelstudien
SC	Sources chrétiennes. Paris: Cerf, 1943–
SHR	Studies in the History of Religions (supplement to *Numen*)
SJ	Studia judaica
SJLA	Studies in Judaism in Late Antiquity
SPAW	Sitzungsberichte der preussischen Akademie der Wissenschaften
SR	*Studies in Religion*
ST	*Studia theologica*
STDJ	Studies on the Texts of the Desert of Judah
StPB	Studia post-biblica
SVTP	Studia in Veteris Testamenti pseudepigraphica
TA	*Tel Aviv*
TADAE	*Textbook of Aramaic Documents from Ancient Egypt: Newly Copied, Edited, and Translated into English.* Edited by Bezalel Porten and Ada Yardeni. Vols. A–D (Hebrew) = 1–4 (English). Texts and Studies for Students. Jerusalem: The Hebrew University, Department of the History of the Jewish People, 1986–99
TBü	Theologische Bücherei
TDOT	*Theological Dictionary of the Old Testament.* Edited by G. Johannes Botterweck, Heinz-Josef Fabry, and Helmer Ringgren. Translated by J. T. Willis, G. W. Bromiley, and D. E. Green. 15 vols. Grand Rapids, MI: Eerdmans, 1974–2006
ThSt	Theologische Studiën

ThWAT	*Theologisches Wörterbuch zum Alten Testament.* Edited by G. Johannes Botterweck, Heinz-Josef Fabry, and Helmer Ringgren. 10 vols. Stuttgart: Kohlhammer, 1970–
Transeu	*Transeuphratène*
TRE	*Theologische Realenzyklopädie.* Edited by G. Krause and G. Müller. Berlin: de Gruyter, 1977–
TRu	*Theologische Rundschau*
TSAJ	Texte und Studien zum antiken Judentum
TZ	*Theologische Zeitschrift*
UF	*Ugarit-Forschungen*
VT	*Vetus Testamentum*
VTSup	Vetus Testamentum Supplements
WBC	Word Biblical Commentary
WDSP	Wadi ed-Daliyeh Samaria Papyri
WMANT	Wissenschaftliche Monographien zum Alten und Neuen Testament
WUNT	Wissenschaftliche Untersuchungen zum Neuen Testament
ZA	*Zeitschrift für Assyriologie*
ZABR or *ZAR*	*Zeitschrift für Altorientalische und Biblische Rechtsgeschichte*
ZAH	*Zeitschrift für Althebräistik*
ZAW	*Zeitschrift für die alttestamentliche Wissenschaft*
ZBKAT	Zürcher Bibelkommentare: Altes Testament
ZDMG	*Zeitschrift der deutschen morgenländischen Gesellschaft*
ZDPV	*Zeitschrift des deutschen Palästina-Vereins*
ZTK	*Zeitschrift für Theologie und Kirche*

How, When, Where, and Why Did the Pentateuch Become the Torah?

GARY N. KNOPPERS and BERNARD M. LEVINSON

Introduction

The origins of this volume lie in the four special panels on Biblical and Ancient Near Eastern Law that convened at the 2006 International Meeting of the Society of Biblical Literature in Edinburgh (2–6 July). The panels were organized to investigate the promulgation and acceptance of the Pentateuch as a prestigious writing in the late Persian and early Hellenistic periods. Drawing on the talents of a distinguished body of internationally-recognized scholars, the four special sessions were designed to obtain a better grasp of the means, circumstances, factors, and setting of the Pentateuch's rise to prominence as a foundational collection of Scriptures in early Judaism and Samaritanism. In setting a thematically coherent research project as the goal of the program unit, we sought to continue the approach employed so productively by the Biblical and Ancient Near Eastern Law section at earlier international SBL meetings (Berlin in 2002 and Cambridge in 2003). The panels there dealt with the challenges in interpreting the multiple and overlapping roles played by the book of Deuteronomy in biblical literature.[1] These earlier sessions dealt with Deuteronomy and the Tetrateuch, Deuteronomy as part of a Pentateuch, Deuteronomy as part of a Hexateuch, Deuteronomy as part of a larger and later Deuteronomistic History, and Deuteronomy as part of an Enneateuch. The research goals of the sessions in Edinburgh extended the methodological concerns of these earlier sessions while embarking in new directions. The Pentateuch (or Proto-Pentateuch) as an existing literary entity served as the point of departure as we sought to investigate its growing acceptance as a prestigious and constitutional document in the larger life of the community during the Achaemenid and Hellenistic periods.

---

1. The proceedings were later published as *Deuteronomium zwischen Pentateuch und Deuteronomistischem Geschichtswerk* (ed. Eckart Otto and Reinhard Achenbach; FRLANT 206; Göttingen: Vandenhoeck & Ruprecht, 2004).

There is no doubt that the reception of the Pentateuch as authoritative *tôrâ* ('instruction') led to this *tôrâ*'s becoming one of the defining pillars of the religious practices of Jews and Samaritans. Since antiquity, the five books of Moses have served as a sacred constitution, foundational for both belief and practice. However long the process of authorization took, this was, by all accounts, a monumental achievement in the history of these peoples and indeed an important moment in the history of the ancient world. In the long development of Western societies, the Pentateuch has served as a major influence on the development of law, political philosophy, and social thought. The question is: when, how, where, and why did the rise of the Torah occur?

There are several related issues in addressing this important, highly debated, and very complex question. Before discussing the individual essays included in this volume, we may find it useful to sketch the larger issues that lie at the background (in some cases, the foreground) of our contributors' work. It is impossible in this context to provide anything even approaching a full history and critical review of modern scholarship. Entire volumes have been written on this topic.[2] It will only be possible to introduce some of the major points of contention and debate. Some issues pertain to ancient historical, religious, and social matters; others relate more to the history of modern scholarship and its critical interpretations of the development of "the five books of Moses." In either case, to appreciate the new models proposed by the contributors to this volume, the reader will find it helpful to situate these new perspectives in the context of the broader scholarly debate.

First, how does one explain the composition of the Pentateuch as a heterogeneous work, not only including sizable portions of narrative and law but also incorporating two or more major sources? How is it that several distinct law collections (e.g., the Covenant Code, Deuteronomy, the Priestly Code, and the Holiness Code) were combined and integrated into a larger narrative structure to form a single document—the Torah? These are fundamentally literary questions, but they have a bearing on our understanding of the larger historical process by which the Pentateuch was formed and came to enjoy a well-regarded status in the community. To complicate matters further, we may inquire as to why this was done and when. What was the historical, social, religious, or economic impetus to compile and promote one written corpus of law, however multilayered, over against many?

Second, should one think of the promulgation of the Pentateuch as originally occurring within the confines of a small Judean elite? That is, are we dealing with basically a very limited inner-Judean phenomenon? If so, is the formulation of the Pentateuch (or Proto-Pentateuch) basically the result of the work of

---

2. For references, readers are referred to the erudite notes of the contributors to this volume.

one author/editor, who edited, integrated, and supplemented earlier material? In such a scenario, the Pentateuch may be viewed as the product of the last person (or persons) who worked on it. Or, perhaps scribes at the Jerusalem temple had to work with both extensive Priestly and Deuteronomic (or Deuteronomistic) texts. In this scenario, scribes had a considerable task before them in coordinating and integrating two essentially separate corpora.

Other scenarios are also possible. For instance, did the promulgation of the Torah have to do with the revision and transformation of an elite scribal curriculum at the Jerusalem temple? It may have been the case that sometime in the postexilic period the Torah served as foundational educational material—copied and committed to memory and recitation—that eventually became normative law. If so, when did this occur? Did this transformation take place in the Persian period? Or was it an act of communal self-definition undertaken later as a reaction to an ongoing process of Hellenization in the southern Levant? Either way, should the broad acceptance of the Torah as a kind of constitutional document for the community be distanced from its putative use as the foundational core of an elite scribal curriculum?

Perhaps one should think of the priests as having a substantial and foundational role in the process of promulgation. If so, is the rise of written (and recited) Torah to be connected to a broader priestly effort to educate elements of the populace in a common tradition? Perhaps the priestly leaders of the Jerusalem temple promoted what they regarded as a foundational document as an essential literary work that needed to be copied, memorized, and recited. In any case, how did an elite document come to enjoy a more widely-recognized status within the community? Or does the broad acceptance itself constitute evidence that could challenge the assumption of a "top-down" imposition of the Torah by an elite?

Third, in thinking about the promulgation of the Pentateuch, some legal historians have envisioned something taking place more broadly than a long series of internal developments at the Jerusalem temple. Perhaps priestly groups negotiated not only with other priestly groups at the temple but also with prominent lay leaders within Judean society to advance a certain set of documents (over others) as normative for the community. In this scenario, the Pentateuch may be regarded as a compromise document, the result of protracted societal negotiations and concessions.[3] The very existence of a Pentateuch containing different

---

3. Stimulating in this regard is the often-overlooked work of Morton Smith, "Pseudepigraphy in the Israelite Literary Tradition," in *Pseudepigrapha I: Pseudopythagorica, Lettres de Platon, Littérature pseudépigraphique juive* (ed. Kurt von Fritz; Entretiens sur l'antiquité classique 18; Vandoeuvres, Geneva: Fondation Hardt, 1972) 191–215. The panel debate following his article addresses the idea that the Pentateuch's redaction is inconceivable without a compromise having taken place between competing social elements.

legal collections is thus direct evidence for the process that led to the Pentateuch's compilation. If so, what was the internal or external stimulus that triggered this societal compromise and the ensuing elevation in status for what came to be known as "the five books of Moses"?

Fourth, was the rise of the Pentateuch related to the rise or demise of other important writings in the community? For example, some have hypothesized over the course of the last centuries that the rise of the Pentateuch (Genesis through Deuteronomy) as the normative set of Scriptures for Jews (and Samaritans) was connected to the rejection of a slightly larger corpus that included the book of Joshua (the Hexateuch). In this respect, the provocative title of the paper delivered by A. Graeme Auld at the conference is most apt: "When Did the Pentateuch Become the Torah? or When Did the Torah Become the Pentateuch?"[4] In the rivalry between the Hexateuch and the Pentateuch, the Pentateuch eventually emerged victorious. The issue is not simply one of length—a preference for a shorter rather than a longer corpus. The Hexateuch incorporates the detailed story of Israel's actual entrance into the land repeatedly promised in the Pentateuch and includes many references and allusions to this fact. Is the choice of the Pentateuch over against the Hexateuch to be connected to the international (or transnational) nature of Judaism in the Neo-Babylonian, Persian, and Hellenistic eras?

The same issue can be seen from another vantage point. At the very close of the last book in the Pentateuch (Deut 34:10–12), we read that the revelation bestowed to Moses was unparalleled and unrivaled among all those who followed him. Does this unequivocal declaration about Moses' unique standing serve not only as a demarcation of the Pentateuch as a unrivaled set of Scriptures over against the book which follows (Joshua) but also as a demarcation of the Torah from the sort(s) of revelation that we find in the prophetic books, such as Hosea, Amos, Isaiah, Jeremiah, and Ezekiel? If Moses is upheld as the very embodiment of an archetypal and incomparable prophet, are all the other (later) Israelite prophets revered in the community inevitably consigned to secondary and tertiary roles? By the same token, is not the revelation (the Pentateuch) associated with Moses, whom Yhwh "knew face to face" (Deut 34:10), by definition, superior to all of the revelations received by Joshua and the prophets?

A fifth issue has to do with the growth of the Jewish religion in other lands. What role (if any) did Judean leaders who lived in the diaspora play in the rec-

---

4. The editors extend their profound thanks to Professor Auld of the University of Edinburgh, who stepped in at the last minute in the wake of an unanticipated cancellation and delivered his fine paper in our first session. Due to time constraints and the press of other commitments, Auld was unable, unfortunately, to include his paper in this volume.

ognition and acceptance of the Torah as a prestigious document? By the time that the Pentateuch became recognized as a foundational document for the life of the community, Judaism itself had already become an international religion. By the end of the 6th century B.C.E., there were Judean communities in Babylon and Egypt in addition to the Yahwistic community centered in Jerusalem. In this respect, there was not one Judaism but several Judaisms that coexisted during the Neo-Babylonian, Persian, and Hellenistic periods. From the epigraphic remains found at one of these communities (Elephantine in Egypt), from other material evidence, and from the biblical literature itself, we know that there were some contacts, travel, and correspondence among the members of these communities. Did any of the Babylonian or Egyptian communities (and others we do not know about) have a role, whether direct or indirect, to play in the Torah's rise to authoritative status? That is, are we to think of an international diaspora that led to the need for some sort of unifying set of Scriptures, or are we to think of a very diverse international setting that hindered and delayed the rise of a commonly accepted group of prestigious writings? To complicate matters even further, are we to imagine that the Pentateuch (or Proto-Pentateuch) arose in Judah, or are we to imagine that it was brought to Judah from one of the Judean communities in the diaspora (as implied by Ezra 7)? Or are we to think of an even lengthier and more complicated process by which writings from different communities were edited and reedited in new settings before being compiled and integrated into a larger whole?

The sixth question is very much connected to the fifth. How can we best explain the Samarian (or Samaritan) acceptance of basically the same Pentateuch as the one that was accepted in Judah? Recent studies have shed welcome new light on the development of the Yahwistic community to the north of Yehud. This community was neither insubstantial nor a newcomer to the scene. In fact, many archaeologists believe that the population of the province of Samaria was larger than that of Yehud in the Persian period. The remains of the Yahwistic Temple recently excavated on Mt. Gerizim date back to approximately the mid-5th century B.C.E. These historical facts have a bearing on our theories about the acceptance of the Pentateuch as a prestigious writing. Should the Samarian acceptance of the Pentateuch be construed as a later and secondary development, beholden to and significantly later than the acceptance of the Torah in postexilic Judah? Or should one think of a related, if not intimately related, historical process in the province to the north of the Persian province of Yehud that was parallel to what may have been occurring within Yehud itself? Or should one entertain a more radical question, namely, that the Torah was originally a predominately Northern document that came to be accepted in Judah as an authoritative writing at some later time?

The seventh issue has to do with the transition (if there was such a transition) between the use of the Pentateuch as descriptive law and the use of the Pentateuch as prescriptive law. How is it that the Pentateuch (or the Proto-Pentateuch) achieved a kind of normative or legal (*lato sensu*) canonicity?[5] The issue is not simply one of sacral standing. It is perfectly imaginable, after all, that the Pentateuch could have been regarded as sacred Scripture in the sense of embodying a set of much-respected didactic tales and edifying laws. It is another thing for those laws to be regarded constitutionally as legally binding norms for all members of the community. Especially when seen in the context of the ancient Near Eastern world, this was a highly unusual and significant development.

To appreciate this pivotal transformation of the Pentateuch, it is relevant to recall that a transformation of this sort never took place in the case of other ancient Near Eastern law collections. There were a number of prestigious law collections compiled in the (late) third, second, and first millennia, such as the Laws of Ur-Namma (ca. 2100 B.C.E.), the Laws of Lipit-Ishtar (ca. 1900 B.C.E.), the Laws of Eshnunna (ca. 1770 B.C.E.), the Laws of Hummurapi (ca. 1750 B.C.E.), the Middle Assyrian Laws (ca. 1400–1300 B.C.E.), and the Neo-Babylonian Laws (ca. 700–600 B.C.E.). All of these impressive law collections stem from the great city-states of ancient Mesopotamia, although there is also one important collection of laws attested from ancient Anatolia (the Hittite Laws, ca. 1600–1200 B.C.E.). Over the past century, scholars have debated the original function and purpose of these important ancient law codes. Were these legal collections, so important to the history of Western judicial thought, originally created to serve as royal propaganda, judicial philosophy, scribal curricula, or some other purpose? In any event, most legal historians do not believe that these law collections actually served as public law, because, among other reasons, they are not normally cited in court cases. Nor, for the most part, do the penalties stipulated in actual court dockets that have been recovered correspond to penalties stipulated within the various law collections. The situation with the Pentateuch is different, however. Whatever its origins and original status, the Pentateuch did eventually become prescriptive law, normative for all Jews and Samaritans. When did this occur and under what circumstances? What made Judah and Samaria a special case in this regard?

The eighth issue is related to practically all of the previously mentioned issues. Was there some sort of external stimulus that led to or facilitated the rise of the Torah? For some in the late-19th, 20th, and early 21st centuries of the Common Era, the answer to this question was sought in the unique administrative apparatus of the Achaemenid Empire (ca. 550–330 B.C.E.). For these

---

5. Legal canonicity may be linked to but also distinguished from textual canonicity (which involves a process of textual standardization).

scholars, the theory of a Persian imperial authorization (*Reichsautorisation*) has been an attractive way to explain the formation and adoption of the Torah as an authoritative set of Scriptures in the province of Yehud. In this view, the compilation and edition of the Pentateuch were very much linked to the rise of the Pentateuch as authoritative law. Persian authorities (or their local representatives) were said to have launched a new administrative and legal process by which communities in the Persian Empire could (or were expected to) gain legal recognition for their local laws. The written legal traditions of these communities were, in effect, adopted as Persian laws for the local areas affected by such statutes. In the past dozen years or so, there has been a notable reaction against the tenability of this hypothesis.[6] Nevertheless, some would argue that a more limited and nuanced version of the theory is still the best explanation for the promulgation and acceptance for the Pentateuch in the Persian period.

The imperial authorization theory focuses on the ancient Near East, specifically the legal policies of the far-flung Achaemenid regime, as the key trigger to elucidate the compilation of the Torah.[7] Indeed, the diverse and, in the recent past, mostly negative reactions to this theory were a major impetus to our holding the special sessions at the Edinburgh International Meeting of the Society of Biblical Literature in 2006. There is, however, another external context that may shed some welcome light on the rise of Torah in the southern Levant. The period from the late 7th through the mid-4th centuries B.C.E. witnessed the creation of many written statutes and collections of law in a variety of contexts throughout the Mediterranean world. The instances of Athens and Rome are well known, but public laws were also promulgated in urban centers ranging from sites in the small Aegean islands to Crete, southern Italy, and Sicily. Is it simply happenstance that the codification of the Torah may have taken place at roughly the same time? This broader ancient Mediterranean context needs to be more fully explored.

Finally, an essential part of the larger story of the Pentateuch is the story of its afterlife in the history of Judaism, Samaritanism, Christianity, and (indirectly)

6. Full references to the imperial authorization hypothesis of Peter Frei, those who extended his work, those who were skeptical about some particular aspects of the hypothesis, and those who rejected it outright may be found in the discussions and footnotes of the contributors to this volume (but especially in the essay of Konrad Schmid).

7. One of the research goals for the Edinburgh meeting (Biblical and Ancient Near Eastern Law section) was to procure papers on the subject of Achaemenid law and legal procedures from specialists in the area. That goal was unfortunately unrealized. The press of other commitments made it impossible, for example, for Professor Amélie Kuhrt (University College, London) to participate in the conference. Perhaps in a future year we will be able to revisit this question with more success. It was similarly impossible for Professor Erhard Blum (Eberhard Karls University, Tübingen), who played a key role in the development of the Persian imperial authorization hypothesis, to participate.

Islam. There is no doubt that the reception history of the Pentateuch as well as the translation of the Pentateuch into Greek (in the Septuagint) tell us a great deal about how this corpus was treated and viewed in the immediate centuries after which it was formulated and accepted in the community. But do the re-interpretation, translation, and application of texts from the Pentateuch in late biblical and postbiblical literature shed any light on the composition of the Pentateuch itself? Do the Septuagint, the Dead Sea Scrolls, the Apocrypha (or Deu-tero-Canon), and the Pseudepigrapha help us to understand the process that led to the Pentateuch's becoming the Torah?

Ratifying Local Law Codes in an International Age

A number of our essays explore the phenomenon and ramifications of publishing collections of local law in international contexts. The local circum-stances, geographic settings, and international contexts are all imagined some-what differently, however. In his erudite essay, "The Persian Imperial Authori-zation as a Historical Problem and as a Biblical Construct: A Plea for Distinctions in the Current Debate," Konrad Schmid helpfully revisits a number of the issues relating to a possible Persian imperial authorization of the Torah in postexilic Judah. In many ways, Schmid's treatment responds to the criticisms leveled at the imperial authorization hypothesis over the past dozen years. Schmid's essay sets up the entire trajectory of how the model came to play the dominant role in the field that it long held, how the model was challenged, and how a more nuanced and qualified understanding of that model might help give it new life. Because the author had personal access to Peter Frei, he was able to review with him in considerable detail the original intent of the influential theory of impe-rial authorization. In seeking thereby to reground and revitalize the hypothesis, Schmid's essay makes a welcome contribution to the ongoing debate.

Schmid reminds readers that a number of the problems that Frei brought forward in his research about the process leading to the formation and accep-tance of the Torah as an authoritative body of writings continue to bedevil He-brew Bible scholarship, even for those (or especially for those) who reject Frei's thesis outright. For instance, he observes that Ezra 7 presents the Torah as hav-ing been authorized by the Persian rulership. This literary account constitutes an important piece of historical evidence for biblical scholarship, even if the at-tribution to Artaxerxes is a complete fiction. Why did the author of this Ezra text choose to present the authoritative promulgation of the Torah as intimately connected to and resulting from an external, foreign stimulus? Schmid also calls attention to the different levels of Persian governance within the larger empire (central regime, satraps, provinces, and subprovinces) and argues that a local satrap could sanction the implementation of a local law without also involving the central government somehow in the process.

In "The Rise of Torah," David Carr thoughtfully traces a number of external and internal factors at work in the rise of the Torah to fundamental importance across Second Temple Judaism. Among the internal factors Carr discusses, a critical one is the intimate link he sees between the growing importance of the Pentateuch as a foundational document in education and the rise of the Pentateuch as a community-forming law. His wide-ranging work emphasizes the role of elites and of scribal schools in the formation of the Torah, in its acceptance as normative law, and in the reciprocal influence that it exerted in allowing communities to define themselves and to construe their identities. Among the external factors discussed by Carr are Persian administrative policies. Like Schmid, Carr thinks that the particular form of Achaemenid governance played an important role in facilitating the consolidation of local legal traditions. More specifically, Carr thinks that politically insecure, Persian-sponsored returnees drew on a more widely attested pattern of Persian textual sponsorship to secure their position and the position of their Torah texts (*tôrôt*). To accomplish this feat, they created a consolidated version of their Torah traditions and merged them into a larger corpus for which they then sought imperial recognition. This critical step toward the legal founding of Judaism on the foundational Mosaic 'teaching' (*tôrâ*) was presupposed, refracted, and developed in multiple Hellenistic period traditions. From a long-term perspective, the consolidation of the Torah was a critical step in consolidating a transnational community of Jews otherwise not united by typical national-ethnic institutions.

The contribution by Anselm Hagedorn, "Local Law in an Imperial Context: The Role of Torah in the (Imagined) Persian Period," creatively reexamines a number of important issues surrounding the emergence of an authoritative law code in postexilic Judah within a larger international setting. Particularly helpful is the fact that the writer brings many insights of recent anthropological and postcolonial theory to bear on this long-contested issue. These insights have rarely been brought into the discussion of the codification of legal material within an imperial Persian and post-Persian setting. Hagedorn's essay falls into two parts. In the first, he discusses various definitions of empire and how each leads to distinct conceptions of colonial rule. He points out, for instance, that while the structure of Persian foreign policies may have departed from some older patterns of imperial rule, it is still necessary to consider colonial impact, especially in the realm of law, as a critical factor in assessing how local communities adapted to imperial rule. To put matters somewhat differently, a larger Persian and Hellenistic imperial context must be taken into consideration, even if one does not subscribe to the imperial authorization theory.

In the second part of his essay, Hagedorn argues that the larger Persian context shaped the codification of biblical legal material but that this shaping was done by the biblical authors themselves in that they created a legal corpus that could plausibly function within a larger imperial context. In putting together this particular legal code, the biblical writers created a new order that enabled the community to function as part of a larger empire without coming into conflict with it.

Like Carr and Hagedorn, Reinhard Kratz is concerned with the status of the Pentateuch in both Persian and Hellenistic times. His provocative and extensive study, "Temple and Torah: Reflections on the Legal Status of the Pentateuch between Elephantine and Qumran," brings a broad international setting and extensive historical perspective to bear on the ascent of Torah. Kratz contends that one must think not only of a late Persian context but also of Hellenistic and Hasmonean contexts for the process leading to the codification of biblical legal material as authoritative Torah. The writer approaches his subject matter through a detailed comparative analysis of three different but related communities, Elephantine, Jerusalem, and Samaria, and argues that the Elephantine papyri can be seen as reflecting traditional Israelite religion (which he defines as the religion prior to the distinctive Torah-conception of Deuteronomy) in a way that was fairly representative of mainstream Judaism in the 5th century B.C.E. What one sees in the book of Ezra-Nehemiah with respect to the enforcement of Torah by Ezra and Nehemiah is thus a later retrojection into a past age.

Kratz works with *Torah* and *temple* as two distinct, heuristic concepts and attempts to discover at what point they became intimately linked. In his view, a major impetus in the move toward a fixation on Torah (as opposed to temple) may have been Samaritan competition. Kratz boldly contends, in fact, that the Judeans may have derived their Torah from the Samaritans. Like Carr, Kratz makes the case that the movement toward an authoritative Torah was intensified by the pressure of the Hellenization of Judaism. The era of the Maccabees represents the end of this long historical process. The Hasmoneans employ the Torah in their rebellion against Seleucid rule and demand a careful conformity to Torah—if need be, even by force. The answer to the question of how the Pentateuch reached its prominence as Torah (that is, "the official authoritative foundation document of Judaism") thus involves a prolonged historical process extending into the last few centuries before the Common Era. In this reconstruction, the close connection between temple and Torah only reaches its official status in the Maccabean era.

The programmatic essay of Gary Knoppers and Paul Harvey, "The Pentateuch in Ancient Mediterranean Context: The Publication of Local Lawcodes," discusses the promulgation of the Pentateuch as a prestigious writing from a somewhat different perspective. As in the case of Frei's work, Knoppers and Harvey find it useful to look at the publication of local laws within a broader international context. The larger context they examine is, however, the Greek and Roman states during the late archaic and classical eras. The period from the late 7th through the mid-4th centuries B.C.E. witnessed the creation of many written statutes and collections of law in a variety of contexts throughout the Mediterranean world. The instances of Athens and Rome are well known, but public laws were also promulgated in urban centers ranging from sites in the small Aegean islands to Crete, southern Italy, and Sicily. As Knoppers and Harvey observe, the growth in public legislation included considered reflection on and systemization of legislation itself.

Surveying the spread of written law in the ancient Mediterranean world, the authors focus on three particular sites: Athens with a view to Solon's legal reforms, Gortyn (in Crete) with a view to the long series of public laws found there, and Rome with a view to the so-called "Twelve Tables." Having discussed these particular forms of written legislation, Knoppers and Harvey evaluate the different ways in which classical historians have sought to understand the growing popularity and widespread distribution of written laws in the 6th and 5th centuries B.C.E. The essay advocates a Mediterranean-wide perspective in which a number of factors contribute in one way or another to the publication of written laws and law collections in different settings. The authors conclude that the promulgation of written Torah in Judah and Samaria needs to be seen in a broader historical and geographic setting in which many, but by no means all, Mediterranean societies were investing in written law during this period.

Prophets, Polemics, and Publishers:
The Growing Importance of Writing in Persian-Period Judah

The second section of the volume addresses questions of how the formation of the Pentateuch may be related to its acceptance in Yehud. Different and evolving concepts of revelation, writing, scribes, publication, and the relationships between the writings found in the Pentateuch and other writings, especially the writings of the prophets, all come into play. The background to Jean-Louis Ska's richly textured and carefully developed essay, "From History Writing to Library Building: The End of History and the Birth of the Book," lies in recent studies analyzing the complex relationships between oral and literate cultures in the ancient world. Ska is specifically interested in the complex interplay within the same society of a great majority of people living within and relying upon an oral world and the growing importance of a tiny minority of people who are able to read and to write. In the case of Ska's concern with postexilic times, this leads to a focus on the particular nature of Judah's scribal culture. The author's thesis is that the origin of the Pentateuch should be linked to two related developments: the constitution of a library in Jerusalem during postexilic times and the rise of an elite scribal culture specifically dedicated to writing down the most important traditions of Israel, in particular, the Torah.

Ska argues his nuanced thesis in three steps. First, he contends that, after the Neo-Babylonian era, the interest in history, especially recent history, slowly ebbs away and eventually disappears. Second, he ties the demise of an interest in recent history to a growing fascination with the remote past, an interest that leads to the collection, preservation, and editing of ancient traditions in temple archives. Third, the author examines a particular passage, Exod 24:3–8, which he deems to be a very late text, a work that bears the signature of some of the writers responsible for the compilation and redaction of the Pentateuch. The author's creative proposal is that the postexilic scribes responsible for the preservation of the most sacred and authoritative traditions of Israel, for writing them down and reading them in public, are scribes similar to the presentation of Moses as a scribe in Exod 24:3–8. In this exemplary passage, the divine tradition passes from God to Moses and then from Moses to the scroll.

At the beginning of his essay, Eckart Otto reminds readers that the theory of a Persian imperial authorization of local law assumed that the formation of the Pentateuch was the result of a historic compromise between priestly and non-priestly lay perspectives. In his innovative and suggestive study, entitled "Scribal Scholarship in the Formation of Torah and Prophets: A Postexilic Scribal Debate between Priestly Scholarship and Literary Prophecy—The Example of the Book of Jeremiah and Its Relation to the Pentateuch," Otto argues differently. He sees the Pentateuch as the result of a post-Priestly scribal effort to mediate between the Priestly work and a Deuteronomistic edition of Deuteronomy. In this process, the editors of the Pentateuch developed scribal techniques that subsequently became the foundation for rabbinic interpretations and reapplications of Scripture.

Otto's contribution specifically addresses a number of related issues in the editing of the Pentateuch and the editing of the book of Jeremiah. One critical part of the overall argument is that the postexilic formations of the Pentateuch and the book of Jeremiah were each the result of intensive endeavors of scribes, who employed the same sorts of exegetical techniques. A second, equally critical part of the argument is that the Priestly scribes who were responsible for the formation of the Pentateuch were avidly debating critical tenets of the nature and extent of revelation, as well as the hermeneutics of revelation, with scribes belonging to the postexilic prophetic schools. The implication of Otto's study is that the formation of the larger prophetic books, especially Jeremiah, influenced the formation of the Pentateuch and vice versa. In this way, "the Law and the Prophets" do not appear as two diametrically opposed sets of literary works, separated from one another by genre, date, and content. They appear, rather, as two related sets of writings in conversation, albeit in some instances in heated conversation, with one another.

Joachim Schaper's well-documented investigation, "The 'Publication' of Legal Texts in Ancient Judah," like Otto's essay, takes a great interest in writing, editing, and book formation in the Persian period. Yet Schaper's essay takes a different course. He thinks that the increasing importance of fixing laws in writing results from, in part, a massive transition in the conceptualization of law and in its practice. Although classical studies have explored this phenomenon to a considerable degree, the same cannot be said of biblical studies. Schaper aims to rectify this deficiency by focusing on three key texts (Deut 1:5, 27:8; and Hab 2:2) that employ the Piel of the verb באר. He devotes considerable attention to the proper meaning and translation of this verb and calls for a correction of the conventional understanding. He also addresses its use. He argues that the verb is used cataphorically in Deut 1:5 (pertaining to the literary material that follows in Deut 5:1–26:19) and thus provides an insight into the Judean practice of publishing legal and other important texts. This process, consisting of oral and written elements, involves both publishing and confirming legal texts in the community.

Central to the publication process is the public inscription of the text, which effectively documents the text as a legal document. Seen from this perspective, the two acts of inscribing the text on the tablets and then reading the tablets publicly in Deuteronomy constitute the implementation of that text. One of these actions is not enough. They must occur together. In sum, the formulations of Deut 1:5, 27:8; and Hab 2:2 may shed significant light on how the Pentateuch was promulgated or, more precisely, put into force legally during the postexilic period.

The Torah as a Foundational Text in Judah and Samaria

While some of the studies in the present volume focus on the ascent of the Torah in Yehud, others take the ascent of the Torah in Samaria directly into account. The finely argued essay of Christophe Nihan, "The Torah between Samaria and Judah: On Shechem and Gerizim in Deuteronomy and Joshua," assails the common assumption that the various passages in Deuteronomy (11:26–31, 27:1–26) and Joshua (8:30–35) pertaining to a covenant ceremony in or near Shechem represent an ancient North-Israelite tradition. In Nihan's view, these texts evince different attempts to acknowledge Samaria's religious and political role at the time of the Torah's composition. For Nihan, the Pentateuch is an intercommunity (both Judean and Samarian) document.

According to Nihan, the literary setting of Joshua 24—a text that once served as the conclusion of a post-Priestly Hexateuch—at Shechem is not simply a concession made to a traditional cultic center in the heartland of Samaria. The intertextual connection with the story of the division of the kingdom following Solomon's death (1 Kgs 12:1–20) suggests that the Torah is presented in Joshua 24 as the true foundation for a new national unity between Judeans and Samarians in the wake of the fall of both the (Northern) Israelite (722 B.C.E.) and Judahite (586 B.C.E.) kingdoms. Nihan contends that the postexilic insertion of an explicit reference to Mt. Gerizim in what he regards as the second redactional layer of Deuteronomy 27 (vv. 4–8, 11–13 [14–26]) is tied to the redaction of the Pentateuch and should be viewed as a concession to the newly built Gerizim sanctuary (mid-5th century B.C.E.).

The author discerns in the very composition of Deuteronomy 27 a sensitivity to both Northern and Southern concerns. For instance, to preserve the legitimacy of the Jerusalem temple, an editor phrased his allusion to the Gerizim sanctuary in Deuteronomy 27 according to the language of the altar law of Exod 20:24–26 (see Deut 27:5–7) and not according to the language of the centralization legislation in Deuteronomy 12. Finally, Nihan argues that the replacement of "Mt. Gerizim" by "Mt. Ebal" in Deut 27:4 (compare and contrast the MT, the LXX, the Samaritan Pentateuch, and the Old Latin) represents a late polemical, anti-Samaritan textual change that postdates the redaction of the Pentateuch and has as the source of its inspiration Josh 8:30–35 (so the MT; similarly, LXX Josh 9:2^{a-f}). Hence, even though the Jerusalem temple probably remains the most likely place for the composition of the Torah during the second half of the Persian period, Nihan suggests that throughout this literary process the Torah was never written for one community in isolation from the other but was intended to be accepted by both Judeans and Samarians.

The judicious study of Reinhard Pummer deals directly with the Samarian (or Samaritan) community in antiquity. Entitled "The Samaritans and Their Pentateuch," his essay reinvestigates a number of important issues concerning the emergence of the Samaritan Pentateuch. His work engages not only contemporary scholarship but also the entire history of scholarship on the Samaritans over the course of the last few centuries. One of the contributions of Pummer's work is to provide readers with a comprehensive review of the entire Samaritan question, including the date of the origin of the community and the date and context for the formation of their Pentateuch, in relation to Judaism's Pentateuch. Along the way, the author is able to point out that many of the current debates and positions were already anticipated in older scholarship.

The study begins with a helpful overview of the textual character of the Samaritan Pentateuch (set against the background of current insights into the editing of pentateuchal manuscripts in Qumran studies) and its close relationship to other harmonistic pentateuchal texts. He points out that the zeal to document scattered harmonistic additions in the Samaritan Pentateuch has had the unintended effect of obscuring the great extent to which the Samaritan Pentateuch and the Jewish Pentateuch represent the same text. Pummer proceeds to discuss recent research on the origin of the Samaritans, contending (along with others) that they were the descendants of the remnants of the (Northern) Israelite tribes, who remained in the land following the Assyrian conquests. Positing close relations between Samaria and Judah throughout much of their history, he situates the parting of the ways between the Judeans and the Samaritans in the 2nd century B.C.E. following the campaigns of John Hyrcanus. It is this long-term relationship that explains the rise of a common scripture (Pentateuch) shared by both groups.

In the programmatic essay of James Watts, "The Torah as the Rhetoric of Priesthood," due attention is devoted to the priesthoods of both Judah and Samaria. One of his major concerns is to argue that the Torah gained canonical authority during the Second Temple period by means of its association with the priesthoods of the Jerusalem and Samaritan temples. The Torah, in turn, legitimized these priests' control over both the temples and, for much of the period, over the territory of Judah as well. One original function of the Pentateuch was to legitimize the religious and, by extension, the political claims of priestly dynasties.

Watts boldly claims that, although scholarship usually links Torah with temple, the emphasis should be shifted to the Torah's crucial ties to the priesthood. He argues, in fact, that scholars have historically undervalued, ignored, or belittled Priestly contributions to the development of Israelite religion. He points out that a single family of Aaronide priests led not one but two religious and ethnic communities (Judah and Samaria) of increasing size and influence in the last five centuries B.C.E. Sharing a common priesthood and a common Torah can hardly have been a coincidence. Aaronide priests of Joshua's family also later founded and directed a Jewish temple in Leontopolis, Egypt. Watts contends that the Aaronide priests, or at least some of them, were far less committed to Deuteronomy's doctrine of the geographical centralization of cultic worship in Jerusalem than they were to the Priestly doctrine of the Aaronides' monopoly over the conduct of all cultic worship, wherever it might take place. In this, he sees the Torah (or the Priestly interpretation thereof) as advocating a stance of political accommodation. Watts concludes that the priesthood was not simply important to Judean and Samaritan worship but also, and perhaps more importantly, to the survival and benefit of the entire Israelite people.

The Translation, Interpretation, and Application of the Torah

In the final section of the book, a number of scholars examine early reactions to, interpretations of, and extensions of the Torah in early Judaism.[8] In the very interesting essay of Sebastian Grätz, "The Second Temple and the Legal Status of the Torah: The Hermeneutics of the Torah in Ezra and Ruth," the author considers two different ways in which the Torah is interpreted and applied in the postexilic period. Two sections of the essay address the question of the importance of the Torah as a written and authoritative document in the postexilic era on the basis of examples from Ruth and Ezra. A third section engages a historical and social issue: whether the Torah enjoyed an unquestioned status in postexilic Judean society as a public and authoritatively binding set of laws.

Grätz contends that the author of the Ezra narrative presents the Torah as the authoritative constitution for Judean society, a legally-binding set of norms for the people. The author of Ruth follows a different path, however. He feels free to draw from the wisdom tradition to make a different point in his narrative, even though his work also alludes to select narrative details found in the Pentateuch. Like the editors of the Pentateuch, the writer of Ruth regarded the Torah as a valuable and dignified writing. Nevertheless, the author of Ruth did not regard the Torah as the official and authoritative collection of statutes for the community. Grätz concludes that the evidence provided by Ezra and Ruth shows that there were a variety of attitudes in Yehud toward the Torah.

"The Septuagint of the Pentateuch and Ptolemaic Rule," the erudite essay by Arie van der Kooij, investigates the intriguing question of what social and historical issues prompted the initiative to translate the Hebrew Torah into the Greek Septuagint. He systematically reassesses the historical significance of the *Letter of Aristeas* and other ancient evidence to search for the social location and cultural trigger for this important new initiative. Van der Kooij argues that the Jewish community in Alexandria was not initially involved in the project to produce a Greek version of the Torah. Rather, it was a matter of two parties:

---

8. Chronicles represents an important example of the application and reinterpretation of Torah in the Second Temple period. At the conference in Edinburgh, John W. Wright presented an energetic and stimulating paper on this topic: "As It Is Written in the Law of Moses: King, Torah, and Temple in the Book of Chronicles." Unfortunately, a heavy teaching and advising load made it impossible for Professor Wright to submit his revised paper to the volume.

the Ptolemaic court on the one hand and the Jewish authorities in Jerusalem on the other.

In the second section of his paper, the author discusses the viability of four hypotheses made by scholars as to which of these two parties took the initiative and why. Van der Kooij thinks that the Septuagint of the Pentateuch was not produced for religious or liturgical (synagogal) use. Nor was it produced, first and foremost, for the benefit of the Ptolemaic administration, although the Ptolemaic court may have initiated the actual translation project. Instead, scholarly interests within the cultural context of Alexandria at that particular time (3rd century B.C.E.) represented the driving force. Because the authorities in Jerusalem were the other major party involved, it stands to reason that the translators came from Jerusalem. In all likelihood, these translators belonged to circles in which the books of the Torah were read and studied. In other words, these translators were priests and scribes. The writer thus concludes that the promulgation of the Septuagint does not shed any direct light on the larger question of what might have led to the promulgation and acceptance of the Pentateuch itself.

In her carefully considered essay, Sidnie Crawford examines the reception history of the Torah in the Dead Sea Scrolls. As the title suggests, "The Use of the Pentateuch in the *Temple Scroll* and in the *Damascus Document* in the Second Century B.C.E.," she is concerned to compare and contrast the interpretation of the Pentateuch in the *Temple Scroll* and the *Damascus Document*. Crawford helpfully introduces the hermeneutics of the Rewritten Bible, distinguishes key sub-genres (scriptural versus explicitly exegetical formats), and situates this literature in the cultural world of the Second Temple period. One of the contributions of Crawford's essay is to provide an overview of the exegetical techniques and concerns shared by the *Temple Scroll* and the *Damascus Document*, such as the attempt to "close the gaps" in earlier foundational texts through harmonization and a desire to maintain the purity of the temple.

In spite of these similarities, Crawford observes that there are also some important differences between the two. In particular, she contends that the first-person style of the *Temple Scroll*, which became less popular than and ultimately gave way to the third-person style of the *Damascus Document*, has important hermeneutical implications for the way that the authors of this document wished for readers to construe its divine voice. She thinks, however, that both works ultimately stem from the same Priestly-Levitical milieu in the mid–Second Temple period. The literature from this group, which Crawford believes later evolved and became part of the broader Essene movement, is extant at least beginning with the 3rd century B.C.E., and the same circle may also be responsible for the version of the Torah called the pre-Samaritan version, with its concern to

eliminate any perceived gaps or difficulties in the Scriptures by the use of harmonization. The careful analysis of these texts from the caves at Qumran thus
shines welcome new light on the history of the Pentateuch and its interpretation in the late Second Temple period.[9]

Concluding Thanks

Our primary debt of thanks goes to our authors for their sustained commitment to this project despite the "slings and arrows of outrageous" editors. From
the outset, we wanted the essays to appeal to a large scholarly audience consisting not only of readers in biblical and ancient Near Eastern studies but also
readers in ancient history, classics, Jewish studies, legal history, religious studies,
and Samaritan studies. We wanted to open up new disciplinary conversation
and felt strongly that the perspectives of the various texts and versions of the
Pentateuch, of research on the Dead Sea Scrolls, and of current work in empire
theory all have their place in attempting to understand the promulgation of the
Pentateuch. With this goal in mind, we asked contributors to move outside
their own normal "comfort zone" of specialized knowledge so as to address the
relevance of their specific case study for the larger topic of the volume. We
asked everyone to open up their writing to nonspecialists, by explaining terms
and concepts that might otherwise be assumed by those within their discipline.

Although this volume began from the papers presented in Edinburgh,
therefore, it is far from a conventional "conference proceedings." The articles
have all been doubly refereed. They have been extensively revised, sometimes
more than once, in light of the lengthy comments made by the referees and editors. There were also a number of formal matters to address. We asked that all
quotations (even from modern European languages) be translated, so as to
make the volume as accessible as possible to a broad readership. Finally, despite
equal regard for European conventions of academic writing and format, we
asked everyone to follow the Society of Biblical Literature norms. As a result,
the editors would be the first to acknowledge that they tested the patience of
some contributors on both sides of the Atlantic with annoying regularity.
There were teasing (and sometimes not so teasing) e-mail exchanges about
"this is version 47 of the article"; there were repeated plaintive requests from
the editors, "just one more revision please" or "slight tweaking needed here."

---

9. Readers interested in the question of the translation, interpretation, and application of the
Torah in the Second Temple period will want to know that a series of special sessions devoted to
the use of the Torah in late biblical literature, the Apocrypha (or Deutero-Canon), and the Pseudepigrapha was organized at the 2007 Vienna meeting of the International SBL. A number of the
papers presented there will be compiled into a published volume (edited by Eckart Otto and Reinhard Achenbach) or published as articles in *ZAR*.

We created a lot of extra work for our contributors. Nonetheless, what finally emerged was a real intellectual exchange: a dialogue about the substantive issues and growth of understanding, as ideas were thought through and debated. In this way, we also grew through the intellectual process of editing these essays. For this sustained support, we thank our authors.

The editors would be remiss if they did not also extend their gratitude to a number of people who helped make both the Edinburgh sessions and the resulting book a reality. First, we wish to thank Reinhard Achenbach for his timely help in organizing and managing the four special Edinburgh sessions. Second, we thank Eckart Otto, one of the principal founding members of the Biblical and Ancient Near Eastern Law section, for his engagement and for his willingness to chair the open session of our program. Third, a debt of gratitude is owed to Matthew Collins, as Director of Congresses and Professions of the Society of Biblical Literature, for his enthusiastic encouragement and support. As the original idea grew by leaps and bounds, he took unprecedented steps to sustain its intellectual coherence. He scheduled four of the five Biblical and Ancient Near Eastern Law sessions in a continuous sequence over the course of two days for the benefit of presenters and conference attendees.

Fourth, the editors would like to express their sincere thanks to the publisher and chief editor of Eisenbrauns, Jim Eisenbraun. Jim graciously gave us every encouragement as we planned this volume. He affirmed his strong support for our process of vetting and editing the submissions. He worked with us on the copy editing and generously agreed to help with setting the extensive Greek and Hebrew citations. He has been unstinting in his support of the international scholarship represented in this volume. Andy Kerr, with his talent for design, color, and typography, generously solicited our input on the cover and worked closely with us. Finally, we thank Mrs. Beverly McCoy and the rest of the Eisenbrauns staff, who have been very attentive to the details of transforming disparate manuscripts into a coherent book. It has been a true pleasure working with such a well-informed, courteous, and professional editorial staff.

PART 1

Ratifying Local Law Codes in an International Age

The Persian Imperial Authorization as a Historical Problem and as a Biblical Construct: A Plea for Distinctions in the Current Debate

KONRAD SCHMID

University of Zurich

I. The Current Debate

The theory of a "Persian imperial authorization" of the Torah has become one of the most successful hypotheses of Old Testament scholarship during the past twenty years.[1] The theory has primarily been associated with the name of

Author's note: I am grateful to Gary N. Knoppers and Bernard M. Levinson, as the organizers of the Edinburgh session and the editors of this volume, for their help with the literary expression and scholarly content of this article.

1. See Rainer Albertz, *Religionsgeschichte Israels in alttestamentlicher Zeit* (GAT 8/1–2; Göttingen: Vandenhoeck & Ruprecht, 1992) 497–504; translated, idem, *A History of Israelite Religion in the Old Testament Period*, vol. 2: *From the Exile to the Maccabees* (trans. John Bowden; London: SCM, 1994) 466–71. See also Joseph Blenkinsopp, *The Pentateuch: An Introduction to the First Five Books of the Bible* (ABRL; New York: Doubleday, 1992) 239–42; David M. Carr, *Reading the Fractures of Genesis: Historical and Literary Approaches* (Louisville: Westminster, 1996) 324–33; Frank Crüsemann, "Das 'portative' Vaterland," in *Kanon und Zensur: Archäologie der literarischen Kommunikation II* (ed. Aleida and Jan Assmann; Munich: Fink, 1987) 63–79; idem, *Die Tora: Theologie und Sozialgeschichte des alttestamentlichen Gesetzes* (Munich: Chr. Kaiser, 1992); idem, "Der Pentateuch als Tora: Prolegomena zur Interpretation seiner Endgestalt," *EvT* 49 (1989) 250–67; Reinhard G. Kratz, *Translatio imperii: Untersuchungen zu den aramäischen Danielerzählungen und ihrem theologiegeschichtlichen Umfeld* (WMANT 63; Neukirchen-Vluyn: Neukirchener Verlag, 1991) 233–55; Ernst Axel Knauf, *Die Umwelt des Alten Testaments* (Neuer Stuttgarter Kommentar, Altes Testament 29; Stuttgart: Katholisches Bibelwerk, 1994) 171–75; Jon L. Berquist, *Judaism in Persia's Shadow: A Social and Historical Approach* (Minneapolis: Fortress, 1995) 138–39; Horst Seebass, "Pentateuch," *TRE* 26.185–209 (at 26.189–90); Konrad Schmid, *Erzväter und Exodus: Untersuchungen zur doppelten Begründung der Ursprünge Israels innerhalb der Geschichtsbücher des Alten Testaments* (WMANT 81; Neukirchen-Vluyn: Neukirchener Verlag, 1999) 291 n. 658; Odil Hannes Steck, *Der Abschluß der Prophetie im Alten Testament: Ein Versuch zur Frage der Vorgeschichte des Kanons* (Biblisch-theologische Studien 17; Neukirchen-Vluyn: Neukirchener Verlag, 1991) 13–21; idem, "Der Kanon des hebräischen Alten Testaments: Historische Materialien für eine ökumenische Perspektive," in *Verbindliches Zeugnis I: Kanon—Schrift—Tradition* (ed. Wolfhart Pannenberg and Theodor Schneider; Dialog der Kirchen 7; Freiburg: Herder / Göttingen: Vandenhoeck & Ruprecht, 1992) 11–33 (at 16); James W. Watts, *Reading Law: The Rhetorical Shaping of the Pentateuch* (BiSe 59; Sheffield: Sheffield Academic Press,

Peter Frei.[2] But it is important to recognize that the theory was independently formulated by Erhard Blum in the mid-1980s, although he did not publish his results until 1990.[3] Neither Frei nor Blum *invented* this theory, however; it had earlier been proposed by Eduard Meyer, Hans Heinrich Schaeder, Martin Noth, Edda Bresciani, Ulrich Kellermann, Wilhelm In der Smitten, and others. This earlier history of the model has been recognized by Frei and Blum, as well as by Udo Rüterswörden.[4] Indeed, Meyer had already contended in 1896:

> Die Einführung eines derartigen Gesetzbuchs [i.e., Esras Gesetz] für einen bestimmten Kreis von Unterthanen ist nur möglich, wenn es vom Reich sanktionirt, wenn es königliches Gesetz geworden ist. Das wird in v.26 [i.e., Esr 7,26] ausdrücklich ausgesprochen.[5]

> The introduction of such a law book [i.e., Ezra's law] for a certain number of subjects is only possible if it is authorized by the empire itself, if it has become the law of the king. This is explicitly said in v. 26 [i.e., Ezra 7:26].

After enjoying wide reception and agreement, this positive attitude toward the theory seems to have changed in recent scholarship. Following the critical dis-

---

1999) 137–44; Erich Zenger, *Einleitung in das Alte Testament* (Stuttgart: Kohlhammer, 1995) 39–42 (but see the adjustments in the 5th ed. [2004] of his *Einleitung*, 129–31); idem, "Der Pentateuch als Tora und als Kanon," in *Die Tora als Kanon für Juden und Christen* (ed. Erich Zenger; Herders Biblische Studien 10; Freiburg: Herder, 1996) 5–34. Hans G. Kippenberg uses the stronger term "Reichssanktionierung," but he reckons with a similar phenomenon (*Die vorderasiatischen Erlösungsreligionen in ihrem Zusammenhang mit der antiken Stadtherrschaft* [Suhrkamp Taschenbuch Wissenschaft 917; Frankfurt: Suhrkamp, 1991] 181–82).

2. Peter Frei, "Zentralgewalt und Lokalautonomie im Achämenidenreich," in Peter Frei and Klaus Koch, *Reichsidee und Reichsorganisation im Perserreich* (OBO 55; 2nd ed.; Fribourg: Universitätsverlag / Göttingen: Vandenhoeck & Ruprecht [1984] 1996) 5–131; idem, "Zentralgewalt und Lokalautonomie im achämenidischen Kleinasien," *Transeu* 3 (1990) 157–71; idem, "Die persische Reichsautorisation: Ein Überblick," *ZABR* 1 (1995) 1–35. (See also the Eng. trans.: "Persian Imperial Authorization: A Summary," in *Persia and Torah: The Theory of Imperial Authorization of the Pentateuch* [ed. James W. Watts; SBLSymS 17; Atlanta: Scholars Press, 2001] 5–40.)

3. Erhard Blum, *Studien zur Komposition des Pentateuch* (BZAW 189; Berlin and New York: de Gruyter, 1990) 333–60 (see esp. the statement in p. 345 n. 42); idem, "Esra, die Mosetora und die persische Politik," in *Religion und Religionskontakte im Zeitalter der Achämeniden* (ed. Reinhard G. Kratz; Veröffentlichungen der Wissenschaftlichen Gesellschaft für Theologie 22; Gütersloh: Gütersloher Verlagshaus, 2001) 231–55 (at 250 n. 80).

4. Frei, "Zentralgewalt und Lokalautonomie im Achämenidenreich," 16 n. 19; Blum, *Studien zur Komposition des Pentateuch*, 346–47 and nn. 44 and 52 there; idem, "Esra," 250 n. 78; Udo Rüterswörden, "Die persische Reichsautorisation der Thora: Fact or fiction?" *ZABR* 1 (1995) 47–61 (at 51 nn. 17–20).

5. Eduard Meyer, *Die Entstehung des Judenthums: Eine historische Untersuchung* (Halle: Max Niemeyer, 1896) 66 (additions mine). Translations and parenthetical insertions, unless otherwise stated, are mine.

cussion of this theory in the first volume of the *Zeitschrift für altorientalische und biblische Rechtsgeschichte* (1995), additional objections rapidly followed by Eckart Otto, Hans-Christoph Schmitt, and Amélie Kuhrt, as well as the objections included in the anthology *Persia and Torah*, compiled by James W. Watts.[6] Consequently, the majority of current scholarship seems to have distanced itself from the theory. Eckart Otto, for example, arrives at a decisive conclusion when he states in his review of the volume *Persia and Torah* that "die These . . . durch die Fachiranisten einhellig abgelehnt worden [ist]" ("the theory . . . has been unanimously rejected by experts in the field of Iranology").[7] His review concludes:

> Damit ist nun auch in der Alttestamentlichen Wissenschaft das Urteil, das die Iranistik längst gefällt hat, gesprochen. Der Pentateuch, das ist die Konsequenz, ist nicht Ergebnis persischer 'Geburtshilfe', sondern jüdischer Schriftgelehrsamkeit in persischer Zeit.[8]

> The judgment, long after Iranology came to it, has thus also been pronounced in the field of Old Testament scholarship. The Pentateuch (this is the conclusion) is not the result of Persian "midwifery" but rather of Jewish scribal scholarship during the Persian era.

---

6. Eckart Otto, "Kritik der Pentateuchkomposition," *TRu* 60 (1995) 163–91 (at 169 n. 5); idem, "Die nachpriesterschriftliche Pentateuchredaktion im Buch Exodus," in *Studies in the Book of Exodus: Redaction—Reception—Interpretation* (ed. Marc Vervenne; BETL 126; Leuven: Peeters, 1996) 61–111 (at 66–70); idem, "Gesetzesfortschreibung und Pentateuchredaktion," *ZAW* 107 (1995) 373–92 (at 375 and n. 14 there); idem, *Die Tora des Mose: Die Geschichte der literarischen Vermittlung von Recht, Religion und Politik durch die Mosegestalt* (Berichte aus den Sitzungen der Joachim Jungius-Gesellschaft der Wissenschaften; Hamburg: Joachim Jungius Gesellschaft der Wissenschaften, 2001) 51–52; Hans-Christoph Schmitt, "Die Suche nach der Identität des Jahweglaubens im nachexilischen Israel: Bemerkungen zur theologischen Intention der Endredaktion des Pentateuch," in *Pluralismus und Identität* (ed. Joachim Mehlhausen; Veröffentlichungen der Wissenschaftlichen Gesellschaft für Theologie 8; Gütersloh: Gütersloher Verlagshaus, 1995) 259–78 (at 263–67); idem, "Das spätdeuteronomistische Geschichtswerk Gen I–2 Regum XXV und seine theologische Intention," in *Congress Volume: Cambridge 1995* (ed. J. A. Emerton; VTSup 66; Leiden: Brill, 1997) 261–79. Amélie Kuhrt, "The Persian Kings and Their Subjects: A Unique Relationship?" *OLZ* 96 (2001) 166–73. But see the short discussion in Konrad Schmid, "Persische Reichsautorisation und Tora," *TRu* 71 (2006) 494–506. The present essay draws upon and significantly elaborates the analysis provided there.

7. Eckart Otto, "Review of James W. Watts (ed.), *Persia and Torah*," *ZABR* 8 (2002) 411–14.

8. Ibid., 413. See idem, "Rechtshermeneutik des Pentateuch und die achämenidische Rechtsideologie in ihren altorientalischen Kontexten," in *Kodifizierung und Legitimierung des Rechts in der Antike und im Alten Orient* (ed. Markus Witte and Marie Theres Fögen; Beihefte zur Zeitschrift für Altorientalische und Biblische Rechtsgeschichte 5; Wiesbaden: Harrassowitz, 2005) 71–116 (at 105–6). This judgment is not unique. See, for example, Christoph Dohmen and Manfred Oeming, *Biblischer Kanon: Warum und wozu? Eine Kanontheologie* (QD 137; Freiburg: Herder, 1992) 91 and n. 3 there; Norbert Lohfink, "Gab es eine deuteronomistische Bewegung?" in *Jeremia und die "deuteronomistische Bewegung"* (ed. Walter Groß; BBB 98; Weinheim: Beltz Athenäum, 1995)

However, the issue is not as simple as Eckart Otto maintains. In section II, I shall demonstrate that the objections raised by Josef Wiesehöfer, the Iranologist cited so frequently by the critics of Frei's position in the German realm, arise from a misreading of Frei's actual theory.[9] They do not, therefore, invalidate the theory itself. Moreover, the two "opposing" positions are not so far apart as commonly assumed.

The present discussion of the "Persian imperial authorization" of the Torah demands some basic clarification. Foremost, one has to introduce a fundamental distinction between two different issues that are best discussed separately: On the one hand, the question arises whether there ever was such a legal institution in the Persian Empire. On the other hand, there is the debate as to whether the completion of the Torah (or rather the formation of relevant literary precursors) might be connected to such a process of imperial authorization of local laws. Both questions need to be differentiated further. The dichotomy

---

313–82 (at 369–70) (article republished in Norbert Lohfink, *Studien zum Deuteronomium und zur deuteronomistischen Literatur III* [SBAB 20; Stuttgart: Katholisches Bibelwerk, 1995] 65–142); Titus Reinmuth, "Reform und Tora bei Nehemia: Neh 10,31–40 und die Autorisierung der Tora in der Perserzeit," *ZABR* 7 (2001) 287–317; Horst Seebass, "Das Erbe Martin Noths zu Pentateuch und Hexateuch," in *Martin Noth—aus der Sicht der heutigen Forschung* (ed. Udo Rüterswörden; Biblisch-theologische Studien 58; Neukirchen-Vluyn: Neukirchener Verlag, 2004) 21–59 (at 25 n. 13) (*contra* his own position in Seebaß, "Pentateuch," 205); Pierre Briant, "Histoire impériale et histoire régionale: A propos de l'histoire de Juda dans l'empire achéménide," in *Congress Volume: Oslo 1998* (ed. André Lemaire and Magne Sæbø; VTSup 80; Leiden: Brill, 2000) 235–45 (at 241–42); Ernst Baltrusch, *Die Juden und das Römische Reich: Geschichte einer konfliktreichen Beziehung* (Darmstadt: Wissenschaftliche Buchgesellschaft, 2002) 162 n. 57; Hugh Godfrey Maturin Williamson, "Review of J. Schaper, *Priester und Leviten im achämenidischen Juda: Studien zur Kult- und Sozialgeschichte Israels in persischer Zeit,*" *JTS* 54 (2003) 615–20; Wolfgang Oswald, *Israel am Gottesberg: Eine Untersuchung zur Literargeschichte der vorderen Sinaiperikope Ex 19–24 und deren historischem Hintergrund* (OBO 159; Fribourg: Universitätsverlag / Göttingen: Vandenhoeck & Ruprecht, 1998) 224–29; Juha Pakkala, *Ezra the Scribe: The Development of Ezra 7–10 and Nehemiah 8* (BZAW 347; Berlin and New York: de Gruyter, 2004) 38; Erhard S. Gerstenberger, *Israel in der Perserzeit: 5. und 4. Jahrhundert v.Chr.* (Biblische Enzyklopädie 8; Stuttgart: Kohlhammer, 2005) 320–21.

9. Josef Wiesehöfer, "'Reichsgesetz' oder 'Einzelfallgerechtigkeit'? Bemerkungen zu P. Freis These von der achaimenidischen 'Reichsautorisation,'" *ZABR* 1 (1995) 36–45. Hilmar Klinkott largely follows his teacher Wiesehöfer in rejecting the theory of a Persian imperial authorization of local laws (*Der Satrap: Ein achämenidischer Amtsträger und seine Handlungsspielräume* [Oikumene 1; Frankfurt: Antike, 2005] 133–34). Additionally, he strictly distinguishes between *dāta* as "imperial law" and *dīnu* as "local law." This strict thesis, however, can easily be disproven by the use of *dāta* in line 19 of the Letoon Trilingual (see n. 10 below). Here Satrap Pixodarus publishes the local decree of the Xanthus community as his own: "He has written this law (*dāta*)." For a discussion of the term *dāta*, see R. Schmitt, "*dāta*," in *Encyclopaedia Iranica* (ed. Ehsan Yarshater; Costa Mesa: Mazda, 1996) 7.114–15; Gregor Ahn, "'Toleranz' und Reglement: Die Signifikanz achaimenidischer Religionspolitik für den jüdisch-persischen Kulturkontakt," in *Religion und Religionskontakte in Zeitalter der Achämeniden* (ed. Reinhard G. Kratz; Veröffentlichungen der Wissenschaftlichen Gesellschaft für Theologie 22; Gütersloh: Gütersloher Verlagshaus, 2001) 202–4; Otto, "Rechtshermeneutik," 86–89.

between a *pro* or *contra* stance toward "Persian imperial authorization" that dominates recent scholarly discussions is too simplistic. In most cases where this theory is rejected, the rejection does not apply to more than *a specific version of this theory*.

There is no reason to deny that at least some local laws indeed were authorized by higher authorities such as the satraps. This is the unavoidable minimal interpretation of the trilingual inscription of Xanthus, which prompted Frei to develop his theory.[10] On the front face of the stele, the satrap Pixodaros publishes the decision of the community of Xanthus to establish a cult for two Carian deities *as his own decree*, in Aramaic, the imperial language. This provides clear evidence for the elevation of local legislation to imperial legislation. This kind of decentralized legal system is only to be expected within the Persian Empire, especially for such highly developed cultures as Greece, Asia Minor, Judah, and Egypt. The successful administration of an ancient empire necessitated that local autonomy be permitted at key junctures. The administrative effort of introducing and enforcing a centralized legal corpus would be prohibitively high. Scholars have nonetheless searched for this body of law.[11] The search is most likely in vain.[12] Such an attempt at creating a centralized legal corpus could hardly meet with success. Our question cannot be: "Did a 'Persian Imperial Authorization' exist?" but must be, rather: "How can we best describe processes whereby Persian authorities created local autonomy—processes that are only to be expected and that can be substantiated beyond any doubt?"

Accordingly, we have to differentiate the issue of the relation between the establishment of the Torah and Persian policy. Here, too, the question is not whether this relation is to be assumed or rejected *as a whole* but *how and in what manner* the Torah is connected to its historical Persian context, and what political forces influenced its creation.

II. What Peter Frei Originally Meant by "Imperial Authorization" and How His Critics Understood His Theory

Peter Frei defined the Persian Imperial Authorization as follows:

> Zu definieren ist [die Reichsautorisation] als ein Verfahren, durch das die von einer lokalen Instanz gesetzten Normen von einer Instanz der Zentrale nicht einfach gebilligt und akzeptiert, sondern übernommen

---

10. Henri Metzger et al., *Fouilles du Xanthos VI: La stèle trilingue du Létôon* (Paris: Klincksieck, 1979).

11. See especially the theory of Albert T. Olmstead, *A History of the Persian Empire* (Chicago: University of Chicago Press, 1948) 119–34; and idem, "Darius As Lawgiver," *AJSL* 51 (1934/1935) 247–49. Note the discussion of Olmstead by Otto, "Rechtshermeneutik," 85.

12. See Richard Nelson Frye, *The History of Ancient Iran* (Handbuch der Altertumswissenschaft 3/7; Munich: Beck, 1984) 119.

und zur eigenen Norm gemacht werden. Die lokale Norm wird dadurch im Rahmen des gesamten staatlichen Verbandes, eben des Reiches, als Norm höheren Ranges für alle verbindlich gemacht und gesichert.[13]

By definition it [i.e., the Persian imperial authorization] is a process by which the norms established by a local authority are not only approved and accepted by a central authority but adopted as its own. The local norms are thereby established and protected within the framework of the entire state association, that is, the empire, as higher-ranking norms binding all.[14]

These statements have given rise to misunderstandings that have led some to reject the theory *as a whole*. Frei was primarily interested in *qualitative* aspects of the central administration's adoption of local norms and the elevation of these norms to the status of imperial law. Scholars have presumed, however, that Frei's interest indicated something he never intended: that the local norms were *centrally registered and codified as "imperial law."* In a contribution to the discussion of Persian imperial authorization that has been influential in at least the German-speaking realm, Josef Wiesehöfer seems to have understood Frei in exactly this sense: "[A]uf ein Reichszentralkataster, ein Reichszentralarchiv, das auch die speziellsten lokalen Regelungen notiert, gibt es keinen Hinweis."[15] ("There is no indication that a central register, a central archive containing the specific local regulations, ever existed.")

Wiesehöfer concedes, however, that the central authority of the Persian Empire did have processes to ratify local norms. Insofar as he makes this concession, he is quite close to Peter Frei's argument. His main objection concerns this very point of central registration and codification of the approved local norms. Wiesehöfer himself repeats it again:

Jedoch sehe ich, zumindest in den nichtalttestamentlichen Texten und in Esra, keinen Hinweis darauf gegeben, dass es so etwas wie ein 'persisches Reichsgesetz' gegeben hat, in das auch die lokalen Normen—nun als Reichsnormen—aufgenommen waren.[16]

---

13. Frei, "Die persische Reichsautorisation," 3. Compare also p. 29: "Anzunehmen ist, daß durch [die Reichsautorisation] die von einer lokalen Körperschaft, die lediglich Untertanenstatus hatte, gesetzte Norm auf die Stufe der Reichsgesetzgebung gehoben wurde und dadurch entsprechende Autorität genoß." ("It is apparent, however, that through it, the legal norms of a local body with subordinate status were elevated to the status of imperial legislation and so enjoyed corresponding authority" [Frei, "Persian Imperial Authorization," 38].)

14. Ibid., 7.

15. Wiesehöfer, "'Reichsgesetz' oder 'Einzelfallgerechtigkeit'?" 44.

16. Ibid., 44. In a similar vein, see Ahn, "'Toleranz' und Reglement," 194 n. 18; Gary N. Knoppers, "An Achaemenid Imperial Authorization of Torah in Yehud?" in *Persia and Torah* (ed. J. W. Watts; SBLSymS 17; Atlanta: Scholars Press, 2001) 115–34 (at 134); Ludwig Massmann, "Persien und die Tora," *ZABR* 9 (2003) 238–50 (at 249).

But I do not see any indication, in texts outside the Old Testament and in Ezra, that there ever existed something resembling a "Persian imperial law" that also included local norms turned into imperial norms.

Frei, however, had never made this claim. He was interested in the legal *status* of the local norms authorized by the central administration, not in their central codification and archiving. For Frei, "imperial authorization" refers to a specific quality of the relevant laws, not to a process of establishing a central Persian law out of several local regulations. Furthermore, he did not claim that regulations that went through the process of an "imperial authorization" became binding norms in all parts of the empire. Rather, he thought of "lokal gültiges Reichsrecht" ("locally valid imperial law").[17] He admits, however, that his phrasing was not completely clear and that it was part of the reason for Wiesehöfer's misreading.[18]

But Wiesehöfer's criticism went on to develop its own tradition. Gregor Ahn, for example, offers a criticism of Frei's theory in the mood of Wiesehöfer:

Auch die Annahme, die achämenidische Zentralverwaltung habe einen das gesamte Reich umfassenden Prozeß der lokalen Rechtskodifizierung ("Reichsautorisation") initiiert, der in Judäa die Kompilation des Pentateuch katalysorisch ausgelöst habe, verkennt die (wie im Fall der sog. "Trilingue vom Letoon") von lokalen Anfragen ausgehende und nicht zentral gesteuerte pers. Religionspolitik.[19]

The suggestion that the Achaemenid central administration should have initiated an all-encompassing process of local law codification ("imperial authorization") misinterprets the Persian policy. It was not centrally steered but reacted to local queries. Neither the case of the so-called "Letoon Trilingual" nor the compilation of the Pentateuch in Judah provides any evidence for such a suggestion.

One can find here a misunderstanding similar to Wiesehöfer's. Ahn seems to identify "Persian imperial authorization" with the process of a central codification of local laws. If imperial authorization is (mis)understood in this way, of course, there is no evidence to postulate this legal institution. However, Thierry Petit assumed such a central codification for the notice found in the Demotic Chronicle (as well as in Diodorus Siculus 1.94–95), according to which King Darius collected and recorded Egyptian laws.[20] The historical reliability of the

---

17. Frei, "Zentralgewalt und Lokalautonomie im Achämenidenreich," 13.

18. Peter Frei, oral communication with author, 3 November 2003. See especially his phrases quoted above in n. 13: "adopted as its own," and "higher-ranking norms binding all."

19. Gregor Ahn, "Israel und Persien," *RGG* (4th ed.) 4.309–11 (at 310).

20. See Wilhelm Spiegelberg, *Die sogenannte Demotische Chronik des Pap. 215 der Bibliothèque Nationale zu Paris nebst den auf der Rückseite des Papyrus stehenden Texten* (Demotische Studien 7; Leipzig:

Demotic Chronicle is, however, contested.[21] At any rate, Frei did not have such a central archive in mind. Ahn's second objection likewise fails to match Frei's intentions. Ahn thinks that Persian imperial policy functioned bottom-up and not top-down. Local authorities, rather than the central administration, initiated processes for the acceptance of local laws. This suggestion completely concurs with Frei's interpretation of the trilingual inscription of Xanthus:

> [D]aß man die Autorisation einholen wolle, ist ein Teil des Volksbe-schlusses. . . . [D]as Ersuchen um die Autorisation [war]. . . . demnach nicht selbstverständlich und also nicht obligatorisch.[22]

> The desire to obtain an authorization is part of the community's de-cree. . . . The attempt to have an authorization issued was neither taken for granted nor obligatory.[23]

Frei remains uncertain about but did not preclude the possibility of top-down processes of imperial authorization, as was the case in the recording of Egyptian laws by Darius I (522–486 B.C.E.).

Another of Wiesehöfer's objections addresses the fact that not all of Frei's examples indicate that the Persian king himself was involved.[24] This observation is correct, but one should not overestimate its importance. Outside of the homeland, the satrap clearly represents the central government and attends to its interests in the particular satrapy.[25] However, for Darius's legislation in Egypt and Ezra's mission in Judah, the sources (Diodorus 1.95.4 and Ezra 7) explicitly mention and even stress that the central government was involved in the process.[26] These two cases in particular, however, at least in their literary presen-

---

Hinrichs, 1914); Thierry Petit, *Satrapes et satrapies dans l'empire achéménide de Cyrus le Grand à Xerxes Ier* (Liège: Bibliothèque de la Faculté de Philosophie et Lettres de l'Université de Liège 254, 1990).

21. Donald B. Redford holds the reports in the Demotic Chronicle to be of little value for the historical reconstruction of Achaemenid Egypt (idem, "The So-Called 'Codification' of Egyptian Law under Darius I," in *Persia and Torah* [ed. J. W. Watts; SBLSymS 17; Atlanta: Scholars Press, 2001] 135–59). Diodorus presents Persian-period Egypt in a Hellenistic fashion, therefore with its own legislation. The Demotic Chronicle, according to Redford, is not a witness to an imperial authorization or codification of Egyptian laws but might reflect the historical translation of economic documents of Egyptian temples into Aramaic, the lingua franca of the Persian Empire, which allowed the Persian authorities to tax and administer these temples.

22. Frei, "Die persische Reichsautorisation," 27.

23. Idem, "Persian Imperial Authorization," 36.

24. Wiesehöfer, "'Reichsgesetz' oder 'Einzelfallgerechtigkeit'?" 44.

25. On the relation between the satraps and the king of kings, see Pierre Briant, *From Cyrus to Alexander: A History of the Persian Empire* (Winona Lake, IN: Eisenbrauns, 2000) 338–47. For this question, see especially Klinkott, *Satrap*, 134. As a rule, satraps were in charge of legal matters; the king of kings could get involved at any point if the local population appealed to him (Briant, *From Cyrus to Alexander*, 345).

26. Frei, "Persian Imperial Authorization," 9–12.

tation, are suspect: they may very well be fictitious, so that one might assume that, *historically*, the involvement of the satrap was the normal case. This stands to reason: the satrap's task in matters of legislation was not only to implement the will of the central government but also to respect local demands. The satrap's duty was to mediate between local and central interests.[27] The explicit involvement of the Persian king in the process might (or might not) be a special feature of literary presentations such as Diodorus and Ezra 7, which have a special interest in highlighting the imperial status of the legislation in relevant parts of the Persian Empire.

Thus far, one may conclude the following: the criticisms that Iranologists such as Wiesehöfer and Ahn make against Frei's theory of the imperial authorization of local laws contain objections based on some *misreadings* of the theory but are not objections to the fundamental theory itself. Therefore, it is only appropriate that contributors to the *Persia and Torah* volume edited by Watts do not unanimously argue *against* the Persian imperial authorization. Gary Knoppers, for example, opts for a more open definition of the process referred to as "imperial authorization." He does not assume a highly centralized and uniform Persian policy of authorizing local norms but recognizes different forms of tolerance toward local autonomy.[28] Joseph Blenkinsopp distances himself to a certain degree from his former support of the theory of "imperial authorization" without rejecting it as a whole.[29] He acknowledges the main evidence for the "imperial authorization" put forward by Frei in the Trilingual of Xanthus and views this process as one of several instruments of the Persian administration that probably was not that important on a large scale.[30]

Knoppers argues that it is indeed prudent to reject a uniformly reductionist notion of "Persian imperial authorization" connected to the idea of a central archive, a central administration, and the central role of the king of kings (instead of a satrap). But his argument would still be in keeping with Peter Frei's theory. Serious problems would arise for Peter Frei, however, if the new monograph by Sebastian Grätz is correct in its objections to the theory of Persian imperial authorization.[31] Grätz builds on the work of his teacher Udo

27. Klinkott, *Satrap*, 148.
28. Knoppers, "Achaemenid Imperial Authorization," 134.
29. Joseph Blenkinsopp, "Was the Pentateuch the Civic and Religious Constitution of the Jewish Ethnos in the Persian Period?" in *Persia and Torah* (ed. J. W. Watts; Atlanta: Scholars Press, 2001) 41–62. For Blenkinsopp's earlier stance, see n. 1, above.
30. Idem, "Was the Pentateuch the Constitution?" 46.
31. Sebastian Grätz, *Das Edikt des Artaxerxes: Eine Untersuchung zum religionspolitischen und historischen Umfeld von Esra 7,12–26* (BZAW 337; Berlin and New York: de Gruyter, 2004); idem, "Esra 7 im Kontext hellenistischer Politik: Der königliche Euergetismus in hellenistischer Zeit als ideeller Hintergrund von Esr 7,12–26," in *Die Griechen und das antike Israel: Interdisziplinäre Studien zur Religions- und Kulturgeschichte des Heiligen Landes* (ed. Stefan Alkier and Markus Witte; OBO

Rüterswörden.[32] He suggests that Ezra 7:12–26 is a Hellenistic deed of donation, because it reflects the Hellenistic praxis of *euergesis*: that is, the practice of
beneficence often undertaken by Hellenistic kings to present themselves as gen-
erous donors to their subdued population. The edict in Ezra 7:12–26 is important especially for the final invocation of sanctions for any infraction: "All who
will not obey *the law of your God and the law of the king*, let judgement be strictly
executed on them, whether for death or for banishment or for confiscation of
their goods or for imprisonment" (Ezra 7:26). This statement has gained a lot of
attention in the discussion about Persian imperial authorization, because scholars have often interpreted the direct juxtaposition of "the law of your [that is,
Ezra's] God" and "the law of the [Persian] king" in 7:26 to indicate that both
entities were identical—in the sense of a Persian authorization of Ezra's law.[33]
"The law of the king" is nowhere introduced in the preceding context, so this
proposal could be an elegant solution to clarifiy the phrase's ambiguity.

According to Grätz, however, Ezra 7:12–26 cannot be evaluated to reconstruct Persian imperial policy. Grätz argues that the edict of Artaxerxes preserved in Ezra 7:12–26 is a Hellenistic fiction. His proposals are unconvincing.
He himself admits that there are very few analogies to the supposed genre of
"endowment grants" that he introduces in his analysis of Ezra 7:12–26.[34] In
addition, the statements in Ezra 7:25–26 have concerns other than an endowment. The sanction mentioned in Ezra 7:26 does not fit the genre, and Grätz
has to explain it away by assuming the textual influence of Deut 17:11–12.[35]
Finally, Grätz's theory depends on his cross-checking of whether there are any
external parallels to Ezra 7:12–26 available in Achaemenid texts:

> Konkret ausgedrückt: Hat es einen persischen "Euergetismus" gege-
> ben, dem sich das Zeugnis Esr 7,12ff z.B. als Schenkung persischer Pro-
> venienz zuordnen lassen könnte?[36]

> Stated concretely: Was there ever a Persian "euergetism," an institu-
> tion to which Ezra 7:12–26 could be a witness, as a donation of Persian
> provenance?

201; Fribourg: Academic Press / Göttingen: Vandenhoeck & Ruprecht, 2004) 131–54. See also
Ernst Baltrusch, "Review of Sebastian Grätz, *Das Edikt des Artaxerxes: Eine Unterschung zum religionspolitischen und historischen Umfeld von Esra 7,12–26* (BZAW 337; Berlin and New York: de Gruyter,
2004)," http://hsozkult.geschichte.hu-berlin.de/rezensionen/2004-4-129.pdf (accessed 29 January
2007).

32. See Rüterswörden, "Die persische Reichsautorisation der Thora."

33. See, for example, Thomas Willi, *Juda–Jehud–Israel: Studien zum Selbstverständnis des Judentums in persischer Zeit* (FAT 12; Tübingen: Mohr Siebeck, 1995) 91–117 and the bibliography provided there.

34. Grätz, *Das Edikt*, 139–40; the examples from Ezra 6:7–13, 8:9–24, and Josephus (*Ant.* 12
§§138–44) are not conclusive.

35. Grätz, ibid., 181.

36. Ibid., 215.

However, this cross-check would only be valid if Ezra 7:12–26 indeed constitutes a "royal endowment," as Grätz maintains. Exactly this point is disputable. Furthermore, it is astonishing that Grätz does not allow the Cyrus Cylinder, the Udjahorresnet naophoros, or the edict by Cyrus in Ezra 6 (compare Ezra 1:1–3) any relevance as possible analogies. This oversight creates the impression that his argumentation involves a *petitio principii*.[37] Even if Grätz is right that Ezra 7 is a Hellenistic text, it still might be possible that Ezra 7 refers to known Persian processes of "imperial authorization" that could be transferred on a literary level in the introduction of the Torah in Judah.

Therefore, Ezra 7 may or may not be a Hellenistic text, and the letter of Artaxerxes may or may not be a fiction, but this is, in any case, not a conclusive argument against the suggestion that Ezra 7 may reflect Persian-period institutions. For example, we know today that Josephus faked the documents he provides in books 14–16 of his *Antiquities*. Still, they contain historically reliable information.[38] Therefore, even if Grätz's dating and interpretation of Ezra 7 were correct, this would not provide a cogent argument against the institution of Persian imperial authorization.[39]

III. The Imperial Authorization of the Torah as a Historical Problem and as a Biblical Construct

If we should (or, better), if we must assume processes whereby local norms were authorized by the Persian Empire—however these processes are identified and determined in detail—then we are now faced with the question of the degree to which the formation of the Torah must be connected with these processes.

---

37. Grätz states that the Cyrus Cylinder is not a "typisches Zeugnis achämenidischer Politik" ("specific witness to Achaemenid policy"). Instead, he argues as follows: "[Kyros hat sich] wie bereits Assurbanipal wesentlicher Motive [neu]babylonischer Königsideologie bedient, um die Anerkennung v.a. der Marduk-Priesterschaft von Esagila zu erlangen" ("[Cyrus] used, as did Ashurbanipal before him, crucial motifs of [Neo-]Babylonian royal ideology in order to gain approval especially from the Marduk priesthood of Esagila") (Grätz, ibid., 222–23). In relation to the Udjahorresnet naophoros, Grätz remarks, "Kambyses agiert in der Udjahorresnet-Inschrift . . . zunächst als ägyptischer Pharao und nicht als persischer König, so dass sich eine besondere Förderung fremder Kulte als Folge der spezifisch persische [sic] Königsideologie nicht nachweisen lässt" ("In the Udjahorresnet inscription . . . Cambyses foremost acts as Egyptian Pharaoh and not as the Persian king. Therefore, a peculiar promotion of foreign cults as a specific consequence of Persian royal ideology cannot be proven") (Grätz, ibid., 233).

38. See, for example, Baltrusch, *Die Juden*, 94, 96 n. 47, 109 n. 123. Compare, however, Grätz, *Das Edikt*, 164 n. 540, with reference to Bernd Schröder, *Die 'väterlichen Gesetze': Flavius Josephus als Vermittler von Halachah an Griechen und Römer* (TSAJ 53; Tübingen: Mohr, 1996).

39. This argument is also valid regarding Lester L. Grabbe, "The Law of Moses in the Ezra Tradition: More Virtual than Real?" in *Persia and Torah* (ed. J. W. Watts; Atlanta: Scholars Press, 2001) 91–113 (at 92–94).

Several possibilities can be imagined in this regard. Aside from the simple question most often debated in current scholarship whether the formation of the Torah (or a literary precursor) should be connected historically with the process of an imperial authorization, we should also discuss whether the Old Testament, most explicitly Ezra 7, interprets the legal implementation of the Torah according to the known model of Persian imperial authorization.

The first possibility is very much disputed. To be sure, Peter Frei himself never proposed that the formation of the Torah should be explained by the theory of imperial authorization. This is one of the most important differences between Frei and Blum. Blum is most explicit on this issue when he places the decisive steps in the composition of the Pentateuch within the context of Persian policies. He postulates two main compositional layers in the Torah, a "Deuteronomistic" (KD) and a "Priestly" (KP) layer.[40] The compositional activities behind these two layers led to the establishment of a proto-Pentateuch in the early Achaemenid period, and part of the motivation behind these activities was, according to Blum, the requirements of Achaemenid politics: "(KD und) KP [wurde] unter anderem auch unter der Perspektive der 'Reichsautorisation' gestaltet."[41] ("(KD and) KP [were] also formed within the perspective of 'imperial authorization.'")

This is especially true for the inclusion of "KP," the "Priestly" compositional layer in the Torah. Blum maintains that, without some external trigger, the process that led to the integration of these two compositional layers into a single Torah could never have taken place of its own accord. In their theological orientation, after all, the two compositional layers relate to each other like fire and ice. I basically agree with Blum's assertion of a "discontinuous composition" that characterizes the combination of Deuteronomistic and Priestly material on a textual level. The different perspective of these texts is so obvious that it has been almost universally recognized, even within the widely diffuse state of current pentateuchal research.

The argument, however, is not conclusive when it comes to its position regarding the lack of analogies for the composition of the Pentateuch out of theologically divergent material. Although other areas of the Old Testament also

---

40. See Erhard Blum, *Die Komposition der Vätergeschichte* (WMANT 57; Neukirchen-Vluyn: Neukirchener Verlag, 1984); and idem, *Studien zur Komposition des Pentateuch*. In these works, KD and KP both are supposed to have a literary extension from Genesis to Deuteronomy. Blum now limits KD to Exodus–Deuteronomy; see his article "Die literarische Verbindung von Erzvätern und Exodus: Ein Gespräch mit neueren Endredaktionshypothesen," in *Abschied vom Jahwisten: Die Komposition des Hexateuch in der jüngsten Diskussion* (ed. Jan Christian Gertz et al.; BZAW 315; Berlin/New York: de Gruyter, 2002) 119–56.

41. Blum, *Studien zur Komposition des Pentateuch*, 358 (parentheses in original; brackets added). Similarly, p. 360 and n. 96 there. See also idem, "Esra," 235–46.

combine diametrically opposed positions, this has not led biblical scholars to conclude that the combination could only have occurred as a result of external pressure. Some passages from the prophetic books provide especially clear examples of this. The process of innerbiblical reinterpretation often leads to theologically conflicting statements. Certain "diaspora-oriented" texts in the book of Jeremiah (for example, Jer 24:8–10 or 29:16–19) announce the dispersion to all regions of the world of those parts of Judah's and Jerusalem's population that were not deported to Babylon in 597 B.C.E.[42] These texts focus on the primacy of the Babylonian diaspora originating from the 597 B.C.E. deportation. However, there is another set of "diaspora-oriented" texts in the book of Jeremiah, including 23:7–8 and 29:14, that disavow such judgment texts and envisage the return of the whole diaspora to Israel's homeland.[43] They argue against the exclusive primacy of the Babylonian golah. Instead, they focus on the worldwide diaspora as a whole as the legitimate "Israel." Therefore, the *combination of conflicting or opposing concepts* within the Torah does not *have* to have occurred due to external pressure. It might be explained with the help of the theory of Persian imperial authorization, but there is no need to do so.

Another problem is the formation of the Pentateuch as Torah. Why have these five books been transformed into a self-contained canonical entity? Here, it might be helpful at least to *discuss* a certain influence from outside to understand why Genesis through Deuteronomy have been segregated as Torah from the larger context of the narrative books reaching from Genesis to Kings.[44] Scholars who deny an influence of this sort need to propose an alternative explanation.

A more specific problem lies in the question how to explain the adoption of the Pentateuch as the Torah by the Samaritans. Did the Samaritans adopt a

---

42. See Konrad Schmid, *Buchgestalten des Jeremiabuches: Untersuchungen zur Redaktions- und Rezeptionsgeschichte von Jer 30–33 im Kontext des Buches* (WMANT 72; Neukirchen-Vluyn: Neukirchener Verlag, 1996) 253–67. The terms "golah orientation" and "diaspora orientation" were introduced by Karl-Friedrich Pohlmann. See idem, *Studien zum Jeremiabuch* (FRLANT 118; Göttingen: Vandenhoeck & Ruprecht, 1978); and idem, *Ezechielstudien: Zur Redaktionsgeschichte des Buches und zur Frage nach den ältesten Texten* (BZAW 202; Berlin: de Gruyter, 1992). See also the acceptance of this distinction by Christoph Levin, *Die Verheißung des neuen Bundes: In ihrem theologiegeschichtlichen Zusammenhang ausgelegt* (FRLANT 137; Göttingen: Vandenhoeck & Ruprecht, 1985).

43. See Schmid, *Buchgestalten*, 270–74.

44. For discussion of some problems of the formation of the Torah, its theological shape, and its historical circumstances, see my *Erzväter und Exodus*, 290–301. See also my "Pentateuchredaktor: Beobachtungen zum theologischen Profil des Toraschlusses in Dtn 34," in *Les dernières rédactions du Pentateuque, de l'Hexateuque et de l'Ennéateuque* (ed. Thomas Römer and Konrad Schmid; BETL 203; Leuven: Peeters, 2007) 183–97; and idem, "The Late Persian Formation of the Torah: Observations on Deuteronomy 34," in *Judah and the Judeans in the Fourth Century B.C.E.* (ed. Oded Lipschits, Gary Knoppers, and Rainer Albertz; Winona Lake, IN: Eisenbrauns, 2007) 237–51.

Torah that the Judeans had already accepted as a normative text? Or should one think instead of a parallel process in Samaria that led to the adoption of the To-rah as a normative text there? If things are complicated for the case of Judah, this is the more true for Samaria, because historical data for this community and its textual basis in ancient times are hard to determine. Traditionally, scholars have postulated a schism between Judeans and Samaritans in the Persian or early Hellenistic period and have claimed that the introduction of the Torah in Judah was a *terminus a quo* for this schism, which was followed by a final split in the pe-riod of the Hasmoneans or even later.[45] More recent research tends to avoid the "schism" terminology, because it presumes a former unity. On a related note, the archaeological evaluation of the excavations on Mount Gerizim in search of a Samaritan temple or cult place seem to have radically changed in the last few years. In the early 1990s, Yitzhak Magen stated that there were no remnants discernible on Mount Gerizim that antedate the 2nd century B.C.E.[46] Now he claims that the origins of the cult place on Mount Gerizim have to be dated as early as the 6th century B.C.E.[47] Given these recent changes in scholarship, it is no longer possible to adhere to a simple "schism" theory of Samaritan origins, which in turn has repercussions for how to determine the Samaritans' introduc-tion of the Torah. At any rate, further treatments of the promulgation of the Torah in Judah cannot proceed *etsi Samaria non daretur.*

Be this as it may, for the Ezra narratives—especially in Ezra 7–10 but also in Nehemiah 8—one point is clear: the logic of the story aims at presenting Ezra's law as a document equipped with the authority of the Persian Empire.[48] And this is the reason that Meyer in 1896 and Hans Heinrich Schaeder in 1941 could conceive of the institution of Persian imperial authorization.[49] Therefore it is necessary to explain why it is that Ezra 7 can argue in this way. And here again, several possibilities must be considered: (1) Ezra 7 correctly reports the imperial authorization of the Torah, (2) Ezra 7 is a late text but still correctly re-

---

45. See the discussion in Ingrid Hjelm, "What Do Samaritans and Jews Have in Common? Recent Trends in Samaritan Studies," *CurBR* 3 (2004) 9–59 (at 14). See also Alan D. Crown and Reinhard Pummer, *A Bibliography of the Samaritans* (Lanham, MD: Scarecrow, 2005).

46. See Ephraim Stern and Yitzhaq Magen, "Archaeological Evidence for the First Stage of the Samaritan Temple on Mount Gerizim," *IEJ* 52 (2002) 49–57.

47. Hjelm, "Samaritans," 19–20. See the report in the e-newsletter, "The Samaritan Update," http://shomron0.tripod.com/2004/jul29.html (accessed 29 January 2007).

48. See Kratz, *Translatio imperii*, 233–41 (especially 236); Grabbe, "The Law of Moses in the Ezra Tradition." On Rolf Rendtorff, "Esra und das 'Gesetz,'" *ZAW* 96 (1984) 165–84, see Kratz, *Translatio imperii*, 238 n. 380, and Rendtorff's own clarifications in "Noch einmal: Esra und das 'Gesetz,'" *ZAW* 111 (1999) 89–91. See also Bob Becking, "The Idea of Torah in Ezra 7–10: A Functional Analysis," *ZABR* 7 (2001) 273–86; Willi, *Juda–Jehud–Israel*, 90–91.

49. See the quotation from Meyer, *Die Entstehung des Judenthums*, given above, p. 24. See also Hans Heinrich Schaeder, *Das persische Weltreich* (Breslau: Korn, 1941).

ports the imperial authorization of the Torah, or (3) Ezra 7 is a late text and presents the imperial authorization of the Torah as fiction. Which option is the right one? For the moment, it is impossible to determine.[50] But it must be stressed again: Ezra 7 assumes the imperial authorization of the Torah, whether this account is historically true or not.[51]

IV. Conclusions

What conclusions can be drawn from this discussion? If the theory of Persian imperial authorization is evaluated apart from its reduction by its critics, then it should have become clear that mere rejection is too simple an option. The sources clearly are witness to varying processes of authorization of local norms by the Persian authorities. These processes of authorization do not imply the creation and maintenance of a central archive for authorized norms, the personal involvement of the Persian king in each act of authorization, or the necessary initiation of this sort of process by the Persians. Still, this does not mean that little remains of the theory—we must continue to emphasize that no analogy exists in the ancient Near East for the fact that the central Persian government lent its authority to local norms.

How the formation of the Torah should be connected with these processes of authorization currently remains an open question. It is unlikely that this formation had *nothing* to do with these processes. This basic assumption is made clear

---

50. Especially problematic for the option of a "historical" imperial authorization of the Torah could be the fact that the Torah, at least in its main parts in Exodus 19 to Numbers 10, is presented as God's law: "Indem die Autoren des Pentateuch JHWH zur Rechtsquelle der für 'Israel' als Gottesgesetz verbindlichen Sinaitora einsetzen . . . widersprechen sie dem Anspruch des achämenidischen Großkönigs, Dekrete im Namen des persischen Großen Gottes als Schöpfergottes in der Welt zu verkünden" ("Because the authors of the Pentateuch enlisted YHWH as the legal source for the Torah from Sinai that is authoritative for 'Israel' as divine law . . . they opposed the claim of the Achaemenid Great King to promulgate decrees to the world in the name of the Persian Great God as the creator God"; Otto, "Rechtshermeneutik," 105–6). Nevertheless, according to the Priestly notion, it is clear that "God" in the Pentateuch is an inclusive concept; see my "Differenzierungen und Konzeptualisierungen der Einheit Gottes in der Religions- und Literaturgeschichte Israels: Methodische, religionsgeschichtliche und exegetische Aspekte zur neueren Diskussion um den sogenannten 'Monotheismus' im antiken Israel," in *Der eine Gott und die Götter: Polytheismus und Monotheismus im antiken Israel* (ed. Manfred Oeming and Konrad Schmid; ATANT 82; Zürich: Theologischer Verlag, 2003) 11–38. Therefore, in this perspective, "Elohim" can be understood as an inclusive cipher for Ahura-mazda, Zeus, or YHWH. Israel, according to its own tradition, follows "God's" own Law which is, however, mediated by its Mosaic interpretation in Deuteronomy.

51. Here, I cannot discuss the problem of various possible layers in Ezra 7, as, for example, Pakkala suggests (see *Ezra the Scribe*, 301–9). Pakkala's proposal might lead to different perceptions of the Torah in various stages of the literary development of Ezra 7. Pakkala holds the Artaxerxes rescript to be a (multilayered) redactional expansion of Ezra 1–6 (pp. 45–49, 297), but he does not preclude the possibility that it reworked authentic material.

by the Artaxerxes decree in Ezra 7, completely independent of whether the text is authentic or not or whether it is Persian or Hellenistic. Ezra 7 shows us that the author of this text was familiar with processes of authorizing local norms and that he described Ezra's presentation of the Torah to his readers in this context. It is also important not to forget the difficulties that arise if the theory is cast aside altogether: Why did the closure of the Pentateuch occur, to a large degree, during the Persian era? Better theories must be brought forward to explain how the Pentateuch could have gained the status of the Torah. The statement that the Torah is a product of Jewish scribal scholarship will not suffice, for this is true of the entire Hebrew Bible.

The Rise of Torah

David M. Carr

Union Theological Seminary, New York

I. The Question of the Rise of Torah

This essay attempts to answer a particular, strategically important question about the rising status (and the function) of the pentateuchal Torah (hereafter usually "Torah") in later periods of Israel's history.[1] In particular, the focus is on the rise of the Torah to fundamental importance across Second Temple Judaism, where it enjoyed a status not just as a foundational educational document but as a law that forms a community. This question has assumed particular importance for two reasons. The first is that recent developments in pentateuchal scholarship have shown that the Pentateuch—as a narrative extending from creation to wilderness—was not formed as such until the exilic and postexilic periods. Up through the late 1980s and early 1990s, many scholars still assumed that, at the start of the history of Judah and Israel as states, there already were proto-Torah documents, for example, the Yahwistic (J) and Elohistic (E) sources. According to this older consensus, the Pentateuch had always been a part of Israel's written history; the only question was under what circumstances and why its different sources were combined and authorized as foundational for Second Temple Judaism.

In recent years, at least for pentateuchal specialists, that consensus is now a thing of the past. Very few scholars active in the study of the composition of

Author's note: As with other essays in this volume, this one grows out of an oral presentation at the International Meeting of the Society of Biblical Literature in Edinburgh, Scotland, in July of 2006. It builds on prior publications by the author, along with work in progress that will be presented in full in other contexts, particularly a long-term project on the history of Israelite literature. It was not possible—given space constraints of the essay form and time constraints of the author—to eliminate the dependence of these parts of the essay on arguments presented more fully in other contexts. I thank the organizers and participants in the sessions at Edinburgh for this opportunity to formulate, refine, and receive feedback on this initial synthesis, and I thank the editors for their very careful work in suggesting additional bibliography and other revisions to the essay.

1. *Pentateuchal* is used as an initial modifier for *Torah* to recognize the fact that the word *Torah* is used in Judaism to refer to other wholes as well, particularly the *oral Torah* tradition as reflected in the Mishnah and other authoritative Jewish documents. The focus of this essay, however, is on the "Torah" in the sense of the written, pentateuchal Torah.

the Pentateuch advocate the idea of a preexilic J source, let alone an E source of any kind. Instead, as the recent books about the end of the "Yahwist" hypothesis have made clear, there appears to be an increasing consensus that major parts of the Torah tradition—especially the ancestral history and the Moses story—were not joined until a late point in Israel's history, either just before P or by P in the exilic period.[2] If this new consensus holds, it would mean that there was no creation-to-wilderness proto-pentateuchal document to be authorized and focused on until the 6th century. The time of basic composition of such a document and authorization of it are compressed, so that the exilic and postexilic periods appear to be the central times for the rise of a Torah document, both for its existence as a connected narrative and its rise to fundamental legal status.

Furthermore, I maintain that one of the most important developments in the history of Israelite literature, if not the most important, is the rise of the Torah to the point where it became the foundation of Second Temple Jewish education, replacing the sorts of foundational wisdom materials that previously played this role and serving as a document that helps constitute the postexilic Jewish community. The background for this approach to the question is given in my book *Writing on the Tablet of the Heart*.[3] There I argue that literary-theological texts of the sort seen in the Bible, including the Torah, were used primarily in a process of education of royal, priestly, military, and bureaucratic elites. This is not to deny the existence of many other forms of written textuality or the initial formation of some pentateuchal traditions in other contexts. There is epigraphic and other evidence of administrative texts (for example, the Samaria ostraca), graffiti, correspondence, display texts, and other documents in ancient Israel. Moreover, past scholarship was on target in suggesting that some traditions now in the Pentateuch—for example, songs or cultic instructions—had their original home in clan, temple and other institutional contexts. Nevertheless, administrative and display texts generally were not transmitted as such in scroll form to later generations, and not all songs and institution-bound texts found their way into corpora transmitted in book form over a long period of time—long-duration texts. Rather, if such a text entered what Oppenheim aptly called the "stream of tradition," for example, becoming part of the Pentateuch, it was moved from its original clan, temple, or other Sitz im Leben to a context of

---

2. The growing literature coming to this conclusion is discussed and summarized in two volumes: Jan Christian Gertz et al., *Abschied vom Jahwisten: Die Komposition des Hexateuch in der jüngsten Diskussion* (BZAW 315; Berlin: de Gruyter, 2002); and Thomas B. Dozeman and Konrad Schmid, eds., *A Farewell to the Yahwist? The Composition of the Pentateuch in Recent European Interpretation* (SBLSymS 34; Atlanta: Society of Biblical Literature, 2006).

3. David M. Carr, *Writing on the Tablet of the Heart: Origins of Scripture and Literature* (New York: Oxford University Press, 2005).

ongoing oral–written education and (more limited and occasional) communal presentation.[4]

This claim is based on three types of evidence: comparative models from outside Israel, textual indicators in both biblical and nonbiblical Israelite texts, and text-critical evidence in the transmission of biblical traditions. Models outside Israel show that the primary context for transmission of long-duration "literary" texts (thus not documentary or display texts) was education and enculturation. Those who would argue for other contexts' being primary for textuality in Israel must bear the burden of proof.[5] Furthermore, the more we understand the character of this sort of education in the ancient world, the clearer it becomes that the Bible itself and other texts from the Levant point to the existence of text-supported literary education in and around Israel.[6] Finally, parallel traditions in the Bible display the kinds of variants typically found in written traditions that are memorized, again probably in the context of literary education.[7]

To avoid misunderstanding, I should note that this was not education merely of those who would later function as textual professionals—"scribes" in the

---

4. For Oppenheim's phrase, see A. Leo Oppenheim, *Ancient Mesopotamia: Portrait of a Dead Civilization* (rev. and ed. Erica Reiner; Chicago: University of Chicago Press, 1977) 13. In a recent review of my book *Writing on the Tablet of the Heart,* James A. Sanders states in a note that "Norbert Lohfink some twenty-five years ago noted the role of wisdom schools in canon formation in his *Kohelet* (Wurzburg: Echter, 1980)—the place Carr starts but does not mention" (James A. Sanders, review of David M. Carr, *Writing on the Tablet of the Heart, Review of Biblical Literature* [October 2006], accessed 30 January 2007. Online: http://www.bookreviews.org/pdf/4703_5599 .pdf, 2 n. 1). Yet Lohfink was working with a concept of separate "wisdom" schools that this author does not share. Rather than seeing Scripture as formed in separate "schools," let alone separate "wisdom schools" for some kind of separate class of sages, I work with a model in which various elites educated their children (and some others) in family or pseudofamily contexts (in which a teacher served as a teaching "father" to his "sons"). This model comes from new analyses of education elsewhere in the ancient Near East that were not available to Lohfink and others at the time of his writing. For more on familial and nonfamilial contexts of schooling, see my *Writing on the Tablet of the Heart,* 20–21, 66–68, and 113. For more on the problem of separate classes of "scribes" behind the Bible, see below in this essay.

5. The comparative argument is the focus of ibid., 17–109, 177–99.

6. Many of the relevant texts from the Bible are discussed in ibid., 111–73. Note also extensive evidence of this sort of education in the Second Temple period (ibid., 201–72). In addition, I have written a preliminary survey of evidence for text-supported literary education in the Levant that will be a chapter in a book (in progress), tentatively entitled *Studies in the History of Israelite Literature.*

7. The discussion of the research on these variants and a survey of them is likewise part of my book in progress, *Studies in the History of Israelite Literature.* A preliminary discussion of relevant literature and examples of these variants is in my "Empirische Perspektiven auf das Deuteronomistische Geschichtswerk," in *Die deuteronomistischen Geschichtswerke: Redaktions- und religionsgeschichtliche Perspektiven zur 'Deuteronomismus' Diskussion in Tora und Vorderen Propheten* (ed. Marcus Witte et al.; BZAW 365; Berlin: de Gruyter, 2006) 3–5.

narrower sense. Rather, comparative evidence, even from supposedly "scribal" cultures such as Egypt and Mesopotamia, indicates that literary production and reception happened primarily in education of future priestly, royal-bureaucratic, military and other elites—including but not limited to the sorts of full-time textual professionals that many associate with the word *scribe*. In these cultures, words for *scribe* often designated something equivalent to a term such as "college graduate" (theoretically capable of a variety of upper-level professions) rather than just *scribe* in the sense of a textual-administrative professional.[8] The focus of literary education on a variety of sorts of elites is yet more clear in ancient Greek education, a culture in which the terms equivalent to "scribe" (e.g., γραμματεύς) are more clearly limited to—often lower-level—textual professionals. For these reasons, it often is misleading to speak of literary education in the ancient world as "scribal" education. Instead, the common denominator—whether in cultures that focused on the education of "scribes" in a broad sense or in cultures, such as Greece, that used other labels for their elites—was a focus on use of literary education to separate out from broader society a minority group who could fill a variety of bureaucratic and leadership positions.[9]

The significance of the rise of Torah becomes clearer when we examine the educational curricula of better-documented systems in Mesopotamia, Egypt, and Greece. These ancient societies typically used certain types of texts in a particular order. The educational process started with the mastery of the sign system through sign lists or abecedaries. Next came "transitional materials": that is, explicitly pedagogical instructions, gnomic collections, and hymns. Whether Egyptian instructions, Mesopotamian proverb collections, or Greek

---

8. As pointed out by Sumerologists and Assyriologists, the term *scribe* functions in a broader sense than is often assumed in Mesopotamia; see Piotr Michalowski, "Charisma and Control: On Continuity and Change in Early Mesopotamian Bureaucratic Systems," in *The Organization of Power: Aspects of Bureaucracy in the Ancient Near East* (ed. M. Gibson and R. D. Biggs; SAOC 46; Chicago: Oriental Institute, 1987) 62; Herman L. J. Vanstiphout, "On the Old Edubba Education," in *Centres of Learning: Learning and Location in Pre-Modern Europe and the Near East* (ed. Jan Willem Drijvers and Alisdair A. MacDonald; Brill's Studies in Intellectual History 61; Leiden: Brill, 1995) 7–8, 15; Niek Veldhuis, *Elementary Education at Nippur: The Lists of Trees and Wooden Objects* (Groningen: Styx, 1997) 143–44; Petra Gesche, *Schulunterricht in Babylonien im ersten Jahrtausend v. Chr.* (AOAT 275; Münster: Ugarit-Verlag, 2001) 14–16. The same is true in Egypt: Jac J. Janssen and Rosalind M. Janssen, *Growing Up in Ancient Egypt* (London: Rubicon, 1990) 67–68; John Baines and Christopher Eyre, "Four Notes on Literacy," *Göttinger Miszellen* 61 (1983) 87; Jan Assmann, "Kulturelle und literarische Texte," in *Ancient Egyptian Literature: History and Forms* (ed. Antonio Loprieno; Probleme der Ägyptologie 10; Leiden: Brill, 1996) 66–71.

9. Some maintain that Greece or Israel or both achieved something approaching universal literacy. This idea has been shown in a variety of areas to be highly anachronistic for the ancient world. For discussion and an overview of the relevant studies see my *Writing on the Tablet of the Heart*, 13, 20, 70–71 n. 43, 102–4, 115–22, 165–66, 172–73, 187–91, 247, 271, and 278.

gnomic sayings, these transitional materials taught basic social values and served as a foundation for later study. The student then progressed to a broader array of genres of literature: pro–royal propaganda, royal legal decree literature, myths of origins, love songs, and so on.[10]

This overview of ancient educational curricula is the background for consideration of the emerging role of the Torah in ancient Israelite education.[11] If the Bible started out as a collection of educational texts, the single most important development in the formation of the Hebrew Bible is the rise of the Torah to fundamental prominence, including cultic-legal prominence, in a variety of parts of Judaism widely conceived: from Jerusalem to the diaspora, from the temple leadership to outlying groups such as the Samaritans and Qumran community. This development involves not just the writing of major parts of the Torah, not just the joining of these parts and strands into the complex whole of the present Torah, not just their inclusion in the stream of Jewish educational tradition, not just their placement at the foundation of Judean education, but the composition and establishment of the composite Torah as the constitutive legal foundation of education in Judah, most parts of the Jewish diaspora, and even what would become the Samaritan community.

Judging from comparative evidence, "in the beginning" there were various forms of textual "wisdom" in which Torah is either not reflected at all or is reflected in very subtle ways. Indeed, at the outset of Israelite textuality, sometime in the preexilic period, Israel's educational system probably was most similar to older Mesopotamian and Egyptian systems on which it was initially built. Just as Mesopotamian and Egyptian systems began with proverbs, instructions, and hymns as their foundational texts, it is likely that Israel—at least in its earliest stages when it was most dependent on outside models—likewise started with *some* of the texts we now see in Proverbs and Psalms, these texts serving as foundational texts for the rest of the curriculum, teaching basic social values. The pre-Torah origins of these materials would explain the remarkable lack of reference to Torah (or prophetic) themes in many of these texts.[12]

Nevertheless, by the 2nd century B.C.E., things have changed. Authors of wisdom texts, such as Ben Sira and the Wisdom of Solomon, present "wisdom" as founded first and foremost on the Torah of Moses, and the constitutive role of the Torah is obvious among late Second Temple communities, for example, the Qumran community, Samaritans, Sadducees and Pharisees, the Alexandrian

---

10. Ibid., 22–27, 68–70, 178–84.

11. For some qualifications about this kind of use of the word *curriculum* for these ancient practices, see ibid., 12.

12. The issue of dating Proverbs and other texts relevant here is fraught and will be engaged at length in another context. At the very least, the potential early origin of major swathes of Proverbs 10–24 is widely recognized.

diaspora, and the Hasmonean monarchy as ideologically represented in texts such as 1 and 2 Maccabees.[13] The Pentateuch is the first of the biblical corpora to be translated into Greek, Moses is the Jewish "Homer," and the law is the Jewish correlate to the Stoic *nomos*. Moreover, in most of these traditions the *legal* status of the Torah as "law," "laws of the fathers," and so on, has risen to the forefront.

This reflects a shift in the educational system for literate elites across various sectors of Judaism. Not the "wisdom" of a sage like Solomon but the law mediated through Moses has become the source of fundamental values on which the rest of Jewish literary education is built. Eventually, in later rabbinic-period education, Jewish students start with Leviticus, not Proverbs, at the outset of their literary education. In other words, the Torah becomes the first and most foundational text in the Jewish educational curriculum—a curriculum extending to include non-Torah writings as well, writings now understood as "prophecy."[14]

As Reinhard Kratz argues in his essay for this volume, this focus on the Torah was not a universal phenomenon early on (for example, in Elephantine), and this rise of pentateuchal instruction took different forms in different parts of Second Temple Judaism. Nevertheless, the redating of pentateuchal literature and other research makes it ever more clear that this centering of Jewish education on the Torah, which is a nonroyal instruction placed outside the land in a distant past, was a massive *innovation*. Now all who are educated start with the Torah. Only once they memorize it (or a portion of it) do they progress to non-Torah holy writings, "Prophets," and possibly (for some elites) more esoteric writings, for example, the Pseudepigrapha and other instructional texts of the sort found at Qumran.

To be clear, all this pertains to education of elites. Nevertheless, by the Second Temple period, the composition of this elite in ancient Israel has shifted and narrowed. Previously, the elites educated in preexilic Israel were leaders in the royal bureaucracy, military, and priesthood. This was a minority, however much this group of literate elites may have expanded in the later preexilic period.[15] Yet the constitution of a postmonarchic, postexilic "Israel" out of for-

---

13. Carr, *Writing on the Tablet of the Heart*, 209–14, 225–34, 245, 247.

14. For a discussion of how this category encompasses books in both the present "Prophets" and "Writings" category of the Jewish Tanach, see ibid., 167, 209–10, 213, 234–36, 264–67.

15. As suggested by William Schniedewind, Lachish 3 (along with other evidence) points to broadening literacy toward the end of the preexilic period. See idem, "Sociolinguistic Reflections on the Letter of a 'Literate' Soldier (Lachish 3)," *ZAH* 13 (2000) 157–67; and my *Writing on the Tablet of the Heart*, 165–66. I would not go as far as Schniedewind does, however, in positing that "basic literacy became commonplace" (William Schniedewind, *How the Bible Became a Book* [Cambridge: Cambridge University Press, 2004] 91). Though there were utopian visions of general

merly exiled Judean elites produced—at least temporarily—a new situation in which a majority of the males of a part of Israel (in exile) were literate. Insofar as "Israel" eventually was redefined as being constituted by this returnee community (of largely literate elite families), there was potential at the outset of the Persian period for a much higher level of literacy than was typical in the ancient world. Later in the Hellenistic period, this may have been encouraged yet further by Jewish engagement with Hellenistic ideals of general education. These factors may explain the unusually specific descriptions of general education found in Philo (*Hypothetica* 7.10–13) and especially Josephus (*Ag. Ap.* 1.60; 2.204) toward the end of the Second Temple period.[16]

Meanwhile, with the end of the monarchy, literacy is increasingly centered in the one institution still under continuing Judean control: the temple with its priesthood. Though groups formerly associated with nonpriestly groups probably persisted into the early postexilic period, it appears that literacy—particularly literacy in Hebrew literary-theological texts of the sort found in the Bible—became increasingly exclusively connected to members of Priestly families.[17] We see this emphasis on the particularly Priestly locus of textuality and education in late biblical writings, Ben Sira, and various pseudepigraphic and other writings found at Qumran and elsewhere, Josephus, Philo, early Christian writings, and Hecataeus of Abdera (as quoted by Diodorus of Sicily 40.3–5), among other loci.[18] The significance for my purposes is the following: the Torah stands at the outset of an educational curriculum primarily intended for (a) members of priestly families (whether cultic professionals or not) and (b) an Israel that is increasingly understood as a holy, priestly nation.

This does not mean that the Torah now served as a priestly how-to manual to a group of cultic professionals. Rather, it means that the Torah was the kind of oral-written literature that was used to enculturate and shape various sorts of students in Second Temple Judah. Whether they were children of acting priests, members of priestly families who did not work in the temple cult, or other Judeans who partook of (largely) priestly education, these students appear to have been educated in a curriculum that started with the Torah before proceeding to the non-Torah books (Prophets) and, possibly, other literature.

---

education of some kind in Deuteronomy (for example, Deut 4:6–8; see also 6:6, 11:18), a variety of kinds of evidence suggests that Israel, like all other ancient cultures, enjoyed only limited male literacy among its leadership elites (Carr, *Writing on the Tablet of the Heart*, 115–22).

16. Ibid., 244–47.

17. On the persistence of these groups, see Schniedewind, *How the Bible Became a Book*, 158–64.

18. Carr, *Writing on the Tablet of the Heart*, 201–39. Much of this discussion builds on a superb but, sadly, unpublished essay by Stephen Fraade: "'They Shall Teach Your Statutes to Jacob': Priests, Scribes, and Sages in Second Temple Times," unpublished essay (2003).

So far, this essay merely proposes posing the "Torah question" a certain way: the history of Israelite literature can be conceived as the move from older forms of educational literature to a distinctive curriculum centered on the Torah. It is this fundamental move—the reorganization of Jewish education and Jewish community around the Torah—that is the foremost datum that must be explained in a history of Israelite literature. The question now is: how and why did this recentering occur?

II. When and How Did the Torah Rise to Prominence?

The balance of this essay will venture a preliminary answer to this question, tracing three major stages in the composition and rise of the Torah: the initial composition of separate narratives, the creation of the first creation-to-wilderness (non-P and P) proto-pentateuchal narratives in the Exile, and the eventual combination of those narratives during the Postexilic Period into a Torah at the center of late Second Temple Judaism.

1. Preexilic Beginnings

One might begin the story of the rise of the Torah with a discussion of its composition, whether of the whole or its parts. It seems, however, that the field of Hebrew Bible scholarship is farther than it once was from a clear picture of the origins of the Pentateuch. This is due partly to above-mentioned developments in pentateuchal scholarship and partly to the fact that the date and composition of nonpentateuchal evidence (for example, Hosea) is also subject to significant debate. Nevertheless, there are a number of indicators that point to probable Northern origins for early pentateuchal traditions: internal evidence of place- and personal names in Genesis 25–50, parallels between Moses and the picture of Jeroboam in Exodus 2–5, tantalizing references to Northern place-names at the heart of Deuteronomy (Deut 27:11–12), and the earliest possible external testimony to traditions now found in our Torah in a Northern prophet, Hosea, in Hosea 12.[19] Yet, even if one were to look to the preexilic

---

19. The place to go both for earlier literature and excellent textual observations, despite refinements, many introduced by the author himself, is Erhard Blum's discussion of Northern elements throughout *Die Komposition der Vätergeschichte* (WMANT 57; Neukirchen-Vluyn: Neukirchener Verlag, 1984) 66–203, 234–44, 250–57. On the parallels between Moses and the picture of Jeroboam, see Rainer Albertz, *Religionsgeschichte Israels in alttestamentlicher Zeit*, vol. 1: *Von den Anfängen bis zum Ende der Königszeit* (GAT 8/1; Göttingen: Vandenhoeck & Ruprecht, 1992) 215–19; John Van Seters, *The Life of Moses: The Yahwist as Historian in Exodus–Numbers* (Louisville, KY: Westminster John Knox, 1994) 32; James Nohrnberg, *Like unto Moses: The Constituting of a Literary Interruption* (Indiana Studies in Biblical Literature; Bloomington, IN: Indiana University Press, 1995) 282–96. Note also David Damrosch's observation about the agreement in the names of Jeroboam I's and Aaron's sons in "Leviticus," in *The Literary Guide to the Bible* (ed. Robert Alter and Frank Kermode;

North for the origins of the Torah traditions (in the plural!), those origins would be mere fragments of what later becomes the Pentateuch, not much like the full span of the Torah of Moses, the complex whole whose rise is the focus of this investigation.

As the majority of scholars would recognize, the earliest probable beginnings of the story of the rise of the Torah lie in the reign of Josiah, with his apparent reform of the state and cult around centralization and purification regulations found in the Deuteronomic version of the Mosaic Torah (2 Kgs 22:3–23:20//2 Chr 34:14–33). Yet even the Josiah narratives, particularly the expanded account now provided in 2 Kings, are historically questionable on a number of counts.[20] Moreover, even if Josiah's reform did involve the first instantiation of Torah as a legal document that shaped the Israelite community, this move apparently did not persist. Whereas the Deuteronomistic Historian(s) occasionally praise kings up to and including Josiah, the history following Josiah has nothing good to say about the faithfulness of his successors, and this is corroborated by narrative traditions found in Jeremiah.

At the very least, the Torah of Moses that was eventually accepted by Judaism included a variety of traditions beyond Josiah's lawbook: for example, the Covenant Code on which parts of Deuteronomy depended, narrative traditions of various sorts, and Priestly materials. Furthermore, if the substance of the biblical account of the kings that followed Josiah is reliable, his "reform" was relatively short-lived, with the scribes that stood behind his reform marginalized and the law at the center of the reform ignored. Nevertheless, the importance of Josiah's reform grew in the collective memory, as reflected in the expansive coverage of him in 2 Kings 22–23, and in the parallel made between him and Ezra in 1 Esdras. Whatever Josiah's reform once was, it later became cause to understand the postexilic installation of a broader Torah as a *restoration* of a former state of things, rather than as an innovation.[21]

Cambridge, MA: Belknap, 1987) 70–71. For a discussion of another way of understanding the significance of place-names and other potential Northern elements in Deuteronomy, see the essay by Nihan in this volume. I am not as inclined as some recent authors to date these and other elements of the Hosea tradition to a very late period of Israel's history.

20. See, for example, Philip R. Davies, *In Search of "Ancient Israel"* (JSOTSup 148; Sheffield: JSOT Press, 1992) 40–41; idem, *Scribes and Schools: The Canonization of the Hebrew Scriptures* (Library of Ancient Israel; Louisville: Westminster John Knox, 1998) 96–99. For discussion of the problem of the expanded version of this story in Kings, see preliminarily Steven McKenzie, *The Chronicler's Use of the Deuteronomistic History* (HSM 33; Atlanta: Scholars Press, 1984) 168–69.

21. On this see Gary N. Knoppers, *Two Nations under God: The Deuteronomic History of Solomon and the Two Monarchies*, vol. 2: *The Reign of Jeroboam, the Fall of Israel, and the Reign of Josiah* (HSM 53; Atlanta: Scholars Press, 1994) 221–28.

2. The Formation and Rise of Pentateuchal Corpora in the Diaspora

The next major period in the story of the rise of Torah is the period of Exile of large numbers of Judean elites by the Neo-Babylonians. As in the case of Josiah's "reform," the case of the "Exile" (with an end) seems as much a development in collective memory as an actual event, because the concept of a period of "Exile" is itself an ideological product of the elites who gained control of Persian-period Yehud and depicted their story as one of return and retrieval.[22] Certainly our resources for studying this time are limited, aside from a few laments explicitly related to the destruction and diaspora (Psalm 137 and Lamentations), Ezekiel, and some prophecy that seems to date to this time (for example, Isaiah 40–55). There are no narratives to work with between the story of Jehoiachin's being raised in status in 577 (2 Kgs 25:27–30) and the Cyrus edict located in 539 (2 Chr 36:22–23//Ezra 1:1–4). Between these two events, there probably was nothing to be placed in a Judean royal history to be used for education and enculturation, and thus no history-like prose account was written about the period itself. Within the ancient Near East, extended historical writing is virtually always the account of institutions and their leaders for education and enculturation of leaders in a monarchal state.[23] If the state is lacking, there is little to no creation of "history."[24]

That said, there are internal indicators that this period was important in Judah's shaping of its stories about its prestate history, particularly the Pentateuch. Already there are hints of the increasing importance of pre-land traditions in

---

22. Daniel Christopher-Smith, "Reassessing the Historical and Sociological Impact of the Babylonian Exile (597/587–539 B.C.E.)," in *Exile: Old Testament, Jewish and Christian Conceptions* (ed. James M. Scott; Supplements to the Journal for the Study of Judaism 56; Leiden: Brill, 1997) 23–35; Steed V. Davidson, *Finding a Place: A Postcolonial Examination of the Ideology of Place in the Book of Jeremiah* (Ph.D. diss., Union Theological Seminary, New York, 2005) 221–26.

23. To be sure, the earliest chronicles in Mesopotamia were created for various purposes. For recent coverage of early Mesopotamian material, see Jean-Jacques Glassner, *Mesopotamian Chronicles* (ed. Benjamin Foster; SBLWAW 19; Atlanta: Society of Biblical Literature / Leiden: Brill, 2004). Nevertheless, the observation made here refers to more-extended historical narratives, such as the *Epic of Tukulti-Ninurta*, which are more analogous to the extended narratives found in the Hebrew Bible. On this text, see Peter Machinist, "Literature as Politics: The Tukulti-Ninurta Epic and the Bible," *CBQ* 38 (1976) 455–74.

24. The word "history" is in quotation marks to indicate the problematic character of applying this term to many of the narrative materials under discussion. The above point is illustrated by the gaps in the biblical record. The only information communicated about the exilic period is the above-mentioned fragment about Jehoiachin's being raised in status (2 Kgs 25:27–30) and some fragments about the postdestruction government of Judah (2 Kgs 25:22–26; Jer 40:7–16, 51:1–18). This issue of the Sitz im Leben of ancient Near Eastern history will be a topic in my previously mentioned book in progress, *Studies in the History of Israelite Literature*. For now, some preliminary reflections (and bibliography) are in my *Royal Ideology and the Technology of Faith: A Comparative Midrash Study of 1 Kgs 3:2–15* (Ph.D. diss., Claremont Graduate University, 1988) 134–39.

the reflections of semi-pentateuchal materials in Ezekiel (for example, 20:1–26) and Deutero-Isaiah (for example, Isa 43:16–21, 51:1–2). Furthermore, the Exile provides the most plausible context for a number of developments seen in the pentateuchal traditions themselves. These include the transfer of royal attributes to a landless ancestor in the form of the Abrahamic promise, the extension to Abraham of foundational traditions of the Jacob cult (with the proviso that he only "called on YHWH's name" at non-Jerusalem cult sites [Gen 12:8, 13:4, 21:13]), and certain features of the broader Priestly narrative tradition that are best placed in the diaspora.[25]

These and other indicators support the hypothesis that this period of Exile was the time when the various fragments of pentateuchal tradition became the founding story for what were then Judean exiles. At the very time they were landless and in the diaspora, these authors transformed what were once stories of patriarchs gaining land into a prologue to Israel's sojourn in Egypt. Before, stories such as the Jacob narrative told of ancestors gaining a claim to the land directly. But once these stories were placed in a sequence that led to wilderness wandering, these ancestral traditions were transformed into a broader story of Israel's pre-land beginnings, with the ancestors living as strangers in the land that will become their children's only later, after the Egyptian oppression, Exodus, and wilderness wandering. In other words, the construction of a connected Torah out of separate ancestral and Exodus traditions is a crucial move in the transformation of those once separate traditions into a continual story of Israel's origins *outside the land*, from Abraham's reception of the promise in Haran to the reception of legal instructions on Mount Sinai and in the wilderness.

Indeed, this move toward the joining of ancestral and Exodus-wilderness traditions was so natural and compelling that it took place on the level of the non-P traditions and of the P traditions, both of which reflect probable origins in the experience of the diaspora of various waves of Judean elites.[26] It was these pre-land traditions that drew the sustained attention of literate Judeans in the diaspora. Moreover, the diaspora was the point at which these traditions—

---

25. For a summary of major features of the broader Priestly narrative tradition pointing to this, see my *Reading the Fractures of Genesis: Historical and Literary Approaches* (Louisville, KY: Westminster John Knox, 1996) 137–40; and Matthias Köckert, "Die Geschichte der Abrahamüberlieferung," in *Congress Volume: Leiden, 2004* (ed. André Lemaire; VTSup 109; Leiden: Brill, 2006) 120–25.

26. Again, see my *Reading the Fractures*, 229–32. For an argument that this move took place first in the non-P traditions, before the counterpresentation found in P, see my "Genesis in Relation to the Moses Story: Diachronic and Synchronic Perspectives," in *Studies in the Book of Genesis* (ed. A. Wénin; BETL 155; Leuven: Peeters and Leuven University Press, 2001) 273–95; and idem, "What Is Required to Identify Pre-Priestly Narrative Connections between Genesis and Exodus? Some General Reflections and Specific Cases," in *A Farewell to the Yahwist? The Composition of the Pentateuch in Recent European Interpretation* (ed. Thomas B. Dozeman and Konrad Schmid; SBLSymS 34; Atlanta: Society of Biblical Literature, 2006) 159–80.

in the plural—became a connected and foundational whole around which Judah's non-land elite could orient themselves. They focused on the shaping of multiple visions of Israel's distant past, P and non-P, rather than creating a historical narrative that described Israel's diaspora present.

3. Ezra Traditions and the Gradual Rise of the Torah to Dominance

The first major section of this essay included a summary of data that indicates a virtually universal dominance that the Torah (in the singular) achieved across various strains of Judaism by the late Second Temple period. This dominance is reflected in a number of loci, such as Hecataeus, the (formation of) the Septuagint, the *Letter of Aristeas*, and 1 and 2 Maccabees. By this point, not only were blocks of pentateuchal traditions joined into an overall pre-land history, but a Pentateuch (in the singular) appears to have achieved the kind of foundational status that Homer's epics had in Greek tradition, Kemyt or Kheti had at points in Egyptian tradition, and the ur_5-ra = *ḫubullu* lexical list or *Gilgamesh* had in Mesopotamia.

That said, there are some indicators that it took a while for the Pentateuch to achieve this dominance, especially across some parts of Judaism. For example, the Torah does not feature prominently in the Egyptian diaspora Elephantine texts, despite an apparent correspondence with Jerusalem (and Samaria!). Closer to Jerusalem, postexilic prophetic traditions in Isaiah and Haggai–Zechariah, along with the Nehemiah memoir (Neh 1:1–7:4, 12:27–43, 13:4–31), for example, lack the kind of Torah focus seen in later texts.[27] And the poetic material of Job could be added to the list of early postexilic books that show intertextual dependence on a broad range of prophetic and psalmic literature, perhaps even a reflection of the Holiness Code, but still *not* a clear orientation to Torah traditions as foundational.[28]

The next, best, and yet problematic witness to the rise of the Torah is the Ezra tradition seen in the MT Ezra–Nehemiah complex and the Old Greek 1 Esdras. These traditions are "next" because they represent a later postexilic stratum than texts discussed so far, even as they probably predate more clearly Hellenistic traditions such as *Jubilees*, the *Temple Scroll*, and others. These traditions are "problematic" because of issues of dating them and relating them to each other, let alone interpreting them. Perhaps controversially, the treatment

---

27. One significant exception to this is the apparent interpretation of Deut 23:4–9 in Nehemiah 13. See the discussion of this in Michael Fishbane, *Biblical Interpretation in Ancient Israel* (Oxford: Clarendon, 1985) 124–28. For a survey of literature and analysis of the growth of Neh 13:23–26 and its relationship to Ezra 9:12, see Jacob Wright, *Rebuilding Identity: The Nehemiah-Memoir and Its Earliest Readers* (BZAW 348; Berlin: de Gruyter, 2004) 244–57, 268–69.

28. This latter assertion about Job is based on my research in progress on allusions to earlier literature in Job and other "wisdom" books of the Hebrew Bible.

here focuses on Ezra material shared between the books of 1 Esdras and Ezra–Nehemiah.[29] And these traditions are "best" because the Ezra traditions attest to three developments that were not clear at earlier stages: (1) the existence of a Pentateuch consisting of both Priestly and non-Priestly elements; (2) the placement of this Pentateuch at the head of other Jewish writings in a clearly privileged position (as is also evident in a different form that is more difficult to date for the Deuteronomistic Torah and Prophets); and (3) the understanding of this combination of narrative and law as a legal orientation point of the Jewish people.[30]

The main interest for this discussion is the way in which the Ezra traditions represent the Torah as the legal foundation of postexilic Judah. This represents a particular construal of the Torah, one that privileges its legal elements over others. Most synchronic analyses of the Pentateuch agree that it is first and foremost a narrative, with its legal parts embedded into and organized by a broader plot leading from creation to the death of Moses. Nevertheless, the shared Ezra traditions, like many other Second Temple traditions, construe this narrative-legal complex as "law" or "commandment." The Torah that appears there directs how offerings are to be performed (Ezra 3:2, 1 Esd 5:48[5:49 ET]). It is the "law"/Aramaic דת that Ezra studies so that he can teach God's commandments to Israel (Ezra 7:6, 10//1 Esd 8:3, 7; cf. דת ["of God" or "of heaven"] in Ezra 7:12, 14, 21, 25, 26 [the latter alongside "law of the king"]//1 Esd 8:9, 12, 19, 23, 24). The Torah is the rule that leads to the divorce and expulsion of foreign wives (Ezra 10:3//1 Esd 8:90[ET 8:93–94]) before Ezra reads the whole of the law before them (Neh 8:1–8//1 Esd 9:38–48), and the people weep when they hear it (Neh 8:9//1 Esd 9:50) before feasting and rejoicing (Neh 8:10–11//1 Esd 9:51–55).

---

29. Most scholars would understand the 1 Esdras traditions to be a later transformation of traditions found in another form in Chronicles and Ezra–Nehemiah. Dieter Böhler, however, has made a persuasive case for 1 Esdras reflecting an earlier, pre-Nehemiah stage of the Ezra tradition, with the MT Ezra–Nehemiah reflecting a number of changes to accommodate the insertion of Nehemiah material (along with material added presupposing both blocks of material). See Dieter Böhler, *Die heilige Stadt in Esdras α und Esra–Nehemia: Zwei Konzeptionen der Wiederherstellung Israels* (OBO 158; Fribourg: Universitätsverlag / Göttingen: Vandenhoeck & Ruprecht, 1997). For a vigorous critique, see particularly Zippora Talshir, "Ezra–Nehemiah and First Esdras: Diagnosis of a Relationship between Two Recensions," *Bib* 81 (2000) 566–73, though in my view Talshir's objections are not sufficient to disprove Böhler's case. Fuller treatment of this must await another context and is not directly pertinent to the question at hand.

30. On the existence of a Pentateuch with Priestly and non-Priestly elements, see Joseph Blenkinsopp, "Was the Pentateuch the Civic and Religious Constitution of the Jewish Ethnos in the Persian Period?" in *Persia and Torah: The Theory of Imperial Authorization of the Pentateuch* (ed. James Watts; SBLSymS 17; Atlanta: Society of Biblical Literature, 2001) 41–62.

Indeed, these Ezra traditions represent a particular way of understanding Israel and its law, implying that Torah is not only construed as "law" but as "cultic law" for a holy people. In this case, such cultic law consists not so much in instructions for sacrifices as in a vision of Israel as a "holy seed" (זרע הקדש) who must be properly separated from "the peoples of the lands" (עמי הארצות) (Ezra 9:2//1 Esd 8:67[ET 8:70]). After being authorized by Artaxerxes to investigate the land in light of the law, in Ezra 9:10, 14 (//1 Esd 8:79, 84[ET 8:82, 87), Ezra speaks of how Israel has broken God's "commands" (מצות) through the prophets not to intermarry with or to "seek the well-being of" (דרש שלום) the peoples of the lands. Ezra represents this mixing as exemplary of the disobedience to the Torah that led to the Exile in the past (Ezra 9:7//1 Esd 8:73[ET 8:76]). The continuance of intermarriage threatens Judah's tenuous postexilic existence as a remnant granted by God a brief respite under the Persians to live in the land as their slaves (9:8–9//1 Esd 8:75–78[ET 8:78–81]) only to risk it all by repeating the mistakes of the past (9:10, 13–14//1 Esd 8:79, 83–85[ET 8:82, 86–88]).[31]

In so construing Israel as properly a "holy seed," these Ezra traditions pick up on an emphasis in both major strands of the Torah on Israel's status as a holy, priestly people. The non-P strand reflects this idea most clearly in the Sinai pericope, particularly Exodus 19, which promises that Israel will be a priestly people, and Exodus 24, which shows a realization of that promise in a sacrifice performed by Moses and the young men.[32] The P strand reflects this idea of national holiness in its picture of the camp gathered around the tabernacle and in the so-called H elements that extend priestly purity regulations to the people as a whole. The P/non-P Torah combines these two visions of a holy, priestly Israel into one fractured whole in which the non-P promise of Israel's status as a holy nation is fulfilled by P and H instructions for turning Israel into a tabernacle-centered, purified people led by the Aaronic priests.

These Ezra traditions represent an important stage in the rise of Torah. This is reflected not only in the centrality of Torah in the Ezra traditions themselves but also in the way the Ezra α tradition juxtaposes Josiah on the one hand and Ezra on the other.[33] Later Jewish exegetes understood Ezra to be a virtual second Moses. Sadly, we lack nonbiblical narrative testimony to the period of Ezra, so the most we can discuss are hints of history and historical memory in the biblical books of Ezra/1 Esdras. Yet, even if these biblical traditions are his-

---

31. For earlier discussion of interpretation of the Torah in this portion of Ezra, see Fishbane, *Biblical Interpretation*, 114–21.

32. Here, see the exegesis in Erhard Blum, *Studien zur Komposition des Pentateuch* (BZAW 189; Berlin: de Gruyter, 1990) 52–54.

33. This is an interesting witness, no matter what its relationship to the material in Chronicles and Ezra–Nehemiah.

torically unreliable vis-á-vis an actual Ezra, they represent a compelling picture
of a formerly exiled community—a community of "slaves" (עבדים) to foreign
kings (Ezra 9:9; cf. 1 Esd 8:79[ET 8:80])—coming to center itself, as a holy
people, around God's *law* as seen in the Torah.

This distinguishes the pentateuchal Torah—construed as "law"—from the
foundational pedagogical wisdom texts, which it displaced from the primary
position they once occupied. Not only does this Torah now stand at the head
of an educational process where wisdom and hymnic texts probably once
stood, but it is understood as a *law* that constitutes the formerly exiled remnant
of Israel as a holy people. Whatever the Torah's history and actual contents, it
is construed as a cultic-legal instruction mediated by Moses, disobeyed before,
and now present to the postexilic remnant community as its last chance to
avoid another experience of exile.

There will be many later similar representations of the centrality of Torah as
a cultic-legal center of Israel in the books of Maccabees, *Jubilees*, the *Letter of
Aristeas*, Ben Sira, Wisdom of Solomon, and so forth. Nevertheless, few of
these later representations have the close connections to issues of Exile and
coming to terms with foreign domination seen in these Ezra traditions. Among
these various representations of the Torah's centrality, the shared Ezra traditions
(both Ezra and 1 Esdras) are unique in their thematization of Israel as a remnant
community of formerly exiled Judeans, a community who—by virtue of
God's grace—is allowed to live as "slaves" to foreign kings in the land, rather
than being dispersed or utterly destroyed for their Torah disobedience. It is in
this context that the Ezra of these shared Ezra traditions blesses God (Ezra
7:27–28a//1 Esd 8:25–26) for ensuring that the foreign, Persian, king authorized him to investigate Judah and Jerusalem vis-á-vis the Torah, to bring offerings to the temple, teach the Torah to the people of the Transeuphrates, and
enforce the law of God and the law of the king (Ezra 7:12–26//1 Esd 8:9–24).

As others have observed, the pro-Persian stance of these Ezra traditions is
shared with strands of material in Deutero-Isaiah, but it contrasts with later
Hellenistic materials. Unlike the celebration of freedom in Maccabees (see also
Neh 9:32–37), the shared Ezra traditions justify Persian domination theologi-
cally. As indicated by these Ezra traditions, the Persians are not opponents of
God's Torah but supporters of it, enabled by God.[34]

This leads from a discussion of internal factors in the rise of the Torah to a
consideration of external factors in the rise of the Torah, in this case some sort of
involvement of the Persians in support of the kind of legal refocusing of Jewish

---

34. For a persuasive argument that the later materials in Nehemiah (not from the shared Ezra
or Nehemiah memoir) were composed in the Hasmonean period, see Böhler, *Die heilige Stadt*,
374–97.

community around the Torah that is depicted in the shared Ezra traditions. This is not a question of "a highly centralized, constant, and tightly defended Persian policy," in which local elites across the Persian king's empire were impelled by the Persians to collect and publish their indigenous traditions as Persian law.[35] Nor is the suggestion here that there was some sort of central Persian text production and censorship office that was responsible for producing, collecting, and evaluating the contents of the traditions thus authorized. Instead, what is of interest is the multiple and varied documentation for Persian recognition, probably by local Persian authorities (albeit in the name of the king) of locally produced texts as valid Persian law.[36] This fits with a more broadly documented trend of the particularly local orientation of the Persian Empire, especially in areas along its western contact point with Greek spheres of influence.

Once we free ourselves, as Konrad Schmid advocates, from the weaker parts of the governmental hypothesis (along with misreadings of it) and focus on the most plausible elements initially advanced by its advocates, it seems eminently plausible that the returnee community would have sought, of their own initiative, Persian recognition of their exilic Torah traditions as Persian law for Jews.[37] Moreover, this community then claimed Persian recognition in texts, such as the shared Ezra traditions, especially Ezra 7//1 Esd 8:1–27. Judging even from the testimony of traditions such as these that appear to have been produced by returnees from Babylon, this community was in a tenuous relationship vis-à-vis the people already living in the land when they returned. Ethnographic surveys have shown that this is an endemic problem for returnee communities. They require outside power support in order to take control of the community and replace leaders already in their homeland.[38] In this case, it

---

35. See Gary Knoppers, "An Achaemenid Imperial Authorization of Torah in Yehud?" in *Persia and Torah: The Theory of Imperial Authorization of the Pentateuch* (trans. and ed. James Watts; SBLSymS 17; Atlanta: Society of Biblical Literature, 2001) 134. See further, underscoring this point, Konrad Schmid, "Persische Reichsautorisation und Tora," *TRu* 71 (2006) 494–506, and the further elaboration by Schmid in this volume.

36. These include a letter found at Elephantine (*AP* 21), the Demotic papyrus 215 from the Paris National Library, the Letoon Inscription from Xanthus, and a 2nd-century copy of an earlier Persian text found at Sardis. For a review of these and other materials that might point to Persian governmental recognition of local texts, see Peter Frei, "Persian Imperial Authorization: A Summary," in *Persia and Torah* (SBLSymS 17; Atlanta: Society of Biblical Literature, 2001) 5–40. For a review of responses to this hypothesis, see Schmid, "Persische Reichsautorisation."

37. Previous critiques of this hypothesis have helped clarify that there is little chance that the Persians themselves forced a process of governmental authorization on local elites as part of a central state policy. Rather, it appears that local elites loyal to Persia could receive Persian recognition for certain local regulations, particularly regarding the cult, if they so chose. On this, see especially the helpful clarification by James Watts, "Introduction" in *Persia and Torah* (SBLSymS 17; Atlanta: Society of Biblical Literature, 2001) 3–4.

38. For a survey of some studies, see Daniel Smith, *The Religion of the Landless: The Social Context of Babylonian Exile* (Bloomington, IN: Meyer-Stone, 1989) 63–65.

appears that Persian sponsorship was key to this returnee community's securing its political position in Yehud. More specifically, it seems likely that this community would have known of one potential way in which the Persians could support their takeover of Yehud: through the recognition of their exilic traditions as the Persian-recognized local "law."

Thus, the initiative and execution of this move is local—related to the rise of the Torah in the community of exiles and the insecure political position of returning as formerly exiled elites to Yehud. The solution is partly external—taking advantage of a feature of Persian imperial rule, where the Persian local authorities, especially in the west, "recognized" the local law of Persian-sponsored indigenous elites, giving certain local traditions a privileged, official legal status.

This is the most plausible setting for two developments in the rise of the Torah. First, this move helped ensure that the Torah was not just a foundational educational document in Jewish education, which it was, but also the legal foundation for those in Judah and (at least for a while) related communities based in Samaria as well. The foundational educational function of the Torah continues, of course, as is seen in the contours of later Second Temple and post–Second Temple rabbinic literature. Nevertheless, this central educational/formational role of Torah is connected to a yet broader social complex in which Torah eventually serves as a center of the postmonarchic Jewish community. It is one thing for a text to serve as a foundation for the education of elites in a broader royal-temple institutional complex, such as was found in various forms in Egypt and Mesopotamia. Texts of this sort play an important but supportive role in forming elites to function in various parts of a broader state. It is quite another for a text such as the Torah to achieve such cultic-legal status. Within this context, in which the Torah is a document that helps constitute a community, the educational process centered particularly on the Torah helps shape members of this transnational community of Jews both in Judah and throughout other parts of the Mediterranean and Near Eastern world.

Second, the move toward Persian authorization may have influenced the shaping of the tradition itself. The local elites who sought Persian recognition of their traditions would have been impelled to achieve a certain unity in the tradition for which they sought recognition. It would not have been enough to have the Persians recognize as Persian law a variety of local traditions, say a "P" and "non-P" rendering of the Torah tradition. Instead, despite often substantial differences in Torah traditions, postexilic Judean elites—both priestly and lay —had to meld diverse pentateuchal materials into a single whole that could then gain the status of the one "law" uniting the peoples of the area. This impetus, again oriented toward outside recognition, can explain the remarkable combination of highly divergent P and non-P traditions in the Torah, indeed a combination unprecedented in a text of legal character and gaining legal status. In this sense, Blum's arguments for the governmental authorization hypothesis on the basis of sharp contrasts between P and non-P material remain compelling, especially given the difference between the kind of combination of originally separate legal (and narrative) traditions in the Torah under discussion here and the combination of divergent redactional layers seen in prophetic and other texts.[39]

III. Conclusion

In sum, there are a number of internal factors, starting in the late preexilic period and culminating in the exilic period, that lead to the rise of Torah traditions in Jewish education. Nevertheless, some external factors related to Persian policy appear to be important in the consolidation of these traditions and their legal construal and social function in undergirding a transnational community of Jews otherwise not united by typical national-ethnic institutions. More specifically, this essay has advanced the case that politically insecure, Persian-sponsored returnees drew on a more widely attested pattern of Persian textual sponsorship to secure their position and the position of their Torah texts. To do this, they created a consolidated version of their Torah traditions, forming them into a single whole for which they then sought imperial recognition. This step toward the legal founding of Judaism on the foundational Torah-teaching (now in the singular) then was presupposed, refracted, and developed in the multiple Hellenistic-period traditions surveyed previously.

The educational and legal dominance of this primarily exilic document is so firmly established by the early 2nd century B.C.E. that this postmonarchic Torah, long ago shaped and promoted by (former) exiles, is the focal point for an emergent Jewish monarchy under the Hasmoneans, a monarchy that might otherwise have preferred privileging more explicitly monarchic traditions that would have directly legitimated them. They do not initiate a Jewish educational system focused on royal hymns, instructions, and the narratives of the Maccabees. Instead, as argued in *Writing on the Tablet of the Heart*, it appears that the Hasmoneans consolidated a preliminary Jewish scriptural corpus consisting of Torah and Prophets.[40] By this point, there is no turning back: Judaism is a community of the risen Torah.

---

39. See Blum, *Studien*, 333–38, 358. This is in contrast to arguments advanced by Schmid both in the essay for this volume and in his earlier treatment, "Reichsautorisation und Tora."

40. Carr, *Writing on the Tablet of the Heart*, 253–72.

Local Law in an Imperial Context:
The Role of Torah in the (Imagined) Persian Period

ANSELM C. HAGEDORN

Humboldt-Universität zu Berlin

for H. G. M. Williamson on the occasion of his 60th birthday

I. Introduction

Peter Frei's theory of a Persian imperial authorization (*persische Reichsautho-risation*) of local laws and stipulations in the provinces of the Persian Empire assumed that the Persians had a genuine interest in the laws and customs of their subjects. Applied to the shaping of the Pentateuch, the theory suggests that much of the codification of biblical legal material was mainly undertaken because of external pressure from the Persians.[1] For various reasons, this theory has been difficult to sustain, and it has become increasingly clear that different processes were at work during the codification of the legal material in the Hebrew Bible.[2]

This essay will *not* resurrect the theory of a Persian imperial authorization but instead asks the question how local law (that is, the Pentateuch or at least parts

Author's note: My sincere thanks to Sally E. Merry (New York University) for making much of her own material on postcolonial law available to me that was difficult to access in Berlin, and to Gary N. Knoppers and Bernard M. Levinson for both the invitation to participate in the panel that led to this essay and their many helpful comments. All remaining shortcomings are, of course, my own.

1. See Peter Frei, "Zentralgewalt und Lokalautonomie im Achäemenidenreich," in *Reichsidee und Reichsorganisation im Perserreich* (ed. Peter Frei and Klaus Koch; OBO 55; 2nd ed.; Fribourg: Universitätsverlag / Göttingen: Vandenhoeck & Ruprecht, 1994) 5–131; and idem, "Persian Imperial Authorization: A Summary," in *Persia and Torah: The Theory of Imperial Authorization of the Pentateuch* (ed. James W. Watts; SBLSymS 17; Atlanta: Society of Biblical Literature, 2001) 5–40. For the role of Persia during the formation of the Pentateuch, see Erhard Blum, *Studien zur Komposition des Pentateuch* (BZAW 189; Berlin: de Gruyter, 1990) 333–60.

2. See especially Joseph Wiesehöfer, " 'Reichsgesetz' oder 'Einzelfallgerechtigkeit'? Bemerkungen zu Peter Freis These von der achämenidischen Reichsautorisation," *ZABR* 1 (1995) 36–46; and Udo Rüterswörden, "Die Persische Reichsautorisation der Torah: Fact or Fiction?" *ZABR* 1 (1995) 47–61. With a different view, Konrad Schmid, "Persische Reichsautorisation und Tora," *TRu* 71 (2006) 494–506.

57

thereof) functioned within a larger imperial context.[3] By using aspects of social theory and current legal anthropology, especially from a colonial–postcolonial context, I hope to provide an appropriate theoretical framework to demonstrate that the Persian context actually did shape the codification of biblical legal material. But I shall argue that this shaping was done by the biblical authors themselves, who created a legal corpus that functioned in a wider imperial context by maintaining local order. Thus they created an order that allowed postexilic Israel to operate as part of the Persian Empire without entering into conflict with it. In other words, these authors almost voluntarily made the decisive step toward a colonial existence.

This contribution falls into two parts. First, I will evaluate what speaking of an "empire" entails and how imperial conceptions relate to questions of colonial rule. The test case will be the Persian Empire, because it provides the historical and literary backdrop against which the current biblical narrative is set. This part of the essay also shows where the so-called "Persian Empire" departs from traditional notions of imperial power, while still having a colonial impact. Because law has been seen as a classic tool to implement colonial rule, the second goal of my essay will be to show how local law is shaped in an environment that is part of a (colonial) empire but not subject to the pressure of colonial law.[4]

Overall, the essay reflects the renewed interest in the application of insights from critical and postcolonial theory to ancient history.[5] In contrast to other studies, however, mine will not depart from the historical dimension of the en-

---

3. This does not imply that I am disputing the existence of Persian involvement in local affairs, because the evidence from Elephantine and Xanthus points to the contrary. However, as the so-called Passover Letter from Elephantine and the Trilingual Inscription from Xanthus demonstrate, these involvements were individual (legal) stipulations of the Persian court in response to certain specific requests, rather than reflecting an overarching imperial concept. Documents of this sort are not found in Palestine, in contrast to Asia Minor and Egypt. For the Aramaic text and English translation of the Passover Letter, see Bezalel Porten and Ada Yardeni, eds., *Textbook of Aramaic Documents from Ancient Egypt, Vol. 1: Letters* (Jerusalem: Hebrew University, 1986) 54. For the Xanthus Trilingual Inscription (in Aramaic, Lycian, and Greek), see Henri Metzger, Ernest Laroche, and Auguste Dupont-Sommer, eds., *La stèle trilingue du Létôon* (Fouilles de Xanthos 6; Paris: Klincksieck, 1979).

4. On this, see below and Sally E. Merry, "Law and Identity in an American Colony," in *Law and Empire in the Pacific: Fiji and Hawai'i* (ed. Sally E. Merry and Donald Brenneis; School of American Research Advanced Seminar Series; Santa Fe: School of American Research / Oxford: James Currey, 2004) 123–52. This is not the place to evaluate and assess the complicated and often difficult relationship between anthropology, history, and critical theory. On the problem, see Michael Herzfeld, *Anthropology: Theoretical Practice in Culture and Society* (Oxford: Blackwell, 2001).

5. See Neville Moreley, *Theories, Models and Concepts in Ancient History* (Approaching the Ancient World; London: Routledge, 2004); and Sally E. Merry, "Ethnography in the Archives," in *Practicing Ethnography in Law* (ed. June Starr and Mark Goodale; New York: Palgrave Macmillan, 2002) 128–42.

terprise.[6] Despite the increasingly "fashionable orthodoxy" of (post-)colonial studies in rewriting and representing the past in order to reconfigure the present, in this study I will use insights from a theoretical framework but disregard our own present.[7] It is my goal to evaluate how an interpretive framework derived from the social sciences can contribute to a better understanding of the historical and literary processes at work during the formation of the Pentateuch.[8]

II. Persia: Mixing Imperial and Colonial Rule

> Because it is a systematic negation of the other person and a furious determination to deny the other person all attributes of humanity, colonialism forces the people it dominates to ask themselves the question constantly: "In reality, who am I?"[9]

Before embarking on a quest for the role of (parts of) the Torah during the Persian period, I should briefly reevaluate what is actually meant when I refer to the Persian "Empire."[10] Following recent theoretical considerations from the fields of archaeology and anthropology, I define an empire:

> as a territorially expansive and incorporate kind of state, involving relationships in which one state exercises control over other sociopolitical entities . . . and . . . imperialism as the process of creating and maintaining empires. The diverse polities and communities that constitute an empire typically retain some degree of autonomy in self- and centrally-

6. On an approach of this sort, see Uriah Y. Kim, *Decolonizing Josiah: Toward a Postcolonial Reading of the Deuteronomistic History* (The Bible in the Modern World 5; Sheffield: Phoenix, 2005). For the classical world, see the essays collected in Barbara Goff, ed., *Classics and Colonialism* (London: Duckworth, 2005).

7. Ian Chambers, "Off the Map: A Mediterranean Journey," *Comparative Literature Studies* 42 (2005) 318.

8. As far as I am aware, only one study has devoted its attention to the application of critical theory to (parts of) the Pentateuch. See Cheryl B. Anderson, *Women, Ideology, and Violence: Critical Theory and the Construction of Gender in the Book of the Covenant and the Deuteronomic Law* (JSOTSup 394; London: T. & T. Clark, 2004).

9. Frantz Fanon, *The Wretched of the Earth* (trans. Constance Farrington; New York: Grove, 1963) 250. On Fanon's political thought, see Nigel C. Gibson, *Fanon: The Postcolonial Imagination* (Key Contemporary Thinkers; Cambridge: Polity, 2003). On his life, see the personal and often sentimental portrait by Alice Cherki, *Frantz Fanon: A Portrait* (Ithaca, NY: Cornell University Press, 2006).

10. On this subject, see the introductory remarks in Pierre Briant, *From Cyrus to Alexander: A History of the Persian Empire* (Winona Lake, IN: Eisenbrauns, 2002) 1; and Erhard S. Gerstenberger, *Israel in der Perserzeit: 5. und 4. Jahrhundert* (Biblische Enzyklopädie 8; Stuttgart: Kohlhammer, 2005) 45–55. For a different outlook, see Muhammad A. Dandamaev (*A Political History of the Achaemenid Empire* [Leiden: Brill, 1989]), who does not address the question of *empire* but simply uses the term throughout his study.

defined cultural identity, and in some dimensions of political and economic decision making.[11]

Any narrative of empire needs to be aware of the "imperfect geography" and its productive force in the shaping of an empire of any kind.[12] By "imperfect geography," I mean the interplay between territorial and cultural expansion in relation to the resistance of territories and humans to submit fully to imperial rule. This resistance is facilitated by the fact that the extent of an empire, one of its defining features, is the main agent for weakening imperial rule. Xenophon already observed this aspect of the Persian Empire:

καὶ συνιδεῖν δ᾽ ἦν τῷ προσέχοντι τὸν νοῦν τῇ βασιλέως ἀρχῇ πλήθει μὲν χώρας καὶ ἀνθρώπων ἰσχυρὰ οὖσα, τοῖς δὲ μήκεσι τῶν ὁδῶν καὶ τῷ διεσπάσθαι τὰς δυνάμεις ἀσθενής, εἴ τις διὰ ταχέων τὸν πόλεμον ποιοῖτο.

Furthermore, one who observed closely could see at a glance that while the King's empire was strong in its extent of territory and number of inhabitants, it was weak by reason of the greatness of the distances and the scattered condition of its forces, in case one should be swift in making his attack upon it. (Xenophon, *Anab.* 1.5.9)[13]

My emphasis on imperfect geography draws new attention to the fact that territorial control was only one of the main features of many empires in world history. Lauren Benton rightly stresses that:

Empires did not cover territory evenly but composed a fabric that was full of holes, stitched together out of pieces, a tangle of strings. Even in its most paradigmatic cases, empire's spaces were interrupted, politically differentiated, and encased in irregular and sometimes undefined borders. Though empires did lay claim to vast stretches of territory, the nature of these claims was tempered by control that was exercised mainly over narrow bands, or corridors, of territory and over enclaves of various sizes and situations.[14]

This fragmentation of any empire allows for varying degrees of local specificities and poses the question as to how the gap between the "local" and the

---

11. Carla M. Sinopoli, "The Archaeology of Empires," *Annual Review of Anthropology* 23 (1994) 160; compare Norman Yoffe, *Myths of the Archaic State: Evolution of the Earliest Cities, States, and Civilizations* (Cambridge: Cambridge University Press, 2005).

12. See Lauren Benton, "Legal Spaces of Empire: Piracy and the Origins of Ocean Regionalism," *Comparative Studies in Society and History* 47 (2005) 700.

13. Xenophon, *Xenophon: Hellenica Books VI–VII; Anabasis Books I–III* (trans. Charleton L. Brownson; LCL 90; Cambridge: Harvard University Press 1921) 290–91.

14. Benton, "Legal Spaces of Empire," 700.

"global" is bridged, and how the imperial rulers and the imperial ruled subjects construct their territoriality.[15]

Here, one should remember that even the smallest empire or state only exists as an "imagined community," because members will never know all their fellow-members but nevertheless imagine themselves (or are imagined by others) as forming a community.[16] The stress on regional variations and heterogeneity must not cloud the vision of the impact of any imperial policy on the conquered subjects. Keeping this in mind, we will find it useful to supplement a theory of empire with questions of colonialism.[17]

Colonialism is generally defined as expressing domination and hegemony in the classic form of political rule and economic control by a European power (state) over territories and people outside Europe.[18] Here, it is not enough simply to note that the European hegemony was by no means a monolithic entity and that it constantly provoked resistance.[19] One has to understand that

> [w]ith colonialism, the transformation of an indigenous culture of a colonial regime, or the superimposition of the colonial apparatus into which all aspects of the original culture have to be reconstructed, operate as processes of translational dematerialization.[20]

Additionally, the colonial encounter shapes the understanding of colonialism by both the colonizers and the colonized, giving rise to a complex dialectic.[21]

---

15. On human territoriality, see Robert D. Sack, *Human Territoriality: Its Theory and History* (Cambridge: Cambridge University Press, 1986).

16. See Benedict Anderson, *Imagined Communities: Reflections on the Origin and Spread of Nationalism* (2nd ed.; London: Verso, 1991). Additionally, anthropological research into modern empires has drawn attention to the fact that empires and imperialism are able to "[entail] culturally constructed emotions, ambivalences, and ambiguities" (Catherine Lutz, "Empire Is in the Details," *American Ethnologist* 33 [2006] 595).

17. It remains unclear why Jon L. Berquist employs the term "postcolonial" in the title of his study and then proceeds to investigate the structures that are common and defining features of *colonial* existence. See idem, "Constructions of Identity in Postcolonial Yehud," in *Judah and the Judeans in the Persian Period* (ed. Oded Lipschits and Manfred Oeming; Winona Lake, IN: Eisenbrauns, 2006) 53–66.

18. See the definition offered by Nicholas Dirks, "Colonialism," in *New Keywords: A Revised Vocabulary of Culture and Society* (ed. Tony Bennett, Lawrence Gossberg, and Meaghan Morris; Oxford: Blackwell, 2005) 42–45; and the discussion in Homi K. Bhabha, *The Location of Culture* (London: Routledge, 1994) 123–38.

19. See Talal Asad, "Afterword: From the History of Colonial Anthropology to the Anthropology of Western Hegemony," in *Colonial Situations: Essays on the Contextualization of Ethnographic Knowledge* (ed. George W. Stocking; History of Anthropology 7; Madison: University of Wisconsin Press, 1991) 322–23.

20. Robert J. C. Young, *Postcolonialism: A Very Short Introduction* (Oxford: Oxford University Press, 2003) 139–40.

21. See the classic expression of this sort of view in Edward W. Said, *Orientalism: Western Conceptions of the Orient* (London: Penguin, 1979).

The first traces of this dialectic are already noted by Herodotus when he mentions that the Persians readily adopt customs and dresses of their conquered subjects:

> Ξεινικὰ δὲ νόμαια Πέρσαι προσίενται ἀνδρῶν μάλιστα. καὶ γὰρ δὴ τὴν Μηδικὴν ἐσθῆτα νομίσαντες τῆς ἑωυτῶν εἶναι καλλίω φορέουσι, καὶ ἐς τοὺς πολέμους τοὺς Αἰγυπτίους θώρηκας· καὶ εὐπαθείας τε παντοδαπὰς πυνθανόμενοι ἐπιτηδεύουσι κτλ.

But of all men the Persians most welcome foreign customs. They wear the Median dress, deeming it more beautiful than their own, and the Egyptian cuirass in war. Their luxurious practices are of all kinds, and all borrowed. (*Hist.* 1.135)[22]

This welcoming (προσίενται) of other customs (νόμαια) is probably not an expression of a religious or another kind of tolerance but simply Herodotus's way of contrasting the mixed setting of the Persian state with his view of a homogenous Greece.[23]

Herodotus teaches us that any imperial (or colonial) empire creates "contact zones." Such a zone, as Sally E. Merry explains, is not simply a place "where one system is collapsing in favor of another, but a place of intersections located within unequal and shifting power relations."[24] This view is supported by the results of Elspeth Dusinberre's careful study *Aspects of Empire.* This study shows how the presence of an imperial power in a city such as ancient Sardis tends to affect all strata of society, even if the colonial rule is not overly active.[25]

Furthermore, these contact zones can either follow or precede the actual colonial rule and tend to appear in anticipation of colonial rule in the near future. This tendency is evident in the often-cited arbitration between Miletus and Myus (391–388 B.C.E.). The inscription shows Persian involvement in Greek affairs during a period when Persia did not rule over the cities in Asia Minor. The poleis of Miletus and Myus, situated on the Latmian Gulf, referred their border conflict to the Persian king Artaxerxes II, who in turn commanded his satrap Struses to deal with the problem. Struses "arranged for the dispute to be heard by a jury of fifty, comprising five men from each of the remaining states

22. Herodotus, *Herodotus Books I and II* (trans. Alfred D. Godley; LCL 117; Cambridge: Harvard University Press, 1990) 175–77.

23. On the question of (religious) tolerance within the Achaemenid Empire, see Gregor Ahn, "'Toleranz' und Reglement: Die Signifikanz achaimenidischer Religionspolitik für den jüdisch-persischen Kulturkontakt," in *Religion und Religionskontakte im Zeitalter der Achämeniden* (ed. Reinhard G. Kratz; Gütersloh: Chr. Kaiser, 2002) 191–209.

24. See Sally E. Merry, *Colonizing Hawai'i: The Cultural Power of Law* (Princeton Studies in Culture/Power/History; Princeton: Princeton University Press, 2000) 35.

25. Elspeth M. Dusinberre, *Aspects of Empire in Achaemenid Sardis* (Cambridge: Cambridge University Press, 2003).

sharing in the Panionium."[26] Though the use of external arbitrators was not uncommon in the Greek world, it is striking that the two cities here consult the Persian king rather than appealing to a Spartan court—even more striking because Sparta was at war with Persia on behalf of the Greek cities of Asia Minor when the dispute arose:[27]

> ... καὶ τ[ε]θείσης τῆς δίκη-
> ς ὑπὸ Μιλησίων καὶ Μυησίων καὶ τῶμ
> [μ]αρτύρωμ μαρτυρησάντων ἀμφοτέρ-
> [ο]ις καὶ τῶν οὔρων ἀποδεχθέντων τῆ-
> 35 [ς] γῆς, ἐπεὶ ἔμελλον οἱ δικασταὶ δικ-
> ᾶν τὴν δίκην, ἔλιπον τὴν δίκημ Μυή[σ]-
> [ι]οι. οἱ δὲ προδικασταὶ ταῦτα γράψ[α]-
> [ν]τες ἔδοσαν ἐς τὰς πόλεις αἵτινε[ς]
> τὴν δίκην ἐδίκαζομ, μαρτυρίας εἷν-
> 40 αι. ἐπεὶ δὲ Μυσήσιοι τὴν δίκην ἔλιπο-
> ν, Στρούσης ἀκούσας τῶν Ἰώνων τῶν [δ]-
> [ι]καστέων, ἐξαιτράπης ἐὼν Ἰωνίης, [τ]-
> [έ]λος ἐποίησε τὴγ γῆν εἶναι Μιλησ[ί]-
> ων ...

[31]The lawsuit having been undertaken by the | Milesians and Myesians, the witnesses having | witnessed for each party and the boundaries of | the land having been displayed, when the jurors | were about to judge the suit, the Myesians | abandoned the suit. The *prodikastai* wrote this | and gave it to the cities which were judging | the suit, to be a witness. When the Myesians | had abandoned the suit, Struses the satrap of | Ionia heard the Ionians' jurors and made the | final decision that the land should belong to the Milesians.[28]

It becomes apparent that the possibility of imperial rule of a state is recognized by others not yet under imperial rule and used as a kind of higher and independent authority that helps to regulate local conflicts. This shows that, in a sense, one may speak of a precolonial imperialism instigated by conflicts that seem to be irresolvable within one's own ethnic group.

---

26. Peter J. Rhodes and Robin Osborne, *Greek Historical Inscriptions 404–323 BC* (Oxford: Oxford University Press, 2003) 74. The Panionium is a central sanctuary of Poseidon shared by twelve Ionian cities; see Herodotus, *Hist.* 1.142.

27. For the use of foreign judges, see Rhodes and Osborne, *Greek Historical Inscriptions 404–323 BC*, 526–33, no. 101. Similarly, the Persian satraps could approach the Greek cities to solicit support against the Persian king; see Rhodes and Osborne, *Greek Historical Inscriptions 404–323 BC*, 214–17, no. 42.

28. Greek text and English translation according to Rhodes and Osborne, *Greek Historical Inscriptions 404–323 BC*, 72–73, no. 16.

The reason for the often-postulated "freedom" of the conquered subjects within the Achaemenid Empire can probably be found in the Persian view of the world order created by them.[29] Within Persian ideology, it is enough to establish the (conquered) people in their places, as §14 of the Behistun Inscription emphasizes: "I reestablished the people (*kāra-*) on its foundation (*gathu-*), both Persia and Media and the other provinces (*dahyāva-*)."[30]

As long as the colonized stay in the prescribed place (and pay their taxes and bring their gifts to the king), there is no need for the Persians to tighten the imperial grip.[31] Whether this sort of indifference necessarily leads to a fully developed tolerance toward other religions or to a certain respect for the legal traditions of the conquered people remains doubtful.[32] Nevertheless, one has to note that the obvious noninvolvement of the Persians in local religious and legal affairs on a day-to-day basis must have been understood by the ruled nations as a certain degree of freedom, previously unknown to them.

Similar things can be said about the Persian demand for earth and water (γῆν τε καὶ ὕδωρ) reported in Herodotus.[33] This demand can be seen as an alternative to direct military confrontation, because the givers of earth and water acknowledged the superiority of the Persians. As such, the gesture served as a preliminary to any detailed agreement that might follow:

> [E]arth and water played a role in initiating a relationship of ruler/subject in some sense and appears to have been a prime strategy used by the Persian king to attach areas to himself without resorting to military tactics. It allowed him to expect loyalty and material support from states so attached, so that failure to render either could create the justification for the military to bring the erring partner to heel.[34]

---

29. On the question of the religious legitimating of the Persian rulers, see Gregor Ahn, *Religiöse Herrschaftslegitimation im Achämenidischen Iran: Die Voraussetzungen und die Struktur ihrer Argumentation* (Acta Iranica 31; Leiden: Brill / Louvain: Peeters, 1992).

30. Paragraph 14 of the Behistun Inscription (Behistun Inscription of Darius I 1.61–71), along with the English translation, are quoted from Diana Edelman, *The Origins of the "Second" Temple: Persian Imperial Policy and the Rebuilding of Jerusalem* (BibleWorld; London: Equinox, 2005) 354.

31. See Herodotus, *Hist.* 3.90–97, which lists the tribute for the provinces of the Persian Empire. Transeuphrates had to pay 350 talents, apparently regardless of the harvest (3.91).

32. See the debate about the concept of * x̌war'nā* in Eckart Otto, "Die Rechtshermeneutik des Pentateuch und die achämenidische Rechtsideologie in ihren altorientalischen Kontexten," in *Kodifizierung und Legitimierung des Rechts in der Antike und im Alten Orient* (ed. Markus Witte and Marie Theres Fögen; Beihefte zur Zeitschrift für altorientalische und biblische Rechtsgeschichte 5; Wiesbaden: Harrassowitz, 2005) 89–90; and in Ahn, *Religiöse Herrschaftslegitimation,* 199–208.

33. Herodotus, *Hist.* 4.126–32, 5.17–19, 5.73, 6.48–49, 6.94, 7.32, 7.131, 7.133, 7.163, 7.233. The meaning of the phrase is explored in Amélie Kuhrt, "Earth and Water," in *Achaemenid History III: Method and Theory* (ed. Amélie Kuhrt and Heleen Sancisi–Weerdenburg; Leiden: Neederlands Instituut voor het Nabije Oosten, 1988) 86–99.

34. Ibid., 94.

Again, it fits well with Persian ideology—the people who offer earth and water are placed within the Persian cosmos, thus fulfilling the order given by Darius according to the Behistun Inscription. If the ruled subjects follow their obligations, their continued existence is guaranteed:

> Saith Darius the King: "By the favor of Ahuramazda there are the countries which I seized outside of Persia; I ruled over them; they bore tribute to me; what was said to them by me, that they did; my law (*dāta*)— that held them firm."[35]

Due to this view of the world ruled by the Persians, the Persian Empire defies classical notions of imperialism and colonialism (i.e., neglecting to focus on the colonial involvement of every aspect of life of their conquered subjects), while at the same time subscribing to concepts and definitions intrinsic to more traditional empires. The selective disengagement from law that empowers other agents on the local level to fill the vacuum left by the Persian nonregulation creates a new form of colonial imperialism giving rise to a more complex legal development.[36] Because the "grandiose grammar" of Achaemenid imperial interest did not extend beyond the political or fiscal contact zones, the ruled subjects had quite a bit of room to maneuver.[37] The extent of this "freedom" was probably difficult to assess due to the absence of any overarching legal system that would provide a mode of control and trigger a certain degree of resistance. How law is shaped in an environment that does not provide the pressure of colonial law will be the concern of the second part of my essay.

III. Local Law and Global Law

It is by now a commonplace in almost all scholarly works on ancient Persia and its social, economic, and legal institutions to stress that the Achaemenid

---

35. Naqš-i-Rustam Inscription of Darius I (copy A), 15–22; translation according to Roland G. Kent, *Old Persian Grammar, Texts, Lexicon* (AOS 33; New Haven, CT: Yale University Press, 1953) 138.

36. On the concept, see David Guillet, "Rethinking Legal Pluralism: Local Law and State Law in the Evolution of Water Property Rights in Northwestern Spain," *Comparative Studies in Society and History* 40 (1998) 42–70.

37. See Charles E. Carter, *The Emergence of Yehud in the Persian Period: A Social and Demographic Study* (JSOTSup 294; Sheffield: Sheffield Academic Press, 1999); and Oded Lipschits, "Achaemenid Imperial Policy, Settlement Processes in Palestine, and the Status of Jerusalem in the Middle of the Fifth Century B.C.E.," in *Judah and the Judeans in the Persian Period* (ed. O. Lipschits and M. Oeming; Winona Lake, IN: Eisenbrauns, 2006) 19–52. The term "grandiose grammar" is taken from Michael Herzfeld, "Political Philology: Everyday Consequences of Grandiose Grammars," *Anthropological Linguistics* 39 (1997) 351–75. Herzfeld uses the term to describe a form of "political philology," where language is tied to the ruling power but seldom extends beyond it because it contains certain ambiguities for the members of society that are not part of the ruling class.

Empire did not possess a collection of laws comparable to the Babylonian, Akkadian, and even biblical collections.[38] The often-cited exception to the rule is a Persian codification of Egyptian laws, based on a remark in Diodorus Siculus.[39] This process, however, apparently supported by the so-called *Demotic Chronicle*, appears to be not so much a codification of legal stipulations as a translation of Pharaonic decrees that were significant for the economy of Egypt.[40]

Nevertheless, the Persian Empire was hardly a law-free or even a lawless entity.[41] If law can be defined as an imaginative structure of meaning with symbols providing the material for the creation, communication, and imposition of such structures, it is not necessarily the legal code that has to effect these binding arrangements.[42] Naturally, a concept of this sort is difficult to grasp in rela-

---

38. Out of the plethora of studies, see Joseph Blenkinsopp, "Was the Pentateuch the Civic and Religious Constitution of the Jewish Ethnos in the Persian Period?" in *Persia and Torah: The Theory of Imperial Authorization of the Pentateuch* (ed. James W. Watts; SBLSymS 17; Atlanta: Society of Biblical Literature Press, 2001) 41–43; Otto, "Die Rechtshermeneutik des Pentateuch," 85–90. A different point of view can be found in Muhammad A. Dandamaev and Vladimir G. Lukonin, *The Culture and Social Institutions of Ancient Iran* (Cambridge: Cambridge University Press, 1989) 115–30. They acknowledge the extremely diverse character of the legal systems and institutions that existed within the Achaemenid Empire, as well as noting that the Persian conquests did not lead to any dramatic changes in the legal traditions of the conquered peoples. Yet, they also state that "[i]ntensive work on the codification of the laws of the conquered peoples was carried out during the reign of Darius I. . . . The laws existing in various countries were made uniform within the limits of a given country, while where necessary they were also changed according to the policy of the king" (p. 117).

39. ἕκτον δὲ λέγεται τὸν Ξέρξου πατέρα Δαρεῖον τοῖς νόμοις ἐπιστῆναι τοῖς τῶν Αἰγυπτίων κτλ. "A sixth man to concern himself with the laws of the Egyptians, it is said, was Darius, the father of Xerxes" (Diodorus Siculus, 1.95.4, in *Diodorus of Sicily: Vol. I. Books I and II, 1–34* [trans. Charles H. Oldfather; LCL 279; New York: Putnam's, 1931] 325).

40. See Donald B. Redford, "The So-Called 'Codification' of Egyptian Law under Darius I," in *Persia and Torah: The Theory of Imperial Authorization of the Pentateuch* (ed. James W. Watts; SBLSymS 17; Atlanta: Society of Biblical Literature, 2001) 135–59. The text of the *Demotic Chronicle* can be found in Wilhelm Spiegelberg, ed., *Die sogenannte Demotische Chronik des Pap. 215 der Bibliothèque Nationale zu Paris: Nebst den auf der Rückseite stehenden Texten* (Demotische Studien von Wilhelm Spiegelberg 7; Leipzig: Hinrichs, 1914) 30–31. It is surprising that the most recent German introduction to the Hebrew Bible still propagates the notion that Darius I acted as a lawgiver; see Angelika Berlejung, "Geschichte und Religionsgeschichte des Alten Israel," in *Grundinformation Altes Testament: Eine Einführung in Literatur, Religion und Geschichte des Alten Testaments* (ed. Jan Christian Gertz; Göttingen: Vandenhoeck & Ruprecht, 2006) 146.

41. The evidence (apart from the royal inscriptions) seems, however, to point to individual enactments rather than to an overarching code; see the use of *dāta* in the Trilingual Inscription from Xanthus (the text can be found in Henri Metzger, Emmanuel Laroche, and André Dupont-Sommer, eds., *La stèle trilingue du Létôon* (Fouilles de Xanthos 6; Paris: Les Belles Lettres, 1979). Compare Briant, *From Cyrus to Alexander*, 707–9.

42. On this definition of law, see Clifford Geertz, "Local Knowledge: Fact and Law in Comparative Perspective," in *Local Knowledge: Further Essays in Interpretive Anthropology* (New York: Basic Books, 1983) 67–234. See Susan B. Coutin, "Enacting Law through Social Practice: Sanctuary

tion to societies in contact with Persia that placed enormous importance on the role of a codified law or a legal corpus, such as Greece and biblical Israel.[43] Even if one does not postulate that the Pentateuch served as the constitution for a Jewish community or state during the Persian period, it can hardly be denied that extensive writing and reworking of older material took place during the Persian period, prompting the question why this literary activity was possible and overlooked by the imperial authorities.[44]

It is one of the main insights of current legal anthropology that, even in non-colonized states, law is deeply pluralized.[45] These pluralities arise out of various factors, such as different ethnicities within different legal systems or ideas and are supplemented in a colonial context with the encounter between colonizer and colonized. The struggle to maintain separate legal orders—already detectable in noncolonized societies—thus increases. Sally Merry explains:

> A focus on the dialectic, mutually constitutive relations among global law, nation-state law, customary law, and other normative orders emphasizes the interconnectedness of social orders and the vulnerability of local places to structures of domination far outside their immediate worlds.[46]

Because laws and legal practice within colonial and imperial contexts tend to travel and to cross boundaries, they have a tendency to become an important part of the social construction of territories and regions.[47]

---

as a Form of Resistance," in *Law and Anthropology: A Reader* (ed. Sally Falk Moore; Oxford: Blackwell, 2005) 278–88.

43. Probably one of the earliest (Greek) references that attributes the giving of laws to Darius is a difficult and rather obscure passage from Aeschylus, *Persians* 858–59: πρῶτα μὲν εὐδοκίμους στρατιᾶς ἀπε- | φαινόμεθ', ἠδὲ †νομίσματα πύργινα πάντ' ἐπεύθυνον†, "First we proved ourselves glorious on military campaigns, and then a system of laws, steadfast as towers, regulated everything" (Edith Hall, trans., *Aeschylus: Persians* [Warminster: Aris & Phillips, 1996] 89). On the problematic phrase νομίσματα πύργινα, see J. D. Rogers, "On the νομίσματα πύργινα of Aeschylus, Pers. 859," *AJA* 7 (1903) 95–96. For Israel, see Sebastian Grätz, *Das Edikt des Artaxerxes: Eine Untersuchung zum religionspolitischen und historischen Umfeld von Ezra 7, 12–26* (BZAW 337; Berlin: de Gruyter, 2004); and Reinhard G. Kratz, "Ezra—Priest and Scribe," in *Sages, Scribes, and Seers: The Sage in the Eastern Mediterranean World* (ed. Leo G. Perdue; FRLANT 219; Göttingen: Vandenhoeck & Ruprecht, 2007).

44. On the formation of the Pentateuch, see Reinhard G. Kratz, *The Composition of the Narrative Books of the Old Testament* (London: T. & T. Clark, 2005); and further, Eckart Otto, "Der Zusammenhang von Herrscherlegitimation und Rechtskodifizierung in altorientalischer und biblischer Rechtsgeschichte," *ZABR* 11 (2005) 51–92.

45. Sally E. Merry, "Colonial and Postcolonial Law," in *The Blackwell Companion to Law and Society* (ed. Austin Sarat; Oxford: Blackwell, 2004) 570.

46. Ibid., 571.

47. Benton, "Legal Spaces of Empire," 701.

Generally speaking, law represents a central aspect of the way (emerging) nations tell their stories—who they are and how their ethnic identities have been forged.[48] This aspect is the reason why, in the perspective of others (especially the Greeks and Jews), the Persians must have had a set of laws; if law represents identity and a certain degree of equality, any group that claims to be an ethnic community must have a set of laws that helps to maintain its ethnic status. Therefore, it is hardly surprising that Plato attributes the function of law-giver to Darius, whom he credits with reestablishing the Persian Empire.

Δαρεῖος γὰρ βασιλέως οὐκ ἦν υἱὸς παιδείᾳ τε οὐ διατρυφώσῃ τεθραμ-
μένος, ἐλθὼν δ᾽ εἰς τὴν ἀρχὴν καὶ λαβὼν αὐτὴν ἕβδομος διείλετο ἑπτὰ
μέρη τεμόμενος, ὧν καὶ νῦν ἔτι σμικρὰ ὀνείρατα λέλειπται, καὶ νόμους
ἠξίου θέμενος οἰκεῖν ἰσότητά τινα κοινὴν εἰσφέρων, καὶ τὸν τοῦ Κύρου
δασμὸν ὃν ὑπέσχετο Πέρσαις εἰς τὸν νόμον ἐνέδει, φιλίαν πορίζων καὶ
κοινωνίαν πᾶσι Πέρσαις, χρήμασι καὶ δωρεαῖς τὸν Περσῶν δῆμον προ-
σαγόμενος. (*Laws* 695c)

Darius was not a king's son, nor was he reared luxuriously. When he came and seized the kingdom, with his six companions, he divided it into seven parts, of which some small vestiges remain even to this day; and he thought good to manage it by enacting laws into which he introduced some measure of political equality, and also incorporated in the law regulations about the tribute-money which Cyrus had promised the Persians, whereby he secured friendliness and fellowship amongst all classes of the Persians, and won over the populace by money and gifts.[49]

For Plato, the origin of empire is intrinsically linked to the giving of laws, which in turn ensure some form of political equality (καὶ νόμους ἠξίου θέ-μενος οἰκεῖν ἰσότητά τινα κοινὴν εἰσφέρων). Of course, the concept behind Plato's argument is the Greek notion that the existence of laws creates a certain degree of equality within society.[50]

The legal narrative of ethnic identity enables the biblical narrators to bracket out the actual colonial presence, evoking a picture of an autonomous creation of the present, while neglecting the external (colonial) forces that helped to

---

48. See Herodotus, *Hist.* 7.104, where Demartus explains the bravery of the Greeks (Spartans) to Xerxes, a bravery that does not result from fear of a king or of any other worldly authority but from the supremacy of law: ἐλεύθεροι γὰρ ἐόντες οὐ πάντα ἐλεύθεροι εἰσί· ἔπεστι γάρ σφι δεσπότης νόμος, τὸν ὑποδειμαίνουσι πολλῷ ἔτι μᾶλλον ἢ οἱ σοὶ σέ, "Free they are, yet not wholly free; for law is their master, whom they fear much more than your men fear you" (*Herodotus: Books V–VII* [trans. Alfred D. Godley; LCL 119; Cambridge: Harvard University Press, 1922] 409).

49. Plato, *Plato: Laws Volume I, Books I–VI* (trans. Robert G. Bury; LCL 187; Cambridge: Harvard University Press, 1926) 229–31.

50. See Solon, *fr.* 36 (West): θεσμοὺς δ᾽ ὁμοίως τῷ κακῷ τε κἀγαθῷ εὐθεῖαν εἰς ἕκαστον ἁρ-μόσας δίκην ἔγραψα ("Laws I wrote for the lower and upper classes alike, providing a straight legal process for each person"); and Euripides, *Suppliant Women*, 433–34.

shape this identity. During this process, the colonial period is transcended by denying its very existence, and thus it becomes the productive force for the postcolonial future.[51] What is often portrayed as a subversive reception of some form of Persian imperial ideology appears to be the first steps toward the creation of an ethnic identity of Israel in post-Persian and postcolonial times.[52]

These theoretical considerations, combined with the nonexistence of any documents supporting Persian pressure toward the codification of the legal material of their conquered subjects, allow us to reevaluate the status of the Torah during the Persian period.[53] First of all, the lack of official interest in the Pentateuch or, more precisely, in the legal material does not automatically preclude the existence of external force. The complex dialectic within any colonial context as discussed above allows for an imagined pressure felt by the colonized subjects to avoid conflict with the hegemonic power. The legal system is therefore both a mode of control and a place of resistance.[54]

Before turning our attention to the Pentateuch, I would like to approach the problem from the margins, briefly looking at a text that belongs to the narrative of the promulgation of the Pentateuch, the so-called Artaxerxes rescript in Ezra 7:12–26. According to Ezra 7:7 (בשנת שבע לארתחשסתא המלך, "in the seventh year of Artaxerxes the king"), this letter from Artaxerxes to Ezra must be dated to the year 458 B.C.E., in the reign of Artaxerxes I (465–424 B.C.E.), and is written in Aramaic, thus interrupting the Hebrew narrative.[55] This change in language as well as Ezra's authority in the sacred and profane sphere undoubtedly give the text the authoritative character of an official Persian document.[56]

---

51. Ronen Shamir investigates why Israeli histories tend to neglect the impact of the British government in the early phases of Zionist settlement: *The Colonies of Law: Colonialism, Zionism and Law in Early Mandate Palestine* (Cambridge Studies in Law and Society; Cambridge: Cambridge University Press, 2000).

52. Against Otto, "Die Rechtshermeneutik des Pentateuch," 91–106. On the question of identity formation in the Persian period, see John Kessler, "Persia's Loyal Yahwists: Power Identity and Ethnicity in Achaemenid Yehud," in *Judah and the Judeans in the Persian Period* (ed. O. Lipschits and M. Oeming; Winona Lake, IN: Eisenbrauns, 2006) 91–121.

53. It remains unclear why Erhard S. Gerstenberger continues to speak of a "liberation" by the Persians that was the driving force behind the origin of the Torah: "Es liegt aber in der Natur der Sache, dass die Konstitution der Jahwegemeinden um ihr religiöses Rückrat, die Tora, herum erst nach der Befreiung durch die Perser im Jahre 539 v. Chr. gleichzeitig mit der Entstehung der Heiligen Schriften voll einsetzte und im 5. Jh. v. Chr. zu einem guten Ende gebracht wurde" (*Israel in der Perserzeit*, 295).

54. Merry, "Colonial and Postcolonial Law," 576.

55. Questions of chronology cannot be addressed here; see Joseph Blenkinsopp, *Ezra–Nehemiah: A Commentary* (OTL; Philadelphia: Westminster, 1988) 139–44; H. G. M. Williamson, *Ezra, Nehemiah* (WBC 16; Waco, TX: Word, 1985) xxxix–xliv.

56. The exact nature of Ezra's mission is notoriously difficult to determine; see the proposals offered in Joseph Blenkinsopp, "The Mission of Udjahorresnet and Those of Ezra and Nehemiah," *JBL* 106 (1987) 409–21; Lester L. Grabbe, "What Was Ezra's Mission?" in *Second Temple Studies, 2:*

As Bob Becking argues, "The text functions as an imperial legitimation of Ezra's deeds and actions in both fields."[57] In a way, the text itself provokes the question that dominates scholarship: the problem of the authenticity of the Artaxerxes rescript. Despite numerous parallels from Aramaic letters, it is difficult to use language and form as a conclusive argument for the authenticity of Ezra 7:12–26, precisely because this letter does not fit the normal structure of a standard letter.[58] Furthermore, the rescript's content poses a challenge to its authenticity as a Persian document, a challenge that literary-critical arguments cannot meet. Thus, one is forced to offer additional hypotheses, such as postulating the Persian ratification of a document originally drafted by Ezra or by some other Jewish scribes.[59] From there, it is but a small step to ascribing some cunning move to Ezra and writing a psychological portrait of Artaxerxes.[60]

These methodological difficulties have once again strengthened the position of arguing for authenticity or fictionality based on the literary context of the

---

Temple Community in the Persian Period (ed. Tamara C. Eskenazi and Kent H. Richards; JSOTSup 175; Sheffield: JSOT Press, 1994) 286–99; David Janzen, "The 'Mission' of Ezra and the Persian–Period Temple Community," *JBL* 119 (2000) 619–43.

57. Bob Becking, "The Idea of *Thorah* in Ezra 7–10: A Functional Analysis," *ZABR* 7 (2001) 273–86 (quotation from p. 281).

58. See the detailed analysis in Dirk Schwiederski, *Handbuch des nordwestsemitischen Briefformulars: Ein Beitrag zur Echtheitsfrage der aramäischen Briefe des Esrabuches* (BZAW 295; Berlin: de Gruyter 2000) 344–82. For a different perspective, see Bezalel Porten, "המסמכים בספר עזרא ושליחותו של עזרא," *Shnaton* 3 (1978–79) 174–96.

59. Thus, Eduard Meyer observed: "Das kann allerdings kein Perser aus eigener Kentniss geschrieben haben. Aber es liegt doch auf der Hand, dass Artaxerxes' Rescript nichts anderes ist als die Redaction einer Vorlage, die Ezra und seine jüdischen Genossen . . . den Ministern vorgelegt haben. Der König hat . . . befohlen, dass das Gesetz, welches sich im Besitz Esras befindet . . . bei den Juden eingeführt und zum Grundgesetz der jüdischen Gemeinde gemacht werden soll. Das kann die persische Regierung nicht aus eigener Initiative gethan haben, denn sie konnte davon nichts wissen." ("No Persian could have written this based on his own knowledge. But it is quite obvious that the Artaxerxes rescript is nothing other than a redaction of a Vorlage provided for the officials by Ezra and his Jewish companions. The king commanded . . . that the law that is in Ezra's possession be introduced to the Jews and made into the constitution of the Jewish community. This, the Persian administration could not have done on its own initiative, because it was not aware of it") (*Die Entstehung des Judenthums:Eine historische Untersuchung* [Halle: Max Niemeyer, 1896] 65). On the debate surrounding Meyer's view, see Fausto Parente, "*Die Entstehung des Judenthums*: Persien, die Achämeniden und das Judentum in der Interpretation von Eduard Meyer," in *Eduard Meyer: Leben und Leistung eines Universalhistorikers* (ed. William M. Calder III and Alexander Demandt; Mnemosyne Supplement 112; Leiden: Brill, 1990) 329–43; Reinhard G. Kratz, *Das Judentum im Zeitalter des Zweiten Tempels* (FAT 42; Tübingen: Mohr Siebeck, 2004) 6–22.

60. "Esra erfaßte den günstigsten Augenblick für sein Werk. Artaxerxes war ein beeinflußbarer Mann, unter dem erreicht werden konnte, was noch ein Xerxes schwerlich gewährt hätte" ("Ezra seized the moment. Artaxerxes was a corruptible person under whose rule one could accomplish what would have been impossible under Xerxes") (Hans Heinrich Schaeder, *Esra der Schreiber* [BHT 5; Tübingen: Mohr Siebeck, 1930] 62).

pericope itself.[61] Here Reinhard Kratz, Juha Pakkala, and Sebastian Grätz, among others, have shown that much of the rescript of the Artaxerxes letter is closely connected to the narrative framework and shaped with knowledge of Ezra 1–6 and Nehemiah 2–6. It is therefore difficult to assume the existence of an authentic document that has been incorporated into the narrative.[62] Limited space does not allow for a detailed discussion of such arguments. In the following, I will assume that the rescript is indeed a "historical fiction" (*Geschichtsfiktion*).[63] I assume further that it was written by an author who had "wide confidence in the Achamenid authority in providing security and order in the land."[64] However, this author uses formulations and information known in the Persian period, so a certain knowledge of Persian imperial structures can be assumed.[65] This knowledge is independent of any actual date of the Ezra narrative. In other words, even if one favors a Hellenistic composition of the Ezra narrative or, in fact, a compilation of the Pentateuch, the context provided by the biblical documents themselves still remains Persian. The passage from the rescript addressing the role of the law reads as follows:

> [14]For you are commissioned by the king and his seven advisors to regulate (לבקרא) Judah and Jerusalem according to the law of your God which is in your care (בדת אלהך די בידך). . . . [25]And you, Ezra, by the divine wisdom you possess, appoint magistrates and judges (שפטין ודינין) to judge (דאנין)[66] all the people in the province Beyond the River who know the laws of your God (לכל־ידעי דתי אלהך), and to teach those who do not know them. [26]Let anyone who does not obey the law of your God and the law of the king (דתא די־אלהך ודתא די מלכא) be punished with dispatch, whether by death, corporal punishment, confiscation of possessions, or imprisonment. (Ezra 7:14, 25–26 [NJPS])

61. See Klaus Koch, "Der Artaxerxes-Erlaß im Esrabuch," in *Meilenstein: Festgabe für Herbert Donner zum 16. Februar 1995* (ed. Manfred Weippert and Stefan Timm; Ägypten und Altes Testament 30; Wiesbaden: Harrassowitz, 1995) 87–98.

62. See Kratz, *Composition of the Narrative Books*, 68–80; Juha Pakkala, *Ezra the Scribe: The Development of Ezra 7–10 and Nehemia 8* (BZAW 347; Berlin: de Gruyter, 2004) 22–56; Grätz, *Das Edikt des Artaxerxes*, 80–83. Furthermore, Sara Japhet has shown that one of the main emphases of Ezra 1–6 is to demonstrate that the will of God is equated with the will of the Persian king; see her "Sheshbazzar and Zerubbabel against the Background of the Historical and Religious Tendencies of Ezra–Nehemiah," *ZAW* 94 (1982) 66–98 (repr. in Japhet, *From the Rivers of Babylon to the Highlands of Judah: Collected Studies on the Restoration Period* [Winona Lake, IN: Eisenbrauns, 2006] 53–95).

63. Grätz, *Das Edikt des Artaxerxes*, 294.

64. Pakkala, *Ezra the Scribe*, 39.

65. Kratz rightly states: "Ohne die persische Reichsidee und spezielle Art der Reichsverwaltung sind die Dokumente im Esrabuch nicht zu verstehen" (*Judentum*, 20).

66. The LXX translates κατάστησον γραμματεῖς καὶ κριτάς, ἵνα ὦσιν κρίνοντες παντὶ τῷ λαῷ κτλ., probably thinking of ספרין. Changing the MT is unnecessary; compare Grätz, *Das Edikt des Artaxerxes*, 77.

According to Ezra 7:14, Ezra is sent (שלח) by the king to set up a judicial inquiry (בקר) according to the divine law (בדת אלהך),[67] which must be distinguished from the law of the king. This first action of Ezra must be separated
from the simple teaching of the law and the appointment of judges and officials, issues that only follow in vv. 25–26. Maybe, Ezra 7:14 is a necessary pre-
requisite for the teaching of the law and the upholding of the royal order in
Yehud.[68]

It is striking that Ezra 7:25–26, using language reminiscent of Deuteronomy,
places the Law of God and the Law of the King in parallel, thus assuming equality of both legal corpora.[69] This parallelism has—within the Ezra narrative—
consequences for the political and religious institutions, because in Ezra 7:25–
26 the judges guard the proper execution of the Law of God *and* the Law of the
King.[70] If one is concerned with finding any historical reality, this identification
of divine and Persian law poses a series of problems.[71] However, this concern
for historicity overlooks the fact that Ezra 7:12–26 as well as the *Letter of Aristeas*
simply provide a Jewish etiology for the advent or promulgation of the Hebrew
Torah and the Greek *Nomos* in postexilic Judaism.[72] Therefore, it is futile to enter here into the debate about which part of the Pentateuch Ezra carried with
him as "Law." As far as the narrative is concerned, this Law is clearly supposed
to be the Pentateuch as a whole, because Ezra functions as a second Moses, who
brings the Torah in its entirety to the Jews in Yehud.

---

67. The extensive debate about the character of דת and its relationship to תורה cannot be
repeated here; see Reinhard G. Kratz, *Translatio imperii: Untersuchungen zu den aramäischen Danielerzählungen und ihrem theologiegeschichtlichen Umfeld* (WMANT 63; Neukirchen-Vluyn: Neukirchener Verlag, 1991) 233–41.

68. See Williamson, *Ezra, Nehemiah*, 101.

69. The closest parallels can be found in the laws regulating the offices of Israel in Deut 16:18–
18:22; see Blenkinsopp, *Ezra–Nehemiah*, 150–51; Williamson, *Ezra, Nehemiah*, 104; and Pakkala
(*Ezra the Scribe*, 39), who assumes the direct influence of Deut 16:18. This parallelism is still reflected
in the Septuagint, which translates the phrase τὸν νόμον τοῦ θεοῦ καὶ τὸν νόμον τοῦ βασιλέως.

70. Grätz, *Das Edikt des Artaxerxes*, 99.

71. Lisbeth S. Fried ("'You Shall Appoint Judges': Ezra's Mission and the Rescript of Artaxerxes," in *Persia and Torah: The Theory of Imperial Authorization of the Pentateuch* [ed. James W. Watts;
SBLSymS 17; Atlanta: Society of Biblical Literature, 2001] 63–89) argues that Ezra appointed Persian judges that would have then judged according to the *dāta* of the king and according to the
dāta of the god, both being Persian concepts. Fried seems to overlook the fact that the closeness of
Ezra 7 to Deut 16:18–18:22 makes this proposal unlikely, because the Deuteronomic text (on
which much of the Ezra narrative is modeled) does not allow for the investiture of a "foreign" judiciary. Also, why would a Persian king send a Jewish envoy to one of his provinces to appoint
Persian judges? Furthermore, where would the Persian judges come from, and would it be likely
that they would support the issues concerning the "marriage crisis"?

72. On the relationship between the role of the *Letter of Aristeas* and Ezra 7, see Reinhard G.
Kratz, "Temple and Torah: Reflections on the Legal Status of the Pentateuch between Elephantine and Qumran," in this vol., pp. 77–103.

The authors of Ezra and Nehemiah counter any (imagined future) Persian pressure by a preemptive strike, inventing a document that fits well into Persian ideology and that avoids any conflict with it. This avoidance of conflict leads to the self-portrait of postexilic Judaism as founded by a decree of the Achaemenid Empire, which in turn will guarantee its continued existence.[73] Following the internal logic of the narrative, it is hardly surprising that aspects of the Persian penal code were used even for infractions of traditional Jewish law.[74] Resorting to the Persian penal code is clearly an effort to avoid predictable tensions with the colonial ruler.

For the Ezra-narrative, it must be stressed that it is not a direct act by the Persians that helps to promulgate the Torah in Yehud but, rather, an imagined process of a Jewish group that envisages an initiation by the imperial court.[75] In passing, I will note that this literary fiction also fulfills an inner-group purpose: by attributing a quasi-double legitimation to the Pentateuch, that is, by both a divine and a political authority (YHWH and the Persian king), the authors of Ezra 7 remove the Torah from any future criticism. In the current setting, any opposition to the Torah from within the group will be an offense against God and king. This protective purpose of the text persists, even if one argues for a later setting of Ezra 7.[76]

If "[c]olonial rule magnified jurisdictional tensions and gave greater urgency and symbolic importance to the task of defining the interactions of various legal forums, sources, and personnel,"[77] it is hardly surprising that, for example, the authors of Deuteronomy carefully avoided the regulation of any problems or concepts outside the narrow confines of Judean territory. Here, the law of kingship in Deut 17:14–20 might be a good test case.[78] Both the setting of the law

---

73. See Kratz, "Das nachexilische Judentum sieht sich nach Lage der Quellen aus eigenem Antrieb vom persischen Weltreich begründet und garantiert" (*Judentum*, 22).

74. Blenkinsopp, *Ezra–Nehemiah*, 152.

75. See Titus Reinmuth, "Reform und Tora bei Nehemia: Neh 10, 31–40 und die Autorisierung der Tora der Perserzeit," *ZABR* 7 (2001) 287–317.

76. In other words, if the author is lying, he uses the "lie" of an imperial authorization to legitimate his theological concept. If, in turn, the text was created in the Hellenistic period (as argued by Grätz), Ezra 7 serves the same purpose as does 2 Kgs 22:3–13: an old and therefore valid document is invented to promulgate reforms. In contrast to the time of Josiah, divine support no longer seems enough. The new cosmopolitan existence of Judaism in the postexilic period reflected in the books of Ezra, Daniel, and Esther is now in need of the additional support of the worldly ruler, even if this ruler is only imagined.

77. Laura Benton, *Law and Colonial Cultures: Legal Regimes in World History 1400–1900* (Studies in Comparative World History; Cambridge: Cambridge University Press, 2002) 253.

78. On Deut 17:14–20, see most recently Bernard M. Levinson, "The Reconceptualisation of Kingship in Deuteronomy and the Deuteronomistic History's Transformation of Torah," *VT* 51 (2001) 511–34; idem, "The First Constitution: Rethinking the Origins of Rule of Law and Separation of Powers in Light of Deuteronomy," *Cardozo Law Review* 27 (2006) 1853–88; Ernest W.

הָאָרֶץ אֲשֶׁר יהוה אֱלֹהֶיךָ נֹתֵן לָךְ, "the land, that Yʜwʜ your God will give you")
as well as the stipulation who the king shall be (לֹא תוּכַל לָתֵת עָלֶיךָ אִישׁ נָכְרִי, "you
shall not set a foreigner over you") seem to fit well in the context of Achaemenid ideology in which the (conquered) people are put in their place within the
Persian world order (*arta*). The obvious lack of any law-giving authority in the
hands of the king—a major revolution within the ancient Near Eastern legal
context—probably allows a community to live by its local laws, while at the
same time suggesting that any stipulation drafted by a global authority can still
be followed.[79]

Here, the authors responsible for writing or placing the law in its current
context seem to fulfill a double task: on the one hand, any clash with a higher
authority outside the narrow confines of the designated place is carefully
avoided by limiting an institution to a local level. On the other hand, the foundations are set for an existence after kingship or colonial rule. What we have
here can probably be described as a "harmony ideology."[80] This implies that the
presence of colonial or imperial rule evokes strategies avoiding conflict and favoring compromise and harmony between ruler and ruled subject. This drive
for harmony is often performed on a nonofficial level because these approaches

> are either counter-hegemonic political strategies used by the colonized
> groups to protect themselves from encroaching superordinate power-
> holders or hegemonic strategies the colonizers use to defend themselves
> against organized subordinates.[81]

How harmony is maintained depends entirely on the seekers of a harmonious
state. The biblical view of avoiding conflicts by limiting regulations to a local
level may be contrasted with the local involvement of individual Persians in
Greek cults in cities, such as Sardis, as apparent from the first half of the Droaphernes inscription:

> Ἐτέων τριήκοντα ἐννέα Ἀρτα-
> ξέρξεω βασιλεύοντος τὸν ἀν-
> δριάντα Δροαφέρνης *vac.*

Nicholson, "Do Not Dare to Set a Foreigner over You: The King in Deuteronomy and 'The
Great King,'" *ZAW* 118 (2006) 46–61; Gary N. Knoppers, "The Deuteronomist and the Deuteronomic Law of the King: A Reexamination of a Relationship," *ZAW* 108 (1996) 329–46.

79. "Das Spezifikum der Rechtskodifikationen im Pentateuch der Hebräischen Bibel ist es, daß
hier erstmals im Alten Orient Rechtssätze zu Programmtexten redigiert werden, die sich von der
königsideologischen Herrscherlegitimation lösen" (Otto, "Die Rechtshermeneutik des Pentateuch,"
91).

80. See Laura Nader, *Harmony Ideology: Justice and Control in a Zapotec Mountain Village* (Stanford: Stanford University Press, 1990).

81. Ibid., 1.

Βαρ(ά)κεω Λυδίης ὕπαρχος Βαρα-
5 δάτεω Διί. *feuille.* Προστάσσει τοῖς
εἰσπορευομένοις εἰς τὸ ἄδυ-
τον νεωκόροις θεραπευ-*vac.*
ταῖς αὐτοῦ καὶ στεφανοῦσι τὸν θε-
ὸν μὴ μετέχειν μυστηρίων Σαβα-
10 ζιου τῶν τὰ ἔνπυρα βασταζόν-
των καὶ Ἀνγδίστεως καὶ Μᾶς.Προσ-
τάσσουσι δὲ Δοράτη τῷ νεωκόρω τού-
των τῶν μυστηρίων ἀπέχεσθαι. *feuille.*

In the thirty-ninth year of Arta- | xerxes' ruling, the statue of a | man Droaphernes (set up), | the son of Bar(a)kes, hyparch of Lydia, to | Zeus of Baradatas. [*leaf ornament*] He orders those | who have entered into the adyton, | the neokoroi therapeuthes [those who serve the god and temple] | of him, and who garland the god | that they do not take part in the mysteries of Saba- | zios, of those who lift up the burnt | offerings either of Angidistis or Ma. They | order the neokoros for Dorates | to abstain from these mysteries.[82]

The Droaphernes inscription manifests a certain Persian presence that moves beyond the official involvement in the running of the province.[83] Contacts of this sort would certainly increase the pressure with regard to the ideal of a strict separation of colonizers and colonized, a separation that could no longer be maintained, except on an imaginary level.

The authors of the Pentateuch seem to fulfill a double task. On the one hand, they create a document that can be understood within the Persian context, because it limits legal procedure and legal claims to a certain locality, most likely only Persian Yehud—that is, to the place ascribed to Judeans. The apparent nonuse or non-validity of the Torah at Elephantine seems to prove the point.[84] Just in passing, I would like to stress that this function of local law in a larger imperial context does not, of course, presuppose the existence (or creation) of a "Citizen-Temple-Community."[85]

---

82. Greek text according to L. Robert, "Une nouvelle inscription de Sardes: Règlement de l'autorité perse relatif à un culte de Zeus," *CRAIBL* (1975) 306–30; the English translation is from Dusinberre, *Aspects of Empire*, 233.

83. Dusinberre (ibid., 118) rightly speaks of a "degree of acculturation at Sardis."

84. See Kratz, "Temple and Torah," 77–103.

85. On the concept, see Joel Weinberg, "The Agricultural Relations of the Citizen-Temple Community in the Achaemenid Period," *The Citizen-Temple Community* (JSOTSup 151; Sheffield: JSOT Press, 1992) 92–104; and the justified criticism of Weinberg's view in H. G. M. Williamson, "Judah and the Jews," *Studies in Persian Period History and Historiography* (FAT 38; Tübingen: Mohr Siebeck, 2004) 25–45.

On the other hand, the authors of the Pentateuch create a narrative that confers identity and seems to ignore the political surroundings and, in doing so, submits itself to external pressure. It is an external pressure that is not officially sanctioned but simply generated by the colonial existence within an imperial structure. The authors of the Pentateuch meet this pressure by creating an ideology of harmony that allows them to use the "freedom" granted by the Persians to a maximum extent, while avoiding open resistance. It seems that the lessons learned from the Assyrian and Babylonian periods resulted in a new approach to a life under foreign rule and might be a reason why much of the pentateuchal narrative is situated in the distant past.[86] The Persian presence and pressure triggers harmony and is therefore responsible for the shaping of the Pentateuch—even though Persia never officially sanctioned the process.

---

86. See Jean-Louis Ska, *Introduction to Reading the Pentateuch* (trans. Sr. Pascale Dominique; Winona Lake, IN: Eisenbrauns, 2006) 185–87. This volume is a translation and revision of *Introduction à la lecture du Pentateuque: Clés pour l'interprétation des cinq premiers livres de la Bible* (Le livre et le rouleau 5; Brussels: Éditions Lessius, 2000) 320–21.

Temple and Torah:
Reflections on the Legal Status of the
Pentateuch between Elephantine and Qumran

REINHARD G. KRATZ
Göttingen

The main question of this essay is: how did the Pentateuch reach its prominence as Torah; that is, how did it become the official, binding, and foundational document of Judaism? I shall argue that one must think not only of a late Persian context but also of Hellenistic and Hasmonean contexts to understand the process leading to the codification, distribution, and acceptance of the Pentateuch as Torah. This historical process took place between Elephantine and Qumran—"in between," not only in terms of geography and chronology, but also in terms of the acknowledgement and acceptance of the Pentateuch as Torah. A distinction should be made between "torah" as cultic and legal custom practiced at the temple(s) and the Pentateuch as the Torah of Moses, which presupposes the temple but goes far beyond its needs and was not necessarily practiced there. I shall demonstrate that asking how the Pentateuch reached its prominence as Torah means asking how the temple and the Torah of Moses came together.

1. The Problem

At first, the answer to the question how the Pentateuch became Torah seems fairly simple. It happened because God revealed his Torah to Moses on Mt. Sinai. This answer, however, provided by the document itself, obviously did not

---

Author's note: My sincere thanks to Anselm C. Hagedorn (Berlin) for his valuable help in preparing the English version of this article. I also would like to express my gratitude to the editors of this volume, Gary Knoppers and Bernard Levinson, for their help in improving the argument, as well as the language.

survive the deconstruction of 18th- and 19th-century historical criticism.[1] The scholarship of this period demonstrated that ancient Israelite religion and Judaism certainly did not arise all of a sudden but gradually—despite the general objection of Jacob Bruckhardt.[2] In other words, neither Torah nor Judaism— and still less, their close connection to one another—arrived in the world fully formed. Even Noth's hypothesis of the basic form of the Pentateuch (*Grundlage*, G) via the detour of an oral tradition of the pentateuchal themes could not give back to the Torah of Moses its early origin.[3] Rather, the Torah of Moses evolved over several centuries and does not mark the beginning but the end of the history of ancient Israel, while at the same time introducing the epoch generally known as Judaism.[4] To place the Torah at the very beginning of Israel's history is already an evaluation of its status, but this does not tell us anything about how the Pentateuch came to have this particular role.

The answers usually provided by critical biblical scholarship about how the Torah became so central to Judaism do not satisfy either. Scholars refer to Josiah's reform as reported in 2 Kings 22–23 and to the book of Deuteronomy, which served as the basis for that report and supposedly served also as the basis of the reform itself. Or one thinks of Ezra—returning from the Golah in Babylon and organizing life in Judah with the "Law of the God of heaven" in his hands, reading and teaching the Torah to the people of Jerusalem—as one reads Ezra 7–10 and Nehemiah 8. However, both of these texts, the Josiah account as well as the Ezra legend, already presuppose the general acceptance of the Torah and, therefore, cannot be trusted as reliable witnesses.

More likely, an analysis of the Pentateuch revealing the gradual literary growth of the text itself will provide the answer to our question. The hypothe-

---

1. See the classic position in Julius Wellhausen, *Die Composition des Hexateuchs und der historischen Bücher des Alten Testaments* (4th ed.; Berlin: de Gruyter, 1963); idem, *Prolegomena zur Geschichte Israels* (6th ed.; Berlin: Reimers, 1905; reprinted from the 6th ed. of 1927, with an index of scriptural citations, Berlin: de Gruyter, 2001; ET: *Prolegomena to the History of Ancient Israel* [trans. J. Sutherland Black and Allan Menzies; Edinburgh: Black, 1885; reissued, with a foreword by D. A. Knight: Scholars Press Reprints and Translation Series 17; Atlanta: Scholars Press, 1994]).

2. See Jacob Burckhardt, *Über das Studium der Geschichte* (ed. Peter Ganz; Jacob Bruckhardt Werke: Kritische Gesamtausgabe 10; Munich: Beck, 2000) 381 (see also pp. 170, 332: "Religions can hardly *have come into existence in a gradual way*. . . . There may have been transformations and reunions, partly sudden, partly gradual; however, (there is) no (such thing as) gradual origin" (*Allmählich* können die Religionen *nicht* wohl *entstanden* sein. . . . Es waren teils plötzliche, teils allmähliche Wandlungen und Reunionen, aber kein allmähliches Entstehen).

3. Martin Noth, *Überlieferungsgeschichte des Pentateuch* (Stuttgart: Kohlhammer, 1948; ET: *A History of Pentateuchal Traditions* [trans. with an introduction by Bernhard W. Anderson; Englewood Cliffs, NJ: Prentice Hall, 1972; reissued, Atlanta: Scholars Press, 1981]).

4. As for the distinction between "ancient Israel" and "Judaism," I refer to Wellhausen, *Prolegomena*, 1, 361–424 [ET: 1, 363–425] as well as to his *Israelitische und jüdische Geschichte* (10th ed.; Berlin: de Gruyter, 2004).

sis of a Priestly compromise determining the composition of the Pentateuch as Torah is one attempt to provide the answer.[5] However, too many uncertainties remain in this area. The diachronic analysis of the Pentateuch—if one does not abandon this enterprise entirely—yields only a relative chronology of its literary strata.[6] Therefore, one must be very careful to correlate the data and historical constructions given by the individual literary layers of the Pentateuch itself and other biblical sources with historical circumstances and must not simply project a biblical historical fiction onto history. This suggests that we must rely on additional information and hypotheses when searching for the historical circumstances under which the Pentateuch literary corpus evolved and eventually became the Torah.

Scholars have always assumed that information about the historical circumstances of this transformation could be found in the epigraphic sources. Ever since the time of Eduard Meyer, legal documents from the Persian period have been used as analogies to the Aramaic documents in the book of Ezra.[7] They still provide the basis for Peter Frei's thesis of an imperial authorization that was adapted by biblical scholars to explain how the Pentateuch became Torah.[8] The texts upon which this hypothesis depends do not need to be listed here.[9] A study of their historical setting and value demonstrates, however, that we must be very careful when drawing such far-reaching conclusions from them.

---

5. For the suggestion of a priestly compromise caused by internal and external factors (including the Persian imperial authorization), see Erhard Blum, *Studien zur Komposition des Pentateuch* (BZAW 189; Berlin: de Gruyter, 1990) 333–60; idem, "Esra, die Mosetora und die persische Politik," in *Religion und Religionskontakte im Zeitalter der Achämeniden* (ed. Reinhard G. Kratz; Veröffentlichungen der Wissenschaftlichen Gesellschaft für Theologie 22; Gütersloh: Gütersloher Verlag, 2002) 231–56. An innerpriestly "compromise" dominated by Zadokites (without any Persian participation or imperial authorization) is suggested by Eckart Otto, *Das Deuteronomium im Penatetuch und Hexateuch: Studien zur Literaturgeschichte von Pentateuch und Hexateuch im Lichte des Deuteronomiumrahmens* (FAT 30; Tübingen: Mohr Siebeck) 234–73.

6. My view on the matter is presented in detail in my *Komposition der erzählenden Bücher des Alten Testaments: Grundwissen der Bibelkritik* (Göttingen: Vandenhoeck & Ruprecht, 2000) [ET: *The Composition of the Narrative Books of the Old Testament* (London: T. & T. Clark / Continuum, 2005)].

7. Eduard Meyer, *Die Entstehung des Judenthums* (Halle a.d.S.: Max Niemeyer, 1896; reissued, Hildesheim: Olms, 1987); idem, *Der Papyrusfund von Elephantine* (Leipzig: Hinrichs, 1912). On this issue, see my "Entstehung des Judentums: Zur Kontroverse zwischen E. Meyer und J. Wellhausen," in *Das Judentum im Zeitalter des Zweiten Tempels* (2nd ed.; FAT 42; Tübingen: Mohr Siebeck, 2006) 3–22.

8. Peter Frei, "Zentralgewalt und Lokalautonomie im Achämenidenreich," in *Reichsidee und Reichsorganisation im Perserreich* (ed. Peter Frei and Klaus Koch; OBO 55; Fribourg: Universitätsverlag / Göttingen: Vandenhoeck & Ruprecht, 1984) 7–43; second revised edition (1996) 5–131. For the reception of Frei's hypothesis by biblical scholarship, see Blum, *Studien zur Komposition* 345–60; idem, "Esra, die Mosetora und die persische Politik," 246–54.

9. See my view in *Translatio imperii: Untersuchungen zu den aramäischen Danielerzählungen und ihrem theologiegeschichtlichen Umfeld* (WMANT 63; Neukirchen-Vluyn: Neukirchener Verlag, 1991) 246–57.

Frei's hypothesis initiated a lively scholarly debate.[10] In the course of this discussion, several things became confused. Therefore, it might be useful to point
out what is the indisputable basis of his hypothesis and what seems to be rather
questionable.[11]

The indisputable fact upon which Frei's thesis rests—and a fact supported
by external evidence, moreover—is that the Persian imperial authority granted
certain privileges and occasionally also seems to have authorized local institutions, customs, and laws of the people under Persian rule. This authorization
served as a quasi-legal acceptance of these institutions or customs. This is the
legal procedure that Frei calls imperial authorization, no more and no less. So
far the argument of Frei is quite strong, regardless of whether the evidence is of
a historical or a literary-fictitious nature. Because there is, in this case, some external historical evidence, perhaps one can go on to conclude that the pertinent
literary or possibly literary-fictitious witnesses, such as Ezra 7 and Daniel 6, also
testify to the existence of the legal procedure practiced by Persian authorities
within their provinces.

There are, however, two major objections to Frei's hypothesis and its application to the Torah. The question arises whether one is able to deduce from a
variety of kinds of local evidence a generally approved and universally valid legal
practice or legal understanding within the broader Achaemenid Empire. Here
the use of the term "law" (Persian *dāta*, borrowed in Semitic languages) in the
Achaemenid royal inscriptions must be taken into consideration. It reveals a
kind of consciousness of a global legal order.[12] Still, the question remains to
what extent, if any, the conceptual framework of the royal inscriptions was connected with the process of rendering individual legal decisions. Furthermore,
one must address the question whether it is indeed possible to adapt the procedure of imperial authorization to apply to the Torah of Moses. It seems highly
speculative to deduce from the legal practice in this or that specific location in
the Persian Empire the route that the Pentateuch took to become the Torah.

Thus, the thesis of the Persian imperial authorization is highly disputed.
Furthermore, no clear indications of a connection between Persian legal prac-

---

10. See the contributions in *ZABR* 1 (1995) and in *Persia and Torah: The Theory of Imperial Authorization of the Pentateuch* (ed. James W. Watts; SBLSymS 17; Atlanta: Society of Biblical Literature, 2001). In both publications, Peter Frei provides a summary of his original hypothesis: "Die
persische Reichsautorisation: Ein Überblick," *ZABR* 1 (1995) 1–35; ET: "Persian Imperial Authorization: A Summary," in *Persia and Torah*, 5–40.

11. For a more extensive treatment of this question, see the contribution by Konrad Schmid in
this volume (pp. 23–38).

12. See Klaus Koch, "Weltordnung und Reichsidee im alten Iran," in *Reichsidee und Reichsorganisation im Perserreich* (ed. Peter Frei and Klaus Koch; OBO 55; 2nd ed.; Fribourg: Universitätsverlag / Göttingen: Vandenhock & Ruprecht, 1996) 133–337, esp. 149–53; Kratz, *Translatio
imperii*, 205–6, 253–54.

tice and the Pentateuch can be found. It is, therefore, necessary to develop alternative models. I would like to approach the problem from a different angle and broaden the question of the legal status of the Pentateuch by asking about the distribution and validity of the Pentateuch as Torah within Judaism itself. It is within this broader perspective that the role of the temple comes into play. It was at the temple of Jerusalem and possibly the schools related to it that the Pentateuch (or the Torah of Moses) reached its prominence and legal status as Torah.

I approach this broader question from two avenues: first, by looking at the situation of Judaism as represented in the archives from Elephantine (Jeb); and second, by focusing on the situation documented in the Dead Sea Scrolls (Qumran). Both cases have a distinct advantage in that the sources from these sites can be dated almost exactly: the papyri from Elephantine around 400 B.C.E., the manuscripts from Qumran from about 150 B.C.E. to 150 C.E. Without resorting to an uninspired positivism, I would like to evaluate whether sources from two different regions and phases in the history of ancient Judaism can be used to draw conclusions about what happened in the period between these two phases.

Furthermore, I would like to evaluate how the biblical material relates to the available external evidence.[13] In the case of Elephantine, the evidence consists of private and official documents including information concerning matters of religion. At Qumran, the evidence consists mainly of religious documents, including biblical manuscripts. In between these two archives, there is the Pentateuch, the Mosaic Law, which became Torah and was accepted as the foundational document of Judaism not only in the Second Temple of Jerusalem but also in the Samaritan community as well as in the Egyptian (and Babylonian) diaspora. So I shall ask how this document, the Torah of Moses, relates to the archives of Elephantine and Qumran and whether this relationship tells us something about the ascent of the Pentateuch as Torah.

---

13. Both the literary tradition and the external evidence have to be taken into account for the purposes of historical reconstruction. In this respect, I disagree with Lester L. Grabbe, who in his review of my book *Das Judentum im Zeitalter des Zweiten Tempels* (RBL 06/2005) finds a "clear Christian orientation" in my approach. Despite the indisputable fact that I am a Christian, I actually do not know what he wanted to say with this characterization. But I insist that—apart from its historicity or fictitiousness—the biblical tradition as such (including the Apocrypha and Pseudepigrapha, the Septuagint, the Qumran literature, and the writings of the New Testament, which, as far as I know, were written by Jews) must be taken seriously as a historical phenomenon in reconstructing the history of ancient Judaism. A pure positivistic reconstruction that only relies on the *realia* provided by external evidence and on the few historical data that can be extracted from the biblical and nonbiblical literature misses the most important factor of the history of ancient Judaism in the Persian and Hellenistic–Roman periods: the religious and theological (or—if you like—ideological) thoughts that, as their outcome shows, obviously influenced history.

2. The Situation at Elephantine

Writing about the Jews living on Elephantine, Julius Wellhausen describes them as a "strange vestige of pre-legal Hebraism" and a "fossil remnant of not yet reformed Judaism in a distant land." He continues that these were Jews who "in a distant corner of the globe maintained their old nature" on a "pre-legal level, quite similar to the Jewish pagans whom the members of the Golah encountered in the land."[14] These are unmistakably clear and undoubtedly provocative words that Wellhausen added to the seventh edition of his *Israelitische und jüdische Geschichte* in 1914, immediately after the discovery of the papyri. These words seemed apt and find support in the sources themselves.[15] Nevertheless, this view did not prevail. Discoveries of new texts and a different perspective on the sources led to the view that the Jews of Elephantine, some syncretistic peculiarities notwithstanding, were not so far removed from the Judaism known from biblical sources and later Jewish texts.[16] The discussion about the religion of the Jews at Elephantine continues.[17] The crucial question

---

14. See Wellhausen, *Israelitische und jüdische Geschichte*, 176–78: "Von einem merkwürdigen Überrest des vorgesetzlichen Hebraismus, der sich über die Zeit Ezras und Nehemias hinaus an der Grenze Ägyptens und Nubiens erhalten hatte, haben wir jüngst durch glückliche Funde Kenntnis bekommen" (p. 176). "Im Unterschied von den sogenannten Zehn Stämmen sind diese Juden nicht in dem Heidentum, das sie umgab, aufgegangen, sondern haben in einem entlegenen Winkel der Welt ihr altes Wesen behauptet" (p. 177). "Sie standen noch auf der vorgesetzlichen Stufe, ähnlich wie die jüdischen Paganen, welche die Bne haGola im Lande vorfanden" (pp. 177–78). "Dieser fossile Überrest des unreformierten Judentums in fernem Lande liefert demnach eine willkommene Bestätigung dessen, was schon vorher als Ergebnis der kritischen Untersuchung der israelitischen Religionsgeschichte fest stand" (p. 178).

15. See Meyer, *Der Papyrusfund*, 38–67; Arthur E. Cowley, *Aramaic Papyri of the Fifth Century B.C.E.* (Oxford: Clarendon, 1923 [repr. Osnabrück: Otto Zeller, 1967]) xiii–xxviii; Albert Vincent, *La religion des Judéo-Araméens d'Éléphantine* (Paris: Geuthner, 1937).

16. See Bezalel Porten, *Archives from Elephantine: The Life of an Ancient Jewish Military Colony* (Berkeley: University of California Press, 1968); idem, "The Religion of the Jews of Elephantine in Light of the Hermopolis Papyri," *JNES* 28 (1969) 116–21. The edition used in this essay is Bezalel Porten and Ada Yardeni, *Textbook of Aramaic Documents from Ancient Egypt*, vols. A–D (Jerusalem: Academon, 1986–99; hereafter, *TADAE*).

17. See Peter Bedford, "Jews at Elephantine," *Australian Journal of Jewish Studies* 13 (1999) 6–23; Paul-Eugène Dion, "La religion des papyrus d'Éléphantine: Un reflet du Juda d'avant l'exil," in *Kein Land für sich allein: Studien zum Kulturkontakt in Kanaan, Israel/Palästina und Ebirnâri für Manfred Weippert zum 65. Geburtstag* (ed. Ulrich Hübner and Ernst Axel Knauf; OBO 186; Fribourg: Universitätsverlag / Göttingen: Vandenhoeck & Ruprecht, 2002) 243–54; Bob Becking, "Die Gottheiten der Juden in Elephantine," in *Der eine Gott und die Götter: Polytheismus und Monotheismus im alten Israel* (ed. Manfred Oeming and Konrad Schmid; ATANT 82; Zurich: Theologischer Verlag, 2003) 203–26; Reinhard G. Kratz, " 'Denn dein ist das Reich': Das Judentum in persischer und hellenistisch-römischer Zeit," in *Götterbilder—Gottesbilder—Weltbilder: Polytheismus und Monotheismus in der Welt der Antike* (2 vols.; ed. Reinhard G. Kratz and Hermann Spieckermann; FAT 2/17–18; Tübingen: Mohr Siebeck, 2006) 1.347–74.

remains: what was the status of the Torah among the "Judeans" (יהודיא) or "Arameans" (ארמיא), as the Jews of Elephantine also called themselves? It is unnecessary to examine all of the available data relevant to our question here; instead, the most important evidence will suffice.[18] One consideration in estimating the importance of the Torah to the Jews at Elephantine is to consider not just what has been found but also what has not been found among the documents collected there. Copies of the biblical texts were not found among the papyri from Elephantine. This evidence is significant, because the considerable finds from Elephantine include not only private archives but also the official archive of Yedaniah concerning matters of religion. Here, we would expect to find corresponding texts or at least references to the Torah if the Torah was in use in Elephantine.

To complicate matters somewhat, the preserved texts dealing with matters of the temple and of religious practice (especially the correspondence regarding the destruction and rebuilding of the temple at Elephantine) contain many details that can also be found in the Hebrew Bible. However, these details are restricted to phraseology and religious customs, such as mourning and fasting in the light of the destruction of the temple—things that are quite common. Therefore, they simply serve as a phenomenological analogy to the phraseology and customs also found in the Hebrew Bible. Moreover, in contrast with the Hebrew Bible, and more specifically, in contrast with the correspondence provided in the book of Ezra about the rebuilding of the temple in Jerusalem, the correspondence from Elephantine makes no reference to the Torah.[19]

Furthermore, the lack of copies of the Torah at Elephantine is even more striking because there is evidence that other literature was used in the schools there. This literature included the history and the proverbs of the wise scribe Ahiqar, who had not yet been transformed into a pious Jew, as is the case in the book of Tobit.[20] This literature includes also the Aramaic version of the

---

18. See Ernst Axel Knauf, "Elephantine und das vor-biblische Judentum," in *Religion und Religionskontakte im Zeitalter der Achämeniden* (ed. Reinhard G. Kratz; Veröffentlichungen der Wissenschaftlichen Gesellschaft für Theologie 22; Gütersloh: Gütersloher Verlag, 2002) 179–88.

19. See *TADAE* A 4.3, 4.5, 4.7–8, 4.9, 4.10. On this issue, see my "Second Temple of Jeb and of Jerusalem," in *Judah and the Judeans in the Persian Period* (ed. Oded Lipschits and Manfred Oeming; Winona Lake, IN: Eisenbrauns, 2006) 247–64 [German version in idem, *Das Judentum im Zeitalter des Zweiten Tempels* (2nd ed.; FAT 42; Tübingen: Mohr Siebeck, 2006) 60–78]. The lack of references to the Torah in this correspondence was already noticed and discussed at length by Cowley, *Aramaic Papyri*, xxiii–xxviii; see esp. p. xxviii: "Regarded without prejudice, these texts lead to the conclusion that the Pentateuch, both in its historical and legal aspects, was unknown in the fifth century to the Jews at Elephantine, and it is probable that the populace in Judaea in the seventh century was no better informed." See also Dion, "La religion d'Éléphantine," 250, 252.

20. Tob 1:21–22, 2:10, 11:18, 14:10. See Max Küchler, *Frühjüdische Weisheitstraditionen* (OBO 26; Fribourg: Universitätsverlag / Göttingen: Vandenhoeck & Ruprecht, 1979) 364–70.

Behistun Inscription of Darius the Great, a piece of royal propaganda that was read or, at least, was supposed to be read at Elephantine. These two documents show what it meant for the Jews of Elephantine to fear God (or gods) and the Persian king (see Prov 24:21).[21]

The first commandment and especially the legislation regarding the centralization of worship in Deuteronomy 12 and Leviticus 17 also seemed to be unknown to the Jews on Elephantine. It is well known that they swore by other gods in addition to YHW, or even worshiped them, and that they had their own temple in which they offered—supervised by priests—their sacrifices to YHW (including the burnt offering).[22] The correspondence regarding the destruction and rebuilding of this temple does not seem to indicate that the Jews in Elephantine felt any embarrassment that they swore to or worshiped more than one god at a temple outside Jerusalem or indeed that they even felt the need for any embarrassment on this front. Therefore, one should not place too much importance in the fact that the burnt offering—mentioned in the letters from Elephantine—is missing in the memorandum sent by the governors of Judah and Samaria, who agreed with the rebuilding of the temple.[23] After all, it was a prestigious Jewish messenger, Hananiah, who addressed the Jews of Elephantine as his "brothers" and told them the dates for the Festival of Mazzoth celebrated at the temple on Elephantine.

Indeed, the celebrations of Mazzoth (Unleavened Bread) and Passover at Elephantine also provide clues about the status of the Torah there. Originally Passover and Mazzoth were separate rites (see Exod 12:1–14, 21–27 and Exod 12:15–20; 13:3–10; 23:15; 34:18). Only Deuteronomy integrates the two rites and gives them a new meaning in its festival legislation (Deut 16:1–8; cf. Exodus 12–13 as a whole).[24] In contrast, Elephantine seems to know only the earlier

---

21. See Cowley, *Aramaic Papyri*, xiv–xv: "The literary pieces, it is true, are evidently of non-Jewish origin, but they show nevertheless the kind of literature which was current in the community. And their interest consists not only in what they say but in what they omit: in the light they give and in the darkness in which they leave us." See also Dion, "La religion d'Éléphantine," 251–52.

22. On the archaeological evidence, see Cornelius von Pilgrim, "Textzeugnis und archäologischer Befund: Zur Topographie Elephantines in der 27. Dynastie," in *Stationen: Beiträge zur Kulturgeschichte Ägyptens, Rainier Stadelmann gewidmet* (ed. Heike Guksch and Daniel Polz; Mainz: von Zabern, 1998) 485–97; idem, "Tempel des Jahu und 'Straße des Königs': Ein Konflikt in der späten Perserzeit auf Elephantine," in *Egypt—Temple of the Whole World / Ägypten—Tempel der gesamten Welt (Festschrift J. Assmann)* (ed. Sibylle Meyer; SHR 97; Leiden: Brill 2003) 303–17. On the textual evidence, see n. 19.

23. For the discussion of this question, see Ingo Kottsieper, "Die Religionspolitik der Achämeniden und die Juden von Elephantine," in *Religion und Religionskontakte im Zeitalter der Achämeniden* (ed. Reinhard G. Kratz; Veröffentlichungen der Wissenschaftlichen Gesellschaft für Theologie 22; Gütersloh: Gütersloher Verlag, 2002) 150–78, esp. 169–75.

24. See Bernard M. Levinson, *Deuteronomy and the Hermeneutics of Legal Innovation* (Oxford: Oxford University Press, 1997) 53–97.

state of affairs, pertaining to the two distinctive rites, and shows an awareness neither of the Deuteronomic interpretation nor of the combination of the two rites in Exodus 12–13 within the larger Torah of Moses.

It should be known by now that the so-called Passover Letter found at Elephantine—as much of the letter as is extant—does not deal with Passover but only with the Festival of Unleavened Bread or Mazzoth. In the main edition of Porten and Yardeni, it is labeled document A 4.1 and is translated by the editors as follows (*TADAE* 1.54–55):

> RECTO [1][To my brothers Je]daniah and his colleagues the Jewish ga[rrison,] your brother Hanan[i]ah. May God/the gods [seek after] the welfare of my brothers [2][at all times]. And now, this year, year 5 of King Darius, it has been sent from the king to Ar[sames . . .]. [3][. . .] . . . Now, you thus count four[teen [4]days of Nisan . . .] and from the 15th day until the 21st day of [Nisan . . .[5]. . .] be pure and take heed. Any work do n[ot do [6]. . .] do not drink, anything of leaven do not [eat. VERSO [7] . . .] sunset until the 21st day of Nisa[n . . .[8]. . . b]ring (sc. the leaven) into your chambers and seal (them) up during [these] days [9][. . .] . . . [10][To] my brothers Jedaniah and his colleagues the Jewish garrison, your brother Hananiah s[on of PN].

This document contains stipulations for the Festival of Unleavened Bread, some of which are found in the Torah of Moses, some only in the Mishnah, and some of which were later outlawed.[25] At the beginning of the letter, Hananiah refers to a certain message from the Persian king (Darius II) to Arsames, the satrap in Egypt, that is unfortunately not preserved.[26] However, both the stipulations themselves and their close connection with a command of the king indicate that the festival practice followed not the stipulations of the Torah of Moses but the custom sanctioned by the Persians, a custom that did not need the Torah of Moses.

In addition, there are two ostraca that do mention the Passover. But, again, one must pay attention to what they mention and what they fail to mention.[27] Like the Passover Letter, but unlike Deuteronomy 16, these ostraca do not establish whether Passover and Mazzoth are celebrated together or where Passover should be celebrated—in the family (Exodus 12–13) or at the temple (Deuteronomy 16). One can only say this: at Elephantine, Mazzoth was probably celebrated at the temple, and Passover was a specific day of the year. This

---

25. See Knauf, "Elephantine und das vor-biblische Judentum," 186, with reference to Bezalel Porten et al., *The Elephantine Papyri in English* (DMOA 22; Leiden: Brill, 1996) 126.

26. See Kottsieper, "Die Religionspolitik der Achämeniden," 150–58.

27. See *TADAE* D 7.6:9–10 (convex); 7.24:5 (concave); and Porten, *Archives from Elephantine*, 131–32.

practice reflects a situation that the Torah of Moses also discusses and regulates in a certain way. But it is equally clear that in Elephantine—as far as we can see—this situation was not based on the stipulations of the Torah of Moses and, furthermore, that this situation existed earlier than the regulations pertaining to Mazzoth found in the so called Passover Letter.

The same can be said of the Sabbath, which is again only documented in ostraca, the documents of daily life on Elephantine.[28] Here, too, the biblical tradition combines what were originally two customs, the feast of Sabbath (often mentioned together with the new moon; see 2 Kgs 4:23) and the prohibition of work on every seventh day of the week (see Exod 23:12).[29] On Elephantine, both customs were known but, as far as we can see, not yet combined. In the ostraca, the Sabbath is mentioned as a certain date.[30] The Passover Letter also tells us that the prohibition of work was known at Elephantine, at least for the evening before the Festival of Mazzoth. But according to the ostraca, the prohibition of work apparently does not seem to apply to the Sabbath. Rather, we are told that on the Sabbath the Jews of Elephantine engaged in trade and transportation and also stocked the warehouses. In this respect, they were no different from the Judeans or the people of Tyre mentioned in Neh 13:15–16 or from the kings of Judah and the people of Jerusalem addressed in Jer 17:19–27. However, the Jews of Elephantine, unlike the Judeans and the people of Tyre, are never accused of disobeying a law of the Mosaic Torah.

Finally, the contracts found at Elephantine do not show any signs of a specific jurisdiction based on the Torah of Moses but instead seem to follow common customs and practices. In several instances, such as in regard to the social position of women and the possibility of a divorce instigated by the wife, we do find certain parallels to biblical passages.[31] However, these parallels, again, simply reflect commonly held views and customs that were also incorporated into the biblical tradition but that do not depend on the Torah of Moses.

The result of this brief survey seems to be quite clear: the documents found at Elephantine provide evidence of a form of Judaism that worshiped YHWH

---

28. See *TADAE* D 7.10:5, 7.12:9, 7.16:2, 7.35:7, maybe also 7.28:4, 7.48:5. With respect to this issue, see Lutz Doering, *Schabbat: Sabbathalacha und -praxis im antiken Judentum und Urchristentum* (TSAJ 78; Tübingen: Mohr Siebeck, 1999) 23–42.

29. See Johannes Meinhold, *Sabbat und Woche im Alten Testament* (FRLANT 5; Göttingen: Vandenhoeck & Ruprecht, 1905); idem, "Die Entstehung des Sabbats," *ZAW* 29 (1909) 81–112; idem, "Zur Sabbathfrage," *ZAW* 48 (1930) 121–38; Gnana Robinson, *The Origin and Development of the Old Testament Sabbath: A Comprehensive Exegetical Approach* (Frankfurt a.M.: Peter Lang, 1988).

30. Whether this date is (still) the full moon (equivalent to Akkadian *šab/pattum*) or (already) the weekly seventh day is very much in dispute. It is by no means as clear as Doering (*Schabbat*, 34–35, on the basis of the expression עד ערובה, "until the evening [before a certain event]" and the supposed Hebrew and Greek equivalents ערב שבת, προσάββατον, and πρασκευή) asserts.

31. See Porten, *Archives from Elephantine*, 260–62.

(YHW or YHH) and maintained a temple. But this form of Judaism did not follow the Torah of Moses and most likely did not even know it. Thus far, Wellhausen's verdict—that the Jews of Elephantine operated at a "pre-legal level," that is, without the Torah of Moses—seems to be correct. The question remains, however, whether this form of Judaism simply represented a marginal group in a "distant corner of the globe" or whether the situation reflected in the documents from Elephantine was representative of the Egyptian diaspora as well as (major parts of) Judaism in Palestine. This question will be the basis of a comparison with the situation at Qumran and in Jerusalem.

This question, too, can be answered definitively. The "Judeans" of Elephantine do not just represent an earlier form of the religion of preexilic Israel or preexilic Judah, respectively.[32] The close connections kept by the Jewish garrison not only with the Persian authorities but also with the ruling people in Jerusalem and Samaria in matters regarding the rebuilding of the temple seem to suggest that, even for their own time, they were not exceptional. Rather, they seem to have been compatible with the Jewry represented by the leading figures in Jerusalem and Samaria to whom they addressed their letters. This, in turn, allows conclusions to be drawn regarding the situation in Palestine.[33] It appears that there, too, the Torah of Moses did not play an important role yet —at least for major parts of Jewish society in the Persian provinces of Yehud and Samaria.

As far as the comparison between Elephantine and Palestine is concerned, the analogy to the situation regarding the Sabbath described in Neh 13:15–16 and the role of the messenger Hananiah are crucial. Hananiah visited Elephantine at least once and sent the Passover Letter (covering a message from the Persian king and the stipulations for the Festival of Mazzoth) there. Both the analogy of Nehemiah 13 and the role of Hananiah reinforce the impression that the situation in Jerusalem and Samaria was not too different from the situation on Elephantine. Whoever this Hananiah was, he did not come from Elephantine but from the motherland or even from the Babylonian Golah. He, nevertheless, addressed the Jews of Elephantine as "my brothers" and acted as a

---

32. For an Israelite (Ephraimite?) descent of the "Judeans" at Elephantine, see Manfred Weippert, "Synkretismus und Monotheismus: Religionsinterne Konfliktbewältigung im alten Israel," in *Jahwe und die anderen Götter: Studien zur Religionsgeschichte des antiken Israel in ihrem syrisch-kanaanäischen Kontext* (FAT 18; Tübingen: Mohr Siebeck, 1997) 1–24, esp. 15. For a Judahite descent, see Cowley, *Aramaic Papyri*, xv–xvi, xviii, xix–xx, xxii, xxviii; Dion, "La religion d'Éléphantine," 252–53.

33. For a reconstruction of the historical situation mainly based on the data of the Elephantine papyri and the epigraphic evidence from Judah and Samaria, see my "Statthalter, Hohepriester und Schreiber im perserzeitlichen Juda," in *Das Judentum im Zeitalter des Zweiten Tempels* (2nd ed.; FAT 42; Tübingen: Mohr Siebeck, 2006) 93–119.

mediator between the Persian administration and the Jews of Elephantine in matters of religion.[34] He may even have been the one who managed to negotiate the privileged status of a "Jewish garrison" (חיל יהודיא) for them.[35] Hananiah was for the Judeans at Elephantine what, according to the biblical account, Ezra and Nehemiah were for the Judeans in the province of Judah. However, Hananiah did not bring a law book to Elephantine but simply a single stipulation that confirmed or introduced a custom and was somehow connected with a command from the Persian king. The Torah of Moses, then, does not seem to have played an important role and, according to the available external evidence, knowledge of the Torah of Moses was not widespread either inside or outside the community on Elephantine. In comparison with this evidence, the biblical figures of Ezra and Nehemiah are exceptional and seem to represent a marginal group or party within Judaism of the late Persian period.

Finally, we must turn to the question of the legal status of the Torah. Simply put, in the areas where it was unknown, the Torah could not have had any legal status at all. Rather, the legal situation of the Jews of Elephantine corresponds to the general situation in the ancient Near East and, specifically, in the Persian Empire.[36] Single enactments of local (Jewish or Persian) judges and other officials ("scribes") were crucial for legal practice and are amply documented.[37] These officials were bound by a higher norm, such as the "Law of the King," the "natural law," or just a custom (*Gewohnheitsrecht*) but not by a legal code.[38] A legal code unknown to the Achaemenids may have existed among individual ethnic groups within the empire and perhaps also among the Jewish people. Indeed, it might have been carefully composed and studied within scholarly circles, such as the later Qumran communities of the *Yaḥad*. But, as far as one can see, it apparently did not possess any practical cultic or legal significance for the official circles within the provinces of Yehud and Samaria. The only possible exception to this generalization might be the stance of individuals, such as Ezra and Nehemiah, if both of them or at least Nehemiah ever had an official position and if it was actually true what the books of Ezra and Nehemiah re-

---

34. On the question of Hananiah's identity, see my chapter "The Second Temple," 253 [German version in *Das Judentum*, 65].

35. *TADAE* A 4.1:1, 10; C 3.15:1. On this issue, see Kottsieper, "Die Religionspolitik der Achämeniden," 157.

36. See Lisbeth S. Fried, "'You Shall Appoint Judges': Ezra's Mission and the Rescript of Artaxerxes," in *Persia and Torah: The Theory of Imperial Authorization of the Pentateuch* (ed. James W. Watts; SBLSymS 17; Atlanta: Society of Biblical Literature, 2001) 63–89.

37. See, for example, the list of officials in *TADAE* 4.5:9–10 or 4.6:5–6; and Porten, *Archives from Elephantine*, 45–53; Fried, "Ezra's Mission," 65–67; Kratz, "Statthalter, Hohepriester und Schreiber."

38. See Fried, "Ezra's Mission," 68, 79–80, 83 where, however, the distinction of "positive" and "natural law" is often blurred. For the "Law of the King," see above, n. 12.

port, that Nehemiah not only was responsible for rebuilding the wall but also was sent, like Ezra, to reorganize the province of Yehud according to the Torah of Moses.

3. The Situation at Qumran

The situation reflected in the texts from the Dead Sea (Qumran) is entirely different.[39] Here, it is completely unnecessary to embark on the laborious task of gathering clues to prove that the Torah of Moses was known and widely used. Several copies of the Torah (and other biblical books) point in this direction.[40] Countless references to the Torah in the pre- and non-Qumranic Apocrypha and Pseudepigrapha confirm the point.[41] Similarly, Qumranic (Essene) writings show that the Torah was well known and often cited.[42] But what exactly is the significance of this intensive attestation of the Torah of Moses in the Dead Sea Scrolls? What is under discussion here is not the knowledge of the Torah but the legal or, at least, official status of the Torah inside and outside the community of Qumran, which called itself "the *Yaḥad*" (היחד).[43]

Within the Qumran community, the Torah played an absolutely dominant role, because it regulated everything from the organization of the community and the administration of justice to the practice of religion and private conduct of life.[44] One has only to open any of the community rules (1QS, CD) to realize that almost every sentence seems to refer to God's commandments and

---

39. A complete list of the texts can be found in Emanuel Tov, *The Texts from the Judaean Desert: Indices and Introduction to the Discoveries in the Judaean Desert Series* (DJD 39, Oxford: Clarendon, 2002). On the state of research, see the contributions in *The Dead Sea Scrolls after Fifty Years: A Comprehensive Assessment* (2 vols.; ed. Peter Flint and James C. VanderKam; Leiden: Brill, 1998–99).

40. See Eugene Ulrich, "The Dead Sea Scrolls and the Biblical Text," in *The Dead Sea Scrolls after Fifty Years,* 1.79–100; Leonard J. Greenspoon, "The Dead Sea Scrolls and the Greek Bible," in ibid., 1.101–27.

41. See Peter Flint, "'Apocrypha,' Other Previously-Known Writings, and 'Pseudepigrapha' in the Dead Sea Scrolls," in ibid., 2.24–66.

42. On the differentiation, see Armin Lange, "Kriterien essenischer Texte," and Charlotte Hempel, "Kriterien zur Bestimmung 'essenischer Verfasserschaft' von Qumrantexten," both of which are published in *Qumran kontrovers: Beiträge zu den Textfunden vom Toten Meer* (ed. Jörg Frey and Hartmut Stegemann; Einblicke 6; Paderborn: Bonifatius, 2003) 59–69 and 71–85, respectively.

43. For introductory primers, see Hartmut Stegemann, *Die Essener, Qumran, Johannes der Täufer und Jesus* (4th ed.; Freiburg: Herder, 1994; ET: *The Library of Qumran: On the Essenes, Qumran, John the Baptist and Jesus* [Grand Rapids: Eerdmans, 1998]); James C. VanderKam, *The Dead Sea Scrolls Today* (Grand Rapids: Eerdmans, 1994; GT: *Einführung in die Qumranforschung* [Göttingen: Vandenhoeck & Ruprecht, 1998]); Timothy H. Lim, *The Dead Sea Scrolls: A Very Short Introduction* (Oxford: Oxford University Press, 2005). On the archaeology of the site, see Jodi Magness, *The Archaeology of Qumran and the Dead Sea Scrolls* (Grand Rapids: Eerdmans, 2002).

44. But see also Johann Maier, "Pentateuch, Torah und Recht zwischen Qumran und Septuaginta," in *Studien zur Jüdischen Bibel und ihrer Geschichte* (SJ 28; Berlin: de Gruyter, 2004) 111–24.

the Torah. For example, the *Community Rule* (1QS) stresses right at the beginning that it was written "in order to seek God with [all the heart and with al]l soul doing what is good and right before him, as he commanded through Moses and through all his servants the prophets" (1QS I 1–3). Further on, regarding admission to the community, the *Rule* stipulates:

> [E]very one who enters in the Council of the Community *shall enter into the covenant of God in the sight of all those who devote themselves*, he shall take upon his soul by a binding *oath* to return to the Torah of Moses *according to all which he has commanded* with all heart and with all soul, according to everything which he has been revealed from it *to the Sons of Zadok, the priests who keep the covenant and seek his will* and according to the multitude of the (Council of the men of Community) *men of their covenant who devote themselves together to his truth and to walking in his will*. (1QS V 7–9)[45]

The differences between this situation and that of Elephantine, a Judaism roughly 250 years older, could hardly be more significant. At Elephantine, the Torah of Moses was apparently unknown; here at Qumran, it is absolutely binding. And one other thing is striking. At Elephantine, we find a temple and everything that belongs to it, including cultic and legal customs, but no Torah of Moses. Of course, some of the cultic and legal customs that were practiced at Elephantine show a certain resemblance to the material (such as the Covenant Code) that was integrated into the Pentateuch. Nevertheless, they do not represent the Torah of Moses or any forerunner of the Torah of Moses. Only within the Torah of Moses did these customs, as well as any other cultic or legal material, reach their theological status as the Law of the Lord. In contrast, at Qumran one finds the Torah of Moses but no real temple. The temple in Jerusalem was not ignored by any stretch of the imagination but was frowned upon by the Qumran community, which believed that the Torah was not kept or at least not kept properly at this temple. Hence, as a substitute, the community regarded itself as a sanctuary in which worship was practiced that complied with the Torah.[46] Moreover, the community was convinced that this worship

---

45. My translation follows Elisha Qimron and James Charlesworth's translation in *The Dead Sea Scrolls: Hebrew, Aramaic, and Greek Texts with English Translations*, vol. 1: *Rule of the Community and Related Text* (ed. James H. Charlesworth with Frank M. Cross et al.; Princeton Theological Seminary Dead Sea Scrolls Project; Tübingen: Mohr Siebeck / Louisville: Westminster John Knox, 1994). Asterisks ** indicate omissions, while parentheses ( ) indicate variants in the parallel manuscripts B (4Q256) and D (4Q258), which offer a shorter version.

46. See 1QS VIII 1–7 (trans. Qimron and Charlesworth): "In the Council of the Community there (are to be) twelve (lay)men and three priests, perfect in everything which has been revealed from the whole Torah, to perform truth, righteousness, justice, merciful love, and circumspect walking, each one with his fellow to keep faithfulness in the land with a steadfast purpose and a broken spirit, to pay for iniquity by works of judgment and suffering affliction, and walk with all

was also practiced by the angels in heaven and that, at the end of time, true worship would be practiced again even at the temple in Jerusalem.

As in the case of Elephantine, it is necessary to ask to what extent the Judaism of the Second Temple period is represented by the evidence of Qumran. An answer to this question is not as simple as it may appear, because everything outside the Qumran community is labeled outside the Torah of Moses by the Qumran community itself. However, the acceptance of the Torah could not have been so unusual, because the so-called nonsectarian (non-Qumranic) texts found in the caves at the Dead Sea—that is, the biblical writings themselves as well as the Apocrypha and Pseudepigrapha (among them works, such as Ben Sira, *1 Enoch*, and the book of *Jubilees*)—all point beyond the narrow circle of the community of Qumran. Unfortunately, however, these texts (with the sole exception, perhaps, of Ben Sira) do not tell us much about the legal status and the actual use of the Torah in the temple in Jerusalem. We have to admit, difficult as it may be, that, despite the sheer magnitude of information presented by the Apocrypha and Pseudepigrapha, it is impossible to extract any evidence regarding the spread and the status of the Torah and the other biblical books in other groups or communities of ancient Judaism, especially the leading circles at the temple of Jerusalem. It is similarly impossible to do so from the biblical books themselves.

Two texts from the Qumran community, then, take on special significance for the question whether Qumran was part of the mainstream or, at least, in agreement with other groups of ancient Judaism with respect to the Torah. These documents take on significance because they are addressed explicitly to the outside world—that is, to the aristocracy at the Jerusalem temple. The two documents are: the *Prayer for the Welfare of King Jonathan* (4Q448) and the halakic letter 4QMMT (4Q394–4Q399), the addressee of which remains anonymous but seems to have been a person of high status who had special responsibilities for the people.

The two texts are quite similar, which is the reason for a recent hypothesis that they belong to the same work.[47] In both cases, it remains unclear and hence disputed who the addressee is. It might be Jonathan, the son of Mattathias, and brother of and successor to Judas Maccabee, and the leader of the Maccabees from 160/159 to 142 B.C.E., who, as the first Hasmonean, seized the

---

by the measure of truth and the norm of the Endtime. When these become in Israel—the Council of the Community being established in truth—an eternal plant, the House of Holiness (בית קדש) consisting of Israel, a most holy assembly for Aaron, (with) eternal truth for judgment, chosen by (divine) pleasure to atone for the earth and to repay the wicked their reward."

47. Annette Steudel, "4Q448: The Lost Beginning of MMT?" in *From 4QMMT to Resurrection: Mélanges qumraniens en hommage à Émile Puech* (ed. Florentino García Martínez et al.; STDJ 61; Leiden: Brill, 2006) 247–63.

office of high priest in 152 B.C.E. Or the addressee might have been Alexander Jannaeus, son of Hyrcanus, who reigned as king and high priest from 103 to 76 B.C.E. However one decides this issue, both texts are addressed to a representative of the Hasmonean Dynasty, who—at least nominally—held aloft the banner of the fight for the Torah. It appears that the authors of both texts hoped that the Hasmoneans would help to lead the Qumran community to victory in their agenda of promulgating obedience to the Torah within Second Temple Judaism.

This hope is especially expressed in the halakic letter 4QMMT, which informs its addressee about several details regarding the proper exegesis and practice of the Torah of Moses. In this context, the Halakah about the place of sacrifice is of particular interest.[48] It is the only place in 4QMMT where a direct quotation (from the Hebrew Bible) is the object of a halakic interpretation. The discussion focuses on Lev 17:3–4 and the question of exactly where the sacrifices should be slaughtered. On this matter, the author of 4QMMT takes a remarkably strict position by limiting the sacrifice only to the sanctuary. In the same context, he refers to Deuteronomy 12 and stresses that "the place that he (YHWH) has chosen" is clearly Jerusalem and its temple.

This passage is interesting for two reasons. First, it shows that 4QMMT assumes that the addressee of the letter is familiar with the quotation from the Torah and that its validity is generally accepted, despite differing opinions about how to practice the law under discussion. Second, it is striking that the text that alludes to the Torah explicitly stresses that only Jerusalem is the legitimate place for the sanctuary and not Khirbet Qumran or some other place. Both matters reflect a complete change in the earlier circumstances represented by the documents from Elephantine. Despite the rejection of the Jerusalem temple as legitimate under the circumstances at the time of the author of 4QMMT, remarkably—according to what one reads in the halakic letter— centralization of worship was not questioned at all, either by the author or its addressee. All this leads to the question what happened to the Torah of Moses and to the relationship between Torah and temple in the period between the situation at Elephantine in 400 and at Qumran in 150 B.C.E., not only in Jerusalem but also—when looking at Alexandria and the Septuagint—in the Egyptian diaspora.

---

48. 4QMMT B 27–35 (Elisha Qimron and John Strugnell in consultation with Yaʿakov Sussmann and with contributions by Yaʿakov Sussmann and Ada Yardeni, *Miqṣat Maʿaśe Ha-Torah* [DJD 10; Oxford: Clarendon, 1994] 48–52). See my "'Place Which He Has Chosen': The Interpretation of Deuteronomy 12 and Leviticus 17 in 4QMMT" (Meghillot: Studies in the Dead Sea Scrolls; Jerusalem: Bialik / Haifa: Haifa University, forthcoming).

4. The Situation in Between

Simply put, the results of our investigation of the external evidence are the following: (1) the temple without the Torah of Moses (but with cultic and legal customs) in the documents of Elephantine; (2) the Torah of Moses without the temple (but with a decisive ideological claim on the temple) in the Dead Sea Scrolls from Qumran. Both archives are chronologically far removed from one another, but both contain important hints about contacts with Jerusalem. Perhaps these hints can help to illuminate the history of Judah during the late Persian and Hellenistic-Roman periods.

The comparison between Elephantine and Qumran suggests that the circumstances in Jerusalem underwent a dramatic change. In the course of only 100 years (between 400 and 300 B.C.E.), the editorial process of the Torah—itself composed from the several different traditions—must have been finished. The finished product must have gained so much ground that, if we believe the evidence found in Diodorus and Josephus, by around 300 B.C.E. a Greek historian, Hecataeus of Abdera, could already use the Mosaic history as a source for his description of Judaism.[49] Another 150 years later, the Torah of Moses was a document that was accepted and interpreted by various groups within ancient Judaism. So, what happened?

Looking back from the outcome, it is clear what must have happened: temple and Torah, two entities that do not necessarily belong together, must by one path or another have been joined together. To avoid any misunderstandings here, again, it should be stressed that this conclusion does not mean that Torah and temple were previously not connected. However, "torah" was originally something other than the written, Mosaic Torah as we know it from the Hebrew Bible. Naturally, the oral (or even written) torah of the priest—containing cultic and legal material such as, for example, information about what was clean and what was unclean—had its place at the temple. But this "torah" was in no way identical with the Torah of Moses found in the Pentateuch. Therefore, the crucial point is the link between the temple and the Torah of Moses.

It cannot be disputed that the Torah of Moses also had an oral and literary prehistory. However, it would be short-sighted to identify the prehistory of the

---

49. For the Greek witnesses, see the relevant texts in Menahem Stern, ed., *Greek and Latin Authors on Jews and Judaism* (3 vols.; Jerusalem: Dorot, 1974–84) 1.20–44. Here, as well as in reference to Hecataeus's contemporary Theophrastus, the question regarding the sources used has not been sufficiently solved. Therefore, it is exceedingly difficult to evaluate how reliable and representative notes are that are derived from second- and third-hand sources. The characterization of the Jews as "philosophers" found in all sources from Theophrastus to Manetho is quite remarkable and in need of a detailed study, because it probably provides insights into the nature of the sources. The legends that have grown around Judaism in the Greek tradition should not be used too hastily as historical proof or as independent witnesses to an ominous "cultural memory."

Mosaic Torah simply with the practices of priests and prophets in the First and Second Temples, and to place it institutionally—be it in the form of a "school" or of any other system of education—within the official archive or library of the temple.[50] There might be one or two clues for a view of this sort in the biblical literature itself but not any conclusive evidence. On the contrary, the evidence from the archives of Elephantine and from the "library" from Qumran leads, instead, to the conclusion that the Torah of Moses as well as the other biblical books did not belong to the official canon of Jewish educational literature.

The process of the oral and literary origin of the Mosaic Torah—and this is what is at stake here—might have begun in preexilic times and come to a close during the Persian period. But this process does not provide us with any reliable information about the status of the Torah at the temple and its dissemination within Jewish society in the preexilic and postexilic periods. A common knowledge and practice of the Torah of Moses cannot just be taken for granted simply because the biblical literature and the tradition of biblical Judaism presuppose it. For this reason, we must pose the question how the Temple of YHWH and the Torah of Moses were connected, in Judah and Jerusalem as well as in the Egyptian diaspora.

The biblical tradition itself still shows quite clearly that this connection between the temple and the Torah of Moses was hardly taken for granted. How the connection happened is described in Ezra 7 for the Hebrew Torah and in the *Letter of Aristeas* for its translation, the Greek *Nomos*. Like Hananiah, Ezra is a Jewish envoy of the Persian king. In contrast to Hananiah, who simply brought a single enactment, Ezra would promulgate in Judah the "Law of the God of heaven"—that is, a jurisdiction based on the Torah and, as such, the Torah itself.[51] This "Law of the God of heaven" is regarded as the "Law of the

---

50. On this question, see most recently David Carr, *Writing on the Tablet of the Heart: Origins of Scripture and Literature* (Oxford: Oxford University Press, 2005) and the secondary literature provided and discussed on pp. 299–305.

51. The relationship between the "Law of the God of heaven" and the Torah is disputed. Rolf Rendtorff argues for a strict separation of both but has to admit that the current composition of Ezra–Nehemiah (that is, the canonical final form to which he is usually referring) seems to favor an identification between the two ("Esra und 'das Gesetz,'" *ZAW* 96 [1984] 165–84; idem, "Noch einmal: Esra und 'das Gesetz,'" *ZAW* 111 [1999] 89–91). The identification results from the Hebrew variants of the Aramaic title of Ezra (Ezra 7:12, 21) in Ezra 7:6, 10–11. Only for a postulated preliminary stage of Ezra 7:12–26 could one argue for a differentiation, but Rendtorff does not seem to take that into account and does not make any reference to such a stage. Needless to say, he does not offer any explanation for the expression "Law of the God of heaven." Against Rendtorff, see my *Translatio imperii*, 288–89; and Thomas Willi, *Juda—Jehud—Israel: Studien zum Selbstverständnis des Judentums in persischer Zeit* (FAT 12; Tübingen: Mohr Siebeck, 1995) 90–91, 101–17. Whether one identifies דת and תורה, or whether one determines the relationship (as proposed by Willi, *Juda*, 113) as exegesis, whereby "Law of the God of heaven" describes an early form of the halakic interpretation of Torah, the identity remains the same. See my *Translatio imperii*, 235–39.

King" or at least as being under the protection of the king.[52] At the same time, Ezra's orders are to hand over the collection of the king to the temple in Jerusalem, which means that temple and Torah are supported equally by the Persian king. The unity is stressed by both titles attributed to Ezra: he is "priest" and "scribe" at the same time.[53] However, the literary tradition places different emphasis on the issues of temple and Torah. While the mission of Ezra in Ezra 7–8 reaches its climax in the praise of God and in the glorification of the temple (7:27–28), the further narrative (Ezra 9–10) places greater emphasis on the Torah of Moses—a process that reaches its closure in Nehemiah 8, where the public reading of the Torah almost seems to replace worship at the temple.

Similar things can be said of the *Letter of Aristeas*, which traces the Greek translation of the Torah back to an order issued by Ptolemy II. The translation is connected to the temple by the fact that a message is sent to Jerusalem to request 72 priests as translators. These translators gain the respect of the king through dialogue and by accurately translating. This, in turn, is the reason for the authority of the Greek Torah—the Septuagint being named, of course, for the seventy(-two) priests. It must be stressed that, for the *Letter of Aristeas*, the temple in Jerusalem is the distinctive reference point and not a temple in Elephantine or elsewhere in the diaspora. The Torah brought to the Ptolemaic king is legitimated by its connection with the Jerusalemite priesthood and can serve as a complete substitution for the missing temple. Thus, here too the difference between the temple and the Torah of Moses is still perceivable and both reports—the Ezra legend and the *Letter of Aristeas*—seek to demonstrate how temple and Torah came together.

Old Testament scholars tend to use both of these texts—Ezra 7 and the *Letter of Aristeas*—for a historical reconstruction, even though both documents are highly disputed as far as their authenticity and historical value are concerned.[54] Despite all the historical coloring in Ezra 7 and in the Ezra narrative as a whole,

---

52. The relationship depends on whether one understands the "Law of the King" in Ezra 7:25 as an equivalent to the "Law of the God of heaven" in the hand of Ezra or simply equates it with the order of the king; on the question, see my *Translatio imperii*, 233–35 (with further bibliography).

53. See my "Ezra—Priest and Scribe," in *Sages, Scribes, and Seers: The Sage in the Eastern Mediterranean World* (ed. Leo G. Perdue; FRLANT 219; Göttingen: Vandenhoeck & Ruprecht, 2007).

54. The Ezra legend is used for historical reconstruction extensively by Koch, "Weltordnung und Reichsidee im alten Iran," 206–307. See also Rainer Albertz, *Religionsgeschichte Israels in alttestamentlicher Zeit* (ATD Ergänzungsreihe 8/2: Grundrisse zum Alten Testament; Göttingen: Vandenhoeck & Ruprecht 1992) 497–99 [ET: *A History of Israelite Religion in the Old Testament Period* (2 vols.; OTL; Louisville, KY: Westminster / John Knox, 1994) 2.466–68]. For a different view, however, see Erhard S. Gerstenberger, *Israel in der Perserzeit: 5. und 4. Jahrhundert v. Chr.* (Biblische Enzyklopädie 8; Stuttgart: Kohlhammer, 2005) 82–85. For the *Letter of Aristeas*, see the contribution of Arie van der Kooij in this volume (pp. 289ff.).

the report is highly suspicious. Its authenticity is questioned for literary-histori-
cal reasons.[55] Moreover, the comparison with Hananiah confirms the literary-
critical result.[56] The only reason for arguing for historicity here seems to be the
fact that the Ezra narrative is found in the Bible; the *Letter of Aristeas* is obviously not, thus making it much easier to argue that it is fictitious in character
and late in origin.[57] Both documents present the promulgation of the Torah
and its translation, respectively, as a royal favor. More likely, both the promulgation and the translation of the Torah involved a longer historical process.
Moreover, they probably came about for reasons other than simply the dedication of the Achaemenid king to the God of heaven or the Ptolemaic king's desire to read good books. Moreover, both legendary reports reflect this historical
process and formulate it—as is common in legends—as an exceptional historical act.[58]

But what does this historical process of making the Torah of Moses the Torah of the Jerusalem temple and the foundational document of Judaism look
like? As far as I am aware, no authentic records of this process exist. Therefore,
a hypothesis is necessary, and the adoption of Peter Frei's theory of an imperial
authorization is just one of several possibilities. Looking for an alternative, we
could begin with the tension detected between the two poles of Elephantine on
the one side and Qumran on the other. At Elephantine, one finds a temple and
religious customs in conflict with other (Egyptian) interests, within the larger
framework of the Achaemenid bureaucracy. At Qumran, during the Hellenistic
period, there is evidence of an inner-Jewish conflict about the proper interpre-

---

55. See my *Composition of the Narrative Books*, 68–83; idem, "Ezra—Priest and Scribe."

56. Contrast Fried, "Ezra's Mission," 88–89. She does not realize, however, that the mission
of Ezra does not correspond to the normal legal practices in the ancient Near East so compellingly
reconstructed by her. Rather, it is based on the "Law of your God," which cannot be the Persian
"natural law" but must be identical with the Jewish Torah (or at least deduced from it) that is employed by Ezra (Ezra 7:14 and chaps. 10–11) and promulgated to the people by the "judges."

57. See André Pelletier, *Lettre d'Aristée a Philocrate* (SC 89; Paris: Cerf, 1962); German translation with introduction and notes by Norbert Meissner, "Aristeasbrief" (2nd ed.; JSHRZ 2/1; Gütersloh: Gütersloher Verlag, 1977) 35–87; English translation in R. J. H. Shutt, "Letter of Aristeas"
(OTP 2; Oxford: Clarendon, 1913) 7–34.

58. Examples of this principle—the formulation of a historical process as an exceptional historical act— are to be found in all parts of the Hebrew Bible as well as in the apocryphal literature
of the genre Rewritten Bible. Thus, the ancestral narratives in Genesis reflect relations between
families and clans that were living as neighbors throughout the history of Israel and Judah, the
story of the exodus reflects experiences of the Shasu and Hapiru in the second and first millennia
B.C.E., the stories of the Judges reflect the circumstances of tribal life in certain territories within
the monarchic period, the story of Joseph and the tales of Daniel, Esther, and Tobit reflect experiences of Jewish people in the diaspora. In the same way, Ezra and Nehemiah represent certain
groups and their interests in the Persian and Hellenistic periods and reflect the outcome of history
that went in their direction.

tation of the Torah. In the time between these two stages of development, I suggest that a certain degree of reflection occurred dealing with the significance of the community's own customs.

Indeed, to understand the development of the relationship between Torah and temple, it is necessary to look once again at the difference between the religious customs taught by the priests as part of their Priestly "torah," and the Torah of Moses. In fact, it was the religious custom of the Priestly Torah practiced at the temple that became part of the Mosaic Torah. In so doing, this custom was systematized and interpreted in the particular theological manner that we find in the various literary layers of the Pentateuch. Law corpora, such as the so-called Covenant Code (Exodus 20–23) and its reinterpretation, the book of Deuteronomy, were incorporated into the narrative of the Pentateuch. Priestly and cultic materials were collected in the Priestly writing and also incorporated into the Pentateuch. Later redactions expanded the legal and cultic material and tried to interpret and harmonize it. The whole process of making the Pentateuch can be understood as an ongoing theological reflection upon the meaning of the community's own customs. This long process led to the continual rewriting and innerbiblical interpretation of the legal materials within the Pentateuch itself.

In turn, there must also have been reflection upon existing customs within the leading circles at the temple and even within other groups of Judean society. As a result, the Torah of Moses began to replace the old customs long practiced at the temple. This caused a number of difficulties, however. The Torah of Moses is not made to serve just as a handbook for priests or judges going about their daily tasks, offering sacrifices, practicing rituals, and speaking about law. Thus, questions about the proper application of the Torah of Moses arose and ignited a dispute about the halakic exegesis of the Torah. Only as part of the customs at the temple did the Torah gain its legal status within Judaism under Persian or Hellenistic rule.

Again, for this transition from religious custom to the Torah of Moses and vice versa, we have no historical evidence. It is only reflected in legendary form. For example, in Dan 6:6, דת אלהה, "the law of his [Daniel's] God," seems to stand for "his religion" and refers to the prayer practices of Jews in the Golah. Furthermore, דת, "law," in Esth 3:8 describes the way of life of the Jews. Nevertheless, the transition obviously must have taken place, as the legendary witnesses suggest. What exactly provoked such a reflection on the religious customs at the temple—a reflection that would lead to the replacement of the original customs at the temple by the Torah? That is, why (or how) did the Torah become normative not only for particular groups or sects that lived away from the temple or in the diaspora but also for groups at the temple itself?

What was the attraction of the Torah of Moses for the temple? I argue that we should look for external factors in this case, and the following two seem to suggest themselves.

First, there were two provinces, Yehud and Samaria, each of them having its own temple: the temple of Jerusalem and the temple on Mt. Gerizim (the foundation of which, as shown by recent archaeological discoveries, probably should be dated earlier than generally assumed based on the information given in Josephus).[59] Despite the fact that the two provinces (according to the archaeological evidence) shared much in common and had quite normal relations, they were divided into two administrative units of different demographic, economic, and political weight. This division must have led to a degree of competition and, finally, to the enmity that is attested in biblical literature (esp. Chronicles, Ezra–Nehemiah, and Sir 50:25–26) and in Josephus. It is this ideological enmity that is the basis for what is sometimes called the "Samaritan Schism."[60]

Under these historical circumstances, "attempts at self-definition may have been necessary," not only for the elite in Jerusalem, but also for the Yahwistic community in Samaria, "precisely because of the similarities between the Yahwists living in the two territories."[61] It is obvious that the Pentateuch, the Torah of Moses, and especially the claim for the centralization of the cult (Deuteronomy 12) were used for the self-definition of "Israel" in Judah as well as in Samaria. However, because a common knowledge of the Pentateuch and its traditions in Judah as well as in Samaria cannot simply be presupposed, the question arises whether the Pentateuch (wherever it was composed and whoever was responsible for its transmission) became popular and reached its status as To-

---

59. Josephus, *Ant.* 11.8.2 §310, 11.8.4 §324, 11.8.6 §346, 12.5.5 §259, 13.9.1 §§254–56. For the following, see Gary N. Knoppers, "What Has Mt. Zion to Do with Mt. Gerizim? A Study in the Early Relations between the Jews and the Samaritans in the Persian Period," *Studies in Religion / Sciences Religieuses* 34 (2005) 307–36; idem, "Revisiting the Samarian Question in the Persian Period," in *Judah and the Judeans in the Persian Period* (ed. Oded Lipschits and Manfred Oeming; Winona Lake, IN: Eisenbrauns, 2006) 265–89 (both articles provide further references).

60. There is no consensus on when the breach between Judaism and Samaritanism occurred or even whether there ever was a "schism." For the discussion, see Ronald J. Coggins, *Samaritans and Jews: The Origins of Samaritanism Reconsidered* (Oxford: Blackwell, 1975), who argues for a gradual separation. Hans G. Kippenberg (*Garizim und Synagoge: Traditionsgeschichtliche Untersuchungen zur samaritanischen Religion der aramäischen Periode* [Religionsgeschichtliche Versuche und Vorarbeiten 30; Berlin: de Gruyter, 1971]) and James D. Purvis (*The Samaritan Pentateuch and the Origin of the Samaritan Sect* [HSM 2; Cambridge: Harvard University Press, 1968]; idem, "The Samaritan Problem: A Case Study in Jewish Sectarianism in the Roman Era," in *Traditions in Transformation: Turning Points in Biblical Faith* [ed. Baruch Halpern and Jon D. Levenson; Winona Lake, IN: Eisenbrauns, 1981] 323–50) date the breach to the early 2nd century or at the end of the 2nd century B.C.E., respectively. Alan D. Crown ("Redating the Schism between the Judaeans and the Samaritans," *JQR* 82 [1991] 17–50) does not see any clear evidence for a real separation until the 3rd or 4th century C.E.

61. See Knoppers, "Revisiting the Samarian Question," 279.

rah for the first time at the temple in Judah and Jerusalem or at the temple in Samaria and Shechem. Only with the Torah and the idea of the centralization of the cult did the (perhaps competitive but generally peaceful) relations between the two sanctuaries in Jerusalem and on Mt. Gerizim (and elsewhere, such as Bethel) become a matter of religious rivalry and of *status confessionis*.[62]

Within modern scholarly discourse, Judah and Jerusalem are normally understood to be the milieu within which the Pentateuch was composed and established as the Torah. Jerusalem's attempt to obtain a political and economic advantage over its stronger competitors, the sanctuaries in Bethel (which may have been located in the province of Yehud itself) and Shechem (in the province of Samaria), may have been the reason why the Jerusalem authorities laid claim to the Torah of Moses and cited the exclusive demands for centralization in Deuteronomy 12 for their own temple.[63] With this step (expressed time and time again in the biblical literature that greatly influenced the course of modern scholarly opinion), the "Samaritan religion was a Jewish heresy whose basic institutions (temple, priesthood, Scriptures) were derived from the Jerusalem cultus."[64]

However, as far as the establishment of the Pentateuch as Torah is concerned, the alternative viewpoint is also conceivable.[65] The claim of the Samarians (or Samaritans) to be descendants of "Israel" was in a certain sense more justified than the claim made by the Judeans. Thus, it may be that the Samaritans were the first to refer to the centralization of worship according to Deuteronomy 12, elevate the status of the Torah to holy Scripture, and use the Torah to distinguish themselves from their counterparts in Jerusalem. The reason for doing so may have been the fact that the Samaritan temple on Mt. Gerizim—in contrast to Bethel and Jerusalem—was a new foundation that needed special legitimation. Perhaps this new foundation was supported by groups or sects that had separated themselves from the temple in Jerusalem and were in favor of the Torah of Moses. If so, the interpretation of Deuteronomy 12 as referring to Jerusalem, an interpretation that became the prevalent view in Jewish tradition, would not have been the cause of but a reaction against the growing self-consciousness of the people in the province of Samaria and, in particular, of the religious community on Mt. Gerizim.

---

62. For relations between Jerusalem and Samaria, see Oded Lipschits, "Achaemenid Imperial Policy, Settlement Processes in Palestine, and the Status of Jerusalem in the Middle of the Fifth Century B.C.E.," in *Judah and the Judeans in the Persian Period* (ed. Oded Lipschits and Manfred Oeming; Winona Lake, IN: Eisenbrauns, 2006) 19–52. For relations between Jerusalem and Bethel, see Ernst Axel Knauf, "Bethel: The Israelite Impact on Judean Language and Literature," ibid., 291–349.

63. For the identification of the cultic place with Jerusalem, see my "Place Which He Has Chosen."

64. Purvis, "The Samaritan Problem," 330. See also idem, *Samaritan Pentateuch*, 93.

65. See Etienne Nodet, *A Search for the Origins of Judaism: From Joshua to the Mishna* (JSOTSup 248; Sheffield: Sheffield Academic Press, 1997) esp. 122–53, 154–201.

This conclusion fits very well with the explicit references to Mt. Gerizim in Deut 11:29–30; 27:4–8, 11–13, and Josh 8:30–35. In general, scholarship tends to take the Judaic position and explains these references either as fossil remnants of an old Northern Israelite tradition used by the Deuteronomists or as late additions with a pro- or anti-Samaritan tendency.[66] Both views pose great difficulties. On a literary level, an old tradition seems impossible, because all passages in Deuteronomy and Joshua are secondary additions. However, there is no indication of a Judean debate on the Samaritan question. The Judean position itself—the identification of the chosen place as Jerusalem—is missing in the Pentateuch and only reaches prominence in the course of the narratives of the Former Prophets. The so-called compromise between Judean and Samaritan interests that is often postulated for the pentateuchal redaction is rather difficult to detect in these passages from Deuteronomy and Joshua as well as other passages of the Pentateuch.[67]

It is possible, however, that both positions contain some truth. Although the references to Mt. Gerizim are certainly not part of an old Northern tradition, they nevertheless may represent the earliest explicit identification of the chosen cultic place mentioned in Deuteronomy 12. If so, the Samaritan perspective most likely would have been inserted by the Samaritans themselves, not by the Judeans, and only later corrected and reinterpreted by the Judean redaction of the Torah.

Following this path, we find the interesting fact that among the three passages in question only two, Deut 27:5–7 and Josh 8:30–35, speak of the building of an altar. In describing this construction, the passages refer to formulations in Exodus 20 (altar law) and—most likely—Deuteronomy 12 ("joy" in Deut 27:7) but not to the centralization formula. If the reading "on Mt. Gerizim" in Deut 27:4 that is preserved in the Samaritan Pentateuch and the Old Latin (*Vetus Latina*) is the original reading, one would have here the original Samaritan gloss. This reading was then changed in the report of the completion of the altar in Josh 8:30–35, a text that originally may have been placed before Josh 5:1 (see 4Q47) and in the Greek version (Septuagint) is placed after 9:1–2. In Josh 8:30–35, this reading was changed to "on Mt. Ebal" by groups supporting the Judean tradition, who then also corrected the text in Deut 27:4.[68] Due to this

---

66. See for the first option, Eduard Nielsen, *Deuteronomium* (HAT 1/6; Tübingen: Mohr Siebeck, 1995) 128–30, 243–49; Martin Noth, *Das Buch Josua* (3rd ed.; HAT 1/7: Tübingen: Mohr Siebeck, 1971) 51–53. For the second option, see Timo Veijola, *Das 5. Buch Mose Deuteronomium* (ATD 8/1; Göttingen: Vandenhoeck & Ruprecht, 2004) 258–59; Volkmar Fritz, *Das Buch Josua* (HAT 1/7; Tübingen: Mohr Siebeck, 1994) 93–99.

67. For a different view, see the contribution of Christophe Nihan in this volume (pp. 187ff.).

68. See, earlier, Noth, *Das Buch Josua*, 5; and for the text-critical evidence, including the versions of Qumran and the testimony of Josephus, see Heinz-Josef Fabry, "Der Altarbau der Samaritaner—ein Produkt der Text- und Literargeschichte?" in *Die Textfunde vom Toten Meer und der Text*

correction in the text, only the blessing and the curse happen on the mountains of Gerizim and Ebal.[69] The place of sacrifice and the place where the Law was written down is no longer Mt. Gerizim but only the (less-important) Mt. Ebal, which will become—like the altars of patriarchal times—a stopover on the road to the chosen cultic place in Jerusalem.

The existence of the Samaritan community and its temple is one external factor to consider in the increasing importance attached to the Torah. A second and equally or even more important factor is the transition from Persian to Hellenistic foreign rule, as well as the growing Hellenization of Judaism that went with it. However, the historical reconstruction of this period is in no respect easier than the reconstruction of the former Persian period. Regarding the status of the Torah of Moses, the edict of Antiochus III that gave special treatment to the Jews, the events (entirely opposing the edict of Antiochus III) transpiring under Antiochus IV, and the subsequent renewal of privileges for the Jews are of particular relevance.[70] Again, scholars remain uncertain to what extent the reports of Josephus and other sources (Daniel, 1 and 2 Maccabees) are of historical value. As in the case of Ezra 7 and the *Letter of Aristeas*, it is appropriate to assume that the diverse reports echo a complex and diverse historical process and, further, that these reports aim at presenting this process as a simple and continuous chain of events. Be that as it may, all these reports reflect the indisputable fact that the status of the Torah became a major subject of public discourse in the 3rd and 2nd centuries B.C.E.

Within these reports, it is striking that Josephus, when talking about Antiochus III, refers only to the "paternal laws" or the "paternal law." In contrast, when speaking of Antiochus IV, he explicitly distinguishes "the (Book) of

---

der Hebräischen Bibel (ed. Ulrich Dahmen et al.; Neukirchen-Vluyn: Neukirchener Verlag, 2000) 35–52; for discussion, see also Ed Noort, "4QJoshua[a] and the History of Tradition in the Book of Joshua," *JNSL* 24 (1998) 127–44; idem, *Das Buch Josua: Forschungsgeschichte und Problemfelder* (EdF 292; Darmstadt: Wissenschaftliche Buchgesellschaft, 1998) 56–57. The Samaritan version of the book of Joshua reads, as one might expect, Mt. Gerizim in Joshua 8 (IX:14–18); see Moses Gaster, "Das Buch Josua in hebräisch-samaritanischer Rezension," *ZDMG* 62 (1908) 209–29, 494–549; here 502–3; on this source, see Noort, *Das Buch Josua*, 58–59.

69. According to Deut 11:29–30, Joshua (5 and) 8, and later Jewish and Christian tradition, the two mountains are to be located somewhere in the region of Gilgal, Jericho, and Ai, not at Shechem. This, too, is probably an anti-Samaritan polemic that eventually led to the puzzling twofold location on the Madeba map. On this whole matter, see Ed Noort, "The Traditions of Ebal and Gerizim: Theological Positions in the Book of Joshua," in *Deuteronomy and Deuteronomic Literature: Festschrift C. H. W. Brekelmans* (ed. Marc Vervenne and Johan Lust; BETL 133; Leuven: Peeters, 1997) 161–80, and the references mentioned in n. 68.

70. For the edict of Antiochus III, see Josephus, *Ant.* 12.3.3–4, §§138–153. For the events under Antiochus IV, see Daniel 7–12; 1 Maccabees 1; 2 Maccabees 5–7; *Ant.* 12.5.1–4, §§237–256. For the renewal of privileges, see 2 Macc 11:13–38.

Law" from the "paternal customs."[71] It is conceivable, of course, that this terminological distinction is not strictly relevant, because Josephus—like the text of 2 Maccabees (6:1; 11:25, 31)—identifies the "paternal laws" and the "paternal customs" with the Torah; this is dealt with in the common source of both, 1 Maccabees (1:49, 52, 56–57). Nevertheless, this terminological distinction could reflect an earlier distinction between customs and Torah—a distinction that can still be felt in the literature of the Qumran community. Also, the *Yaḥad* lived by this difference and regarded the Torah of Moses to be in competition with the temple (the temple's customs and the exegesis of Torah being practiced in the temple there).

Perhaps similar things can be said of the Egyptian diaspora in Alexandria, which (in contrast to Elephantine and Leontopolis) did not have a temple but instead had a synagogue and relied on the Greek translation of the Torah.[72] In 2 Maccabees 1–2, this community is courted by the Jerusalemites to celebrate the festival of the dedication of the temple with them. Thus, the difference between the Torah of Moses and the temple was still perceptible, but the Torah of Moses increasingly became a unifying document that brought together different groups within ancient Judaism and gathered them together "under a common roof." These groups included people who were closely affiliated with the temple and people who were less so.

All of this, of course, does not constitute historical proof of the way that the Torah of Moses and the temple came together but simply comprises pieces of circumstantial evidence drawn from the literary tradition. However, this circumstantial evidence may lead to a historical path that can tell us how the Pentateuch, the Torah of Moses, was distributed widely and how it achieved common acceptance even among the groups affiliated with the Jerusalem temple.

To sum up, I shall sketch a possible scenario. Apart from the religious practice at the temple or perhaps originating as an alternative to it, and at a very late stage, the Torah of Moses became the mandatory custom. This mandatory custom eventually was also practiced at the temple. The leveling of the differences between the Torah and the temple was probably not accomplished in a single act. Rather, it was a slow progressive process that began in the late Persian period and continued into Hellenistic times. It may have been triggered by the Samaritan competition, but it was certainly intensified by the pressure of Hellenization on Judaism.

---

71. See *Ant.* 12.3.3 §142, and 12.3.4 §§145, 150; and *Ant.* 12.5.4 §§251, 253, 255–56, respectively.

72. See Jörg Frey, "Temple and Rival Temple: The Cases of Elephantine, Mt. Gerizim, and Leontopolis," in *Gemeinde ohne Tempel / Community without Temple: Zur Substituierung und Transformation des Jerusalemer Tempels und seines Kults im Alten Testament, antiken Judentum und frühen Christentum* (ed. Beate Ego et al.; WUNT 118; Tübingen: Mohr Siebeck, 1999) 171–203.

Of course, various forces were active in this process, first and foremost the circles that handed down the Torah and kept it sacred. It is hard to say who these circles were. There is no external or other indisputable evidence for the assumption that they consisted of the priests in the Jerusalem temple. The multitude of priests and other groups mentioned in the Hebrew Bible cannot simply be projected onto history. However, the evidence from Elephantine and Qumran supports the suggestion that the circles responsible for the composition and distribution of the Pentateuch were not or were no longer primarily affiliated with the ruling class at the temple or in the province. Of course, it is true that the priests at the temple and the political representatives of the province were needed to give the Mosaic Law the status of Torah at the temple. They would have felt more and more the need to connect the religious customs at the temple and beyond with the Torah of Moses. This need would have been intensified by historical circumstances, such as Samaritan competition, the Hellenization of Judaism, and the religious crisis under Antiochus IV.

The Maccabees and the Hasmoneans represent the end of this process. They used the Torah of Moses in their insurgence against Seleucid rule and proclaimed a rigorous obedience to it, an obedience that, if necessary, was put into practice by force, even against their own population. The incipient connection of temple and Torah reached its official status in the Hasmonean Kingdom, with the high priest Jonathan. Only from this moment onward can the Torah be said to have been the "official" law and binding basis of Judaism. From then on, at the latest, temple and Torah were no longer alternatives. What was important from this time forward was the proper interpretation of the Torah, with or (after 70 c.e.) without the temple.

The Pentateuch in Ancient Mediterranean Context: The Publication of Local Lawcodes

GARY N. KNOPPERS AND PAUL B. HARVEY JR.
The Pennsylvania State University

One of the commendable features of Peter Frei's imperial-authorization theory is the extent to which he attempts to contextualize the process leading to acceptance of the Pentateuch as law by leaders of the Judean community within a much larger international context.[1] One may take issue with several of his claims.[2] Yet, insofar as Frei draws connections between legal developments in postexilic Judah and legal developments that were occurring elsewhere within the Achaemenid Empire, he provides scholars with some very useful comparisons for the study of ancient law.[3] This essay also discusses the promulgation of the Pentateuch as a prestigious writing but from a somewhat different perspective. As in the case of Frei's work, we find it useful to look at the publication of local laws within a broader international context. In this essay, we advocate a Mediterranean-wide perspective in which a number of factors may contribute in one way or another to the publication of written laws and law collections in various societal settings. The specific context we examine is the Greek and Roman states during the late archaic and classical eras.[4] The period from the late 7th through the mid-4th centuries B.C.E. witnessed the creation

Authors' note: We would like to thank Bernard M. Levinson for his helpful comments and observations on an earlier draft of this essay. We would also like to convey our thanks to Ms. Cara B. Fraser for her assistance with various bibliographical and editorial matters.

1. Peter Frei and Klaus Koch, *Reichsidee und Reichsorganisation im Perserreich* (2nd ed.; OBO 55; Freiburg: Universitätsverlag / Göttingen: Vandenhoeck & Ruprecht, 1996); Peter Frei, "Die persische Reichsautorisation: Ein Überblick," *ZABR* 1 (1995) 1–35 [trans. "Persian Imperial Authorization: An Overview," in *Persia and Torah: The Theory of Imperial Authorization of the Pentateuch* (ed. James W. Watts; SBLSymS 17; Atlanta: Society of Biblical Literature, 2001) 5–40].

2. See Gary N. Knoppers, "An Achaemenid Authorization of the Torah in Yehud?" in *Persia and Torah: The Theory of Imperial Authorization of the Pentateuch* (ed. James W. Watts; SBLSymS 17; Atlanta: Society of Biblical Literature, 2001) 115–34, and the references cited there.

3. In this context, see also the essay by Konrad Schmid in this volume (pp. 23–38).

4. Abbreviations of ancient Greek and Roman works follow the *Oxford Classical Dictionary* (ed. Simon Hornblower and Antony Spawforth; 3rd ed.; Oxford: Oxford University Press, 1996) xxix–liv.

of many written statutes and collections of law in a variety of contexts throughout the Mediterranean world. The instances of Athens and Rome are well known, but public laws were also promulgated in urban centers ranging from sites in the small Aegean islands to Crete, southern Italy, and Sicily.

Our study will begin by surveying the spread of written law in the ancient Mediterranean world from the late 7th century to the 5th century B.C.E., paying attention to three particular sites: Athens, with a view to Solon's legal reforms; Gortyn, with a view to the long series of public laws found there; and Rome, with a view to the so-called Twelve Tables.[5] Having briefly discussed these particular forms of written legislation, we will evaluate the various ways in which classical historians have sought to understand the growing popularity and widespread distribution of written laws in the 6th and 5th centuries. Our essay will then explore what may be learned from the promulgation of law collections within these diverse contexts for understanding the promulgation of the Pentateuch within Yehud and Samaria.

I. The Growing Popularity of Written Legislation in the Greco-Roman World in the Late Archaic and Classical Periods

The earliest examples of written laws from the Greek states in the archaic period date to the mid- to late 7th century B.C.E.[6] Because the ancient Greeks used the same word for "law" and for "custom" (*nomos*), the beginning of ancient Greek law is difficult to define with precision.[7] During the archaic period and early classical period, written documentation is not well attested in the material record, but one does see the appearance of a good number of different

---

5. This essay is part of a larger project. Unfortunately, space limitations preclude our delving into the topic at hand at any great depth. We plan to devote a monograph to the issues raised in this study in the near future.

6. Greek law, if one can even speak of such a thing as a single entity (a major point of contention), was not a national system of laws but a family of systems (Stephen C. Todd, *The Shape of Athenian Law* [Oxford: Clarendon, 1993] 16). On the question, see also Moses I. Finley, *The Use and Abuse of History* (London: Penguin, 1990) 134–46; Stephen C. Todd and Paul C. Millet, "Law, Society and Athens," in *Nomos: Essays in Athenian Law, Politics and Society* (ed. Paul Cartledge, Paul C. Millett, and Stephen C. Todd; Cambridge: Cambridge University Press, 1990) 1–18; Raphael Sealey, *The Justice of the Greeks* (Ann Arbor: University of Michigan Press, 1994) 59–89; Michael Gagarin, "The Unity of Greek Law," in the *Cambridge Companion to Greek Law* (ed. Michael Gagarin and David Cohen; Cambridge: Cambridge University Press, 2005) 29–40, and the references cited there.

7. What constitutes *law*, broadly speaking, is a difficult issue (Sealey, *Justice of the Greeks*, 3–12; C. L. van der Vliet, "Justice and Written Laws in the Formation of the Polis," in *The Law's Beginnings* [ed. Ferdinand J. M. Feldbrugge; E. J. M. Meijers Instituut M-65; Boston: Martinus Nijhoff, 2003] 23–43, esp. 25–26).

legal texts from a wide variety of sites in the form of public inscriptions.[8] Most of these legal inscriptions, which do not survive except in fragmentary form, regulate judicial procedures and the holding of public office.[9]

A number of features of these early inscriptions stand out. First, these inscribed laws are impressive for their public and monumental character. The ordinances were not simply written but were carefully inscribed on stone or on some other relatively durable material and were (apparently) displayed in a public place, whether in the *agora*, a community gathering place, or on the walls of a temple. Associations with sanctuaries and explicit references to a deity or deities in the inscriptions are important, because these religious elements suggest the divine sanction and protection of the laws themselves.[10]

Second, many are presented self-consciously as communal legislation. That is, they do not represent private inscriptions displayed in a public setting but are presented as civil or state legislation.[11] Nevertheless, the ordinances deal as much with judicial process and the administration of justice as they do with formulating substantive law. As such, these written texts may presuppose existing custom or traditional law.

Third, some care seems to have been taken, within the limits of early writing abilities, to make these laws clear and accessible to the members of the elite who might need or want to know them. In this context, it is appropriate to call attention to some recently published curses from Teos, dating to approximately 475–470 B.C.E.[12] A fragmentary inscription records curses to be pronounced

---

8. See Russell Meiggs and David Lewis, *A Selection of Greek Historical Inscriptions to the End of the Fifth Century B.C.* (rev. ed.; Oxford: Clarendon, 1988), hereafter ML. For early Greek legal enactments inscribed and displayed publicly, see, for instance, ML, no. 8, pp. 14–17 (Chios), no. 13, pp. 22–25 (West Locris), no. 20, pp. 35–40 (Naupaktos?). We shall discuss these and other texts in the more extensive work noted above.

9. In the context of this overview, it may be the better part of wisdom to concentrate on the existing evidence, rather than to become unduly entangled in the important ongoing debate about the putative existence of law collections associated with various legendary Greek lawgivers. On this matter, see the foundational studies of Karl-Joachim Hölkeskamp, "Arbitrators, Lawgivers and the 'Codification of Law' in Archaic Greece," *Métis: Revue d'anthropologie du monde grec ancien* 7 (1992) 55–57; idem, *Schiedsrichter, Gesetzgeber und Gesetzgebung im archaischen Griechenland* (Stuttgart: Franz Steiner, 1999) 60–261.

10. Karl-Joachim Hölkeskamp, "Written Law in Archaic Greece," *Proceedings of the Cambridge Philological Society* 38 (1992) 87–117, esp. 99–102; idem, *Schiedsrichter*, 278–79.

11. A point repeatedly underscored by Michael Gagarin, *Early Greek Law* (Berkeley: University of California Press, 1986) passim; idem, "Early Greek Law," in the *Cambridge Companion to Greek Law* (ed. Michael Gagarin and David Cohen; Cambridge: Cambridge University Press, 2005) 82–94.

12. Teos, one of the 12 cities in the Ionian League was located on the Anatolian coast of the Aegean, north of Ephesus. The text (ML 30 [pp. 62–66]: Henri van Effenterre and Françoise Ruzé, *Nomima, I: Recueil d'inscriptions politiques et juridiques de l'archaïsme grec* [Collection de l'École

publicly each year by certain magistrates (B.29–35) against individuals who might endanger the interests of the community. The curses include a clause against public officials who do not read aloud the writing on the stele "by (the statue) of Dynamis" (ἐπὶ Δυνάμει) and other deities.[13] Hence, apart from acknowledging the symbolic value of these public writings, we find evidence that they were also designed to be read and recited.

Fourth, at least some of the inscriptions self-referentially allow for the possibility of emendation, if certain conditions are met. This suggests that they were intended to function as genuine legislation and not simply to reflect the judicial ideals of a writer or a community at a particular time. Finally, written laws seem to have increased during a time of growing urbanization, an era in which the Greek city-states were developing more-formal political systems in a process of state (trans)formation. In this respect, it is worth noting that many early written laws imposed checks on officials in the *poleis*. Whether these particular city-states were especially prone to civil strife is unclear.[14] But at least some of these statutes seem to mark the attempt by some members of the elite to limit or demarcate carefully the powers of others within the elite.[15]

Having briefly introduced the appearance of early Greek legal inscriptions, we will find it useful to survey a few specific cases in more detail. In each instance, the subject of discussion is not simply a singular law or legal decree of some sort but, rather, a collection of laws. The first two case studies involve Greek cities that are geographically far apart (Athens and Gortyn) but deal with temporal settings that are similar—the late archaic period and the early classical period. The third deals with the mid-5th-century compilation of laws in Rome known as the Twelve Tables. In each of these three cases, we are dealing with more than the publication of a few short statutes or a single ordinance on a particular topic, subdivided into several provisions.

A. Solon's Reforms in Athens

An Athenian politician, reformer, and poet, Solon served as *archon* in Athens in 594/3 B.C.E. Although many link his reforms to his archonship, some situate

---

française de Rome 188; Paris: de Boccard, 1994] no. 104 [pp. 366–70]) consists of fragments, labeled A (12 lines) and B (41 lines) from one or two steles found near the city.

13. Reading line 31 with Carl D. Buck, *The Greek Dialects* (Chicago: University of Chicago Press, 1955) 187; ML 30 (p. 65). Some would translate "to the best of their power" (ἐπὶ δυνάμει) or something similar (van Effenterre and Ruzé, *Nomima,* no. 104 [pp . 366–68]). Given the context, the former interpretation seems more cogent (ML 30.31 [p. 65]). The text also includes a severe penalty for anyone who broke the stele or cut out or obliterated the letters (B.35–41).

14. So Rosalind Thomas, "Writing, Law, and Written Law," in the *Cambridge Companion to Greek Law* (ed. Michael Gagarin and David Cohen; Cambridge: Cambridge University Press, 2005) 43.

15. Ibid., 46, 54–55.

his reforms about 20 years later.[16] His laws did not survive except as they are quoted, discussed, and reformulated in a variety of other texts, such as the rhetoric of the 4th-century orators, the elegiac tradition, the Athenian Constitution (*Athēnaiōn politeia*), and the works of other literary, historical, and philosophical writers.[17]

In the work of Herodotus (1.29–33, 2.177), Solon appears as a preeminent sage, lawgiver, and poet. As *archon*, Solon mediated among various factions within Athenian society.[18] When Solon took office, "many were the slaves of the few," and "strife was fierce" (*Ath. pol.* 5.1). The poetry accredited to Solon reveals that he tried to achieve some sort of compromise between the demands of the wealthy and the underprivileged.[19] According to the author of the Athenian Constitution, Solon "wrote laws for lowborn and noble alike, fitting straight justice to each" (*Ath. pol.* 12.4).[20] Historically speaking, however, Solon may have satisfied neither party.

Solon's reforms seem to have consisted of two related elements. The first was judicial and political. He weakened the power of the aristocracy by strengthening the power of the *ekklēsia* (assembly) and the judicial system.[21] He is credited with creating a new council of 400 to prepare business for the assembly (*Ath. pol.* 8.4; Plutarch, *Vita Solon.* 8.2; 14; 19.1–2). He formulated a

---

16. See Charles Hignett, *A History of the Athenian Constitution to the End of the Fifth Century* B.C. (Oxford: Clarendon, 1962) 316–21; Gagarin, *Early Greek Law*, 51–80.

17. Plutarch, *Vita Solon*; Diogenes Laertius 1.53–57, 1.63 (= *Anthologia Palatina* 7.87); Eberhard Ruschenbusch, Σόλωνος νόμοι: *Die Fragmente des solonische Gesetzeswerkes mit einer Text- und Überlieferungsgeschichte* (Historia Einzelschriften 9; Wiesbaden: Franz Steiner, 1966) 1–58; Mortimer H. Chambers, *Aristoteles Athēnaiōn politeia; accedunt tabulae* (Bibliotheca scriptorum Graecorum et Romanorum Teubneriana; Leipzig: Teubner, 1994) §§2–13; Martin L. West, *Iambi et elegi Graeci ante Alexandrum cantata, 2: Aucta atque emendata* (Oxford: Clarendon, 1992) 139–65. See especially André P. M. H. Lardinois ("Have We Solon's Verses?" in *Solon of Athens: New Historical and Philological Approaches* [ed. Josine H. Blok and André P. M. H. Lardinois; Mnemosyne, bibliotheca classica Batava, Supplementum 272; Leiden: Brill, 2006] 15–35), who argues that the poetic diction of Solon's poems was transmitted through the semantic and political filters of later Greek traditions.

18. The divisions were not simply between rich and poor but also within the elite itself (Hignett, *History*, 86–107; Hölkeskamp, "Arbitrators," 65–72; Hans-J. Gehrke, "Gesetz und Konflikt: Überlegungen zer frühen Polis," in *Colloquium um aus Anlaß des 80 Geburtstages von Alfred Huess* [ed. Jochen Bleicken; Frankfurter althistorische Studien 13; Kallmünz: Lassleben, 1993] 49–67).

19. Solon, *Athēnaiōn politeia* 11.2, 12.4–5; see Joseph A. Almeida, *Justice as an Aspect of the Polis Idea in Solon's Political Poems: A Reading of the Fragments in Light of the Researches of New Classical Archaeology* (Mnemosyne, Bibliotheca Classica Batava, Supplementum 243; Leiden: Brill, 2006), as well as the references cited there.

20. The Athenian Constitution, traditionally associated with Aristotle, may well have been written by one of his pupils (Peter J. Rhodes, *A Commentary on the Aristotelian Athenaion Politeia* [rev. ed.; Oxford: Clarendon, 1993]).

21. West, *Iambi et Elegi, fr.* 4.7–10, 35–36 (= Demosthenes 19.254ff.); Solon, *Ath. pol.* 11.2–12.1; 12.3; Aristotle, *Politics* 1274a 15; 1281b 32.

category of public lawsuits in which any citizen might prosecute, in contrast with private lawsuits in which only the injured party or his family could prosecute (Solon, *Ath. pol.* 9.1, Plutarch, *Vita Solon.* 18.6–7). Solon also provided for appeals to the *ēliaia* against the verdicts of magistrates.[22]

The second element of his reforms was legislative.[23] Many of the laws ascribed to Solon deal with issues such as murder, manslaughter, severe bodily injury, and inheritance, involving claims on property by kin, the consequences of marriage in these situations, and the role of the *epiklēros*, the so-called heiress through whom (landed) property was transmitted in the absence of a brother as a male heir.[24] Other laws attributed to Solon include regulations concerning the cultic calendar and cultic practices, including matters related to sacrifice.[25]

As with the laws of the earlier Athenian reformer Drakon, Solon's laws were written on numbered *axones* (ἄξονες, "axles"). The *axones* were probably three- or four-sided wooden pillars, mounted on a vertical axis so that readers could turn them.[26] It is quite possible that the *axones* could still be read and studied in the 4th century.[27] But in the later period in which Plutarch wrote, only small

---

22. Solon, *Athēnaiōn politeia* 9.1. The *ēliaia* (sometimes spelled the *hēliaia*) was a meeting of Athenian citizens to try a legal case, or a building in which these meetings were held (D. M. McDowell, "*ēliaia*," *Oxford Classical Dictionary*, 520–21). It has been generally thought that when Solon introduced trials by the people in the early 6th century B.C.E., the *ēliaia* was simply the *ekklēsia* called by this different name (when it was performing a judicial function). A second view holds that Solon established it as a separate body, consisting of citizens selected by lot. This second theory is based primarily on passages in which Aristotle (and one of his students) attribute to Solon the establishment of the law court or law courts (*Politics* 1273b 35–1274a 5, 17; 1281b 32–34; *Ath. pol.* 7.3, 9.1). In the traditional view, these passages merely signify that Solon's innovation eventually led to the law courts of the 4th century.

23. To Solon's critics, his laws lacked clarity, thus generating disputes. But some (not including the author of the Athenian Constitution) thought that this was by design to give the *dēmos* more power and to put it in charge of the trials (*Ath. pol.* 9.2).

24. Van der Vliet, "Justice," 35.

25. Adele C. Scafuro would add more measures to this list ("Identifying Solon's Laws," in *Solon of Athens: New Historical and Philological Approaches* [ed. Josine H. Blok and André P. M. H. Lardinois; Mnemosyne, Bibliotheca Classica Batava, Supplementum 272; Leiden: Brill, 2006] 175–96). Others would add the prohibition of political passivity, the refusal to take sides in political strife (*Ath. pol.* 8.5; Plutarch, *Vita Solon.* 20.1; Cicero, *Epistulae ad Atticum.* 10.1.2; Ruschenbusch, Σόλωνος νόμοι, 82–83 [F 38]), but the reliability of this claim is in doubt.

26. Ronald S. Stroud, *The Axones and Kyrbeis of Drakon and Solon* (University of California Publications: Classical Studies 19; Berkeley: University of California Press, 1979).

27. If 4th-century writers had access not only to Solon's poems but also to the *axones* on which the laws were written, they would have had a solid basis for their portrayals of him. This does not mean, of course, that they interpreted the *axones* properly or that they attempted in a serious manner to understand the decrees in their original historical context. These writers had their own interests and naturally displayed their own selectivity in treating their sources. In this respect, note the cautions of Lardinois ("Have We Solon's Verses?" 15–33) and Eva Stehle ("Solon's Self-Reflexive Political Persona and Its Audience," 79–113) both in *Solon of Athens: New Historical and*

fragments survived.[28] Solon's laws were eventually transferred to stone, and many alterations and additions were made to them. It seems, then, that Solon's legislative reforms consisted of repealing certain older laws, extending some existing laws, revising others, and instituting some new statutes. He did not create a new law code in the sense of generating a full-scale and systematic set of laws.[29] At the end of the 5th century, however, democrats in Athens thought of him as their founding hero. In the times that followed, his reputation increased further. During the 4th century, orators in Athens simply seem to have assumed that virtually all the laws current in their time, in spite of all the later additions, changes, and deletions, were the "laws of Solon" (Demosthenes 20.92).[30] In later centuries, Athenians continued to refer to their law code as the laws of Solon (Plutarch, *Vita Solon.* 18).

B. Gortyn

Although the laws of Solon are much discussed and cited in ancient literary, historiographical, and philosophical texts but are otherwise lost to us in direct textual transmission, the opposite is true of the Gortyn laws. From the important urban site of Gortyn in central Crete, there is a copious amount of epigraphical material. Approximately one-quarter of all surviving Greek Cretan inscriptions stem from Gortyn. Moreover, Gortyn is only one of some 11 cities in Crete from which at least fragments of early legal inscriptions survive.[31]

The Gortyn texts are thoroughly impressive. The largest collection of legal inscriptions from anywhere in the Greek-speaking world has been preserved at this site. The inscriptions contain frequent references to antecedent law that assume some knowledge on the part of readers of older statutes. Although scholars often speak of the "law code of Gortyn" or the "Great Code of Gortyn," these epithets are, in certain respects, misleading. Actually, the "Great Code" (*IC* IV 72) is only one, but by far the longest of a lengthy series of inscriptions grouped together by Guarducci as *IC* IV 1–159, all dating to the archaic and

---

Philological Approaches (ed. Josine H. Blok and André P. M. H. Lardinois; Mnemosyne, Bibliotheca Classica Batava, Supplementum 272; Leiden: Brill, 2006).

28. Solon, *Athēnaiōn politeia* 7.1; Plutarch, *Vita Solon.* 25; Ruschenbusch, Σόλωνος νόμοι, 46–47.

29. In this respect, the reservations of Hölkeskamp ("Arbitrators," 56–57) and Sealey (*Justice of the Greeks*, 25–58) about Solon's "Code" have merit. But even Hölkeskamp acknowledges that Solon was responsible for formulating a variety of legal statutes (*Schiedsrichter*, 262–85).

30. For instance, according to the author of the Athenian Constitution (*Ath. pol.* 35.2), the oligarchy of the Thirty in its consolidation of power (ca. 404/3 B.C.E.) "removed the laws of Ephialtes and Archestratos about the Areopagus and annulled the laws of Solon that had ambiguities" (*diamphisbētēsis*).

31. See van Effenterre and Ruzé, *Nomima*, 46–52, 56–75, 114–30, 192–204, 222–23, 244–47, 276–77, 280, 306–16; James Whitley, "Cretan Laws and Cretan Literacy," *AJA* 101 (1997) 635–61.

classical periods and all except one (*IC* IV 50) dealing in some way with public law.[32] The earlier statutes were only slightly reorganized when they were (re)inscribed in approximately 450 B.C.E. (ML 41).[33] In addition to speaking of the "Great Code," one may also speak of "little codes" (e.g., *IC* IV 41 and *IC* IV 75), shorter texts that like the longer text of *IC* IV 72 show some planning for units.

Written *boustrophedon*, the Great Code runs to 12 columns of 53–56 lines each, engraved on the inner surface of a circular wall, following in sequence from right to left (a total of about 30 feet of lines).[34] Inscribed in stone and displayed in public, the inscription appeared along the walls of the 5th-century Temple of Apollo Pythios.[35] The fact that visitors to the temple were confronted by a massive inscribed wall must have seemed symbolic of both the grandeur of the inscription and the power of its creators.[36] There are no long preambles at the beginning of the laws. Column 1 begins, *thioi*, "gods," and there is some unused space at the end of the last column, suggesting that some effort had been expended to provide a measure of unity to the whole. Yet these Gortyn laws do not constitute a complete, ordered code.[37] One finds overlap, repetition, and inconsistencies among the laws within this part of the larger Gortynian corpus of legal inscriptions.[38]

Taken as a whole, the Gortyn legislation deals with a variety of topics: family and family property, slaves, surety, contracts, donations, mortgages, procedure

---

32. Margarita Guarducci, *Inscriptiones Creticae, IV: Tituli Gortynii* (Rome: Libreria dello Stato, 1950) 40–219 [hereafter, *IC* IV]. John K. Davies provides a helpful overview and discussion ("The Gortyn Laws," in the *Cambridge Companion to Greek Law* [ed. Michael Gagarin and David Cohen; Cambridge: Cambridge University Press, 2005] 305–28). Anselm C. Hagedorn makes a number of important comparisons between the laws found at Gortyn, especially the "Great Code," and the laws found in Deuteronomy (*Between Moses and Plato: Individual and Society in Deuteronomy and Ancient Greek Law* [FRLANT 204; Göttingen: Vandenhoeck & Ruprecht, 2004]).

33. The format of *IC* IV 72 is quite lucid, even though it contains no headings, indentations, or new line beginnings. Individual sections on identifiable topics are separated by asyndeton (Ronald F. Willetts, *The Law Code of Gortyn: Edited with Introduction, Translation and a Commentary* [Kadmos Supplement 1; Berlin: de Gruyter, 1967] 3–4; Michael Gagarin, "The Organization of the Gortyn Law Code," *Greek, Roman, and Byzantine Studies* 23 [1982] 130–37).

34. Guarducci, *IC* IV, 123–71. In the mid-4th century, *boustrophedon* was abandoned (*IC* IV 160).

35. Most of the blocks of the inscription were found built into a wall supporting an odeum constructed in the 1st century C.E. on one side of the *agora* in Gortyn, but the inscription had probably always been displayed in this general area (Willetts, *Law Code*, 3–4).

36. Whitley, "Cretan Laws," 660.

37. The prescript of *IC* IV 78.1, "Gods. The following were pleasing to the *Gortynoi* voting . . . ," confirms that an enactment could emanate from the citizen assembly and may indicate that the prescript "Gods" elsewhere (*IC* IV 43 Ba.1, Bb.2; 51.1; 64.1; 65.1; 72.1) also reflects an assembly decision (Davies, "Gortyn Laws," 309).

38. Willetts, *Law Code*, 8; Davies, "Deconstructing Gortyn," 36–53.

in trials, crime, and other issues.[39] One finds among the laws detailed regulations on adoption, the property rights of heiresses, and the property rights of divorced wives of citizens. Two terms for the state as a collective appear: *polis* and *Gortynoi*. In charge as the principal magistracy was the *kosmos*, but the use of the term bears some ambiguity, suggesting either a collective management group or a single individual. Other types of officials are also named.

There is evidence in the inscriptions to suggest that the Gortynian legislative body did not act to create a comprehensive set of laws. Important questions are dealt with only cursorily, while other questions are wholly neglected—for example, homicide. Over the course of time, the Gortynians did not systematically revise their laws but did occasionally reinscribe and reorganize them by means of amendments and supplements added to the end of earlier laws.[40] The writers responsible for the later material do not seem to have attempted to integrate the newer provisions into a larger and more coherent whole.[41] Indeed, the question may be raised whether one should regard the new material as supplements or as new laws. Hence, Willetts can state, "The Gortyn Code is really a codification, not of law, but of laws."[42] Davies puts matters a little differently: "The Code has to be seen as part of a corpus of documentation," and "its format has to be seen in a framework of revision of law that both moves away from and toward codification."[43] In short, when speaking of a Gortyn code, scholars are actually dealing with a variety of laws that were enacted over the course of 200 to 250 years (early 6th century to the 4th century).[44]

Having looked at some aspects of the Gortyn inscriptions, we should comment on their larger significance. To begin with, one is struck by the monumental and public character of the Gortyn laws. Like many other legal inscriptions, the Great Code evinces careful craftsmanship. A deliberate effort has been made to render these laws in clear script in prominent places within a central area of the city. In discussing legal texts from a variety of sites in the ancient Mediterranean world, scholars have long debated whether certain texts,

---

39. Josef Kohler and Erich Ziebarth, *Das Stadtrecht von Gortyn und seine Beziehungen zum gemeingriechischen Rechte* (Hildesheim: Gerstenberg, 1972 [orig. Göttingen, 1912]).

40. Willetts, *Law Code*, 27; Davies, "Deconstructing Gortyn," 37–40.

41. So Willetts, *Law Code*, 9; Gagarin, "Organization," 145.

42. Willetts, *Law Code*, 34. See also Hölkeskamp, "Written Law," 90; "Arbitrators," 55–56; *Schiedsrichter*, 262–66.

43. Davies, "Deconstructing Gortyn," 33. By this, Davies means that the legal material from Gortyn shows two contradictory processes at work: (1) codification or systemization and (2) continual amendment or decodification via generalized case law in operation at the same time ("Deconstructing Gortyn," 56). Davies thinks that the process of codification that the Gortyn materials reflect may be closer to the process of the Roman praetor's edict or of the activity of the *nomothetai*, who recodified so much material in Athenian law in 410–399 B.C.E. ("Gortyn Laws," 305–28).

44. Guarducci, *IC* IV, 208–19; Jeffery, *Local Scripts*, 309–16.

such as Hammurapi's Code, the Laws of Eshnunna, and the Law Code of Lipit-Ishtar represent legal rhetoric, royal propaganda, illustrative guidance, or enforceable statute.[45] In the case of the Gortyn laws, the last option (enforceable statute) is the most likely possibility, not only for the reasons outlined above, but also because the laws themselves state that certain regulations are to be valid from the time in which they were written (e.g., *IC* IV 72 II.19–23). If these statutes self-referentially prohibit retroactive effect, they must have been written to function as a guide for actual judicial activity.[46] Provisions specifying that a certain law is not retroactive are only needed when a law is intended to be used in actual cases.[47] In this context, Lemosse has argued that the Gortyn laws constitute a law code, not in the sense of being a systematic, coherent, and comprehensive collection of laws, but in the sense of being an authoritative publication of laws.[48]

C. Rome: The Twelve Tables

We now turn to perhaps the best example, within the historical horizon here under consideration, of legal codification in a western Mediterranean society: the Twelve Tables (*Lex duodecim tabularum*) in mid-5th-century Rome. There is no doubt that by ca. 500 B.C.E. central Italic Latin society was, at least on an elite level, fairly literate. A well-studied dedication from Satricum (immediately to the south of Rome), the "Lapis Satricanus," reveals Roman elites dedicating a temple to an Italic deity.[49] In Rome itself, an archaic Latin text, the "Lapis

---

45. Fritz R. Kraus, "Ein zentrales Problem des altmesopotamischen Rechtes: Was ist der Codex Hammu-rabi?" *Geneva* 8 (1960) 183–96; Jacob J. Finkelstein, "Ammiṣaduqa's Edict and the Babylonian 'Law Codes,'" *JCS* 15 (1961) 91–104; Bernard S. Jackson, *Essays in Jewish and Comparative Legal History* (SJLA 10; Leiden: Brill, 1975) 26–34; Eckart Otto, "Kodifizierung und Kanonisierung von Rechtssätzen in keilschriftlichen und biblischen Rechtssammlungen," in *La Codification des Lois dans l'Antiquité: Actes du Colloque de Strasbourg, 27–29 novembre 1997* (ed. Edmond Lévy; Travaux du Centre de recherché sur le Proche-Orient et la Grèce antiques 16; Strasbourg: Université Marc Bloch, 2000) 77–124; Gonzalo Rubio, "From Sumer to Babylonia: 6. The Mesopotamian Law Collections: Were They Really Legal Codes?" in *Current Issues and the Study of the Ancient Near East* (ed. Mark W. Chavalas; Publications of the Association of Ancient Historians 8; Claremont, CA: Regina, 2007) 31–34.

46. Davies, "Gortyn Laws," 309. Although most scholars view the texts as genuine law, the existing data do not provide sufficient evidence about whether the laws were applied and how they were enforced (if they were enforced) in practice. On the difficult question of normativity in ancient law, see Bernard S. Jackson, *Studies in the Semiotics of Biblical Law* (JSOTSup 314; Sheffield: Sheffield Academic Press, 2000) 114–207.

47. Raymond Westbrook, "Cuneiform Law Codes and the Origins of Legislation," *ZA* 79 (1989) 201–22.

48. M. Lemosse, "Les lois de Gortyne et la notion de codification," *RIDA* 3/4 (1957) 131–37. Gagarin's line of argumentation differs somewhat, but he arrives at a similar conclusion ("Organization of the Gortyn Law Code," 129–46).

49. See the *Corpus Inscriptionum Latinarum, volumen primus, editio altera, addenda tertia* (ed. Attilio Degrassi and Joannes Krummrey; Berlin: de Gruyter, 1986) [hereafter, *CIL* I² 3], no. 2832

Niger," plausibly dated to the decades of the late 6th to early 5th century, sets out civic rules and regulations concerning the office of a high religious officer.[50]

What survives from the mid-5th-century Twelve Tables is not the code itself but hundreds of quotations and paraphrases of its provisions, along with a rich literary dossier of *testimonia*.[51] Those quotations, paraphrases, and literary notices permit a general description of the code. The code was set out on twelve tablets displayed publicly (in the forum) at Rome.[52] The code seems to have been organized in such a way that each tablet dealt with a discrete general topic (the individual tablets were not necessarily of equal length). The first tablet, for example, contained provisions for procedure at law; the final tablet, sumptuary legislation. Other tablets dealt with, for example, debt, family relations (especially marriage), rural and urban real estate issues, and so forth.[53] The scope of the code was considerable: the extant fragments (quotations and paraphrases of individual provisions) constitute the equivalent of about ten pages of text.

It is important to observe that our *fragmenta et testimonia* for the Twelve Tables are not quoted in the archaic Latin of the mid-5th century B.C.E., as the early epigraphic texts mentioned above, the "lapis Satricanus" and the "lapis niger," amply demonstrate. Many of the *fragmenta* are indeed in archaic Latin, but it is the Latin of the late 3rd to early 2nd centuries B.C.E.[54] This situation probably

---

(pp. 857–58). The recent work of Elisa Lucchesi and Elisabetta Magni is relevant, *Vecchie e nuove (in)certeszze sul Lapis Satricanus* (Pisa: ETS, 2002); along with Paul B. Harvey Jr., "Review of Elisa Lucchesi and Elisabetta Magni, *Vecchie e nuove (in)certeszze sul Lapis Satricanus*," *Archivio Glottologico Italiano* 80 (2004) 128–36.

50. *CIL* I² 3, no. 1 (pp. 854–55). See especially Robert E. A. Palmer, *The King and the Comitium: A Study of Rome's Oldest Public Document* (Historia Einzelschriften 11; Wiesbaden: Franz Steiner, 1969).

51. The law of the Twelve Tables was, of course, not systematic enough to be called a code in a technical sense (that is, an authoritative, comprehensive, and systematic set of laws). When we refer to the Twelve Tables as a code, we are using the term in a broader sense to indicate a significant collection of legal stipulations. On the complex issue of what (if anything) constitutes codification in antiquity, see the nuanced study of Martha T. Roth, "The Law Collection of King Hammurabi: Toward an Understanding of Codification and Text," in *La Codification des Lois dans l'Antiquité: Actes du Colloque de Strasbourg, 27–20 novembre 1997* (ed. Edmond Lévy; Travaux du Centre de recherché sur le Proche-Orient et la Grèce antiques 16; Strasbourg: Université Marc Bloch, 2000) 9–31.

52. Sextus Pomponius (Roman jurist of the 2nd century C.E.), as quoted in Justinian's *Digest* (1.2.4), thought of "ivory tablets"; one might more plausibly think of (typical for Rome) whitewashed (gypsum) tablets.

53. In this discussion of the Twelve Tables, we have followed the text, arrangement, and translation of the *testimonia et fragmenta* in the now-standard edition of Michael H. Crawford, *Roman Statutes* (2 vols.; London: University of London, Institute of Classical Studies, 1996) 2.555–721 (no. 40).

54. Michael C. Alexander ("Law in the Roman Republic," in *A Companion to the Roman Republic* [ed. Nathan Rosenstein and Robert Morstein-Marx; Oxford: Blackwell, 2006] 238–39) observes that the language of the fragments is not the "form of Latin . . . in which they must have

reflects the work of the Roman politician and jurist Sextus Aelius Paetus Catus (consul in 198 B.C.E.). Aelius Paetus produced a work entitled the "Tripertita," the "Three-Part Work," in which, it seems, he quoted the original provisions of the Twelve Tables, then a "modern" interpretation (in contemporary Latin), followed by a notation of subsequent legislation and modifying decisions (the *legis actiones*).[55]

Some comments may be in order about the character of this particular collection of laws. The code was presented to later readers as the transaction and result of an early Latin/Rome political struggle among social-status groups. This legendary, romantic, folkloric historical tradition (as set out esp. in Livy 3.30–55; compare the more sober, didactic explication in Cicero, *de republica* 2.25–27 [61–63]) has led some critics to dismiss the functionality of the code because of the later historiographic (in many respects, "novelistic") tradition.[56]

---

originally been written." A striking illustration of this circumstance appears in the occurrence of the exceptional morphology of the second/third-person singular deponent imperative *-mino*. This verbal form is attested in the Twelve Tables (I.1: *antestamino*: see Crawford, *Roman Statutes*, 2.578; 2.584–85), Plautus (*Epidicus* 695: *arbitramino*; *Pseudolus* 859: *progredimino*), and the elder Cato (*de agri cultura* 141.2: *praefamino*). This imperative form also appears in an epigraphic text: *CIL* I[2] 3, no. 584, line 32: *fruimino*. This text records the settlement of a land dispute among folk around Genua in 117 B.C.E.; the arbitrators were the Roman senators Q. and M. Minucius Rufus. The terms of the settlement may well reflect, here as elsewhere in the text, the language of an earlier settlement in 197 B.C.E., by the ancestor of the Minucii, Q. Minucius Rufus (see Livy 32.22–23). This exceptional imperative form, *-mino*, does not appear in the surviving texts and fragments of Latin prior to the age of Plautus (ca. 205–184 B.C.E.).

55. See, above all, Pomponius, as quoted (in excerpt) in Justinian's *Digest* (1.2.38): "Sextus Aelius . . . whose book entitled the *Tripertitia*, survives and contains the elements, so to speak, of law. This book, moreover, is so called (the 'three-part thing'), because an interpretation is added to the Law of the XII Tables, followed by the [relevant] legal procedures." For the date of Aelius Paetus, see T. Robert S. Broughton, *Magistrates of the Roman Republic* (3 vols.; Philological Monographs 15; New York: American Philological Association, 1951–1986) 1.330 (sub anno 198). On the scope and significance of Aelius Paetus's *Tripertita*, see Alan Watson, *Law Making in the Later Roman Republic* (Oxford: Oxford University Press, 1974) 112–16, 134–36.

56. Contrast the discussion of Dionysius of Halicarnassus in the *Roman Archaeology* (*Ant. Rom.* 10.54–60). For the highly romanticized literary tradition of the redaction of the Twelve Tables, see R. M. Ogilvie, *A Commentary on Livy: Books 1–5* (rev. ed.; Oxford: Oxford University Press, 1970) 445–503. For agnosticism on the tradition, see, for example, Gary Forsythe, *A Critical History of Early Rome: From Prehistory to the First Punic War* (Berkeley: University of California Press, 2005) 201–33. Marie Theres Fögen offers a careful and convincing dissection of the literary, especially the Livian, tradition of the redaction of the Twelve Tables, noting very well the romantic/novelistic elements of this tradition (*Römische Rechtsgeschichten: Über Ursprung und Evolution eines sozialen Systems* [Göttingen: Vandenhoeck & Ruprecht, 2002] 61–124). In her analysis, she does not, in our opinion, sufficiently distinguish the social and political contexts for a legal code of this sort in the mid-5th century from the later historiographic tradition: see esp. Fögen, *Römische Rechtsgeschichten*, 63–69. For further relevant bibliography, see the references in Crawford, *Roman Statutes*, 1.555.

Scholars well versed in the history of Roman law have recognized well, however, the social and political plausibility of a mid-5th-century legal enactment, apart from any (later) literary coloring and semantic modernizing of the traditional text of the Twelve Tables.[57]

The extant provisions reflect a society in transition. As in other law codes intended, we believe, for practical, vernacular use (at Gortyn and elsewhere), the Twelve Tables begin with pragmatic stipulations: for example, how to go to a judicial forum and ensure a defendant's presence.[58] Many regulations concern rural (agricultural) issues; others, urban settings. The code often contains alternative punishments for an action: older "eye-for-eye" (*lex talionis*) justice, along with compensatory/symbolic punishments (fines instead of physical harm, for example). This circumstance suggests a society moving from traditional forms of "self-help justice" to a more institutional system of adjudication and justice suitable for a more complex urban environment.[59]

The code also exhibits a strong interest in property issues and the role of the senior male head of a kinship group (the *paterfamilias*). Hence, a remarkable number of provisions are concerned with marriage (and the transfer of property among generations), debt, and "sumptuary" issues—that is, rules clearly aimed at maintaining the integrity of family goods from one generation to the next, rather than ostentatious expenditure of family property.[60]

The code is not comprehensive: the surviving provisions suggest a combination of traditional rules to encourage the maintenance of property rights and (perhaps) newer formulations aimed at providing for all Roman citizens some degree of equity in legal matters. One interesting aspect of this collection of laws is the repeated encouragement to settle disputes out of court. Hence, one finds a recurring preference for compromise and a local (neighborhood) resolution of disputes.[61] This situation suggests a society in which, again, various

---

57. For discussion of the fundamental authenticity of the Twelve Tables as distinguished from legends and literary coloring, see, for example, Gaetano de Sanctis, *Storia dei Romani, II* (2nd ed.; Pensiero storico 38; Florence: La Nuova Italia, 1960) 39–84 (esp. 59–79); Alan Watson, *Rome of the XII Tables: Persons and Property* (Princeton: Princeton University Press, 1975) ix, 166–86; Tim J. Cornell, *The Beginnings of Rome: Italy and Rome from the Bronze Age to the Punic Wars (c. 1000–264 BC)* (Routledge History of the Ancient World; London: Routledge, 1995) 272–88. On the antiquity of many of the social, religious, and political institutions of the Twelve Tables, see, e.g., Robert E. A. Palmer, *The Archaic Community of the Romans* (Cambridge: Cambridge University Press, 1970) 194–98, 220–21.

58. Twelve Tables: Crawford, *Roman Statutes*, 2.578–9. For Gortyn, see above, section I B.

59. For recent, critical discussion of these issues in the formation (and character) of the Twelve Tables, see especially Michel Humbert, "La codificazione decemvirale: Tentative d'interpretazione," in *Le Dodici Tavole: Dai Decemviri agli Umanisti* (ed. Michel Humbert; Pavia: IUSS, 2005) 3–50.

60. Crawford, *Roman Statutes*, 2.580–83 (specifically, IV.2; V.3–7; V.2–7; VI.5; X.1–10).

61. Ibid., 2.578–83 (specifically, III.1–7; VI.6–9; VIII.2–6; I.12–13; XII.3).

kinship groups live in proximity, but laws discourage the overuse of public institutions (that is, formal public courts) to resolve disputes.

In approximately 52 B.C.E., Cicero remarked, "As boys, we used to learn the Twelve Tables as a required text; now no one does" (*de legibus* 2.59). There were several reasons that, by the time of Cicero's maturity, "no one" learned the Twelve Tables. First, by the time of Cicero, discussion of individual provisions in the code—and subsequent legislation and decisions modifying the code, as well as reinterpretations of the code—was available.[62] More importantly, the code by design was not intended to be nor did it become an unchangeable text. Continual amendment and revision to the provisions of the code engendered, by the late 1st century B.C.E., a presumption that the code had included a provision that "whatever the people most recently decide is binding."[63] This presumption—of dubious historical authenticity—was, however, a reflection of the historical reality that the code had been continually revised. The Twelve Tables served the Romans as a legal touchstone and a guide, not as an inflexible set of rules. Hence, even centuries later (in the 2nd–4th centuries C.E.), legal scholars would often, as numerous examples in Justinian's *Digest* of Roman law illustrate, begin with a consideration of what the Twelve Tables said on a given topic and then proceed to exegesis from that point.[64] To that extent, a set of rules for an emerging urban center of the mid-5th century B.C.E. served as a foundation for the later, continually-evolving structures of Roman civil law. Even though much of the material in the Twelve Tables became obsolete, it remained an authoritative reference for Roman civil law until Justinian's legislation of 528–534 C.E.

D. Some Common Factors and Themes

We have been discussing the phenomenon of written public law at a variety of sites in the late archaic and early classical periods. It may be useful, at this

---

62. For example, Q. Mucius Scaevola (consul, 95 B.C.E.) produced, before his death in 82, 18 books on Roman civil law (Frantz Peter Bremer, *Iurisprudentia Antehadriana* [2 vols.; Leipzig: Teubner, 1896–1901] 1.48–104). Cicero's contemporary, the jurist Servius Sulpicius Rufus, wrote a book on the Twelve Tables. The fragments suggest his concern to clarify archaic language and procedures (Bremer, ibid., 1.228–30). A few decades later, the jurist M. Antistius Labeo (dead 10/11 C.E.) produced a treatise "On the Twelve Tables" (Aulus Gellius, *Noctes Atticae* 6.15.1; Bremer, *Iurisprudentia Antehadriana*, 2.81–83). See also Watson, *Law Making*, 111–68, and Elizabeth Rawson, *Intellectual Life in the Late Roman Republic* (Baltimore: Johns Hopkins University Press, 1985) 201–14.

63. Twelve Tables XII.5; see Crawford, *Roman Statutes*, 2.721.

64. See, for example, Justinian, *Digest* 1.2.2.23–24; 27.10.1, 13; 38.16.3.9.11 (Paul Krüger and Theodor Mommsen, *Corpus Iuris Civilis I: Institutiones; Digesta* [Berlin: Weidmann, 1877]). These citations could be multiplied tenfold. See also Crawford, *Roman Statutes*, 2.564–67; Fögen, *Römische Rechtsgeschichten*, 70 (nn. 65–66).

point, to step back and look at the larger picture. In ancient Greece, the transition to written public law began in the 7th century B.C.E. and was not completed until the end of the 5th century in Athens (and later in other cities). Of course, customary law and the oral dimension of law never disappeared, because students were taught to memorize and recite a variety of important scribal texts.[65] Moreover, written laws could often presuppose existing (oral) laws and focus on procedures or penalties. In this respect, the written was "grafted onto" the oral.[66]

Yet, in observing the many close connections between unwritten and written law, one must also do justice to a historical trend that favored the composition and inscription of legal texts. From a relatively early time, writing was employed in some fashion for the promulgation of public laws, and this practice rapidly proliferated in a variety of Greek states. The coexistence of a variety of *poleis*, each with its own polity (aristocratic, oligarchic, democratic, tyrannical), history, traditions, customs, and rules, meant that *polis* laws and their attendant institutions could vary immensely. In any event, by the 5th century, most independent Greek cities had developed well-established legal systems of their own. In some cases (e.g., Athens and Gortyn), significant collections of written law are attested. The growth in public legislation included considered reflection on and systemization of legislation itself.

The importance and impact of written law can be seen in another development. The phrase "unwritten law" (*agrapta nomima*) begins to appear in the late 5th century, indicating that most laws were considered to be written laws at this time.[67] In Athens, another development took place that coincided with the establishment of democracy and Athens' recovery from military defeat. In the years following 410 B.C.E., an effort was made to deal with the problematic areas within current law. Existing laws were revised to remove contradictions, obscurities, and inconsistencies. New laws were made by vote of the *ekklēsia*

---

65. In this respect, it is misleading to pit written texts against oral texts, because the two could often be employed in a complementary fashion (Rosalind Thomas, *Oral Tradition and Written Record in Classical Athens* [Cambridge Studies in Oral and Literate Culture 18; Cambridge: Cambridge University Press, 1989]; eadem, *Literacy and Orality in Ancient Greece* [Key Themes in Ancient History; Cambridge: Cambridge University Press, 1992]; Susan Niditch, *Oral World and Written Word: Ancient Israelite Literature* [Library of Ancient Israel; Louisville, KY: Westminister John Knox, 1996]; David M. Carr, *Writing on the Tablet of the Heart* [New York: Oxford University Press, 2005]).

66. A point stressed by Thomas, *Oral Tradition*, 34–94; eadem, "Writing, Law," 53–54. Select written texts could be profitably used in a variety of (oral) performative contexts. Indeed, the fact that writings could often be supplemented by oral communication and recitation may well have enhanced their status. See section III below.

67. So, for example, see Sophocles, *Antigone* 454–55 (ca. 442 B.C.E.). Later references may be found in Aristophanes' *Acharnians* 532 (425 B.C.E.) and the Periclean funeral speech (Thucydides 2.37).

("assembly"). Henceforth, no uninscribed law was to be enforced and no de-cree (*psēphisma*) could override a law (*nomos*).[68] The judicial revision eventually resulted in a revised law code on the *Stoa Basileios*. How much effect this large-scale revision of older law had in actual legal practice over the long term is open to question. In any case, "the 'codification' of law was seen at that time to be both the means to achieve this end (*eunomia*, 'good order') and the end itself."[69]

II. The Rise of Written Legislation:
An Assessment of Some Current Theories

How is one to explain the appearance and growth of written legislation within a variety of Greek city-states and within Rome, as well? There are a va-riety of theories, some of which overlap, deserving serious consideration, but there is no scholarly consensus.[70] In what follows, we will briefly review some of the major theories. At the outset, we should state that there may be at least some merit in each of these views and that this may be a case in which a num-ber of different factors contributed to the end result. Depending on political, economic, and social contexts, the publication of written laws did not have identical implications everywhere.[71] It also seems probable that at least some states adopted written laws as a copy-cat phenomenon within Greece itself.[72]

A. Near Eastern Influence

The theory of Near Eastern influence would readily explain how the ancient Greeks derived the idea of writing law and displaying it prominently in urban

---

68. Andokides, *On the Mysteries*, 85–87. See Douglas MacDowell, *Andokides: On the Mysteries* (Oxford: Clarendon, 1962) 125–29, 194–99. For much of the 5th century, no distinction was made between a permanent rule (*nomos*) and a decree (*psēphisma*) for a specific occasion (Martin Ostwald, *Nomos and the Beginnings of Athenian Democracy* [Oxford: Oxford University Press, 1969] 20–54; idem, *From Popular Sovereignty to the Sovereignty of Law* [Berkeley: University of California Press 1986] 85–94). Hans J. Wolff claims that the new policy only applied to office holders, who were exercising their duty to protect the reestablished democracy ("Vorgeschichte und Enstehung des Rechtsbegriffs im frühen Griechentum," in *Enstehung und Wandel rechtlicher Traditionen* [ed. Wolfgang Fikentischer, Herbert Franke, and Oskar Köhler; Veröffentlichungen des "Instituts für Historische Anthropologie e.V." 2; Munich: Alber, 1980] 566).

69. Hölkeskamp, "Written Law," 87.

70. Stephen C. Todd, "Law in Greece," *Oxford Classical Dictionary* (ed. Simon Hornblower and Antony Spawforth; 3rd ed.; Oxford: Oxford University Press, 1996) 834–35.

71. A point stressed by Thomas, "Writing, Law," 42.

72. On the phenomenon of competitive emulation in ancient Greece, see the overview of Colin Renfrew, "Introduction: Peer Polity Interaction and Socio-political Change," in *Peer Polity Interaction and Socio-political Change* (ed. Colin Renfrew and John F. Cherry; Cambridge: Cambridge University Press, 1986) 1–18.

contexts.[73] If a variety of states in the ancient Near East had written laws long before the Greeks did and the Greeks borrowed other things from their eastern neighbors, it seems quite plausible that the Greeks also borrowed the notion of written laws. Hence, there is some merit in this view insofar as it goes.

Nevertheless, in the case of most, if not all, ancient Near Eastern states, law codes served as illustrative guidance, royal propaganda, or as a kind of judicial philosophy but not as actual legislation. Even though the great urban centers of ancient Mesopotamia were responsible for many important technological and intellectual innovations, their leaders never seem to have employed law codes to create actual public law. For the impetus to this development, we must look elsewhere and recognize that, just as the Greeks took over other eastern inventions, such as the alphabet, and put them to work for their own purposes, the same be true for the concept of written legislation.[74]

B. Trade and Colonization

In the age of colonization (late 8th–early 6th century B.C.E.), many new city-states were founded around the Mediterranean and Black Seas. These *poleis* often imitated the institutions of their mother *poleis* yet innovated further by adapting to local conditions.[75] Because some of these sites contained colonists who themselves originated from different cities, the leaders of these *poleis* may not have found any particular advantage in duplicating the institutions of only one site.[76] In the trade-and-colonization theory, lawgiving and the idea of creating a social order through lawgiving were inextricably bound up with

73. Max Mühl, *Untersuchungen zur altorientalischen und althellenischen Gesetzgebung* (Klio Beiheft 29, n.s. 16; Leipzig: Dieterich, 1933); Lilian H. Jeffery, *Archaic Greece: The City-States, c. 700–500 B.C.* (New York: St. Martin's, 1976) 189. More generally, John Boardman, *The Greeks Overseas: Their Early Colonies and Trade* (4th ed.; New York: Thames & Hudson, 1999).

74. Walter Burkert observes, "Cultural predominance remained for a while with the Orient, but Greeks began to develop their own distinctive forms of culture through an astonishing ability to adopt and transform what they had received" (*The Orientalizing Revolution: Near Eastern Influence on Greek Culture in the Early Archaic Age* [2nd ed.; Revealing Antiquity 5; Cambridge: Harvard University Press, 1992] 128). In this context, see also the comments of Kurt Raaflaub, "Poets, Lawgivers, and the Beginnings of Political Reflection in Archaic Greece," in the *Cambridge History of Greek and Roman Political Thought* (ed. Christopher Rowe and Malcolm Schofield; Cambridge: Cambridge University Press, 2000) 50–57.

75. Some writers (e.g., Gagarin, *Early Greek Law*, 129–30) would separate these two factors (trade and colonization) and speak of them as distinct theories. In the present context, we find it convenient to combine them, because the two are often related.

76. Thomas J. Dunbabin, *The Western Greeks: The History of Sicily and South Italy from the Foundation of the Greek Colonies to 480 B.C.* (Oxford: Oxford University Press, 1948) 10–11; Graham, *Colony and Mother City*, 1–68.

colonization and may well have had their very beginnings in these so-called colonies.[77]

One could cite in support of this theory the fact that some of the earliest public inscriptions are legal texts stemming from Greek colonies, especially the western colonies. However, some of the other affected communities, such as Gortyn, Athens, and Rome were not colonies. Moreover, trade and traders do not seem to have concerned the early legislators. Hence, this theory may provide insight into one of the factors contributing to the rise of written law, but it does not fully account for the phenomenon.

C. The Rise of Law as a Key Factor in the Growth of the Polis

In this hypothesis, the development of the Greek *polis* is a correlate to the rule of law. To quote van der Vliet, "Lawgiving was instrumental to the creation and legitimation of the institution of the *polis* as a state."[78] Seen from this perspective, the emergence of a central authority in an increasingly complicated state and writing go together; one is a corollary of the other.[79] The development of written law strengthened and refined the public judicial process and restricted traditional means of familial self-help.[80] According to Gagarin, the growth of the Greek city-states led to greater opportunities for conflict and a breakdown of the older *oikos*-based social structure.[81] The composition and inscription of public law, displayed in a public setting, represented a crucial means by which the *polis* was able to exercise its authority over its own inhabitants.

In fact, a case can be made that the modern differentiation between the archaic period and the classical period in ancient Greece is based in large part on positing a major transformation of society from an age of unwritten law that could be distorted, forgotten, or manipulated by unjust judges to a new age in which law and codification of law played a central role in the transformation of society.[82] The development of written law (not necessarily democracy) is construed to be a formative influence in the transition from one epoch to an-

---

77. Robert J. Bonner and Gertrude Smith, *The Administration of Justice from Homer to Aristotle* (2 vols.; Chicago: University of Chicago Press, 1930–38) 1.69; Willetts, *Law Code,* 8–9; idem, *The Civilization of Ancient Crete* (London: Batsford, 1977) 168; Giorgio Camassa, "Leggi orale e leggi scritte: I legistori," in *I Greci: Storia Cultura Arte Società; II: Une storia greca, 1: Formazione* (ed. Salvatore Settis; Turin: Einaudi, 1996) 561–76.

78. Van der Vliet, "Justice," 24.

79. C. L. van der Vliet and Ferdinand J. M. Feldbrugge, "Law's Beginnings: Some Concluding Reflections," in *The Law's Beginnings* (ed. Ferdinand J. M. Feldbrugge; E. J. M. Meijers Instituut M-65; Boston: Nijhoff, 2003) 279.

80. Gagarin, *Early Greek Law,* 135–46.

81. Ibid., 118, 136–41.

82. Hölkeskamp, "Arbitrators," 77–81; idem, *Schiedsrichter,* 280–85.

other.[83] The world of the classical *polis* was a world in which written law came to function as a ruling principle.[84]

There are many insights afforded by this theory. Its advocates point to a number of ways in which the formulation of written law played an important, perhaps even instrumental role in the construction of a new political order in certain city-states. However, one must recognize that the phenomenon in question was by no means universal. There were other contexts of urban growth and increased complexity in the ancient world in which written law did not become such an important feature of public state polity. The major states of ancient Mesopotamia developed elaborate legal systems and, indeed, witnessed the creation of royally sponsored legal codes without employing these codes to structure the governance of their societies. Closer to Greece, there were ancient Mediterranean societies that do not seem to have developed written law codes in the time frame addressed by our study.[85] Hence, while affirming the important role that written law played in the public sphere in transforming certain communities, one must also acknowledge that other communities never saw either the need or the desire to resort to it. The question that should be addressed, then, is what the elites of certain states saw in the possibilities of public written law that others did not. We will return to this matter below.[86]

D. Written Law as a Catalyst for Social Reform

In the social-reform theory, the driving force behind legal reform and the rise of written law is thought to be rising social tensions and increasing social inequality.[87] In the view of one scholar, "The increasing certainty of law and elimination of arbitrariness on the part of judges and officials served both the elite and the non-elite by reducing the potential for conflict and lowered the risk of losing their collective power to a tyrant."[88] The rule of inscribed public legislation is thus deemed to be the answer to the problems posed by "gift-devouring men" serving as magistrates, as depicted in Hesiod's *Works and Days*,

---

83. In fact, most of the *poleis* were not democracies but took other political forms; for what can be said of early Greek democracies apart from Athens, see Eric W. Robinson, *The First Democracies: Early Popular Government outside Athens* (Historia Einzelschriften 107; Stuttgart: Franz Steiner, 1997).

84. Wolff, "Vorgeschichte und Enstehung," 560–61; Gagarin, *Early Greek Law*, 140–46; Thomas, "Writing, Law," 58.

85. Looking at the larger context of contemporary societies in the western Mediterranean, for instance, we see that Carthage and other Phoenician-founded emporia and urban centers offer no evidence of law codes and no tradition of law givers.

86. See section II E below.

87. So John B. Bury and Russell Meiggs, *A History of Greece to the Death of Alexander the Great* (4th ed.; London: Macmillan, 1975) 104; van der Vliet, "Justice," 27.

88. Raaflaub, "Poets, Lawgivers," 44.

who openly defied Zeus and slandered his daughter Dike with their unjust and "crooked judgments" (*Op.* 220–21).[89]

The social-reform thesis assumes that the development of written legislation functioned as a major means to resolve harmful conflicts, reducing "the officials' freedom of decision and, by implication, the power of established families from among whom these officials were chosen."[90] That early Greek legislation was prominently displayed in major public areas within the society, such as in the agora or a major sanctuary, suggests associations of written laws with both state and divine authority.[91]

The social- and political-reform theory exhibits some useful traits in that it helps to explain the development of written law at Athens. There, as we have seen, Solon's legal and political reforms addressed social frictions that required major adaptations to the customary order. The impulse toward more accountability in communal polity may be helpful in understanding the appearance of written laws in new colonies, because some of the important monuments of early law in these locales were evidently the result of negotiated settlement.[92] The theory also has some merit when applied to the example of Rome, although the situation there was complex, involving the expulsion (traditionally dated to 510/9 B.C.E.) of an Etruscan monarchy and the foundation of the oligarchic "*Res publica*," increased urbanization, and political and social conflicts within Roman society between the (land-owning) traditional Latin clans—the self-styled "patricians"—and other Roman citizens, the "plebeians."[93] The struggle on the part of the plebeians to attain equality with the patricians, especially access to religious and political offices and equitable treatment in legal affairs, was not resolved for centuries (until ca. 281 B.C.E.). An early stage of this struggle for equality seems to have occasioned the redaction of Rome's fundamental law code, the Twelve Tables.[94]

One drawback to the social-reform theory is its general application to all circumstances.[95] That is, the problem with the theory is not so much what it

---

89. Martin L. West, *Hesiod: Works and Days* (Oxford: Clarendon, 1978) 211–12.

90. Raaflaub, "Poets, Lawgivers," 43–44.

91. The association of written laws with divine authority would hold even if many of the laws were not specifically religious in nature.

92. Van der Vliet and Feldbrugge, "Law's Beginnings," 255–80 (esp. 280). It must be underscored, however, that a good number of negotiated settlements seem to have involved various groups within the elites of the affected societies.

93. See Livy, *Ab urbe condita libri* 3.30–55; and above, n. 56.

94. Literary traditions explained the process of redaction in terms of plebeian opposition to arbitrary patrician behavior, leading to a civic strike (a plebeian "secession" from public activity), resolved by the appointment of an authoritative board of ten, charged with compiling a law code. See n. 93.

95. Gagarin offers other criticisms of the hypothesis (*Early Greek Law*, 121–26).

affirms as what it implicitly denies. Written law may have been a positive force for social change in Athens, Rome, and some of the Greek colonies, but it does not seem to have functioned in the same way in Gortyn and in some other locales. Whether written law always functioned as an effective instrument for impartial justice is most doubtful.[96] On the contrary, written law could be used in certain contexts as a vehicle to protect privilege, social standing, and wealth. In some circumstances, laws were inscribed to protect, if not reinforce aristocratic and patriarchal privileges in family, community, and property law. As Davies points out, the Gortyn laws constituted a "system of protecting privilege, of safeguarding the ownership and transmission of property (including 'slaves'), and of ensuring the continuance of male lineages."[97] The very fact that these laws were publicly inscribed may have inhibited attempts to reform them. Hence, within the ancient world, written law may have served as a catalyst for social justice in one setting but may have served the consolidation of aristocratic power in another.[98]

E. "Put That in Writing": A New Function for a Valued Technology

By the time writing was introduced as an appropriate medium for inscribing Greek and Roman law, writing had already served a number of public and private functions in the ancient world. The decision to employ writing for inscribing public laws in ancient Greece and Rome may well have been linked to the prestige and importance already attributed to writing in society, especially in elite circles.[99] There is literary evidence from the 5th and 4th centuries to suggest that many elites did place an emphasis on the value of written law. As Thomas writes: "By the time of the classical period, written law was widely regarded as *in itself* conducive to fairness, justice, and equality—not only democracy."[100] To quote an early-5th-century treaty between Gortyn and Rhittena, "Let what is written be valid, but nothing else."[101]

---

96. Hölkeskamp, *Schiedsrichter*, 262–85.

97. Davies, "Gortyn Laws," 327.

98. Hence, we can agree with the broad assertion that "writing was used in all these contexts to construct power," with the understanding that such constructions served a wide variety of purposes (Alan K. Bowman and Greg Woolf, "Literacy and Power in the Ancient World," in *Literacy and Power in the Ancient World* [ed. Alan K. Bowman and Greg Woolf; Cambridge: Cambridge University Press, 1994] 2).

99. Rosalind Thomas argues that the increased public use of writing might well have been stimulated by the private use of writing in memorial inscriptions ("Law and the Lawgiver in the Athenian Democracy," in *Ritual, Finance, Politics: Athenian Democratic Accounts Presented to David Lewis* [ed. Robin Osborne and Simon Hornblower; Oxford: Clarendon, 1994] 119–33).

100. Eadem, "Writing, Law," 43 (italics hers).

101. *IC* IV 80.12. We are following the translation of Michael Gagarin ("Letters of the Law: Written Texts in Archaic Greek Law," in *Written Texts and the Rise of Literate Culture in Ancient Greece* [ed. Harvey Yunis; Cambridge: Cambridge University Press, 2003] 72).

Why did ancient Greeks and Romans view traditional custom and unwritten law as insufficient to meet their needs? In the case of Athens, it is quite possible that customary laws had been applied arbitrarily or were manipulated unscrupulously by the oligarchy.[102] Inconvenient and awkward laws could be omitted or forgotten. In the case of the establishment of an unwritten law, reforms and new measures could be agreed to by various parties in a dispute, but these agreements would be of little use if they were easily forgotten or conveniently misquoted by one or more of the parties subscribing to the norm. Even settled customary laws could be ignored or countermanded by the very officials who were supposed to enforce them, because the laws were dependent on social memory and on the officials and judges responsible for settling disputes.

By contrast, writing seemed to offer permanence, stability, and security for the laws so affected.[103] If desired, inscribed statutes could be distanced from older traditional rules and customs (*themistes*) to convey the sense of a new beginning. Written law could include small details of procedure that could easily be lost or altered in oral transmission. Putting something down in writing promised to give a norm an enduring, if not unchanging, status. From the point of view of individuals who were in favor of employing written law, writing appeared to be a medium that could stabilize, if not fix both substantive regulations and judicial procedure. Written laws were potentially accessible to everyone in the public domain and could be employed to penalize arbitrary judgment. In this way, written law was perceived as a symbol and bulwark of proper political organization. As such, written law was thought to be a source for the good order (*eunomia*) and stability of the *polis*.

One of the merits of the prestige-of-writing theory is that it acknowledges a variety of motives at work in the codification of law in various times and circumstances, while underscoring the importance of written law itself. The exploitation-of-writing theory has been subject to some criticism, namely, that it rests on anachronistic assumptions about the nature and spread of writing. There is some justification to this criticism. Indeed, in certain cases, inscriptions were so long or placed so high that hardly anyone could or, probably, wanted to read them. It is also true that, in some older formulations of this theory, proponents spoke of a tremendous growth in literacy during the classical and Hellenistic eras. The recent study of Harris suggests, however, that the maximum literacy achieved in certain Hellenistic cities was 20–30%.[104] However, the theory does not or should not depend on widespread literacy. Instead, it de-

---

102. Thomas, "Writing, Law," 51.

103. Ibid., 49.

104. William V. Harris, *Ancient Literacy* (Cambridge: Harvard University Press, 1989). For informed discussion of Harris's work, see the various essays (ranging far beyond the geographical

pends on the increasing importance of and prestige attached to writing itself in the late archaic and classical periods in a number of different societies, even though most people in these settings were functionally illiterate. Publishing the laws ensured that they were available to the community or at least to the part of the community's literate elite who might need to have recourse to them.

It has occasionally been claimed that writing in itself did not confer any special status on a law (as opposed to leaving an ordinance as an unwritten law), but this does not seem to have been the case.[105] To begin with, one must ask why scribes would go through all the trouble of writing something down or engraving it on stone and situating the inscription in a carefully chosen public setting if the statute was not significant (that is, of import for the literate local community).[106] If the act of writing did not lend any status to a given ordinance, why would scribes add proscriptions in many archaic legal inscriptions instructing readers not to deface the writing and charging the people to adhere to "what is written"?

In historical retrospect, some citizens of Greek city-states may have had unrealistic expectations of what writing public laws could achieve for them. It may well be that written law promised much more than it could really provide in practice.[107] Written laws, like customary laws, could be manipulated by judicial officials. The public inscription of laws could have consequences unforeseen by the authorities responsible for the inscription. Like customary law, written law could be subject to manipulation, uneven enforcement, nonenforcement, or the political bias of judges and officials.[108] Written laws, like unwritten laws, could be partial and unfair. Moreover, the same medium (writing) that exemplified strength, permanence, and stability could inhibit change when there was an obvious need for change, because of the very nature of the new medium (stone or bronze). The great 4th-century Athenian orator Demosthenes (24.139–41) cites as a cautionary tale a Locrian ordinance, elsewhere attributed to Zaleucus

---

scope the title suggests) in Mary Beard et al., *Literacy in the Roman World* (Journal of Roman Archaeology, Supplementary Series 3; Ann Arbor, MI: Journal of Roman Archaeology, 1991).

105. For an example of this view, see Whitley, "Cretan Laws," 640.

106. The deliberate selection of sites for various legal inscriptions based on their intended audiences is emphasized by M. B. Richardson ("The Location of Inscribed Laws in Fourth-Century Athens, IG II² 244, on Rebuilding the Walls of Peiraieus (337/6 BC)," in *Polis and Politics: Studies in Ancient Greek History Presented to Mogens Herman Hansen on His Sixtieth Birthday* [ed. Pernille Flensted-Jensen, Thomas H. Nielsen, and Lene Rubinstein; Copenhagen: Museum Tusculanum Press, 2000] 601–16).

107. Thomas, "Writing, Law," 60.

108. Indeed, this may help explain why many written laws seek to control both public behavior and the procedures to be employed by officials to enforce the new (or, at least, newly written) statutes. See further Gagarin, "Early Greek Law," 82–94; and Thomas, "Writing, Law," 59.

(Polybius 12.16), that anyone who wished to propose a new law had to do so with a halter around his neck.[109]

All of this may be true, but the insights gained through historical experience and sustained philosophical reflection on the use and abuse of written law may not have been apparent to proponents of written law in the late 7th, 6th, and 5th centuries. If expectations that written law could achieve great things for a society proved in later years to be overly optimistic, naïve, and simplistic, this fact does not negate the fact that citizens of the same society in an earlier time held to these hopeful convictions.

In any case, it would be a mistake to consider the impact of writing law based only on the content of public legal inscriptions. Both Greeks and Romans, like many other peoples in the ancient Mediterranean world, gave writing a magical and nonfunctional role, as well as its more familiar role of preserving literature, records, and inscriptions. Writing operates both as a form of communication and as a symbol, comparable to images, such as monumental statues and icons.[110] Indeed, many public laws were, as we have seen, inscribed on monuments and preserved in sacred places. To engrave legislation in stone or bronze represented a serious investment of time and expense. Given their prominent settings, public inscriptions conveyed the authority and communal power deemed critical to the success of the legislation. To focus exclusively on the question how many citizens could actually read the entirety of these inscriptions may miss the larger point.

F. Common Factors and Themes

Before turning to a consideration of the rise of written legislation in Judah and Samaria, we may find it helpful to summarize some common factors and themes emerging from the previous discussion of Greek and Roman legal texts. First, the texts and traditions here discussed may be located within a fairly limited historical horizon (late 7th to the 4th century B.C.E.). Second, these texts and traditions reflect a degree of literacy in the societies from which they emanate and illustrate a movement from orality to greater literacy. They also, thus, illustrate and reflect an impulse to record *and* display regulations for a specific community or society. These texts—and the traditions about them—also demonstrate a medium and a message by which the specific society or community expressed and defined its identity.

Third, the law collections appeared in an era of a particular community's (increased) urbanization. None of these texts was found in or associated with rural

---

109. Thomas comments that it is no wonder that the Locrians gained only one new law in over two hundred years (ibid., 60)!

110. See, for instance, Whitley, "Cretan Laws," 640–61.

locales, although all—in greater or lesser measure—reflect both urban and rural concerns (the latter especially in matters of real property and its use and disposition). Fourth, these law codes appeared at a time of transition in the particular society from a monarchical or, at least, a highly authoritarian polity to a society governed by a stratum of society broader than a single ruler, family, or narrow caste.[111] This consideration should be qualified, however, in the instance of Gortyn. We do not have sufficient evidence of any sort to know with certainty the form of government in Gortyn prior to the earliest stratum (early 6th century B.C.E.) of the extant inscribed laws. The factors and themes common to the Greek and Roman texts we have discussed may be kept in mind when considering the emergence of written law in Judean and Samarian contexts.

III. The Rise of Written Legislation in Judah and Samaria

In his recent study of the character and types of ancient Near Eastern law, Westbrook comments that only in the 7th century B.C.E. does one begin to see a movement toward the employment of a traditional law collection as a source of authoritative law.[112] He points out that this "revolution in ideas" occurs, not within one of the great centers of power in ancient Mesopotamia and Egypt, but within the peripheral land of ancient Judah.[113] The how, when, and why of this extensive historical process are vexing questions that continue to challenge scholars.[114] Given the legal history of the East Semitic world, one could say that the "rise of Torah" in the West Semitic world of Judah and Samaria was by no means a necessary development.[115] Full discussion of the complicated problems

---

111. This consideration may also apply to the law from Chios or Erythrae (ML 8, pp. 14–17) and possibly also to the curses from Teos (ML 30, pp. 62–66).

112. Raymond Westbrook, "The Character of Ancient Near Eastern Law," in *A History of Ancient Near Eastern Law* (ed. Raymond Westbrook; 2 vols.; Handbook of Oriental Studies/Handbuch der Orientalistik, 1: The Near and Middle East/Der Nahe und Mittlere Osten 72; Leiden: Brill, 2003) 1.1–90.

113. Ibid., 21. In addition to Westbrook's geopolitical focus on Judah, we want to focus attention on Samaria as well.

114. This is not to imply that there were no important developments in cuneiform law through the millennia. On some of the changes, reforms, and developments, see Eckart Otto, *Rechtsgeschichte der Redaktionen im Kodex Ešnunna und im "Bundesbuch": Eine redaktionsgeschichtliche und rechtsvergleichende Studie zu altbabylonischen und altisraelitischen Rechtsüberlieferungen* (OBO 85; Göttingen: Vandenhoeck & Ruprecht, 1989); idem, *Körperverletzungen in den Keilschriftrechten und im Alten Testament: Studien zum Rechtstransfer im Alten Testament* (AOAT 226; Kevelaer: Butzon & Bercker / Neukirchen-Vluyn: Neukirchener Verlag, 1991); idem, "Aspects of Legal Reforms and Reformulations in Ancient Cuneiform and Israelite Law," in *Theory and Method in Biblical and Cuneiform Law: Revision, Interpolation and Development* (ed. Bernard M. Levinson; JSOTSup 181; Sheffield: Sheffield Academic Press, 1994 [repr. Sheffield: Sheffield Phoenix, 2006]) 160–96.

115. To borrow from the title of the essay by David Carr (in this volume, pp. 39–56).

associated with explaining the use of Torah as written law would require at least a book-length study and thus lies beyond the scope of this essay. Nevertheless, a few comments may be made, especially as they relate to wider developments in the ancient Mediterranean world.

First, there is much that remains unclear about the way that individual law collections were authored, edited, and used in ancient Judah. Presumably, the legal collections were primarily (and originally) employed in scribal exercises, as they were in the city-states of ancient Mesopotamia. But historical reconstruction is complicated by the fact that Judaism had become an international religion already in the 6th century B.C.E. (if not earlier). In the Neo-Babylonian, Persian, and Hellenistic periods, one is dealing with a variety of Judaisms and not simply with the Judaism practiced in Yehud. The degree to which scribes in Jerusalem may have communicated and cooperated with scribes in the diaspora (e.g., Babylon) in composing or editing certain laws or law collections is not known. Certainly there are texts, such as the rescript of Artaxerxes (Ezra 7:12–26), that suggest a close connection between the Babylonian and Jerusalemite communities.[116]

By the same token, it would be useful to attain a better knowledge of to what extent the Judean communities in Jerusalem, Babylon, and Elephantine differed from each other in legal traditions, practices, and attitudes.[117] To complicate matters further, the extent to which scribes in Judah may have collaborated with scribes in Samaria in authoring or editing portions of the Pentateuch is an interesting puzzle. The fact that these two communities ended up with virtually the same Pentateuch and viewed this corpus as authoritative is highly significant and can hardly be viewed as accidental, but historians would like to know much more about the social, political, and religious factors that contributed to this result.[118] In any event, the very development of the Covenant

---

116. In fact, much of the book of Ezra–Nehemiah has to do with the successful initiatives undertaken by members of the eastern diaspora to influence the course of events within Yehud during the Persian period (Peter Ross Bedford, *Temple Restoration in Early Achaemenid Judah* [Supplements to the Journal for the Study of Judaism 65; Leiden: Brill, 2001]). In the case of Ezra's journey to Jerusalem on behalf of the Achaemenid "king of kings," Ezra's charge includes investigating Yehud and Jerusalem "with the law of your God (בדת אלהך), which is in your possession" (די בידך; Ezra 7:14). Our concern in this context is not so much the historical veracity of the claim made about Ezra as the claim itself and the link (if not outright identity) the authors posit between the law of God that Ezra takes with him from the Judean community in Babylon and the law of God that Ezra is to implement in Judah and Jerusalem. The authors of the Ezra narrative (Ezra 7–10) seem to identify the "law of your God" with the Torah. See the discussion below, as well as the essay by Anselm Hagedorn in this volume (pp. 57–76).

117. The issue is highlighted in a very careful and provocative way in the essay of Reinhard Kratz (in this volume, pp. 77–103).

118. Questions of composition, cooperation, and development are dealt with in the essays by Christophe Nihan (pp. 187–223), Reinhard Pummer (pp. 237–269), and James Watts (pp. 319–

Code, Deuteronomy, the Priestly Code, the Holiness Code, and other legal collections embedded within the Pentateuch, whatever the respective dates assigned to the composition and rewriting of these literary works, is testimony to the growing importance of written law in ancient Judah.

Second, the long-standing question of precisely how individual law collections were collected and combined with disparate narratives into the larger corpus that later became known as the Pentateuch or Torah continues to occasion much debate.[119] Nevertheless, the final result is not in doubt. The various corpora ultimately became one corpus, and the legal sections of this corpus were related to the life, struggles, and efforts of one human legislator. This in itself is very significant. As in many centers in the ancient Greek and Roman world, disparate precepts, some of which themselves drew heavily on earlier statutes, were presented with prospective force as if they were promulgated in a single act of legislation.[120] In this typical literary conceit, laws dating to various times were associated with divine authority, projected back into an earlier age, and bestowed to the body politic by a trusted lawgiver (Moses). The association with an ancient heroic figure lent authority and a sense of unity to the law collection itself.

Third, the transformation of the legal sections of the Pentateuch (or even of the Pentateuch as a whole) from what has been described as descriptive law to prescriptive law is a fascinating, albeit highly complicated historical process, the dimensions and timing of which are not particularly well understood.[121] How

---

331) in this volume. On the relations between the two communities, see Gary N. Knoppers, "What Has Mt. Zion to Do with Mt. Gerizim? A Study in the Early Relations between the Jews and the Samaritans in the Persian Period," *SR* 34 (2005) 307–36; idem, "Revisiting the Samarian Question in the Persian Period," in *Judah and the Judeans in the Persian Period* (ed. Oded Lipschits and Manfred Oeming; Winona Lake, IN: Eisenbrauns, 2006) 265–89.

119. See the recent treatments of Eckart Otto, *Das Deuteronomium im Pentateuch und Hexateuch* (Tübingen: Mohr Siebeck, 2000); Reinhard Achenbach, *Die Vollendung der Tora: Studien zur Redaktionsgeschichte des Numeribuches im Kontext von Hexateuch und Pentateuch* (Beihefte zur Zeitschrift für altorientalische Rechtsgeschichte 3; Wiesbaden: Harrassowitz, 2003); Jean-Louis Ska, *Introduction to Reading the Pentateuch* (Winona Lake, IN: Eisenbrauns, 2006), and the references cited in these works.

120. Bernard M. Levinson discusses in considerable detail Deuteronomy's dependence upon, reuse of, and revision of earlier legislation, *Deuteronomy and the Hermeneutics of Legal Innovation* (New York: Oxford University Press, 1997); idem, "Is the Covenant Code an Exilic Composition? A Response to John Van Seters," in *In Search of Pre-exilic Israel: Proceedings of the Oxford Old Testament Seminar* (ed. John Day; JSOTSup 406; London: T. & T. Clark, 2004) 272–325.

121. The recent study of Michael LeFebvre provides a useful discussion of the issues, although we disagree with some of his analyses and conclusions (*Collections, Codes, and Torah: The Re-characterization of Israel's Written Law* [Library of Hebrew Bible/Old Testament Studies 451; New York: T. & T. Clark, 2006] 1–54). See also the earlier study of Philip R. Davies ("'Law' in Early Judaism," in *Judaism in Late Antiquity, 3: Where We Stand—Issues and Debates in Ancient Judaism* [ed.

did *tôrâ* ("instruction") become law? It would be helpful to have surviving temple archives, palace archives, court dockets, and the like from the Neo-Assyrian, Neo-Babylonian, Persian, Hellenistic, and Hasmonean periods in the southern Levant to shed light on this long process. The evidence we do possess is mainly biblical evidence, the dating and interpretation of which vary.

Fourth, in addressing the difficult question of normativity there is some evidence available outside the Pentateuch itself. The historiographic literature dating to the late preexilic, exilic, and postexilic eras gives prominence to the role (or non-role) of Torah in the histories of ancient Israel and Judah.[122] The Deuteronomistic authors selectively employ standards of *Ur-Deuteronomium* to evaluate, criticize, and commend the actions of the leaders and monarchs portrayed in their work. The kings of Israel and Judah are subjected to a written normative standard external to and in some respects subversive of their own authority. The citation of specific texts from Deuteronomy as an authority to justify the fact that certain legal actions were (or were not) taken in the history of Judah is one important development.[123] The Deuteronomistic writers promote the use (or reuse) of a prestigious collection of statutes in their society.

In one case (the case of the king who was touted by the Deuteronomists as the nation's best reformer, 2 Kgs 22:2, 23:25), Josiah reads the scroll that he considers normative for the community to the assembled masses (2 Kgs 23:1–3). It is true that this pious king makes no attempt to display the Torah permanently as a public inscription, but the Torah scroll is kept in the Jerusalem temple. In any event, the public display of law in the time of Josiah is telling. In the epilogue to the Laws of Hammurapi, one finds the invitation to any "wronged man" (*awīlum ḫablum*) to come before Hammurapi's statue and have his laws read to him so that he might "examine his case" (*likallimšu dīnšu*) and "calm his heart" (*libbašu linappišma*).[124] In Kings, the same sort of sequence (public reading and implementation of written laws) is said to have happened in the history of Judah, however partially, temporarily, and selectively (2 Kgs 23:4–20, 21–23).[125]

Jacob Neusner and Alan J. Avery-Peck; 4 vols.; Handbook of Oriental Studies/Handbuch der Orientalistik, 1: The Near and Middle East/Der Nahe und Mittlere Osten 40, 41, 49, 53; Leiden: Brill, 1998–2001] 1.4–33), although (again) we disagree with some of his analyses and conclusions.

122. In his recent book, Thomas C. Römer advances the case for preexilic (Josianic), exilic, and postexilic editions of the Deuteronomistic work (*The So-Called Deuteronomistic History: A Sociological, Historical, and Literary Introduction* [London: T. & T. Clark, 2005]).

123. Westbrook calls attention to the example of Amaziah's refusal to subject the sons of his father's assassins to capital punishment (2 Kgs 14:5–6) on the basis of a stipulation found in the "Scroll of the Torah of Moses" (Deut 24:16) ("Character of Ancient Near Eastern Law," 19–21).

124. Following the translation of Martha T. Roth, *Law Collections from Mesopotamia and Asia Minor* (SBLWAW 6; Atlanta: Scholars Press, 1995) §xlviii 3–19 (p. 134).

125. It is relevant that in the later version of Josiah's reforms found in the Chronicler's work, the tension between publicly mandated prescriptions of Deuteronomy and the royal implementation of

One can argue whether the highly selective citation of Deuteronomy that we find in the Deuteronomistic History of the monarchies, focusing as it does on the royal implementation (or, more often, nonimplementation) of cultic prescriptions having to do with centralization, amounts to a very selective use, reuse, or misuse of the older work.[126] But, in any case, the very (re)citation of *Ur-Deuteronomium* suggests that *Ur-Deuteronomium* had acquired a certain amount of cultural capital in the circles within which the Deuteronomists worked.[127] It is precisely because *Ur-Deuteronomium* evidently enjoyed a prestigious status that the Deuteronomistic writers found it advantageous to employ it as a standard within their own work.

To be sure, there is no external evidence to suggest that *Ur-Deuteronomium* achieved anything near the force of statutory law in 7th–6th-century Judah. Whatever one makes of the historicity of Josiah's reforms and the reforms of Hezekiah before him (2 Kgs 18:4), the Deuteronomistic text itself makes clear that these were exceptional, if highly laudable incidents. There are no indications that customary laws existing in a number of Judahite and Samarian locales were suddenly overturned by royal officials and replaced by a central constitution. Moreover, other literature (prophetic and sapiential) found within the Hebrew Bible does not point clearly in this direction.[128] What one can say on the basis of the testimony found in the Deuteronomistic historical work is that there was an effort on an elite level to argue for a selective implementation of certain cultic demands found in the old Deuteronomic law.

these statutes (in Kings) is somewhat alleviated by the claim that the people themselves actively participated in Josiah's reforms (2 Chr 34:4, 9, 29; 35:8–9, 18). See Sara Japhet, *The Ideology of the Book of Chronicles and Its Place in Biblical Thought* (BEATAJ 9; Frankfurt am Main: Peter Lang, 1989) 308–24; eadem, *I and II Chronicles* (OTL; Louisville: Westminster John Knox, 1993) 1017–37. The very reworking and democratizing of the older Kings account by the Chronicler is indicative of the force that Deuteronomy carried among the elite in the Chronicler's own time.

126. Gary N. Knoppers, *Two Nations under God: The Deuteronomistic History of Solomon and the Dual Monarchies* (HSM 53–54; Atlanta: Scholars Press, 1993–94); idem, "The Deuteronomist and the Deuteronomic Law of the King: A Reexamination of a Relationship," *ZAW* 108 (1996) 329–46; idem, "Rethinking the Relationship between Deuteronomy and the Deuteronomistic History: The Case of Kings," *CBQ* 63 (2001) 393–415; Bernard M. Levinson, "The Reconceptualization of Kingship in Deuteronomy and the Deuteronomistic History's Transformation of Torah," *VT* 51 (2001) 511–34.

127. For this reason (among others), the discrepancies between Deuteronomy and the Deuteronomistic History need not be seen as disproving the authoritative status of Deuteronomy, as LeFebvre seems to imply in his recent study (*Collections, Codes, and Torah*, 55–95). The repeated, albeit dialectical recourse to *Ur-Deuteronomium* in the Deuteronomistic historical work indicates that *Ur-Deuteronomium* was a judicial writing esteemed by the Deuteronomists, a work that could be profitably employed in their own extensive and highly charged presentation of the past. Indeed, the very appeal to a prestigious older document could enhance the value of the writers' new work.

128. See, for instance, the essays by David Carr (pp. 39–56) and Sebastian Grätz (pp. 273–287) in this book.

Fifth, we find an intensification of the promotion of written law in the historiographic literature of Judah dating to the late Persian and early Hellenistic
periods. The point requires some discussion with reference to Chronicles and
Ezra–Nehemiah. In Chronicles, for instance, the author cites and alludes to
"the Torah," "the (book of the) Torah of Moses," and "the Torah of Yhwh" as
an authority much more often than the Deuteronomists do in their history of
the monarchy.[129] In Chronicles, we even find a king aptly named "Jehoshaphat" (יהושפט), who launches a campaign to educate the Judean people in "the
scroll of the Torah of Yhwh" by sending royal officers, Levites, and priests
throughout the cities of Judah to teach Torah (2 Chr 17:7–9). A variety of earlier biblical traditions depict the judicial responsibilities of monarchs (e.g.,
2 Sam 8:15–18, 1 Kgs 3:16–28) or express a desire for royal justice (e.g., 1 Sam
8:5, Psalm 72), but Chronicles is most unusual in its depiction of a king explicitly mandating the dissemination of Torah to effect this result. Set against the
background of ancient Near Eastern legal tradition, the Chronicler ingeniously
presents a king promulgating not his own royal code but God's law. The result
is something unprecedented in Israelite history: a monarch mandating education in Torah to his people.[130]

Of specific interest to us in analyzing the Chronicler's work is his citation of
both the Deuteronomic and the Priestly works as normative for Israelite practice. To take just one example, the account of Josiah's national Passover (2 Chr
35:12–13) harmonizes the Priestly (Exod 12:8–9) and Deuteronomic (Deut
16:7) regulations pertaining to the preparation of the Passover lamb by asserting
that the priests and Levites, in complying with the "scroll of Moses, . . . boiled
(בשל) the Passover lamb with fire (באש), according to the custom."[131] Both
the reuse and the harmonization of this earlier legal material indicate that the
proto-Pentateuch (the combination of P and D) employed by the Chronicler
enjoyed a prestigious status among the elite for whom the Chronicler wrote.

---

129. See 1 Chr 16:40; 22:22; 2 Chr 6:16; 12:1; 14:3; 15:3; 17:9; 19:10; 23:18; 25:4; 30:16;
31:3, 4, 21; 33:8; 34:14, 15, 19; 35:26. The point has been long noted by scholars. Recent studies
(with further references) include Judson R. Shaver, *Torah and the Chronicler's History Work: An Inquiry into the Chronicler's References to Laws, Festivals, and Cultic Institutions in Relationship to Pentateuchal Legislation* (BJS 196; Atlanta: Scholars Press, 1989); Kevin L. Spawn, *As It Is Written and
Other Citation Formulae in the Old Testament: Their Use, Development, Syntax and Significance* (BZAW
311; Berlin: de Gruyter, 2002).

130. In a later initiative, Jehoshaphat overhauls the system of justice within his land by ap-
pointing judges in every town and by establishing a central court in Jerusalem staffed by ancestral
heads, priests, and Levites (2 Chr 19:4b–11). Although instituted by a reformer king, this new national system of jurisprudence actually features little or no direct royal involvement (Gary N.
Knoppers, "Jehoshaphat's Judiciary and the Scroll of Yhwh's Torah," *JBL* 113 [1994] 87–108).

131. On the sophisticated exegetical techniques evident in this text, see further Fishbane, *Biblical Interpretation in Ancient Israel* (Oxford: Clarendon, 1985) 134–38.

Within the book of Ezra–Nehemiah, the appeal to Torah and to the precedent of Torah is especially prominent in Ezra.[132] There, the "Torah of Moses, the man of God," is appealed to in connection with the sacrifice of burnt offerings at the Jerusalem altar (Ezra 3:2–3). The celebration of the Festival of Sukkoth is said to occur "as it is written" (ככתוב; Ezra 3:4).[133] When narrating the arrival of Ezra, the scribe, "skilled in the Torah of Moses" in Jerusalem (Ezra 7:6–9), the author comments that Ezra "set his heart to seek out the Torah of Yhwh to observe and to teach law and custom in Israel" (Ezra 7:10). In the rescript of King Artaxerxes (Ezra 7:12–26) given to Ezra, "the scribe of the words of the commandments of Yhwh and his statutes concerning Israel" (Ezra 7:11), the "law of your God" (דת אלהך) seems to be equated with the Torah (Ezra 7:14, 21, 25, 26). Officials in the community cleverly allude to, combine, and extend stipulations in earlier laws (Exod 34:11–16; Deut 7:1–5, 23:4–9) in alerting Ezra to the problem of foreign wives (Ezra 9:1–2). So that "the Torah might be practiced" (כתורה יעשה; Ezra 10:3), the foreign wives are subsequently divorced and expelled (Ezra 10:4–44).[134] In the narrative world of Ezra, it seems that the Torah does not simply function as some sort of descriptive ideal but as a body of prescriptive legal literature, the statutes of which are to be followed in the community. In other words, the law collections embedded within the Torah no longer represent scribal exercises without public impact.

---

132. Space restrictions do not allow a discussion of the development of Ezra–Nehemiah. Recent scholarship has argued for a complicated process of composition and redaction, although scholars disagree quite substantially about the number and extent of the stages involved in the editorial process. See Dieter Böhler, *Die heilige Stadt in Esdras α und Esra–Nehemia: Zwei Konzeptionen der Wiederherstellung Israels* (OBO 158; Göttingen: Vandenhoeck & Ruprecht, 1997); Titus Reinmuth, *Der Bericht Nehemias: Zur literarischen Eigenart, traditionsgeschichtlichen Prägung und innerbiblischen Rezeption des Ich-Berichts Nehemias* (OBO 183; Göttingen: Vandenhoeck & Ruprecht, 2002); Juha Pakkala, *Ezra the Scribe: The Development of Ezra 7–10 and Nehemia 8* (BZAW 347; Berlin: de Gruyter, 2004); Jacob Wright, *Rebuilding Identity: The Nehemiah-Memoir and Its Earliest Readers* (BZAW 348; Berlin: de Gruyter, 2004); Reinhard G. Kratz, *The Composition of the Narrative Books of the Old Testament* (trans. John Bowden; London: T. & T. Clark, 2005) 49–86.

133. The literary evidence within Ezra–Nehemiah plays a substantial role in the reconstructions of Westbrook, "Character of Ancient Near Eastern Law," 16–21; and in the earlier studies of Michael Fishbane, *Biblical Interpretation*, 107–34, 539–40; ibid, "From Scribalism to Rabbinism: Perspectives on the Emergence of Classical Judaism," in *The Sage in Israel and the Ancient Near East* (ed. John G. Gammie and Leo G. Perdue; Winona Lake, IN: Eisenbrauns, 1990) 439–56; ibid., "Midrash and the Meaning of Scripture," in *Interpretation of the Bible* (ed. Jože Krašovec; JSOTSup 289; Sheffield: Sheffield Academic Press, 1998) 539–63; Jackson, *Studies*, 141–42, 161–62; Anne Fitzpatrick-McKinley, *The Transformation of Torah from Scribal Advice to Law* (JSOTSup 287; Sheffield: Sheffield Academic Press, 1999).

134. Baruch Halpern makes a detailed comparison with the 5th-century citizen reforms in Athens ("Ezra's Reform and Bilateral Citizenship in Athens and the Mediterranean World," in *Egypt, Israel, and the Ancient Mediterranean World: Studies in Honor of Donald B. Redford* [ed. Gary N. Knoppers and Antoine Hirsch; Probleme der Ägyptologie 20; Leiden: Brill, 2004] 439–53).

Quite the opposite; the rules that may have been originally composed as elite scribal exercises now appear as written laws that are publicly enforced for the entire community under the aegis of a scribal priest.

Given that the end result is not in doubt—namely, that the Pentateuch eventually became normative Scripture in both Judah and Samaria—it does not seem unreasonable to conclude that the promulgation of texts such as Chronicles and Ezra–Nehemiah played a role in this process. More than that, these books were not created as disembodied literary entities floating freely in space. They were written and edited by authors with certain goals in view. As such, they reflect the tenets of certain groups in the community. The same texts also note opposition to the positions of the leaders that the book promotes.[135] Hence, while it is not possible to determine when a number of practices and views advanced by late texts (such as Chronicles and Ezra–Nehemiah) about the Torah came to dominate Judean society, the texts themselves provide important clues about this historical process. If there existed a process at certain times in the Persian period whereby communities could seek Achaemenid affirmation and ratification of their legal (mostly cultic) traditions from local Achaemenid officials, this process may have aided the efforts of the Judean leaders who were promoting the public authority of certain stipulations found in the Torah.[136] Based on the examples usually cited in support of the imperial-authorization hypothesis, local recognition of this sort was, however, probably addressed to a specific issue or to a set of regulations dealing with a disputed intercommunity matter, rather than to an entire collection of laws.

Sixth, there is another feature of postexilic historiographic literature that deserves careful attention in relation to the use of written law in postmonarchic Judah: the phenomenon of public readings of the Torah in the community. The increasing weight attributed to written law in the history of ancient Judah may thus be seen from another vantage point. The most famous example is Ezra's reading to the assembly from the "scroll of the Torah of Moses by which YHWH charged Israel" (Neh 8:1–8), but there are three other examples found in Ezra–Nehemiah. One relates to the educational activities of Ezra, the ancestral heads, the priests, and the Levites when the people observed Sukkoth (Neh

---

135. See further, Gary N. Knoppers, "Nehemiah and Sanballat: The Enemy Without or Within?" in *Judah and the Judeans in the Fourth Century B.C.E.* (ed. Oded Lipschits, Gary N. Knoppers, and Rainer Albertz; Winona Lake, IN: Eisenbrauns, 2007) 305–31.

136. A scaled-down version of the imperial-authorization hypothesis is advocated by David Carr (pp. 39–56) and Konrad Schmid (pp. 23–38) in their essays in this volume. See also Joseph Blenkinsopp, "Was the Pentateuch the Civic and Religious Constitution of the Jewish Ethnos in the Persian Period?" in *Persia and Torah: The Theory of Imperial Authorization of the Pentateuch* (ed. James Watts; SBLSymS 17; Atlanta: Society of Biblical Literature, 2001) 41–62; Konrad Schmid, "Persische Reichsautorisation und Tora," *TRu* 71 (2006) 494–506.

8:13–18). Another relates to the Israelites' public confession of sins (9:1–3) preceding the long Levitical prayer (9:4–37). Yet another serves as a prelude to the priests' and Levites' separating "everything foreign from Israel" (13:1–3).[137]

One of the fascinating features of the public readings is not simply that law is being conceived of as a written text but also that these texts need to be recited and performed in a public setting.[138] Oral readings, group discussions, and public recitations of prestigious older texts affirm the authority of the written word for the life of the community.[139] In these cases, we can discern a transition, not from the oral to the written, but from the written to the oral. The oral presupposes the written and represents a staged performance of it. The two exist in a reciprocal relationship in which the oral affirms and publicly ratifies the written. The recitation and practice of the written word bind the people to the written word.[140] Here, one can notice the effort to differentiate between a written document without public impact as a select text for the literati and a written document that does have a broader social impact.

Finally, it may be no accident that one finds a special concern with the public functions of written law in the biblical (historiographic) texts that are normally dated to the postmonarchic period. In this context, our comparative study of the increased use of written law within a number of other ancient Mediterranean societies may be of relevance. Surveying the rise of written law in Athens, Gortyn, and Rome, we observed that the promulgation of law collections in these societies did not occur in monarchical or tyrannical contexts. Rather, the rise of public written law seems to have been facilitated by the transition in a particular society from a monarchic or highly authoritarian polity to a polity that involved some degree of shared rule by a number of different parties or office holders. The issue was not democracy as opposed to all other forms of governance, because relatively few *poleis* were democracies. Rather, the issue was some diffusion of power among the elite within a number of different types of societies.

---

137. The number of public readings is stressed by Michael W. Duggan (*The Covenant Renewal in Ezra–Nehemiah* [*Neh 7:72b–10:40*]: *An Exegetical, Literary, and Theological Study* [SBLDS 164; Atlanta: Society of Biblical Literature, 2001] 108).

138. See our discussion of the rise of written law in the Greco-Roman world (above, section I) and also the discussion of Joachim Schaper in this volume (pp. 225–236).

139. In other words, the oral dimension of texts and textual transmission ably discussed in the studies of Susan Niditch (*Oral World and Written Word*), Thomas (*Oral Tradition and Written Record*; eadem, *Literacy and Orality*), Carr (*Writing on the Tablet of the Heart*), and others does not disappear but takes on a new function.

140. As the essay by Jean-Louis Ska (in this volume, pp. 145–169) points out, certain texts within the Pentateuch contain markers pointing to the special importance of written law and to the authority of these inscribed regulations.

The polities of the ancient Mediterranean civilizations embracing the rule of written law varied (aristocratic, democratic, oligarchic, etc.), but in each case the social order involved the active participation of a broader range of leaders than a single monarch, dictator, or family would normally allow.[141] One function of written law in this sort of postmonarchic setting was to bring (or add) definition, unity, and structure to the society itself. A related function was a limiting of the prerogatives of some members of the elite by other members of the elite. There were, as we have seen, some cases in which class struggles may have also played a role in advancing the cause of public, written legislation.[142]

In the case of postmonarchic Judah, one is dealing with a (sub-)province in the larger context of an immense Persian Empire. Some scholars have described the leadership structure of Yehud simply as a diarchy (governor and high priest). While it is true that the two posts of governor and high priest feature prominently in the texts of Ezra–Nehemiah, Haggai, and Zechariah, there are other leaders clearly visible as well, such as priests, Levites, elders, nobles, heads of ancestral houses (ראשי האבות), and prophets and prophetesses. It is unimaginable that a scribal priest, such as Ezra, who does not seem to have been a high priest himself (Neh 12:10–11), could have played as large a role as he is said to have played (Ezra 7–10; Neh 8:1–18, 12:26), unless there was some diversity and flux in the leadership structure of the province itself.[143]

The conflicts depicted or referred to in late narratives and prophetic texts (e.g., Haggai, Zechariah, Malachi) dealing with the postexilic period point in the same direction. The point in this context is neither to sort out what the conflicts and disagreements all involved nor to identify each of the relevant parties but to observe that the existence of open struggles suggests the emergence of a diversity of opinion and of leadership in the province of Yehud.[144] Based

---

141. It would be very illuminating to have more historical information about the mechanics of judicial enforcement in Gortyn and about the larger social structure of Gortyn (see section I B above). The references in the Gortyn laws to the *polis* and to the *Gortynoi* (Gortynians) as a citizen body, to the *kosmos* as a magistrate (or a group of magistrates), and to other officials suggest some diversity in the leadership of what is thought to be an aristocratic society. It is impossible to say much more, given the paucity of available evidence.

142. See sections I C and II B above.

143. See further, Erhard Blum, *Studien zur Komposition des Pentateuch* (BZAW 189; Berlin: de Gruyter, 1990); Rainer Albertz, *A History of Religion in the Old Testament Period* (2 vols.; OTL; Louisville: Westminster John Knox, 1994) 2.437–522; Joseph Blenkinsopp, *Sage, Priest, Prophet: Religious and Intellectual Leadership in Ancient Israel* (Library of Ancient Israel; Louisville, KY: Westminster John Knox, 1995); Joachim Schaper, *Priester und Leviten im achämenidischen Juda* (FAT 31; Tübingen: Mohr Siebeck, 2000); Lester L. Grabbe, *A History of the Jews and Judaism in the Second Temple Period* (Library of Second Temple Studies 47; London: T. & T. Clark, 2004).

144. On the reconstruction of the various parties, see the disparate treatments of Otto Plöger, *Theokratie und Eschatologie* (Neukirchen-Vluyn: Neukirchener Verlag, 1959); Paul D. Hanson, *The Dawn of Aocalyptic: The Historical and Sociological Roots of Jewish Apocalyptic Eschatology* (rev. ed.;

on comparative study of other societies in the ancient Mediterranean world, we submit that this social and religious setting in Yehud was one factor favoring the development of written law. If the historical, social, and religious situation in Yehud also involved some degree of contacts of the elite with Yahwists both in the diaspora (e.g., Babylon, Egypt) and in Samaria, this might have intensified the need to resort to a common set of sacred Scriptures (or more narrowly, of sacred laws) that could be affirmed as foundational by all concerned. In a diverse international setting, the development of a common set of written laws would have served to unify Yahwists scattered in a variety of lands.

Conclusion

In this essay, we have advocated a Mediterranean-wide perspective in which a number of factors may have contributed in one way or another to the publication of written laws and law collections in various societal settings. In referring to the development of written laws at these sundry sites, we are not claiming that the leaders of Yehud and Samaria were somehow directly influenced by developments within the various Greek and Roman states and their assorted colonies. Nevertheless, the possibility of indirect knowledge of trends and events elsewhere in the Mediterranean world cannot be ruled out.[145]

Philadelphia: Fortress, 1979); Morton Smith, *Palestinian Parties and Politics That Shaped the Old Testament* (2nd ed.; London: SCM, 1987); Jon L. Berquist, *Judaism in Persia's Shadow: A Social and Historical Approach* (Minneapolis: Fortress, 1995); Joseph Blenkinsopp, *A History of Prophecy in Israel* (rev. ed.; Louisville, KY: Westminster John Knox, 1996); Lester L. Grabbe, *Judaic Religion in the Second Temple Period: Belief and Practice from the Exile to Yavneh* (London: Routledge, 2000); Reinhard G. Kratz, *Das Judentum im Zeitalter des Zweiten Tempels* (FAT 42; Tübingen: Mohr Siebeck, 2004).

145. Deut 27:1–4, 8 (cf. 27:5–7) may provide an example of this awareness: Moses enjoins the inscription of the law on large, plastered stones. Compare Joshua's order that 12 stones (one for each tribe) be erected (Josh 4:2–9, 20–24) on the other side of the Jordan and his later inscription of a "copy (מִשְׁנֶה) of the Torah of Moses, which he wrote in the presence of the Israelites" on the stones of the altar he erected at Shechem (Josh 8:30–35; cf. LXX Josh 9:2ᵃ⁻ᶠ; 4QJoshᵃ). Josh 8:30–35 is surely presented as the fulfillment of the Mosaic injunctions of Deuteronomy and seems to reflect, in its present wording, a combination of Deut 27:1–4, 8 and 27:5–7. (On this matter, see the detailed essay of Christophe Nihan elsewhere in this volume, pp. 187–223). In both instances (Deut 27:1–8 and Josh 8:30–35), we suggest, the writer exhibits an awareness of the wider Mediterranean practice of recording legal texts pertinent to a particular community in monumental format. The Mosaic curses set out in Deut 27:14–26, in turn, find a parallel in a fragmentary Greek stone inscription (ca. 475–70 B.C.E.) from Teos (an Ionian city on the coast north of Ephesus). This text records the community's curses against poisoners and people who interfere with the city's grain trade. See ML 30 (pp. 62–66) and above, n. 12. For a detailed discussion of Deuteronomy 27, with reference to the inscription from Teos, see Anselm C. Hagedorn, "Wie flucht man in östlichen Mittelmeer? Kulturanthropologische Einsichten in die *Dirae Teiae* und das Deuteronomium," in *Kodifizierung und Legitimierung des Rechts in der Antike und im Alten Orient* (ed. Markus Witte and Marie Theres Fögens; Wiesbaden: Harrassowitz, 2005) 117–31. The people of Teos, incidentally, were aware of eastern elements in their own culture: the letters of the inscription (lines 37–38) are *phoinikeia*, attested elsewhere (Herodotus 5.58.2) to indicate the Phoenician origin of the Greek alphabet.

One channel for the transmission of developments elsewhere in the Mediterranean world was, of course, trade, especially sea trade.[146] Popham has reviewed the physical evidence for a revival of trade with the Levant in the Aegean Greek world during the Early Iron Age, while Morris points out that, due to technical advances in shipbuilding and navigation during the latter part of the Iron Age, the Mediterranean became a smaller place.[147] In his recent survey of the intermittent Greek presence in the eastern Mediterranean world during the Iron Age, Fantalkin identifies five distinct stages.[148] In discussing the last stage, which actually extended beyond the Iron Age into the Persian period, he notes the presence not only of eastern Greek imports but also of amphoras from Chios, Samos, and other locales.[149] The distribution of these material remains is considerably wider than was the case in the late Neo-Assyrian period.[150] In the 5th century, eastern Greek pottery in the southern Levant was slowly replaced by Attic imports.[151] This material evidence suggests the possibility, even the probability, of cross-cultural contact during the historical period under discussion.

---

146. Trade operated, of course, in more than one direction; hence the contacts and influences among ancient Mediterranean cultures neither functioned in simply one particular way nor led to identical results in the societies affected by the commercial ventures.

147. Mervyn Popham, "Precolonization: Early Greek Contact with the East," in *The Archaeology of Greek Colonisation* (ed. Gocha R. Tsetskhladze and Franco De Angelis; Oxford: Oxford University Committee for Archaeology, 1994) 11–34. The advances in shipbuilding had occurred already by the end of the 8th century (Ian Morris, *Archaeology as Cultural History: Words and Things in Iron Age Greece* [Malden, MA: Blackwell, 2000] 257). On the significance of maritime transport for spreading goods and ideas in the ancient Mediterranean, see Nicholas Purcell, "Colonization and Mediterranean History," in *Ancient Colonizations: Analogy, Similarity and Difference* (ed. Henry Hurst and Sara Owen; London: Duckworth, 2005) 115–39.

148. Alexander Fantalkin, "Identity in the Making: Greeks in the Eastern Mediterranean during the Iron Age," in *Naukratis: Greek Diversity in Egypt* (ed. Alexandra Villing and Udo Schlotzhauer; London: The British Museum, 2006) 199–208. See also Jane C. Waldbaum, "Early Greek Contacts with the Southern Levant, 1000–600 B.C.: The Eastern Perspective," *BASOR* 293 (1994) 53–66; eadem, "Greeks in the East or Greeks and the East? Problems in the Definition and Recognition of Presence," *BASOR* 305 (1997) 1–17; Boardman, *The Greeks Overseas*, 102–53; idem, "Aspects of 'Colonization,'" *BASOR* 322 (2001) 33–42.

149. Fantalkin, "Identity in the Making," 204.

150. Ephraim Stern, "Between Persia and Greece: Trade, Administration and Warfare in the Persian and Hellenistic Periods," in *The Archaeology of Society in the Holy Land* (ed. Thomas E. Levy; London: Leicester University Press, 1995) 432–45; idem, *Archaeology of the Land of the Bible, II: The Assyrian, Babylonian, and Persian Periods, 732–332 BCE* (ABRL; New York: Doubleday, 2001) 217–27, 283–86, 518–59.

151. Fantalkin, "Identity in the Making," 204. See also Ephraim Stern, "The Beginning of the Greek Settlement in Palestine in the Light of the Excavations at Tel Dor," in *Recent Excavations in Israel: Studies in Iron Age Archaeology* (ed. Seymour Gitin and William G. Dever; AASOR 49; Winona Lake, IN: Eisenbrauns, 1989) 107–24.

Indeed, some of the examples of local law often cited in connection with the Persian imperial-authorization theory, such as the trilingual (Lycian, Aramaic, Greek) Letoon Inscription from the Xanthus Valley in Lycia and the Miletus Inscription adjudicating a border dispute between Miletus and Myus, bear witness to the international tenor of this age.[152] The Persian period was an age of cultures in contact, a time of unprecedented multilateral trade and travel. To be sure, this was also an age punctuated by a series of international wars. Yet, even during these conflicts, trade continued and, in some cases, grew. Given the location of mainland Greece in the eastern (and not western) Mediterranean world, some have argued for a reconsideration (or reconceptualization) of the traditional categories used to separate the geopolitical realities of the ancient Mediterranean world into an Aegean world, on the one hand, and an Egyptian and Near Eastern world, on the other hand. Instead, some prefer to speak of an eastern Mediterranean world that comprised various adjoining societies.[153]

In any case, the larger point remains. In discussing the promulgation of the Pentateuch as Torah, we will find an advantage in examining a wider range of evidence than is possible if one limits the investigation to the confines of the Persian imperial network. Historical analyses of the acceptance of the Torah as a prestigious writing within the postexilic community may produce some valuable information about this process through comparative study of the publication of written laws in a variety of other societies within the ancient Mediterranean world. Judah and Samaria were only two of many (but by no means all) Mediterranean societies investing in written law during the mid- to late centuries of the first millennium B.C.E.

---

152. Henri Metzger et al., *Fouilles de Xanthos 6: La stéle trilingue du Létôon* (Paris: Klincksieck, 1979); Peter J. Rhodes and Robin Osborne, *Greek Historical Inscriptions: 404–323 BC* (Oxford: Clarendon, 2003) 70–74 (no. 16); Frei and Koch, *Reichsidee und Reichsorganisation* (2nd ed.) 12–16, 39–47, 96–97. Other epigraphic evidence pointing to contacts among a variety of societies in the ancient Mediterranean world is cited in Gary N. Knoppers ("Greek Historiography and the Chronicler's History: A Reexamination," *JBL* 122 [2003] 627–50).

153. Hagedorn discusses this issue at some length in *Between Moses and Plato*, 14–38.

PART 2

Prophets, Polemics, and Publishers:
The Growing Importance of Writing
in Persian Period Judah

From History Writing to Library Building: The End of History and the Birth of the Book

JEAN-LOUIS SKA

Rome

In recent discussions about the formation of the Pentateuch, scholars have often looked for a concrete Sitz im Leben that could explain the reason why the first five books of the Bible were gradually compiled and arranged in a way that is similar to the organization that we know today. In the past two decades, much has been said about "Persian imperial authorization" but, to say the least, this proposal has not been greeted with the same enthusiasm by all scholars— either in North America or in Europe.[1] In my first, very short section, I will present a few additional marginal comments on this topic (§1). My main intention in this essay, however, is to explore new avenues of research in a field that has had some success in recent years—namely, the complex relationships between oral and literate cultures or, rather, the complex interplay within the same society between a majority of people relying only on orality and the growing importance of a tiny minority able to read and to write.[2] My main

---

1. See especially the contributions in James W. Watts, ed., *Persia and Torah: The Theory of Imperial Authorization of the Pentateuch* (SBLSymS 17; Atlanta: Society of Biblical Literature, 2001). For the original publication on this topic, see Peter Frei and Klaus Koch, *Reichsidee und Reichsorganisation im Perserreich* (2nd ed.; OBO 55; Fribourg: Universitätsverlag / Göttingen: Vandenhoeck & Ruprecht, 1996); Peter Frei, "Die Persische Reichsautorisation: Ein überblick," *ZABR* 1 (1995) 1– 35. For other recent publications in this area, see the volume edited by Reinhard G. Kratz, *Religion und Religionskontakte im Zeitalter der Achämeniden* (Veröffentlichungen der Wissenschaftlichen Gesellschaft für Theologie 22; Gütersloh: Chr. Kaiser, 2002), in particular, the article by Erhard Blum, "Esra, die Mosetora und die persische Politik," 231–56. See also Lisbeth S. Fried, *The Priest and the Great King: Temple-Palace Relations in the Persian Empire* (Biblical and Judaic Studies from UCSD 10; Winona Lake, IN: Eisenbrauns, 2004). It is perhaps interesting to recall that this theory goes back to Eduard Meyer, *Die Entstehung des Judenthums: Eine historische Untersuchung* (Halle: Niemeyer, 1896) 65–66: "Die Einführung eines derartigen Gesetzbuchs [das Gesetzbuch Ezras] ist nur möglich, *wenn es vom Reich sanktionirt, wenn es königliches Gesetz geworden ist*" ("The introduction of such a code of law [Ezra's code of law] *is only possible if it is approved by the empire, if it becomes a royal law*," p. 66; italics mine).

2. See the important publications by three North American scholars: Susan Niditch, *Oral World and Written Word: Ancient Israelite Literature* (Library of Ancient Israel; Louisville, KY: Westminster

---

thesis, which I will develop in a second, longer section is that the birth of the Torah should be linked with two related developments (§2). The first is the rise of a scribal culture dedicated to the writing of ancient, "paradigmatic," traditions, especially the Torah. The second is the constitution of a library in the Jerusalem temple in the postexilic period. I will develop this idea in three steps. First, I will show that, after the Exile, the interest in "history" as such, especially recent history, slowly dwindled and eventually disappeared during the Roman period (§2.1). Second, another phenomenon is a correlate to the first. The interest in the *remote* past increased a great deal. This led to the so-called *antiquarian interest* mentioned by several authors and to the collection, compilation, and safeguarding of ancient traditions, which were then preserved in archives and libraries (§2.2).[3] Third, I will analyze one text in particular, Exod 24:3–8, which is in my opinion a very late text that bears the signature of some of the "writers" responsible for the redaction and transmission of the "Teaching/Law of Moses" to future generations; who were, in other words, the first "editors" or compilers of the present Pentateuch (§2.3).[4]

1. Persian Imperial Authorization

Regarding Persian imperial authorization, I have nothing essential to add to what I have already written elsewhere.[5] That there had been some kind of decision taken by Persian authorities on the constitution of the province of Yehud

---

John Knox, 1996); William M. Schniedewind, *How the Bible Became a Book: The Textualization of Ancient Israel* (Cambridge: Cambridge University Press, 2004); David M. Carr, *Writing on the Tablet of the Heart: Origins of Scripture and Literature* (New York: Oxford University Press, 2005).

3. On the *antiquarian* as such, see Arnaldo Momigliano, "The Rise of Antiquarian Research," in *The Classical Foundations of Modern Historiography* (Berkeley: University of California Press, 1990) 54–79; Mark Salber Phillips, "Reconsiderations on History and Antiquarianism: Arnaldo Momigliano and the Historiography of Eighteenth-Century Britain," *Journal of the History of Ideas* 57 (1996) 297–316. On *antiquarian interest* in the Bible, see, among others, John Van Seters, *In Search of History: Historiography in the Ancient World and the Origins of Biblical History* (New Haven: Yale University Press, 1983 [repr. Winona Lake, IN: Eisenbrauns, 1997]) 96–98; Thomas L. Thompson, "Historiography (Israelite)," in *ABD* 3.206–12, esp. 209; Baruch Halpern, *The First Historians: The Hebrew Bible and History* (San Francisco: Harper, 1988) 11, 97, and passim.

4. For a sharp (but also somewhat one-sided) critique of the use of the terms *editors* and *redactors* in biblical criticism, see John Van Seters, *The Edited Bible: The Curious History of the "Editor" in Biblical Criticism* (Winona Lake, IN: Eisenbrauns, 2006). For a short response, see Jean-Louis Ska, "A Plea on Behalf of the Biblical Redactors," *ST* 59 (2005) 4–18. See also Bernard M. Levinson, "Is the Covenant Code an Exilic Composition? A Response to John Van Seters," in *In Search of Pre-exilic Israel: Proceedings of the Oxford Old Testament Seminar* (ed. John Day; JSOTSup 406; London: T. & T. Clark, 2004) 272–325 (at 275–88).

5. Jean-Louis Ska, "'Persian Imperial Authorization': Some Question Marks," in *Persia and Torah: The Theory of Imperial Authorization of the Pentateuch* (ed. James W. Watts; SBLSymS 17; Atlanta: Society of Biblical Literature, 2001) 161–82.

or on the reconstruction of Jerusalem and the temple is obvious (e.g., Ezra 7). What I contest, however, is the notion that one should consider the *Pentateuch* to be this document of authorization. The objections are serious and numerous. One of them, which is often either forgotten or forsaken, is that a long document in Hebrew was of no use to Persian authorities. We should have at least a document or a copy of the document in Aramaic. Another objection that should be taken more seriously is that there are in the Pentateuch very few clear and explicit (or even implicit) allusions either to Persia or to Persian authorities, let alone to the new political situation of the province of Yehud in the Persian Empire.[6] For these and other reasons, I have preferred to adopt a different line of thought. I have tried to understand the formation of the Pentateuch within the multifarious interactions among the various groups that made up the postexilic community.[7]

2. The Birth of the Torah

2.1. The End of History Writing

In his discussion of the concept of the "history of salvation" and the theology of the "God who acts in history," James Barr makes the very interesting remark that the idea of *history* is surely not the unique, fundamental idea of biblical theology.[8] The significance of "the history of salvation" slowly diminished after the Exile, whereas the interest in wisdom literature, among other things, noticeably increased. Along the same lines, Arnaldo Momigliano noted some years ago that there was no real historical research coming from Israel or Israelite authors between the *Jewish War* (around 75 C.E.) and the *Jewish Antiquities* (around 93 C.E.) by Josephus, on the one hand; and the work of Josippon (or Joseph ben Gorion; 10th century) or, even, *Me'or 'Enayim* by Azariah de Rossi, a Jewish Italian humanist born in Mantova around 1511, on the other.[9] It is worth quoting a few sentences from Momigliano in this respect:

> if by research we mean care in depicting a contemporary political situation, the Books of Ezra and Nehemiah and the First Book of Maccabees are fine specimens. They give us a coherent picture of a political development, and they allow us to see what actually happened. They are more

---

6. See, however, Jacques Vermeylen, "La 'table des nations' (Gn 10): Yaphet figure-t-il l'Empire perse?" *Transeu* 5 (1992) 113–32.

7. See on this point my *Introduzione alla lettura del Pentateuco* (4th ed.; Bologna: Dehoniane, 2004) 245–58 [trans.: *Introduction to Reading the Pentateuch* (Winona Lake, IN: Eisenbrauns, 2006) 217–29].

8. James Barr, "Story and History in Biblical Theology," *The Scope and Authority of the Bible* (Explorations in Theology 7; London: SCM, 1980) 1–17, esp. 10–11.

9. Momigliano, *Classical Foundations*, 22, 27.

than material for future historians. They are thought-out historiography.
There was nothing wrong with this Jewish historiography, except, quite
simply, that it died out and did not become part of the Jewish way of
life. The Jews did not go on writing history. Even the First Book of
Maccabees ceased to be a Jewish book. Its original Hebrew text was
allowed to fade out, and the Greek translation was preserved by the
Christians.[10]

A little further on, he makes this significant statement: "The very way in
which history is treated in the Books of Daniel, Esther, Judith, and, one could
add, Tobit, shows that by the second century B.C. the interest in history was at
a very low level."[11] Today, some would be even more skeptical about "history
writing" in Israel as such, but Momigliano's observations remain altogether
valid.[12]

For Momigliano, moreover, the rabbinic tradition was fundamentally ahis-
torical, according to the well-known aphorism "*in the Torah there is no before
and no afterwards*" (*b. Pesaḥ.* 6b).[13] A few more examples will buttress this idea.
The Chronicler, for instance, did not write the history of the reconstruction of
the temple and the reorganization of its cult. He adopted another method, a
midrashic retelling of ancient history and a retrojection of contemporary issues
into a "mythical past," especially the time of David and Solomon.[14] Ben Sirach (Ecclesiasticus), in chaps. 44–50 ("The Praise of the Ancestors"), concentrated his attention less on events than on personalities.[15] The apocryphal (or

---

10. Ibid., 21.

11. Ibid., 22.

12. See, among others, Marc Zvi Brettler, *The Creation of History in Ancient Israel* (London:
Routledge, 1995); Lester L. Grabbe, ed., *Did Moses Speak Attic? Jewish Historiography and Scripture
in the Hellenistic Period* (JSOTSup 317; Sheffield: Sheffield Academic Press, 2001); Daniel Doré,
ed., *Comment la Bible saisit-elle l'histoire?* (LD 215; Paris: Cerf, 2007).

13. The saying applies, in the Talmud, to the lack of chronological order in the book of Numbers. There is a tension between the date given in Num 1:1, "Yhwh spoke to Moses [. . .] on the
first day of the *second* month of the second year after [the Israelites] had come out of Egypt," and
Num 9:5 (also see 9:1), where the Israelites celebrated Passover on the fourteenth of the *first* month.
Thus chap. 9 should chronologically precede chap. 1. The solution to this problem, according to
the rabbis, is that there is no chronological order in the Torah. The rabbis used this principle in several similar instances. Momigliano himself uses it to illustrate his thesis about the relative lack of interest in history as such in rabbinic literature (Momigliano, *Classical Foundations*, 23).

14. See Gary N. Knoppers, *1 Chronicles 1–9: A New Translation with Introduction and Commentary* (AB 12; New York: Doubleday, 2004) 129–34. See, however, the final statement: "Chronicles is more than a paraphrase or literary elaboration of the primary history. Chronicles needs to
be understood as its own work" (p. 134).

15. On this text, see, among others, Alon Goshen-Gottstein, "Ben Sirah's Praise of the Fathers:
A Canon-Conscious Reading," in *Ben Sira's God: Proceedings of the International Ben Sira Conference*

Deuterocanonical) Wisdom of Solomon 16–19 offered a long midrashic med-
itation on Exodus and some episodes of the sojourn of Israel in the desert. *Jubilees* (135–105 B.C.E.) is another midrashic retelling of Genesis and the early
chapters of Exodus (Exodus 1–14). Only 1–2 Maccabees, under Hellenistic
influence, attempted to recount recent history, as James Barr noted.[16] And we
know that 1 and 2 Maccabees were excluded from the Jewish canon. Josephus
too was influenced by Greek culture, with which he was in constant dialogue.
The rabbis, in the Mishnah and Talmud, were not very interested in history as
such but much more in anecdotes.[17] Toward the end of this period, we find
the harsh judgment of the great Maimonides (1135–1204), who bellieved that
occupying oneself with history is a sheer waste of time (*bizbuz zēmān*).[18]

To be sure, I must add a few qualifications to Momigliano's and Barr's statements. First of all, the change did not happen all of a sudden. There were historical works in the postexilic period, regardless of the definition we give to the
word *historical*. But there was no attempt to write a complete history of postexilic Israel, whether during the Persian, the Hellenistic, or the Roman period.
History writing became sporadic and was restricted to a short period of time, as
in the case of Ezra and Nehemiah, 1 and 2 Maccabees, and the *Jewish War* of Josephus, or it was concentrated on an ideal past, as in the case of 1–2 Chronicles,
Jubilees, and the *Antiquities* of Josephus. Second, it is clear that after the time of
Josephus Israel did not produce any real historical work until the Renaissance.
Third, and I insist on this point, the change was gradual and extended from the
return from Exile to the Roman period, which means more or less five centuries. In any case, I am speaking here of the orthodox Jewish tradition, which
had a different approach to Scripture than the first Christian community did.

What are the reasons for this growing lack of interest in history writing in
postexilic Israel? After the traumatic experience of the Exile, and even more
after 70 C.E. and 135 C.E., it seems that official Judaism tried, for obvious reasons, to remain aloof to recent history and preferred to dedicate more and more
energy to the study of the Torah, which means that a kind of atemporal wisdom gradually replaced an interest in recent history. One could say that history
had proved to be too cruel and too ruthless. Israel, apart from some exceptions,
preferred to remain at a distance from actual history and to find vital space in

---

(Durham, 2001) (ed. Renate Egger-Wenzel; BZAW 321; Berlin: de Gruyter, 2001) 244–60; Jean-
Louis Ska, "L'éloge des pères dans le Siracide (Si 44–50) et le canon de l'Ancien Testament," in
Treasures of Wisdom: Festschrift Maurice Gilbert (ed. Nuria Calduch-Benages and Jacques Vermeylen;
BETL 143; Leuven: Peeters, 1999) 188–91.

16. Barr, "Story and History," 15.

17. Ibid.

18. Maimonides, *Perush ha-Mishnah, Sanhedrin* 10; see Momigliano, *Classical Foundations*, 22.

less perilous areas.[19] Conversely, an interest in past history, especially in a "glorious" past, removed from recent tragedies, grew rapidly. This means, according to Momigliano, that "history" became after awhile a "complete history" or a history superior to any other kind of history.[20] History, in other words, became, for the most part, an "ideal history" or a "paradigmatic history."[21] This evolution started soon after the Exile, with the creation of the Torah, which unites history and law, and the important historical complexes we find now in Joshua–2 Kings. With this, however, I come to my second point: the collection of ancient valuable documents about this "paradigmatic" and "etiological" past in archives and libraries.

2.2. Library Building

2.2.1. The Reasons for Collecting Ancient Documents

In this section, I rely on several recent studies on orality and literacy, and the creation of archives and libraries in the ancient Near East and in Israel.[22] The thesis I want to defend is that there was a connection in postexilic Israel between the gradual creation of an "ideal history" and the creation of "libraries"

---

19. This does not mean, as Martin Noth states in the introduction of his *Geschichte Israels* (Göttingen: Vandenhoeck & Ruprecht, 1950) 15 (trans. *The History of Israel* [London: Black, 1958] 7), that Israel's history comes to an end in 135 C.E., with the defeat of Bar Kochba and that Israel is "replaced" by Christianity on the world's scene: "It is these revolts which may be said to have brought the history of 'Israel' to its close, and the treatment of the insurrections of A.D. 66–70 and 132–135 may therefore form the appropriate conclusion for a presentation of the history of 'Israel'" (p. 7). On this point, see the important reflections by Rolf Rendtorff, "Das 'Ende' der Geschichte Israels," in his *Gesammelte Studien zum Alten Testament* (TBü 57; Munich: Chr. Kaiser, 1975) 267–76.

20. Momigliano, *Classical Foundations*, 23.

21. On the paradigmatic character of history in the Bible, see, among others, Rudolf Smend, *Elemente alttestamentlichen Geschichtsdenkens* (ThSt 95; Zurich: EVZ, 1968) 18–23; Jacob Neusner, "Paradigmatic versus Historical Thinking: The Case of Rabbinic Judaism," *History and Theory* 36 (1997) 353–77; Susan Boorer, "The 'Paradigmatic' and 'Historiographical' Nature of the Priestly Material as a Key to Its Interpretation," in *Seeing Signals, Reading Signs: The Art of Exegesis—Festschrift A. F. Campbell* (ed. Mark A. O'Brien and Howard N. Wallace; JSOTSup 415; London: T. & T. Clark, 2004) 45–60.

22. Fundamental to my argumentation in this section are, in particular, Susan Niditch, *Oral World and Written Word*, 60–69; Philip R. Davies, *Scribes and Schools: The Canonization of the Hebrew Scriptures* (Library of Ancient Israel; Louisville, KY: Westminster John Knox, 1998); Schniedewind, *How the Bible Became a Book*; Carr, *Writing on the Tablet of the Heart*, although I might insist somewhat more than David Carr does on the growing importance of writing, libraries, and books in the late postexilic period. For more information on libraries and archives, see Jeremy A. Black and William J. Tait, "Archives and Libraries in the Ancient Near East," in *CANE* 4: 2197–2209; Olof Pedersén, *Archives and Libraries in the Ancient Near East, 1500–300 B.C.* (Bethesda, MD: CDL, 1998). On the phenomenon in the ancient world, see Lionel Casson, *Libraries in the Ancient World* (New Haven: Yale University Press, 2001).

or "archives." The main reason for seeing a connection between the two phenomena is that the interest not in the recent but in the remote past naturally led to an interest in the remnants of this past, especially the old traditions and written documents. This obliges us to speak of the formation of libraries and archives. Usually one distinguishes libraries from archives, the first containing scholarly and literary texts and the second preserving diplomatic and administrative documents.[23] In common with most specialists, I do not think that there was a real difference between archives and libraries in the ancient Near East, apart from a few exceptions.[24] Documents of all kinds were gathered—first of all administrative documents, then literary texts.

The reasons that documents were gathered and preserved are many. The first reason is, of course, usefulness. Good administration requires the ability to keep track of various political, financial, and commercial transactions, especially letters, contracts, treaties, deeds, dockets, and records of various kinds, such as payment of taxes, fulfillment of regular services, and so on.[25] To this first obvious reason, one can add a second: prestige. The importance of an archive is naturally proportionate to the importance of a city, kingdom, or empire; the more transactions, the more documents, and quantity proved the richness and power of a political, economic entity. The possession of literary texts was a status symbol in ancient times, as well as today.[26] The "book" had a prestige that is difficult to appreciate in a modern culture where books can be found, sold, and bought almost everywhere. In antiquity, all scrolls or books were "rare books," which means that all books were very precious and therefore were preserved with great care. A narrative such as 2 Kings 22, for instance, underlines in many ways the awe that surrounded the book discovered in the temple.[27]

---

23. See, in particular, Davies, *Scribes and Schools*, 17–18.

24. See Niditch, *Oral World*, 61: "in the better represented parts of the ancient Near East the distinction between archive and library is sometimes blurred"; and especially Carr (*Writing on the Tablets of the Heart*, 19, 303), who disagrees with Menahem Haran ("Archives, Libraries, and the Order of the Biblical Books," *JANESCU* 22 [1993] 51–61) and Davies (*Scribes and Schools*), insofar as they maintain a sharp distinction between archives and libraries. For Carr and others, the only exceptions are Assurbanipal's library and later Hellenistic libraries.

25. These documents are mostly for immediate use. Recording older documents often has a different purpose. See Niditch, *Oral World*, 62–63.

26. "The private libraries may have had pragmatic function as aids in their owners' works but were also tributes to their work, identifying them as possessors of a special sacred arcane knowledge. The texts are on some level signets and markers of status" (ibid., *Oral World*, 67).

27. See the analysis by Norbert Lohfink, "Die Gattung der 'Historischen Kurzgeschichte' in den letzten Jahren von Juda und in der Zeit des Babylonischen Exils," *ZAW* 90 (1978) 319–47, esp. 320–22 [repr. in his *Studien zum Deuteronomium und zur deuteronomistischen Literatur*, vol. 2 (SBAB 12; Stuttgart: Katholisches Bibelwerk, 1991) 55–86, esp. 56–58].

Texts, especially literary texts, were also preserved for ritual, liturgical, judicial, and educational purposes.[28] The Hebrew Bible contains several allusions
to public readings of the Torah in a setting that was at the same time didactic,
liturgical, and judicial.[29] In all these cases, ancient traditions were put in writing because they were deemed essential for a culture. Conversely, the very fact
that they were written down also added to their prestige and relevance. Sometimes, according to Niditch, the written word acquired a sacral, even magical
value.[30] One should perhaps mention the idea, widespread in antiquity, that
written works, like monuments, preserve the memory of great personalities or
important events.[31] *Verba volant, scripta manent* ("spoken words fly away, written
words remain"), one medieval Latin motto states.[32]

Written texts have different functions from oral traditions, as I just stated,
but I do not think that one can set the two in opposition to one another. The
presence of a text in a library does not mean that the tradition was no longer
accessible or that it stopped being part of an oral, educational curriculum or,
more simply, of the world of living folklore.[33] It may simply mean that, at a

---

28. See Bernard S. Jackson (*Studies in the Semiotics of Biblical Law* [JSOTSup 314; Sheffield:
Sheffield Academic Press, 2000] 129–41), who mentions three functions of written literature: ar-
chival, ritual, and didactic. See also Carr, *Writing on the Tablets of the Heart*, 201–14, 241–51, 253–
85. Carr insists very much on the educational and didactic aspect of Scripture, as for instance in
this critique of Philip Davies's theory: "The Hebrew Bible, I would argue, is an example of such
an educational corpus, not the remnant of a library" (p. 303). These aspects are connected, however, as other parts of the book make clear. See, for instance, pp. 262–63, where Carr quotes
2 Macc 2:13–14 and says that the Hasmoneans reconstituted a library in their endeavor to introduce an anti-Hellenistic educational curriculum. The founding of a library and an education program often go hand in hand.

29. See especially James W. Watts, in particular, *Reading Law: The Rhetorical Shaping of the Pentateuch* (Biblical Seminar 59; Sheffield: Sheffield Academic Press, 1999).

30. Niditch, *Oral World*, 44, 81–84, and passim; also see Schniedewind, *How the Bible Became a
Book*, 24–34 ("The Numinous Power of Writing").

31. See Stephen J. Liebermann, "Canonical and Official Cuneiform Texts: Toward an Understanding of Assurbanipal's Personal Tablet Collection," in *Lingering over Words: Studies in Ancient
Near Eastern Literature in Honor of William L. Moran* (ed. Tzvi Abusch, John Huehnergard, and
Piotr Steinkeller; Atlanta: Scholars Press, 1990) 311, about Assurbanipal, who wanted his library
to be a monument to preserve his memory. Hammurapi's stele had a similar function, which was
to preserve the king's judicial reform for posterity. About the same function of the written text,
see, for instance, Job 19:23–24; Isa 30:8; Jer 17:1; cf. John 19:22. With regard to a monument's
perpetuating someone's memory, see 2 Sam 18:18. Nevertheless, in some contexts, one finds a
critical attitude toward the power of written words (e.g., Isa 10:1–2, Jer 8:8). We will come back
to this point in our analysis of Exod 24:3–8 (see §2.3.3).

32. However, the original meaning of the saying seems to be that words can circulate, whereas
writings remain immobile in the dust of archives and libraries. This was true in a predominantly
oral society, in which literacy was the privilege of a tiny minority.

33. This is a major thesis defended by Niditch, *Oral World*, 83–88, 97–98, and passim.

certain point, someone recognized the worth of this tradition for present and for future generations.[34]

2.2.2. Books and Libraries in Postexilic Israel

But did ancient Israel build libraries for literary texts?[35] First of all, we must remember that there is no archaeological evidence whatsoever that there were libraries in Israel, and I mean *libraries* in the strict sense of the word.[36] Moreover, the Bible itself is almost completely silent about the creation of archives and libraries.[37] We cannot conclude, however, that there were no libraries in Israel. The simple mention of the "books of the chronicles of the kings of Judah/Israel," whatever they may have contained and whatever historical value they may have had must preserve a kernel of truth and refer to some reality. The discovery of ostraca and bullas also confirms the existence of "archives" in the kingdoms of Israel and Judah.[38]

If we turn to the Bible itself, there is an interesting phenomenon noticed by some authors. At one point in the history of Israel, books were more and more frequently mentioned.[39] The exact dates of the texts are obviously disputed, but most of them were not earlier than the end of the monarchy. They belong, at the earliest, to the so-called "Deuteronomic Reform," which means the reign of Josiah. Some of them are, of course, later and go back only to the exilic or postexilic (Persian) period. Let us mention, among more important texts, Josh 24:26, 2 Kings 22, Jeremiah 36, Nehemiah 8, and the several references to

---

34. Thus, one can understand why the Code of Hammurapi and the *Gilgamesh Epic* were found in many libraries in ancient Mesopotamia. See, on this point, Carr's clarifications in his discussion with Davies (Carr, *Writing on the Tablet of the Heart*, 303).

35. The idea of the existence of a library or an archive in Jerusalem's temple in which old documents were preserved is not new. It goes back at least to Richard Simon (*Histoire critique de l'Ancien Testament* [Paris, 1678; Rotterdam: Reiniers Leers, 1685] foreword), who speaks of the "archives de la république des Hébreux" ("the archives of the Hebrews' republic"). The idea was adopted by Karl David Ilgen in the title of his work *Die Urkunden des Jerusalem'schen Tempelarchivs in Ihrer Urgestalt* (Halle: Hemmerde & Schwetschke, 1798). It is also found in Johann Gottfried Eichhorn's *Introduction to the Study of the Old Testament* (trans. G. T. Gollop; London: Spottiswoode, 1888) §3, pp. 15–16. On this, see Van Seters, *The Edited Bible*, 185–86, 192, 198.

36. Archaeologists have found traces of archives but not of libraries in Israel. For a summary, see Niditch, *Oral World*, 61–63; Carr, *Writing on the Tablet of the Heart*, 161, 166.

37. Ibid., 160–61.

38. See Niditch, *Oral World*, 61–63.

39. Jean-Pierre Sonnet, "'Le livre trouvé': 2 Rois 22 dans sa finalité narrative," *NRTh* 116 (1994) 836–61, and more importantly by the same author, "'Lorsque Moïse eut achevé d'écrire . . .' (Dt 31,24): Une théorie narrative de l'écriture dans le Pentateuque," *RSR* 90 (2002) 509–24. Archaeologists note that literacy started spreading in the late 8th and 7th centuries B.C.E. For a summary, see Schniedewind, *How the Bible Became a Book*, 91–117. Schniedewind tends, however, to overemphasize the importance of Hezekiah's and Josiah's times, especially with respect to the composition of the Pentateuch.

a book or a scroll (*sēper*) in Deuteronomy, in particular Deut 17:18; 28:58, 61; 29:19, 20, 26; 30:10; 31:24, 26.[40] More interestingly, the word *sēper* is often associated with the root *ktb*, "to write," for instance, in Deut 17:18; 28:58, 61; 29:20, 26; 30:10.[41]

Two things must be noted. First, the "written" book is always the book of the Torah. Only in Deut 24:1, 3, is the written document different, but it still belongs to the same, judicial realm because it is with regard to a "bill of divorce."[42] In other words, the documents that, according to the book of Deuteronomy, are written down contain mostly legal or judicial material. Nowhere does Deuteronomy indicate that mere epic or "historical" documents are written down. The only possible exception is the "song" that Moses was to write for the Israelites and teach them (Deut 31:19, 22). This song, found in Deuteronomy 32, nonetheless has many points in common with the law because its main purpose is to exhort Israel to remain faithful to the Lord and to the law.[43] If there is one text that must be written down, it is the Torah of Moses.

Second, there is a shift in the book of Deuteronomy. In the beginning, it normally speaks of a "proclaimed" torah and its content. At the end, we find more and more references to the "written" torah.[44] Most of the uses of the verb *ktb* appear in the last chapters of the book, especially after chap. 30.[45] This means that we have, for the most part, late (postexilic) texts.[46]

2.3. The Book of the Torah

Why was there this shift to a "written torah"? The exact reasons for this phenomenon are not very clear. One could say that, in the absence of the monarchy, the basic institution supporting the law, there was a need for a sub-

---

40. In Deut 24:1, 3, the terminology *sēper kērîtut* means "bill of divorce." On some of these passages, but from a different perspective, see Geert Johan Venema, *Reading Scripture in the Old Testament: Deuteronomy 9–10, 31; 2 Kings 22–23; Jeremiah 36; Nehemiah 8* (OtSt 48; Leiden: Brill, 2004).

41. The same holds true for Deut 24:1, 3. For the importance of Deuteronomy in this respect, see Carr, *Writing on the Tablet of the Heart*, 166–67.

42. See Jean-Pierre Sonnet, *The Book within the Book: Writing in Deuteronomy* (Biblical Interpretation 14; Leiden: Brill, 1997) 83–84.

43. On this text, see ibid., 117–98.

44. Ibid., 2–3.

45. Ibid., 85.

46. Deuteronomy 31–34 is usually considered to be a later Deuteronomistic text. See, in particular, Martin Noth, *The Deuteronomistic History* (2nd ed.; JSOTSup 15; Sheffield: JSOT Press, 1991) 59–60; and, more recently, Richard D. Nelson, *Deuteronomy: A Commentary* (OTL; Louisville, KY: Westminster John Knox, 2002) 8–9. Deut 31:1 could have functioned at an earlier stage as a first conclusion to the whole book if one accepts the reading of the LXX and of 1QDeut[b], which read: "And Moses finished speaking," instead of "Moses went out and spoke." See Nelson, *Deuteronomy*, 353. For a more complete study of this problem, see Carmen M. Carmichael, *Deuteronomy* (Biblia Hebraica Quinta; Stuttgart: Deutsche Bibelgesellschaft, 2007) 133*.

stitute. The narrative that illustrates this idea is 2 Kings 22–23, the discovery of the "the book of the law" in the temple and the ensuing reform introduced by Josiah in accordance with this "book."[47] Most scholars today think that the part of the narrative describing the discovery of the book postdates the destruction of the temple and the end of the monarchy, because the text presupposes the loss of both institutions.[48] Be that as it may, the point of this narrative that deserves our attention is that the most important "character" in the whole story is the book itself.[49] Moreover, the "book" and the "scribe" are the only elements of this narrative that will survive the destruction of Jerusalem. King, temple, and priesthood will either disappear (kingship) or go through a long eclipse (temple and priesthood). Even prophecy is destined to dwindle and eventually vanish. As Thomas Römer puts it, "The 'cleansing' of the temple was indeed of not much use, since it was destroyed a few decades later. But the discovery of the book offered a possibility to *understand* this destruction, and to worship Yahweh *without any temple*."[50] I would add that what was at stake was not only the temple but above all the institution of the monarchy, the Kingdom of Judah itself and all that was linked with the temple and the monarchy, such as for instance prophecy. In the ancient mind, a destroyed thing revealed its fragility and its human origin. After reading 2 Kings 22–23, one can conclude that only the book was not destroyed, and it therefore was of "divine" origin. The book,

---

47. On "book-findings" in temples, see Bernhard-Dieter Diebner and C. Nauerth, "Die Inventio des *sefer hattorah* in 2 Kön 22: Struktur, Intention und Funktion von Auffindungslegenden," *DBAT* 18 (1984) 95–118; Thomas Römer, "Transformations in Deuteronomistic and Biblical Historiography: On 'Book-Finding' and Other Literary Strategies," *ZAW* 109 (1997) 1–11; Katie Stott, "Finding the Lost Book of the Law: Re-reading the Story of 'The Book of the Law' in Light of Classical Literature," *JSOT* 30 (2005) 153–70. For Thomas Römer (*The So-Called Deuteronomistic History: A Sociological, Historical and Literary Introduction* [London: T. & T. Clark, 2006] 49–56), the tendency is to see 2 Kings 22 as a postexilic text, even in its earlier kernel.

48. See, for a summary, ibid., 53–56. For more details on this text, see Norbert Lohfink, "The Cult Reform of Josiah of Judah: 2 Kings 22–23 as a Source for the History of Israelite Religion," in *Ancient Israelite Religion: Essays in Honor of Frank Moore Cross* (ed. Patrick D. Miller, Paul D. Hanson, and S. Dean McBride; Philadelphia: Fortress, 1987) 459–75; William M. Schniedewind, "History and Interpretation: The Religion of Ahab and Manasseh in the Book of Kings," *CBQ* 55 (1993) 649–61; Lowell K. Handy and Herbert Niehr, "Der Reform des Joschija: Methodische, historische und religionsgeschichtliche Aspekte," in *Jeremia und die "deuteronomistische Bewegung"* (ed. Walter Gross; BBB 98; Weinheim: Beltz Athäneum, 1995) 33–56; Erik Eynikel, *The Reform of King Josiah and the Composition of the Deuteronomistic History* (OtSt 33; Leiden: Brill, 1996); Marvin Sweeney, *King Josiah of Judah: The Lost Messiah of Israel* (New York: Oxford University Press, 2001). For the date of the "discovery report" (mainly 22:8, 10, 11, 13*, 16–18, 19*, 20*; 22:1–3), see, for instance, Christoph Levin, "Joshija im deuteronomistischen Geschichtswerk," *ZAW* 96 (1984) 351–71; reprinted in his *Fortschreibungen: Gesammelte Studien zum Alten Testament* (BZAW 316; Berlin: de Gruyter, 2003) 198–216 (at 201, 213–15). This layer is the latest part of the text, which means, for Levin, that it is later than 1–2 Chronicles—and this is very late indeed!

49. Lohfink, "Der Gattung der 'Historischen Kurzgeschichte,'" 321–22 (= *Studien*, 2.57–58).

50. Römer, *The So-Called Deuteronomistic History*, 51.

not the temple or the king, was the solid cornerstone on which Israel could build its existence and identity, and it was the cornerstone of Yahweh's true worship.[51] And this was recognized by all: king (Josiah), priest (Hilkiah), and prophetess (Huldah).[52]

There is another aspect of this text that must be underscored. This aspect is related to the first aspect, even linguistically, because the narrative itself connects the book (*sēper*) with the scribe (*sōpēr*; 2 Kgs 22:8, 10). The "mediators of this 'book-religion' are neither the king nor the priest and their sacrificial cult, but the scribes who produce and read these books," to quote Thomas Römer again.[53] He insists, with good reason, on the book's superiority to the cult of the temple. It seems to me, however, that the text underscores even more the book's superiority to the king himself, who is present in the whole narrative, whereas the temple and the priest are mentioned only at random. Josiah was a great king, of course, but this is because he recognized the essential relevance of the "book of the covenant" (2 Kgs 23:2; cf. Exod 24:7) and acted according to its content.

I will add another explanation that does not exclude the first but completes it. This explanation is linked with the high standing of books in other cultures, especially in Mesopotamia and in Egypt. The most famous example is of course the library of Assurbanipal in Nineveh.[54] It is my contention that Israel, stimulated by its neighbors' artistic and intellectual achievements, tried by every means to prove that it was not inferior to the impressive cultures of Egypt and Mesopotamia. This is evident in the statement "And what other great nation has statutes and ordinances as just as this entire law that I am setting before you today?" (Deut 4:8). This assertion is remarkable in several respects, but one is more relevant to our discussion: Israel ought to be proud in relation to other

---

51. Ibid., 53.

52. In this section, I analyze 2 Kings 22–23 as "narrative," and I speak of the "intention of the text." I must set aside many questions—for instance, questions about the very nature of Josiah's reform, about the historical value of the text, and about the implementation of the reform. With good reason, some scholars underline the important differences between what Deuteronomy requires and what "happens" in 1–2 Kings. See Gary N. Knoppers, *Two Nations under God: The Deuteronomistic History of Solomon and the Dual Monarchies* (HSM 52–53; Atlanta: Scholars Press, 1993–94); idem, "The Deuteronomist and the Deuteronomic Law of the King: A Reexamination of a Relationship," *ZAW* 108 (1996) 329–46; idem, "Rethinking the Relationship between Deuteronomy and the Deuteronomistic History: The Case of Kings," *CBQ* 63 (2001) 393–415; Bernard M. Levinson, *Deuteronomy and the Hermeneutics of Legal Innovation* (New York: Oxford University Press, 1997) 95–97; and idem, "The Reconceptualization of Kingship in Deuteronomy and the Deuteronomistic History's Transformation of Torah," *VT* 51 (2001) 511–34.

53. Römer, *The So-Called Deuteronomistic History*, 53.

54. On Assurbanipal's library, see in particular Liebermann, "Canonical and Official Cuneiform Texts," 305–36.

nations because of its Torah.[55] What makes Israel unique and, moreover, superior to other nations is not its long history of conquests and victories or mag-
nificent monuments or the splendor of its economic and commercial richness
but its Torah. The same chapter of Deuteronomy adds this statement: "You
must observe the[se statutes and ordinances], for this will show your wisdom
and discernment to the peoples, who, when they hear all these statutes, will say,
'Surely this great nation is a wise and discerning people!'" (Deut 4:6). The
unique quality of Israel's law is the source of Israel's "wisdom" and "discernment" (or "intelligence"), if the people choose to observe the Torah. Again,
we can notice that Israel's pride is neither in political and military glory nor in
economic wealth but in "wisdom." To come back to our topic, I think that this
is the chief reason why there is so much stress put on the "book of the Torah,"
which is the main, and often the only, item mentioned when the Bible and
postbiblical literature speak of the most impressive accomplishments of its culture and history. Apart from Deut 4:6, 8, which is the clearest statement in this
respect, one should mention Deut 26:19, which links the glory and superiority
of Israel over all the other nations not to military power or political supremacy
but to the observance of the Torah. In Ezra–Nehemiah, the proclamation of
the Torah in Neh 8:1–18 is described with much more emphasis than the reconstruction of the temple in Ezra 6:13–18. The praise of the Torah is present
in texts such as Psalms 1, 19:8–15, 119 (especially vv. 46, 72, 96); Sir 24:23–
34; Bar 3:9–4:4. These texts are late, especially the apocryphal books of Ben
Sirach (ca. 190–180 B.C.E.) and Baruch (ca. 50 B.C.E.).[56] Bar 4:1–5 is particularly telling:

> [Wisdom] is the book of the commandments of God, the law that en-
> dures forever. All who hold her fast will live, and those who forsake her
> will die. Turn, O Jacob, and take her; walk toward the shining of her
> light. Do not give your glory to another, or your advantages to an alien
> people. Happy are we, O Israel, for we know what is pleasing to God.
> Take courage, my people, who perpetuate Israel's name!

For these reasons, one could say that after the Exile the Torah increasingly became the "portable homeland" of Israel, to use an expression coined by the

---

55. See Nelson, *Deuteronomy*, 65: "What is at issue here is religious and ethical greatness,
something pertinent even for dispossessed exiles." Also see Moshe Weinfeld (*Deuteronomy and the
Deuteronomic School* [Oxford: Clarendon, 1972; repr. Winona Lake, IN: Eisenbrauns, 1992] 150–
51), who sees in Deut 4:8 a possible echo of the Code of Hammurapi, especially in the expression
"righteous statutes and ordinances," and in Deut 4:6, "a polemic note against the Hammurabi
Code, which at that time was widely studied in the ancient Near East" (p. 151).

56. In the book of *Jubilees* (ca. 50 B.C.E.), the Torah was considered eternal and was written on
heavenly tablets (1:29, 3:31, 6:17).

Jewish poet Heinrich Heine (1797–1856).[57] This became even more true after 70 B.C.E. and 135 B.C.E.

The Torah has a privileged position in postexilic times, but this does not mean that other basic elements of Israel's tradition ebb away and disappear. There is hope in the return to the land, in the reconstruction of the temple, and in the restoration of the monarchy. The temple, for instance, does not lose its significance, even after its destruction.[58] Altogether, the Torah, especially the "book of the Torah," enjoys a privileged position in postexilic Israel, but one cannot speak of a monopoly. However this may be, to come back to our topic, the position of the Torah becomes unique in several ways. It can be compared, for instance, with the Code of Hammurapi or the *Epic of Gilgamesh* in Mesopotamia or with Homer in Greek and Hellenistic culture. But two main differences emerge when it is compared with these other examples. First, the Torah of Moses contains both narrative and judicial material, whereas the documents from Mesopotamia or Greece are either narrative or legal but never both. In Egypt, on the other hand, we have mostly wisdom literature. Torah is inseparably narrative and law, a series of laws inserted into a "paradigmatic" and "etiological" history, a kind of "protohistory" or a "myth of foundation" that precedes any other "history" and provides its readers with all the keys to understanding their past and present. It helps them, moreover, to build their future.[59]

---

57. The quotation is found in a letter addressed to Betty Heine in 1853. It is used by Rainer Albertz, "Das 'portative Vaterland': Struktur und Genese des alttestamentlichen Kanons," in *Kanon und Zensur* (ed. Aleida Assmann and Jan Assmann; Beiträge zur Archäologie der literarischen Kommunikation 2; Munich: Fink, 1987) 63–79.

58. On the ongoing significance of the temple, see, for instance, Gary N. Knoppers, "Prayer and Propaganda: The Dedication of Solomon's Temple and the Deuteronomist's Program," *CBQ* 57 (1995) 229–54; idem, "Yhwh's Rejection of the House Built for His Name: On the Significance of Anti-temple Rhetoric in the Deuteronomistic History," in *Essays on Ancient Israel in Its Near Eastern Context: A Tribute to Nadav Naʾaman* (ed. Y. Amit et al.; Winona Lake, IN: Eisenbrauns, 2006) 221–38. On the complex situation during the postexilic period, especially the Persian period, see, among many other recent publications, the essays in Oded Lipschits and Joseph Blenkinsopp, eds., *Judah and the Judeans in the Neo-Babylonian Period* [Proceedings of the Conference Held at Tel Aviv University, May 2001] (Winona Lake, IN: Eisenbrauns, 2003); Lester L. Grabbe, *A History of the Jews and Judaism in the Second Temple Period*, vol. 1: *Yehud: A History of the Persian Province of Judah* (Library of Second Temple Studies 47; London: T. & T. Clark, 2004); Oded Lipschits, *The Fall and Rise of Jerusalem* (Winona Lake, IN: Eisenbrauns, 2005); Jill Middlemas, *The Troubles of Templeless Judah* (Oxford Theological Monographs; Oxford, Oxford University Press, 2005).

59. On the importance of the simultaneous presence of narrative and law in the Torah, see in particular Bernard M. Levinson, " 'The Right Chorale': From the Poetics of Biblical Narrative to the Hermeneutics of the Hebrew Bible," in *"Not in Heaven": Coherence and Complexity in Biblical Narrative* (ed. Jason P. Rosenblatt and Joseph C. Sitterson; Bloomington: Indiana University Press, 1991) 129–53 (notes: pp. 242–47). Also see Eckart Otto, "Gesetzesfortschreibung und Pentateuchredaktion," *ZAW* 107 (1995) 373–92; idem, "Kritik der Pentateuchkomposition," *TRu* 60

Second, as David Carr clearly demonstrates, the Torah occupies a unique position in Israel's education and culture.[60] There are, to be sure, other texts or traditions besides the Torah. Nonetheless, Deuteronomy's statements are so strong that one must say that the Torah itself provides Israel with all that is necessary for its survival. Its life and welfare depend only on the Torah, not on any other "book" or tradition, such as an old epic, a royal chronicle, a mere collection of laws, or an anthology of wisdom sayings. I return here to my first observation, that Torah—"teaching" par excellence—is more important than "history." The Torah alone is sufficient, whereas "history" is secondary and dispensable. The Deuteronomistic History is a clear demonstration of this truth, because Israel's history is judged according to the Torah's canons, and consequently, Torah itself is above history and other educational materials.[61] Postexilic Israel had enough reasons, it seems to me, to write down the content of its "Torah" and to keep it in a "library," most likely in the temple, as one of the most precious and prestigious treasures of its culture.[62]

There remain many questions about the Pentateuch, of course, but I would say at this stage that the Torah was the core of Israel's tradition, and this is the reason that it was written down. It is clear that the actual structure of the Bible emphasizes the central position of the Pentateuch and creates connections (perhaps contrived in certain cases) with the Torah of Moses or the Torah of God. Josh 1:8–9 at the beginning of the prophetic books and Psalm 1 at the beginning of the Psalter manifest that the center of the *Tanakh* is the Torah of Moses. This has been amply demonstrated elsewhere and we do not need to belabor the point.[63]

(1995) 163–91; idem, *Der Pentateuch* (Erträge der Forschung; Darmstadt: Wissenschaftliche Buchgesellschaft, 2004).

60. Carr, *Writing on the Tablet of the Heart,* 141–42: "What makes the D vision unique, especially in Deuteronomy itself, is the totalizing claim it makes for the instruction advocated in it" (p. 141).

61. Ibid., 166–67: "This elevation of Mosaic Torah appears to have been connected with a radical reconceptualization of the educational-enculturational corpus. In contrast to comparable educational curricula, the ascendant Mosaic Torah was placed first in the educational process (as envisioned in Deuteronomy), while older introductory proverbial and instructional materials were relegated to a later point." See also Carr's contribution in this volume. Carr insists on the educational part of the question with good reason. I have tried to draw some complementary aspects into the picture.

62. Temples were the normal places to keep books, especially for liturgical and educational purposes; see Carr, *Writing on the Tablet of the Heart,* 198–99, 267–71.

63. On the secondary character of Josh 1:7–8, see Rudolf Smend, "Das Gesetz und die Völker: Ein Beitrag zur deuteronomistischen Redaktionsgeschichte," in *Probleme biblischer Theologie: Gerhard von Rad zum 70. Geburtstag* (ed. Hans Walter Wolff; Munich: Chr. Kaiser, 1971) 494–97 [trans., "The Law and the Nations: A Contribution to Deuteronomistic Tradition History," in *Reconsidering Israel and Judah: Recent Studies on the Deuteronomistic History* (ed. Gary N. Knoppers and J. Gordon McConville; Sources for Biblical and Theological Study 8; Winona Lake, IN: Eisenbrauns, 2000) 96–98]; Michael Fishbane, *Biblical Interpretation in Ancient Israel* (Oxford: Clarendon, 1986) 384. For

The precise way in which the various books were composed and integrated into the Pentateuch and the rest of the Bible is a process that remains, for the most part, a matter of conjecture. One thing remains certain, however: the Torah is the book most often mentioned in the Pentateuch itself. But who were the people responsible for the writing of the Torah? To answer this question, I propose to analyze Exod 24:3–8 more closely.

2.3. Exodus 24:3–8 and the Signature of the "Writers" of the Law of Moses

Exod 24:3–8 is undoubtedly one of the most discussed passages in the book of Exodus.[64] In this short essay, my purpose is not to offer a complete exegesis of this text but only to underscore some of its features that are sometimes neglected in favor of other debated problems. But I must first clarify some of my presuppositions about its composition, dating, and origin.

2.3.1. The Basic Literary Unity of Exodus 24:3–8

This text has been studied again and again.[65] First of all, in spite of many attempts to find different layers in this short text, I am convinced that there are no solid grounds for doing so.[66] There may be some short additions. In v. 3, the expression *wĕkol hammišpāṭîm* ("all the ordinances") comes too late after "all the

---

the interpretation of the text, see Thomas Römer, "Josué, lecteur de la Tora (Jos 1,8)," in *"Lasset uns Brücken bauen . . ."*: Collected Communications to the XVth Congress of the International Organization for the Study of the Old Testament, Cambridge 1995 (ed. Karl-Dietrich Schunck and Matthias Augustin; BEATAJ 42; Frankfurt am Main: Peter Lang, 1998) 117–24; Carr, *Writing on the Tablet of the Heart*, 139–40; Erich Zenger, "Heilige Schrift der Juden und der Christen," in *Einleitung in das Alte Testament* (ed. Erich Zenger; 5th ed.; Studienbücher Theologie 1/1; Stuttgart: Kohlhammer, 2005) 25.

64. The list of publications on this passage is endless. For this reason, I will only mention the works and studies that are directly relevant to my topic. For a more complete bibliography, see Ludwig Schmidt, "Israel und das Gesetz: Ex 19,3b–8 und 24,3–8 als literarischer und theologischer Rahmen für das Bundesbuch," *ZAW* 113 (2001) 167–85, esp. 168 n. 11. To this may be added, among others, Dennis J. McCarthy, *Treaty and Covenant: A Study in Form in the Ancient Oriental Documents and in the Old Testament* (2nd ed.; AnBib 21A; Rome: Pontifical Biblical Institute, 1978); Adrian Schenker, "Les sacrifices d'alliance, Ex XXIV, 3–8 dans leur portée narrative et religieuse: Contribution à l'étude de la *bᵉrît* dans l'Ancien Testament," *RB* 101 (1994) 481–94; John A. Davies, *A Royal Priesthood: Literary and Intertextual Perpectives on an Image of Israel in Exodus 19.6* (JSOTSup 395; London: T. & T. Clark, 2004); Christoph Dohmen, *Exodus 19–40* (Herders theologischer Kommentar zum Alten Testament; Freiburg: Herder, 2004) 196, 200–204; William H. C. Propp, *Exodus 19–40: A New Translation with a Introduction and Commentary* (AB 2A; New York: Doubleday, 2006) 293–96, 308–9. Fundamental is the article by Ernest W. Nicholson, "The Covenant Ritual in Exodus 24:3–8," *VT* 32 (1982) 74–86.

65. Two studies remain basic in this regard: Lothar Perlitt, *Bundestheologie im Alten Testament* (WMANT 36; Neukirchen-Vluyn: Neukirchener Verlag, 1969); and McCarthy, *Treaty*.

66. This is confirmed in the recent study by Schmidt, "Israel und das Gesetz," 171–72.

words of Yhwh" and, moreover, is repeated neither in the people's answer at the end of the same verse nor in the next verse, where Moses writes down only the "words."[67] The phrase is also absent in v. 8, where Moses concludes the covenant on the basis of the "words" but does not mention the "ordinances."[68] Another clear addition is the word *pārîm* ("young bulls," "steers") at the end of v. 5. The word makes little sense where it stands and seems to be there only to clarify the nature of the sacrifice and assure the reader that Moses offered a "first-class" holocaust.[69]

Many authors see a doublet in the second answer of the people in v. 7b, which repeats v. 3b.[70] The differences between the two verses are minimal. In v. 7b, we do not find *dĕbārîm* ("words") used as in v. 3b, and v. 7b adds the verb *wĕnišmaʿ* ("and we will hear/listen") at the end. Is this a doublet? Some, for instance Adrian Schenker, doubt that it is a doublet.[71] Schenker says that the two answers have different functions. In v. 3, Moses informs the people about God's law, and the people give their approval. In v. 7b, the situation differs, because in this case the people agree not only to observe the law but also to *listen* in the future to these words. The presence of *wĕnišmaʿ* ("and we will hear/listen") is essential, because in v. 7, the people promise to hear again and again the content of the *book* whenever is read, and to act accordingly. In this way, they declare their readiness to listen to the book as they listened to Moses, identifying the content of the book with Moses' teaching and God's words (cf. v. 3).

I would like to add one further observation to Schenker's convincing explanation. This observation is based on a difference between the judicial value of

---

67. It would have been more normal to find a sentence like this: "Moses told the people all the words and all the ordinances *of Yhwh,* and all the people answered in one voice and said, 'All the words and *all the ordinances* that *Yhwh* said we will observe.'"

68. See Schmidt, "Israel und das Gesetz," 171, with bibliography (n. 26).

69. Ibid., 171 n. 24, with Erich Zenger, *Die Sinaitheophanie* (FB 3; Würzburg: Echter, 1971) 75. The word *šĕlāmîm* in Exod 24:5b is also sometimes considered to be a later addition (see Schmidt, "Israel und das Gesetz," 171 n. 24). But the expression *zebaḥ šĕlāmîm* (usual translation: "sacrifices of communion") is found in 1 Sam 11:15, and the expression *zĕbāḥîm šĕlāmîm* ("sacrifice of communion") in Lev 3:1, 19:5, 22:21; Num 6:17, 15:8; with the verb *zbḥ,* "to sacrifice," in Lev 19:5. Most of these texts are late, but, as we will see, Exod 24:3–8 is also very late. For these reasons, I consider the word *šĕlāmîm* to be original.

70. For instance Heinrich Holzinger, *Das zweite Buch des Mose oder Exodus,* in *Die Heilige Schrift des Alten Testaments* (ed. Emil Friedrich Kautzsch and Alfred Bertholet; 4th ed.; Tübingen: Mohr Siebeck, 1922) 133; Bernard Renaud, *La théophanie du Sinaï, Ex 19–24: Exégèse et théologie* (CahRB 38; Paris: Gabalda, 1991) 68; Perlitt, *Bundestheologie,* 191–96.

71. Adrian Schenker, "Drei Mosaiksteinchen: 'Köngreich von Priestern,' 'Und ihre Kinder gehen weg,' 'Wir tun und wir hören' (Exodus 19,6; 21,22; 24,7)," in *Studies in the Book of Exodus: Redaction—Reception—Interpretation* (ed. Marc Vervenne; BETL 126; Leuven: Leuevn University Press, 1996) 367–80, esp. 378–80. Rabbinic scholars discussed this text at length. For a summary, see for instance, Benno Jacob, *The Second Book of the Bible: Exodus* (Hoboken, NJ: KTAV, 1992 [original Hebrew: 1945]) 743–44.

Israel's two answers in Exod 24:3 and 24:7. The terms of the contract are read for the first time in v. 3, to provide information and prior agreement, and are read again when the people, so to speak, "sign" the contract. Moreover, for the validity of this contract (*bĕrît*, "covenant"), in v. 7 the people must identify the "words" written in the book with Yhwh's "words" spoken by Moses in v. 3. The phrasing of the sentences is very precise, and this element is too often overlooked in the exegesis of the text. In v. 3, actually, Moses "tells"—*waysappēr*—the people Yhwh's "words," and in v. 7a, he "reads"—*wayyiqrāʾ*—the words written in the book. After the reading, in v. 7b, the people promise again as in v. 3b to observe all the words *that Yhwh said* (*kol ʾăšer-dibber yhwh*)—not "the words that Moses read." This means that they identify the "words" written in the book with the words reported by Moses in v. 3b and, equally, with Yhwh's words. For Israel, there is an identity between the words written in the book and the words spoken by Moses at the outset of the narrative, and these words are identified as Yhwh's words. This is not just stated by the narrator but recognized by the people. Only on this basis is the contract valid: the people recognize the identity between what they hear read to them and the content of the book.[72] For this particular reason, added to others mentioned before, I do not think that vv. 3b and 7b are doublets.[73]

Some authors also try to find here two liturgies that were combined at a later date by a redactor, a liturgy of the word (24:3–4aα, 7, 8bβ) and a liturgy of the blood (24:4aβb, 5–6, 8abα).[74] But it is difficult to separate the two accounts for several reasons. First, v. 4 can hardly be separated into two parts, because all the verbs have the same subject, Moses, who is referred to only once, at the beginning of the verse.[75] Second, the expression *wayyaškēm babbōqer*, "and he rose up in the morning," which is often considered the beginning of a new narrative[76] describing the blood liturgy, can also appear in the middle of a narrative (e.g., Gen 20:8, 21:14, 22:3, 28:18; Exod 34:4; Josh 6:12, 8:10; Judg 19:8) or at the

---

72. This fact is noted by Jacob, ibid., 743.

73. The unity of the text is also defended by Martin Noth, *Exodus: A Commentary* (OTL; London: SCM, 1962) 197–99; Brevard S. Childs, *Exodus: A Commentary* (OTL; London: SCM, 1974) 505; McCarthy, *Treaty*, 266–69: "It is, in fact, a coherent unit, not a redactional *mixtum gatherum*" (p. 266); Erhard Blum, *Studien zur Komposition des Pentateuch* (BZAW 189; Berlin: de Gruyter, 1990) 51; Wolfgang Oswald, *Israel am Gottesberg: Eine Untersuchung zur Literaturgeschichte der vorderen Sinaiperikope Ex 19–24 und deren historischen Hintergrund* (OBO 159; Fribourg: Universitätsverlag / Göttingen: Vandenhoeck & Ruprecht, 1998) 58–59.

74. See, among others, Zenger, *Sinaitheophanie*, 74; Perlitt, *Bundestheologie*, 195–203; Schniedewind, *How the Bible Became a Book*, 124–25. For Schniedewind, vv. 4–8 "add a Deuteronomic interpretative layer to the covenant ceremony" (p. 124).

75. Schmidt, "Israel und das Gesetz," 171.

76. See, among others, Zenger, *Sinaitheophanie*, 74; Perlitt, *Bundestheologie*, 195.

end of a narrative (e.g., 1 Sam 29:11).[77] The expression may simply indicate the beginning of a new phase in the same action. Fourth, the book written by Moses in v. 4 that contains Yhwh's words is called "the book of the covenant" (v. 7a) and, in this context, this clearly refers to the covenant concluded in v. 8, when Moses sprinkled the second portion of the blood on the people. Therefore, it is impossible to separate v. 7 from the first part of v. 8.[78] Fifth, dividing v. 8 into two parts causes difficulties. How can we understand the expression "in accordance with all these words," if it does not refer to the covenant just concluded? And if v. 8 is a unity, then "blood" on the one hand and "book" or "words" on the other belong to the same liturgy.[79] In conclusion, we are on firm ground when we assert that Exod 24:3–8 is a unified text, apart from two glosses in v. 3 (*wĕkol hammišpāṭîm*, "and all the ordinances") and v. 5 (*pārîm*, "young bulls").[80]

2.3.2. The Late Date of Exodus 24:3–8

Several solid arguments can be put forward in favor of a late date for Exod 24:3–8.[81] First, this text has a sophisticated liturgy; it is very unusual and without parallel in the rest of the Bible. In other texts, for instance in Jeremiah 34, we find a ritual that is attested elsewhere in the ancient Near East, the cutting up of one or more animals into two parts and the passage of the contracting partners (or the vassal) through the midst of these animals. In addition to this, the very fact that the covenant is based on the reading of a book supposes that we are in a culture where literacy is vital. This is usually a sign of a later date.[82]

---

77. See Hans-Winfried Jüngling, *Richter 19: Ein Plädoyer für das Königtum* (AnBib 84; Rome: Pontifical Biblical Institute, 1981) 125–27.

78. See Norbert Lohfink, "Bundestheologie im Alten Testament: Zum gleichnamigen Buch von L. Perlitt," *Studien zum Deuteronomium und zur deuteronomistischen Literatur I* (SBAB 8; Stuttgart: Katholisches Bibelwerk, 1990) 325–61, esp. 356. He also distinguishes different phases in the conclusion of a covenant, where others see doublets. In Exod 19:7–8, the covenant is proposed; in 24:3, the terms are accepted and then written down in the "book." Eventually, the "book" is once more read publicly, when the covenant is solemnly concluded.

79. It is not possible to isolate 4aβ–6 from the rest of the ritual, as Perlitt (*Bundestheologie*, 195–203), for instance, proposes to do. In this case, the buckets of blood would be "left over for no reason and contrary to Israelite feeling expressed in Dt 12" (McCarthy, *Treaty*, 268 n. 52).

80. For more details, see Eckart Otto, "Die nachpriesterschriftliche Pentateuchredaktion im Buch Exodus," in *Studies in the Book of Exodus: Redaction—Reception—Interpretation* (ed. Marc Vervenne; BETL 126; Leuven: Peeters, 1996) 61–112, esp. 79–80.

81. See, for instance, Schmidt, "Israel und das Gesetz," 177–78.

82. See Michael D. Coogan, "Literacy in Ancient Israel," in *The Oxford Companion to the Bible* (ed. Bruce M. Metzger and Michael D. Coogan; Oxford: Oxford University Press, 1993) 437–38; Niditch, *Oral World*, 83. See also André Lemaire, "Schools and Literacy in Ancient Israel and Early Judaism," in *The Blackwell Companion to the Hebrew Bible* (ed. Leo G. Perdue; Blackwell Companions to Religion 3; Oxford: Blackwell, 2001) 207–17; Seth L. Sanders, "What Was the

Second, the closest parallel to the sprinkling of the blood, first on the altar, then on the people, is found in late Priestly texts, in the ritual for the consecration of Aaron and his sons as priests (Exod 29:19–21 and Lev 8:22–24, 30).[83] Only in these two rituals is the blood divided into two parts: the first part is sprinkled on the altar, and the second part is used for people—in the case of Exodus 29 and Leviticus 9, the priests; and in the case of Exodus 24, the whole nation. Third, the text combines elements that are present in two important traditions, the "book" or "scroll" (*sēper*) and the "blood" (*dām*). The "book" or "scroll," as we have seen, belongs mostly to the latest part of the book of Deuteronomy, hence to the Deuteronomistic tradition. The "blood," on the other hand, belongs to the Priestly tradition, especially to fundamental rituals found in the book of Leviticus (see Leviticus 17). Usually, the combination of elements stemming from two different traditions is later than the traditions. Eventually, Exod 24:3–8 was inserted into another text describing the ascension of Mount Sinai by Moses, Aaron and his two sons, and 70 elders of Israel, who contemplate God and eat in front of him on the mountain.[84] This text also was rather late, as was recognized by several authors. Its purpose was to legitimate the authority of the two main institutions of the postexilic Israel: the priesthood and the elders. More important, however, was the insertion of Exod 24:3–8 into this late text. Most of the time, the inserted text is later than the one into which it is introduced. There are exceptions to this rule of thumb, of course, but, all in all, I must say that it is unlikely that Exod 24:3–8 was a very early text.

Alphabet For? The Rise of Written Vernaculars and the Making of Israelite National Literature," *Maarav* 11 (2004) 25–56.

83. See Eberhard Ruprecht, "Exodus 24,9–11, als Beispiel lebendiger Erzähltradition aus der Zeit des babylonischen Exils," in *Werden und Wirken des Alten Testaments: Festschrift Claus Westermann* (ed. Rainer Albertz et al.; Göttingen: Vandenhoeck & Ruprecht, 1980) 138–73, 167; Erhard Blum, *Studien,* 50–52. The idea of a consecration of Israel in Exod 24:8 is also advocated by Propp, *Exodus 19–40,* 309; Dohmen (*Exodus 19–40,* 203) rejects the idea and prefers to speak of "Israel's closeness to God," which is another very similar element of Priestly theology. In my opinion, the use of blood in rituals of consecration (Exod 29:19–21; Lev 8:14–15, 22–24, 30) and the close parallelism between Exod 24:3–9 and Exod 19:3b–8 are strong arguments in favor of the view that 24:8 describes the consecration of a "priestly kingdom" (19:6). I cannot develop this point in this essay, however. See, for instance, McCarthy, *Treaty,* 266–69; Ronald S. Hendel, "Sacrifice as the Cultural System: The Ritual Symbolism of Exodus 24,3–8," *ZAW* 101 (1989) 366–90; Adrian Schenker, "Les sacrifice d'alliance, Ex XXIV,3–8 dans leur portée narrative et religieuse: Contribution à l'étude de la berît dans l'Ancien Testament," *RB* 101 (1994) 481–94, and the studies mentioned in nn. 67 and 76.

84. On Exod 24:9–11, see, among others, my "Repas de Ex 24,11," *Bib* 74 (1993) 305–27, and the article by Ruprecht quoted there in n. 86.

2.3.3. Exodus 24:3–8 and the Custodians of Israel's Library

Exod 24:3–8 is interesting in many respects.[85] In the present discussion about the origin and composition of the Pentateuch, it seems to me that this particular text has much to offer, although very few scholars have taken advantage of its potential. In my opinion, we somehow find here the "signature" of the men who were responsible for the composition of the Torah, which means the main part of the Pentateuch.

First, it is essential to observe that this text uses the root *spr* ("to tell") several times. The verb is used in 24:3, whereas the verbs *qr'* (Qal, "to proclaim," "to read") and *ngd* (Hiphil, "to report," "to inform") are more frequently used in the same contexts. In Exod 19:7, for instance, we find the first verb and in 19:9b, the second. The use of the root *spr* ("to tell") is most likely intentional, because it is related to the word *sēper* ("scroll," "book") which appears in v. 7. The same root, as we know, is present in the noun *sōpēr*, "scribe," which does not appear in this context but is probably in the background of the scene. Moses, who writes Yhwh's words, is of course a "scribe," a "writer." To put it differently, Moses is the first *sōpēr* and can be seen as the model and ancestor of all the *sōpĕrîm* of Israel.

This first aspect is substantiated by another observation. This is the only case in the whole Bible that offers a complete description of all the different procedures connected with a *sēper*, a "scroll." These procedures are the following: Moses *tells* (*waysappēr*) the people or reports to them Yhwh's words, which means he transmits to them the content of an oral, divine tradition, and the people *answer* (*wayya'an* . . . *wayyō'mĕrû*; 24:3). Then, he *writes down* (*wayyiktōb*, v. 4) these same words, Yhwh's words, in a *sēper* (although the word itself is not used in v. 4). After the first part of the ritual of the blood, Moses proceeds to the *reading* of the *book/scroll* (*wayyiqrā'* and *sēper*, v. 7), and the people *answer* (*wayyō'mĕrû*). To sum up the whole procedure in a few words, the narrative describes a process that begins with an oral performance (Moses *tells* the people Yhwh's words in v. 3) and finishes with the oral *response* of the people in v. 7. In between, we have the passage from *oral* performance to *writing* and from *writing* to *reading* (vv. 4 and 7).

The main point that I want to underscore is that this unit provides a clear example of the passage from orality to literacy. There have been several works on this topic in recent years, especially by Susan Niditch.[86] These studies show

---

85. On the importance of the "book" in this text, but from a different perspective, see Jean-Pierre Sonnet, "Le Sinaï dans l'événement de sa lecture: La dimension pragmatique d'Ex 19–24," *NRTh* 111 (1989) 321–44, esp. 338–43.

86. Niditch, *Oral World and Written Word*, 83–88, 97–98; also see Carr, *Writing on the Tablet of the Heart*, 4–8.

that, contrary to what earlier scholars claimed, orality and literacy are not mutually exclusive.[87] Oral traditions can coexist with written tradition, and both can develop side by side. Our text, however, describes a different phenomenon, which is the (basic) identity of the written tradition with the oral tradition. This is underlined in our text by the repetition of the formula *kol-dibrê yhwh*, "all of Yhwh's words," in vv. 3a and 4a, and of the expression *kol (haddĕbārîm) 'ăšer-dibber yhwh*, "all that Yhwh said," in vv. 3b and 7b. In this narrative, what Moses *says* in v. 3, what he *writes* in v. 4, and what he *reads* in v. 7 are equivalent. For this reason, the people's answer in v. 7b is identical with their answer in v. 3b. The text stresses in a very striking way that there is no difference between what Yhwh revealed to Moses and what Moses wrote in the *sēper* (Exod 24:4, 7). The reader, naturally, knows this *sēper* or "scroll," and the intention of Exod 24:3–8 is obvious to its addressees. They know that the "scroll" of the Law is reliable for two main reasons: its content is of divine origin, and its "writer" is Moses, the most faithful custodian of this divine tradition. This also means that there is no opposition between oral and written tradition.[88] Both coincide in the *sēper habbĕrît* (Exod 24:7). The following figure illustrates these correspondences:

24:3a	ויספר משה לעם את כל־דברי יהוה	Moses told the people all the words of Yhwh
24:3b	כל־דברים אשר־דבר יהוה נעשה	all the words that Yhwh said, we will do
24:4	ויכתב משה את כל־דברי יהוה	and Moses wrote all of Yhwh's words
24:7	כל־דברים אשר־דבר יהוה נעשה	all the words that Yhwh said, we will do
24:8	על כל־דברים האלה	in accordance with all these words

Some texts show that this perfect equivalence of orality and literacy, of the oral word of God and the written *sēper habbĕrît* ("book/scroll of the covenant") as it is described in Exod 24:3–8, is not as evident as it may appear at first sight. There are some texts that place oral tradition in opposition to written law, for instance, Isa 10:1–2: "Ah, you who make iniquitous decrees, who write op-

---

87. In contemporary studies, the idea of a sharp dichotomy between orality and literacy has been put forward mainly by Albert B. Lord, *The Singer of Tales* (Cambridge: Harvard University Press, 1960) 129; idem, *The Singer Resumes the Tale* (Ithaca, NY: Cornell University Press, 1995) 212–37; the idea, however, is already present in Hermann Gunkel, *Genesis* (3rd ed.; Göttingen: Vandenhoeck & Ruprecht, 1910) lxxx. Quoting from the English translation (*Genesis* [Macon, GA: Mercer University Press, 1997] lxix): "For its part, literary fixation will have contributed to the death of the other surviving remnants of oral tradition much as the written law ended the institution of the priestly torah and the New Testament canon put an end to the early Christian charismatics ['Geistesträger']."

88. We may also find here the origin of the rabbinic tradition about the written law and the oral law as both going back to Moses.

pressive statutes, to turn aside the needy from justice and to rob the poor of my people of their right, that widows may be your spoil, and that you may make the orphans your prey!" [89] Or, consider Jer 8:8, "How can you say, 'We are wise, and the law of Yhwh is with us,' when, in fact, the false pen of the scribes has made it into a lie?" In these two texts, it seems that the prophet is contrasting an inner sense of justice, the unwritten law of the people's conscience, with the laws written by scribes. [90] Exod 24:3–8 excludes this possibility, especially because it attributes the writing of the scroll/book to Moses himself and invites the people to certify that there are no discrepancies between the oral word of God and the written scroll.

There is another point that deserves some attention, although I have already mentioned it in passing. The book written by Moses and read aloud to the people contains "Yhwh's words." Yet nowhere is the reader told the exact content of this scroll. The addressees of the narrative must know it, and the modern reader immediately identifies it with the law revealed by God to Moses in the preceding chapters. The phrasing of v. 3 as it now stands makes the identification of its content even easier. The "words" are of course the "words" of the so-called Decalogue, Exod 20:1–17 (see Exod 20:1, *kol-haddĕbārîm hā'ēlleh*), and the "ordinances" are the laws of the so-called "Book of the Covenant" (Exod 20:22–23:19; cf. 21:1, *wĕ'ēlleh hammišpāṭîm*). There is no doubt that this scroll contains legal material that forms the judicial basis of the covenant concluded between Yhwh and the people of Israel. This is relevant to our discussion because it means that Israel grants more importance to its legal tradition and written law than to its history or poetry. Moses does not write Israel's epic tradition—Moses is not Homer. Neither does Moses record Israel's past history—Moses is not Herodotus. And Moses does not write only poetry, as Pindar did, or tragedies, as the great Greek tragedians Aeschylus, Sophocles, and Euripides did. Here we have the core of what will become the Pentateuch, which is rightly called *Torah* in Hebrew.

As a writer, Moses is also a *sōpēr*, a "scribe," as we saw above. But his role is different from that of Shaphan, who in 2 Kgs 22:10 read the "scroll" discovered in the temple to Josiah. In Jer 36:21, 23, the scribe Jehudi also read to the king, this time a scroll written by Baruch at the dictation of prophet Jeremiah. In Exod 24:7, however, Moses reads to the people, as Josiah himself does in 2 Kgs 23:2. The "scroll" read by Josiah is, moreover, very similar to the scroll written by Moses, because the king is said to read *bĕ'oznêhem 'et-kol-dibrê sēper habbĕrît*, "in their hearing, all the words of the book of the covenant." The phrasing is very close to Exod 24:7, where we find the verb *qr'*, "to read," the expression

---

89. The translations are from the NRSV, with a few slight variations.
90. On Jer 8:8, see Schniedewind, *How the Bible Became a Book*, 115–17.

bĕ'oznê, "in the hearing [of]," and the syntagma *sēper habbĕrît* ("book/scroll of the covenant"), which is common only to Exod 24:7 and 2 Kgs 23:3, 21 (see its parallel in 2 Chr 34:30). The parallelism between Josiah and Moses is striking.[91] Both are official "readers" of the "book of covenant" and mediators of a covenant between God and the people (Exod 24:8, 2 Kgs 23:3). Does this mean, as some suggest, that Moses is a royal figure or that he subsitutes for the king? In my opinion, these texts affirm the opposite. The king himself is described in 2 Kings 22–23 (or in Deut 17:18) as a "scribe." To use a German expression, the king is no longer a king, he is a *Schriftgelehrter,* "a doctor of the law."

Another official reader of the law is of course Ezra, the "scribe" (*sōpēr;* Neh 8:4, 13). The public reading presented in Nehemiah 8 (even though there is no clear echo of Exod 24:3–8 or 2 Kgs 23:1–3 in this passage) has a similar function. Exod 24:3–8 is the moment at which Israel officially becomes Yhwh's people for the first time. 2 Kgs 23:1–3 depicts the rediscovery of the book of the covenant and the renewal of this covenant. Nehemiah 9 narrates the foundation of the postexilic community around the Torah of Moses after the reconstruction of Jerusalem and its temple. Here again the key person is a "scribe" who "reads" the Torah (Neh 8:3).

Of course Exod 24:3–8 is not just presenting Moses in anticipation of or as a model for kings, in particular for Josiah, or for Ezra the scribe. We can assume, rather, with some probability, that Moses is a model for every "scribe" in Israel, especially in the postexilic period.[92] Scribes are responsible for both oral and written tradition, oral and written law, and for the conformity of the written tradition to the oral. They can write down Yhwh's words and read them

---

91. This is underlined in a particular way by Schniedewind, *How the Bible Became a Book,* 126. But his conclusion that the Torah must have been written down under Josiah is, in my opinion, somewhat hasty. Should we take the narrative in 2 Kings 22–23 at face value?

92. Here we rely on several works by Eckart Otto. See, among others, "Pentateuch," *Religion in Geschichte und Gegenwart,* vol. 6 (ed. Hans-Dieter Betz et al.; 4th ed.; Tübingen: Mohr Siebeck, 2003) 1089–1102 (with bibliography); idem, *Die Tora des Mose: Die Geschichte der literarischen Vermittlung von Recht, Religion und Politik durch die Mosegestalt* (Göttingen: Vandenhoeck & Ruprecht, 2001); idem, "Mose, der erste Schriftgelehrte: Deuteronomium 1,5 in der Fabel des Pentateuch," in *L'Écrit et l'Esprit: Études d'histoire du texte et de théologie biblique en hommage à Adrian Schenker* (ed. Dieter Böhler, Innocent Himbaza, and Philippe Hugo; OBO 214; Fribourg: Academic Press / Göttingen: Vandenhoeck & Ruprecht, 2005) 273–84; Timo Veijola, "Die Deuteronomisten als Vorgänger der Schriftgelehrten: Ein Beitrag zur Entstehung des Judentums," in *Moses Erben: Studien zum Dekalog, zum Deuteronomismus und zum Schriftgelehrtentum* (BWANT 149; Stuttgart: Kohlhammer, 2000) 29–47; and idem, "The Deuteronomistic Roots of Judaism," in *Sefer Moshe: The Moshe Weinfeld Jubilee Volume—Studies in the Bible and the Ancient Near East, Qumran, and Post-Biblical Judaism* (ed. Chaim Cohen, Avi Hurvitz, and Shalom M. Paul; Winona Lake, IN: Eisenbrauns, 2004) 459–78. The role of the scribes connected with the temple is also emphasized by Carr, *Writing on the Tablet of the Heart,* 267–85.

"in the hearing of the people" (Exod 24:7, 2 Kgs 23:2; cf. Neh 8:3b). In short, the "Book of the Covenant" contains the key tradition of Israel, the tradition that deserves to be written down, and the individuals who are responsible for it are "scribes," the true heirs of Moses. With them abides the most important and most prestigious symbol of Israel's religion, the "book," which bears the seals of divine and Mosaic authority. When, in Exod 24:7 Israel promises to "listen" to the reading of the book, they actually promise to listen to these heirs of Moses.[93]

Conclusion

The formation of the Pentateuch that along with an increasing number of scholars I place during the Persian period is enshrouded in mystery. In this inquiry, I examined the hypothesis that the origin of the Pentateuch should be linked to the founding of a "library" in Jerusalem in the postexilic period and the writing down of the most important traditions of Israel, in particular the *torah*, although it is difficult to be much more precise about its original content. The officials responsible to the people for the preservation of the most sacred and authoritative traditions of Israel—for writing them down and reading them in public—are "scribes" similar to Moses in Exod 24:3–8. In this text, we can see how the divine tradition passes from God to Moses and from Moses to the "book" to which the people promise to listen again and again, because listening to the reading of the book means listening to Moses, and to God himself.

---

93. See, among others, Sonnet, "Lorsque Moïse eut achevé d'écrire," 524: "En présentant le Dieu d'Israël et Moïse, le médiateur, sous les traits de scribes, en les 'surprenant' dans des pratiques scribales, les scribes, auteurs du Deutéronome, ont, pour ainsi dire, autorisé leur propre pratique" ("In presenting Israel's God and Moses, the mediator, in the guise of scribes and 'catching' them in scribal activities, the scribes who were the authors of Deuteronomy authorized, so to speak, their own practice"). In my view, this is even more striking in the case of Exod 24:3–8.

Scribal Scholarship in the Formation of Torah and Prophets:

A Postexilic Scribal Debate between Priestly Scholarship and Literary Prophecy— The Example of the Book of Jeremiah and Its Relation to the Pentateuch

ECKART OTTO

Munich

This essay intends not only to demonstrate that the postexilic formations of the Pentateuch and the book of Jeremiah were each the result of an intensive endeavor of scribes using the same techniques but also that Priestly scribes who were responsible for the formation of the Pentateuch were discussing critical theologoumena of revelation and the hermeneutics of revelation in a disputatious way with scribal authors who belonged to postexilic prophetic schools. These scribal authors viewed themselves as connected to and ultimately deriving from preexilic prophets, such as Isaiah and Jeremiah. This means that the formation of prophetic books, especially the book of Jeremiah (which was the result of the work of the Jeremianic school), influenced the formation of the Pentateuch and vice versa.

Author's note: Abbreviations that are unique to this essay are:

D/Dtr	Deuteronomistic Deuteronomy (exilic period)
DtrD	Horeb-redaction of the exilic Deuteronomy (Deuteronomy 5–28)
DtrL	Moab-redaction of the exilic Deuteronomy and book of Joshua (Deuteronomy 1–Joshua 23) following the Horeb-redaction
HexRed	hexateuchal redaction of Genesis 1 to Joshua 24 in the period of Nehemiah (ca. 450 B.C.E.)
PentRed	pentateuchal redaction of Genesis 1 to Deuteronomy 34 in the period of Ezra (ca. 400 B.C.E.) following the hexateuchal redaction and the exclusion of the book of Joshua
P	Priestly Code, Genesis 1–Exodus 29 (exilic)
P^S	*P-Sondergut*: early postexilic supplement to P in Genesis 1–Leviticus 9

I. The Formation of the Pentateuch:
Beyond the "Compromise Hypothesis" of an Imperial Authorization
of the Torah by the Persian Government

After the breakdown of the classical Documentary Hypothesis of JEP and its derivate of J as an exilic "redactor" or a "historian," there remains one decisive starting point for the future of pentateuchal research—that is, the fact that there are two literary layers in the Pentateuch, Priestly and non-Priestly.[1] One option in thinking about this starting point for a literary history of the Pentateuch is the hypothesis of two redactions, Deuteronomistic and Priestly, which were combined by means of a literary compromise between priests and laymen.[2] This hypothesis is characterized by the same shortcoming as the old Documentary Hypothesis. Its construction was based mainly on Genesis as the beginning of the Pentateuch without considering Deuteronomy as the final section of this corpus. Taking into account that Deuteronomy is an integral part of the Pentateuch (a Pentateuch that does not "function" without this final book), we can see a different perspective emerging instead of the compromise hypothesis. During the so-called exilic period of the 6th century B.C.E., the two rivaling conceptions of Israel's origins were written down by two different Priestly factions: the Priestly code (Genesis 1–Exodus 29 [Leviticus 9; P^S]) of the Aaronides, on the one side, and Deuteronomistic Deuteronomy, on the other.[3] The Priestly work ended with the Sinai pericope, whereas Deuteronomy started with the Horeb motif. Each of the two literary conceptions represented a critical reaction to the other's work.[4] After the Exile, when the different Priestly factions responsible for P and D (Dtr) were reunited under the label of Aaron, it became necessary to conflate these two competing conceptions of Israel's origins and identity.[5] This was not only an institutional matter but also a theological necessity. With the success of the idea of monotheism in the exilic and postexilic period, there was also a theological need to unify the

---

1. For a survey of the state of discussion in pentateuchal research, see Erich Zenger, *Einleitung in das Alte Testament* (6th ed.; Stuttgart: Kohlhammer, 2006) 99–135.

2. See, for instance, Erhard Blum, *Studien zur Komposition des Pentateuch* (BZAW 189; Berlin: de Gruyter, 1990).

3. See my *Deuteronomium im Pentateuch und Hexateuch: Studien zur Literaturgeschichte von Pentateuch und Hexateuch im Lichte des Deuteronomiumrahmens* (FAT 30; Tübingen: Mohr Siebeck, 2000) 234–75 (summary).

4. See, e.g., Hermann-Josef Stipp, "'Meinen Bund hat er gebrochen' (Gen 17,14): Die Individualisierung des Bundesbruchs in der Priesterschrift," *Münchner Theologische Zeitschrift* 56 (2006) 290–304. Appropriating a term that I used in another context, Stipp speaks of a "subversive reception" of Deuteronomistic theology in P.

5. For the Priestly background of the postexilic formation of the Pentateuch, see my "Vom biblischen Hebraismus der persischen Zeit zum rabbinischen Judaismus in römischer Zeit: Zur Geschichte der spätbiblischen und frühjüdischen Schriftgelehrsamkeit," *ZA(B)R* 10 (2004) 1–49.

two conceptions of P and D because, if there was only one God, there could only be one history of God with Israel.

But the authors of the postexilic Pentateuch of the 5th century B.C.E. did not simply connect P and D, creating a narrative beginning with the creation of the world and ending with Moses' death (a combination easily effected, because the one conception began where the other ended). These postexilic authors also used the sources of their sources P and D, something we can observe, for example, in the Covenant Code, which as a preexilic source of Deuteronomy was incorporated into the Sinai pericope by the post-Deuteronomistic and post-Priestly authors of the Pentateuch.[6] The same was true for the two versions of the Decalogue in Deuteronomy 5 and Exodus 20, the Deuteronomistic framework of Deuteronomy, the post-Priestly and post-Deuteronomistic formation of the Sinai pericope, and parts of the book of Numbers.[7]

When this is kept in mind, it shows that there was some truth in the traditional Documentary Hypothesis of Julius Wellhausen and Abraham Kuenen, who reckoned with the existence of preexilic sources older than D and P in the Hexateuch and the Pentateuch. Nevertheless, the preexilic texts in the Pentateuch formed not continuous sources but separate blocks of texts that were used by D and P and incorporated by the postexilic authors into the Pentateuch.[8] These authors, who were also "redactors" of their source material, used this preexilic material to create a literary layer mediating between D and P.[9]

---

6. On the Covenant Code as a preexilic source of Deuteronomy, see my *Deuteronomium: Politische Theologie und Rechtsreform in Juda und Assyrien* (BZAW 284; Berlin: de Gruyter, 1999) 203–364.

7. See Reinhard Achenbach, *Die Vollendung der Tora: Studien zur Redaktionsgeschichte des Numeribuches im Kontext von Hexateuch und Pentateuch* (Beihefte zur Zeitschrift für altorientalische und biblische Rechtsgeschichte 3; Wiesbaden: Harrassowitz, 2003) 173–442.

8. The most important criterion for source divisions in Genesis, the change of the divine names, is not actually a criterion, because there is a well-defined logic implicit in the use of the divine names. The authors of the Pentateuch differentiated very precisely between their "time of narration," that is, the postexilic period; and the "narrated time," that is, the fictitious time of Moses. In the time of narration, the reader of the Pentateuch was of course aware from the very beginning that YHWH is the God of Israel, but on the level of narrated time the divine name was not revealed before the encounter portrayed in Exodus 3. The changing of the divine names was an intentional measure employed by the authors of the Pentateuch as one means of creating space between the time of narration and the narrated time. See my "Hidden Truth behind the Text or the Truth of the Text: At a Turning Point of Biblical Scholarship Two Hundred Years after de Wette's *dissertatio critico exegetica*, in *The Pentateuch* (ed. Jurie Le Roux and Eckart Otto; London: T. & T. Clark, forthcoming).

9. The objection of John Van Seters (*The Edited Bible: The Curious History of the "Editor" in Biblical Criticism* [Winona Lake, IN: Eisenbrauns, 2006]) is not convincing, because he overestimated the influence of the field of classics on biblical scholarship, especially of the interpretation of Homer since the time of the 18th century, and the meaning of its development in the 19th and 20th centuries for biblical studies; see my review in *RBL* (http://www.bookreviews.org/bookdetail .asp?TitleId=5273), May 12, 2007.

This redaction was not just a mechanical exercise but a creation of something new in the form of a Hexateuch and then later a Pentateuch. The authors of the Hexateuch adopted the Deuteronomistic Moab redaction of Deuteronomy and Joshua as a literary unit (DtrL; Deuteronomy 1–Joshua 23), which was focused on Israel's return to its land. Working in the 5th century B.C.E. during the period of Nehemiah's activity in Jerusalem, these authors underscored Israel's possession of its land, which was in their opinion the aim of God's history of salvation with Israel (Joshua 24).[10]

Priestly scholars during the diaspora took charge of the literary history of the work and created the Pentateuch in the time of Ezra. Working against the background of the diaspora, these scholars were of the opinion that the Torah, not Israel's possession of the land, was the decisive gift of God's history of salvation to His people. They expanded the Sinai pericope by a number of means but especially by forming the Holiness Code and by cutting off the book of Joshua from the Pentateuch. These authors used as a prototype for their redaction the Deuteronomistic Horeb (DtrD) redaction in Deuteronomy 5–28 underlying the Deuteronomistic Moab redaction, which was used by the postexilic authors of the Hexateuch.[11]

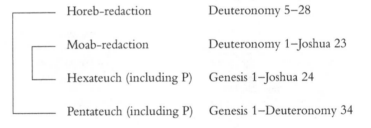

Horeb-redaction	Deuteronomy 5–28
Moab-redaction	Deuteronomy 1–Joshua 23
Hexateuch (including P)	Genesis 1–Joshua 24
Pentateuch (including P)	Genesis 1–Deuteronomy 34

Thus, the Deuteronomistic Deuteronomy was the cradle of the Pentateuch, not just the Priestly Code.

The postexilic literary mediations between the exilic conceptions of the Deuteronomistic Deuteronomy and the Priestly Code involved profound postexilic theological discussions about Israel's identity as it related to God's history of salvation.[12] The scribal techniques used by these Priestly authors who formed

10. For the following, see my *Deuteronomium im Pentateuch*, 110–233.

11. For a literary differentiation of the two Deuteronomistic-exilic redactions and the post-deuteronomistic edition of Deuteronomy as part of the Hexateuch and Pentateuch, see ibid., 1–233; and Thomas Römer, *The So-Called Deuteronomistic History: A Sociological, Historical and Literary Introduction* (London: T. & T. Clark, 2005) 56–65, 123–36, 170–72.

12. Even after the formation of the Pentateuch at the end of the 5th century B.C.E., a number of late supplements were incorporated into the Pentateuch, especially into the book of Numbers (Achenbach, *Vollendung der Tora*, 443–634). The Pentateuch redaction (PentRed) was not at all a

the post-Deuteronomistic and post-Priestly "narratives" of the Hexateuch and the Pentateuch can best be observed in the legal material of the Covenant Code: the authors supplemented an early legal collection with a postexilic interpretation in the context of the Sinai pericope in Exod 20:22–23; 21:2; 22:19b, 20aβb, 21, 23, 24bα, 30; 23:13–33,[13] on the one hand; and they formed the Holiness Code (Leviticus 17–26) out of Deuteronomy 12–26 and P with the Covenant Code as a hermeneutical key, on the other hand.[14] The Pentateuch itself represents a kind of monument to these scribal activities: it interprets Moses not only as the first scribe (aside from God himself, who transcribed only the Decalogue, whereas Moses wrote down the other legal sections of the Torah, including the Covenant Code and Deuteronomy [Exod 24:4, 7; Deut 31:9, 19, 22, 24])[15] but also as the person who expounded on the laws of the Sinai pericope in the land of Moab (Num 36:13, Deut 1:5).[16] With Moses' death, the period of direct revelation to God's prophet Moses came to an end (Deut 34:10–12). From then on, the written Torah (which went across the river Jordan with the people after Moses' death) took over the function of representing God's revelation to Israel. In this sense, one can say that Moses' function as a mediator of revelation was "resurrected" in the form of the Torah, which after his death had to be expounded as he had done; this was accomplished by

---

"final redaction," as is occasionally claimed, although this redaction was responsible for the formation of the "fable" of the pentateuchal narrative in Genesis 1–Deuteronomy 34. See my "The Pentateuch in Synchronical and Diachronical Perspective: Protorabbinic Scribal Erudition Mediating between Deuteronomy and the Priestly Code," in *Das Deuteronomium zwischen Pentateuch und Deuteronomistischem Geschichtswerk* (ed. Eckart Otto and Reinhard Achenbach; FRLANT 206; Göttingen: Vandenhoeck & Ruprecht, 2004) 14–35.

13. See my "Nachpriesterschriftliche Pentateuchredaktion im Buch Exodus," in *Studies in the Book of Exodus: Redaction—Reception—Interpretation* (ed. Marc Vervenne; BETL 106; Leuven: Peeters, 1996) 61–111.

14. Idem, "Innerbiblische Exegese im Heiligkeitsgesetz Levitikus 17–26," in *Levitikus als Buch* (ed. Heinz-Josef Fabry and Hans-Winfried Jüngling; BBB 119; Berlin: Philo, 1999) 125–96.

15. The idea that Moses transcribed the whole Pentateuch from Genesis to Deuteronomy was a postbiblical idea.

16. See my "Mose, der erste Schriftgelehrte: Deuteronomium 1,5 in der Fabel des Pentateuch," in *L'Écrit et l'Esprit: Études d'histoire du texte et de théologie biblique en hommage à Adrian Schenker* (ed. Dieter Böhler and Innocent Himbaza; OBO 214; Fribourg: Academic Press / Göttingen: Vandenhoeck & Ruprecht, 2005) 273–84; pace Georg Braulik and Norbert Lohfink, "Deuteronomium 1,5 *b'r 't htwrh hz't*: 'Er verlieh dieser Tora Rechtskraft,'" in *Textarbeit: Studien zu Texten und ihrer Rezeption aus dem Alten Testament und der Umwelt Israels—Festschrift für Peter Weimar* (ed. Klaus Kiesow and Thomas Meurer; AOAT 294; Münster: Ugarit Verlag, 2003) 35–51. A correct interpretation of Deut 1:5 also depends on the interpretation of the colophons in Lev 26:46, 27:34, and Num 36:13; see my "Ende der Toraoffenbarung: Die Funktion der Kolophone Lev 26,46 und 27,34 sowie Num 36,13 in der Rechtshermeneutik des Pentateuch," in *Auf dem Weg zur Endgestalt von Genesis bis II Regum: Festschrift für Hans-Christoph Schmitt zum 65. Geburtstag* (ed. Martin Beck and Ulrike Schorn; BZAW 370; Berlin: de Gruyter, 2006) 191–202.

applying the Torah to life in the promised land by expounding on the Sinaitic Torah in Deuteronomy.[17]

II. The Hermeneutics of Revelation in the Postexilic Formation of the Pentateuch and the Book of Jeremiah

The hermeneutics employed by the prophetic schools in postexilic times was entirely different from Priestly hermeneutics of the Pentateuch. Postexilic discourse in the prophetic schools was no longer the kerygmatic type of prophecy observable in the preexilic period but was instead a literary process that Odil Hannes Steck once called *Tradentenprophetie*.[18] As we shall see, postexilic literary discourse employed the same literary techniques as were employed by the authors of the postexilic Pentateuch. The reflexive literary theory of the Pentateuch is important to our understanding of the processes involved in the literary formation of the Pentateuch.[19] Similar things could be said about the book of Jeremiah. In this context, Jeremiah 36 is a good starting point. There are hints in Jer 36:1, 9, and 32b (*wĕ'ôd nôsap 'ălêhem dĕbārîm rabbîm kāhēmmâ*) of a complicated literary history behind the formation of the book of Jeremiah.[20]

These transcription notices (compare the transcription notices that appear in Jer 29:1, 30:1–2 in relation to Jer 32:1, 51:59–64) had the same function as the notices that appear in the Pentateuch. There, they are part of a classification system with regard to the legal authority of *tôrôt* together with a system of superscriptions and subscriptions.[21] The transcription notices in the book of Jeremiah also formed a system of defining a graduated scale of authority of prophetic texts within this book. The "book of consolation" in Jeremiah 30–31, which ostensibly was written by Jeremiah himself during the period of Zedekiah's tenure,

---

17. Eckart Otto, "Das postdeuteronomistische Deuteronomium als integrierender Schlußstein der Tora," in *Die deuteronomistischen Geschichtswerke: Redaktions- und religionsgeschichtliche Perspektiven zur "Deuteronomismus"—Diskussion in Tora und Vorderen Propheten* (ed. Jan Christian Gertz and Konrad Schmid; BZAW 365; Berlin: de Gruyter, 2006) 71–102.

18. See Odil Hannes Steck, *Bereitete Heimkehr: Jesaja 35 als redaktionelle Brücke zwischen dem Ersten und dem Zweiten Jesaja* (SBS 121; Stuttgart: Katholisches Bibelwerk, 1985) 81–99; idem, *Studien zu Tritojesaja* (BZAW 203; Berlin: de Gruyter, 1991) v–vi, 26–27, 270–77; idem, *Der Abschluß der Prophetie im Alten Testament: Ein Versuch zur Frage der Vorgeschichte des Kanons* (BibS[N] 17; Neukirchen-Vluyn: Neukirchener Verlag, 1991) 61–63, 167–70.

19. See my "Wie 'synchron' wurde in der Antike der Pentateuch gelesen?" in *Das Manna fällt auch heute noch: Beiträge zur Geschichte und Theologie des Alten, Ersten Testaments—Festschrift für Erich Zenger* (ed. Frank-Lothar Hoßfeld and Ludger Schwienhorst-Schönberger; Herders Biblische Studien 44; Freiburg: Herder, 2004) 470–85.

20. Hermann-Josef Stipp speaks of a *redaktionelle Autolegitimation* in Jer 36:32b, "Baruchs Erben: Die Schriftprophetie im Spiegel von Jer 36," in *"Wer darf hinaufziehen zum Berg JHWHs?": Beiträge zu Prophetie und Poesie des Alten Testaments* (ed. Hans Irsigler; St. Ottilien: EOS, 2002) 166.

21. Otto, "Ende der Toraoffenbarung."

should have more authority than the words of the prophet that someone else recorded in 605 and 604 B.C.E., during the reign of Jehoiakim. In other words, the transcription notices in the book of Jeremiah did not aim at the legal authority of *tôrôt* but at the revelational authority of prophetic words during the conception of the book.[22] The fact that the same technique for structuring books with transcription notices was used in both the postexilic Pentateuch and the book of Jeremiah raises the question whether there are additional hints at correlations between these two literary works.

The authors of Jeremiah 36 were scribal scholars of a postexilic purely literary prophecy who carried on an intensive discourse with the scribal authors of the postexilic Pentateuch. There are critical indications of this scribal discussion. Jer 36:3 quotes Jer 26:3:[23]

Jeremiah 26:3

אולי ישמעו וישבו איש מדרכו הרעה ונחמתי אל־הרעה אשר אנכי חשב לעשות להם
מפני רע מעלליהם

Jeremiah 36:3

אולי ישמעו בית יהודה את כל־הרעה אשר אנכי חשב לעשות להם
למען ישובו איש מדרכו הרעה וסלחתי לעונם ולחטאתם

Moreover, in Jer 36:3, two sources (Jer 26:3 and Exod 34:9) have been conflated:

Jeremiah 36:3bβ

וסלחתי לעונם ולחטאתם

Exodus 34:9bβ

וסלחת לעוננו ולחטאתנו ונחלתנו

Jer 36:3, which combines two texts from different contexts, is surely the derivative text, while Jer 26:3 and Exod 34:9 are the source texts. The synchronic direction of reading from Jer 26:3 to Jer 36:3 is also the diachronic. Exod 34:8–9 is linked together with the "formula of grace" in Exod 34:6–7, which is part of the postexilic redaction of the Pentateuch in the late 5th century B.C.E.[24]

---

22. Idem, "Der Pentateuch im Jeremiabuch: Überlegungen zur Pentateuchrezeption im Jeremiabuch anhand neuerer Jeremia-Literatur," *ZA(B)R* 12 (2006) 245–306. For a discussion of the text-critical problems of the book of Jeremiah, see this article and also William McKane, *Jeremiah* (ICC; Edinburgh: T. & T. Clark, 1996); and Hermann-Josef Stipp, *Das masoretische und alexandrinische Sondergut des Jeremiabuches: Textgeschichtlicher Rang, Eigenart, Triebkräfte* (OBO 136; Fribourg: Universitätsverlag / Göttingen: Vandenhoeck & Ruprecht, 1994).

23. See Georg Fischer, *Jeremia 26–52* (HTKAT; Freiburg: Herder, 2006) 288–89.

24. Otto, "Pentateuchredaktion," 92–98; see also Reinhard Achenbach, "Grundlinien redaktioneller Arbeit in der Sinaiperikope," in *Das Deuteronomium zwischen Pentateuch und deuteronomistischem Geschichtswerk* (ed. Eckart Otto and Reinhard Achenbach; FRLANT 206; Göttingen: Vandenhoeck & Ruprecht, 2004) 56–80.

The authors of Jeremiah 36 put Moses' words in Jeremiah's mouth as transcribed by Baruch. Exod 34:9 enhances the lexeme *nḥm* in Exod 32:12–14 by
use of the lexeme *slḥ*. Jer 26:3, for its part, quotes Exod 32:(12), 14:[25]

Jeremiah 26:3bα

ונחמתי אל־הרעה אשר אנכי חשב לעשׂות להם

Exodus 32:12

והנחם על־הרעה לעמך

Exodus 32:14

וינחם יהוה על־הרעה אשר דבר לעשׂות לעמו

Exod 34:8–9 is also linked to the covenant motif in Exod 34:10. The final
remark in Jer 31:34, כי אסלח לעונם ולחטאתם לא אזכר־עוד, quotes Exod 34:9
and hints at Jer 36:3.[26] The complex linkages among Jeremiah 26, 31, and 36
were structured by the reception of the post-Deuteronomistic and post-Priestly
Sinai pericope of the Pentateuch redaction in the 5th century B.C.E.[27] There is
no doubt that what we find in Jeremiah 36 in relation to chap. 26 and to chap.
31 is no longer the transcription of a vivid "kerygmatic" prophecy but the result of scribal scholars quoting and conflating texts from different fields of literature using techniques that the Priestly scribes also used for the formation of
the Pentateuch in linking D and P.[28]

The postexilic Priestly and "prophetic" circles were as close to each other in
their use of the same scribal techniques as they were different from each other
in their hermeneutical approaches. The authors of these Jeremiah texts did not
simply quote the Sinai pericope in order to confer Moses' authority on Jere-

---

25. For Exod 32:12, 14 as part of the postdeuteronomistic redaction of the Pentateuch, see
Erik Aurelius, *Der Fürbitter Israels: Eine Studie zum Mosebild im Alten Testament* (ConBOT 27;
Stockholm: Almqvist & Wiksell, 1988) 91–100; Hans-Christoph Schmitt, "Die Erzählung vom
Goldenen Kalb Ex 32* und das Deuteronomistische Geschichtswerk," in *Rethinking the Founda-
tions: Historiography in the Ancient World and in the Bible—Essays in Honour of John Van Seters* (ed.
Steven L. McKenzie and Thomas Römer; BZAW 294; Berlin: de Gruyter, 2000) 311–25; Otto,
Deuteronomium im Pentateuch, 40–43; Achenbach, "Grundlinien," 74–76.

26. Konrad Schmid is correct in refuting the thesis that Exodus 32–34 was dependent on Jeremiah 31: *Buchgestalten des Jeremiabuches: Untersuchungen zur Redaktions- und Rezeptionsgeschichte von
Jer 30–33 im Kontext des Buches* (WMANT 72; Neukirchen-Vluyn: Neukirchener Verlag, 1996)
77 n. 123.

27. Even the motif of the two transcriptions of Jeremiah's words by Baruch in Jeremiah 36
finds its closest parallel in the two transcriptions of the Decalogue in the Sinai pericope; see William
L. Holladay, *Jeremiah 2: A Commentary on the Book of the Prophet Jeremiah Chapters 26–52* (Herme-
neia; Minneapolis: Fortress, 1989) 254; Fischer, *Jeremia 26–52*, 304.

28. See my "Rechtshermeneutik in der Hebräischen Bibel: Die innerbiblischen Ursprünge
halachischer Bibelauslegung," *ZA(B)R* 5 (1999) 75–98.

miah.[29] The text of Jer 31:31–34, in particular, contradicts this theory.[30] No, the authors of Jeremiah 36 created a counterposition to the hermeneutics of the Pentateuch. Quoting the postexilic Sinai pericope implies that they presupposed the epitaph of the Pentateuch, which is part of the same postexilic Pentateuch redaction as the verses in Exodus 32 and 34 that were quoted in the book of Jeremiah.[31] For the Priestly authors of the postexilic Pentateuch, prophetic speech revealed by God "face to face" had come to an end with Moses' death. In Jer 31:31–34, the pentateuchal theory of a transcription of the Torah by Moses (Exod 24:4, Deut 31:9) was refuted by the prophetic theory of a divine transcription of the Torah on the people's hearts. Similarly, the pentateuchal idea of teaching and learning the Mosaic Torah (Deut 31:12–13) was refuted by the prophetic idea that there would no longer be any necessity for teaching and learning the Torah, because every Israelite would have internalized it. Finally, the pentateuchal idea of a Mosaic covenant at Sinai and in Moab as the only covenant(s) was refuted by the idea that these covenants were broken by the people so that there would be a need for a New Covenant.[32]

In addition to these Jeremianic countermotifs to important concepts found in the postexilic Pentateuch, there also was a decisive hermeneutical difference between the Priestly authors of the postexilic Pentateuch and the scribal authors of the Jeremianic literary prophecy. In Jer 36:3, the authors of this prophetic circle put Moses' words into Jeremiah's mouth, declaring them to be God's own words in Jer 36:4: "Baruch wrote upon the scroll all the words Jeremiah had dictated that YHWH had spoken to him." For this postexilic scribal circle of a Jeremianic *Tradentenprophetie*, divine revelation did not come to an end with Moses' death but went on until the time of Jeremiah in the exilic period. Hence, this sort of divine revelation continued even after the destruction of the temple in Jerusalem. Although the Priestly authors of the postexilic Pentateuch were of opinion that after Moses' death there was only one access to God's revelation, by interpretation of Moses' Torah, the scribal authors of the

---

29. Pace Christl Maier, *Jeremia als Lehrer der Tora: Soziale Gebote des Deuteronomiums in Fortschreibungen des Jeremiabuches* (FRLANT 196; Göttingen: Vandenhoeck & Ruprecht, 2002).

30. See my *Deuteronomium im Pentateuch*, 153–54; idem, "Old and New Covenant: A Postexilic Discourse between the Pentateuch and the Book of Jeremiah—Also a Study of Quotations and Allusions in the Hebrew Bible," *Old Testament Essays* 19 (2006) 939–49.

31. For Deut 34:10–12 as part of the Pentateuch redaction of the 5th century B.C.E., see my *Deuteronomium im Pentateuch*, 215–16, 228–30.

32. LXX and MT Jer 31:31–34 disagree about whether Israel alone gave up on these Mosaic covenants or whether YHWH also gave up on them; see Adrian Schenker, *Das Neue am neuen Bund und das Alte am alten: Jer 31 in der hebräischen und griechischen Bibel—Von der Textgeschichte zur Theologie, Synagoge und Kirche* (FRLANT 212; Göttingen: Vandenhoeck & Ruprecht, 2006) 15–69. The LXX represents the original text, whereas the Masoretic Text tradition was revised to be nearer to the Pentateuch during the formation of the canon.

postexilic Jeremiah school claimed that divine revelation of the highest author-ity, given "face to face," did not come to an end with Moses' death at all.[33]

The scribal authors of this prophetic school could even use tensions within the Mosaic Torah of their Priestly opponents to argue against their hermeneu-tical claims for scribal exegesis of the Torah as the only access to God's revela-tion. Deut 18:18 as part of the Deuteronomistic Deuteronomy of the exilic period proclaims that YHWH will raise up a prophet like Moses and put His words in his mouth so that he will speak to them all that YHWH commands him. For the postexilic authors of the Pentateuch, God's revelation came to an end with Moses' death so that, as Deut 34:10 proclaims, "There did not arise again in Israel a prophet like Moses, whom YHWH knew face to face." The scribal authors of the postexilic *Tradentenprophetie* used this contradiction within the Priestly Torah of the Pentateuch as a decisive argument against the Priestly hermeneutics embedded within this Torah.

This technique of scribal scholarship may be observed in many postexilic texts embedded within the book of Jeremiah. The writers of these texts in Jeremiah argued against the hermeneutics of the Pentateuch. In what follows, I will deal with Jer 26:1–5 as a good example of this type of text. In an earlier part of this essay, I dealt with the relationship of Jer 26:1–5 to 36:3 and 31:31–34. For the task of dating Jeremiah 26, it is not only important that in this chap-ter (as we have seen) the postexilic interpretation of the Sinai pericope is quoted in v. 3 but also that v. 4bβ alludes to Deut 4:8 and 11:32. The phrase ללכת בתורתי אשר נתתי לפניכם finds a close parallel in Deut 4:8 and 11:32 (us-ing the expression Torah + *ntn lpn*). The expression *hlk bĕtôrātî* has a close par-allel in Exod 16:4. All these texts of the Pentateuch are postdeuteronomistic and are part of the postexilic Hexateuch and Pentateuch.[34] Jer 26:4bβ is a con-flation of these postdeuteronomistic texts of the Pentateuch.

---

33. From the point of view of these Priestly authors, Moses himself had engaged in this sort of interpretation in the context of the postexilic Pentateuch, as is evident from Deuteronomy. See my "Rechtshermeneutik im Pentateuch und in der Tempelrolle," in *Tora in der Hebräischen Bibel: Studien zur Redaktionsgeschichte und zur synchronen Logik diachroner Transformationen* (ed. Reinhard Achenbach, Martin Arneth, and Eckart Otto; Beihefte zur Zeitschrift für altorientalische und bib-lische Rechtsgeschichte 6; Wiesbaden: Harrassowitz, 2007) 72–122. For a different approach, see Norbert Lohfink, "Prolegomena zu einer Rechthermeneutik des Pentateuch," in *Das Deuterono-mium* (ed. Georg Braulik; ÖBS 23; Frankfurt/Main: Peter Lang, 2003) 11–55. But see already my "Mose, der erste Schriftgelehrte," 273–84; as well as "Das postdeuteronomistische Deuterono-mium," 71–102.

34. Otto, *Deuteronomium im Pentateuch*, 24, 36–38, 54, 58, 101, 164–75. For the post-Priestly interpretation of Exod 16:1–15, see idem, "Forschungen zur Priesterschrift," *TRu* 62 (1997) 14–15. For the post-Deuteronomistic origin of Deut 4:1–44 as part of the postexilic redaction of the Pentateuch, see idem, "Deuteronomium 4: Die Pentateuchredaktion im Deuteronomiumsrahmen,"

Jer 26:3–4 formulates the central theme of Jeremiah's theology in a post-exilic perspective, employing words of the Priestly Torah in its postexilic shape. This means that the scribal authors of Jer 26:1–5 also presupposed Deut 34:10–12 as the hermeneutical key to the Priestly Pentateuch, which was part of the same literary layer as Deut 4:1–44. Jer 26:5 alludes to the Deuteronomistic theory of prophetic revelation in 2 Kgs 17:13, which is related to the Deuteronomistic law pertaining to prophets in Deut 18:18. But Jer 26:1–19 argues theologically far beyond this Deuteronomistic theory. For Deut 18:22, as part of the larger Deuteronomistic (exilic) law of the prophets in Deut 18:9–22, the fulfillment of prophetic predictions should be the decisive criterion for differentiating between true and false prophecies. Jer 26:19 falsifies this criterion, quoting Exod 32:14. Micah's prediction of the destruction of Zion was not fulfilled in the days of Hezekiah, because YHWH "relented of the evil and reversed the decision that He had pronounced against them." The Deuteronomistic theory of true and false prophecy had deliberately renounced the Torah as a criterion for approving prophecies.[35] Instead of the Deuteronomistic criteria in Deut 18:22 for Jer 26:4–6, the Torah represents the decisive criterion of true prophecy by allusion to Deut 4:8, 11:32, and Exod 16:4–6: "And you shall say to them, thus says YHWH: If you will not obey me, to walk in my Torah, which I have set before you and obey the words of my servants the prophets, whom I sent to you persistently, though you have not obeyed, then I will make this house like Shiloh."[36]

Jer 26:4 argues against the horizon of the postexilic postdeuteronomistic theory of prophecy in Deut 34:10–12. True prophecy for the Priestly authors of the Pentateuch was only Mosaic prophecy—that is, prophecy according to the Torah. The scribal authors of the postexilic Jeremianic *Tradentenprophetie* agreed with this point made by the scribal authors of the postdeuteronomic Pentateuch and refuted the Deuteronomistic criterion of fulfillment of prophetic predictions as decisive for the approval of true prophecy, as well.[37] But

---

in *Das Deuteronomium und seine Querbeziehungen* (ed. Timo Veijola; Göttingen: Vandenhoeck & Ruprecht, 1996) 196–222. Knut Holter also interprets Deut 4:1–44 as a well-structured literary unit of late origin presupposing P and Isaiah 40–55; see his *Deuteronomy 4 and the Second Commandment* (Studies in Biblical Literature 60; New York: Peter Lang, 2003). See my review in *ZA(B)R* 12 (2006) 397–400.

35. See my "'Deuteronomium krönt die Arbeit der Propheten': Gesetz und Prophetie im Deuteronomium" in *"Ich bewirke das Heil und erschaffe das Unheil" (Jesaja 45,7): Studien zur Botschaft der Propheten—Festschrift für Lothar Ruppert zum 65. Geburtstag* (ed. Friedrich Diedrich and Bernhard Willmes; FB 88; Würzburg: Echter Verlag, 1998) 277–310.

36. For the literary relations between Jer 7:1–8:3 and 26:1–5, see Maier, *Jeremia als Lehrer,* 161–63.

37. The same attitude can be found in 2 Kgs 22:16–20, which also derived from postexilic circles of a scribal prophetic nature. The theological value of the Torah was confirmed, but the

arguing with Deut 34:10–12 in view, in this particular instance, they opposed the hermeneutical implication that there was no prophet like Moses since Moses (whom YHWH knew face to face), by putting the words of Moses into Jeremiah's mouth, stating that he, Jeremiah, received this word directly from YHWH (Jer 26:1–2). The scribal authors of Jeremiah 26 took up the canonical formula employed by the postexilic authors of the Pentateuch in Deut 4:2 (cf. 13:1): "You shall not add to the word that I command you, neither shall you omit it, that you may keep the commandments of YHWH your God, which I command you."[38]

But the authors of Jeremiah 26 quoted only the second part of this formula in Jer 26:2: "Thus says YHWH: Stand in the court of YHWH's house and speak to all the towns of Judah that came to worship in YHWH's house all the words that I command you to speak to them; *do not omit a word.*" The postexilic Priestly authors of the Pentateuch claimed that with Moses' death the Torah was completed so that nothing should be added or taken away. But the authors of the book of Jeremiah refuted this Priestly theory by their claim that God's revelation went on until Jeremiah, who was the last prophet in a long chain of prophets (Jer 26:5) who received their words directly from God. These words should not be diminished, but again and again new words of God followed and were added, contradicting the Priestly canonical formula and its hermeneutical implications relating to the Priestly theory of divine revelation in the Pentateuch. The prophetic circles were convinced of the divine authority of the words of prophets, which should not be considered inferior to the words of the Torah. Hence, in Jeremiah's trial (Jer 26:10–19), the prophetic word of Micah of Moresheth and its interpretation in Jer 26:18–19 had authority as a basis for sentencing Jeremiah to life or death. From the Priestly perspective of the authors of the Pentateuch, only YHWH's Torah could fill this function. The authors of Jer 26:10–19 connected the decision of Jeremiah's trial to a traditional prophetic word, thus underlining the divine authority of prophets. They looked to the law concerning prophets in Deut 18:19–20, which they used as the basis for

---

prediction of Josiah's death was false. For the postexilic shape of 2 Kings 22, see also Römer, *Deuteronomistic History,* 152. Here in 2 Kings 22, these authors saw good reason that it should not be Jeremiah whose prediction was falsified but an unknown prophetess called Huldah. Thus, the often observed parallels between 2 Kings 22–23 and Jeremiah 36 receive an entirely new meaning. For the relationship between 2 Kings 22–23 and Jeremiah 36, see also G. J. Venema, *Reading Scripture in the Old Testament: Deuteronomy 9–10 – 2 Kings 22–23 – Jeremiah 36 – Nehemiah 8* (OtSt 48; Leiden: Brill, 2004) 75–137. Pace Venema's conclusion (pp. 220–24) regarding the nonreferential character of these texts as pertaining to "external facts," I argue that the cross-references in the prophetic texts to the Pentateuch reflect the postexilic discussion between Priestly and prophetic circles. Hence, it does not suffice to negate the different interests behind these texts.

38. For this formula in the context of the postexilic period, see my *Deuteronomium im Pentateuch,* 164–65, 273.

their claim to authority.[39] And it was the literary Jeremiah himself who interpreted Deut 18:19–20 and applied it to his own case, doing just what the postdeuteronomistic authors of the Pentateuch opined that Moses had done in Deuteronomy.

Many other late texts in the book of Jeremiah exhibit signs of the same discussions with the Priestly authors of the Pentateuch that Jeremiah 26 and 36 do.[40] Nevertheless, the attitude of other prophetic circles, such as the Isaiah tradition regarding the Mosaic Priestly circle of the Pentateuch, was not nearly as critical as the Jeremiah school was. Isaiah 40–66 was much closer to the Pentateuch than Jeremiah 26 and 36, which were influenced by the discussions about the hermeneutical claims of the Torah.[41] What was true of the Isaiah circle was also true of the school of the postexilic Ezekiel tradition, which was closely related to the Pentateuch's redaction of the Holiness Code in Leviticus 17–26.[42]

But what united all of these prophetic schools during the postexilic period was their position in the controversy that Otto Plöger once characterized as the opposition between "theocracy" and "eschatology."[43] Paul Hanson adopted this approach and demonstrated the different interests of the Priestly-hierocratic circles represented by P and the prophetic circles responsible for the chapters of Trito-Isaiah.[44] What I have tried to demonstrate in this essay is the fact that all of the post-Priestly Pentateuch, not only P, was involved in this debate and that the book of Jeremiah had an important position in this controversy. Jeremiah demonstrates more clearly than any other prophetic book what

---

39. Comparison with Neh 8:1–8 demonstrates analogies and differences between postexilic prophetic and Priestly hermeneutics. In this text, the Priestly interpretation of Torah took the place of the prophet in Jeremiah 26, and the Torah itself took the place of the authoritative tradition of prophetic words (Otto, *Deuteronomium im Pentateuch*, 196–211).

40. See my "Pentateuch im Jeremiabuch," 245–306.

41. See Benjamin D. Sommer, *A Prophet Reads Scripture: Allusion in Isaiah 40–66* (Contraversions; Stanford: Stanford University Press, 1998) 132–51. The connection between Isaiah 40–66 and the Pentateuch will be even closer if one realizes that Isa 56:1–8 does not argue against Numbers 18, because this chapter is a supplement to the postexilic Pentateuch and much later than Isaiah 56. For the literary history of Numbers 18, see Achenbach, *Vollendung der Tora*, 141–72. Sommer demonstrates the wide range of allusions and (although he argues against this term) quotations of the Pentateuch in Isaiah 40–66. This means that the literary method in Isaiah 40–66 corresponds to the method used in the book of Jeremiah. Fischer, in his commentary on Jeremiah, also demonstrates the wide range of allusions to and quotations of the Pentateuch in nearly every chapter of the book of Jeremiah. But although the literary techniques are identical in both prophetic books, their applied hermeneutics differ.

42. Otto, *Deuteronomium im Pentateuch*, 258–59.

43. Otto Plöger, *Theokratie und Eschatologie* (WMANT 2; Neukirchen-Vluyn: Neukirchener Verlag, 1959).

44. Paul D. Hanson, *The Dawn of Apocalyptic: The Historical and Sociological Roots of Jewish Apocalyptic Eschatology* (rev. ed.; Philadelphia: Fortress, 1979). But see Sommer, *A Prophet Reads Scripture*, for Isaiah 56–66.

the kernel of this postexilic discussion was: the Priestly authors of the Pentateuch pleaded for a Torah that was literarily closed by the time of Moses' death because there should be no divine revelation after Moses. Hence, from this point forward, it was the task of Priestly scribal scholars to interpret the Torah as the only divine basis for Jewish life.

However, all of the prophetic circles of the postexilic period claimed that divine revelation went on until the days of the prophets, who founded their schools—whether Jeremiah, Isaiah, or Ezekiel. But the reason for this claim was theological: these circles were convinced that there would be new interventions of God in favor of his people, fulfilling the promises of the prophets. The authors of the postexilic Pentateuch responded by underlining the prophetic abilities of Moses, predicting the catastrophe of the exilic period and the survival of Israel after this catastrophe (for example, in Leviticus 26).[45] But what they described in these *vaticinia ex eventu* of the postexilic period was not a new intervention by Yhwh to change Israel's life fundamentally for the better but only Israel's restitution as it became reality in postexilic Yehud, which they projected back onto the Pentateuch. As we have seen, both sides, the Priestly and prophetic circles, used the same scribal techniques to argue against each other.

---

45. Of special importance in this respect is the interpretation of the covenant in Lev 26:42. See the discussion of Hans-Ulrich Steymans, "Verheißung und Drohung: Lev 26," in *Levitikus als Buch* (BBB 1119; Berlin: Philo, 1999) 299–300, and Walther Gross, "'Rezeption' in Ex 31,12–17 und Lev 26,39–45: Sprachliche Form und theologisch-konzeptionelle Leistung," in *Rezeption und Auslegung im Alten Testament und in seinem Umfeld: Ein Symposion aus Anlaß des 60. Geburtstags von Odil Hannes Steck* (ed. Reinhard G. Kratz and Thomas Krüger; OBO 153; Göttingen: Vandenhoeck & Ruprecht, 1997) 61, on the one side; and Graham Davies, "Covenant, Oath, and the Composition of the Pentateuch," in *Covenant as Context: Essays in Honour of Ernest W. Nicholson* (ed. A. D. H. Mayes and R. B. Salters; Oxford: Oxford University Press, 2003) 82–86, on the other side. See also my discussion of these approaches in "Der Bund im Alten Testament: Eine Festschrift für E. W. Nicholson," *ZA(B)R* 11 (2005) 364.

PART 3

The Torah as a Foundational Document in Judah and Samaria

The Torah between Samaria and Judah: Shechem and Gerizim in Deuteronomy and Joshua

CHRISTOPHE NIHAN

University of Geneva

1. Introduction:
The Place of Samaria in New Models
for the Acceptance of the Pentateuch as "Torah"

Possibly one of the most significant developments in pentateuchal scholarship these past decades has been the growing interest in the redactional process that led to the composition of the Pentateuch and the historical background underlying this process. The classic models inherited from the 19th century focused on the isolation of earlier, discrete sources. Today, in spite of all the differences among more-recent models, most scholars acknowledge that the combining of various conflicting traditions into a unified narrative and elaborating on them was a scribal achievement per se.[1] The Pentateuch is not simply a collection of various sources compiled by a "final redactor" in an almost

---

Author's note: I would like to thank my colleagues in Geneva and Lausanne, Jean-Daniel Macchi and Thomas Römer, who read an earlier draft of this paper and offered many suggestions. I have also benefited from discussions with Jean-Daniel Macchi at an early stage of my work on this topic. I also want to express my gratitude to the editors, Gary N. Knoppers and Bernard M. Levinson, for help with revising my paper and for offering many valuable suggestions. Unless otherwise specified, all translations of the biblical texts are my own.

1. For technical reasons, it is unlikely, however, that this document was initially written on a single scroll. See the comments on the *status quaestionis* by Konrad Schmid, *Buchgestalten des Jeremiabuches: Untersuchungen zur Redaktions- und Rezeptionsgeschichte von Jer 30–33 im Kontext des Buches* (WMANT 72; Neukirchen-Vluyn: Neukirchener Verlag, 1996) 38–39. Besides, there are numerous indications that the division between the first five books was not made on merely "practical" grounds, as it was classically assumed (thus still recently, John Van Seters, *The Pentateuch: A Social-Science Commentary* [Trajectories 1; Sheffield: Continuum, 1999] 15–19, esp. 16–17), but is *editorial* in nature. That is, it reflects the understanding of the final editors of the Torah themselves. For a recent discussion, refer to my *From Priestly Torah to Pentateuch: A Study in the Composition of the Book of Leviticus* (FAT; Tübingen: Mohr Siebeck, 2007) 69–76.

mechanical way.[2] Rather, it is a sophisticated composition that, on the basis of earlier traditions, defines a new legend establishing the origins of "Israel," a legend capable of rivaling other prestigious national traditions inside the Achemenid Empire, as is apparent, for instance, in Deut 4:8: "And what great nation has statutes and ordinances as equitable as this whole law that I am setting before you today?"

In the 1990s, the so-called imperial-authorization (*Reichsauthorisation*) hypothesis identified an external factor behind the creation of the Pentateuch and its acceptance as "Torah"—namely, the willingness of the Achemenid administration to acknowledge the Pentateuch as the *nomos* of the Persian province of Yehud.[3] In recent years, however, growing skepticism has been voiced, and legitimately so, about the application of the imperial-authorization hypothesis to the Pentateuch and even about the general validity of the hypothesis itself.[4] As a result, in recent scholarly treatments the Pentateuch is regarded first and foremost as an *inner-Judean* compromise, a synthesis of various scribal traditions aimed at redefining the identity of "Israel" in the complex situation following

---

2. See characteristically, Martin Noth, *A History of Pentateuchal Traditions* (trans. Bernhard W. Anderson; Atlanta: Scholars Press, 1981). On the shift of paradigm described here, and, consequently, the most recent concern for so-called post-Priestly redactions within the Torah, see in particular the *Forschungsbericht* by Eckart Otto, "Forschungen zum nachpriesterschriftlichen Pentateuch," *TRu* 66 (2001) 1–31.

3. See Peter Frei and Klaus Koch, *Reichsidee und Reichsorganisation im Perserreich* (2nd ed.; OBO 55; Freiburg: Universitätsverlag / Göttingen: Vandenhoeck & Ruprecht, 1996). Erhard Blum, on the basis of what he regarded as a "legitimate working hypothesis" (*begründete Arbeitshypothese*), sought a balance between "internal" and "external" factors behind the publication of the Pentateuch and its acceptance as Torah. He thus initiated a view that was to become quite popular in the 1990s, that the Pentateuch was the result of a "coalition" of sorts between landowners and (reforming?) priests. This coalition would have known of the institution of the imperial authorization and composed the Pentateuch with the expectation that it would be acknowledged as the *nomos* of the Achemenid province of Yehud. See Erhard Blum, *Studien zur Komposition des Pentateuch* (BZAW 189; Berlin: de Gruyter, 1990) 333–60, especially pp. 345–60 (thus on p. 360: the Pentateuch was reworked "from the perspective of an 'imperial authorization' from the central Persian authority" ["mit der Perspektive einer 'Reichsautorisation' durch die persische Zentralgewalt"]). For a similar view, see, for example, Rainer Albertz (*A History of Israelite Religion in the Old Testament Period* [2 vols.; London: SCM, 1994] 2.466–70), who adopted Blum's understanding of the imperial-authorization hypothesis for the creation of the Pentateuch.

4. For criticism, see Josef Wiesehöfer, "'Reichsgesetz' oder 'Einzelfallgerechtigkeit'? Bemerkungen zu Peter Freis These von einer achaimenidischen Reichsautorisation," *ZAR* 1 (1995) 36–46; Udo Rüterswörden, "Die persische Reichsautorisation der Tora: Fact or Fiction?" *ZAR* 1 (1995) 47–61. See now also the studies in *Persia and Torah: The Theory of the Imperial Authorization of the Pentateuch* (ed. James W. Watts; SBLSymS 17; Atlanta: Scholars Press, 2001), especially the essays by Joseph Blenkinsopp ("Was the Pentateuch the Civic and Religious Constitution of the Jewish Ethnos in the Persian Period?" [pp. 41–62]), Gary N. Knoppers ("An Achaemenid Imperial Authorization of Torah in Yehud?" [pp. 115–34]), and Jean-Louis Ska ("'Persian Imperial Authorization': Some Question Marks" [pp. 161–82]).

the state's collapse.[5] Even though external factors behind the creation of the Pentateuch as a unified document should not be entirely precluded, there is clearly some plausibility in the present approach. In the latest parts of the Torah, such as the so-called Holiness Code (Leviticus 17–27), and especially in the book of Numbers, the complex discussion behind the creation of the Pentateuch as a scribal synthesis is still evident in many places.[6]

What remains to be clarified is the intended audience of the Pentateuch during the main stages of its composition. Most recent models assume that the Pentateuch, because it is likely to have been composed in the library of the Second Temple in Jerusalem, was addressed first and foremost to residents of the Persian province of Yehud. Some scholars have recently observed nonetheless that the decision to close the Torah with Moses' death *outside* the land in Deuteronomy 34 (thus deliberately *not* including the fulfillment of the divine promise to Abraham and his offspring as recounted in the book of Joshua) probably means that, for one thing, a concession was being made to the already

---

5. See characteristically the model sketched by Jean-Louis Ska, *Introduction à la lecture du Pentateuque: Clés pour l'interprétation des cinq premiers livres de la Bible* (Le livre et le rouleau 5; Brussels: Lessius, 2000) 310–21; ET: *Introduction to Reading the Pentateuch* (Winona Lake, IN: Eisenbrauns, 2006) 219–29.

6. On the so-called Holiness Code in Leviticus 17–26, see Eckart Otto, "Innerbiblische Exegese im Heiligkeitsgesetz Levitikus 17–26," in *Levitikus als Buch* (ed. Heinz-Josef Fabry and Hans-Winfried Jüngling; BBB 119; Bodenheim: Philo, 1999) 125–96; Christophe Nihan, "The Holiness Code between D and P: Some Comments on the Function and Significance of Leviticus 17–26 in the Composition of the Torah," in *Das Deuteronomium zwischen Pentateuch und Deuteronomistischem Geschichtswerk* (ed. Eckart Otto and Reinhard Achenbach; FRLANT 206; Freiburg: Universitätsverlag / Göttingen: Vandenhoeck & Ruprecht, 2004) 81–122. On the case of the book of Numbers, see programmatically, Thomas C. Römer, "Das Buch Numeri und das Ende des Jahwisten: Anfragen zur 'Quellenscheidung' im vierten Buch des Pentateuch," in *Abschied vom Jahwisten: Die Komposition des Hexateuch in der jüngsten Diskussion* (ed. Jan Christian Gertz, Konrad Schmid, and Markus Witte; BZAW 315; Berlin: de Gruyter, 2002) 215–31. For a detailed analysis, see now Reinhard Achenbach, *Die Vollendung der Tora: Studien zur Redaktionsgeschichte des Numeribuches im Kontext von Hexateuch und Pentateuch* (Beihefte zur Zeitschrift für altorientalische und biblische Rechtsgeschichte 3; Wiesbaden: Harrassowitz, 2003). For instance, the story of Numbers 11 (at least in its present shape) climaxes with a statement by Moses expressing the hope that the people as a whole might become a "people of prophets" and partake of his (Yahweh's) spirit (Num 11:29). This corresponds to the reception, inside the Torah, of a central belief of postexilic eschatological prophecy (see Isa 32:15, 44:3; Ezek 36:27, 39:29; Joel 3:1–2). Note, also, that Numbers 11 is the *only* text in the Pentateuch to use the root nb᾽ ("prophecy") as a verbal form, a usage frequently found in the Latter Prophets. The story immediately following in Numbers 12, on the contrary, reasserts Moses' absolute superiority over the entire prophetic tradition (see Num 12:6–8). As such, it corrects Numbers 11 from a perspective that anticipates the concluding summary of the entire Torah in Deut 34:10–12. On the conflict between Numbers 11 and 12, see further Thomas C. Römer, "Nombres 11–12 et la question d'une rédaction deutéronomique dans le Pentateuque," in *Deuteronomy and Deuteronomic Literature: Festschrift C. H. W. Brekelmans* (ed. Marc Vervenne and Johan Lust; BETL 133; Leuven: Peeters, 1997) 481–98.

well-established Judean diaspora.[7] Even more intriguing evidence comes from the province of Samaria, because we know that very early on the Samarians adopted the Pentateuch as Torah and, conversely, did not accept the other books now contained in the canon of the Hebrew Bible.[8]

Today, there appears to be general agreement among specialists that the so-called Samaritan schism cannot be situated before the end of the 2nd century B.C.E. and probably occurred in connection with the destruction of the sanctuary on Mount Gerizim by John Hyrcanus in 112–111 B.C.E. Others, however, would date it still later or even dispute the very notion of a sudden, unique "break" between Jews and Samari(t)ans.[9] The books of Ezra and Nehemiah do suggest intense conflicts between Judeans and Samarians already during the Persian and early Hellenistic periods (as does also the late, polemical account of 2 Kgs 17:24–41).[10] However, the book of Chronicles implies a much more conciliatory perspective, the best example of which is the account of Hezekiah's invitation to the Northern tribes to celebrate the Passover in 2 Chronicles 30.[11]

---

7. See Thomas Römer, "La fin de l'historiographie deutéronomiste et le retour de l'Hexateuque?" *TZ* 57 (2001) 269–80, here 280; as well as Eckart Otto, *Das Deuteronomium im Pentateuch und Hexateuch: Studien zur Literaturgeschichte von Pentateuch und Hexateuch im Lichte des Deuteronomiumsrahmen* (FAT 30; Tübingen: Mohr Siebeck, 2000) 247–48.

8. As do several other authors, I shall use the terms *Samarians* and *Judeans* here in order to distinguish them from the *Samaritans* and *Jews* of later periods (late Hellenistic and Roman times), even though, admittedly, there is necessarily some kind of continuity between the two sets of terms.

9. For a dating in the 2nd century B.C.E., see in particular Ferdinand Dexinger, "Der Ursprung der Samaritaner im Spiegel der frühen Quellen," in *Die Samaritaner* (ed. Ferdinand Dexinger and Reinhard Pummer; Wege der Forschung 604; Darmstadt: Wissenschaftliche Buchgesellschaft, 1992) 67–140, here 136; and earlier James D. Purvis, *The Samaritan Pentateuch and the Origins of the Samaritan Sect* (HSM 2; Cambridge: Harvard University Press, 1968); idem, "The Samaritan Problem: A Case Study in Jewish Sectarianism in the Roman Era," in *Traditions in Transformation: Turning Points in Biblical Faith* (ed. Baruch Halpern and Jon D. Levenson; Winona Lake, IN: Eisenbrauns, 1981) 323–50. For the scholarly development situating the final break between Jews and Samaritans in the Maccabean/Hasmonean period, rather than in the Persian era as was previously thought, see earlier, the *Forschungsbericht* by Reinhard Pummer, "The Present State of Samaritan Studies: I," *JSS* 21 (1976) 39–61, here 48–51. See also Richard J. Coggins, *Samaritans and Jews: The Origins of Samaritanism Reconsidered* (Oxford: Blackwell, 1975). For a recent review, see Ingrid Hjelm, "What Do Samaritans and Jews Have in Common? Recent Trends in Samaritan Studies," *CurBR* 3/1 (2004) 9–59, here 13–30. Among scholars who would place the Samaritan schism still later, see especially Alan D. Crown, "Redating the Schism between the Judeans and the Samaritans," *JQR* 82 (1991) 17–50 (not before the 2nd century C.E.).

10. On 2 Kgs 17:24–41 as a late, polemical fiction, postdating the Deuteronomistic redaction of the Former Prophets, see the detailed analysis by Jean-Daniel Macchi, *Les Samaritains: Histoire d'une légende. Israël et la province de Samarie* (Le Monde de la Bible 30; Geneva: Labor & Fides, 1994) 47–72, especially 59–69; and more briefly, for example, Erik Eynikel, *The Reform of King Josiah and the Composition of the Deuteronomistic History* (OtSt 33; Leiden: Brill, 1996) 94 with n. 209.

11. On the Chronicler's positive attitude toward the province of Samaria during the Persian period, see now the fine article by Gary N. Knoppers, "Mt. Gerizim and Mt. Zion: A Study in the

Most significantly, the account of 2 Macc 15:1 shows that in the 2nd century B.C.E. Samaria was apparently still the most natural place for outcast Jews seeking refuge.[12]

Furthermore, we also have evidence suggesting at least occasional exchange between Jerusalem and Samaria during the Persian period. In particular, one of the Aramaic papyri found at Elephantine (= Cowley, *AP* 32) suggests that the governor of the province of Yehud, Bagôhî, and one of the sons of the governor of Samaria, Dalayah, managed to achieve a common position on the issue of the rebuilding of the temple on Elephantine after receiving a letter that had been sent to them separately in 407 B.C.E.[13] More indirectly, a tradition of administrative correspondence between the provinces of Yehud and Samaria may be reflected in 2 Chronicles 30, which reports that Hezekiah sent letters to all the tribes of Israel for his Passover invitation.

2. Reconsidering Samaria's Role in the Composition of the Pentateuch and Its Adoption as "Torah": The Case of the So-Called Shechemite Covenant Tradition

In light of our review above, we may consider the classic view—according to which the Pentateuch was composed for Judeans mainly, if not exclusively, before being adopted later by Yahwists in Samaria—to be unsatisfactory from a historical perspective. In what follows, I would like to propose that it is actually possible to identify some instances of concessions made to Samarians at the time of the Torah's redaction in the Persian period. This suggests in turn that the Torah, though probably compiled in Jerusalem, was nonetheless intended to be adopted by Yahwists in Samaria, as well, *from the very time of its inception*. Probably one of the most interesting instances concerns the so-called Shechem covenant tradition in Deuteronomy and in Joshua, because it is linked very tightly to

---

Early History of the Samaritans and Jews," *Studies in Religion / Sciences Religieuses* 34 (2005) 309–38, with further references. On Samaria in the Persian period, see also idem, "Revisiting the Samarian Question in the Persian Period," in *Judah and the Judeans in the Persian Period* (ed. Oded Lipschits and Manfred Oeming; Winona Lake, IN: Eisenbrauns, 2006) 265–89.

12. As noted, for instance, by Macchi, *Les Samaritains*, 41.

13. Two copies of the letter initially sent to the governor of Yehud by the Elephantine community have been found (= *AP* 30 and 31); the first is apparently only a draft, while the second is much better written. No copy of the letter sent to the two sons of the governor of Samaria has been discovered, but reference is made to it in *AP* 30, line 29 and *AP* 31, line 28. For the original edition see Arthur E. Cowley, *Aramaic Papyri of the Fifth Century B.C.* (Oxford: Clarendon, 1923) (= *AP*). See further, for instance, Pierre Grelot, *Documents araméens d'Egypte* (LAPO 5; Paris: Cerf, 1972) 406–16; James M. Lindenberger, *Ancient Aramaic and Hebrew Letters* (SBLWAW 4; Atlanta: Scholars Press, 1994 [2nd ed., Leiden: Brill, 2003]) 63–68.

the Torah, covenant ceremonies, and a cultic site in Samaria near Shechem. It is to this issue, therefore, that this section is devoted.

In Deut 11:29–30, chap. 27, and Josh 8:30–35 (MT), one finds a set of texts referring to a public exposition of the Torah in connection with the building of an altar in the vicinity of Shechem, on either Mount Gerizim or Mount Ebal. In Joshua 24, moreover, Joshua performs a covenant ceremony in Shechem in addition to the two former covenants concluded at Mount Sinai / Mount Horeb (Exod 24:1–8, Deuteronomy 5) and in the Plains of Moab (Deuteronomy 28–29). Like its forerunners, this covenant is connected to the revelation of additional laws and instructions (see Josh 24:25). Given the importance of Shechem as a cultic location in Deuteronomy and Joshua, and following Martin Noth's thesis of a twelve-tribe "amphictyony," scholars have assumed that Shechem was once the site of the annual covenant ceremony of the twelve tribes and that all the above-quoted passages preserved (albeit fragmentarily) the memory of this institution.[14] Gradually, however, with scholars questioning Noth's amphictyony theory, the connection between these two sets of texts (Deut 11:29–30, chap. 27, and Josh 8:30–35 MT on the one hand; and Joshua 24 on the other) has become an issue.[15] Recently, Nadav Na'aman has returned to the question of Shechem in Deuteronomy 27 and Joshua 24.[16] Although he

14. See Martin Noth, *Das System der zwölf Stämme Israels* (2nd ed.; Darmstadt: Wissenschaftliche Buchgesellschaft, 1966) 133–51. It is also taken up in his *Geschichte Israels* (Göttingen: Vandenhoeck & Ruprecht, 1986). See also Gerhard von Rad, "The Form-Critical Problem of the Hexateuch" (1938) in his *Problem of the Hexateuch, and Other Essays* (trans. E. W. Trumena Dicken; London: SCM, 1984) 37. This view was quite popular for some time in the middle of the 20th century, and it was often adopted by others; see, for example, Carl-A. Keller, "Über einige alttestamentliche Heiligtumslegende I," *ZAW* 67 (1955) 141–68, here 145–48.

15. Thus, in several studies the problem of the relationship between Deut 11:29–30, chap. 27, and Josh 8:30–35 is addressed separately from Joshua 24. See in particular Moshe Anbar, "The Story about the Building of an Altar on Mount Ebal: The History of Its Composition and the Question of the Centralization of the Cult," in *Das Deuteronomium: Entstehung, Gestalt und Botschaft* (ed. Norbert Lohfink; BETL 68; Leuven: Peeters, 1985) 304–9; Paolo Sacchi, "Ideologia e varianti della tradizione ebraica: Deut 27,4 e Is 52,14," in *Bibel in jüdischer und christlicher Tradition: Festschrift Johann Maier* (ed. Helmut Merklein, Karlheinz Müller, and Günter Stemberger; BBB 88; Frankfurt am Main: Hain, 1993) 13–32, here 14–25; Ed Noort, "The Traditions of Ebal and Gerizim: Theological Positions in the Book of Joshua," in *Deuteronomy and Deuteronomic Literature: Festschrift C. H. W. Brekelmans* (ed. Marc Vervenne and Johan Lust; BETL 133; Leuven: Peeters, 1997) 161–80; idem, "4QJoshua and the History of Tradition in the Book of Joshua," *JNSL* 24 (1998) 127–44. Most recently, see Michaël N. van der Meer, *Formation and Reformulation: The Redaction of the Book of Joshua in the Light of the Oldest Textual Witnesses* (VTSup 102; Leiden: Brill, 2004) 479–522, especially 498–504.

16. Nadav Na'aman, "The Law of the Altar in Deuteronomy and the Cultic Site near Shechem," in *Rethinking the Foundations: Historiography in the Ancient World and in the Bible. Festschrift John Van Seters* (ed. Steve L. McKenzie and Thomas C. Römer; BZAW 294; Berlin: de Gruyter, 2000) 141–61. Actually, J. L'Hour ("L'alliance de Sichem," *RB* 69 [1962] 5–36, 161–84,

rightly questions the antiquity of this tradition, he still assigns these texts to a single, comprehensive redaction. However, even though the location of both Deuteronomy 27 and Joshua 24 in or near Shechem cannot be a coincidence, the two texts actually deal with distinct sacred sites and do not evince any cross-referencing going on between them. In what follows, I shall seek to show that Deuteronomy 27 and Joshua 24, though both of late origin, correspond to two distinct stages in the composition of the Torah, a Hexateuch and a Penta-teuch, and that they actually reveal concessions that were made to the Yahwis-tic community in the Persian province of Samaria so that the Torah would be just as acceptable to Samarians as to Judeans.

3. Joshua 24:
The Shechem Covenant Ceremony
and the Finale of the Post-Priestly Hexateuch

The account of the conquest of the promised land in Joshua ends in chap. 24 with the report of a covenant ceremony in the town of Shechem (see vv. 1 and 25). The ceremony involves a summary of the Torah's narrative from Abraham to the conquest (vv. 2–13). It is followed by an exhortation to follow Yahweh rather than other gods (vv. 14–15); a solemn pledge by the people to serve Yahweh (vv. 16–24); the conclusion of the covenant itself and Joshua's disclosure of additional "statutes" and "ordinances," חק ומשפט, in Shechem (v. 25); and, finally, the writing down of "these words" in a "book of the Law of God," ספר תורת אלהים, as well as the erection of a commemorative stone under the oak at Shechem's sanctuary (vv. 26–27).

The brief exchange between Joshua and the people in vv. 19–21 in which Joshua forecasts the people's future apostasy because of their incapacity to re-main faithful to Yahweh looks intrusive. It appears to render pointless the sol-emn engagement that was just taken by the people in v. 18. It could well be a later interpolation, therefore, introduced by the technique of *Wiederaufnahme*, or

---

349–68) had already concluded from his detailed examination of these texts that the Shechem covenant tradition was, in its present state, the work of a late redactor who knew both the Deuter-onomistic and Priestly (P) documents and was close to the pentateuchal redaction, thus anticipat-ing the conclusions of the present study. Nevertheless, in his view, this redactor took up and adapted a very ancient tradition of a covenant ceremony in Shechem that probably went back as far as the time of the conquest. Na'aman, for his part, rightly acknowledges the late, fictitious character of this tradition and views it as a post-Deuteronomistic creation seeking to enhance the role of Shechem's sanctuary after the Judean Exile and before the rebuilding of the Jerusalem temple. He does not connect these texts, therefore, with the redaction of the Torah, as the follow-ing analysis will propose.

repetitive resumption: the people's statement in v. 18, "we will serve Yahweh," נעבד את־יהוה, is repeated verbatim in v. 21 but in reverse order (את־יהוה נעבד).[17] The rest of the chapter does not evidence significant tension and may be regarded a homogeneous composition, except for a few glosses. The LXX has preserved a number of significant variants, and in several instances it appears to reflect an earlier textual tradition than the MT. This is especially true in the case of a passage from the MT that is missing in the LXX.[18] However, none of these variants is very long (at least with regard to vv. 1–28; the LXX has, however, a long plus in v. 33), and this issue does not need to be addressed in detail in the context of this study.

Joshua 24 has long been assigned by critics to the so-called Elohistic (E) source. However, in his 1938 commentary on Joshua, Noth demonstrated that this view was based on dubious arguments.[19] Noth himself assigned the redaction of Joshua 24 to the Deuteronomist (the redactor responsible for composing the "Deuteronomistic History" comprising the books of Deuteronomy to 2 Kings), even though he noted, as many others did, that this account was isolated to the book of Joshua and had few connections with the previous chapters. For Noth, however, it was obvious that Dtr had made use of a considerably older tradition, the so-called *Landtag von Sichem* ("legal assembly of Shechem"), dating back to the pre-state period, a view that was adopted by many other authors after him.[20] This suggestion was later questioned by other scholars in the 1980s, who noted that the reconstruction of an ancient tradition behind Joshua 24 was arbitrary and that the text was best regarded as the creation of a late

---

17. See already, for instance, Martin Noth, *Josua* (HAT 1/7; Tübingen: Mohr Siebeck, 1938) 105–6. See further for instance Christoph Levin, *Die Verheissung des neuen Bundes: In ihrem theologiegeschichtlichen Zusammenhang ausgelegt* (FRLANT 137; Göttingen: Vandenhoeck & Ruprecht, 1985) 114; Erik Aurelius, *Zukunft jenseits des Gerichts: Eine redaktionsgeschichtliche Studie zum Enneateuch* (BZAW 319; Berlin: de Gruyter, 2003) 175; most recently, Thomas C. Römer, "Das doppelte Ende des Josuabuches: Einige Anmerkungen zur aktuellen Diskussion um 'deuteronomistisches Geschichtswerk' und 'Hexateuch,'" *ZAW* 118 (2006) 523–48. The "repetitive resumption" or *Wiederaufnahme* was an ancient scribal device used to bracket an insertion or digression, and is well attested in a broad range of cuneiform, biblical, and postbiblical literature. See Bernard M. Levinson, *Deuteronomy and the Hermeneutics of Legal Innovation* (New York: Oxford University Press, 1997) 17–20.

18. For a detailed comparison of the MT and the LXX of Joshua 24, see especially Moshe Anbar, *Josué et l'alliance de Sichem (Josué 24:1–28)* (BBET 25; Frankfurt a.M.: Peter Lang, 1992) 23–46. Anbar concludes that in most cases priority must be given to the LXX over the MT.

19. See Noth, *Josua*, 107–8.

20. See Noth, *Josua*, 105–9. See further, for instance, Eduard Nielsen, *Shechem: A Traditio-Historical Investigation* (2nd ed.; Copenhagen: Gad, 1959) 86–141. There are numerous reviews of past scholarship on Joshua 24. See in particular William T. Koopmans, *Joshua 24 as Poetic Narrative* (JSOTSup 93; Sheffield: JSOT Press, 1990); as well as Ed Noort, *Das Buch Josua: Forschungsgeschichte und Problemfelder* (Erträge der Forschung 292; Darmstadt: Wissenschaftliche Buchgesellschaft, 1998).

Deuteronomistic or even post-Deuteronomistic writer.[21] In a detailed 1992 study, Moshe Anbar demonstrated that Joshua 24 was "a pure literary work" (*une pure oeuvre littéraire*). According to Anbar, the scribe who wrote Joshua 24 had at his disposal the main traditions of the Torah, including P (the Priestly document), and combined them freely.[22] This conclusion has been adopted by various other authors.[23]

As a matter of fact, the conflation of Priestly and non-Priestly traditions is unmistakable in some passages of Joshua 24, especially in the historical summary in vv. 2–13. This is obvious, in particular, in the account of the crossing of the Red Sea in vv. 6–7.[24] Verse 6 combines the description found in Exod 14:9 and 22–23, two passages that are classically assigned to P. Verse 7 takes up the Priestly motif of the people crying out to God in Exod 14:10 but combines it with a reference to the non-Priestly tradition of the darkness separating Pharaoh's army from the Israelites, which is taken from Exod 14:20. The reference in this verse to Yahweh's making the Sea "return over" (שוב Hiphil) the Egyptians and "cover" them (כסה Piel) corresponds to Exod 14:28 and is distinctive of the Priestly tradition. But the concluding statement, "Your eyes have seen what I have done to the Egyptians," corresponds to Exod 14:31, which belongs to the non-Priestly account in Exodus and furthermore is often assigned to the redactor of the Pentateuch. Finally, the reference to Israel's sojourn in the wilderness at the end of v. 7 is based on Deut 1:46, a (late) Deuteronomistic passage. Thus, the author of Josh 24:6–7 appears already to know Exodus 14 in its final, redactional shape, as well as the Deuteronomistic edition of the book of Deuteronomy.

Although this is the most telling illustration of the combination of various pentateuchal traditions in Josh 24:2–13, other instances may be mentioned.[25]

---

21. See in particular Andrew D. H. Mayes, *The Story of Israel between Settlement and Exile: A Redactional Study of the Deuteronomistic History* (London: SCM, 1983) 51–53, assigning Joshua 24 to a late Deuteronomistic redactor; as well as John Van Seters ("Joshua 24 and the Problem of Tradition in the Old Testament," in *In the Shelter of Elyon: Essays on Ancient Palestinian Life and Literature in Honor of G. W. Ahlström* [ed. W. Boyd Barrick and John R. Spencer; JSOTSup 31; Sheffield: JSOT Press, 1984]), who argues that Joshua 24 is the work of a postdeuteronomistic Yahwist.

22. Anbar, *Josué et l'alliance de Sichem*.

23. See Thomas Römer, "Pentateuque, Hexateuque et historiographie deutéronomiste: Le problème du début et de la fin du livre de Josué," *Transeu* 16 (1998) 71–86; Konrad Schmid, *Erzväter und Exodus: Untersuchungen zur doppelten Begründung der Ursprünge Israels innerhalb der Geschichtsbücher des Alten Testaments* (WMANT 81; Neukirchen-Vluyn: Neukirchener Verlag, 1999) 209–30; Otto, *Das Deuteronomium im Pentateuch*; Jose Luis Sicre, *Josué* (Estella: Verbo Divino, 2002) 475–98; Na'aman, "The Law of the Altar," 141–43; Achenbach, *Die Vollendung der Tora*, 178 n. 11, 201, 316 n. 46, 394 n. 25.

24. For the following, see also Anbar, *Josué et l'alliance de Sichem*, 90–91.

25. Thus, the reference to the land as ארץ כנען in Josh 24:3 is otherwise exclusively found in the Priestly portions of Genesis. The "mountain of Seir" (הר שעיר) as Esau's home (Josh 24:4) is

The blending of Priestly and non-Priestly language can be found elsewhere in the books of Genesis–Deuteronomy. As critics have observed, this device is distinctive of *redactional* passages in the Torah, such as for instance Num 33:50–56.[26] Thus, Joshua 24 cannot simply be assigned to a late Deuteronomist, a theory that has frequently been proposed since the 1980s.[27] Rather, it should be viewed as a *post-Deuteronomistic* and *post-Priestly* creation that was mediating among various traditions of origins to compose a summary of Israel's past history from Abraham to Joshua. This conclusion is consistent with the observation that our chapter betrays the influence of some of the latest texts in the Torah, such as Genesis 24,[28] and that its closest parallel is found in the postexilic prayer of Nehemiah 9.[29] However, because the historical summary in Joshua 24 covers a period extending from Abraham to *Joshua* (not to Moses), its author cannot be identified with one of the redactors of the Pentateuch. More likely, the author of Joshua 24 sought to create a *Hexateuch* (that is, a work extending from Genesis

---

otherwise mentioned in Gen 36:8–9 only. The mention of "Terah, father of Abraham and father of Nahor" in Josh 24:2 presupposes the Priestly genealogy of Gen 11:10–32. (However, this phrase is generally viewed as an interpolation, because it is at odds with the plural that appears immediately after, in v. 2b; see, for example, Noth, *Josua*, 105.) Similarly, the reference to the sending of Moses and Aaron in v. 5a probably presupposes the Priestly account in Exodus, but this phrase is missing in the LXX and may be a later addition. On the dependence of Joshua 24 on P, see, in addition to Anbar's treatment, Römer, "Pentateuque, Hexateuque et historiographie deutéronomiste," 83 n. 53; as well as Schmid, *Erzväter und Exodus*, 226–27.

26. On Num 33:50–56 as a late redactional passage inside the Torah, blending Priestly and non-Priestly (including Deuteronomistic) traditions, see in particular the detailed analysis by Gary N. Knoppers, "Establishing the Rule of Law? The Composition Num 33,50–56 and the Relationships among the Pentateuch, the Hexateuch, and the Deuteronomistic History," in *Das Deuteronomium zwischen Pentateuch und Deuteronomistischem Geschichtswerk* (ed. Eckart Otto and Reinhard Achenbach; FRLANT 206; Göttingen: Vandenhoeck & Ruprecht, 2004) 135–52.

27. In addition to the authors already mentioned above (n. 21), see, for example, Volkmar Fritz, *Das Buch Josua* (HAT 1/7; Tübingen: Mohr, 1994) 235–49. To achieve this, however, Fritz is forced to sort out all the non-Deuteronomistic elements in Joshua 24 in order to reconstruct a purely Deuteronomistic version of this chapter. The proposed reconstruction is not only arbitrary but is also hardly coherent. Anbar himself still hesitated with a Dtr assignment. But he already noted quite correctly that the "mixing of styles" (*mélange des styles*) between the various pentateuchal sources as well as the general ideology of the chapter favored an attribution to a later, post-Deuteronomistic scribe (Anbar, *Josué et l'alliance de Sichem*, 143–44).

28. The reference to Yahweh's "taking" (לקח) Abraham to lead him out of Mesopotamia is found only in Gen 24:7. See Anbar, *Josué et l'alliance de Sichem*, 89 and 98. On Genesis 24 as a late creation, see for example, Susanne Gillmayr-Bucher, "Genesis 24: Ein Mosaik aus Texten," in *Studies in the Book of Genesis: Literature, Redaction and History* (ed. André Wénin; BETL 155; Leuven: Peeters, 2001) 521–32; pace Gary A. Rendsburg, "Some False Leads in the Identification of Late Biblical Hebrew Texts: The Cases of Genesis 24 and 1 Samuel 2:27–36," *JBL* 121 (2002) 23–46.

29. A point also observed by Römer, "Pentateuque, Hexateuque et historiographie deutéronomiste," 83.

to Joshua), as Thomas Römer, Eckart Otto, and Reinhard Achenbach have recently argued.[30]

The location of the covenant ceremony in Joshua 24 at Shechem partakes of the same compositional logic. The reference to Shechem artfully frames the entire hexateuchal narrative. In Genesis 12, Shechem is the very first place settled by Abraham in his peaceful occupation of the promised land (see vv. 6–7; and note, in addition, how this mirrors the extent of the historical summary in Josh 24:2–13). Somehow, the history of Israel's origins begins in Shechem, *and* it also ends there. Obviously, this was a means of acknowledging in the founding legend of Israel the importance of what had been a major cultic site in the heartland of Samaria, as a concession to Northern Yahwists.[31]

Whether or not the town was still settled at the time of the redaction of Joshua 24 is an issue, although it does not fundamentally alter the interpretation

---

30. Alternatively, it has recently been suggested by some scholars that Joshua 24 was part of an *Enneateuch* (Genesis to 2 Kings), in particular because of the obvious connection between vv. 19–21 and some late texts in Judges, Samuel, and Kings, such as the mention of the אלהי נכר, "foreign gods" (v. 20; compare with Judg 6:7–10, 10:6–16; 1 Sam 7:3–4, 1 Samuel 12). See Schmid, *Erzväter und Exodus*, 228–30; as well as Reinhard G. Kratz, "Der vor- und nachpriesterschriftliche Hexateuch," in *Abschied vom Jahwisten: Die Komposition des Hexateuch in der jüngsten Diskussion* (ed. Jan Christian Gertz, Konrad Schmid, and Markus Witte; BZAW 315; Berlin: de Gruyter, 2002) 295–323. But, as observed above, vv. 19–21 are likely to be a later insertion, so the view connecting Joshua 24 with the creation of a post-Priestly Hexateuch initially seems preferable. Furthermore, the notion that Joshua 24 was intended to conclude the narrative extending from Genesis to Joshua, rather than to introduce the following books of Judges, Samuel, and Kings is corroborated by the doublet that has long been observed between Josh 24:28–31 and Judg 2:6–10. However one assesses this doublet, it is quite problematic for the Enneateuch hypothesis. If, as is generally admitted, Judg 2:6–10 is the older of the two passages (see, for instance, Detlef Jericke, "Josuas Tod und Josuas Grab: Eine redaktionsgeschichtliche Studie," *ZAW* 108 [1996] 347–61), Josh 24:28–31 is manifestly a revision intending to establish that, with Joshua's death, a conclusion has been reached (contrast esp. Josh 24:31 with Judg 2:10). In this case, the editorial willingness to separate Joshua from the following books is apparent. If, however, Josh 24:28–31 was the basis for Judg 2:6–10, this would mean that the late scribe who introduced the passage in Judges 2 sought to resume the narrative after Joshua 24. But in this scenario, the concluding function of Joshua 24 was still obvious to the scribe, and he was forced to correct it by completing the statement in Josh 24:31 by means of Judg 2:10.

31. For this insight, see Erhard Blum, *Die Komposition der Vätergeschichte* (WMANT 57; Neukirchen-Vluyn: Neukirchener Verlag, 1984) 44, 54, 57–79; idem, "Der kompositionelle Knoten am Übergang von Josua zu Richter: Ein Entflechtungsvorschlag," in *Deuteronomy and Deuteronomic Literature: Festschrift C. H. W. Brekelmans* (ed. Marc Vervenne and Johan Lust; BETL 133; Leuven: Peeters, 1997) 181–212, here 200. See also Anbar, *Josué et l'alliance de Sichem*, 117–20; Thomas Römer and Marc Brettler, "Deuteronomy 34 and the Case for a Persian Hexateuch," *JBL* 119 (2000) 401–19, esp. 413. The fact that the LXX reads "Shiloh" instead of "Shechem" in vv. 1 and 25 should be viewed primarily as a later *anti-Samarian* correction (see, for instance, Anbar, *Josué et l'alliance de Sichem*, 30); but it also serves to connect the account of Joshua 24 with the beginning of Samuel (see 1 Samuel 1–3), according to which the ark was preserved in Shiloh before it was brought to Jerusalem by David.

proposed here. Recently, Nadav Na'aman has argued that the composition of Joshua 24, which he also regards as a late, post-Deuteronomistic text, must have predated the town's abandonment, ca. 480–475 B.C.E.,[32] and reflected the viewpoint of a scribe who was keen on emphasizing Shechem's role over other towns, such as Jerusalem, as a cultic and administrative center.[33] Although this interpretation is appealing in some respects, it also leaves many questions unanswered. In particular, Na'aman does not address the meaning of Joshua 24 in the book as a whole. Once it is acknowledged that Joshua 24 is not an ancient Northern tradition but, rather, a late supplement to Joshua intended to create a Hexateuch, the chapter has a central editorial function and cannot be analyzed as a discrete composition (as Na'aman proceeds to do). From this perspective, the assignment of Joshua 24 to a putative Shechemite scribe on the sole basis of Shechem's importance in this chapter appears to rest on a shaky foundation.

There are indications of a pro-Judean stance in Joshua, for example in Joshua 15, suggesting that the book was edited in Jerusalem. Thus, the reference to Shechem could also be a purely literary device by a Judean scribe eager to acknowledge the town's role in the tradition of origins shared by Judah and Samaria, as the inclusio constructed with Genesis 12 already suggests. Eckart Otto and Reinhard Achenbach, for their part, have proposed situating the creation of the Hexateuch (of which this chapter forms the grand conclusion) during the time of Nehemiah's mission to Jerusalem (ca. 445 B.C.E.). This suggestion is tempting and does makes some sense. If the Hexateuch was indeed composed in Jerusalem, an ambitious and sophisticated synthesis of traditions into a unified legend of origins for all "Israel" is unlikely to have taken place before the town's rehabilitation as a major cultic and administrative center—that is, before Nehemiah. If this is true, the composition of Joshua 24 (and of the Hexateuch) would postdate Shechem's abandonment in 480 B.C.E. Actually, emphasizing Shechem in the Hexateuch as well as the town's celebration as a traditional cultic center would have been all the easier for a Judean scribe, because during his time Shechem had already lost all political and economic significance and would therefore no longer have been an object of conflict between Judeans and Samarians.

However, it is likely that there is a reasosn for the location of the ceremony of Joshua 24 at Shechem in addition to the concession being made to Samarian Yahwists. It can hardly be a coincidence that Shechem is also the very place where the biblical tradition in 1 Kings 12 situates the separation of the Northern tribes under the reign of Rehoboam, Solomon's heir and successor, and hence

---

32. See Edward F. Campbell, "Shechem," *NEAEHL* 4:1345–54.
33. Na'aman, "The Law of the Altar."

the division into two kingdoms.[34] In Joshua 24, on the other hand, Shechem is related to the conclusion of a national covenant in the final stage of the history of Israel's origins, according to the Hexateuch, in a foundational and idealized past situated long before the emergence of the state. This contrast is reinforced by the inclusive, "pan-Israelite" perception that characterizes Joshua 24, which has long been observed by scholars. The beginning of chap. 24 specifies that the covenant ceremony involves "all the tribes of Israel" in Shechem (v. 1), which constitute a single nation (עַם), united in its commitment to Yahweh (vv. 16, 19, 21, 22) and its covenant with the deity (vv. 24–27). For the Yahwistic communities of Yehud and Samaria in the Persian period, both of which had experienced the end of kingship and the loss of political autonomy, the Torah is presented in Joshua 24 as the very basis of a new national and religious alliance, intended to overcome the traditional division between the Northern and Southern kingdoms and to re-create the legendary unity of origins.[35]

4. Deuteronomy 27 and the Acknowledgment of the Gerizim Sanctuary in the Context of the Redaction of the Pentateuch

Let us now turn to the other passage mentioning a cultic site in the area of Shechem, namely, Deuteronomy 27 (see also Deut 11:29–30). Discussing this passage as well as its relation to Joshua 24 is complicated by the composite character of chap. 27 and by the textual problem raised by the divergence between the Masoretic Text (MT) and the Samaritan Pentateuch (SP) in Deut 27:4,

---

34. A point also emphasized, for instance, by Anbar, *Josué et l'alliance de Sichem*, 117.

35. As Naʾaman has suggested, it is tempting to assume that, at least in its present form, Gen 35:1–5, which ends with Jacob's burial of the foreign gods previously worshiped by his clan under the terebinth in Shechem (v. 4), is not part of the ancient Jacob narrative but is more likely a late polemic against the covenant in Shechem recounted in Joshua 24 (see Naʾaman, "The Law of the Altar," 160–61 n. 54; following an earlier proposal by Yair Zakovitch, "The Object of the Narrative of the Burial of Foreign Gods at Shechem," *BetM* 25 (1980) 30–37 [Hebrew]). With this interpolation, the very place where Joshua concludes a covenant with the people after the conquest and where a stone is erected as a memorial of this event is delegitimized and presented as a profane, unholy place. Note also that the reference to the "gods of the foreigner" (אלהי הנכר) in Gen 35:2, 4 otherwise plays no role in the Jacob story except to prepare for the motif of the people's forthcoming apostasy in Josh 24:20, 23, using the same terminology. For the redactional character of vv. 2(b) and 4, see also Thomas Nauerth, *Untersuchungen zur Komposition der Jakoberzählungen: Auf der Suche nach der Endgestalt des Genesisbuches* (BEATAJ 27; Frankfurt am Main: Peter Lang, 1997) 120–25. However, this polemical addition in Genesis 35 may even have been acceptable to the Samarians after the elimination of the book of Joshua from the Torah and, above all, the building of the central sanctuary on Mount Gerizim, which I will discuss in the next section. More problematic is the case of the other polemic against Shechem in Genesis 34. Whether the final redaction of this text belongs to the same literary stratum as Gen 35:1–5, as proposed by Naʾaman, is difficult to decide and need not be settled here.

which read "Mount Ebal" and "Mount Gerizim," respectively. I shall briefly address these two issues in turn.

4.1. Redaction Criticism of Deuteronomy 27

The fact that Deuteronomy 27 is clearly not from one hand has long been observed, but there is hardly any agreement about the chapter's redactional history.[36] Here, I shall limit myself to discussing the main aspects of the question. The starting point for any critical analysis of Deuteronomy 27 should be the classic observation of the obvious doublet that appears between vv. 2–3a on one hand and vv. 4 and 8 on the other (see fig. 1, p. 201). Verse 4aα corresponds to v. 2aα; v. 4aβ to 2bα; and v. 4b to v. 2bβ. Similarly, v. 8 repeats v. 3a verbatim. The last phrase of v. 3a, an allusion to Israel's entrance into the land (בעברך, "when you [sing.] pass over"), has no parallel in v. 8 but is repeated at the very beginning of v. 4 (though with a plural form of address).[37] Only v. 4aγ, especially the reference to Mount Ebal (MT) or Mount Gerizim (SP), as well as the last command found in v. 8, באר היטב ("expound it clearly") have no equivalent in vv. 2–3a.

Most commentators of Deuteronomy 27 have noted this doublet, but its meaning for the redaction history of this chapter remains disputed. Earlier critics initially considered vv. 4–8 to be a late insertion by a Deuteronomistic redactor ("Rd"), though vv. 5–7 (or 5–7a) were nonetheless viewed as a fragment of the Elohistic source, because of their similarity to Exod 20:24–26.[38] Gradu-

---

36. The lament over the difficulties raised by the redaction criticism of Deuteronomy 27 has a long tradition and belongs to the genre of the commentary on this chapter. See already, for example, Carl Steuernagel, *Das Deuteronomium* (2nd ed.; HKAT 3; Göttingen: Vandenhoeck & Ruprecht, 1923) 147: "Die Entstehung des gegenwärtigen verwirrten Textes aufzuklären, ist ein aussichtslos Unternehmen" ("Elucidating the development of the present, confused text is a pointless enterprise"). Likewise, Gustav Hölscher, "Komposition und Ursprung des Deuteronomiums," *ZAW* 40 (1922) 161–255; on p. 218: "sehr verwickelte[r] Abschnitt" ("[a] very complex passage"). Noth, *Das System der zwölf Stämme Israels*, 144: "Die Entstehungsgeschichte von Deut 27,1ff. ist sehr kompliziert" ("The compositional history of Deut 27:1ff. is very complicated"), etc.

37. The problems raised by the shift between singular and plural in the address of vv. 2–4 are reflected in the versions. In v. 3, the LXX reads a plural for the phrase בעברך in the MT ("when you [sing.] pass over"). However, this could be harmonizing with בעברכם in v. 4a ("when you [pl.] pass over"). In v. 4aγ; on the other hand, the LXX and the SP have a singular for the MT's אתכם; but this could also be to prepare for the singular address in v. 4b (thus, for instance, Nielsen, *Shechem*, 50).

38. See, for example, August Dillmann, *Die Bücher Numeri, Deuteronomium und Josua* (Kurzgefasstes exegetisches Handbuch zum Alten Testament 13; Leipzig: Hirzel, 1886) 364–66; Carl Steuernagel, *Übersetzung und Erklärung der Bücher Deuteronomium und Josua und allgemeine Einleitung in den Hexateuch* (HAT 3; Göttingen: Vandenhoeck & Ruprecht, 1900) 96–97 (but note his different position in *Das Deuteronomium*, 146–47); also Hölscher, "Komposition und Ursprung des Deuteronomiums," 218 (although he rejects, for the first time, the assignment of vv. 5–7 to E). Alternatively, the redactional homogeneity of vv. 1–8 has been argued by Abraham Kuenen (*Historisch-kritische Einleitung in die Bücher des Alten Testaments*, vol. 1/1 [Leipzig: Schulze, 1885] 120 and 123),

Deut 27:2	**Deut 27:4**
[2aα] והיה ביום אשר תעברו את־הירדן	[4aα] והיה בעברכם את־הירדן
[2aβ] אל־הארץ אשר־יהוה אלהיך נתן לך	[4aβ] תקימו את־האבנים האלה
[2bα] והקמת לך אבנים גדלות	[4aγ] אשר אנכי מצוה אתכם היום
[2bβ] ושדת אתם בשיד	בהר עיבל [MT] / בהר גריזים [SP]
	[4b] ושדת אותם בשיד
[2aα] On the day you pass over the Jordan	[4aα] And when you pass over the Jordan,
[2aβ] to the land that Yahweh your God gives to you,	[4aβ] you shall set up *these* stones—
[2bα] you shall set up for yourself large stones,	[4aγ] which I command you this day
[2bβ] and plaster them with plaster.	—*on Mount Ebal* [MT] / *on Mount Gerizim* [SP],
	[4b] and plaster them with plaster.
Deut 27:3a	**Deut 27:8**
וכתבת עליהן את־כל־דברי התורה הזאת בעברך	וכתבת על־האבנים את־כל־דברי התורה הזאת באר היטב
[3a] And you shall write upon them all the words of this tôrâ, when you pass over . . . [see v. 4aα]	[8] And you shall write upon the stones all the words of this tôrâ; *expound them clearly.* [see Deut 1:5]

Fig. 1. The Parallel between Deuteronomy 27:2–3a and 27:4, 8.

ally, however, various scholars have proposed that the source used by the Deuteronomistic redactor in Deuteronomy 27 should have included vv. 4–8 (and not simply vv. 5–7), mainly because of the observation that the instruction for the building of an altar outside Jerusalem openly contradicts the ideology of centralization and is unlikely to stem from a Deuteronomistic hand.[39]

who was followed by Samuel Rolles Driver (*A Critical and Exegetical Commentary on Deuteronomy* [3rd ed.; ICC; Edinburgh: T. & T. Clark, 1902] 295 [except for vv. 5–7, which would have been an earlier tradition]). However, neither of these two authors really accounts for the doublet observed between vv. 2–3a on one hand and vv. 4 and 8 on the other.

39. See characteristically, Noth, *Das System der zwölf Stämme Israels*, 141–43; Wilhelm Rudolph, *Der "Elohist" von Exodus bis Josua* (BZAW 68; Berlin: Alfred Töpelmann, 1938) 151–55, and on p. 153: "Wenn aber ein Deuteronomist von der Errichtung eines Altars auf dem Ebal spricht, so hätte er das nie von sich aus getan, er muß hier an eine ältere Tradition anknüpfen . . ." ["If, however, a Deuteronomist was speaking of the erection of an altar on Mount Ebal, he would never have done this by himself, and he must have been relying here on an earlier tradition . . ."]. See also Nielsen, *Shechem*, 50–66, esp. 62–66; Gerhard von Rad, *Deuteronomy: A Commentary* (trans. Dorothea Barton; OTL; Philadelphia: Westminster, 1966) 165; and for further references, see L'Hour, "L'alliance de Sichem," 174 nn. 214 and 216. More recently, Henri Cazelles ("Sichem, II: Les textes et l'histoire," *DBSup* 12: col. 1278) identifies a predeuteronomistic text in vv. 4–6a. Eduard Nielsen (*Deuteronomium* [HAT 6; Tübingen: Mohr, 1995] 245) considers vv. 1, 4, 8, 5*, 6–7 to be

Although this latter observation is entirely correct, the assignment of vv. 4 and
8 (setting aside for the moment the problem raised by vv. 5–7) to a *predeuter-*
onomistic source is nevertheless problematic.

First, the wording of vv. 4 and 8 does not justify the assumption of a predeuteronomistic tradition. The mention of "all the words of this *tôrâ*" in v. 8
(את־כל־דברי התורה הזאת) can only refer to Moses' previous discourse in Deuteronomy. Note, similarly, that the reference to the imminent crossing of the
Jordan in v. 4 presupposes a situation of communication matching the situation
laid out in Deut 1:1–5.[40] Finally, in v. 8, the phrase באר היטב, "expound them
clearly," unparalleled in v. 3, is unmistakably reminiscent of Deut 1:5, as some
authors have correctly noted, thus enhancing the connection between 27:4–8
and Deut 1:1–5.[41] Significantly, Deut 1:5 is the only other passage in Deuteronomy that uses the verb באר, and it has a clear editorial function for the whole

---

a "proto-Deuteronomic" tradition. Sacchi ("Ideologia e varianti della tradizione ebraica," 16–17,
22–23) discerns a first layer of Deuteronomistic origin in vv. 4–8, while vv. 1–3 constitute a later,
nomistic revision from the 5th–4th centuries B.C.E. Most recently, van der Meer (*Formation and
Reformulation*, 498–500) sees an earlier, predeuteronomistic instruction in vv. 4–7, whereas vv. 2–
3 and 8 are a Deuteronomistic correction. Note that for some of these authors, vv. 2–3 are Deuteronomistic (thus Rudolph), whereas for others (Nielsen and also apparently von Rad) there are
two parallel recensions in vv. 2–3 and vv. 4–8. Some authors have also suggested that the earliest
layer should be vv. 4 and 8, because v. 8 appears to follow v. 4 immediately. See Noth, *Das System
der zwölf Stämme Israels*, 148–51. For a similar reconstruction, see also Anbar ("The Story about
the Building of an Altar," 307–9), for whom vv. 4 and 8 were gradually supplemented by vv. 2–3
and 5–7, although he offers various alternative models for this development. Note, as well, the
view of Noort ("The Traditions of Ebal and Gerizim," 70–173), who finds a primitive layer in
vv. 4, 8, later supplemented by vv. 5–7, and finally by vv. 2–3; idem, "4QJosh[a] and the History of
Tradition," 140–41.

40. Thus, most of the scholars who assume the existence of a predeuteronomistic tradition in
vv. 4–8 have been forced to acknowledge that vv. 4 and 8 have been heavily edited by the Deuteronomist. See, for example, Nielsen, *Shechem*, 63. Martin Rose (*5. Mose: Teilband 2* [ZBKAT 5;
Zurich: Theologischer Verlag, 1994] 525–27) also correctly concludes that vv. 4 and 8 must be
viewed as late interpolations but proposes that vv. 5–7* would initially have followed immediately
after vv. 2–3*. However, in that case, the command to build an altar "there" (שם) would have
lacked a location, contrary to what is the case with v. 4. A similar criticism applies to the solution
advocated by Heinz-Josef Fabry, "Noch ein Dekalog! Die Thora des lebendigen Gottes in ihrer
Wirkungsgeschichte: Ein Versuch zu Deuteronomium 27," in *Im Gespräch mit dem Dreieinen Gott:
Elemente einer trinitarischen Theologie—Festschrift zum 65. Geburtstag von Wilhelm Breuning* (ed. Michael Böhnke and Hanspeter Heinz; Düsseldorf: Patmos, 1985) 75–96, here 80–83. He maintains
that vv. 5–8 are a supplement to vv. 1–3, with v. 4 being a still later interpolation. However, the
fact that vv. 4 and 8 form *together* a doublet vis-à-vis vv. 2–3a militates against their assignment to
different layers. Hence, it is more satisfactory to regard all of vv. 4–8 as a later addition to vv. 2–3.

41. Thus already, for instance, Nielsen (*Shechem*, 63) and further esp. van der Meer (*Formation
and Reformulation*, 499). Van der Meer rightly concludes from this observation that v. 8 cannot be
part of the earliest layer in Deuteronomy 27 but nevertheless seeks to retain vv. 4–7 as original (see
before him, Cazelles ["Sichem," 1278], who identified a pre-Deuteronomistic text in vv. 4–6a).
Yet, without v. 8, the reason that the stones need to be plastered (v. 4b) remains entirely obscure.

book.[42] If the use of באר Piel in Deut 27:8 refers to 1:5, it also cannot be earlier.

Second, apart from the language of vv. 4 and 8, there is an obvious reference to vv. 2–3 in the mention of "*these* stones" (את־האבנים האלה) in v. 4aβ. Most likely, this is a reference to the "large stones" (אבנים גדלות) mentioned in v. 2bα.[43] This observation, together with the previous remarks on the language of vv. 4 and 8, implies that the assignment of these verses to a predeuteronomistic layer in Deuteronomy is entirely unlikely and that vv. 4 and 8 are derived from vv. 2–3, rather than the opposite scenario.[44]

---

42. The use of באר in the Piel occurs elsewhere in the Hebrew Bible only in Hab 2:2. The exact meaning of this stem is disputed. David T. Tsumura ("Hab 2,2 in the Light of Akkadian Legal Practices," *ZAW* 94 [1982] 295–96) has suggested a comparison with the D-stem of *bâru(m)* III in Akkadian, which has the meaning "to establish the true legal situation (ownership, liability, etc.) by a legal procedure involving ordeal, oath, or testimony." This suggestion has been developed recently by Georg Braulik and Norbert Lohfink, "Deuteronomium 1,5 באר את־התורה: 'er verlieh dieser Tora Rechtskraft,'" in *Textarbeit: Studien zu Texten und ihrer Rezeption aus dem Alten Testament und der Umwelt Israels—Festschrift für Peter Weimar zur Vollendung seines 60. Lebensjahres mit Beiträgen von Freunden, Schülern und Kollegen* (ed. Klaus Kiesow and Thomas Meuer; AOAT 294; Münster: Ugarit-Verlag, 2003) 34–51; reprinted in Norbert Lohfink, *Studien zum Deuteronomium und zur deuteronomistischen Literatur*, vol. 5 (SBAB 38; Stuttgart: Katholisches Bibelwerk, 200) 233–51. Braulik and Lohfink render באר Piel as "he bestowed legal force on this *tôrâ*" (*er verlieh dieser Tora Rechtskraft*). Although this Akkadian parallel is illuminating, it must be observed that early translators and commentators of Deut 1:5 have usually understood באר Piel in the sense of "to comment, expound." See on this the detailed survey by Eckart Otto, "Mose, der erste Schriftgelehrte: Deuteronomium 1,5 in der Fabel des Pentateuch," in *L'Écrit et l'Esprit: Études d'histoire du texte et de théologie biblique en hommage à Adrian Schenker* (ed. Dieter Böhler, Innocent Himbaza, and Philippe Hugo; OBO 214; Fribourg: Academic Press / Göttingen: Vandenhoeck & Ruprecht, 2005) 273–84 (esp. 277–80). In Deut 27:8, in particular, this meaning actually appears to make better sense. For a reexamination of these issues, however, with fresh evidence in support of the position of Tsumura and Braulik/Lohfink, see Joachim Schaper, "The 'Publication' of Legal Texts in Ancient Judah" (in this volume, pp. 225–236). In any event, the editorial function of באר Piel in Deut 1:5, introducing all of Deuteronomy 1–30, is unmistakable, and this has generally been noticed by other commentators. See, for example, Lothar Perlitt, *Das Deuteronomium* (BKAT 5; Neukirchen-Vluyn: Neukirchener Verlag, 1990) 24. See also Richard D. Nelson, *Deuteronomy: A Commentary* (OTL; Louisville, KY: Westminster John Knox, 2002) 17: "The designation of the locale as Moab prepares for 27:69 [ET 29:1]; 34:1, 5, 6, 8. 'Began' forms a unifying bracket with 'finished' in 31:1; 32:45. The phrase 'this law' will be picked up by the new major heading of 4:44." For further detailed discussion, see Otto (*Das Deuteronomium im Pentateuch*, 167–75), who assigns Deut 1:5 to a pentateuchal redactor.

43. Anbar ("The Story about the Building of an Altar," n. 307 n. 17) has proposed that the reference in v. 4 is to the sequel of the instructions in vv. 5–8, rather than to what precedes in v. 2. Nadav Na'aman ("The Law of the Altar," 149) objects to Anbar's proposal, noting that "vv. 4–8 contain no description of the stones upon which the writing must be inscribed." However, Na'aman's criticism is not entirely accurate: compare vv. 5b and 6aα. Still, it is true that the reference in v. 4 is much more obvious if it is to the instruction in v. 2 rather than to what follows, especially when one considers the parallel between vv. 2 and 4.

44. For the rejection of a predeuteronomistic layer in vv. 4–8, see, in addition to the older critics cited above (n. 38), Rosario P. Merendino, "Dt 27, 1–8: Eine literarkritische und überlieferungsgeschichtliche Untersuchung," *BZ* 24 (1980) 194–207 (although he still considers vv. 1a*, 3b, 5a, 7 to be an earlier layer); and, most recently, Na'aman, "The Law of the Altar," 149–50.

Actually, the reason for the repetitive resumption (*Wiederaufnahme*) of vv. 2–3a in vv. 4 and 8 is clear. Indeed, this repetition frames the introduction of two new elements very nicely: the (re-)location on Mount Ebal / Mount Gerizim, on one hand (v. 4aγ), and the lengthy instructions for offering sacrifices to Yahweh in vv. 5–7, on the other.[45] That a later redactor would have omitted *precisely these elements* in order to compose vv. 2–3 on the basis of vv. 4 and 8 is difficult to conceive; this is an observation that corroborates the priority of vv. 2–3 over vv. 4–8.[46] In passing, one may note that the technique used here by the interpolator of vv. 4–8 has parallels in ancient Jewish literature. Interestingly, it is also found in the long plus interpolated by the SP into Exod 20:17, where Deut 11:29a and 30 bracket the interpolation of a passage repeating Deut 27:2b–7.[47] This also shows that, once Deut 27:4 and 8 are recognized as a *Wiederaufnahme* of vv. 2–3, it is no longer necessary to regard vv. 5–7 as a still later addition. Rather, bracketing vv. 5–7 by repeating the content of vv. 2–3a in vv. 4 and 8 would have been an ideal way for a later redactor to insert the

---

45. As well as, of course, the command "expound on them clearly" in v. 8. Recently, Kristin De Troyer ("Building the Altar and Reading the Law: The Journeys of Joshua 8:30–35," in *Reading the Present in the Qumran Library: The Perception of the Contemporary by Means of Scriptural Interpretation* [ed. Kristin De Troyer and Armin Lange; SBLSymS 30; Atlanta: Society of Biblical Literature, 2005] 141–62, here 151) has proposed that the elements in vv. 4 and 8 that are not paralleled in vv. 2–3a should be retained as part of the original material in Deuteronomy 27. In other words, they would have belonged with vv. 2–3a initially and were not added in connection with the repetitive resumption of vv. 2–3a in vv. 4 and 8. This, however, seems quite unlikely. In particular, I do not understand, in this scenario, why these elements would later have been displaced to be associated with vv. 4 and 8. Besides, if they were original to vv. 2–3a, they also should have been duplicated in vv. 4 and 8! Methodologically, therefore, it seems more sensible that the additional material in vv. 4 and 8 was introduced together with the repetitive resumption of vv. 2–3a, as in the case of vv. 5–7 (see below).

46. The classic argument is that the Deuteronomistic redactor responsible for vv. 2–3 would have sought to remove the original command to set up the stones with the law inscribed on them on Mount Ebal / Mount Gerizim and replace it with a command to set them up after the crossing of the Jordan, which may be a reference to the episode recounted in Joshua 4. Thus, among recent authors: Anbar, "The Story about the Building of an Altar," 308; Noort, "The Traditions of Ebal and Gerizim," 177–78; and van der Meer, *Formation and Reformulation*, 499. Although the idea of a reference to Joshua 4 in Deut 27:2–3 is indeed likely, as we shall see below, it is difficult to say that the command to set up stones on Mount Ebal or Mount Gerizim would have been removed with the addition of vv. 2–3. Rather, in the present shape of Deuteronomy 27, vv. 2–3 and 4–8 appear more likely to be two *successive* commands, the fulfillment of which is recounted in two *distinct* places in the book of Joshua: Joshua 4, on the one hand, and Josh 8:30–35 MT, on the other. This point has been correctly perceived, for instance, by Jean-Pierre Sonnet, *The Book within the Book: Writing in Deuteronomy* (Biblical Interpretation Series 14; Leiden: Brill, 1997) 88 n. 5.

47. For an analysis of the insertions and the editorial techniques employed in the Samaritan Tenth Commandment, see Jeffrey H. Tigay, "Conflation as a Redactional Technique," in *Empirical Models for Biblical Criticism* (ed. Jeffrey H. Tigay; Philadelphia: University of Pennsylvania Press, 1985) 78–83.

command to build an altar.[48] Besides, without the instructions for the building of an altar and the offering of sacrifices, the ceremony's relocation on a sacred spot such as Mount Gerizim (or even Mount Ebal) in v. 4 is little more than a blind motif.[49] Finally, one may also note that the corresponding text, Josh 8:30–35 MT, to which we shall return later in this essay (§5), knows Deut 27:4–8 in its present shape.

Once it is acknowledged that vv. 4–8 are necessarily later than (and derived from) vv. 2–3, the composition of the remainder of chap. 27 raises fewer difficulties. Verses 9–10 follow quite logically after vv. 1–3, whereas vv. 11–13 take up the Gerizim/Ebal location introduced by the supplementary vv. 4–8. Note also the reference to Israel's crossing of the Jordan in v. 12aβ, with בעברכם את־הירדן ("when you pass over the Jordan"), which repeats the first words of v. 4. We can thus easily identify two successive redactions in Deuteronomy 27: first, vv. 1–3, 9–10; and later, vv. 4–8, 11–13.[50] The last part of the chapter, the recitation of the curses in vv. 14–26, may belong to this second redaction, though it was more likely an even later supplement. However, discussion of this problem is not necessary to the present argument.[51]

---

48. This was already correctly recognized by Michael Fishbane (*Biblical Interpretation in Ancient Israel* [Oxford: Clarendon, 1985] 162), who noted that the resumption of v. 3a in v. 8 "therewith brackets the secondary (or parenthetical) material," which should then include vv. 4–8, as argued in the present essay. Pace, for example, Anbar, "The Story about the Building of an Altar"; Noort, "The Traditions of Ebal and Gerizim." See also De Troyer, "Building the Altar and Reading the Law," 150. However, on p. 151, following a suggestion by Bernard M. Levinson, De Troyer also acknowledges that one could argue that "the editor who inserted 27:5–7 needed to use the technique of *Wiederaufnahme* to continue the narrative" and that vv. 4a–b and 8a–b "can be credited to the editor who inserted verses 5–7"—a view that agrees with the solution advocated in this essay.

49. This point has often been missed by commentators. As a recent example, see De Troyer ("Building the Altar and Reading the Law," 150), who holds that initially (that is, before the interpolation of vv. 5–7), "the text specified where the stones needed to be erected, namely, on Mount Ebal (27:4). Then an editor connected the stones with the altar by inserting 27:5–7."

50. On the relationship between Deut 27:1–3 and 9–10, see further below. Fabry ("Noch ein Dekalog," 80–83) proposes to dissociate v. 11 from vv. 12–13. According to him, vv. 12–13 together with v. 4 belong to the latest interpolation in Deuteronomy 27. In his model, vv. 9–10 (the Deuteronomistic core of chap. 27) have been supplemented first by vv. 1–3, 11, and 16–25, then by vv. 5–8, 14–15, and 26, and last by vv. 4, 12–13. However, the separation between v. 11 and vv. 12–13 has no textual support. Similarly, the proposed sequence, reading vv. 16–25 (26) immediately after v. 11, seems improbable.

51. The traditional argument relating to the absence of blessings in vv. 14–26 is not convincing because the same device may be found in most Neo-Assyrian treaties. The tension between the mention of Levi's tribe in v. 12 and the Levites in v. 14 is unmistakable but may simply signal that, at the time of the final redaction of Deuteronomy 27, the Levitical priests of Deuteronomy had not yet been fully identified with Levi's tribe, a development that is exclusively found in the latest strata of the book of Numbers (1:48–54, 2:32–34, 3:5–4:49). See Achenbach, *Die Vollendung der Tora*, 443–98. Nonetheless, it is true that the relationship between the command to the twelve tribes in vv. 12–13 and the command to the Levitical priests in vv. 14–26 remains unclear. Most

4.2. The Origin and Purpose of the Two Redactions in Deuteronomy 27

If we seek to locate more precisely the origin and meaning of the two main redactions identified in Deuteronomy 27, then we should assign the first layer to a late Deuteronomistic redaction.[52] Scholars unanimously acknowledge that Deut 27:1–3 interrupts the transition between the short exhortation concluding the Deuteronomic code in Deut 26:16–19 and the blessings and curses of chap. 28. Scholars have also repeatedly noted the analogy between the terminology of 27:9–10 and 26:16–19. Indeed, all of 27:9–10 may be described as a sophisti-cated inversion of 26:16–19 (or, more exactly, 26:16–18), repeating *in reverse order* all the major elements found in this previous passage (see fig. 2, p. 207).[53] After the introduction in 27:9a, v. 9bβ corresponds to 26:18a, whereas 27:10 takes up the beginning and the end of 26:16–17. Verse 10a (שמע, "listen to, obey" + בקל־יהוה, "the voice of Yahweh") corresponds to the last two words of 26:17 (ולשמע בקלו). Verse 10bα–β summarizes, here again in reverse order, the exhortation of 26:16. Verse 10bβ takes up the beginning of 26:16a (see היום הזה יהוה אלהיך מצוך, "on this day, Yahweh your God is instructing you"), while 27:10bα repeats (in shortened form) the instruction found in the rest of 26:16 to "perform" (עשה) the חקים, "statutes," and the משפטים, "ordinances" (although מצוה, "commandment," is used in 27:10 instead of משפטים).

Scholars have traditionally concluded from this that Deut 27:9–10 once fol-lowed immediately after 26:16–19.[54] This solution cannot be excluded. In this

---

problematic, possibly, is the fact that Josh 8:30–35 appears to know Deut 27:1–13 in its present shape (see §5) but not necessarily vv. 14–26 (as already noted by Kuenen, *Historisch-kritische Ein-leitung*, 1/1.124). At any rate, it is clear that the Levites' proclamation in vv. 14–26 has been pre-pared by the interpolation of the reference to the Levitical priests (הכהנים הלוים) alongside Moses in v. 9, as is generally recognized. See on this point especially Ulrich Dahmen, *Leviten und Priester im Deuteronomium: Literarkritische und redaktionsgeschichtliche Studien* (BBB 110; Bodenheim: Philo, 1996) 113–17.

52. Contrary to Fabry ("Noch ein Dekalog") however, I see no reason to assign vv. 1–3 to a pentateuchal redactor. The construction of this passage is typically Deuteronomistic and shows no sign of Priestly influence. Admittedly, the phrase למען אשר ("in order that") in v. 3bα appears mainly in late texts (ibid., 84), but it is also found in Deut 20:18, and this observation alone cannot support the late dating of vv. 1–3. Furthermore, Fabry's assignment to a redactor is entirely based on his reconstruction of the literary genesis of Deuteronomy 27, taking vv. 1–3 together with the series of curses in vv. 16–25. The reasons for rejecting this reconstruction were stated in n. 40.

53. Verse 19, which has no equivalent in Deut 27:9–10, may well be a later insertion. The emphasis on Israel's cultural superiority over other nations is not Deuteronomistic, but is charac-teristic of the latest (postdeuteronomistic) strata in Deuteronomy; see also Deut 4:5–8. Similarly, the reference to Israel's holiness is no longer a motivation for the law's observance, as earlier in D (Deut 7:6; 14:2, 21a). On the contrary, in 26:19 it has become a goal to achieve through obedi-ence to God's commands. See on this also Otto, *Das Deuteronomium im Pentateuch*, 119 and n. 53; as well as my *From Priestly Torah to Pentateuch*, 557 and n. 619.

54. This view was already standard at the end of the 19th century; see Kuenen, *Historisch-kritische Einleitung*, 1/1.121–22; and Driver, *Deuteronomy*, 297, with many other ancient references. For au-thors sharing this view in the first half of the 20th century, see L'Hour, "L'alliance de Sichem," 178

Deut 27:9b	Deut 26:18
9bα הסכת ושמע ישראל 9bβ היום הזה נהיית לעם ליהוה אלהיך	18a ויהוה האמירך היום להיות לו לעם סגלה 18b כאשר דבר־לך ולשמר כל־מצותיו
9bα Keep silence and hear, Israel! 9bβ This day you have become the people of Yahweh your God.	18a Yahweh has caused you to agree <u>this day</u> to be his own personal people 18b as he told you, and to keep all his commandments

Deut 27:10	Deut 26:16–17
	16a היום הזה יהוה אלהיך מצוך לעשות את־החקים האלה ואת־המשפטים 16b ושמרת ועשית אותם בכל־לבבך ובכל־נפשך 17a את־יהוה האמרת היום 17bα להיות לך לאלהים וללכת בדרכיו 17bβ ולשמר חקיו ומצותיו ומשפטיו ולשמע בקלו
10a ושמעת בקול יהוה אלהיך 10bα ועשית את־מצותו ואת־חקיו 10bβ אשר אנכי מצוך היום	
10a You shall obey the voice of Yahweh, your God, 10bα performing his commandment (*Kethiv*) and his statutes 10bβ which I am instructing you this day.	16a <u>On this day</u>, Yahweh your God is <u>instructing you</u> to do these statutes and these ordinances; 16b you shall keep them and <u>perform them</u> with all your heart and all your being. 17a <u>On this day</u>, you have caused Yahweh to agree 17bα that he will be your God and that you will walk in his ways, 17bβ to keep <u>his statutes, his commandments</u> and his ordinances, <u>and to obey his voice.</u>

Fig. 2. Parallels between Deuteronomy 26:16–18 and 27:9–10.

case, vv. 1–3 should be viewed as a still later insertion between Deuteronomy 26, 27:9–10, and 28. However, one wonders what the point of repeating the exhortation of 26:16–18 in a shortened form was *if not to introduce additional material in between*, that is, in vv. 1–3, once again using the well-known technique of repetitive resumption (*Wiederaufnahme*). Additionally, there is one central

---

nn. 233 and 234. More recently, see, for example, Georg Braulik, *Deuteronomium* (2 vols.; NEchtB 28; Würzburg: Echter Verlag, 1986–92) 2.199; Fabry, "Noch ein Dekalog," esp. 90 n. 59; Dahmen, *Leviten und Priester*, 107–39.

aspect of the exhortation in 26:16–18 that is consistently *not* repeated in 27:9–
10—the command to "keep" (שמר) Yahweh's laws (repeated three times in
26:16–18); however, this is precisely the command found in 27:1. This observation makes sense if v. 1 belongs to the same layer as 27:9–10 and was presupposed by the latter. Finally, one may similarly observe that the reference in
27:10 to Yahweh's "commandment," מצוה, singular (according to the conso-
nantal text), has no equivalent in 26:16–18 (always מצות, plural) but is prepared
by the exhortation in 27:1.

Thus, a case can be made for viewing all of 27:1–3, 9–10 (not merely 27:1–
3) as a later insertion between Deuteronomy 26 and 28, bracketed by the repetition of 26:16–18 in 27:9–10.[55] As several scholars have already proposed, the
introduction of vv. 1–3 appears to build a bridge with the Deuteronomistic account in Joshua 4, which reports Joshua's erection of 12 stones at Gilgal as a
memorial of the crossing of the Jordan.[56] With the interpolation of Deut 27:1–
3 and 9–10, however, the episode recounted in Joshua 4 is significantly reinterpreted: the stones are to be plastered and inscribed with Moses' *tôrâ* ("all
the words of this law"; see 27:3a), a notion still unknown to the account of
Joshua 4. As Deut 27:3b makes clear, the purpose is to warrant Israel's possession of the promised land, immediately after the crossing of the Jordan: "in order that you may enter the land that Yahweh, your God, is giving to you."[57]
This, as some scholars have noted, is reminiscent of the ancient practice of
erecting standing stones to establish publicly one's legal rights over a given estate, as in the case of Kassite *kudurrus* in ancient Mesopotamia.[58] What we have
in the first layer of Deuteronomy 27 (vv. 1–3, 9–10) is, therefore, an original
reinterpretation of the account of the erection of standing stones in Joshua 4
that connects it with a concept that transforms the book of Deuteronomy into
a legal document legitimizing Israel's claim to possession of the land.

In the second layer of Deuteronomy 27, which consists of the interpolated
vv. 4–8, 11–13 (and possibly also vv. 14–26), this late Deuteronomistic exegesis
of Joshua 4 is itself reinterpreted in a most creative fashion. As the wording of
v. 4 and the reference to "these stones" (האבנים האלה) indicate, the entire ritual

---

55. Contrary to what is asserted by Kuenen (*Historisch-kritische Einleitung*, 1/1.121–22), 28:1–2
offers a fitting follow-up to 26:16–19 (or better, 26:16–18; see above, n. 53).

56. For this view, see Dillmann, *Die Bücher Numeri, Deuteronomium und Josua*, 364–65; Steuernagel, *Das Deuteronomium*, 147. See further, for instance, Noth, *Das System der zwölf Stämme Israels*,
148; Rudolph, *Der "Elohist,"* 154–55, 165; L'Hour, "L'alliance de Sichem," 175 (with earlier references); Anbar, "Story about the Building of an Altar," 307; Na'aman, "The Law of the Altar," 149.

57. Following the Masoretic division, which places the main caesura in v. 3 between בעברך
("when you [sing.] pass over") and . . . למען אשר ("in order that"), thus connecting למען אשר
with what follows (תבא אל־הארץ, "you may enter the land"), contrary to what one finds in many
modern translations. For a similar rendering, see, for example, Braulik, *Deuteronomium*, 2.200.

58. For analogies in Mesopotamia and in Greece, see especially the discussion by Sonnet, *The
Book within the Book*, 92–95.

commanded in vv. 2–3 is now relocated to either Mount Ebal or Mount Gerizim (vv. 4, 8), while at the same time being developed into a complex ceremony involving the building of an altar and the offering of sacrifices (vv. 5–7, the repetition of vv. 2–3 in vv. 4 and 8 serving also to bracket the interpolation of new material), as well as the recitation of blessings and curses (vv. 11–13). However artful and sophisticated, the relocation in vv. 4–8 of the ceremony initially instructed in vv. 2–3 involves a significant geographical tension. Following v. 2, the erection of stones and the inscription upon them of Moses' law should have occurred not in the area of Shechem but soon after the crossing of the Jordan. This makes sense if, as noted above, the author of Deut 27:1–3, 9–10 had the account of Joshua 4 in mind. A first attempt to harmonize the conflicting geographical indications can be found in the late gloss of Deut 11:30, the complicated formulation of which somehow seeks to connect Shechem's area to Gilgal.[59] At a much later stage, it gave rise to the fanciful yet popular idea in Christian circles of late Antiquity that Mount Gerizim and Mount Ebal were actually located in the vicinity of Gilgal, a view found for the first time in Eusebius's *Onomasticon* (4th century C.E.).[60]

---

59. As several authors have shown, Deut 11:29–30 is clearly interpolated in 11:26–32. See in particular Nielsen, *Shechem*, 43–44; L'Hour, "L'alliance de Sichem," 166–68; Horst Seebass, "Garizim und Ebal als Symbole von Segen und Fluch," *Bib* 63 (1982) 22–31, here 26–27. The interpolation may have been caused, in particular, by the language of vv. 31–32, referring to the imminent crossing of the Jordan, as in Deut 27:2–3, 4a. In any event, the redactor responsible for this interpolation appears to know Deuteronomy 27 in its final shape. The wording of v. 30 is difficult but reads approximately, concerning the location of Mount Gerizim and Mount Ebal (mentioned in v. 29): "Are they not on the other side of the Jordan, toward the setting sun, in the land of the Canaanites who dwell in the Arabah facing Gilgal, near the oaks of Moreh?" As was nicely observed by L'Hour, ("L'Alliance de Sichem," 167): "Le rédacteur de cette glose [. . .] connaît la localisation du Garizim et de l'Ebal près de Sichem, puisqu'il les place à proximité du chêne de Moreh. Cependant, très adroitement, sans dénaturer les faits, il donne des indications très floues pour montrer que, après tout, l'Ebal et le Garizim ne sont pas si éloignés de Gilgal" ("The redactor of this gloss [. . .] is aware of the location of Gerizim and Ebal near Shechem because he places them in the vicinity of the oak of Moreh. Yet, very skillfully, without distorting the facts, he gives very vague indications so as to indicate that, after all, Ebal and Gerizim are not so far away from Gilgal").

60. See on this point already Otto Eissfeldt, "Schechem oder Gilgal," in his *Kleine Schriften* (ed. Rudolph Sellheim and Fritz Maass; 6 vols.; Tübingen: Mohr, 1962–79) 5.165–73; Noort, "The Traditions of Ebal and Gerizim," 162–64. Whether the redactor who introduced vv. 4–8 thought that the stones with which the altar had to be built (vv. 5–6a) were the *same* as the stones upon which the words of "this *tôrâ*" were to be written according to v. 8 is actually difficult to tell, although the latter view is quite popular among exegetes. See, for example, Fishbane, *Biblical Interpretation*, 162; and De Troyer, "Building the Altar," 152. This is apparently how it was interpreted by the author of MT Josh 8:30–35 (vv. 31–32); but, as will be argued in the following section, because Josh 8:30–35 is clearly later than the second layer of Deuteronomy 27 and cannot be from the same hand, this observation is not decisive. On one hand, it would be logical that the stones with which the altar has to be built are identical with the stones upon which the law is to be written. But on the other hand, the syntax of vv. 4 and 5–6a may also suggest distinct types of stones. Moreover, the command in vv. 5–6a to use "perfect" or "complete" stones, upon which

A decisive clue to the origin of this redaction is given in vv. 5–7, which repeats formulations found in two central passages from the Sinai account in Exodus 20–24. The instructions for the building of an altar and the offering of
sacrifices in Deuteronomy 27 is unmistakably reminiscent of Exod 20:24–26
(more precisely vv. 24–25), the law that opens the so-called Covenant Code in
Exod 20:24–23:33 (see fig. 3, p. 211). Here again, a pattern of inverted quotation occurs (in accordance with Seidel's law).[61] Deut 27:5b–6a refers to Exod
20:25, whereas Deut 27:6b–7a cites Exod 20:24a. In Deut 27:7b, finally, the
preceding quotations are artfully combined with a statement characteristic of
the D code, "you shall eat there and you shall rejoice before Yahweh your God"
(see Deut 12:12, 18; 16:11).[62] Furthermore, the combination of the motifs of

---

no iron tool has been lifted, in order to build the altar is difficult to reconcile (from a rituralistic
perspective) with the command to cover the stones with plaster in v. 4. Note, significantly, that
this part of the instruction in Deuteronomy 27 has been omitted in the corresponding account of
Josh 8:31–32 (MT). In fact, the question is probably misleading: the redactor who inserted Deut
27:4–8 did *not* compose freely, but tried to rearticulate two commands that were initially separate—Deut 27:2–3a on the one hand and the altar law of Exod 20:24–25 on the other (see below,
with fig. 3). Because of the redactional technique he used (that is, bracketing the altar section in
vv. 5–7 with the repetitive resumption of vv. 2–3a in vv. 4 and 8), he was forced to juxtapose
these two commands, thus leaving open whether the stones mentioned in vv. 4–8 are identical or
not. The author of Josh 8:30–35 MT, because he was already reinterpreting the text of Deuteronomy 27, was free to choose the former option and therefore did not retain the instructions that
did not fit with this reading, such as the command to cover the stones with plaster.

61. The principle of inverted citation (or "Seidel's Law") is named after its discoverer: Moshe
Seidel, "Parallels between Isaiah and Psalms," *Sinai* 38 (1955–56) 149–72, 229–40, 272–80, 335–
55, at p. 150; reprinted, *Hiqrei Miqra* (Jerusalem: Rav Kook Institute, 1978) 1–97 [Hebrew]. For a
discussion and analysis of this editorial technique, see Levinson, *Deuteronomy and the Hermeneutics
of Legal Innovation*, 17–20.

62. These parallels have long been established, though their interpretation is the real issue. See,
for instance, Fishbane, *Biblical Interpretation*, 160–61; Anbar, "The Story about the Building of an
Altar," 306; Paul Heger, *The Three Biblical Altar Laws* (BZAW 279; Berlin: de Gruyter, 1999) 14–
87, esp. 58–76. It is impossible in this essay to get into the scholarly discussion of the origin of Exod
20:24–26, its literary integrity, and the meaning of this passage in its literary and historical context.
On these questions, see Bernard M. Levinson, "Is the Covenant Code an Exilic Composition? A
Response to John Van Seters," in *In Search of Pre-Exilic Israel: Proceedings of the Oxford Old Testament
Seminar* (ed. John Day; JSOTSup 406; London: T. & T. Clark, 2004) 272–325, esp. 291–315; reprinted in idem, *"The Right Chorale": Studies in Biblical Law and Interpretation* (FAT; Tübingen:
Mohr Siebeck, forthcoming). In any case, the main point for the present discussion is that scholars
agree that Deuteronomy 27 is derived from Exodus 20, rather than vice versa. This is corroborated
by several details, such as the fact that Deuteronomy 27 uses שלמים (to refer to "offerings of well-
being"), a term unknown to Dtr and otherwise never found in Deuteronomy (for this observation,
see Driver, *Deuteronomy*, 297; and Anbar, "The Story about the Building of an Altar," 306 n. 10; it
is also a rare term in the Former Prophets). That there are differences between the two is only logical, given the fact that Deuteronomy 27 was from a later scribe than was Exodus 20 and was already a
creative exegesis of the altar law found in the Covenant Code, applying the latter to a new situation
(more on this below); hence, a term-to-term comparison of the two laws (e.g., Heger) is ultimately

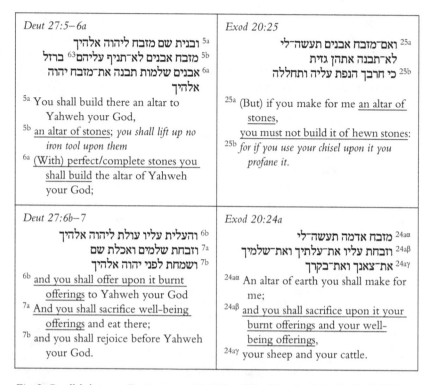

Deut 27:5–6a	Exod 20:25
<div dir="rtl">5a וּבָנִיתָ שָּׁם מִזְבֵּחַ לַיהוה אֱלֹהֶיךָ 5b מִזְבַּח אֲבָנִים לֹא־תָנִיף עֲלֵיהֶם[63] בַּרְזֶל 6a אֲבָנִים שְׁלֵמוֹת תִּבְנֶה אֶת־מִזְבַּח יהוה אֱלֹהֶיךָ</div>	<div dir="rtl">25a וְאִם־מִזְבַּח אֲבָנִים תַּעֲשֶׂה־לִּי לֹא־תִבְנֶה אֶתְהֶן גָּזִית 25b כִּי חַרְבְּךָ הֵנַפְתָּ עָלֶיהָ וַתְּחַלְלֶהָ</div>
5a You shall build there an altar to Yahweh your God,	25a (But) if you make for me <u>an altar of stones</u>,
5b an altar of stones; *you shall lift up no iron tool upon them*	you must not build it of hewn stones:
6a (With) perfect/complete stones you <u>shall build</u> the altar of Yahweh your God;	25b *for if you use your chisel upon it you profane it.*

Deut 27:6b–7	Exod 20:24a
<div dir="rtl">6b וְהַעֲלִיתָ עָלָיו עוֹלֹת לַיהוה אֱלֹהֶיךָ 7a וְזָבַחְתָּ שְׁלָמִים וְאָכַלְתָּ שָּׁם 7b וְשָׂמַחְתָּ לִפְנֵי יהוה אֱלֹהֶיךָ</div>	<div dir="rtl">24aα מִזְבַּח אֲדָמָה תַּעֲשֶׂה־לִּי 24aβ וְזָבַחְתָּ עָלָיו אֶת־עֹלֹתֶיךָ וְאֶת־שְׁלָמֶיךָ 24aγ אֶת־צֹאנְךָ וְאֶת־בְּקָרֶךָ</div>
6b <u>and you shall offer upon it burnt offerings</u> to Yahweh your God	24aα An altar of earth you shall make for me;
7a And you shall sacrifice <u>well-being offerings</u> and eat there;	24aβ <u>and you shall sacrifice upon it your burnt offerings</u> and your <u>well-being offerings</u>,
7b and you shall rejoice before Yahweh your God.	24aγ your sheep and your cattle.

Fig. 3. *Parallels between Deuteronomy 27:5–7 and the "altar law" in Exodus 20:24–25*

altar building, publication of the law, and offering of burnt and well-being sacrifices in Deut 27:4–8 is reminiscent of the covenant ceremony recounted in Exod 24:3–8, which concludes the revelation of the Covenant Code to Moses and forms an inclusio with Exodus 20.[64]

inaccurate. This is obvious, for instance, in the replacement of the prohibition on "hewn" or "cut" stones (verb גזז) in Exodus 20 (a term otherwise never applied to stones in the Pentateuch) with an exhortation to use "perfect," or "complete" stones (for this rendering of שלמים in this context, see Heger, *The Three Biblical Altar Laws*, 50–54), or in the transformation of the prohibition on using a "chisel" (lit., "sword") on the stones into a prohibition on "lifting up" any "iron" (ברזל) in Deuteronomy 27.

63. Thus the MT, but several Hebrew manuscripts correct to עֲלֵיהֶן, with a feminine suffix to make it agree with the Hebrew word for "stones" (see BHS).

64. For this observation, see also Rudolph, *Der "Elohist,"* 153–54; L'Hour, "L'Alliance de Sichem," 177, 359–60. Rudolph even went so far as to suggest that originally the alleged predeuteronomistic layer in Deut 27:1–8 (vv. 1a, 4–8) was situated immediately after Exod 24:1–11 and was only later relocated to its present place by the Deuteronomistic redactor of Deuteronomy 27. For

This fine instance of the innerbiblical reception of Exodus 20–24 in Deuteronomy 27 is unlikely to be the work of a late Deuteronomistic redactor, contrary to what was argued above in the case of the first layer of Deuteronomy 27 (vv. 1–3, 9–10). As earlier commentators correctly observed, the altar law of Exod 20:24–26, which tolerates a multiplicity of altars ("in every place where Yahweh causes his name to be remembered," v. 24b MT), is impossible to reconcile with the Deuteronomistic command of cultic centralization found in Deuteronomy 12. Rather, the reception of the altar law of Exodus 20 in Deuteronomy 27 should correspond to a later stage in the development of biblical literature, when the Covenant Code and the book of Deuteronomy were no longer two *separate* corpora but were now brought together as parts of one document—that is, at the time of the redaction of the Pentateuch.[65] This conclusion would also account for the connection, noted above, between Deut 27:8 and Deut 1:5, also a late redactional passage from the hand of the editor of Deuteronomy.[66]

---

more on Exodus 24, see Jean-Louis Ska, "From History Writing to Library Building: The End of History and the Birth of the Book," in this volume (pp. 145–169).

65. On these two distinct phases of literary history and their implications, see Levinson, *Deuteronomy and the Hermeneutics of Legal Innovation*, 144–50.

66. See above, n. 42. For a similar idea, see Jean L'Hour, "L'Alliance de Sichem," who assigns Deut 27:4–8 to a postdeuteronomistic redactor seeking to unify the Covenant Code and the book of Deuteronomy. However, L'Hour remained vague regarding the relationship between this redactor and the redaction of the Pentateuch. The enumeration of the 12 tribes in vv. 12–13 presents an interesting problem, because it is different from other, similar lists of the 12 tribes in the Pentateuch; however, this issue may be left open here. See provisionally the study by Koichi Namiki, "Reconsideration of the Twelve-Tribe System of Israel," *AJBI* 2 (1976) 29–59, esp. pp. 40 and 55 (with fig. 5). In particular, as Namiki points out, the distribution of the tribes appears to play on the genealogy of Genesis 29–30. Rachel's sons (Joseph, Benjamin) and Rachel's female slave's sons (Dan, Naphtali) are systematically placed last in each of the two groups of 6 tribes standing on the two mountains, thus reflecting the priority of Leah over Rachel. The other 4 tribes standing on the blessing side include all of Leah's sons from the first group of sons (Gen 29:31–35) except for Reuben (in other words, Simeon, Levi, Judah). However, Reuben may have been deliberately set apart to head the group of 6 tribes standing on Mount Ebal for the curse. Why he was chosen for this is difficult to say but, as proposed by Namiki, it probably reflects the biblical tradition of having Reuben head the tribal lists. Simeon, Leah's second son after Reuben, stands as the head of the 6 tribes standing on Mount Gerizim, and the fourth place in the enumeration (before the mention of Rachel's two sons at the end) is then logically occupied by Issachar, the first of Leah's sons from the second list of sons (Gen 30:17–20). In any event, the inclusion of Levi shows that the list of tribes in Deut 27:12–13 is earlier than the 12-tribe system exclusive of Levi, which is only found in the latest stratum of Numbers; see Num 1:5–15, 20–43; 2:3–31; 7:12–83; 10:14–28; 13:4–15; 26:5–51; 34:16–29. On this, see Achenbach, *Die Vollendung der Tora*, 443–98 and passim. Note, finally, that in 1 Kgs 6:7 a late editor has inserted a passage reflecting the influence of the exegesis of Exod 20:24–25 in Deut 27:5–6 to correct the earlier statement that Solomon's temple was built with hewn stones (גזית, 1 Kgs 5:31, prohibited by Exod 20:25a). On this, see further Fishbane (*Biblical Interpretation*, 159–62), who assigns the passage to "the compiler-redactor of the Book of Kings."

4.3. Mount Gerizim in the Postdeuteronomistic
Pentateuchal Revision of Deuteronomy 27

Having clarified the redaction history of Deuteronomy 27, we may now turn to the decisive issue of the variant readings "Mount Gerizim" and "Mount Ebal" in v. 4 of the SP and the MT, respectively. On both internal and external grounds, the Samaritan reading is most likely to be original. If vv. 4–8 and 11–13 are part of the same redactional layer in chap. 27, as argued above, it is entirely unlikely that Mount Ebal, which stands as the place for *curses* in v. 13, would have been chosen for the erection of stones engraved with the Torah and the building of an altar as commanded in vv. 4–8, as scholars have traditionally observed.[67] Furthermore, even if a cultic place existed on Mount Ebal in the early Iron Age (ca. the 10th century B.C.E., although this point is disputed by specialists),[68] we have no evidence whatsoever regarding the cultic function of this site at a later period, contrary to what is true for Mount Gerizim. Once it is acknowledged that Deut 27:4 is not part of an ancient Northern tradition but belongs to a late, Persian-period redaction of the Pentateuch, the very idea of an original reference to Mount Ebal in v. 4 loses all historical likelihood. The classic objection that the Gerizim reading betrays a distinctively Samaritan correction cannot be maintained from a text-critical perspective.[69] The reading "Mount Gerizim" is also supported by an Old Latin Lyon Codex from the 5th- or 6th-century C.E. (reading *in monte Garzin*); it necessarily belongs therefore to a broader Jewish tradition.[70] Considering the above arguments, it is much

---

67. See for example Steuernagel, *Das Deuteronomium*, 146–47; L'Hour, "L'Alliance de Sichem," 177; Sacchi, "Ideologia e varianti della tradizione ebraica," 24–25; Heger (*The Three Biblical Altar Laws*, 45–47), who notes that there are still traces in later Jewish tradition of the problem posed by the location (in the textual tradition from which the MT is derived) of the altar on Mount Ebal, which is the site where curses and not blessings are proclaimed.

68. See the discussion between Adam Zertal ("An Early Iron Age Cultic Site on Mount Ebal," *TA* 13–14 [1986–87] 105–65) and various critics of his proposal, such as Aharon Kempinski ("Joshua's Altar: An Iron Age I Watchtower," *BAR* 12 [1986] 42, 44–49).

69. This view has a long tradition and can still be found among some recent scholars. See, for instance, Nielsen, *Das Deuteronomium*, 246; Noort, "The Traditions of Ebal and Gerizim."

70. On this point, see especially Reinhard Pummer, "Argarizin: A Criterion for Samaritan Provenance?" *JSJ* 18 (1987) 18–25. In his recent study, van der Meer (*Formation and Reformulation*, 501) wants to view the reading *in monte Garzin* in Codex Lugdunensis as "a secondary attempt by the Latin translator, or a Greek or Latin copyist, to make sense of a corrupted Greek/Latin *Vorlage*." However, even though it is correct that the geographical name *Gaibal* (= Hebrew *'ēbāl*) was corrupted into various forms (such as *gabail* or *gebad*) in various manuscripts of the LXX, the proximity of this Old Latin reading with the SP reading גריזים is certainly too great to be explained away so easily. On the Greek fragments of Deuteronomy 24–29 belonging to the lost Greek translation of the Samaritan Pentateuch (the Σαμαρειτικόν), which have preserved the reading *argar(i)zim* in Deut 27:4, see the study by Emanuel Tov, "Pap. Giessen 13, 19, 22, 26: A Revision of the LXX?" *RB* 78 (1971) 355–83.

more likely that it is the Mount Ebal reading that should be considered a later, anti-Samaritan correction. The origin of this anti-Samaritan revision will be explored below in connection with the story of Josh 8:30–35 (MT).

Once it is acknowledged that the SP has preserved the original reading in Deut 27:4, the reinterpretation of the original ceremony of vv. 2–3 in vv. 4–8 (according to the two-stage model for the redaction of Deuteronomy 27 advocated above) and the introduction of a *second* ceremony located, this time not immediately after the crossing of the Jordan, as in Joshua 4, but on *Mount Gerizim* should be viewed as a concession made to the Yahwists residing in Samaria at the time of the redaction of the Torah. This concession clearly presupposes the rebuilding of a sanctuary on Mount Gerizim, as well as its recognition by Samarian Yahwists as their central cultic site. Traditionally, this development was situated in the early Hellenistic period, shortly after Alexander's conquest of Palestine, on the basis of Josephus's account (*Ant.* 11.317–319).[71] But recent archaeological investigations conducted on the Gerizim site have suggested moving this date one century earlier, ca. 450 B.C.E.[72] In this case, the interpretation of Deuteronomy 27 proposed here would remain entirely compatible with the classic view situating the redaction of the Pentateuch in the second half of the Persian period, that is, after Nehemiah, and probably in connection with Ezra's sojourn in Jerusalem in 398 B.C.E., as the tradition preserved in Ezra 7 and Nehemiah 8 suggests.

The introduction of a reference to the Gerizim sanctuary in Deuteronomy 27 is closely connected to the creation of a Pentateuch. The decision by the editors of the Torah to separate the first five books from the following book by adding a subscription in Deut 34:10–12 emphasizing the uniqueness of the revelation made to Moses ("never since has there arisen a prophet in Israel like Moses," v. 10a) had far-reaching consequences. For Judeans, the fact that the Torah concludes with Moses' death and therefore *before* the entrance into the promised land would not have been a problem. For them, the Torah was probably never meant to be read without the body of literature that was later to become the second part of the biblical canon (in the late 3rd or early 2nd century). Although it did not have the same authority as the Torah (and never would), it was also regarded as authoritative in the second half of the Persian period. In this collection, Mount Zion is consistently presented as the one place elected by Yahweh for his sanctuary, as commanded by Deuteronomy 12. The entire

---

71. See, for instance, Menachem Mor, "The Persian, Hellenistic and Hasmonean Periods," in *The Samaritans* (ed. Alan D. Crown, Tübingen: Mohr Siebeck, 1989) 1–18, here 6–8. Similarly, Albertz, *A History of Israelite Religion*, 2.527–28.

72. Yitzhak Magen, "Mt. Gerizim: A Temple City," *Qadmoniot* 33/2 (2000) 74–118 [Hebrew]. See also Yitzhak Magen and Ephraim Stern, "The First Phase of the Samaritan Temple on Mt. Gerizim: New Archaeological Evidence," *Qadmoniot* 33/2 (2000) 119–24.

account in the Former Prophets (Joshua–2 Kings) culminates in Samuel and Kings (= 1–4 Kingdoms in the Greek tradition) with the capture of Jerusalem by David, the bringing of the ark, and, above all, the construction of the temple by Solomon. Zion is also the leading theme of several prophetic books, such as Isaiah and Zechariah, and it can probably even be said to be the dominant theme of the *Nebi'im* as a whole.[73] Samarians, however, apparently had no comparable authoritative literature. Remember that the only Samaritan literature that we know comprises manuscripts from the Middle Ages or even later. Even though it is clear that these manuscripts conflate earlier sources, the attempt to isolate traditions from the Roman, Hellenistic, or even earlier periods that was fashionable in the 1960s and 1970s is now looked on with the greatest skepticism by most scholars.[74] Therefore, for Samarians, the decision to close the Torah with Deuteronomy would automatically have raised a significant problem and would have necessitated inserting a reference to the Gerizim sanctuary in the Pentateuch to demonstrate the legitimacy of the Yahwistic cult practiced there.

The legitimation of the cultic site on Mount Gerizim was introduced in a most thoughtful way, probably reflecting considerable discussion and negotiation among the scribes responsible for the creation of the Torah. The unmistakable reference to the law of Exod 20:24–26 in the formulation of Deuteronomy 27 indicates that the altar built on Mount Gerizim conforms to the prescriptions of the Covenant Code. However, the Covenant Code, contrary to Deuteronomy, does not reckon with a single altar but acknowledges multiple sanctuaries, "in any place where Yahweh causes his name to be remembered" (cf. Exod 20:24b MT). This suggests that for the author of Deut 27:4–8 the altar on Mount Gerizim *was* legitimate *but only in the sense that the Torah preserves a law authorizing multiple sanctuaries* that coexists with the centralization law of Deuteronomy 12. In this regard, the tension created by the de facto existence of *two*

---

73. Not to mention the case of Psalms, where Zion as the place of Yahweh's sanctuary is also a central motif. The existence of *pesharim* on the Psalms at Qumran in addition to various prophetic books may suggest that the Psalms were initially somehow joined to the prophetic corpus. It has frequently been argued that the absence of an explicit reference to Jerusalem as cultic center in the Torah was due to the tradition associating Jerusalem's conquest with David, as related in 2 Samuel 5. However, this need not necessarily be true. The late author of Judges 1 had no difficulty recounting Jerusalem's capture by Judah long before David's reign (Judg 1:8). Even in the Torah one finds veiled allusions either to Jerusalem (שלם ["Shalem"] in Gen 14:18; see Ps 76:3, where this name is parallel with Zion, and the *Genesis Apocryphon* [22:13], where it is identified with Jerusalem) or to Jerusalem's Temple Mount (the mountain of the land of מריה ["Moriah"] in Gen 22:2; see 2 Chr 3:1).

74. For a general survey of Samaritan manuscripts from the Middle Ages, see, for example, the comprehensive article by Paul Stenhouse, "Samaritan Chronicles," in *The Samaritans* (ed. Alan D. Crown; Tübingen: Mohr Siebeck, 1989) 218–65. Interestingly, the Samaritan tradition has retained the notion that only a copy of the Torah and a book of the lives of some of the high priests survived through the Roman period. On this issue, see in detail, ibid., 224–31.

conflicting altar laws inside the Torah, in Exodus 20 and Deuteronomy 12, was brilliantly used by the Judean redactor who inserted Deut 27:4–8 to legitimate the coexistence of two major sanctuaries in his own time that claimed to be the unique sanctuary prescribed by Deuteronomy 12.

Indeed, referring the Gerizim sanctuary to the altar law of Exodus 20 actually leaves entirely open the issue of the identity and location of the unique altar commanded by Deuteronomy 12, which could thus legitimately be claimed by both communities simultaneously. In the context of the pentateuchal narrative alone, the Gerizim altar commanded in Deuteronomy 27 should logically be identified with the unique altar in Deuteronomy 12, and this is how Samarian Yahwists would have interpreted it. But for Yahwists in Judah, on the contrary, it would have been clear that the Gerizim altar was *not* the altar commanded by Deuteronomy 12, which was to be built much later in Jerusalem by Solomon, as the book of Kings demonstrates. This conflicted interpretation, somehow programmed by the very ambivalence of the reference to Mount Gerizim in Deuteronomy 27, is recorded in the text of Deuteronomy 12 itself, as has long been noted. Whereas for Samarians Yahweh has *already* chosen (בחר) the מקום, the "unique place," where he will be revered (Deut 12:5, 11, 14, 18, 21, 26 in the SP), for Judeans it is only in the future that Yahweh will make this choice (יבחר in the MT).[75] The fact that MT Deuteronomy 12 speaks only of a future choice is an obvious reference to the fact that it is only much later, with David and Solomon, that the location of the central sanctuary on Mount Zion will be disclosed.[76]

What we have in Deut 27:4–8 is, therefore, a remarkable instance of innerbiblical exegesis by means of which the presence of two altar laws in Exodus 20 and Deuteronomy 12 was creatively used by a postdeuteronomistic, pentateuchal redactor (1) to mediate between the competing claims of Zion and Gerizim in the late 5th or early 4th century B.C.E. and (2) to reach a compromise that would be acceptable by the two parties involved. The compromise achieved in Deuteronomy 27, introducing Mount Gerizim within the Torah *yet* leaving open the identity of the central altar commanded by Deuteronomy 12, authorized the coexistence of both cultic sites, *despite* the centralization law.

---

75. The ideological drive in the SP to legitimate Gerizim as the sanctuary that was chosen (and rule out Zion as the place to be chosen) can also be seen in its reworking of the altar law of Exod 20:24 itself. In the SP, Exod 20:24 ("the places where I shall cause my name to be remembered"; Hiphil imperfect 1cs) is transformed into an Aphel perfect 1cs, "where I have caused my name to be remembered." See further, Levinson, "Is the Covenant Code an Exilic Composition?" 307.

76. This device actually occurs in all the passages in Deuteronomy where a reference to the *māqôm* chosen by Yahweh is found, as has been long observed: see further Deut 14:23, 24, 25; 15:20; 16:2, 6, 7, 11, 15, 16; 17:8, 10; 18:6; 26:2; 31:11. The use of a past tense (*qatal*) in the SP should probably be viewed as a reference to Gen 12:7, which recounts how Yahweh appeared for the first time to Abraham in Shechem—as argued, for instance, by Reinhard Pummer, *The Samaritans* (Iconography of Religions 23, Judaism 5; Leiden: Brill, 1987) 6.

As such, it legitimized a religious and political situation that would prevail until the end of the 2nd century B.C.E. (and which is still reflected, for instance, in 2 Maccabees). At the same time it made possible the acceptance of the Torah by both Yahwistic communities in the second half of the Persian period.[77]

5. Joshua 8:30–35 MT (Josh 9:2a–f LXX; 4QJosh[a]) and the Anti-Samarian Reception of Deuteronomy 27

The replacement of Mount Gerizim with Mount Ebal at a later stage corresponded to an anti-Samarian reception of Deuteronomy 27 after the main redaction of the Torah, which appears also to be reflected in the late account found in Josh 8:30–35 MT, which describes the fulfillment of Moses' instructions in Deuteronomy 27.

It has long been acknowledged that this brief account appears to know Deuteronomy 27 in its final shape but is probably from a later hand.[78] Actually, Josh 8:30–35 MT follows seriatim the sequence of instructions found in Deut

---

77. In particular, some passages in 2 Maccabees manifest a symmetrical treatment of Zion and Gerizim by Antiochus IV Epiphanes, indicating that, for him (and, possibly, for the author of 2 Maccabees as well), both cultic sites were equally important and legitimate. See 2 Macc 5:22–23 and, above all, 6:2–3, which reports that Antiochus dedicated the Jerusalem temple to "Olympian Zeus," while simultaneously consecrating the Gerizim sanctuary to "Zeus Hospitable" (Διὸς Ξενίου). Unlike the large majority of scholars who identify traces of an ancient tradition in Deut 27:4, Fabry ("Noch ein Dekalog," 93–95) has correctly perceived that Deut 27:4 was a late insertion belonging to the final stages of the redaction of the Torah. Because he recognizes that the Gerizim reading in this verse is original, he also rightly concludes that this interpolation is meant to back Samarian claims after the building of a cultic site on Mount Gerizim in the postexilic period and thus belongs, historically speaking, "in der Phase der jüdisch-samaritanischen Auseinandersetzungen" ("in the stage of Jewish-Samaritan arguments"; Fabry, "Noch ein Dekalog," 93). However, because he misses the deliberate ambivalence of the reference to the altar law of Exodus 20 in Deut 27:4–8 pointed out here, he mistakenly assumes that the acknowledgment of the sanctuary on Mount Gerizim could only be made at the expense of the centralization command in Deuteronomy 12: "Eine solche Versöhnung konnte nur durch Änderung des Grundgesetzes zustande gebracht werden" ("Such a reconciliation could be introduced only through revision of the basic law"; ibid., 95). Yet, the conjecture that the redactors of the Torah explicitly contradicted the central command of Deuteronomy and one of the most important commands within the Torah is unlikely and goes against the harmonizing tendencies that characterize these final redactors, especially with regard to legal material in the Pentateuch.

78. See already Hölscher, "Komposition und Ursprung des Deuteronomiums," 220; Noth, *Das Buch Josua*, 51; Nielsen, *Shechem*, 75–80; Rudolph, *Der "Elohist,"* 198–99; L'Hour, "L'Alliance de Sichem," 178–81; Anbar, "The Story about the Building of an Altar"; Alexander Rofé, "The Editing of the Book of Joshua in the Light of 4QJosh[a]," in *New Qumran Texts and Studies: Proceedings of the First Meeting of the International Organization for Qumran Studies, Paris 1992* (ed. George J. Brooke; STDJ 15; Leiden: Brill, 1994) 73–80, here 76; Noort, "4QJosh[a] and the History of Tradition," 140–41. Most recently, see van der Meer (*Formation and Reformulation*, 498–511), who attributes Josh 8:30–35 MT to a late nomistic revision by "a redactor who had Deut. 27 in its present layered form in front of him" (p. 504).

27:4–8 and 11–13 and in two places even explicitly refers to it in order to emphasize its conformity with Moses' former command (see vv. 31a and 33b). Simultaneously, additional elements are introduced that are mainly taken from other passages in both Deuteronomy and Joshua, suggesting very clearly that a different, later scribe has used this opportunity to amplify the original command, adding various exegetical elements of his own.[79]

In v. 30, the building of an altar on Mount Ebal corresponds to Deut 27:4 MT. It follows in v. 31a with the prescription that the altar be made "of whole/perfect stones upon which you have lifted no iron," which is quoted from Deut 27:5b–6a (itself a reinterpretation of the corresponding prescription in Exod 20:25; see above, fig. 3), "as is written in (the book of) Moses' Torah." [80] The mention of burnt offerings and sacrifices of well-being in the second half of v. 31 matches the remainder of Deut 27:5–7 (see 27:6b–7). In v. 32, the inscription of the Torah on "the stones" (apparently the stones of the altar itself) follows Deut 27:8.[81] The remainder of the ceremony (Josh 8:33–35 MT) similarly agrees with the corresponding instructions found in Deut 27:11–13 (compare Josh 8:33).[82] But the text also introduces many new motifs.[83] In particular, in v. 33a all the political leaders in Deuteronomy ("elders," "officers," and "judges") are specifically mentioned, in addition to "all Israel," as standing near the ark carried by the Levites (see Deut 10:8–9, 31:9–14).[84] The com-

---

79. Pace Naʾaman ("The Law of the Altar," 150–51), who wants to assign Deut 27:4–8 and Josh 8:30–32 to the same hand. In the context of this essay, I cannot address systematically the differences between Josh 8:30–35 MT and Josh 9:2a–f LXX. There are, however, relatively few differences between the two recensions; the most significant differences are discussed in the following footnotes.

80. The phrase ככתוב בספר תורת משה, "as it is written in the book of the Law of Moses." The word בספר ("in the book") is lacking in the corresponding passage in the LXX (Josh 9:2b), which reads merely "the Law of Moses." The same difference appears in Josh 8:34 MT // Josh 9:2e LXX.

81. On the issue of writing on the stones of the altar and on the possible difference between Deut 27:4–8 and Josh 8:30–35 in this respect, see the discussion above, n. 60.

82. As noted above in §4.1., the absence of any clear reference to the blessings and curses pronounced in 27:14–26 is an argument for viewing this section as possibly being later than vv. 11–13.

83. This is, of course, not sufficient reason to consider assigning Josh 8:30–32 and 8:33–35 to two different redactional layers, as has occasionally been proposed (recently by Naʾaman, for example). Without vv. 33–35, Moses' instructions in Deut 27:11–13 (which belong to the same layer in chap. 27 as do vv. 4–8) are not even recounted. Similarly, the suggestion by Fritz (*Das Buch Josua*, 94–99) to retain only vv. 30, 31, and 34 as original is unlikely, because these verses presuppose the corresponding command in Deuteronomy 27. The separation of vv. 32–33 (corresponding to Deut 27:8 and 12–13, respectively) is arbitrary and unjustified. One may only agree here with the earlier judgment by Rudolph (*Der "Elohist,"* 199), when he states that the search for earlier traditions in Josh 8:30–35 is "pointless" (*aussichtslos*).

84. For elders, see in particular Deut 5:23; 27:1; 29:9; 31:9, 28; also Deut 19:12; 21:2, 3, 4, 6, 19, 20; 22:15, 16, 17, 18; 25:8, 9. For "functionaries" (שטרים), see Deut 1:15; 20:5, 8, 9; 29:9. For judges: Deut 1:16; 16:18; 17:9, 12; 19:17, 18; 21:2; 25:2. The OG reads the following sequence:

bined reference to the "resident alien" (גר) and the "native" (אזרח) is not at all Deuteronomistic but betrays the influence of Priestly traditions within the Pentateuch.[85] In v. 34, Joshua's public reading of Moses' Torah may be based on the command of Deut 27:8 to "comment" or "expound" (באר Piel) "all the words of this *tôrâ*," but it is also reminiscent of the command found in Deut 31:9–13, as commentators have noted.[86] Furthermore, the fact that this public reading takes place after v. 33 and the mention of the ark suggests that the ספר התורה, the "Book of the Torah," from which Joshua reads in Joshua 8 (following the MT) is the one preserved inside the ark according to Deut 31:24–26. In v. 35, finally, the mention of the "resident alien," "walking amidst them" (הגר ההלך בקרבם) together with women and children is also specifically reminiscent of Deut 31:12.[87]

In Josh 8:30–35, therefore, one is dealing with a very late supplement that postdates the redaction of the Torah. This late origin is also corroborated by the observation that the MT and the LXX (and to some extent also 4QJosh[a], although the evidence is more complex) disagree regarding the passage's position inside the book of Joshua. In the LXX, it is located after Josh 9:1–2, the notice reporting a coalition of kings against Joshua (see Josh 9:2a–f LXX).

With regard to the location in the MT, Rofé suggests that the logic is topographic: in Josh 8:1–29, Joshua has just conquered Ai, which is "the place nearest to Shechem to be reached by Joshua in his campaigns; later he will go

---

"elders," "judges" (δικασταί), and "scribes" (γραμματεῖς = Heb. שטרים), thereby reversing the order of the last two terms in the MT.

85. See Exod 12:19, 48, 49; Lev 16:29; 17:15; 18:26; 19:33, 34; 24:16, 22; Num 9:14; 15:29; 35:15. All of these passages belong either to the Priestly document (P) or to the Holiness Legislation (H, Leviticus 17–27). Outside the Pentateuch, apart from Josh 8:33, it is found only in Ezek 47:22. Pace van der Meer (*Formation and Reformulation*, 508), who has correctly noted the problem for his own solution, this makes the attribution of Josh 8:30–35 to a late Deuteronomistic redactor all the more unlikely.

86. See, for example, Rudolph, *Der "Elohist,"* 199; Noth, *Das Buch Josua,* 29; Nielsen, *Shechem,* 79, etc.

87. In Deuteronomy, the גר ("resident alien") is usually mentioned either alone (e.g., 1:16; 24:14) or, more frequently, in connection with other *personae miserae*, especially the orphan and the widow (Deut 10:18; 14:29; 24:17, 19, 20, 21; 27:19). In some cases, the Levite is also mentioned in this list (16:11, 14; 26:11, 12, 13). The mention of the גר in connection with women and children occurs otherwise only in 29:10 and 31:12. The reference to resident aliens as "walking" in the midst of Israel (with the verb הלך) is quite unique. Deuteronomy never uses a verb to qualify the resident alien staying with Israelites. The usual construction is אשר בשעריך, "who is within your gates" (Deut 5:14; 14:29; 31:12); in 26:11, we have אשר בקרבך, "who is in your midst"; and in 29:10, אשר בקרב מכניך, "who is in the midst of your camp." The designation used in Josh 8:35 MT appears to be based on Deut 26:11, but the introduction of the verb is reminiscent of the formulation consistently used by (late) Priestly writers, הגר הגר בתוכם / בתוככם, "the resident alien who dwells in your/their midst" (see Exod 12:49; Lev 16:29; 17:12; 18:26; 20:14; 26:11, 12, 25; Num 15:14; 19:10).

to the south (chaps. 9–10) and to the far north (11:1–14)."[88] In addition, the location may be viewed as a way of giving thanks after the capture of Ai in chap. 8, in spite of Achan's crime in chap. 7. That the location in the LXX could be due merely to "an inaccurate copying of the interpolated passage from one manuscript to another" (thus Rofé) is unlikely. It is true that the declaration of war against Israel by a coalition of kings in 9:1–2 hardly calls for a cultic celebration in Shechem, but it must be observed that the story of the Gibeonites immediately following in 9:3–27 forms a delaying element anyway, the war against the allied kings resuming only in 10:1. A possible motivation for the placement of Josh 9:2a–f LXX would be to have the story about the covenant with the Gibeonites preceded by a celebration of the covenant with Yahweh.[89] In any event, there can be no question that both in the MT and in the LXX the account of the building of an altar is only very loosely connected to its narrative context. In the MT, the interpolation of this passage even destroys the syntactical connection between 8:29 and 9:1.

The case of 4QJosh[a] is more complex. Two fragments from 4QJosh[a] (frgs. 1–2) have been found that preserve a text corresponding to Josh 8:34–35* MT, followed by one and a half lines that are unparalleled in the MT and the LXX, and the beginning of Josh 5:2 (MT and LXX). After the publication of these fragments by Eugene Ulrich, most scholars have assumed that they show that, in 4QJosh[a], Josh 8:30–35 MT was actually placed between Joshua 4 and 5, probably immediately after 4:18, and that we must therefore be dealing with three different recensions of this short account (the MT, the LXX, and Qumran).[90] However, as initially noted by Ulrich, we cannot be certain that all of Josh 8:30–35 was actually present in this place in 4QJosh[a].[91] Moreover, it would mean that the scribe responsible for 4QJoshua[a] already considered Ebal and Gerizim to be located in Gilgal rather than in Shechem, as the later tradi-

---

88. Rofé, "The Editing of the Book of Joshua in the Light of 4QJosh[a]," 77.

89. As proposed by L'Hour, "L'Alliance de Sichem," 181. L'Hour makes this suggestion for the MT; however, it is much more apt for the LXX. For a different suggestion, see van der Meer (*Formation and Reformulation*, 519), who thinks that the location in the LXX typically betrays the Greek translator's special interest in military affairs, as elsewhere in Joshua.

90. Eugene Ulrich, "4QJoshua[a] and Joshua's First Altar in the Promised Land," in *New Qumran Texts and Studies: Proceedings of the First Meeting of the International Organization for Qumran Studies, Paris 1992* (ed. George J. Brooke; STDJ 15; Leiden: Brill, 1994) 89–104. For this view, see further Rofé, "The Editing of the Book of Joshua"; A. Graeme Auld, "Reading Joshua after Kings," in *Joshua Retold: Synoptic Perspectives* (Edinburgh: T. & T. Clark, 1998) 102–12, esp. 109–11; Emanuel Tov, "The Growth of the Book of Joshua in Light of the Evidence of the Septuagint," in *The Greek and Hebrew Bible: Collected Essays on the Septuagint* (VTSup 72; Leiden: Brill, 1999) 385–96, here 396 n. 26; Noort, "4QJoshua[a] and the History of Tradition"; and, most recently, De Troyer, "Building the Altar and Reading the Law," 157.

91. Ulrich, "4QJoshua[a]," 91. See also the note of caution voiced by Noort, "4QJoshua[a] and the History of Tradition," 132–34; and similarly by De Troyer, "Building the Altar and Reading the Law," 157.

tion would assume. A completely different view has now been advocated by van der Meer, who holds that 4QJoshua[a] actually never reported the building of an altar after the crossing of Gilgal and that frg. 1 only mentioned the writing of the *tôrâ* on stones (8:32) and its recitation (8:34–35) after 4:18.[92] The purpose of this interpolation would have been to offer a report that complied with the *first* command to plaster stones and inscribe them with the *tôrâ* in Deut 27:2–3. The compliance with Deut 27:4–8 would have been recounted in Josh 8:30–35, as in the MT. If so, 4QJosh[a] frgs. 1–2 may no longer be viewed as an alternative recension vis-à-vis the MT and the LXX. Rather, they would be a creative duplication of existing material in order to answer exegetical concerns. Though the suggestion is quite hypothetical, it is very attractive, in my opinion. It solves the problem raised by the location of Ebal and Gerizim in Gilgal. Otherwise, if one reads 4QJosh[a] frg. 1 immediately after 4:18, this would mean that the two mountains were located in the very middle of the river Jordan, as observed by van der Meer. Furthermore, the notion that the scribe responsible for 4QJoshua[a] would have read Deut 27:2–3 and 4–8 as two distinct, successive commands is entirely consistent with the interpretation proposed throughout §4 of this essay.

There is, however, a related issue that van der Meer unfortunately does not discuss, which is the witness of Josephus, *Ant.* 5.20. Josephus also recounts the building of an altar immediately after the crossing of the Jordan, an observation to which Ulrich and, above all, Rofé give considerable weight. Nevertheless, in a discussion of this problem, Christopher Begg observes that "the lack of any *Rückverweis* to Ant. 4.305–308 (// Deuteronomy 27), such as one does find in 5.68–70 (. . .) here in 5.20 leaves it questionable whether Josephus intends the above notice to be taken as even a partial, initial fulfillment of Moses' earlier injunctions."[93] He then concludes that the whole episode in Josephus cannot be taken to imply that "Josephus made use of a text of Joshua in which the MT 8:30–35 stood after chap. 4"; in his view, therefore, "references to the altar and sacrifices in 5.20 are nothing more than Josephus' *Ausmalung* of the stones of Josh 4:20."[94] If Begg is correct, therefore, Josephus's witness would not be at odds with the interpretation of 4QJoshua[a] that was recently proposed by van der Meer.

Regardless of whether the MT or the LXX is to be preferred (though the former is more likely here, in my opinion),[95] one can only agree with Auld that

---

92. Van der Meer, *Formation and Reformulation*, 511–14.

93. Christopher Begg, "The Cisjordanian Altar(s) and Their Associated Rites according to Josephus," *BZ* 41 (1997) 192–211, here 201–2.

94. Ibid., 202.

95. As noted by van der Meer (*Formation and Reformulation*, 519), the sequence in the LXX restores the syntactical and logical connection between Josh 8:29 and 9:1 that was broken in the

the different locations of this passage show that "it is in fact not original at all, but a latecomer looking for a suitable home."[96] The interpolation of Josh 8:30–35 MT (as well as Josh 9:2a–f LXX) at a very late stage would actually fit with a stage in the editing of the book of Joshua that in a recent contribution Rainer Albertz has proposed designating the "canonical alignment" (*die kanonische Anpassung*) of the book of Joshua. In this late revision of Joshua, the book became the first supplement to the canonical Torah and served to exemplify the faithful fulfillment of the Torah inside the promised land.[97] Contrary to the Torah itself, this postcanonical revision of Joshua was never meant to be received by the Samarian community: it is a distinctively Judean creation. For this reason, the altar specified in Deuteronomy 27 could now be located on Mount Ebal (Josh 8:30), in open criticism of the new Samarian sanctuary on Mount Gerizim. At some point, the reading "Mount Ebal" was eventually received, in Judah within the Torah itself, thus legitimizing a tradition of interpretation hostile to the Gerizim sanctuary that culminated with the campaigns of John Hyrcanus in 112–111 B.C.E.[98]

MT and is therefore suspect, from a text-critical perspective, of being harmonized vis-à-vis the MT. For a contrary view, however, see De Troyer, "Building the Altar and Reading the Law," 158–59.

96. Auld, "Reading Joshua after Kings," 110. See similarly Emanuel Tov, "Some Sequence Differences between the Masoretic Text and the Septuagint and Their Ramifications for Literary Criticism," in *The Greek and Hebrew Bible: Collected Essays on the Septuagint* (VTSup 72; Leiden: Brill, 1999) 411–18, here 413: "the different location of this section in the LXX implies that its placement had not yet been fixed."

97. See Rainer Albertz, "Die kanonische Anpassung des Buches Josua," in *Les rédactions du Pentateuque, de l'Hexateuque et de l'Ennéateuque* (ed. T. Römer and K. Schmid; BETL 203; Leuven: Peeters, 2007) 199–216. For a similar idea, see Ernst A. Knauf, "Towards an Archaeology of the Hexateuch," in *Abschied vom Jahwisten: Die Komposition des Hexateuch in der jüngsten Diskussion* (ed. Jan Christian Gertz, Konrad Schmid, and Markus Witte; BZAW 315; Berlin: de Gruyter, 2002) 275–94, here 279–80 and n. 23. According to a fitting formulation by Knauf, Joshua was devised by its final redactors as "*the first deutero-canonical book attached to a canon of scripture which, by that time, comprised only the Torah*" (emphasis added). This also corresponds to van der Meer's insights about the "nomistic" outlook characterizing Josh 8:30–35 (*Formation and Reformulation*, 504–11), albeit at a later stage in the composition and transmission of the biblical material than the stage he considers.

98. It is difficult to decide whether the introduction of the reading "Mount Ebal" in Deut 27:4 was contemporary with Josh 8:30–35 MT or still later. On one hand, because Josh 8:30–35 MT otherwise presents itself as a faithful execution of Moses' command in Deuteronomy 27, it seems logical to assume that the correction of Mount Gerizim to Mount Ebal in 27:4 MT goes back to the same stage. On the other hand, if the interpolation of Josh 8:30–35 MT postdates the redaction of the Pentateuch, as I have argued here, the two passages need not be placed on the same footing. At that point, the book of Joshua served as a kind of orthodox commentary on the Torah for Judeans exclusively, and the scribe who introduced Josh 8:30–35 could accept leaving the reading "Mount Gerizim" in Deut 27:4 as long as it was corrected in the corresponding account in Joshua.

6. Conclusion:
Samaria and the Reception of the Pentateuch as "Torah"

The various passages in Deuteronomy and Joshua describing a covenant ceremony in or near Shechem do not represent an ancient Northern tradition, as was usually assumed during the 20th century, but correspond to several attempts to acknowledge Samaria's religious and political role at the time of the Torah's composition. Initially, Joshua 24 formed the conclusion of a post-Priestly *Hexateuch* that extended from Genesis to Joshua. The location of this account in Shechem does not simply represent a concession made to a traditional cultic center in the heartland of Samaria. The intertextual connection with 1 Kings 12 also suggests that the Torah is presented here as the true foundation for a new national unity between Judeans and Samarians after the fall of the two kingdoms and the end of the monarchical state.

In the case of Deuteronomy 27, we have seen that the passage prescribing the building of a sanctuary on Mount Gerizim (vv. 4–8, together with vv. 11–13) was introduced in the context of the redaction of the Pentateuch. The decision to end the Torah with Moses' death outside the land created a specific problem for Samarian Yahwists because of the absence of another collection of scrolls that described Gerizim as the place chosen by Yahweh according to Deuteronomy 12 (unlike the choice of Mount Zion in the *Nebi'im*). In order to preserve the legitimacy of the Jerusalem temple, however, the mention of the Gerizim sanctuary in Deuteronomy 27 was deliberately presented as corresponding to the regulation found in the altar law of Exod 20:24–26 (see Deut 27:5–7) and *not* to the Deuteronomistic law of centralization in Deuteronomy 12. This device left the location of the altar commanded by the centralization law of Deuteronomy 12 unspecified, and the location could then be claimed by both communities.

Finally, the replacement of "Mount Gerizim" with "Mount Ebal" in a polemical, anti-Samarian perspective was a still later development that postdated the redaction of the Pentateuch and had its origins in Josh 8:30–35 MT // Josh 9:2a–f LXX. The case of 4QJosh^a probably represents a separate issue, although it also displays the problems raised by Deuteronomy 27 for the editors of Joshua.

On the whole, our analysis of the so-called Shechemite tradition implies that, even though the Jerusalem temple probably was the most likely place for the composition of the Torah during the second half of the Persian period, it was never written for only *one* community but was intended to be accepted by both Judeans *and* Samarians.

The "Publication" of Legal Texts in Ancient Judah

JOACHIM SCHAPER
University of Aberdeen

I. The Problem Addressed and the Methodology Used to Solve It

This essay explores the way that legal texts were published and put into force in postexilic Judah. In order to do so, I shall refer to certain procedures described in texts of the Hebrew Bible and to equivalent procedures in neighboring ancient Near Eastern cultures and in archaic and Classical Greece.[1] I hope to arrive at a more precise understanding of "publication" procedures described in texts of the Hebrew Bible. This analysis may, in turn, help reconstruct the "promulgation" of the Pentateuch: how this "promulgation" took place and the means by which the Pentateuch was declared binding upon its adherents. The significance of legal texts' *being fixed in writing* and the relation between the written texts and their oral proclamation will be at the center of attention.

Some of the key biblical texts providing the material for a reconstruction of the procedure of publishing legal(ly binding) texts in ancient Judah are Deut 1:5; 27:3, 8; Josh 8:32, 34; and Hab 2:2. I am not going to pay much attention to later texts, such as Nehemiah 8 and others. The focus here is on the *origins* of the practice of publishing legal texts, as reflected in texts such as Hab 2:2, rather than on the practices of Persian-period Judaism.

II. Biblical Passages

1. Deuteronomy 1:5 and 27:3, 8

The use of I באר Piel in Deut 1:5, 27:8, and Hab 2:2—the only three places in the entire Hebrew Bible in which it is used—presents exegetes with a

---

1. The importance of *reading* legal texts in ancient Judah has been discussed, with regard to its relevance to the formation of the Pentateuch, by James W. Watts, *Reading Law: The Rhetorical Shaping of the Pentateuch* (Biblical Seminar 59; Sheffield: Sheffield Academic Press, 1999). I, too, am interested in the oral delivery of texts but only as one part of the overall process of the publication of legal texts in ancient Israel. I shall try to reconstruct what elements constituted the actual process of the publication of these texts.

formidable problem. It is commonly assumed to mean "to clarify, to elucidate (a law)."[2] Georg Braulik and Norbert Lohfink have now come up with a new interpretation of the term in Deut 1:5, 27:8, which is partly based on an earlier article on Hab 2:2 by David T. Tsumura.[3] Drawing upon his use of an Akkadian analogy for the verb, they point out that, strictly speaking, Moses does not *promulgate* the Law in Deuteronomy: It is not announced here *for the first time*.[4] In Deuteronomy, no *new* laws are introduced. Rather, Deut 1:3 makes it clear that "Moses spoke to the people of Israel according to all that the LORD had given him in commandment to them" (RSV).[5] This refers back to the laws that are found in the Tetrateuch. If I באר Piel in Deut 1:5 is also understood to refer back to these earlier laws, it will most likely be seen as meaning "to clarify," "to interpret," "to expound"—as it commonly is. But, as Lohfink states, nowhere in the Pentateuch are earlier laws referred to as "this Torah."[6]

This is a centrally important point, a point the significance of which goes well beyond the quest for the correct understanding of the verb I באר Piel. By contrast, some scholars, taking "this Torah" as referring back to Num 36:13 and thus ultimately to Lev 26:46 and 27:34, claim that the verb can only mean "to interpret," "to expound." Thus Jean-Louis Ska concludes, with special reference to Num 36:13 and Deut 1:1–5: "La loi n'est plus proclamée, mais interprétée et expliquée. Avec le Deutéronome, le lecteur passe pour ainsi dire du 'texte' au 'commentaire'" ("The law is no longer proclaimed, but interpreted and explained. With Deuteronomy, the reader passes, so to speak, from the 'text' to the 'commentary'").[7] This kind of argument—also put forward many years ago by Joel Weingreen and, more recently, by the late Timo Veijola—has found an enthusiastic follower in Eckart Otto.[8] Otto recently devoted a whole

---

2. See *HALOT* 1.106.

3. David T. Tsumura, "Hab 2 2 in the Light of Akkadian Legal Practice," *ZAW* 94 (1982) 294–95.

4. See the important article by Georg Braulik and Norbert Lohfink, "Deuteronomium 1,5 באר את־התורה הזאת: 'er verlieh dieser Tora Rechtskraft,'" in *Textarbeit: Studien zu Texten und ihrer Rezeption aus dem Alten Testament und der Umwelt Israels: Festschrift für Peter Weimar zur Vollendung seines 60. Lebensjahres mit Beiträgen von Freunden, Schülern und Kollegen* (ed. Klaus Kiesow and Thomas Meurer; AOAT 294; Münster: Ugarit-Verlag, 2003) 34–51; reprinted in Norbert Lohfink, *Studien zum Deuteronomium und zur deuteronomistischen Literatur*, vol. 5 (SBAB 38; Stuttgart: Katholisches Bibelwerk, 2005) 233–51. Compare with idem, "Prolegomena zu einer Rechtshermeneutik des Pentateuchs," in *Studien zum Deuteronomium*, 181–231 (at 190).

5. Ibid., 191.

6. Ibid., 203.

7. Jean-Louis Ska, "La structure du Pentateuque dans sa forme canonique," *ZAW* 113 (2001) 331–52 (at 351).

8. Joel Weingreen, *From Bible to Mishnah: The Continuity of Tradition* (Manchester: Manchester University Press / New York: Holmes & Meier, 1976) 132–54. Compare with Timo Veijola, *Moses Erben: Studien zum Dekalog, zum Deuteronomismus und zum Schriftgelehrtentum* (BWANT 149; Stuttgart: Kohlhammer, 2000).

article to Deut 1:5 and its significance in the *fabula* (that is, the sequence of events created in the reader's mind in the process of perceiving a narrative text) of the Pentateuch,[9] claiming that Deuteronomy depicts Moses as the "first scribe."[10]

---

9. See N. Lohfink, "Zur Fabel des Deuteronomiums," *Studien zum Deuteronomium und zur deuteronomistischen Literatur*, vol. 4 (SBAB 31; Stuttgart: Katholisches Bibelwerk, 2000) 247–63, at p. 247: "Die Erzählfolge deckt sich also nicht mit der Ereignisfolge, der 'Fabel'" ("The narrative sequence is thus not identical with the [purported] sequence of [the] events [narrated], the 'fabula'").

10. Eckart Otto, "Mose, der erste Schriftgelehrte: Deuteronomium 1,5 in der Fabel des Pentateuch," in *L'Écrit et l'Esprit: Études d'histoire du texte et de théologie biblique en hommage à Adrian Schenker* (OBO 214; Fribourg: Academic Press / Göttingen: Vandenhoeck & Ruprecht, 2005) 273–84. In the title, Otto reiterates Ska, who called Moses "le plus autorisé de tous les commentateurs" ("the most authoritative of all the commentators"), and Veijola, who calls Moses "erster Ausleger der Tora" ("the first expositor of the Torah"; Ska, "Pentateuque," 351; Veijola, *Moses Erben*, 216). See also A. D. H. Mayes, who states that in Deut 1:5 Moses "is presented as a scribe" (*Deuteronomy* [NCB; Greenwood, SC: Attic, 1979] 116). It is important to realize that, apart from its significance for a reconstruction of the process of publishing legal texts, Deut 1:5 is also a key text in Pentateuch theory. This is why Otto, in the above-mentioned article, further develops points that he made in a monograph on the significance of Deuteronomy in Pentateuch/Hexateuch theory (Eckart Otto, *Das Deuteronomium im Pentateuch und Hexateuch: Studien zur Literaturgeschichte von Pentateuch und Hexateuch im Lichte des Deuteronomiumrahmens* [FAT 30; Tübingen: Mohr Siebeck, 2000]). He states: "Die Toraoffenbarung am Sinai wird mit Lev 26,46, die Gebotsoffenbarung insgesamt mit Num 36,13 als Kolophon abgeschlossen, das an Lev 26,46; 27,34 anknüpft und in Dtn 1,1–5 wieder aufgenommen wird" ("The revelation of the Torah at Sinai is concluded with Lev 26:46, the revelation of the commandment in its entirety with Num 36:13 as its colophon, which links up with Lev 26:46; 27:34 and is taken up again in Deut 1:1–5"; idem, "Mose, der erste Schriftgelehrte," 275). Otto's interpretation of I באר Piel and הַתּוֹרָה הַזֹּאת is central to his argument. Otto considers—correctly—that the relation between the law given on Sinai and the law given in the Plains of Moab is central to our understanding of the Pentateuch's *fabula*. On this basis, he attempts to show that this *fabula* depicts the law of Deuteronomy as an *interpretation* of the law of Sinai (Otto, "Mose, der erste Schriftgelehrte," 274–75, 282–83). He states: "Alles kommt in der Fabel des Pentateuch darauf an, daß die von Mose gegebene Toraauslegung (Dtn 1,5) identisch ist mit der von Gott gegebenen Tora" ("In the Pentateuch's *fabula*, everything depends on the interpretation of the Torah given by Moses [Deut 1:5] being identical with the Torah given by God"; ibid., 282). One is tempted to ask: What is the use of a Torah commentary that is *identical* with the Torah on which it builds? But quite apart from this consideration, why is his interpretation of I באר Piel and הַתּוֹרָה הַזֹּאת so important to Otto? It is because his Pentateuch theory as well as his reconstruction of the history of the priesthood hinges upon understanding "this Torah" in Deut 1:5 as referring *back* to the law revealed on Mt. Sinai (instead of being seen as cataphoric, that is, as pointing forward toward Deut 4:44): "Das Volk aber hat die Tora nicht anders als in ausgelegter Gestalt. Damit setzen sich die Schriftgelehrten als Autoren des Pentateuch ein Denkmal und begründen ihren eigenen Berufsstand" ("The people, however, do not have the Torah except in the form of its interpretation. Thus the scribes put up a monument to themselves as the authors of the Pentateuch and give a foundation to their profession"; ibid., 283). The ramifications of this understanding for the reconstruction of the history of priestly groups (*rival* priestly groups, Otto maintains) are important and are developed at some length in the above-mentioned monograph. More importantly still, Deut 1:5 functions as the cornerstone of Otto's reconstruction of the literary history of the Pentateuch. In order for this reconstruction to work, I באר Piel *must* refer back

Because Deut 1:5 has thus been invested with such massive potential importance (not just by Otto but, in similar though not identical ways, also by Ska,
Veijola, and others), I shall have to explore, among other things, whether an interpretation of I באר Piel as "to interpret," "to expound" and thus as referring
back to Num 36:13—the central claim of Ska's, Veijola's, and Otto's argument—will stand up to close scrutiny.

Here it is of paramount importance to realize that "this Torah" is mentioned
in Deut 1:5—that is, in the context of Deut 1:1–5. As Lohfink rightly points
out, Deut 1:1–5 is the introduction *to the first of four parts* of Deuteronomy, not
a "book title" for the whole of Deuteronomy.[11] Lohfink, following Kleinert in
exploring Deuteronomy's *Vierüberschriftensystem* ("system of four superscriptions"), understands this "system" to have been imposed upon Deuteronomy
by a late hand that gave the book its final structure.[12] It consists of Deut 1:1–
5, 4:44–5:1aα, 28:69–29:1a, and 33:1–2aα.[13] That "this Torah" in Deut 1:5 in
fact refers to what *follows*—that is, to Deuteronomy 5–28—becomes obvious
from the fact that Deut 4:44 (part of the second *Überschrift* in Deuteronomy,
which introduces Deuteronomy 5–28) takes up Deut 1:5 ("this Torah") by reversing the word order and saying: "And this is the Torah," and so on.[14] The
significance of I באר Piel, the key term of Deut 1:5, can therefore be properly
grasped only if it is interpreted as an operative part of this system, referring to
texts *within* Deuteronomy, not outside of it.[15]

Another point lends further support to Lohfink's thesis. The deictic reference to הַתּוֹרָה הַזֹּאת, "this Torah," described by Braulik, as a "formula" (*ge-
prägte Wendung*) appears very often in Deuteronomy in conjunction with the
verb כתב, "to write."[16] This indicates that "this Torah" in Deut 1:5 and the use
of the verb I באר Piel in this verse point right from the start to the process of

---

to Num 36:13 and thus be linked further back to the two colophons (Lev 26:46 and 27:34)—
otherwise Otto's concept of the Pentateuch redactor collapses.

11. See Norbert Lohfink, "Die An- und Absageformel in der hebräischen Bibel: Zum Hintergrund des deuteronomischen Vierüberschriftensystems," in *Biblical and Oriental Essays in Memory of
William L. Moran* (BibOr 48; Rome: Pontifical Biblical Institute, 2005) 49–77.

12. See P. Kleinert, *Das Deuteronomium und der Deuteronomiker: Untersuchungen zur alttestamentlichen Rechts- und Literaturgeschichte* (Bielefeld: Velhagen & Klasing, 1872) 166–68; and Lohfink,
"Die An- und Absageformel," 71, and passim. In the same vein, Watts rightly states that "Deuteronomy's laws present themselves as a self-contained, freestanding collection" (Watts, *Reading Law*,
72; Watts is also quoted in Lohfink, "Prolegomena," 203 n. 74).

13. Lohfink, "An- und Absageformel," 71.

14. Idem, "Prolegomena," 199.

15. See idem, "An- und Absageformel," passim.

16. Georg Braulik, *Die Mittel deuteronomischer Rhetorik* (AnBib 68; Rome: Pontifical Biblical Institute, 1978) 117. See my "Tora als Text im Deuteronomium," in *Was ist ein Text? Alttestamentliche,
ägyptologische, und altorientalistische Perspektiven* (ed. Ludwig Morenz and Stefan Schorch; BZAW 362;
Berlin: de Gruyter, 2006) 49–63.

the *textualization* of the Torah.[17] This process of textualization represents a central concern of Deuteronomy and is distinctive to Deuteronomy, as Jean-Pierre Sonnet has demonstrated.[18]

Far from supporting Ska, Veijola, and Otto's claim, therefore, a close reading of Deuteronomy that views Deut 1:5 in its proper context lends further support to Braulik and Lohfink's contention that באר in Deut 1:5 cannot refer back to Numbers and Leviticus but must refer to the "Torah" that *follows*.[19] It is best understood as cataphorically referring to the Torah of Deuteronomy 5–28 (or rather: of Deut 5:1–26:19) and thus *cannot* mean "to interpret" or "to expound."[20]

What *does* the verb mean, then, and do Braulik and Lohfink offer the correct solution? In order to answer this question, we must establish, first, whether (as they argue) *bâru(m)* in the D stem, that is, *burru*, is indeed cognate with the Hebrew term I באר Piel; and second, should this be the case, whether the use of *burru* in Akkadian material can help us to understand the meaning of the Hebrew term.

Regarding the first point, the link between *bâru(m)* and Hebrew I באר has recently been called into question.[21] The claim is that the hollow root *$*b\bar{u}r$ that underlies *bâru(m)* is unlikely to be linked to Hebrew באר; no further reasons are given. However, both the Akkadian and the Hebrew root belong to the same type, as Lohfink, following Wolfram von Soden, rightly points out.[22] There is another objection that might be raised against the theory of a link between *bâru(m)* and באר: the vast majority of ANE texts using *bâru(m)* and *burru* are of Old Babylonian origin, and only a few instances are found in Neo-Assyrian literature. However, this objection is not convincing. Rather, the most likely explanation is that the use of the term in legal practice was so well established and so prominent in the relevant Babylonian literature that it was assimilated into Hebrew during the Babylonian Exile by exiled Judean scholars, who then made use of it when they gave Deuteronomy its final shape.[23]

---

17. See ibid.

18. See Jean-Pierre Sonnet, *The Book within the Book: Writing in Deuteronomy* (Biblical Interpretation Series 14; Leiden: Brill, 1997).

19. On Ska, Veijola, and Otto's claim, see above, nn. 7, 8, and 10.

20. See my "Tora als Text." Deut 1:5 points forward to Deut 4:44. The latter forms, together with Deut 27:3, 8, an inclusio around the "Torah" that is being referred to (Deut 5:1–26:19).

21. Otto, "Mose, der erste Schriftgelehrte," 279.

22. *AHw*, 108. Lohfink states: "Das Phonem 'Länge' ist in diesem Fall im Akkadischen als Länge, im Hebräischen als Stimmabsatz realisiert" ("The phoneme 'length' is realized in this case as [vowel-] length in Akkadian and as the glottal stop in Hebrew"; Lohfink, "Prolegomena," 203 n. 77).

23. See Arnold F. Walther, *Das altbabylonische Gerichtswesen* (Leipziger Semitistische Studien 6/4–6; Leipzig: Hinrichs, 1917; repr. New York: Johnson Reprint, 1968) 225–27.

Regarding the second point, according to *AHw*, Akkadian *bâru(m)* III in the D stem (*burru*) means "make clear, to convict (of)," "render precisely," "establish precisely," "convict someone of something," "prove someone to be something," "confirm to someone," and so on.[24] *CAD* B refers to the verb under *bâru* A, §3a: "to establish the true legal situation (ownership, amounts, liability, etc.) by a legal procedure involving an oath."[25] The use of the term in ancient Near Eastern literature that is most relevant to our understanding of Deut 1:5 is found in an ancient Babylonian text that addresses the confirmation of written testimonies with and without witnesses: "*inūma [tuppum]* . . . *innezbu balum šībū ina nīš ilim ú-bi-ir-ru iššaṭir inanna šībū ina nīš ilim li-bi-ir-ru-šu*, when the written testimony was made out, it was written without witnesses having confirmed it by oath, now let witnesses under oath [also] confirm it."[26] As Tsumura rightly points out with regard to this passage, the use of *burru* here refers to "the confirmation of a legal action after the testimony is written down."[27]

Given the overall *fabula* of Deuteronomy, this ties in very well with the fact that I באר Piel in Deut 1:5 and 27:8 refers to what the Israelites are supposed to do with "this Torah" (התורה הזאת)—the written (!) law (cf. Deut 27:3, 8). These two verses, referring to Deut 4:44 and ultimately Deut 1:5, require the Israelites to inscribe the Torah (that is, Deut 5:1–26:19) on the stones at the crossing of the Jordan and on Mount Ebal. The term I באר Piel is used again in Deut 27:8: וְכָתַבְתָּ עַל־הָאֲבָנִים אֶת־כָּל־דִּבְרֵי הַתּוֹרָה הַזֹּאת בַּאֵר הֵיטֵב. A translation along the lines of *burru*, "to confirm (a written testimony)," both here and in Deut 1:5, makes perfect sense. In Babylonian legal practice, it was precisely this confirmation that put the legal document in force. Therefore, there is really not even a conceptual shift from the meaning of the Akkadian term to the meaning of the Hebrew: both signify confirmation—*confirmation that puts the document in question in force*. This becomes obvious only when the Hebrew term is seen in its overall context within Deuteronomy, and especially within the *Vierüberschriftensystem*, as I have demonstrated here.

These considerations confirm the thesis of Braulik and Lohfink, who translate Deut 1:5 as follows: "Moses began '*to give legal force to this Torah.*'"[28] They render Deut 27:8: "Inscribe onto the stones all decrees of this Torah, thus cor-

---

24. *AHw*, 108–9.

25. *CAD* B 127–30.

26. Transliteration and translation from *CAD* B 129. The cuneiform text is available in Arno Poebel, ed., *Historical and Grammatical Texts* (Publications of the Babylonian Section 5; Philadelphia: University Museum, 1914) pl. 42 (text 100, col. 1, lines 32 and 34).

27. Tsumura, "Hab 2 2," 294.

28. Braulik and Lohfink, "Deuteronomium 1,5," 247: "Mose begann damit, '*dieser Weisung Rechtskraft zu verleihen.*'"

rectly putting them in force."[29] They stress that this putting in force of the *Torah* is enacted "through its public reading, through binding declarations by God and by Israel, through an oath ritual, the writing down of the law and its deposition next to the Ark, through institutionalizing the passing on of the covenant and through decrees concerning the production of an inscription after the crossing of the Jordan."[30]

This is an important observation, because it makes it clear that, according to the final text of Deuteronomy, there are a number of constitutive elements in the process of putting the Torah in force. It seems advisable to search for other examples of these legal practices in the Hebrew Bible. The first conclusion with regard to the publication of legal texts as envisaged in Deuteronomy is therefore that, for the law in question to be put in force, it needed to be published in two ways: through writing it down *and* through reading it aloud publicly. Other texts in the Hebrew Bible that depict these procedures confirm this analysis.

2. Habakkuk 2:2

In the Hebrew Bible, there is one more text, apart from the two Deuteronomic texts just discussed, that employs the term I באר Piel. At issue, as mentioned above, is Hab 2:2: וַיַּעֲנֵנִי יהוה וַיֹּאמֶר כְּתוֹב חָזוֹן וּבָאֵר עַל־הַלֻּחוֹת לְמַעַן יָרוּץ קוֹרֵא בוֹ. The NJPSV translation is a typical example of the traditional understanding of the verse:

> The LORD answered me and said:
> Write the prophecy down,
> Inscribe it clearly on tablets,
> *So that it can be read easily.* (emphasis added)

Hab 2:2 depicts YHWH as ordering that an oracle that the prophet has received from him be written up and officially proclaimed. As I have discussed elsewhere, the final clause should be translated: "so that a *(town-)crier* may run

---

29. Ibid., 249: "Graviere auf die Steine alle Bestimmungen dieser Tora, ihnen so auf korrekte Weise Rechtskraft verleihend." On the meaning of היטב, see ibid. See also my "Living Word Engraved in Stone: The Interrelationship of the Oral and the Written and the Culture of Memory in the Books of Deuteronomy and Joshua," in *Memory in the Bible and Antiquity* (ed. Stephen Barton, Loren Stuckenbruck, and Benjamin Wold; WUNT 212; Tübingen: Mohr Siebeck, 2007) 9–23.

30. Braulik and Lohfink, "Deuteronomium 1,5," 247: "Mose begann damit, 'dieser Weisung Rechtskraft zu verleihen'—und dies, so weiß der Leser, wenn er am Ende des Buches angekommen ist, durch ihren öffentlichen Vortrag, durch bindende Erklärungen Gottes und Israels, durch ein Schwurritual, durch ihre Niederschrift und Deponierung bei der Lade, durch Institutionalisierung der Bundesweitergabe und durch Verfügungen über die Herstellung einer Inschrift nach der Überschreitung des Jordan."

with it"—in order to proclaim the oracle publicly. The participle קוֹרֵא is not in conjunction with בְּ, but stands here as an absolute, as in וּקְרָאתֶם בְּעֶצֶם הַיּוֹם הַזֶּה ("And you shall make proclamation on that very day,"[31] Lev 23:21). The participle קוֹרֵא is the subject, and יָרוּץ is linked with בְּ (here used to refer to the instrument of the action; for examples, see *HALOT* 1.105).[32] The word קוֹרֵא is thus understood as referring to a "town-crier" who publicly reads or announces the text written on the tablets.

If this interpretation is correct, then the aim is to bring the oracle into the public domain by publishing it through having it read publicly by a קוֹרֵא, literally a "reader" or "announcer." My interpretation is supported by the fact that town-criers and heralds—the Akkadian term for them is *nāgiru(m)*—are copiously documented in Mesopotamian literature.[33] So Hab 2:2 provides the element of oral proclamation but also, as another constitutive element of the process of proclamation (or, indeed, promulgation), the writing down of the oracle. However, the term *nāgiru(m)* also denotes that a legal witness is confirming a protocol (as described in Babylonian court documents; for example, in CT 8 40a:2: *na-gi-rum ša Bābilim*).[34] This adds yet another interesting dimension to the significance of the קוֹרֵא in Hab 2:2 and underlines the importance of appreciating the legal "flavor" of Hab 2:2.

Braulik and Lohfink do not discuss the use of I בָאר Piel in Habakkuk. Tsumura in his short note suggests that the verse be translated as follows: "Write and confirm the vision on tablets!"[35] Now as far as the syntax is concerned, an interesting question arises. Wilhelm Rudolph pointed out, in his commentary on Habakkuk, that עַל־הַלֻּחוֹת should be read in conjunction with כְּתוֹב and not with וּבָאֵר. The latter should be interpreted as an interjection interrupting the flow of the sentence, an interjection devised in order to emphasize the importance of בָאר. But Rudolph accepted the usual understanding of בָאר as "to write clearly" and translated: "schreibe die Offenbarung auf, / und zwar deut-

---

31. Compare the KJV and the RSV.

32. See my "Exilic and Post-Exilic Prophecy and the Orality/Literacy Problem," *VT* 55 (2005) 324–42.

33. I thank Karel van der Toorn for drawing my attention to this fact. See *CAD* N/1 116–17.

34. See Walther, *Das altbabylonische Gerichtswesen*, 158; and *CAD* N/1 116.

35. See Tsumura, "Hab 2 2," 294–95. Tsumura can propose this translation because, in his analysis of the syntax, he follows Rudolph's commentary and states: "As Rudolph rightly noted, though for a different reason, עַל־הלחות should be connected directly with כתוב, rather than with באר. Here we propose to recognize an A×B pattern, in which a compound unit כתוב ובאר 'write and confirm' [A&B] is interrupted, as a literary device, by the insertion of חזון (×). Since חזון is the object of כתוב, as far as the surface structure is concerned, the same object could have been understood as having been ellipsized after the second verb באר, thus, as the underlying structure, כתוב חזון ובאר (חזון) [A×&B×]. However, on a contextual basis, על־הלחות should be directly connected with כתוב, especially since באר is to be taken as 'to confirm,' namely as the second stage of the legal procedure."

lich, auf die Tafeln" ("write down the revelation, /—and clearly, to be sure!—on the tablets").[36]

However, according to Braulik and Lohfink's interpretation of the term's meaning in Deuteronomy, and taking seriously Rudolph's insight into the verse's syntax, the clause כְּתוֹב חָזוֹן וּבָאֵר עַל־הַלֻּחוֹת should be understood as follows: "*Write down [the] vision—and put [it] in force!—[write it down] on the tablets, so that a [town-]crier may run with it.*" The definite article has been added *ad sensum* because חָזוֹן refers to the vision in Habakkuk 1, and וּבָאֵר is an interjection that emphasizes the importance of having the written document confirmed (the document to which the word must refer in the context of the sentence). This is why the definite direct object has been added in the translation. By having the vision confirmed, it is put in force; the scarlet thread is taken up again with עַל־הַלֻּחוֹת. What could this actually mean in the given context? If the interpretation of בָּאֵר in a legal sense is correct, how does this fit in with the Habakkuk passage? A closer look at the whole of the vision answers this question. God is depicted as saying,

> For there is yet a prophecy for a set term,
> A truthful *witness* for a time that will come.
> Even if it tarries, wait for it still;
> For it will surely come, without delay. (Hab 2:3)[37]

The aim of the writing down is to make the vision public knowledge and to put it in force as something like a legal witness against the detractors and the defiant. As noted above, the NJPSV convincingly renders יָפֵחַ, on the basis of Ugaritic evidence, as "witness." This is another indication of the legal "feel" of the oracle's wording.

III. Greek and Ancient Near Eastern Material

To summarize what has been argued so far: it seems likely that in Hab 2:2, as in Deut 1:5 and 27:3, 8, we have traces of a legal procedure of putting a law or another publicly relevant document in force. Tsumura, in his interpretation of Hab 2:2, thinks of a two-part process, consisting of the writing down of the document and its confirmation through the act of באר. He does not say what this act entails.[38] I think the process is more complex than Tsumura assumes. The document that is supposed to be put in force needs to exist in written

---

36. Wilhelm Rudolph, *Micha – Nahum – Habakuk – Zephanja: Mit einer Zeittafel von Alfred Jepsen* (KAT 13/3; Gütersloh: Mohn, 1975) 211.

37. Translation from NJPSV, emphasis added.

38. Tsumura states that באר indicates confirmation by witnesses but is unable to say how this confirmation was enacted (Tsumura, "Hab 2 2," 295).

form, a public inscription of the text needs to produced, and it needs to be read publicly ("read out" or "announced"—the Hebrew term קרא is ambiguous). Hab 2:2 implies that the act of באר is enacted through producing the public inscription *and* through reading it aloud or announcing it.

This is essentially the same process as envisaged by Deuteronomy and Joshua. That the same process informs two very different biblical texts from more or less the same period points to an actual practice involving the "publication" of legal texts. This interpretation of the evidence is further supported by the fact that we have archaeological and textual evidence from archaic and Classical Greece as well as from Mesopotamia that proves the existence of inscriptions carrying legal texts and, indeed, prophetic texts with legal implications.[39] The Habakkuk passage, for example, and the way it was supposed to be fixed in writing are not unlike certain Neo-Assyrian prophecies and the way they were put in writing and displayed in the Temple of Aššur in the city of Assur, Ešarra. The oracle ascribed to Aššur (SAA 9 3.3: ii 26–32) is a good example:

> This is the [oracle of] well-being (placed) before the Image.
> This covenant tablet of Assur enters the king's presence on a cushion.
> Fragrant oil is sprinkled, sacrifices are made, incense is burnt, and
>   they read it out in the king's presence.[40]

In the Greek world, the public inscriptions of the *polis* of Teos provide a fine example of the relation between the written and the oral in the publication of legal texts. As Rosalind Thomas points out, "The city of Teos actually propagated a law in the form of a curse and the officials who were to read out the inscription were effectively pronouncing a public curse on offenders."[41] This is of course strikingly reminiscent of passages such as Deuteronomy 27 and Joshua 8. These examples from Greece and Mesopotamia demonstrate that the procedure I have tried to reconstruct on the basis of biblical texts has historical parallels in other ancient cultures. This reinforces the conclusion that the procedure described in the biblical texts discussed here is not a literary fiction but mirrors an actual practice.

---

39. The earliest known Greek written law inscribed in stone is from Dreros on Crete and dates back to 650–600 B.C.E. A particularly well-known example is the so-called Great Code of Gortyn, produced in the middle of the 5th century. On the Code, see the essay by Gary N. Knoppers and Paul B. Harvey in this volume (pp. 105–141).

40. Translation from Simo Parpola, ed., *Assyrian Prophecies* (SAA 9; Helsinki: Helsinki University Press, 1997) 24–25 (bracketed insertions mine).

41. Rosalind Thomas, *Literacy and Orality in Ancient Greece* (Key Themes in Ancient History; Cambridge: Cambridge University Press, 1992) 71.

IV. Conclusion

Analysis of these passages strongly suggests the Judahite practice of "publishing" legal (and other important) texts. Braulik and Lohfink's understanding of באר is correct, as opposed to theories put forward by Ska, Veijola, and Otto.[42] With regard to the central object of the present essay, a number of conclusions can be drawn. The Hebrew verb באר functions technically to denote one part of the process of "publishing" and confirming legal texts. The "publication" of legal texts in ancient Judah involved a process that consisted of oral and written elements. Central to this process was the public inscription that documented the legal text. The perfect example is found in Joshua 8. According to the logic of this narrative in the Deuteronomistic History, the Torah is put in force only when it is finally inscribed on Mt. Ebal *and* read publicly.[43] The same is true, of course, of Hab 2:2: the two acts of inscribing the text on the tablets and reading them aloud publicly constitute, *in conjunction*, the putting into force of the text.

The introduction of this practice may have been the result of a cultural impulse received in the Babylonian Exile, as the relation between Hebrew באר Piel and Akkadian *bâru(m)* III and between the institutions of the *nāgiru(m)* and the קוֹרֵא seem to suggest. From this perspective, Deuteronomy in its final form may well be the key to understanding the "promulgation" of the Pentateuch. The process of publishing legal texts and putting them in force that I have reconstructed on the basis of Deut 1:5, 27:8, and Hab 2:2 may have been the process by means of which the Pentateuch was "promulgated" or, more precisely, legally put into force.

Practices of this sort were also introduced at more or less the same time in archaic Greece. The increasing importance of fixing laws in writing was the result of a massive transition in the conceptualization of law and in its practice. In classics, this phenomenon has been explored to a considerable degree. Old Testament studies is only just beginning to recognize both the fundamental importance of this transition and the extent to which it is bound up with technological developments, such as the rise of the practice of writing.[44] The increasing importance of writing in the publication of legal material provides a focus of special interest. As Rosalind Thomas points out:

---

42. Because באר is used cataphorically, and because "this Torah" refers to Deut 5:1–26:19, neither is Moses "the first scribe," nor does Otto's evaluation of the significance of Deut 1:5 in the context of the work of the "Pentateuch redactor" stand up to scrutiny.

43. See Josh 8:32, 34.

44. See my "Theology of Writing: Deuteronomy, the Oral and the Written, and God as Scribe," in *Anthropology and Biblical Studies: Avenues of Research* (ed. Louise Lawrence and Mario Aguilar; Leiden: Deo, 2004) 97–119; and idem, "Exilic and Post-Exilic Prophecy and the Orality/Literacy Problem."

The problem is that most tend to regard the effects of writing something down as obvious (e.g., justice, or stability), not seeing it in its social and political context. Yet the effect of written law depends rather
heavily on the legal and political system it is part of, as well as contemporary attitudes to writing. We need to ask who decided which laws to
write down, who enforced them, and what role writing could possibly
have in this very earliest stage of public documents.[45]

Rosalind Thomas is right. Her analysis makes it possible to come a bit closer to
understanding the function of law in postexilic Judah and the place of the
Pentateuch in Judahite society.

---

45. Thomas, *Literacy and Orality*, 68.

The Samaritans and Their Pentateuch

REINHARD PUMMER
University of Ottawa

One hundred forty years ago, Abraham Geiger wrote: "May scholars again pay serious attention to the neglected Samaritans!"[1] It took many years after Geiger's plea before his wish was realized. And even when it was, attention to the Samaritans did not reach the wider community of researchers but was largely confined to a few "Samaritanologists." In the recent past, however, this has changed somewhat, and references to matters Samaritan are included in works on the Bible—Old and New Testament alike—and on the history of Palestine.[2] Nevertheless, difficulties with the material remain. The main reason is that the extant Samaritan writings are late, and many have neither been edited critically nor translated into a European language. The one area in which research has intensified the most is the Samaritan Pentateuch (SP in the following). Although a satisfactory critical edition is still lacking,[3] there are now a growing number of works that are devoted to the scholarly study of various aspects of the SP, ranging from paleography to the recitation of the Torah. The greatest impetus comes, of course, from the discovery and study of the Dead

---

1. Abraham Geiger, "Neuere Mittheilungen über die Samaritaner IV," *ZDMG* 19 (1865) 614–15 (original: "Möge die Aufmerksamkeit der Gelehrten den vernachlässigten Samaritanern . . . wieder ernstlich zugewendet werden!").

2. This can be seen when perusing the latest edition of *A Bibliography of the Samaritans* by Alan David Crown and Reinhard Pummer (ATLA Bibliography 51; Lanham, MD: Scarecrow, 2005).

3. The well-known and much-used edition by August von Gall (*Der Hebräische Pentateuch der Samaritaner* [Giessen: Alfred Töpelmann, 1918]) presents an eclectic text. Although it is based on a large number of manuscripts, in many cases von Gall chose the readings that agreed with the Masoretic Text. He also favored readings with *scriptio defectiva* over readings with *scriptio plena*, even in cases in which the majority of the manuscripts have the latter (see the explanation for his editorial principles on pp. lxviii–lxix of his edition). A diplomatic edition of one of the most important manuscripts from 1204 was published by Abraham Tal (*The Samaritan Pentateuch Edited according to MS 6 [C] of the Shekhem Synagogue* [Texts and Studies in the Hebrew Language and Related Subjects 8; Tel Aviv University: Chaim Rosenberg School of Jewish Studies, 1994] Hebrew). Samaritan authors published a parallel edition of the SP and the Masoretic Text (Abraham Nur Tsedaka and Ratson Tsedaka, *Jewish Version / Samaritan Version of the Pentateuch with Particular Stress on the Differences between Both Texts* [Tel Aviv and Holon, 1964–65]). It is not a critical edition but is useful for a first orientation.

Sea Scrolls. They have enabled us to pinpoint the time and manner of the origin of the specifically Samaritan readings in the Pentateuch. However, they have not answered the question how to explain effectively the fact that Samaritans and Jews possess essentially the same text of the Pentateuch. In the following, I will attempt to address this question against the background of what is now known about the origin of the Samaritans and the relationship between Southern and Northern Yahwists after the Assyrian conquests of the 8th century B.C.E.

1. Terminology

In the past, all inhabitants of the city and region of Samaria were simply called "Samaritans." Research into the origin of the Samaritans, however, has achieved greater awareness of the differences in the population of Samaria during the history of the region. Scholars realized that not all inhabitants were Samaritans in the strict sense of the term but that the population consisted of a variety of ethnic and religious groups. In 1971, Hans Gerhard Kippenberg, in his book *Garizim und Synagoge*, introduced the distinction between "Samarians" on the one hand and "Samaritans" on the other. He called the inhabitants of the political district *Samarier*, "Samarians" and the followers (*Anhänger*) of the Gerizim cult *Samaritaner*, "Samaritans."[4] Since then, more and more authors have adopted this distinction, although old habits die hard.

The consequences of an imprecise terminology are by now well known. Applying the name *Samaritans* to all inhabitants of Samaria after the Assyrian defeat of the Northern Kingdom—first documented in Josephus and later in rabbinic and Christian writings—suggests that the followers of the Gerizim cult are descendants of the Assyrian settlers and/or the mixed population described in 2 Kgs 17:24–41. On the basis of this understanding, the adversaries of the returnees from Babylonia in Ezra–Nehemiah were then also seen in this light—that is, as the descendants of semipagans. Both of these assumptions were invalidated by modern research.

The Samaritan community see themselves as the true Israelites. Unlike the Jews with regard to Judea, the Samaritans never felt a special bond with the district or the city of Samaria.[5] They therefore reject the designation שמרונים (*šōměrônîm*), "Samarians," and call themselves שמרים (pronounced by the Sa-

---

4. Hans Gerhard Kippenberg, *Garizim und Synagoge: Traditionsgeschichtliche Untersuchungen zur samaritanischen Religion der aramäischen Periode* (Religionsgeschichtliche Versuche und Vorarbeiten 30; Berlin: de Gruyter, 1971) 34. Kippenberg draws attention to an earlier attempt to distinguish between these two groups by Gerard van Groningen, *First Century Gnosticism: Its Origin and Motifs* (Leiden: Brill, 1967) 135–36.

5. Rightly pointed out by Kippenberg, *Garizim und Synagoge*, 34.

maritans *šāmīrĕm*), that is, "guardians" of the Torah or of the land of Israel or of both, although it is not certain when they first used this term. In any case, it was already in use as early as Origen (ca. 185–ca. 254 C.E.).[6] In two inscriptions, found on Delos and dated on the basis of orthography and paleography to ca. 250–175 B.C.E. and ca. 150–50 B.C.E., respectively,[7] they call themselves "Israelites [on Delos] who make offerings to hallowed, consecrated *Argarizein*."[8] In their medieval chronicles and their correspondence with European scholars, the Samaritans' self-designation is "Israelite Samaritans" (בני ישראל השמרים).[9]

The recent discovery of Persian-period remains on Mount Gerizim, probably belonging to a temple built in the mid-5th century B.C.E., led Oded Lipschits to suggest that the term *Samaritans* should be used "for the population of the area following the foundation of the temple at a much earlier period than we heretofore thought."[10] However, given the fact that the Samaritans rejected Jerusalem and worked out their particular theology only at a much later time, the YHWH-worshiping Samarians in the 5th century B.C.E. should still be called "proto-Samaritans," that is, YHWH worshipers of Samaria who still considered Jerusalem a legitimate place of worship in addition to Mount Gerizim.

2. The Samaritan Pentateuch

It is well known that, for the Samaritans, "Scripture" means the Pentateuch.[11] Although there is a Samaritan *Book of Joshua*, it is not the same as the

---

6. See my *Early Christian Authors on Samaritans and Samaritanism: Texts, Translations and Commentary* (TSAJ 92; Tübingen: Mohr Siebeck, 2002) 7–8.

7. L. Michael White thinks they date to around 165 B.C.E.: *The Social Origins of Christian Architecture; Volume II: Texts and Monuments for the Christian Domus Ecclesiae in Its Environment* (HTS 42; Valley Forge, PA: Trinity Press International, 1992) 341.

8. See my "Samaritan Synagogues and Jewish Synagogues: Similarities and Differences," in *Jews, Christians, and Polytheists in the Ancient Synagogue: Cultural Interaction during the Greco-Roman Period* (ed. Stephen Fine; London: Routledge, 1999) 121.

9. For a discussion of the term, see my *Early Christian Authors*, 7 with n. 32.

10. Oded Lipschits, "Achaemenid Imperial Policy, Settlement Processes in Palestine, and the Status of Jerusalem in the Middle of the Fifth Century B.C.E.," in *Judah and the Judeans in the Persian Period* (ed. Oded Lipschits and Manfred Oeming; Winona Lake, IN: Eisenbrauns, 2006) 31 n. 38.

11. That the Samaritans recognize only the Pentateuch as Scripture was already noted by early Christian authors: Origen (ca. 185–ca. 254), *Comm. Jo.*13.26.154 (for the texts and translations, see my *Early Christian Authors*, 69–70); Cyril of Jerusalem (ca. 315–ca. 386), *Catech.* 18.13 (ibid., 118 and 120); Epiphanius of Salamis (ca. 315–403), *Anaceph. 19*.1 (ibid., 145–46); *Pan.* 9.2.1 (ibid., 149 and 156); 9.5.4 (ibid., 151 and 159); *De gemm.* 88.19 (ibid., 173 and 179); Anastasius Sinaita (ca. 630–ca. 700), *Quaest.* 45 (ibid., 370 and 371), quoting Epiphanius of Salamis. The Samaritan liturgical poet Amram Dare, who lived in the 3rd/4th century, wrote: "There is no god besides our Lord, no scripture like the Torah, no true prophet like Moses" (Arthur E. Cowley, *Samaritan Liturgy* [Oxford: Clarendon, 1909] 38, lines 27–28; Ze᾿ev Ben-Ḥayyim, *The Literary and Oral Tradition of Hebrew and Aramaic amongst the Samaritans, 3/2: The Recitation of Prayers and Hymns* [Jerusalem: Academy of

biblical book by the same name and does not have the same standing as the Pentateuch. The Samaritan *Book of Joshua* exists in an Arabic and a Hebrew version. The core of the Arabic version is derived from a collection of Hebrew, or rather, Aramaic sources.[12] The book was edited, with a Latin translation and a commentary, by Theodoor Willem Jan Juynboll in 1848; an English translation was published by Oliver Turnbull Crane in 1890.[13] In its present form, the book begins with the investiture of Joshua, recounts the Balaam story (Numbers 22–24), the war against the Midianites (Numbers 31), the death of Moses (Deuteronomy 34), and ends with the history of the Samaritan leader of the 3rd/4th century C.E., Baba Rabba.[14] The work was composed no later than the beginning of the 14th century. The Hebrew Samaritan *Book of Joshua* was published, with a German translation, by Moses Gaster in 1908.[15] According to him, this was the original *Book of Joshua*. It begins with the death of Moses and the investiture of Joshua and ends in the 13th year of the entry of the Israelites into Canaan, when Abisha, the great-grandson of Aaron, wrote the most revered Samaritan Torah scroll on Mount Gerizim, at the entrance of the tent of meeting. Gaster's contention was contested by a number of scholars,[16] who claimed that the book was written by the eminent Samaritan author, scribe, and high priest Jacob ben Aaron (1841–1916) in 1902 and that Jacob used for his composition the Arabic *Book of Joshua*, the chronicle of Abū 'l-Fatḥ, and the Masoretic Text of the book of Joshua.[17] Nevertheless, it may be assumed that the Samaritans did possess a *Book of Joshua* at an early period, albeit in a different

the Hebrew Language, 1967] 42, lines 17–19 [Hebrew]). For a German translation, see Hans G. Kippenberg, "Ein Gebetbuch für den samaritanischen Synagogengottesdienst aus dem 2. Jh. n. Chr.," *ZDPV* 85 (1969) 78.

12. See the discussion in Maurice Baillet, "Samaritains," *DBSup* 11.915–16.

13. Theodoor Willem Jan Juynboll, *Chronicon Samaritanum, Arabice conscriptum, cui titulus est Liber Josuae* (Leiden: Luchtmans, 1848); Oliver Turnbull Crane, *The Samaritan Chronicle or the Book of Joshua, the Son of Nun* (New York: Alden, 1890). The translation, with some modifications, was reprinted in Robert T. Anderson and Terry Giles, *Tradition Kept: The Literature of the Samaritans* (Peabody, MA: Hendrickson, 2005) 67–142.

14. For the bibliographical references, see Paul Stenhouse, "Samaritan Chronicles," in *The Samaritans* (ed. Alan D. Crown; Tübingen: Mohr Siebeck, 1989) 219–20.

15. Moses Gaster, "Das Buch Josua in hebräisch-samaritanischer Rezension: Entdeckt und zum ersten Male herausgegeben," *ZDMG* 62 (1908); also reprinted separately (Leipzig, 1908).

16. See especially David Yellin, "Book of Joshua or Chronicle?" *Jerusalem* 6 (1903) 203–5 [Hebrew]; idem, "A Samaritan Book of Joshua in Hebrew," *Jerusalem* 6 (1903) 138–55 [Hebrew]; Paul Kahle, "Zum hebräischen Buch der Samaritaner," *ZDMG* 62 (1908) 550–51; Abraham S. Yahuda, "Über die Unechtheit des Samaritanischen Josuabuches," *SPAW* 39 (1908) 887–914; idem, "Zum samaritanischen Josua: Eine Erklärung," *ZDMG* 62 (1908) 754. See also entry 1733 in Crown and Pummer, *A Bibliography of the Samaritans*.

17. See the discussion in Baillet, "Samaritains," 922–26; and the bibliography in Stenhouse, "Samaritan Chronicles," 220.

form from the present versions.[18] The position and role of Joshua and Mount Gerizim in the "Jewish" book of Joshua would certainly have appealed to the Samaritans.[19]

For a long time now it has been claimed that there are 6,000 differences between the SP and the Masoretic Text (in the following, MT).[20] This number goes back to a list in appendix 4 (pp. 19–34) in the sixth volume of the London Polyglot, published in 1657. The list was drawn up by Brian Walton, Edmund Castell, and John Lightfoot.[21] However, this number should finally be discarded for several reasons. First of all, it is based on one manuscript only, which was acquired by Pietro della Valle in 1616,[22] and was first published, with numerous mistakes, in the Paris Polyglot in 1629, and republished, albeit with corrections, in the London Polyglot (1657). Second, most of the differences concern *scriptio plena* and *scriptio defectiva*. But it is now clear that Samaritan scribes follow no specific norm in this regard. The many manuscripts that have come to the attention of scholars since the days of the Paris and London Polyglots show that individual scribes exercised great freedom in copying the

---

18. Alan D. Crown believes that the Samaritan Hebrew *Book of Joshua* was extant "before the end of the second century A.D." ("The Date and Authenticity of the Samaritan Hebrew Book of Joshua as Seen in Its Territorial Allotments," *PEQ* 96 [1964] 97). Iain Ruairidh Mac Mhanainn Bóid dates the Samaritan *Book of Joshua* to the time of Baba Rabbah but considers it possible that it goes back to the 2nd century C.E.; he believes that the Samaritan text is "a very developed form of a short text that is more primitive in its recensional origin than MT/LXX" ("The Transmission of the Samaritan Joshua–Judges," *Dutch Studies* 6 [2004] 22 and 23).

19. See József Zsengellér, "Canon and the Samaritans," in *Canonization and Decanonization: Papers Presented to the International Conference of the Leiden Institute for the Study of Religions (LISOR), Held at Leiden, 9–10 January 1997* (ed. Arie van der Kooij and Karel van der Toorn; SHR 82; Leiden: Brill, 1998) 166–67.

20. For a recent statement, see, for instance, Esther and Hanan Eshel, "Dating the Samaritan Pentateuch's Compilation in Light of the Qumran Biblical Scrolls," in *Emanuel: Studies in Hebrew Bible, Septuagint, and Dead Sea Scrolls in Honor of Emanuel Tov* (ed. Shalom M. Paul et al.; VTSup 94; Leiden: Brill, 2003) 215.

21. Another lengthy list is by Julius Heinrich Petermann in his work *Versuch einer hebräischen Formenlehre nach der Aussprache der heutigen Samaritaner nebst einer darnach gebildeten Transscription der Genesis und einer Beilage enthaltend die von dem recipirten Texte des Pentateuchs abweichenden Lesarten der Samaritaner* (Abhandlungen für die Kunde des Morgenlandes 5/1; Leipzig: Brockhaus, 1868) 219–326.

22. Through Pietro della Valle, the SP became known again in the West. The last authors to mention it before that were George Syncellus (died after 810 C.E.) in his *Ecloga chronographica* 95.26–32; 99.10–100.16; 100.32–101.3, quoting from Eusebius; and Benjamin of Tudela (second half of the 12th century) in his work ספר מסעות (*Book of Travels* or *Itinerary*), 32. For the texts and English translation of Syncellus, see my *Early Christian Authors*, 402–5; for English translations, see also William Adler and Paul Tuffin, *The Chronography of George Synkellos: A Byzantine Chronicle of Universal History from the Creation* (Oxford: Oxford University Press, 2002) 93–94, 95–96, 99–101. For the Hebrew text and an English translation of Benjamin of Tudela, see Marcus Nathan Adler, *The Itinerary of Benjamin of Tudela* (London: Frowde, 1907) 20.

Pentateuch.[23] In the case of the SP, uniformity exists in the oral transmission instead—that is, in the recitation of the Torah. Therefore, to assess properly the text of the Pentateuch, it is necessary to take into account the reading of the Pentateuch as practiced by the Samaritans.[24] This reveals that "many cases of alleged *scriptio plena* do not use the 'vowel letters' as *matres lectionis* but rather as representations of consonants."[25]

The differences between the SP and the MT have been categorized by a number of scholars. The oldest and best known system is the division into eight categories by Wilhelm Gesenius.[26] Others were proposed by Raphael Kirchheim in his book published in 1851, and by Samuel Kohn in his study of 1865.[27] More recently, Abraham Geiger and Paul Kahle contributed their own

---

23. Alan D. Crown estimates that on the whole there are extant approximately 750 SP manuscripts, *Samaritan Scribes and Manuscripts* (TSAJ 80; Tübingen: Mohr Siebeck, 2001) 35. Freedom in copying the Pentateuch was pointed out by Abraham Tal, "Observations on the Orthography of the Samaritan Pentateuch," in *Samaritan Researches Volume V* (ed. Vittorio Morabito, Alan D. Crown, and Lucy Davey; Mandelbaum Studies in Judaica 10; Sydney: Mandelbaum Publishing, 2000) 35; idem, "Divergent Traditions of the Samaritan Pentateuch as Reflected by its Aramaic Targum," *Journal for the Aramaic Bible* 1 (1999) 299–300.

24. The continuity of the pronunciation by the Samaritans for the last 800 years has been demonstrated by an analysis of medieval grammars by Ze'ev Ben-Ḥayyim in his work *The Literary and Oral Tradition*, vols. 1–2 (Jerusalem: Academy of the Hebrew Language, 1957 [Hebrew]). It is then assumed that the tradition goes back much further. See also idem, "Samaritan Hebrew: An Evaluation," in *The Samaritans* (ed. Alan D. Crown; Tübingen: Mohr Siebeck, 1989) 517 (= Ze'ev Ben-Ḥayyim and Abraham Tal, *A Grammar of Samaritan Hebrew Based on the Recitation of the Law in Comparison with the Tiberian and Other Jewish Traditions: A Revised Edition in English* [Jerusalem: Magnes / Winona Lake, IN: Eisenbrauns, 2000] 333). Other scholars, however, have questioned the tendency to ascribe too much importance to the reading tradition in today's Samaritan synagogue for understanding the Hebrew of the Second Temple, to the detriment of historical-comparative linguistics (so, for instance, Holger Gzella in his review of Moshe Florentin, *Late Samaritan Hebrew: A Linguistic Analysis of Its Different Types* [Studies in Semitic Languages and Linguistics 43; Leiden; Boston: Brill, 2005] in *Mediterranean Language Review* 16 [2005] 227).

25. Tal, "Divergent Traditions," 300. See Stefan Schorch, "The Significance of the Samaritan Oral Tradition for the Textual History of the Pentateuch," in *Samaritan Researches Volume V* (ed. Vittorio Morabito, Alan D. Crown, and Lucy Davey; Mandelbaum Studies in Judaica 10; Sydney: Mandelbaum, 2000) 103–17; idem, "Die Bedeutung der samaritanischen mündlichen Tradition für die Exegese des Pentateuch," *Wort und Dienst* 25 (1999) 77–91; idem, "Die Bedeutung der samaritanischen mündlichen Tradition für die Textgeschichte des Pentateuch (II)," *Mitteilungen und Beiträge der Forschungsstelle Judentum, Theologische Fakultät Leipzig* 12/13 (1997) 53–64; idem, *Die Vokale des Gesetzes: Die samaritanische Lesetradition als Textzeugin der Tora, 1: Das Buch Genesis* (BZAW 339; Berlin: de Gruyter, 2004).

26. W. Gesenius, *De Pentateuchi samaritani origine, indole et auctoritate commentatio philologico-critica* (Halle: Rengerianae, 1815) 24–61. For an English translation, see Samuel Davidson, *A Treatise on Biblical Criticism Exhibiting a Systematic View of That Science* (Edinburgh: Adam and Charles Black / London: Longman, 1854) 79–81. See also the enumeration and discussion of Gesenius's categories in Jean Margain, "Samaritain (Pentateuque)," in *DBSup* 11.763–68.

27. Raphael Kirchheim, כרמי שומרון (Frankfurt am Main: Kaufmann, 1851) 32–48. For a German translation and a short discussion, see Stefan Schorch, "Die (sogenannten) anti-polytheistischen

views regarding the classification.[28] A contemporary list is provided by Bruce Waltke in his unpublished Ph.D. dissertation (1965) and in his later article (1970).[29] The most recent classification is found in Emanuel Tov's special study.[30] It is evident that all classifications select certain differences without being exhaustive, which would be an impossible task. In fact, Abraham Tal has concluded that "we do not know the number of actual differences between the MT and the SP."[31]

Earlier, Abraham Geiger realized that the SP represents "an old version . . . , as it was in general use at that time."[32] This was confirmed by the finds at Qumran, where pentateuchal texts were discovered that are close to the SP. On the whole, approximately five percent of the Torah texts found at Qumran are so-called pre-Samaritan, or harmonizing, texts. Earlier, these texts were called proto-Samaritan texts to indicate their affinity with the SP.[33] It was realized, however, that this designation is misleading because these texts display none of the "sectarian" readings that are distinctive of the SP. Therefore, they are now

---

Korrekturen," *Mitteilungen und Beiträge der Forschungsstelle Judentum, Theologische Fakultät Leipzig* 15/16 (1999) 6–7; Samuel Kohn, *De Pentateucho samaritano ejusque cum versionibus antiquis nexu* (Ph.D. dissertation, Universitas Viadrina; Leipzig: Kreysing, 1865) 9. Kohn believed that Gesenius's eight categories could be reduced to three.

28. Above all, in Abraham Geiger, "Einleitung in die biblischen Schriften, 11: Der samaritanische Pentateuch," in *Abraham Geiger's Nachgelassene Schriften* (5 vols.; ed. Ludwig Geiger; Berlin: Gerschel, 1877) 4.54–67; idem, *Urschrift und Übersetzungen der Bibel in ihrer Abhängigkeit von der inneren Entwicklung des Judentums* (2nd ed.; Frankfurt am Main: Madda, 1928). See Paul Kahle, "Untersuchungen zur Geschichte des Pentateuchtextes," *Theologische Studien und Kritiken* 88 (1915) 399–439. For the latter, see also Margain, "Samaritain (Pentateuque)," 768–69.

29. Bruce Waltke, *Prolegomena to the Samaritan Pentateuch* (Ph.D. dissertation, Harvard University, 1965) 271–338; idem, "The Samaritan Pentateuch and the Text of the Old Testament," in *New Perspectives on the Old Testament* (ed. J. Barton Payne; Evangelical Theological Society Symposium Series 3; Waco, TX: Word, 1970) 212–39.

30. Emanuel Tov, *Textual Criticism of the Hebrew Bible* (2nd rev. ed.; Minneapolis: Fortress / Assen: Van Gorcum, 2001) 84–97. For a critical discussion of Tov's categories, see Schorch, "Die (sogenannten) anti-polytheistischen Korrekturen," 7–9.

31. Tal, "Divergent Traditions," 300.

32. Geiger, "Einleitung in die biblischen Schriften," 67 ("eine alte Recension . . . , wie sie zu jener Zeit allgemeine Verbreitung hat").

33. See James D. Purvis, *The Samaritan Pentateuch and the Origin of the Samaritan Sect* (HSM 2; Cambridge: Harvard University Press, 1968) 80; Emanuel Tov, "The Proto-Samaritan Texts and the Samaritan Pentateuch," in *The Samaritans* (ed. Alan D. Crown; Tübingen: Mohr Siebeck, 1989) 397–407; idem, "The Samaritan Pentateuch and the So-Called 'Proto-Samaritan' Texts," in *Studies on Hebrew and Other Semitic Languages Presented to Professor Chaim Rabin on the Occasion of His Seventy-Fifth Birthday* (ed. Moshe H. Goshen-Gottstein, Shelomo Morag, and S. Kogut; Jerusalem: Academon, 1990) 136–46 [Hebrew]. Maurice Baillet's opinion that these were Samaritan texts ("Le texte Samaritain de l'*Éxode* dans les manuscrits de Qumrân," in *Hommages à André Dupont-Sommer* [ed. André Caquot and Marc Philonenko; Paris: Adrien-Maisonneuve, 1971] 363–81) cannot be accepted because of the very fact that none of the texts contains the "sectarian" expansions.

called pre-Samaritan "on the assumption that one of them was adapted to form the special text of the Samaritans," or "harmonistic," because their main characteristics are harmonizing readings—that is, the tendency to make the pentateuchal text "consistent" from one passage to another.[34] Thus, in 4Qpaleo-Exod[m], for instance, texts from Deuteronomy have been inserted into the text of Exodus.[35] Other differences from the MT that pre-Samaritan texts and the SP have in common relate to linguistic features and the content of certain passages.[36] However, none of the pre-Samaritan texts exhibits the readings that reflect Samaritan ideology, above all the sanctity and centrality of Mount Gerizim expressed in the change of the Deuteronomic formula "the place that the LORD your God *will* choose (יבחר)" to "the place that the LORD your God *has* chosen (בחר)" in all 21 occurrences (Deut 12:5, 11, 14, 18, 21, 26; 14:23, 24, 25; 15:20; 16:2, 6, 7, 11, 15, 16; 17:8, 10; 18:6; 26:2; 31:11),[37] and in the Samaritan Tenth Commandment. Whereas in the MT the unnamed "place that the LORD your God *will* choose" was eventually understood to refer to Jerusalem (which was not yet conquered in the lifetime of Moses and could therefore not be named), the Samaritans claim that the "place" is Mount Gerizim, which was chosen by God from the beginning. The Samaritan Tenth Commandment consists of Exod 13:11a; Deut 11:29b; 27:2b–3a, 4a, 5–7; and 11:30.[38] It was added to both versions of the Decalogue—that is, after Exod 10:17 (MT) and

---

34. For the first position, see Tov, *Textual Criticism*, 97. Tov's study discusses various types of harmonization (ibid., 85–89). On the process of harmonization, see also Esther Eshel, "4QDeut[n]: A Text That Has Undergone Harmonistic Editing," *HUCA* 62 (1991) 80.

35. For the edition of 4QpaleoExod[m], see Eugene Ulrich and Frank Moore Cross, eds., *Qumran Cave 4.VII: Genesis to Numbers* (DJD 12; Oxford: Clarendon, 1994). For a recent study, see Judith E. Sanderson, *An Exodus Scroll from Qumran: 4QpaleoExod[m] and the Samaritan Tradition* (HSS 30; Atlanta: Scholars Press, 1986). For another example of harmonization, see Bernard M. Levinson, "Textual Criticism, Assyriology, and the History of Interpretation: Deuteronomy 13:7a as a Test Case," *JBL* 120 (2001) 211–43.

36. See Tov, *Textual Criticism*, 89–94.

37. Contra Hjelm, there are no exceptions: the MT always has יבחר in these passages and the SP always בחר (see Ingrid Hjelm, *The Samaritans and Early Judaism: A Literary Analysis* [JSOTSup 303; Copenhagen International Seminar 7; Sheffield: Sheffield Academic Press, 2000] 92; and eadem, *Jerusalem's Rise to Sovereignty: Zion and Gerizim in Competition* [JSOTSup 404; Copenhagen International Seminar 14; London; New York: T. & T. Clark, 2004] 295). Nor does the Samaritan chronicle *Kitāb al-Tarīkh* by Abū 'l-Fatḥ employ both tenses, as Hjelm claims (*The Samaritans and Early Judaism*, 92); only the English translation by Paul Stenhouse does. The Arabic text quotes the relevant passages, Deut 12:5, 26, and 15:20 (on pp. 71–76 of the chronicle, the pages referred to by Hjelm), in Hebrew and in Samaritan script and uses the form בחר in every instance (see Paul Stenhouse, *The Kitāb al-Tarīkh of Abū'l-Fatḥ* [Ph.D. dissertation, University of Sydney, 1981] 1/2.72, 74, and 76).

38. See Ferdinand Dexinger, "Das Garizimgebot im Dekalog der Samaritaner," in *Studien zum Pentateuch: Walter Kornfeld zum 60. Geburstag* (ed. Georg Braulik; Vienna: Herder, 1977) 111–33.

Deut 5:18 (MT).[39] In Deut 27:4, it reads "Gerizim" instead of MT "Ebal." The SP reading, also attested in *Vetus Latina*, is probably older than the MT reading. Qumran documents 4Q158 (4QReworked Pentateuch[a]) and 4Q175 (4QTestimonia) have a similar text but do not mention Mount Gerizim. Nor would there have been space in 4QpaleoExod[m] for the insertion of the specifically Samaritan expansion after Exod 20:17 (MT).[40] The Samaritan Tenth Commandment makes it crystal clear that Mount Gerizim is the place chosen by God for sacrifice and worship. Moreover, it specifies the location of the mountain precisely: "beyond the Jordan, some distance to the west, in the land of the Canaanites who live in the Arabah, opposite Gilgal, beside the oak of Moreh in front of Shechem." The final phrase, "beside the oak of Moreh in front of Shechem" (אצל אלון מורא מול שכם), is again part of the Samaritan reading of Deut 11:30. The MT reads "oaks of Moreh" (אלוני מרא) and lacks the addition "in front of Shechem."[41]

Another possibly "sectarian" reading that emphasizes that Mount Gerizim had been selected from the days of the patriarchs is found in Exod 20:24 (21 in some versions), where the SP reads, "in *the* place (במקום) where I *have* caused (אזכרתי) my name to be remembered, I will come to you and bless you," whereas the MT reads, "in *every* place (בכל המקום) where I *will* cause (אזכיר) my name to be remembered, I will come to you and bless you."[42] There are

---

39. Despite this addition, the Samaritans preserve the number ten, because they consider the First Commandment of the MT to be an introduction to the Decalogue. In the Exodus version of the Decalogue, the Samaritans have two more additions. After Exod 10:18 (MT), they insert Deut 5:24–27; and after Exod 20:21 (MT), Deut 5:28b–29, 18:18–22, and 5:30–31. These are, however, not "sectarian" readings. For a discussion, see Dexinger, "Garizimgebot," 126–29; idem, "Samaritan Origins and the Qumran Texts," in *Methods of Investigation of the Dead Sea Scrolls and the Khirbet Qumran Site: Present Realities and Future Prospects* (ed. Michael O. Wise et al.; Annals of the New York Academy of Sciences 722; New York: The New York Academy of Sciences, 1994) 238. See also Sanderson, *Exodus Scroll*, 236–37.

40. See Sanderson, *Exodus Scroll*, 13 and 235, relying on Patrick W. Skehan's reconstruction, "Qumran and the Present State of Old Testament Studies; Text Studies: The Massoretic Text," *JBL* 78 (1959) 23.

41. For an analysis of the conflational technique in the Samaritan Tenth Commandment and its effects, see Jeffrey H. Tigay, "Conflation as a Redactional Technique," in *Empirical Models for Biblical Criticism* (ed. Jeffrey H. Tigay; Philadelphia: University of Pennsylvania Press, 1985) 78–83. See also Innocent Himbaza, *Le Décalogue et l'histoire du texte: Études des formes textuelles du Décalogue et leurs implications dans l'histoire du texte de l'Ancien Testament* (OBO 207; Fribourg: Academic Press / Göttingen: Vandenhoeck & Ruprecht, 2004) 63–66, 183–186, and 198–219.

42. For a thorough, recent, text-critical discussion of the verse, see Bernard M. Levinson, "Is the Covenant Code an Exilic Composition? A Response to John Van Seters," in *In Search of Pre-exilic Israel: Proceedings of the Oxford Old Testament Seminar* (ed. John Day; JSOTSup 406; London: T. & T. Clark, 2004) 297–315.

additional ideological changes that are often enumerated,[43] but in many cases
they may well go back to pre-Samaritan texts and not be specific to the Samaritans.[44] The same is true for phonological and orthographic changes.[45]

As a result of the discovery of the Qumran scrolls, the nature and origin of
the SP have become clearer. The SP is based on a text type that was current
during the last two centuries B.C.E. In the 2nd or 1st century B.C.E., the Samaritans added a small number of changes that reflect their ideology. What the
Samaritans evidently did was to choose one of the harmonistic texts of the Pentateuch and modify it slightly in conformity with their beliefs and practices.
The close affinity between the SP and the MT makes it likely that both go back
to a common text. This common text probably dates to the end of the Persian
period. Certainly by the time of Ben Sira, that is, by approximately 200 B.C.E.,
the Pentateuch "in the same or a similar form to that known today was widely
accepted as authoritative."[46] This means it must have been completed earlier.
Why the Samaritans, or rather the proto-Samaritans, chose one of the harmonistic texts, that is, a pre-Samaritan text as defined above, is difficult to know. In
the words of Tov: "In all probability there was no special reason for this choice,
since texts such as these must have been current in ancient Israel."[47] At the
same time, Tov points out that "the proto-Masoretic text, usually associated
with the temple circles, was not chosen for this purpose." Furthermore, it is
"noteworthy that all five books of the SP bear the same character."[48]

The process of "creating" the SP from an existing text was no different from
what the scribes of pre-Samaritan texts did. This was pointed out by Judith
Sanderson for 4QpaleoExod^m.[49] The Samaritans used the same method for

---

43. For recent lists, see Margain, "Samaritains (Pentateuque)," 767–68; Tov, *Textual Criticism*,
94–95.

44. This was demonstrated, with the help of the Samaritan reading tradition, for so-called an-
tipolytheistic changes, by Schorch in "Die (sogenannten) anti-polytheistischen Korrekturen." He
concludes that it is probable "daß ein schon in weit vor-samaritanischer Zeit als selbstverständlich
vorauszusetzender Henotheismus dazu führte, ein entsprechendes Verständnis dem Text von
vornherein zu unterlegen. In der Folge dieses Verständnisses kam es zum unwillkürlichen Eindrin-
gen entsprechender Lesungen in den Text" (p. 19) (ET: it is probable "that a henotheism that
probably was taken for granted long before the time of the Samaritans was the cause that the text
was understood accordingly. As a consequence, these readings unwittingly entered the text").

45. Tov, *Textual Criticism*, 95–97.

46. Lester L. Grabbe, "The Law of Moses in the Ezra Tradition: More Virtual Than Real?" in
Persia and Torah: The Theory of Imperial Authorization of the Pentateuch (ed. James W. Watts; SLB-
SymS 17; Atlanta: Society of Biblical Literature, 2001) 111.

47. Tov, *Textual Criticism*, 100. Esther and Hanan Eshel believe that the Samaritans chose a harmonistic version because it "corresponded to the Samaritan outlook and in their opinion it could
resolve the inconsistencies in the Bible" ("Dating the Samaritan Pentateuch's Compilation," 239).

48. Tov, *Textual Criticism*, 100.

49. Sanderson, *Exodus Scroll*, 236–37.

their expansions as the others; that is, their scribes copied from other passages of the Bible and inserted the text where they thought it should be.

In sum, there is now a consensus among scholars that the SP is an adaptation of a pre-Samaritan or harmonistic text known from Qumran that was produced in the 2nd or 1st century B.C.E.[50] An analysis of the Samaritan reading tradition arrives at the same time period. Stefan Schorch's investigations into this tradition have shown that it developed at the turn of the 2nd to the 1st century B.C.E. in the general context of the formation of distinct groupings within the Israelite-Jewish tradition, specifically as a consequence of the break between Samaritans and Jews.[51] The question therefore arises: is the origin of Samaritanism as a distinct religion to be dated to this, to an earlier, or to a later time?[52]

3. The Origin of the Samaritans

In trying to find the origin of the Samaritans, we must define even the term *origin*. First, scholars have recognized in modern research that the separation between Jews or Judeans and Samaritans was not a sudden occurrence but a gradual process. Second, it is also clear that there never was a total disengagement or estrangement of one from the other. Nevertheless, in view of the eventual outcome (that is, Samaritanism became an entity separate and distinct from Judaism), we must ask when this separation became apparent to both Jews/Judeans and Samaritans. (As in other similar cases, such as Judaism and Christianity, the

---

50. Esther and Hanan Eshel believe that "the sectarian changes were added to the SP . . . prior to the destruction of the Samaritan temple on Mt. Gerizim in 111 B.C.E." They also believe that, after the Samaritans had chosen their harmonistic version, Jewish scribes continued with "more comprehensive editing than the one documented in the SP," whereas the Samaritans made no further changes ("Dating the Samaritan Pentateuch's Compilation," 238–39).

51. Schorch, *Vokale des Gesetzes*, 61.

52. Most scholars assume that the Samaritan script was developed from the Paleo-Hebrew script in the 1st century C.E. For discussions, see Purvis, *Samaritan Pentateuch*, 18–52; Joseph Naveh, *Early History of the Alphabet: An Introduction to West Semitic Epigraphy and Palaeography* (Jerusalem: Magnes / Leiden: Brill, 1982) 123–24; idem, "Scripts and Inscriptions in Ancient Samaria," *IEJ* 48 (1998) 99–100. William Foxwell Albright recognized that the Samaritan script is close to the script used on the coins from the first Jewish revolt (*From the Stone Age to Christianity* [2nd ed.; Garden City, NY: Doubleday, 1957] 345–46 n. 12). However, only one Samaritan inscription seems to have survived from this period (on a capital from Emmaus-Nicopolis, modern Khirbet ʿImwas), but its dating is uncertain. Only from the Byzantine period do we have datable evidence of the Samaritan script on mosaic floors and on oil lamps; no manuscripts are preserved from this period. For a convenient summary of the question, see Yitzhak Magen, Haggai Misgav, and Levana Tsfania, *Mount Gerizim Excavations, 1: The Aramaic, Hebrew, and Samaritan Inscriptions* (Judea and Samaria Publications 2; Jerusalem: Israel Antiquities Authority, 2004) 35–36. The fact that the Samaritan script and the orthography of the SP cannot be used to date the formation of the SP was shown by Esther and Hanan Eshel, "Dating the Samaritan Pentateuch's Compilation," 222–27.

separation became apparent to outsiders later, as the early Christian writings show.) Everything points to the 2nd/1st centuries B.C.E. as being the period in which the two religions parted ways.[53] Both the destruction of the Samaritan temple by John Hyrcanus and the method of manipulating the text of the Torah employed by the Samaritans to emphasize their distinctiveness speak for this assumption.[54] The harmonistic texts found at Qumran make it more than

---

53. Rainer Albertz's surprise that some scholars of Samaritanism date the "Konstituierung und Abtrennung" of the Samaritans "gar erst in die christliche Zeit" (*Religionsgeschichte Israels in alttestamentlicher Zeit* [2 vols; GAT; ATD—Ergänzungsreihe 8/1 and 8/2; Göttingen: Vandenhoeck & Ruprecht, 1992] 2.577) seems to be based on a misreading of the writings of these scholars (he enumerates Richard J. Coggins, Reinhard Pummer, and Rita Egger); all three date it to the last centuries B.C.E. See Richard J. Coggins, *Samaritans and Jews: The Origins of the Samaritans Reconsidered* (Growing Points in Theology; Oxford: Blackwell, 1975) 115 (it is "surely beyond serious dispute, that a community which we may properly describe as Samaritan was established at Shechem during the third and second centuries"). In "Antisamaritanische Polemik in jüdischen Schriften aus der intertestamentarischen Zeit" (*BZ* 26 [1982] 224–42), the article to which Albertz refers, I am concerned with evidence for *polemics* against Samaritans, as the title indicates; the absence of this sort of polemics in certain intertestamental works does not ipso facto mean that an identifiable Samaritan community did not yet exist. For my dating of the origin of the Samaritans in the 2nd century B.C.E., see my earlier book, *The Samaritans* (Iconography of Religions 23/5; Leiden: Brill, 1987) 3. Rita Egger (*Josephus Flavius und die Samaritaner: Eine terminologische Untersuchung zur Identitätsklärung der Samaritaner* [NTOA 4; Freiburg: Universitätsverlag / Göttingen: Vandenhoeck & Ruprecht, 1986] 106) discusses the Samaritan temple on Mount Gerizim in the time of Hyrcanus (134–104 B.C.E.); on p. 310, she notes that Josephus does not have much to report about the first three centuries of the Samaritan community. For her conclusions regarding the early history of the Samaritans, see pp. 304–7. For the Hasmonean period as the time of the origin of the Samritans, see Purvis, *The Samaritan Pentateuch*, 118.

54. As is well known, the Samaritans themselves have their own beliefs about their origin, the Jews have theirs, and scholarship has several. While the various beliefs and earlier theories cannot be reviewed here, mention should be made of the recent hypothesis of Étienne Nodet insofar as it concerns the Samaritan Pentateuch (see his book *Essai sur les origines du judaïsme: De Josué aux Pharisiens* [Paris: Cerf, 1992], published in a revised English edition under the title *A Search for the Origins of Judaism: From Joshua to the Mishnah* [JSOTSup 248; Sheffield: Sheffield Academic Press, 1997]). Nodet sees the Samaritans as "the most direct heirs of the ancient Israelites and their cult" and maintains "that the material in the Hexateuch should generally be attributed to them, with the conspicuous exception of the weekly Sabbath; that Judaism, dispersed throughout the whole Seleucid Transeuphrates, was an import from Babylon and was made up of ancestral traditions and memories of the Kingdom of Judah; that the union in Judaea between these two, that is to say, between two quite restricted groups, took place a little before 200 BCE, and was followed by an intense literary activity," and so on (p. 12). Regarding the Pentateuch, Nodet concludes: "The first appearance of the Pentateuch as an authoritative compilation able to be called 'law of Moses' is to be situated in Samaria (at Shechem, in connection with Gerizim and its priesthood), a generation or two before the date that Samaritan palaeography calls for it, that is to say, c. 250–200 BCE" (p. 191; see also p. 153). The revision of their own Scripture by the Samaritans became the common Pentateuch. Nodet is aware that these propositions "can appear improbable," but he points out that he sees his work not as a synthesis but its opposite; that is, "it only aspires to open a debate" (p. 12). This is not the place for a detailed critique of Nodet's hypotheses but only for some general comments. One of the major shortcomings is that he uses his sources in such a way

likely that the Samaritan "sectarian" changes date to this period.

The archaeological excavations on Mount Gerizim that were begun in 1982 and are not yet completed[55] show that probably a sanctuary existed on the main peak of the mountain already in the Persian period, that is, in the mid-5th century B.C.E.[56] It was expanded considerably in the Hellenistic period, and the

as to declare elements that do not fit his theory to be later additions. Furthermore, only by combining certain select statements in Josephus and the medieval Samaritan *Book of Joshua* can he conclude that the Samaritan Pentateuch, in an assumed earlier form than the SP in existence now, is the original Pentateuch. Thus, while one must acknowledge that Nodet's hypotheses are bold and apt to stimulate discussion, I must say that they are far too speculative to be convincing. See also the detailed review by Jean-Claude Haelewyck in *RTL* 23 (1992) 472–81. Nodet has reiterated his views on the origins of the Samaritans in his recent book, *La crise macabéenne: Historiographie juive et traditions bibliques* (Paris: Cerf, 2005) 207–9 and 396.

55. The excavator, Yitzhak Magen, along with his colleagues, has published various articles on the excavations in periodicals. See especially the following articles (in Hebrew) in *Qadmoniot* 120 (2000): Yitzhak Magen, "Mt. Gerizim: A Temple City" (pp. 74–118); Ephraim Stern and Yitzhak Magen, "First Phase of the Samaritan Temple on Mt. Gerizim" (pp. 119–24); Yitzhak Magen, Levanah Tsfania, and Haggai Misgav, "The Hebrew and Aramaic Inscriptions from Mt. Gerizim" (pp. 125–32); Yitzhak Magen, "Mt. Gerizim during the Roman and Byzantine Periods" (pp. 133–43). See also Magen's "Mount Gerizim," *NEAEHL* 2.484–92. Recently, Magen has begun to publish the results in book form, *Mount Gerizim Excavations*, a work that contains a brief summary of the excavations and focuses on the inscriptions found on the mountain. Overall, five volumes are planned.

56. Ephraim Stern and Yitzhak Magen believe that there may have been an earlier, 7th-century B.C.E. temple on Mount Gerizim. They base their conjecture on the find of two almost complete limestone capitals and a fragment of a third, unearthed on the eastern slope of the mountain among remains from the Persian and Hellenistic period. All three capitals are proto-Aeolic (also called proto-Ionic) capitals. According to Stern and Magen, they may have been "relics taken from a nearby Israelite sanctuary at Shechem," perhaps by "the first Samaritan settlers brought by the Assyrian kings to replace the exiled Israelites" ("Archaeological Evidence for the First Stage of the Samaritan Temple on Mount Gerizim," *IEJ* 52 [2002] 55–56). In Stern's opinion, "these capitals attest to an early phase of the Temple on Mount Gerizim, before it became a center of monotheistic religion in the Persian Period" ("The Religious Revolution in Persian-Period Judah," in *Judah and the Judeans in the Persian Period* [ed. Oded Lipschits and Manfred Oeming; Winona Lake: IN: Eisenbrauns, 2006] 202–3). With regard to a mid-5th-century Samaritan temple on Mount Gerizim, it is interesting to note that, in a letter written in 408 B.C.E., the Elephantine Jews mention that previously they had written to the governor of Judah and the high priest and other priests in Jerusalem as well as to the political authorities in Samaria, but they do not mention any high priest or other priests in Samaria; see Arthur E. Cowley, ed., *Aramaic Papyri of the Fifth Century B.C.* (Oxford: Clarendon, 1923) no. 30 // 31 (= *Textbook of Aramaic Documents from Ancient Egypt*, vol. 1 [ed. Bezalel Porten and Ada Yardeni; Jerusalem: The Hebrew University, 1986] A4.7 // A4.8). Albrecht Alt concluded from this that, at that time, "unbeschadet der politischen Trennung zwischen Judäa und Samaria die alte Kultgemeinschaft beider über die Grenzen hinweg noch bestand" ("Zur Geschichte der Grenze zwischen Judäa und Samaria," *PJ* 31 [1935] 108 [repr. in idem, *Kleine Schriften zur Geschichte des Volkes Israel* (3 vols.; Munich: Beck, 1953–59) 2.359]; ET: "notwithstanding the political division between Judea and Samaria, the old cultic community of the two still existed across the boundaries"). Kippenberg follows Alt (*Garizim und Synagoge*, 43). Martin Noth thought,

remains of a large temenos and the city surrounding it have been unearthed. Numerous inscriptions dating to different periods have come to light in the course of the excavations. With regard to the question of the origins of the Samaritans, we should underline the fact that the existence of a Samaritan temple on Mount Gerizim was not a sufficient reason for the separation between the YHWH worshipers in Jerusalem on the one hand and the YHWH worshipers in the region of Samaria on the other.[57] As is well known, other Yahwistic temples existed outside Palestine: at Elephantine and Leontopolis.[58] There may also have been a YHWH temple in Khirbet el-Qôm in the 4th century B.C.E. that served the small Jewish community that probably existed in northern

however, that "Den Kolonisten in Elephantine scheint dieser Gegensatz [between Samaria and Jerusalem] verborgen geblieben zu sein," *Geschichte Israels* (6th ed.; Göttingen: Vandenhoeck & Ruprecht, 1966) 319 n. 1 (ET: "It seems that this conflict [between Samaria and Jerusalem] was unknown to the colonists of Elephantine").

57. Thomas C. Römer has noted that "certain texts of the Tetrateuch (but also some texts in Samuel and Kings) assume the existence of several Yahwistic sanctuaries, and this without apparent criticism" ("Cult Centralization in Deuteronomy 12: Between Deuteronomistic History and Pentateuch," in *Das Deuteronomium zwischen Pentateuch und Deuteronomistischem Geschichtswerk* [ed. Eckart Otto and Reinhard Achenbach; FRLANT 206; Göttingen: Vandenhoeck & Ruprecht, 2004] 179). According to Römer, this more open attitude may have come from the Priestly writers.

58. See the article "Sanctuaires juifs" by Mathias Delcor in *DBSup* 11.1296–1329 (he also discusses Arad and Bethel); and the discussion by Gary Knoppers, "'The City Yhwh Has Chosen': The Chronicler's Promotion of Jerusalem in Light of Recent Archaeology," in *Jerusalem in Bible and Archaeology: The First Temple Period* (ed. Andrew G. Vaughn and Ann E. Killebrew; SBLSymS 18; Atlanta: Society of Biblical Literature, 2003) 318–21. On Elephantine, see Stephen G. Rosenberg, "The Jewish Temple at Elephantine," *Near Eastern Archaeology* 67 (2004) 4–13. On Bethel, see also Klaus Koenen, *Bethel: Geschichte, Kult und Theologie* (Freiburg: Universitätsverlag, 2003); Joseph Blenkinsopp, "Bethel in the Neo-Babylonian Period," in *Judah and the Judeans in the Neo-Babylonian Period* (ed. Oded Lipschits and Joseph Blenkinsopp; Winona Lake, IN: Eisenbrauns, 2003) 93–107; Melanie Köhlmoos, *Bet-El—Erinnerungen an eine Stadt: Perspektiven der alttestamentlichen Bet-El-Überlieferung* (FAT 49; Tübingen: Mohr, 2006). See also Edward F. Campbell Jr., "Jewish Shrines of the Hellenistic and Persian Periods," in *Symposia Celebrating the Seventy-Fifth Anniversary of the Founding of the American Schools of Oriental Research (1900–1975)* (ed. Frank Moore Cross; Zion Research Foundation Occasional Publications 1–2; Cambridge, MA: American Schools of Oriental Research, 1979) 159–67; Jörg Frey, "Temple and Rival Temple: The Cases of Elephantine, Mt. Gerizim, and Leontopolis," in *Gemeinde ohne Tempel / Community without Temple: Zur Substituierung und Transformation des Jerusalemer Tempels und seines Kultes im Alten Testament, antiken Judentum und frühen Christentum* (ed. Beate Ego, Armin Lange, and Peter Pilhofer; WUNT 188; Tübingen: Mohr Siebeck, 1999) 171–203. Sometimes ʿAraq el-Emir in Jordan is included among the temples (as in Campbell, "Jewish Shrines," 162–63; and, more recently, Doran Mendels, *The Rise and Fall of Jewish Nationalism* [ABRL; New York: Doubleday, 1992] 150). However, Ernest Will has demonstrated that the building in question was not a temple but a palace (see Ernest Will and François Larché, *ʿIraq al-Amir: Le château du Tobiade Hyrcan* [2 vols.; Bibliothèque archéologique et historique 132, 172; Paris: Geuthner, 1991] 1.255–65). In a lengthy review of Will's and Larché's work, Stephen G. Rosenberg disputes this identification ("Qasr al-Abd: A Mausoleum of the Tobiad Family?" *BAIAS* 19–20 [2001-2] 157–75). He believes that the building was intended as a mausoleum for the Tobiad family. On the presumed function of the Qasr al-Abd, see further idem, *Airaq al-Amir: The Architecture of the Tobiads* (BAR International Series 1544; Oxford: Hedges, 2006) xx.

Idumea.[59] Note also that in 2 Macc 6:2 the temple on Mount Gerizim is mentioned without negative strictures. The phrase is only a factual statement illustrating more of Antiochus IV's evil designs on Judaism—and in 2 Macc 5:22, the Samaritans are considered to be of the same *genos* as the Jews—and its institutions.[60] What brought about or at least precipitated the separation was the destruction of the sanctuary on Mount Gerizim by John Hyrcanus, rather than its construction. But even though both communities now parted ways, contacts between them in various spheres of life, beliefs, and practices did not cease completely. It is therefore problematic to speak of a "final" break.

Rather, the separation between Jews and Samaritans after the destruction of the temple and the city on Mount Gerizim by John Hyrcanus was *final* only in the sense that from then on the Samaritans considered Mount Gerizim to be the only legitimate center of worship. It was not *complete*, however, because interaction between Samaritans and Jews continued for a long time and probably was never totally suspended. This is proved by the rabbinic writings, even if often the Samaritans served only as a foil.[61] Further evidence for this point may be gained from examining the Samaritan synagogues from Byzantine times, which are virtually indistinguishable from Jewish synagogues.[62] Both types of

---

59. So André Lemaire, "Nouveau Temple de Yahô (IVe S. AV. J.-C.)," in *"Basel und Bibel": Collected Communications to the XVIIth Congress of the International Organization for the Study of the Old Testament, Basel 2001* (ed. Matthias Augustin and Hermann Michael Niemann; BEATAJ 51; Frankfurt am Main: Peter Lang, 2004) 265–73; idem, "New Aramaic Ostraca from Idumea and Their Historical Interpretation," in *Judah and the Judeans in the Persian Period* (ed. Oded Lipschits and Manfred Oeming; Winona, Lake, IN: Eisenbrauns, 2006) 416–17.

60. This was pointed out by Jonathan A. Goldstein, *II Maccabees* (AB 41A; Garden City, NY: Doubleday, 1983) 261, 272, 495. The renaming would have been what Greeks and others were used to doing "without changing in any other way the nature of the god or his worship" (p. 273). Others believe that the last part of the verse should be emended from καθὼς ἐτύγχανον οἱ τὸν τόπον οἰκοῦντες, "as the inhabitants of the place happened to be [namely, hospitable]," to καθὼς ἐνετύγχανον οἱ τὸν τόπον οἰκοῦντες "as the inhabitants of the place had requested," as the LXX and the Vg. read. The emendation ἐνετύγχανον has no basis in the manuscript evidence but is influenced by Josephus, *Ant.*12.261, although in Josephus the Samaritans ask that their temple be renamed after Zeus Hellenios, not Xenios. With τυγχάνω, the present participle ὤν may be left out (see William Watson Goodwin and Charles Burton Gulick, *Greek Grammar* [New Rochelle, NY: Caratzas, 1930 (repr. 1988)] §1588). Robert Doran explains the phrase as "an example of brachylogy where the adjective ξένιοι is to be supplied from the context: 'Zeus Hospitable, just as the inhabitants were hospitable'" ("2 Maccabees 6:2 and the Samaritan Question," *HTR* 76 [1983] 483).

61. See my "Samaritanism in Caesarea Maritima," in *Religious Rivalries and the Struggle for Success in Caesarea Maritima* (ed. Terence L. Donaldson; Studies in Christianity and Judaism / Études sur le christianisme et le judaïsme 8; Waterloo, ON: Canadian Corporation for Studies in Religion/ Corporation Canadienne des Sciences Religieuses, 2000) 200–201 and the literature cited there.

62. There is epigraphic evidence for a Samaritan diaspora synagogue from the 2nd century B.C.E. on the Greek island of Delos. However, no building remains have been uncovered so far. See my "Samaritan Synagogues and Jewish Synagogues," 120–21. See also Lee I. Levine, *The Ancient Synagogue: The First Thousand Years* (New Haven: Yale University Press, 2000) 102–3.

buildings are so similar that only the location and/or inscriptions in Samaritan script allow us to identify a synagogue as Samaritan.[63] In general, the material culture of the early Samaritans is indistinguishable from the Jews'. For later times, we find literary influences from Jewish writings on Samaritan works, ranging from the list of 613 Precepts[64] to Torah commentaries and the Arabic translation of the Pentateuch.[65] The Prophets and Writings of the Jewish Scriptures, which are not part of the Samaritans' sacred writings, must have been known by them. They certainly were used in the composition of the *Book of Joshua* and the Samaritan chronicles,[66] although the extant texts date only from the 14th century onward.

4. The Pentateuch among the Samaritans

For a long time, scholars have been asking: How do we explain the Samari(t)an acceptance of basically the same Pentateuch as the Judeans/Jews?[67] Various answers have been proposed. In most reconstructions, the accounts in Neh 13:28 and Josephus, *Ant.* 11.306–312 play a prominent role.

---

63. See my "How to Tell a Samaritan Synagogue from a Jewish Synagogue," *BAR* 24/3 (1998) 24–35; idem, "Samaritan Synagogues and Jewish Synagogues."

64. See Maurice Baillet, "Commandements et lois (*Farâ'id et Tûrot*) dans quatre manuscrits samaritains," in *Études samaritaines. Pentateuque et Targum, exégèse et philologie, chroniques. Actes de la table ronde: "Les manuscrits samaritains. Problèmes et méthodes" (Paris, Institut de Recherche et d'Histoire des Textes, 7–9 octobre 1985)* (ed. Jean-Pierre Rothschild and Guy Dominique Sixdenier; Collection de la Revue des Études Juives 6; Louvain: Peeters, 1988) 259–70; Moses Gaster, "Die 613 Gebote und Verbote der Samaritaner," in *Festschrift zum 75 jährigen Bestehen des Jüdisch-Theologischen Seminars Fraenkelscher Stiftung* (Breslau: Marcus, 1929) 2.393–404 and 35–67 [Hebrew section]; Abraham S. Halkin, "The 613 Commandments among the Samaritans," in *The Ignace Goldziher Memorial Volume* (2 vols.; ed. S. Löwinger, A. Scheiber, and J. Somogyi; Jerusalem: Rubin Mass, 1958) 2.86–100 [Hebrew]; Menahem Haran, "Maimonides' Catalogue of Religious Precepts in a Samaritan Piyyut," *ErIsr* 4 (1956) 160–69 [Hebrew]; idem, "The Song of the Precepts of Aaron ben Manir: A Samaritan Hymn for the Day of Atonement on the 613 Precepts as Listed by Maimonides," *Israel Academy of Sciences and Humanities: Proceedings* 4/15 (1971) 229–80 [Hebrew] and 5/7 (1974) 174–209; Ayala Loewenstamm, "Remarks on the 613 Precepts," *Tarbiz* 41 (1972) 306–12 [Hebrew]; Sergio Noja, "Les préceptes des Samaritains dans le manuscrit Sam 10 de la Bibliothèque Nationale," *RB* 74 (1967) 255–59. See now also Florentin, *Late Samaritan Hebrew*, 53–54. Florentin also discusses (pp. 50–56) other Jewish influences on Samaritanism.

65. For discussion, see my "Greek Bible and the Samaritans," *REJ* 157 (1998) 307–9.

66. The Samaritan chronicles recount the history of the Samaritans from Adam to the Middle Ages or to modern times. For discussion and additional references, see Stenhouse, "Samaritan Chronicles"; idem, "Chronicles of the Samaritans," in *A Companion to Samaritan Studies* (ed. Alan D. Crown, Reinhard Pummer, and Abraham Tal; Tübingen: Mohr Siebeck, 1993) 50–53.

67. As Purvis already pointed out, the Samaritan claim that their Torah is from Moses and was copied by the great-grandson of Aaron, Abisha ben Pinḥas, in the 13th year after the conquest of Canaan is not supported by "the contributions of Pentateuchal criticism" (*The Samaritan Pentateuch*, 93).

a. Nehemiah 13:28 and Josephus, Ant. 11.306–312

In 1894, for instance, Herbert Edward Ryle wrote: "It has been very gener-ally and very naturally supposed, that the Samaritan community obtained their Torah . . . from the renegade priest, of the name, according to Josephus, of Manasseh, who instituted on Mount Gerizim a rival temple worship to that on Mount Moriah (*Jos. Ant. XI. 7 and 8*)."[68] Ryle believed, however, that Jose-phus's dating was wrong and that the incident should be dated to about 423 B.C.E.[69] More than one hundred years after the publication of Ryle's book, the same or similar hypotheses are still being proffered, at least tentatively, by some authors. Interestingly, even modern authors sometimes state categorically that in Josephus's story in *Ant.* 11.306–347 Manasseh "had taken with him from the temple of Jerusalem a Torah scroll which he placed in the sanctuary on Mt. Ge-rizim."[70] Yet, Josephus nowhere mentions the Pentateuch in this narrative.[71]

This solution would conveniently resolve two problems at once. It would not only explain when and how the Pentateuch got to Samaria but also why the Samaritans did not accept the Prophets and the Writings into their canon. In light of more recent research, however, this solution is too facile. It takes Neh 13:28 at face value and, in addition, relies on Josephus's story about the priest who married Sanballat's daughter and whom Josephus called Manasseh (*Ant.* 11.306–312). The Josephan passage is considered by some scholars to be reliable but by others to be an expansion of Neh 13:28. Because of the many improbabilities and inconsistencies in Josephus's story, most authors see it as a "midrash" (by Josephus or his source) on the passage in Nehemiah. The latter is very short on details: "And one of the sons of Jehoiada, son of the high priest Eliashib, was the son-in-law of Sanballat the Horonite; I chased him away from me." Eliashib's descendant remains nameless in the Bible, and in fact the Samari-tan tradition does not know of any high priest by the name of Manasseh.[72] It may well be that the name *Manasseh* was invoked here to discredit the Samaritan

68. Herbert Edward Ryle, *The Canon of the Old Testament: An Essay on the Gradual Growth and Formation of the Hebrew Canon of Scripture* (London: Macmillan, 1892) 91.

69. Ibid., 93.

70. Shemaryahu Talmon, "The Emergence of Jewish Sectarianism in the Early Second Temple Period," in *Ancient Israelite Religion: Essays in Honor of Frank Moore Cross* (ed. Patrick D. Miller Jr., Paul D. Hanson, and S. Dean McBride; Philadelphia: Fortress, 1987) 601.

71. This was already emphasized by John Ebenezer Honeyman Thomson in 1920 ("The Pen-tateuch of the Samaritans: When They Got It, and Whence," *Journal of the Transactions of the Victo-ria Institute* 52 [1920] 145).

72. Admittedly, this fact alone is no proof. Not only are the lists preserved in late sources, but also they would hardly report something that reflects so badly on the Samaritans' early history. For a brief discussion, see Lester L. Grabbe, "Josephus and the Reconstruction of the Judean Restora-tion," *JBL* 106 (1987) 238–41.

priesthood.[73] Certainly, Josephus knows of only one Sanballat, whereas the evidence provided by the Elephantine and Wadi Daliyeh papyri may suggest that there were two or three governors by this name.[74] Josephus's Sanballat lived in the time of Alexander rather than in the time of Nehemiah; he would be Sanballat III, although his existence is only inferred and not documented so far.

The most recent detailed analyses of the matter were undertaken by James VanderKam and Jacob Wright. VanderKam defends the historicity of Josephus's story.[75] In contrast, Wright concludes that Neh 13:28–29 and Josephus, *Ant.* 11.302–312 were originally independent accounts of "an historical struggle for the office of high priest between the great-grandsons of Eliashib or at least a legend which developed about this generation of high priests similar to that of the former generation (*Ant.* §§297ff.)."[76] In the mid-4th century and later, certain Judean circles criticized the aristocracy of Judah and the priests of Jerusalem because they were in league with foreign regimes.[77] In light of the uncertainties regarding the historicity of the narratives in the two passages, it would be imprudent to build a theory on them of how the Pentateuch came to the Samaritans.

Similarly, Henri Cazelles's theory must be rejected in light of recent research on Ezra–Nehemiah. Cazelles claimed that Ezra was sent to unite the returnees to Jerusalem, the *gerim*, and the Samaritans under one legislation. Ezra's law became state law, and the Samaritans accepted the Priestly Code, which explains why Jews and Samaritans have the Pentateuch as canonical law.[78] As

---

73. Francesca Stavrakopoulou, *King Manasseh and Child Sacrifice: Biblical Distortions of Historical Realities* (BZAW 338; Berlin: de Gruyter, 2004) 129. The author observes that "this would also carry ironical undertones, for the Samaritans apparently identified themselves as the descendants of the tribes of Ephraim and Manasseh." See also eadem, "The Blackballing of Manasseh," in *Good Kings and Bad Kings* (ed. Lester L. Grabbe; Library of Hebrew Bible/Old Testament Studies 393; European Seminar in Historical Methodology 5; London: T. & T. Clark, 2005) 256.

74. For summary accounts, see H. G. M. Williamson, "Sanballat," *ABD* 5.973–75; and Douglas M. Gropp, "Sanballat," *Encyclopedia of the Dead Sea Scrolls* 2.823–25. See also the discussion in Menachem Mor, *From Samaria to Shechem: The Samaritan Community in Antiquity* (Jerusalem: Zalman Shazar Center for Jewish History, 2003) 49–52, with a table on p. 53 [Hebrew].

75. James VanderKam, *From Joshua to Caiaphas: High Priests after the Exile* (Minneapolis: Fortress / Assen: Van Gorcum, 2004).

76. Jacob L. Wright, *Rebuilding Identity: The Nehemiah Memoir and Its Earliest Readers* (BZAW 348; Berlin: de Gruyter, 2004) 267.

77. Ibid., 268.

78. Henri Cazelles, "La mission d'Esdras," *VT* 4 (1954) 131. In a similar vein, Albrecht Alt emphasized that, according to Ezra 7:25, Ezra was to carry out his revision of the law and the organization of the courts in the remarkably indeterminate area of the Syrian province ("Zur Geschichte der Grenze zwischen Judäa und Samaria," 104 n. 1 [= repr. 356 n. 1]). See also Jacobus Gerardus Vink, "The Date and Origin of the Priestly Code in the Old Testament," in *The Priestly Code and Seven Other Studies* (ed. Jacobus Gerardus Vink et al.; OtSt 15; Leiden: Brill, 1969) 55–56. For an earlier critique of these views, see Morton Smith, *Palestinian Parties and Politics That Shaped the Old Testament* (New York: Columbia University Press, 1971) 253 n. 116 and 272 n. 101. Concerning

far as the Samaritans themselves are concerned, an echo of the account of the promulgation of the law (whatever is meant by it) by Ezra according to Neh 8:1–12 can be detected in the Samaritans' attitude toward him.

b. Ezra in the Samaritan Tradition

From the Samaritans' point of view, Ezra's part in the establishment of Scripture was negative.[79] The testimonies to this attitude, however, come only from late Samaritan writings. Thus, the 14th-century Arabic chronicle, *Kitāb al-Tarīkh*, compiled by Abū ʾl-Fath ascribes to Ezra and Zerubbabel the creation of "an alphabet of their own, different from the Hebrew alphabet," consisting of 27 letters. Furthermore, "They tampered with the Holy Law, copying it out in the alphabet they had newly created. They cut out many passages of the Holy Law because of the fourth of the ten commandments,[80] and the references to Mount Gerizim in its boundaries. They added to it, cut things from it, changed it and misconstrued it." The text then adds, "May God oppose them. . . . Ezra, may he be cursed, called the Jews together and said to them, 'God said to me yesterday when he gave me this Book, 'This is the Book of God, the authentic truth. Put your faith in it and make copies of this one alone.'"[81] In a later passage of the same chronicle, the Samaritan heretic Dusis is said to have made changes to the Torah just as Ezra did.[82]

Also from the 14th century comes a similar line in the hymn for the Day of Atonement by the Samaritan poet Abisha ben Pinhas (died 1376).[83] In the 19th

---

the intent of Ezra 7:25, see Sebastian Grätz, *Das Edikt des Artaxerxes: Eine Untersuchung zum religionspolitischen und historischen Umfeld von Esra 7, 12–26* (BZAW 337; Berlin: de Gruyter, 2005) 92, 101, 296. According to Grätz, the claim that the administration of justice and the teaching of this law were to extend to the whole of Transeuphratene has "utopische Züge." It harks back to the perfect conditions for the building of the temple and the same space for the rule of the law of God that existed at the time of Solomon and the building of the First Temple, and wants to say: "Auch der zweite Tempel ist damit nicht ein Partikularheiligtum, sondern geistiges und geistliches Zentrum eines geographischen Großraums עבר נהרא wie zu den (Heils-)Zeiten Davids und Salomos" (p. 92; ET: "Thus, the Second Temple, too, is not the sanctuary of a minority but the intellectual and spiritual center of a far-flung geographical area עבר נהרא, as it was during the [salvific] times of David and Solomon).

79. Early Christian authors assert that the name of the priest sent with the law from Assyria or Babylon was Ezra: Epiphanius of Salamis, *Anaceph.* I 9.1 (Pummer, *Early Christian Authors*, 145–46); *Pan.* 8.8.10 (ibid., 147–48); *De gemm.* 91 (ibid., 172 and 178–79); John of Damascus, *De haer.* 9 (ibid., 374–75).

80. In the Sabbath command, the SP has "observe" (שמור) in both passages (that is, in Exod 20:8–11 and Deut 5:12–15), while the MT reads "remember" (זכר) in Exod 20:8.

81. Paul Stenhouse, *The Kitāb al-Tarīkh of Abū ʾl-Fath: Translated into English with Notes* (Studies in Judaica 1; Sydney: Mandelbaum Trust, University of Sydney, 1985) 97–98.

82. Ibid., 217.

83. Cowley, *Samaritan Liturgy*, 514, lines 1–2. See also Ferdinand Dexinger, *Der Taheb: Ein "messianischer" Heilsbringer der Samaritaner* (Kairos: Religionswissenschaftliche Studien 3; Salzburg: Müller, 1986) 118 (text and German translation).

century, the high priest Salama ben Ṭabia (1784–1855) wrote a poem that deals with the future in similar terms as Abisha's hymn.[84] He writes, the Jews will say "we shall join this religion; cursed be Ezra and his word(s) and what he did with us, everything that concerns us is a lie."[85]

Chronicle Adler, a modern work[86] that draws on the earliest Samaritan chronicle, the *Tulida*, and on Abū 'l-Fatḥ's work, states that Ezra, on his arrival in Jerusalem, could not find a copy of the law because the king of Assyria had burned all the books of the Jews. Through a ruse, he obtained an old torn Bible from a Samaritan. Because the Jews no longer knew the sacred language and script, Ezra, Nehemiah, and all the heads of the community wrote the Bible in the Assyrian language and characters. Ezra modified several words by giving them an anti-Samaritan slant, added and deleted many things, and inserted many others from past authors and prophets.[87]

The charge that Ezra introduced a new alphabet is an echo of the rabbinic discussions regarding the change from Paleo-Hebrew to the square Hebrew script, which is called Assyrian script in rabbinic sources.[88] On the whole, the Samaritan image of Ezra is an amalgam of biblical and rabbinic traditions seen from the Samaritans' perspective. For the Samaritans, the figure of Ezra came to embody Judaism and its differences from and antagonism to their own beliefs and traditions. Unfortunately, it is impossible to determine how far back in time this tradition goes, but given that Ezra became even more prominent in early rabbinic writings than he was in the Bible,[89] we may assume that the Samaritans reacted to this elevation of Ezra at a much earlier period than the Middle Ages. Already in the 1st- or early-2nd-century C.E. work of *4 Ezra*

---

84. On Salama, see my *Samaritan Marriage Contracts and Deeds of Divorce* (2 vols.; Wiesbaden: Harrassowitz, 1993–97) 1.152–53.

85. Cowley, *Samaritan Liturgy*, 364, lines 12–13.

86. For a linguistic analysis, see Moshe Florentin, *Late Samaritan Hebrew*, 361–71.

87. Elkan Nathan Adler and Max Séligsohn, "Une nouvelle chronique samaritaine," *REJ* 44 (1902) 221. For an English translation of the passage, see John Bowman, *Samaritan Documents Relating to Their History, Religion and Life* (Pittsburgh Original Texts and Translations Series 2; Pittsburgh, PA: Pickwick, 1977) 102.

88. See Babylonian Talmud, *Sanhedrin* 21b, 22a; Tosefta, *Sanhedrin* 4.7; Jerusalem Talmud, *Megillah* 71a–b. The addition of five letters refers to the introduction of final ך, ם, ן, ף, and ץ (Stenhouse, *Kitāb*, xxv n. 382). Echoes of the talmudic passages can be found in a few of the Church Fathers, such as Epiphanius of Salamis (ca. 315–403) and, in his wake, in John of Damascus (ca. 655–ca. 750), as well as in Jerome (ca. 347–420); see my *Early Christian Authors*, 146, 178, 207.

89. Michael Munk, "Esra Hasofer nach Talmud und Midrasch," *Jahrbuch der Jüdisch-Literarischen Gesellschaft* 21 (1930) 129–98, especially 155–59 (on Ezra and the Samaritans). Giovanni Garbini has pointed out that "no Jewish work, whether in the Bible or not, shows knowledge of the great Ezra before Flavius Josephus: and he speaks of Ezra only as a paraphrase of the biblical text" (*History and Ideology in Ancient Israel* [London: SCM, 1988] 152).

(chap. 14), Ezra receives from God the text of 94 books to replace the law that was burned when the temple was destroyed. Seventy of them he is to hide—the apocalyptic books; and 24 he is to make public—the books of the Hebrew canon. Thus, in later tradition, Ezra becomes a second Moses—an event that would not have been acceptable to the Samaritans, who elevated Moses above all other biblical figures.

To understand better the historical conditions affecting the two communities in biblical times, we must consider the makeup of the population in the North after the Assyrian conquest.

c. The Population of the Former Northern Kingdom and the Pentateuch

Two conclusions from recent research into the history of the Samaritans are now generally accepted: one, there was no schism between Samaritans and Jews in the 5th century B.C.E.; and two, the Samaritan version of the Pentateuch emerged in the 2nd/1st century B.C.E., when the specifically Samaritan readings were introduced into one of the otherwise unchanged texts current also in Judah. Because it is most unlikely that the Northern Yahwists adopted the Pentateuch at this late date and immediately adapted it to their own views, they must have been familiar with it for a considerable amount of time before that. The question is how long?

It is well known that "the extensive theological denigration of the Northern Kingdom throughout Kings"[90] became historical truth for many students of the Bible. Not only is almost every Northern king condemned by Kings, but in 2 Kings 17 the kings and the people are depicted as worshiping other gods (v. 7), walking "in the customs of the nations whom the Lord drove out before the people of Israel" (v. 8), building "for themselves high places at all their towns" (v. 9), setting up pillars and sacred poles (v. 10), making "offerings on all the high places" (v. 11), and serving idols (v. 12). The cause of the North's sins was their falling away from the House of David and following Jeroboam (v. 21). It was the repudiation of the Davidic dynasty and the idolatrous cults instituted

---

90. Stavrakopoulou, "Blackballing of Manasseh," 250. She sees this systematic denigration of the North as an ideological premise for the ostracizing of Manasseh. See also eadem, *King Manasseh*, 63–66. Others read Kings differently. See, for instance, Gary Knoppers: "the Deuteronomist actually commends the creation of two separate states" (*Two Nations under God: The Deuteronomistic History of Solomon and the Dual Monarchies*, vol. 1: *The Reign of Solomon and the Rise of Jeroboam* [HSM 52; Atlanta: Scholars Press, 1993] 9); with regard to 1 Kgs 11:11–13 and 31–36, he writes: Jeroboam, in fact, is "provided with divine legitimation. . . . There is no sedition on his part; he will receive the ten tribes due to Solomon's misconduct" (p. 199); the ten tribes "are not being cast off. Yнwн has called a new leader with whom he has made covenant" (p. 203). Thus, according to Knoppers, the Northern Kingdom is legitimate—Judah and Israel are endorsed by the Deuteronomist as the "two nations under God."

by Jeroboam in Bethel and Dan (1 Kings 12–13) that brought about the rejection of the North by God and led to the exile of the people. This in turn laid the ground for the notion that Judah and Israel are separate from each other.[91] Both 1 Kgs 12:20 and 2 Kgs 17:18 state that only the tribe of Judah followed the House of David. Furthermore, because the North pursued foreign cult practices, it actually became a foreign nation. By taking this theological evaluation by the author of Kings as basically reliable history, authors have found it puzzling that the Samaritans possessed virtually the same Pentateuch as the Judeans.

On the other hand, to a number of scholars it was plain that 2 Kings presents a slanted picture that has influenced our view of the (pre)history of the Samaritans. According to this view, it was mostly the upper classes of Israel that were deported and, while the Assyrians did resettle the land with foreigners, this did not alter the culture and religion of the majority of the indigenous population.[92] Other scholars—the majority—did and do believe, however, that the North was devastated, emptied of the majority of the Israelites, and repopulated with foreigners by the Assyrians.[93] The two views are called "minimalist" and "maximalist," respectively, by Gary Knoppers. He himself presents a middle path.[94] Based on the results of recent archaeological work, including field surveys, and on considerations about the functioning of societies, Knoppers emphasizes that "there is no compelling evidence that the Assyrians systematically imposed their own religious practices on subject peoples."[95] Moreover, he points out that a distinction must be made between Galilee and northern Transjordan on the one hand and the hill country of Ephraim and Manasseh on the other. While the former were severely affected by the Assyrian conquests and deportations, the latter experienced only a "diminution of the local population," probably due to "death by war, disease, and starvation, forced deportations to other lands, and

---

91. Stavrakopoulou, "Blackballing of Manasseh," 251. Again, not all scholars see matters in this way. James Richard Linville argues that, in Kings, "the 'north' does not simply represent that which has so corrupted itself and can no longer be called 'Israel.' Rather, it remains 'Israel,' as its retention of the very name indicates. The 'north' and Judah are each other's alter ego" (*Israel in the Book of Kings: The Past as a Project of Social Identity* [JSOTSup 272; Sheffield: Sheffield Academic Press, 1998] 99–100). Stavrakopoulou recognizes that Kings emphasizes the close interrelationship between the two kingdoms, but she maintains that "this interrelationship harbours a tense ideological negativity, for a distinct anti-Northern polemic pervades Kings" (*King Manasseh*, 64).

92. See above all, Coggins's book *Samaritans and Jews*. See also John Macdonald, *The Theology of the Samaritans* (NTL; London: SCM, 1964) 22–24.

93. See, for instance, Bustenay Oded, "II Kings 17: Between History and Polemic," *Jewish History* 2 (1987) 37–50.

94. Gary Knoppers, "In Search of Post-Exilic Israel: Samaria after the Fall of the Northern Kingdom," in *In Search of Pre-exilic Israel: Proceedings of the Oxford Old Testament Seminar* (ed. John Day; JSOTSup 406; London: T. & T. Clark, 2004) 160–72.

95. Ibid., 162.

migration to other areas, including south to Judah."[96] Foreign importees were not numerous, and "most seem to have been absorbed into the local population."[97] The changes in material culture, such as architecture, were, according to Zertal, limited to administrative and military posts established by the Assyrians. Contra Ephraim Stern, Zertal states that, "in most aspects, life in Iron Age Palestine seems to have continued without much change, as far as daily life is concerned."[98] Furthermore, "most of the Iron Age III [722–535 B.C.E.] ceramic inventory remained local and continued from the eighth into the seventh/sixth centuries, with some modifications and additions. The Assyrian influence is expressed by the addition of a few imported vessels ('palace-ware'), which appear in small quantities."[99] Only a few "Assyrian and Babylonian cuneiform inscriptions, tablets, seals, and other items" were found.[100]

Thus, the continued presence of Israelites in the North accounts for the persistence of the material culture in both the city of Samaria and the highlands. It also "helps to explain the existence of a Yahwistic Samarian community in the Persian period"; they are "descendants of the Israelites who used to have their own kingdom centred in Samaria centuries earlier."[101] This is evident from the attitude displayed in the book of Chronicles and other biblical books.

To begin with the other biblical books, the (Judean) prophets "do not seem to have known of the tradition that Samaria was an impure mixture of pagans and surviving northern Israelites."[102] The texts of Isa 11:12–13; Jer 23:5–6, 31:17–20, and 41:5; Ezek 37:15–28; and Zech 8:13, 9:13, and 10:6–12 presuppose that the inhabitants of Samaria are part of the people of Israel and that the inhabitants of the North share a common faith with the residents of the South. This inspires the hope that one day the unity of Ephraim and Judah will

---

96. Ibid., 170. In 2001, Adam Zertal estimated that the size of the population may have been 70,000–75,000 ("The Heart of the Monarchy: Patterns of Settlement and Historical Considerations of the Israelite Kingdom of Samaria," in *Studies in the Archaeology of the Iron Age in Israel and Jordan* [ed. Amihai Mazar; JSOTSup 331; Sheffield: Sheffield Academic Press, 2001] 44 n. 3). Of these, Sargon II claimed to have deported 27,290. In an essay published in 2003, Zertal estimated the population to be 60,000 to 70,000 ("The Province of Samaria [Assyrian *Samerina*] in the Late Iron Age [Iron Age III]," in *Judah and the Judeans in the Neo-Babylonian Period* [ed. Oded Lipschits and Joseph Blenkinsopp; Winona Lake, IN: Eisenbrauns, 2003] 385).

97. Knoppers, "In Search," 171. Zertal believes that Assyrian authorities chose not to create mixed settlements of Israelites and newcomers ("The Province of Samaria," 404).

98. Ibid., 386; Zertal is referring to Ephraim Stern, *Archaeology of the Land of the Bible, 2: The Assyrian, Babylonian, and Persian Periods (732–332 B.C.E.)* (ABRL; New York: Doubleday, 2001) 18–19.

99. Zertal, "Province of Samaria," 397.

100. Ibid., 399.

101. Knoppers, "In Search," 171–72.

102. Macdonald, *Theology*, 22. See also Coggins, *Samaritans and Jews*, 28–37.

be restored. Had the Northerners been seen as pagans, prophecies of this sort
would not have been enunciated.

The author of Chronicles certainly took for granted the existence of YHWH
worshipers in the North. According to him, priests, Levites, and people "from
all the tribes of Israel [came] to Jerusalem to sacrifice to the Lord" (2 Chr
11:13–17). The Judahite King Abijah addressed the northern Israelites in
2 Chronicles 13 in a major speech; in it, he held out the possibility of repen-
tance for them.[103] Under King Asa, "great numbers had deserted to him from
Israel when they saw that the Lord his God was with him" (2 Chr 15:9). They
gathered around him in Jerusalem, sacrificed to YHWH, and "entered into a
covenant to seek the Lord, the God of their ancestors, with all their heart and
with all their soul" (2 Chr 15:9–15). During the reign of Ahaz, Oded, a
prophet of YHWH, spoke to the Israelites in Samaria, persuading them to release
the Judahite prisoners that they had taken (2 Chr 28:8–15). King Hezekiah
"sent word to all Israel and Judah, and wrote letters also to Ephraim and Manasseh, that they should come to the house of the Lord at Jerusalem, to keep
the passover to the Lord the God of Israel" (2 Chr 30:1).[104] Clearly, the inhabitants of Samaria are addressed as Israelites; there is no trace of forced emigra-
tions or settlements of foreigners in the text. The cultic reforms carried out by
Hezekiah extended to Ephraim and Manasseh (2 Chr 31:1). Similarly, Josiah
implemented his reforms in "the towns of Manasseh, Ephraim, and Simeon,
and as far as Naphtali" (2 Chr 34:6) and "made all who were in Israel worship
the LORD their God" (2 Chr 34:33). Thus, for the Chronicler, the Northerners
were YHWH worshipers, not foreign pagans.[105]

Recent archaeological investigations have shown that the northern and western zones of Samaria soon recovered from the ravages of the Assyrian attacks[106]
and prospered during the Persian period. Settlements increased greatly in numbers, and the system of roads was expanded. Although evidence for the city of
Samaria is sparse, from the fact that the region around it was densely popu-
lated[107] we may infer that it "was one of the most important [cities] in Pales-

---

103. See Gary N. Knoppers's discussion of the speech in "Mt. Gerizim and Mt. Zion: A Study
in the Early History of the Samaritans and the Jews," *SR* 34 (2005) 315–21.

104. On Hezekiah's Passover invitation, see ibid., 321–25.

105. On the attitude of Chronicles toward the Northern Kingdom and the Samarians, see also
Sara Japhet, *The Ideology of the Book of Chronicles and Its Place in Biblical Thought* (2nd rev. ed.;
BEATAJ 9; Frankfurt am Main: Peter Lang, 1997) 308–34.

106. See Adam Zertal, "The Pahwa of Samaria (Northern Israel) during the Persian Period:
Types of Settlement, Economy, History and New Discoveries," *Transeu* 3 (1990) 9–30; idem, "The
Pahwah of Samaria during the Persian and Hellenistic Periods," in *Michael: Studies in History, Epigra-
phy and Scripture in Honor of Professor Michael Heltzer* (ed. Yitzhak Avishur and Robert Deutsch; Tel
Aviv–Jaffa: Archaeological Center, 1999) 75*–87* [Hebrew].

107. See idem, "The Pahwa of Samaria (Northern Israel)," 14.

tine."[108] In comparison with Jerusalem and Judah, Samaria, the region and the city, were not only larger but also more densely settled and were enjoying greater material wealth. In the words of Knoppers, "During the Achaemenid era, members of the Judean elite were not dealing with a depopulated outback to the north. Quite the contrary, they were dealing with a province that was larger, better-established, and considerably more populous than was Yehud."[109] Language and scripts known from papyri, coins, and bullae were substantially the same in Persian Judea and Samaria. Similarly, the two regions shared common proper names.[110]

By way of documentation from the middle of the 4th century B.C.E., we have the Wadi Daliyeh papyri, in particular. The great majority of the wealthy inhabitants of the city of Samaria, who left the documents behind, bore Yahwistic names.[111] One governor (or several governors) of Samaria had an Akkadian name, Sin-uballiṭ (Sanballaṭ), "[the moon god] Sin gives life," but his (or their) sons had Yahwistic names—Delaiah, Shelemiah,[112] and maybe [Yesh]uaʿ/ [Yeshaʿ]yahu (or [Yad]uaʿ).[113] Another governor was named Hananiah.[114]

---

108. Stern, *Archaeology*, 2.424. See also Zertal, "Province of Samaria," 380.

109. Gary Knoppers, "Revisiting the Samarian Question in the Persian Period," in *Judah and the Judeans in the Persian Period* (ed. Oded Lipschits and Manfred Oeming; Winona Lake, IN: Eisenbrauns, 2006) 273.

110. See the material cited in ibid., 273–78.

111. Douglas M. Gropp, *Wadi Daliyeh II* (DJD 28; Oxford: Clarendon, 2001) 6. See also József Zsengellér, "Personal Names in the *Wadi ed-Daliyeh* Papyri," *ZAH* 9 (1996) 182–89; Hanan Eshel, "Israelite Names from Samaria in the Persian Period," in *These Are the Names* (ed. Aaron Demsky, Joseph A. Raif, and Joseph Tabori; Ramat Gan: Bar-Ilan University Press, 1997) 17–31 [Hebrew]; idem, "The Rulers of Samaria during the Fifth and Fourth Century BCE," in *Frank Moore Cross Volume* (ed. Baruch A. Levine et al.; Jerusalem: Israel Exploration Society, 1999) 8–12; André Lemaire, "Das Achämenidische Juda und seine Nachbarn im Lichte der Epigraphie," in *Religion und Religionskontakte im Zeitalter der Achämeniden* (ed. Reinhard G. Kratz; Veröffentlichungen der Wissenschaftlichen Gesellschaft für Theologie 22; Gütersloh: Chr. Kaiser/Gütersloher Verlagshaus, 2002) 220–23; Ran Zadok, "A Prosopography of Samaria and Edom/Idumea," *UF* 30 (1998) 781–85. See now Frank Moore Cross, "Personal Names in the Samaria Papyri," *BASOR* 344 (2006) 75–90.

112. Cowley, *Aramaic Papyri* 30.29 // 31.28, 32.1 = Porten and Yardeni, *Textbook 1* 4.7, 29; 4.8,28; 4.9,1. See also WDSP [Wadi Daliyeh Samaria Papyri] 3 (Delaiah). The names appear also on Samarian coins. For Delaiah, see Yaʿakov Meshorer and Shraga Qedar, *Samarian Coinage* (Numismatic Studies and Researches 9; Jerusalem: Israel Numismatic Society, 1999) 22; for Shelemiah, see ibid., 28.

113. According to Frank Moore Cross, who was followed by many other scholars, there was a dynasty of governors, beginning with Sanballat I in the mid-5th century B.C.E. and ending with Sanballat III in the late 4th century B.C.E. (which he has proposed in a number of articles, two of the latest being "A Report on the Samaria Papyri," in *Congress Volume: Jerusalem, 1986* [ed. J. A. Emerton; VTSup 40; Leiden: Brill, 1988] 19–20; and "A Reconstruction of the Judaean Restoration," *From Epic to Canon: History and Literature in Ancient Israel* [Baltimore: Johns Hopkins University Press, 1998] 151–72). However, not all scholars accept Cross's reconstructions. See, most recently, Lester L. Grabbe, "Pinholes or Pinheads in the *Camera obscura*? The Task of Writing a History of Persian

Moreover, the Judean names Sheshbazzar and Zerubbabel are not Yahwistic either, as has been pointed out repeatedly.[115]

In the 3rd–2nd centuries B.C.E., pilgrims to Mount Gerizim came from the city of Samaria, a fact that we know from votive inscriptions unearthed on Mount Gerizim.[116] These inscriptions show that in the Hellenistic period the names of the persons who worshiped and made donations on Mount Gerizim are indistinguishable from the names in vogue in contemporary Jerusalem.[117] They include the name "Yehudah"/"Yehud"[118] as well as biblical names that are not taken from the Pentateuch but from books that are not part of the Samaritan canon, such as Elnathan (2 Kgs 24:8; Jer 26:22; 36:12, 25; Ezra 8:16), Delaiah (Ezra 2:60; Neh 6:10, 7:62; 1 Chr 3:24), and Zabdi (Josh 7:1, 17–18;

Period Yehud," in *Recenti tendenze nella ricostruzione della storia antica d'Israele (Roma, 6–7 marzo 2003)* (Contributi del Centro Linceo Interdisciplinare "Beniamino Segre" 110; Rome: Accademia Nazionale dei Lincei, 2005) 174–75; and Diana Edelman, *The Origins of the "Second" Temple: Persian Imperial Policy and the Rebuilding of Jerusalem* (Bible World; London: Equinox, 2005) 16, 51–62. See also the caveats of Daniel R. Schwartz, "On Some Papyri and Josephus' Sources and Chronology for the Persian Period," *JSJ* 21 (1990) 175–99.

114. Frank Moore Cross, "Papyri of the Fourth Century B.C. from Dâliyeh: A Preliminary Report on Their Discovery and Significance," in *New Directions in Biblical Archaeology* (ed. David N. Freedman and Jonas C. Greenfield; Garden City, NY: Doubleday, 1969) 47, pls. 34–35; Paul W. Lapp and Nancy L. Lapp, eds., *Discoveries in the Wâdī ed-Dâliyeh* (AASOR 41; Cambridge, MA: American Schools of Oriental Research, 1974) pl. 61; Nahman Avigad and Benjamin Sass, *Corpus of West Semitic Stamp Seals* (Jerusalem: The Israel Academy of Sciences and Humanities, 1997) 176 (no. 419). For Hananiah, see WDSP 7.17 and 9.14, and the Samarian coins discussed by Meshorer and Qedar (*Samarian Coinage*, 23) and Lemaire ("Das Achämenidische Juda," 222).

115. See, for instance, Rainer Albertz, *Religionsgeschichte Israels*, 2.581 n. 25; Ehud Ben Zvi, "Inclusion in and Exclusion from Israel as Conveyed by the Use of the Term 'Israel' in Post-Monarchic Biblical Texts," in *The Pitcher Is Broken: Memorial Essays for Gösta W. Ahlström* (ed. Steven W. Holloway and Lowell K. Handy; JSOTSup 190; Sheffield: Sheffield Academic Press, 1995) 142 n. 112; Knoppers, "Revisiting the Samarian Question," 276. André Lemaire thinks that, even if Sanballat came from Harrān, he was a descendant of Israelites deported to Assyria, and Sheshbazzar and Zerubbabel were descendants of Babylonian exiles ("Épigraphie et religion en Palestine à l'époque achéménide," *Transeu* 22 [2001] 104). Earlier, Lemaire noted that the title "the Horonite" indicates that Sanballat was from Beth-Horon, where the Babylonian exiles could have been installed (Ernest-Marie Laperrousaz and André Lemaire, eds., *La Palestine à l'époque Perse* [Paris: Cerf, 1994] 43 n. 151). See also Ran Zadok, "Samarian Notes," *BO* 42 (1985) 569–70. Edelman points out that the vocalization of Sin-uballit as Sanballat in Nehemiah may indicate that "the connection of the name with the deity Sin was lost in the Jewish environment and the name became 'neutral' and acceptable, especially in Samerina, where a governor bore it" (*The Origins of the "Second" Temple*, 78 n. 21).

116. See Magen, Misgav, and Tsfania, *Mount Gerizim Excavations*, 1.59 (inscription 14) and 60 (inscription 15); see also p. 28.

117. Ibid., 1.25–26 and 85.

118. Ibid., vol. 1, inscriptions 43 and 49. Magen notes that "Yehud(ah)" was used by the Samaritans "despite their enmity toward Judea and the Jews in general during the Hellenistic period" (p. 85).

Neh 11:17; 1 Chr 8:19; 27:27). This usage also continues, however, in much later periods. Several high priests, for instance, are named Hezekiah or Jonathan. Some pilgrims to Mount Gerizim had Greek names[119] (including possibly "Alexander") or Persian and Arabic names. Again, this accords with the use of Arabic names by the Samaritans when they lived among a predominantly Arab population.[120]

If then the theological polemics of the book of Kings is recognized for what it is; if the separateness and foreignness of the North are exposed as myths; and if the continued presence of Yahwists in the North is acknowledged, the fact that the Samaritans have the same Pentateuch as the Judeans should no longer be surprising.[121] The closeness between the North and the South geographically, culturally, and religiously implies that there were contacts and interactions between them, certainly during the Achaemenid and Hellenistic periods, but probably even before.[122] Furthermore, as Knoppers points out, "the links must have been substantial and persistent, rather than superficial and sporadic," such as "trade, travel, migrations, including migrations in time of war, and scribal communications."[123]

Given the shared culture and the longstanding substantial contacts, then, there is no reason that the interactions between the two communities should not have included participation in the development of some of the narrative and legal traditions that came to constitute the Pentateuch. As Joseph Blenkinsopp notes, "It is reasonable to assume that the fall of the Northern Kingdom in the eighth century B.C. would have brought about a more concentrated effort to preserve the common patrimony, including the legal patrimony, in writing."[124]

---

119. Greek names are also found on the inscriptions from Delos, which honor a certain Menippos, son of Artemidoros, for his contribution to the construction of a synagogue; and a Sarapion, son of Jason (see L. Michael White, "The Delos Synagogue Revisited: Recent Fieldwork in the Greco-Roman Diaspora," *HTR* 80 [1987] 144; idem, *Social Origins*, 2.341–2). However, the two persons may have been "pagans" rather than Samaritans (ibid., 2.342 n. 94).

120. See the lists of Samaritan names from medieval to modern times in Edward Robertson, *Catalogue of the Samaritan Manuscripts in the John Rylands Library* (2 vols.; Manchester: John Rylands Library, 1938–62) 1.404–12; 2.297–308; Jean-Pierre Rothschild, *Catalogue des manuscrits samaritains* (Paris: Bibliothèque Nationale, 1985) 159–67; Pummer, *Samaritan Marriage Contracts*, 1.314–43; 2.275–319; Alan D. Crown, "Studies in Samaritan Scribal Practices and Manuscript History, IV: An Index of Scribes, Witnesses, Owners and Others Mentioned in Samaritan Manuscripts, with a Key to the Principal Families Therein," *BJRL* 68 (1985–86) 317–72; idem, *Samaritan Scribes*, 391–463.

121. It should be noted that later Jewish polemics, beginning with Josephus, reinforced the impressions conveyed by the book of Kings.

122. So also Knoppers, "Revisiting the Samarian Question," 278.

123. Ibid.

124. Joseph Blenkinsopp, *The Pentateuch: An Introduction to the First Five Books of the Bible* (ABRL; New York: Doubleday, 1992) 234.

Included in this common legacy were the Jacob traditions connected with Shechem and Bethel.[125] In other words, everything speaks for the assumption that the Northerners did not passively and suddenly accept the Pentateuch from the Judeans, but they must have taken part in its growth. When the Samaritan "sectarian" changes were made, they were made in texts that had circulated among Yahwistic Samarians long before the breach in the 2nd/1st century B.C.E.[126]

If this supposition is correct, exegetical traditions and methods would also have been shared at this early period, not just in postbiblical times.[127] Using Deut 13:7a as a test case, Bernard M. Levinson has shown in a closely argued study that the Second Temple communities behind the Septuagint, the biblical texts discovered at Qumran, and the Samaritan Pentateuch employed the same methods and techniques to interpret and expand the biblical text.[128] With regard to the Samaritan exegetical tradition enshrined in their Pentateuch, however, everything depends on how far they participated in the formation of the Pentateuch, something that we cannot assess at the present time. What we do know is that their version, except for the so-called sectarian readings, is closely akin to the pre-Samaritan versions known from Qumran. At least some of the exegesis in the Samaritan version would then have simply been accepted and assented to by the Samaritans rather than generated by themselves. On the other

---

125. For a detailed study of the tradition-historical, archaeological, and territorial-historical analysis of these traditions, see Eckart Otto, *Jakob in Sichem: Überlieferungsgeschichtliche Studien zur Entstehungsgeschichte Israels* (BWA[N]T 110; Stuttgart: Kohlhammer, 1979).

126. Note the comment of Alt ("Geschichte," 358):

> Denn dieser gemeinsame Besitz [the Pentateuch] kann schwerlich dadurch zustande gekommen sein, daß die Samaritaner, nachdem sie sich einmal von Jerusalem getrennt hatten, den fertigen Pentateuch von dort übernahmen, sonder ist viel wahrscheinlicher als eine Erbschaft aus der Zeit vor der Trennung aufzufassen; dann kann die letztere aber erst geraume Zeit nach Nehemia erfolgt sein, da der Pentateuch erst dann die Juden und Samaritanern gemeinsame endgültige Gestalt gewann.

> ET: For this common possession [the Pentateuch] can hardly have its origin in the adoption of the completed Pentateuch by the Samaritans after they had separated from Jerusalem; rather, it is much more plausible to see it as a patrimony from the time before the separation; in this case, the latter can only have happened a considerable time after Nehemiah, because only then did the Pentateuch achieve the final form common to Jews and Samaritans.

127. For a later period (4th century C.E. on), see Simeon Lowy in his book *The Principles of Samaritan Bible Exegesis* (StPB 28; Leiden: Brill, 1977), who argues that Samaritan exegesis was independent of other exegetical traditions and that parallel explanations are mere coincidences. Although he does admit that there were alien influences on the Samaritans and even cases of plagiarism (pp. 204 and 211), he maintains that "the *content* of their own literature hardly changed" (p. 501; Lowy's emphasis). For a critique of Lowy's views, see my review of the book in *JAOS* 102 (1982) 186–87.

128. Levinson, "Textual Criticism," 211–43.

hand, what is also evident is that, in making their adaptations to assert their identity, they employed the same method as other exegetes at that time.[129]

That the descendants of the Samarian Israelites must have had a part in the *Pentateuch-Kompromiß* was also surmised by, among others, Ernst Axel Knauf, primarily for the following reasons.[130] First, the Samaritans accepted the Torah but not the Prophetic canon from the Maccabean period. Second, the Pentateuch is accommodating toward the Samaritans; that is, despite the demand for cult centralization (Deut 12:5–9, 11–15), it nowhere identifies the "place that YHWH will choose."[131] Furthermore, besides Jerusalem traditions (Genesis 14, 22), traditions about Ebal and Gerizim are also included (Deut 27:4–26). Thus, according to Knauf, the Torah must be seen first and foremost as *Grundgesetz* of the Persian provinces of Yehud and Samaria.[132] Knauf further thinks that the Northern traditions reached Judah via Bethel, "a process that started when Judah incorporated Bethel and its local temple, school, and library" in the course of the 7th century B.C.E.[133]

---

129. Another tradition to be found in both Samaritanism and Judaism is the targumic tradition. The Samaritan Targum was composed in the 3rd or 4th century C.E. and is extant only in a few (late) manuscripts. The most recent edition was published by Abraham Tal (*The Samaritan Targum of the Pentateuch: A Critical Edition* [Texts and Studies in the Hebrew Language and Related Subjects 4–6; Tel Aviv: Tel Aviv University Press, 1980–83]). For a detailed discussion of the various aspects of the Samaritan Targum, see idem, "The Samaritan Targum of the Pentateuch," in *Mikra: Text, Translation, Reading and Interpretation of the Hebrew Bible in Ancient Judaism and Early Christianity* (ed. Martin Jan Mulder; CRINT 2/1; Assen/Maastricht: Van Gorcum / Philadelphia: Fortress, 1988) 189–216. For a short overview, see idem, "Targum," in *A Companion to Samaritan Studies* (ed Alan D. Crown, Reinhard Pummer, and Abraham Tal; Tübingen: Mohr Siebeck, 1993) 226–28.

130. On the compromise hypothesis, see, however, Eckart Otto, "Die Rechtshermeneutik des Pentateuch und die achämenidische Rechtsideologie in ihren altorientalischen Kontexten," in *Kodifizierung und Legitimierung des Rechts in der Antike und im Alten Orient* (ed. Markus Witte and Marie Theres Fögen; BZAR 5; Wiesbaden: Harrassowitz, 2005) 105: "Der Pentateuch ist in diesem Sinne eine Funktion des Ersten Gebotes des Dekalogs und gerade nicht Ausdruck einer von der persischen Reichsregierung inaugurierten Kompromißbildung" (ET: "In this sense, the Pentateuch is a function of the First Commandment of the Decalogue and certainly not the expression of a compromise initiated by the Persian imperial government").

131. On the accommodation of Northern traditions in the Pentateuch, see also Albertz, *Religionsgeschichte Israels*, 1.349 with n. 183. See also Moshe Weinfeld, *Deuteronomy and the Deuteronomic School* (Oxford: Clarendon, 1972; repr. Winona Lake, IN: Eisenbrauns, 1992) 166 n. 3.

132. Ernst Axel Knauf, *Die Umwelt des Alten Testaments* (Neuer Stuttgarter Kommentar: Altes Testament 29; Stuttgart: Katholisches Bibelwerk, 1994) 173. See also Albertz, *Relgionsgeschichte Israels*, 2.588.

133. Ernst Axel Knauf, "Bethel: The Israelite Impact on Judean Language and Literature," in *Judah and the Judeans in the Persian Period* (ed. Oded Lipschits and Manfred Oeming; Winona Lake, IN: Eisenbrauns, 2006) 295; idem, "Towards an Archaeology of the Hexateuch," in *Abschied vom Jahwisten: Die Komposition des Hexateuch in der jüngsten Diskussion* (ed. Jan Christian Gertz, Konrad Schmid, and Markus Witte; BZAW 315; Berlin: de Gruyter, 2002) 275–94.

The question now is whether the factors enumerated above—continuity of YHWH worship in the North, interactions between Samarians and Judeans, accommodation of Samarian traditions in earlier texts of the Pentateuch—explain the fact that the Samaritan and Jewish Pentateuchs are virtually identical, or must we assume a more direct act by a central authority, such as the Persian *Reichsautorisation?*

d. The Samaritan Pentateuch and the Persian Reichsautorisation

As is well known, the hypothesis of the Persian *Reichsautorisation*, in vogue particularly in the 1980s and early 1990s, but based on older suggestions, argued that the Pentateuch as the law for the Jews was endorsed by the Persian authorities as *Reichsgesetz* for the Jews. [134] Assuming that the law was to apply in both Judea and Samaria, the theory would have presented a possible explanation for the two identical Pentateuchs. Newer research, however, is highly skeptical of at least aspects of the hypothesis, [135] and many scholars now reject it in the form in

---

134. See in particular Peter Frei, "Die persische Reichsautorisation: Ein Überblick," *ZABR* 1 (1995) 1–35 (ET: "Persian Imperial Authorization: A Summary," in *Persia and Torah: The Theory of Imperial Authorization of the Pentateuch* [ed. James W. Watts; SBLSymS 17; Atlanta: Society of Biblical Literature, 2001] 5–40); idem, "Zentralgewalt und Lokalautonomie im Achämenidenreich," in Peter Frei and Klaus Koch, *Reichsidee und Reichsorganisation im Perserreich* (2nd ed.; Freiburg: Universitätsverlag / Göttingen: Vandenhoeck & Ruprecht, 1996) 5–131; Erhard Blum, *Studien zur Komposition des Pentateuch* (BZAW 189; Berlin: de Gruyter, 1990) 345–60; idem, "Esra, die Mosetora und die persische Politik," in *Religion und Religionskontakte im Zeitalter der Achämeniden* (ed. Reinhard G. Kratz; Veröffentlichungen der Wissenschaftlichen Gesellschaft für Theologie 22; Gütersloh: Chr. Kaiser/Gütersloher Verlagshaus, 2002) 246–48; Albertz, *Religionsgeschichte Israels*, 2.497–504; Frank Crüsemann, *Die Tora: Theologie und Sozialgeschichte des alttestamentlichen Gesetzes* (Munich: Chr. Kaiser, 1992) 387–93 (ET: *The Torah: Theology and Social History of Old Testament Law* [Minneapolis: Fortress, 1996] 334–39); Blenkinsopp, *The Pentateuch*, 239–43; Knauf, *Die Umwelt des Alten Testaments*, 171–75; Jon L. Berquist, *Judaism in Persia's Shadow: A Social and Historical Approach* (Minneapolis: Fortress, 1995) 138–39. As Grätz (*Edikt des Artaxerxes*, 1 n. 2) has noted, the core of the thesis was already expressed in Hans Heinrich Schaeder, *Der Mensch in Orient und Okzident: Grundzüge einer eurasiatischen Geschichte* (Sammlung Piper; Munich: Piper, 1960) 70. Other authors are cited in Blum, *Studien zur Komposition des Pentateuch*, 346 with n. 44.

135. See Udo Rüterswörden, "Die persische Reichsautorisation: Fact or Fiction?" *ZABR* 1 (1995) 47–61; Josef Wiesehöfer, " 'Reichsgesetz' oder 'Einzelfallgerechtigkeit'? Bemerkungen zu Peter Freis These von der achaimenidischen 'Reichsautorisation,'" *ZABR* 1 (1995) 36–46; as well as the following essays in Watts, ed., *Persia and Torah*: Joseph Blenkinsopp, "Was the Pentateuch the Civic and Religious Constitution of the Jewish Ethnos in the Persian Period?" (41–62); Gary N. Knoppers, "An Achaemenid Imperial Authorization of Torah in Yehud?" (115–34); Donald B. Redford, "The So-Called 'Codification' of Egyptian Law under Darius I" (135–59); and Jean-Louis Ska, " 'Persian Imperial Authorization': Some Question Marks" (161–82). Joseph Blenkinsopp concludes: "Imperial authorization of the laws in the Pentateuch remains a *possible* hypothesis, but for the moment no more than that" (p. 62; emphasis in the original). See also Tamara Cohn Eskenazi, "The Missions of Ezra and Nehemiah," in *Judah and the Judeans in the Persian Period* (ed. Oded Lipschits and Manfred Oeming; Winona Lake, IN: Eisenbrauns, 2006) 509–29; Sebastian Grätz, "Esra 7 im Kontext hellenistischer Politik," in *Die Griechen und das antike Israel:*

which Peter Frei proposed it.[136] Some authors reject the theory altogether. Eckart Otto, for instance, writes: "Apart from numerous Old Testament exegetical and Iranistic arguments, it is above all the Achaemenid ideology of law itself that is at variance with this thesis."[137] Others, however, accept a modified version of the theory.[138] Thus, David M. Carr in his book *Reading the Fractures of Genesis*, concluded that,

> given the parallels to Persian sponsorship of collection and publication of local law elsewhere, and given the highly unusual character of the final redaction of Pentateuchal books like Genesis, it is likely that some kind of Persian collection and publication practice played a role in sponsoring and/or confirming the tensive P/non-P composition that we now have before us.[139]

Carr also points out that "we cannot know exactly how or how much the Persians were involved, and the examples of Persian governmental authorization suggest a broad range of different relationships between local initiative and Persian sponsorship and support."[140]

In this volume, Konrad Schmid also argues for a correct reading of Frei's thesis and pleads for a nuanced view of the toleration or acknowledgment of local regulations by the central Persian authorities. He distinguishes between two problems: on the one hand, there is the question whether historically the Torah was formed as a result of a Persian imperial authorization; on the other hand, we must ask whether the relevant texts in the Bible (e.g., Ezra 7) sought to connect the formation of the Torah with processes of imperial acknowledgment or authorization of local laws.

Interdisziplinäre Studien zur Religions- und Kulturgeschichte des Heiligen Landes (ed. Stefan Alkier and Markus Witte; OBO 201; Fribourg: Academic Press / Göttingen: Vandenhoeck & Ruprecht, 2004) 135–36; and idem, *Edikt des Artaxerxes*, 264–65. See also the references cited in James W. Watts's "Introduction," *Persia and Torah: The Theory of Imperial Authorization of the Pentateuch* (ed. James W. Watts; SBLSymS 17; Atlanta: Society of Biblical Literature, 2001) 2 n. 3.

136. Referring to two collections of articles on the question of *Reichsautorisation* (that is, *Persia and Torah* [ed. James W. Watts] and *Religion und Religionskontakte im Zeitalter der Achämeniden* [ed. Reinhard Kratz]), Grätz remarks: "Die Durchmusterung der Beiträge zeigt, daß sich Freis These im deutschsprachigen Bereich anders als im angelsächsichen einer größeren Zustimmung erfreut" (*Edikt des Artaxerxes*, 2 n. 2; ET: "A perusal of the contributions shows that Frei's thesis enjoys greater acceptance in the German-speaking milieu than in the Anglo-Saxon world").

137. Otto, "Rechtshermeneutik des Pentateuch," 105 ("Gegen diese These spricht neben zahlreichen exegetisch-alttestamentlichen und iranistischen Argumenten vornehmlich die achämenidische Rechtsideologie selbst").

138. For a critique of some of the criticisms leveled against the theory, see Blum, "Esra, die Mosetora und die persische Politik," 248.

139. David M. Carr, *Reading the Fractures of Genesis: Historical and Literary Approaches* (Louisville: Westminster/John Knox, 1996) 330.

140. Ibid., 330–31.

James W. Watts, in his recent book, concluded that "Persian officials frequently provided imperial authorization for written laws governing the cultic
and financial matters of temples. Such authorizations were usually prompted by
local requests and they resulted in the ideological, but not documentary, identification of cultic and imperial law."[141] The advantages of "official recognition
as a 'temple community' provided great legal and financial motivation for Judah's rival legal factions to compose a unified law code."[142] Later, in the summary of his introduction to the collective work *Persia and Torah: The Theory of
Imperial Authorization of the Pentateuch*, Watts suggested that it may be that the
Persian authorities accorded the Pentateuch (in analogy with a modern practice) the designation "official" law of the Jews, but this would have been only
"a token favor, with little or no attention to that law's form or content."[143]

These modifications of the hypothesis of the Persian *Reichsautorisation* to include more-indirect interventions in the formation and promulgation of Jewish
law by the imperial authorities answer some of the concerns raised by the original theory. However, one consequence of the modifications is that the explan-
atory function of the theory for our question regarding the identical Samaritan
and Jewish Pentateuchs is diminished, if not nullified. If the formation of the
Pentateuch was a purely intra-Judean matter or if there was no one authorized
or interested in making the same text binding on the population of both Judea
and Samaria, what motivated the North to adopt the same text as the South? In
fact, does a more diffuse Persian toleration or valorization of the Pentateuch
have any bearing on the *explanandum*—that is, the fact that the two Pentateuchs
are almost identical? Or did the traditions that the two populations had in common and the allowances for Northern beliefs made by the editors of the early
Pentateuch constitute enough of an incentive? At the present time, we simply
do not know.

5. Conclusion

Despite our lack of detailed information about the demography of Samaria
after the Assyrian conquests, it has become more and more evident in recent
years that Samaria was inhabited at all times, even after 722/721 B.C.E., by
YHWH worshipers whose culture and religious outlook were the same as the
Judeans'. Therefore, it stands to reason that the pentateuchal traditions—or at
least some of them—were the common possession of Judahite and Samarian

---

141. James W. Watts, *Reading Law: The Rhetorical Shaping of the Pentateuch* (Biblical Seminar 59;
Sheffield: Sheffield Academic Press, 1999) 142.

142. Ibid., 142–43.

143. Idem, "Introduction," 3.

Yahwists for a long time before the Samarians adapted them to their distinct theology, shortly before the turn of the eras. Unfortunately, the tendentious nature of the biblical writings dealing with the North, the scarcity of extrabiblical sources, and the lack of early nonpentateuchal Samaritan writings make it difficult to be more definitive.

In particular, the realization that there was continuity of YHWH worship in the North, that there were important interactions between Samarians and Judeans, and that some Samarian traditions were accommodated in the early versions of the Pentateuch does not provide an adequate answer to the question how to explain the fact that the pentateuchal texts in Samaria and Judea are virtually identical.

The theories that were put forth and that seemed to account for it can no longer be accepted without qualifications. The earlier hypothesis, based on the combination of Neh 13:28 and Josephus, *Ant.* 11.306–312—that in the 5th or 4th century B.C.E. a priest or a group of priests were expelled and migrated from Jerusalem to Mount Gerizim and took the Pentateuch with them—rests on too many uncertain conjectures about the interpretation of the texts concerned, their time frame, and their referents to be acceptable. The more recent theory of the Persian *Reichsautorisation* would have presented a possible explanation for the identity of the two Pentateuchs. However, it too has come in for criticism and has been rejected by many scholars. A modified version was therefore proposed that allows for a less specific involvement by the Persian government than originally envisaged. If, however, an attenuated contribution from the side of the Persians is assumed, the virtual identity of the Jewish and Samaritan Pentateuch still needs to be explained.

Some of the questions about the prehistory of the Samaritan Pentateuch are the same as questions about the prehistory of the Judean Pentateuch. In both cases, there is still a great deal that is not yet understood regarding the formation of the corpus of writings making up the final product. Progress in these matters will need to come from further close analysis of the biblical texts in conjunction with archaeological surveys and excavations. The discoveries in Elephantine, Qumran and surroundings, and in Wadi Daliyeh, the ongoing excavations on Mount Gerizim, and the surveys and excavations on other sites of Samaria have already deepened our insights into the early history of the Samaritans in previously unexpected ways. We must also hope that further research into the formative process of the Judean Pentateuch will contribute to a better understanding of the circumstances surrounding the origin of the Pentateuch among the Samaritans.

PART 4

The Translation, Interpretation, and Application of the Torah in Early Jewish Literature

The Second Temple and the Legal Status of the Torah: The Hermeneutics of the Torah in the Books of Ruth and Ezra

SEBASTIAN GRÄTZ

Universität Bonn

This essay deals with two important questions concerning the status of the Torah in postexilic times. The first question focuses on the importance of the Torah as a written and authoritative document in the postexilic era on the basis of two examples from the books of Ezra (I) and Ruth (II). The second question addresses the historical problem of the status of the Torah in postexilic Jewish society as a public, binding book of laws (III).

I. Observations on the Use of the Torah in the Book of Ezra

In Ezra 9 and 10, one encounters the so-called prohibition of mixed marriages by Ezra. Ezra is told that some of the people of Israel have taken foreign wives for themselves and their sons (Ezra 9:1, 2). As a consequence, Ezra initiates measures leading to the divorce of the individuals in mixed marriages. According to Ezra 10:3, these measures agree with the Torah: "Now therefore, let us make a covenant with our God to put away all these wives and those who have been born to them, according to the advice of my master and of those who tremble at the commandment of our God; and let it be done according to the law."[1] The English "according to the law" translates the Hebrew כתורה. One wonders which particular law is meant by this wording.

In a very instructive essay in the recent volume *Persia and Torah*, Joseph Blenkinsopp emphasizes that the phrase "according to the law" (כתורה)—linked to the reported measures in Ezra 9–10—does not correspond with any

---

Author's note: I am very grateful to Jochen Schmidt (Bonn) and the editors for their assistance in completing this essay.

1. Read in Ezra 10:3 "my master," following the apparatus of BHS. 1 Esd 8:90 (σοι) implies that Shecaniah's speech refers to the advice of Ezra.

law in the Pentateuch.[2] This observation is undoubtedly correct. There is no law in the Pentateuch commanding the coercive divorce measures taken in Ezra 9–10. But one can ask whether the expression "according to the law" (כתורה) refers to an individual law or to the Torah as an authoritative entity on which the author is focusing. Unfortunately, the expression כתורה appears only four times in the Old Testament (2 Kgs 17:34, Ps 119:85, 2 Chr 30:16, Ezra 10:3), and scholars often interpret it in combination with the more frequent expression "as it is written" (ככתוב). In the words of Thomas Willi, the expression ככתוב does not aim at a literal quotation but at congruence with a written tradition: "The Chronicler is concerned with the preposition of comparison כ and with the idea and the possibility of comparison as such. The point of reference is *the* Scripture as an integrated unity rather than a particular verse or passage."[3]

If we now turn again to Ezra 9–10, it is possible to illustrate Willi's statement as we find allusions to the Holiness Code and to Deuteronomistic phraseology. The first important term to consider is the root בדל "to separate," which appears in Ezra 9:1, as well as its antonym התערב "to mix," which appears in Ezra 9:2.

In the Holiness Code (Lev 20:26), we read the following phrase: "I am the LORD your God, who has separated you from the peoples." The idea of separation (בדל) is constitutive in the Holiness Code (Lev 20:24–26) and also in the material belonging to the Priestly Code in the Pentateuch. The importance of the notion of separation for the Priestly writers can be seen earlier on by the use of the verb "to separate" (בדל) in the Priestly Creation story (Gen 1:4, 7). It seems that, according to the author of Ezra 9, the mixture of human beings who have different origins is theologically unacceptable. To stress his point, the author alludes in Ezra 9:1 to the enumeration of foreign peoples (Canaanites, Hittites, Perizzites, Jebusites, Ammonites, Moabites, Egyptians, and Amorites) that we find especially in Deuteronomistic contexts (e.g., Deut 7:1; Josh 3:10, 9:1), and also to a significant amplification involving the Ammonites, Moabites, and the Egyptians. The list of the latter peoples is taken from Deut

---

2. Joseph Blenkinsopp, "Was the Pentateuch the Civic and Religious Constitution of the Jewish Ethnos in the Persian Period?" in *Persia and Torah: The Theory of Imperial Authorization of the Pentateuch* (ed. James W. Watts; SBLSymS 17; Atlanta: Society of Biblical Literature, 2001) 41–62 (quotation from p. 58).

3. Original: "Dem Chronisten kommt es auf die Vergleichspartikel כ und die Vergleichbarkeit überhaupt an. Bezugsgröße ist *die* Schrift als Einheit und Ganzheit, nicht eine bestimmte Fundstelle oder Textpassage." See Thomas Willi, "Leviten, Priester und Kult in vorhellenistischer Zeit: Die chronistische Optik in ihrem geschichtlichen Kontext," in *Gemeinde ohne Tempel—Community without Temple: Zur Substituierung und Transformation des Jerusalemer Tempels und seines Kults im Alten Testament, antiken Judentum und frühen Christentum* (ed. Beate Ego, Armin Lange, and Peter Pilhofer; WUNT 118; Tübingen: Mohr Siebeck, 1999) 75–98 (quotation from pp. 86–87; italics his).

23:4[ET 23:3], as well as from Deut 23:8[ET 23:9], as Michael Fishbane has shown. The influence of 23:8[9] is evident, because of the mention of the Egyptians in Ezra 9:1.[4] It is very unlikely that the author of Ezra 9 knew any Hittite, Jebusite, or Perizzite personally because it is improbable that any members of these nations still existed in the postexilic context. At this point they existed only textually. Therefore the author seems to quote the Deuteronomistic list as a hermeneutical tool: "there can be little doubt that the reference by Ezra's princes to the intermarriage law in Deut. 7:1–3, 6, *with the notable addition of just those people mentioned in Deut. 23:4–9*, is an intentional exegetical attempt to extend older pentateuchal provisions to the new times."[5] Therefore, one can conclude that the case of the mixed marriages in Ezra 9–10 serves as a textual model for an ideal ("holy" in the sense of "separated") society in postexilic Judah,[6] or, as Joseph Blenkinsopp maintains: "what was at issue here was a matter of the greatest importance for the future: the definition and identity of the Jewish people in its relation to the Gentile world."[7]

---

4. See Michael Fishbane, *Biblical Interpretation in Ancient Israel* (Oxford: Clarendon, 1985) 114–29, with further observations about the "exegetical blendings" of the author of Ezra 9. Fishbane points out that the writer of Ezra 9 is especially indebted to Deuteronomy (7:1–3, 23:4–9) and to the Holiness Code (Leviticus 18): "It is clear from these texts that a corporate holiness is attributed to Israel, and as such, is vulnerable to pollution and desecration" (ibid., 121). It is worth pointing out that 1 Esd 8:66 reads και Ιδουμαιων, "and of (the peoples of) the Edomites" (instead of MT Ezra 9:1, והאמרי, "and the Amorites"). This is in line with Fishbane's reconstruction (note the mention of the "Edomites" in Deut 23:8). This reading may be an interpretation of Deut 23:4–9, however, insofar as it completes the Hebrew Vorlage by mentioning the "Edomites" instead of the expected "Amorites." Nevertheless, the possibility exists not only of a metathesis involving the Hebrew letters ד and מ but also of someone's confusing the ד and the very similar-looking ר in the textual transmission of the passage so that the "Edomites" later became the "Amorites." If Fishbane is right in his observations, one can indeed expect that the author of Ezra 9:1 originally mentioned the "Edomites" side by side with the "Egyptians," both of which he found in Deut 23:8, because the "Amorites" appear in Deut 7:1 without the "Egyptians." See also Joseph Blenkinsopp, *Ezra–Nehemiah: A Commentary* (OTL; London: SCM, 1988) 174.

5. Ibid., 116 (italics original). Deut 7:1–4, in contrast, does not argue its point in line with the motif of "separation," which is typical in the Priestly Code and the Holiness Code, but in line with the motif of serving foreign gods, which is typical in Deuteronomic/Deuteronomistic theology.

6. For "separated," see ibid., 121–23. In this context, it is remarkable that Chronicles, presumably contemporary to Ezra/Nehemiah, clearly displays an inclusive model of Judahite society, as Gary Knoppers has shown. The genealogies of Judah in 1 Chr 2:3–4:23 also draw selectively from pentateuchal genealogies but add to them substantially. Links between Judah (and his descendants) include the Canaanites, Ishmaelites, Edomites, Moabites, and Egyptians. Knoppers summarizes: "If in Ezra (9:10–15) the people's fragile existence in the land is threatened by the phenomenon of mixed marriages, in Chronicles the phenomenon of mixed marriages is one means by which Judah expands and develops within the land." See Gary N. Knoppers, "Intermarriage, Social Complexity, and Ethnic Diversity in the Genealogy of Judah," *JBL* 120 (2001) 15–30 (quotation from p. 30).

7. Blenkinsopp, *Ezra–Nehemiah*, 195.

Seen from a hermeneutical standpoint, the main feature in Ezra 9–10 is, indeed, the claim of conformity to the Torah. That this is true can be seen by the allusions in the initial verses of Ezra 9 (vv. 1–2) and the conclusion of the story in Ezra 10 (v. 3), indicating that the measures undertaken by Ezra are altogether in accordance with the Torah (כתורה). From the perspective of the author of the Ezra narrative, the Torah appears to be the norm for solving problems as they occur in the community. This perspective accords with the high estimation given to the "law" in the letter of Artaxerxes in Ezra 7.[8] The "law" is not quoted or interpreted in a literal sense but in a theological way. The author of Ezra 9–10 takes the theological ideas of "separation" (בדל) and forbidden mixtures (root ערב) from the Torah and applies them to the case of the mixed marriages.[9] This interpretive step indeed amounts to an adaptation—at least by using the same words.[10] And it is also interesting that in the opinion of the author the theological principle of separation between the peoples is more important and foundational than the validity of an individual marriage contract.

The use of כתורה in Ezra 10:3 can be compared with the use of ככתוב in the sense that Willi has suggested—that is, in accordance with an authoritative written tradition. This hermeneutical method opens the possibility of interpreting the Torah in an adaptive manner that brings together the written authoritative tradition on the one hand and the needs of the recipients of this tradition on the other hand. Using this hermeneutical method, the text of Ezra 9–10 introduces a law that is not attested in the Torah (Pentateuch), while nonetheless presenting it as conforming to Torah.[11] Jacob Milgrom has called a

---

8. The meaning of the Aramaic term דת in Ezra 7:12–26, in comparison with the Hebrew term תורה (Ezra 7:6, 10; 10:3), is disputed. The interpretation depends, in part, on one's estimation of the historical value of this text. Among others, Lester L. Grabbe has argued that, "in the context of Ezra 7, there seems little doubt that *torah* and *dat* are to be understood as the same thing" (*Ezra–Nehemiah* [London: Routledge, 1998] 144 [italics his]).

9. As Fishbane (*Biblical Interpretation*, 117–23) has shown, one can easily discern further allusions to the Torah in Ezra 9–10. Note, for instance, the motif of the polluted land in Ezra 9:11 with the Hebrew wording נדה, תועבה, and טמא, referring to the Holiness Code (Leviticus 18). As Bernard M. Levinson ("The Birth of the Lemma: The Restrictive Reinterpretation of the Covenant Code's Manumission Law by the Holiness Code [Leviticus 25:44–46]," *JBL* 124 [2005] 617–39) has pointed out, one can observe the restrictions of older legal material within the Torah. The example of Ezra 9–10 displays a comparable case outside the Torah. Contemporary needs or insights determine the exegesis of the Torah and also create different exegetical tools.

10. See Joachim Schaper, "Reading the Law: Inner-Biblical Exegesis of Divine Oracles in Ezekiel 44 and Isaiah 56," in *Recht und Ethik im Alten Testament: Beiträge des Symposiums "Das Alte Testament und die Kultur der Moderne" anlässlich des 100. Geburtstags Gerhard von Rads (1901–1971) Heidelberg, 18.–21. Oktober 2001* (ed. Bernard M. Levinson and Eckart Otto; Altes Testament und Moderne 13; Münster: LIT, 2004) 125–44. Schaper also speaks of adaptation when he examines the relationship between Deut 23:2–4 and Ezek 44:6–9 (p. 138).

11. Kevin L. Spawn (*"As It Is Written" and other Citation Formulae in the Old Testament: Their Use, Development, Syntax, and Significance* [BZAW 311; Berlin: de Gruyter, 2002] 221–22) draws

comparable interpretive method at Qumran the "homogenization hermeneutic," which was adopted if cases that did not appear in the Torah needed to be anchored therein. Furthermore, the application of this method presupposes an authoritative understanding of the Torah as the origin of any divine law.[12] On the grounds of this understanding of the Torah, the author of Ezra could describe his homogenization in Ezra 9–10 as being "according to the Torah."

II. Observations on the Use of the Torah in the Book of Ruth

I have chosen the example of the mixed marriages in the book of Ezra as a good starting point from which to proceed to my second example, the topic of the foreign woman in the book of Ruth. The book of Ruth presumably stems from the late Persian or early Hellenistic Period and so may be contemporary with the book of Ezra.[13] Very important for the late date of the book are the broad dependencies on the entire Pentateuch. In an article on Ruth, Georg Braulik writes:

> In my article I confine myself to Deuteronomy as the pre-text being decisive for the book of Ruth, though Ruth also refers, for example, to the narratives of Genesis on Israel's arch-parents, to the Manna narrative in Exodus 16, and to the 'kinsman-redeeming' legislation in Leviticus 25. These references show that Ruth probably already presupposes the entire Torah as a canonical entity.[14]

Braulik subsequently shows that the book of Ruth is a "counter story to the 'community law' (Dt 23:4–7)," as well as a "correction of the image of the Moabitesses (Gn 19:30–38)."[15] Finally, he concludes: "All in all, the book of

---

further conclusions when he writes: "In Ezra 10, the writer appears to present Shecaniah as a warning to the reader that shoddy exegetical methods are a threat to the preservation of the traditions of the fathers. . . ." The possible relation between the word "Torah" in Ezra 10:3 and the obvious references to the Torah (Pentateuch) in Ezra 9:1–2 are, however, not taken into account. In the present text (Ezra 9–10), Ezra 10:3 serves in my opinion as a *Wiederaufnahme* to solve the problem of the reported transgressions against the Torah (Ezra 9:1–2) "according to the Torah."

12. See Jacob Milgrom, "The Scriptural Foundations and Deviations in Laws of Purity of the Temple Scroll," in *Archaeology and History in the Dead Sea Scrolls: The New York University Conference in Memory of Yigael Yadin* (ed. Larry H. Schiffman; JSPSup 8; Sheffield: JSOT Press, 1990) 83–99 (quotation from p. 95). See also Bernard M. Levinson, "'You must not add anything to what I command you': Paradoxes of Canon and Authorship in Ancient Israel," *Numen* 50 (2003) 1–51 (esp. 41–43).

13. Irmtraud Fischer, *Rut* (2nd ed.; HTKAT; Freiburg: Herder, 2005) 86–91.

14. Georg Braulik, "The Book of Ruth as Intra-Biblical Critique on the Deuteronomic Law," *AcT* 19 (1999) 1–20 (quotation from p. 3).

15. Ibid., 8.

Ruth changes the Law of Deuteronomy into 'narrative ethics.'"[16] In my opinion, this conclusion is generally correct. The following observations may be
helpful in complementing Braulik's view.

In Ruth 2, we find a scene in which Ruth meets Boaz in his field, and the
following verses, I argue, are important not only for understanding the scene
but also for understanding the narrative as a whole. I quote vv. 10–12, following the NKJV:

> So she fell on her face, bowed down to the ground, and said to him,
> "Why have I found favor in your eyes, that you should take notice of
> me, since I am a foreigner?" And Boaz answered and said to her, "It has
> been fully reported to me, all that you have done for your mother-in-
> law since the death of your husband, and how you have left your father
> and your mother and the land of your birth, and have come to a people
> whom you did not know before. The LORD repay your work, and a
> full reward be given you by the LORD God of Israel, under whose
> wings you have come for refuge."

The quoted section plays an important role in the entire book, because in his
speech Boaz initially looks back to what had happened on the plains of Moab:
"It has been fully reported to me, all that you have done" (הגד הגד לי כל אשר
עשית). Note that the perfect tense is used in the Hebrew.[17] Afterward, the
tense switches to the jussive/future to give an idea of what may happen in the
progression of the plot. The expression "the LORD repay your work" (ישלם
יהוה) employs the jussive, which, in this case, opens a perspective on the expected deeds of God. In recalling the past and pointing to the future, the
speech of Boaz can be understood as the pivotal point of the whole story.[18]
Let me now highlight three main features of the quoted passage by exploring
its content.

At first, Ruth calls herself a "stranger" (נכריה), which seems to be important
for understanding the narrative.[19] Her status as a stranger (נכריה) should have
been the main reason that the encounter with Boaz was unexpected, at least to
her: "Why have I found favor in your eyes?" (Ruth 2:10). The position of Ruth
and her behavior are understandable in different contexts, for example, if one
reads the book against the (fictitious) background of ancient oriental tribal or
clan thinking on which the setting of the Ruth narrative in the time of the

---

16. Ibid., 19.

17. See Fischer, *Rut*, 26.

18. See Kirsten Nielsen, *Ruth: A Commentary* (OTL; Louisville, KY: Westminster John Knox,
1997) 59.

19. Compare with Bernhard Lang, "נכר," *ThWAT* 5.458–59 (= *TDOT* 9.427–28).

Judges is based.[20] Or the story can be read against the contemporary background of a postexilic society in which positions such as we come across in the book of Ezra were apparently common.[21] The crucial theme of the status of foreigners functions well in both contexts. Therefore, one should pay close attention to the status of Ruth as a stranger or foreigner, when interpreting the book of Ruth.

Second, the statement of Boaz evinces the idea of retribution. The key word in Ruth 2:12 is the verb שלם in the Piel stem, which denotes the idea of retribution.[22] In Ruth's commitment to the God of Naomi, her deeds, and her "work" (פעל) for her mother-in-law reported in 1:16–17 and summarized by Boaz in 2:11a, we encounter a concise definition of retribution in word and in action.[23] The definition of retribution by Jan Assmann is useful in this context. He quotes an Egyptian inscription of Neferhotep (1700 B.C.E.), emphasizing: "The reward of one who does is that (things) are done for him."[24] In later times, the social dimension of retribution includes the actions of a deity: "Anybody who does something good is rewarded by god."[25] This view of course has parallels in the Old Testament, as the previously mentioned quotation from Ruth 2:12 also shows. The closest parallel to Ruth 2:12 can be found in the book of Job 34:11: "For He repays (שלם, Piel) a man according to his work (פעל) and enables a man to find a reward according to his way."[26] The speech

---

20. See Fischer, *Rut*, 159; Sebastian Grätz, "Zuwanderung als Herausforderung: Das Rutbuch als Modell einer sozialen und religiösen Integration von Fremden im nachexilischen Judäa," *EvT* 65 (2005) 294–309 (esp. 305–6).

21. We also encounter the use of tribal patterns in Ezra. According to the genealogical principles of this book (Ezra 2, 7:1–5, 8:1–14), the Jewish group that built the Second Temple is called "Judah and Benjamin" (Ezra 1:5, 4:1) in opposition to the "people(s) of the land."

22. See Bernd Janowski, "Die Tat kehrt zum Täter zurück: Offene Fragen im Umkreis des 'Tun-Ergehen-Zusammenhangs,'" *ZTK* 91 (1994) 247–71 (esp. 257–61). The commentary of Jack M. Sasson (*Ruth: A New Translation with a Philological Commentary and a Formalist-Folklorist Interpretation* [2nd ed.; Biblical Seminar 10; Sheffield: JSOT Press, 1989]) seems to underestimate the pivotal character of these verses (Ruth 2:11–12) a little, when he provides just a hint of the Arabic "May God give you" (see p. 52) but does not note the summarizing function of these verses for the whole narrative.

23. See Yair Zakovitch, *Das Buch Rut: Ein jüdischer Kommentar* (SBS 177; Stuttgart: Katholisches Bibelwerk, 1999) 23.

24. Original: "*Der Lohn eines Handelnden liegt darin, dass für ihn gehandelt wird.*" See Jan Assmann, *Ma'at: Gerechtigkeit und Unsterblichkeit im Alten Ägypten* (2nd ed.; Munich: Beck, 1995) 65 (italics in original), 238. [The editors wish to thank Donald B. Redford for his help with translating this saying, as well as for providing his own alternate translation: "The reward of someone who does (something) lies in what (he) has done."]

25. Original: "*Wer etwas Gutes tut, den belohnt der Gott,*" ibid., 67 (italics in original). See also Janowski, "Die Tat kehrt zum Täter zurück," 269–70.

26. Zakovitch, *Das Buch Rut*, 119.

of Elihu can be taken as a classic statement of the idea of retribution, with God as acting subject.[27] The book of Ruth seems to refer to this tradition as well in order to establish the status of Ruth as a member of Israelite society.[28] This may be proved by the second part of Ruth 2:12. Here, Yhwh, who is also the God of Ruth (see her earlier commitment in Ruth 1:16), is clearly identified as "God of Israel" (אלהי ישראל). The social affiliation here is linked to the religious commitment. In Ruth 2:12, the idea of retribution therefore exceeds the narrow bonds of society or, in turn, the relation of Israelites to Moabites according to Deuteronomy 23. It is worth noting that in Deuteronomy 23 the so-called "Law of the Assembly" (Deut 23:2–9[ET 23:1–8]) with its use of the Hebrew term קהל "assembly") refers to Deut 5:22, where the notion of the assembly is closely connected to the covenant at Horeb.[29] This meant, for the reader in Second Temple times, that the peoples mentioned in the Law of the Assembly were excluded from Yhwh's covenant with Israel because they were not allowed to enter the assembly.[30]

The book of Ruth, in contrast, displays another concept of society. The question of her origins notwithstanding, Ruth may be rewarded by Yhwh for her deeds—that is, for her commitment and for treating her mother-in-law in the aforementioned manner.[31] Hence, she has shown her ability to become a

---

27. See Karl-Johann Illman, "שלם," *ThWAT* 8:93–101, esp. 97 (= *TDOT* 15.97–105, esp. 101). Janowski ("Die Tat kehrt zum Täter zurück," 266–70) equates the meaning of שלם Piel/ Pual/Hiphil with שוב Qal/Hiphil and פקד with God as grammatical subject concerning the idea of retribution/reciprocity in the relevant sapiential literature. This means that there are several other instances in the sapiential literature that can be taken into account to gain a deeper understanding of Ruth 2:12. Starting from Prov 24:12 and 25:21–22, Janowski tries to show that the action of God is in line with the social principle of reciprocity. Thus, the sage can reckon that God rewards him for his good deeds. This is precisely the case in the speech of Boaz. Following the principle of reciprocity, Boaz announces God's reward for the deeds of Ruth. As will be shown below, the idea of reciprocity in the book of Ruth is conceptualized beyond the Deuteronomic/Deuteronomistic theology of the covenant.

28. Fischer (*Rut*, 91–92) has suggested that the book of Ruth was written and handed down by "educated circles" that were familiar with the written tradition of the Torah. This also seems to be shown in the previously mentioned article by Braulik, "Book of Ruth." The use of the sapiential tradition seems, in view of Ruth 2:12, to be clear as well. Yet, it remains an open question whether the author is harking back to a written or an oral tradition. The sum of evidence available in the book of Ruth seems to be too scant for drawing further conclusions.

29. See Frank-Lothar Hossfeld and Eva-Martina Kindl, "קהל," *ThWAT* 6.1210–19, esp. 1211–12 (= *TDOT* 12.551–59, esp. 552–54).

30. Though the present connection between Deut 5:22 (קהל) and 23:2–9 (קהל) may be secondary (see Hossfeld and Kindl, "קהל," 1211–12 [*TDOT* 12.552–54]), the author of the book of Ruth must not have been aware of the actual literary stratification of Deuteronomy. In all probability he read the book as a unit.

31. See Lang, "נכר," 458–59 (*TDOT* 9.427–28); Grätz, "Zuwanderung als Herausforderung," 294–309.

member of the Bethlehemite/Israelite society in the full sense. It is clear that the idea of retribution applied in the book of Ruth differs from the idea of retribution in the book of Deuteronomy (7:10: שלם Piel, with God as subject). In Deuteronomy, the idea of retribution is closely linked to obedience to the Deuteronomic/Deuteronomistic Law (Deut 7:11).[32] The feature of God's rewarding or punishing according to a person's deeds operates within the larger context of covenantal theology. Ruth 1–2, as mentioned above, cannot deal with the covenant, because the Deuteronomic/Deuteronomistic notion of the covenant does not include the Moabites.[33] The closest parallel for the idea of retribution in Ruth 2 therefore seems to be the common sapiential insight that God (or society) rewards a person according to her or his deeds.

Now it is appropriate to return to the discussion of Braulik. He convincingly argues that the book of Ruth was created as a counternarrative to the Law of the Assembly in Deuteronomy 23. This also means that the author of Ruth had knowledge of the book of Deuteronomy and, indeed, of the entire Pentateuch, as Braulik claims.[34] And it is interesting to note that the author of Ruth bypasses the well-known verdict of the Law of the Assembly and the Deuteronomic/Deuteronomistic notion of the covenant by choosing to draw from an alternate well-known pattern, the sapiential tradition of retribution or reciprocity.[35] The author appears to have assumed that the sapiential tradition with its international origins and international comprehensibility was a more appropriate context than the Torah within which to address an "international" question such as the problem posed in the book of Ruth. More precisely, it was more appropriate than the covenantal theology anchored in the Torah, with its distinctive conceptions clearly focused on Israel and Israelite society. This means that the author of Ruth found it appropriate to demonstrate an alternative to a clear law written in the Torah by going back to another common tradition in Israel, which may have been as popular or authoritative as the Torah in the time of the author.

Third, we do have a clear reference to the Torah in Ruth (2:11): the author's allusion to two passages in Genesis. The reference is apparent in the following table:

---

32. See Moshe Weinfeld, *Deuteronomy 1–11: A New Translation with Commentary* (AB 5; New York: Doubleday, 1991) 371.

33. Moreover, the imagery in Ruth 2:12b (God's protecting "wings"; see Ps 36:8, 63:8) does not point to the covenant.

34. Braulik, "Book of Ruth," 3.

35. The discussion of Schaper ("Exegesis," 125–44) deals with the reception of the "Law of the Assembly" in the prophetic tradition (Isa 56:1–8, Ezekiel 44). His study is based extensively on the insights of Fishbane, *Biblical Interpretation*, 138–43.

Ruth 2:11b	Gen 2:24a	Gen 12:1
ותעזבי אביך ואמך וארץ מולדתך ותלכי אל עם אשר לא ידעת	על כן יעזב איש את אביו ואת אמו	ויאמר יהוה אל אברם לך לך מארצך וממולדתך ומבית אביך אל הארץ אשר אראך
"and that you have left your father and your mother and the land of your family, and have come to a people whom you did not know before."	"Therefore a man shall leave his father and mother."	"Now the LORD had said to Abram: 'Get out of your country, from your family, and from your father's house, to a land that I will show you.' "

Boaz uses the exact Hebrew terminology of the quoted Yahwistic passages with the reference to the "leaving" (עזב) of "father" (אב), "mother" (אם), and "family" (מולדת), as well as the motif of the "unknown country."[36] This does not seem to be accidental.[37] It shows that the behavior of Ruth, who left her home country and her family, may appear illogical only at first glance, because she behaved exactly as Abram did when he trusted in God. It also shows that, according to Gen 2:24, it is necessary to establish or, in the case of Ruth, to preserve a family.[38] From this point of view, the deeds of Ruth are in line with the Torah, so that both motifs are linked together: the all-embracing idea of retribution is being realized by means of deeds that are according to the Torah. This shows that the book of Ruth is far from arbitrary in its stance toward the Torah and the question of foreigners. But the main feature, the integration of Ruth into Israelite society, is clearly demonstrated by using the idea of retribution in accordance with narrative parts of the Torah and not by adapting or reinterpreting legal material written in the Torah.

Thomas Krüger has shown in an article about the reception of the Torah in Ecclesiastes that "the conceptualization of the Torah as normative canonical direction for the conduct of human life is being criticized theologically. None-

---

36. The late (postexilic) date of the book of Ruth assumed here makes it possible to avoid commenting on the crucial question of the dating of J. Because the author of Ruth seems to know an entire Torah, one may assume that the different sources or fragments had already been compiled and edited into an entire opus.

37. Fischer, *Rut*, 176–77.

38. It even seems possible to go one step further. According to the biblical narrative, the behavior of Abram/Abraham leads to the birth of Israel. According to the present book of Ruth, the comparable behavior of Ruth leads not only to the preservation of Naomi's family but also to the emergence of the Davidic dynasty.

theless, one can gain essential elements of a theological interpretation of human life from the Torah and particularly from the Primeval History and develop these in more detail."[39] This conclusion in Krüger's essay may be compared with the attitude toward the Torah that we find in Ruth. The Torah as an entity was well known, but it was not accepted as the only normative source for answering current questions.[40] Krüger's notion of a "development" may address the issue very well. The author of Ruth intended to criticize current customs or the kind of Torah-exegesis that served to establish certain practices as they are depicted in Ezra 9–10. And in doing so, he also felt comfortable in criticizing a particular law of the Torah—in this case, of Deuteronomy.

At this point in the discussion, it may be helpful to return to the observations of Michael Fishbane about the supplementation of the Deuteronomistic list of foreign nations with the Ammonites and Moabites (taken from Deut 23:4[ET 23:3]) in Ezra 9:1. In a short footnote, Fishbane addresses both the Ezra narrative and the book of Ruth together: "Reconsideration of the status of the Moabites and Ammonites was a major postexilic preoccupation: the genealogical legitimacy of the Moabites is the theme of the Book of Ruth."[41] Both narratives clearly deal with the same issue in different ways and employ different means to apply the Torah.

Before I move to my second main point, the historical question, let me give a short summary of my arguments thus far. The writers of the books of Ezra and Ruth were probably familiar with the Torah. Both deal with the marriage of foreign women in Israel, but in the end they give contradictory answers to a question that may have been current in the time they wrote. The author of Ezra solves the problem "according to the Torah" (כתורה) by alluding to and combining legal material from the Pentateuch. In contrast, the author of Ruth focuses more on the sapiential tradition with its idea of retribution, involving both God and society. This idea of retribution, is used to advance an alternative

---

39. Original: "Das Konzept der Tora als einer letztinstanzlich-normativen, 'kanonischen' Weisung Gottes für die menschliche Lebensführung wird theologisch kritisiert und relativiert. Das hindert aber nicht daran, der Tora—und hier insbesondere der Urgeschichte—wesentliche Elemente einer theologischen Deutung der menschlichen Erfahrungswirklichkeit zu entnehmen und diese kreativ weiterzuentwickeln." See Thomas Krüger, "Die Rezeption der Tora im Buch Kohelet," in *Das Buch Kohelet: Studien zur Struktur, Geschichte, Rezeption und Theologie* (ed. Ludger Schwienhorst-Schönberger; BZAW 254; Berlin: de Gruyter, 1997) 303–25. The essay is reprinted in and cited according to Krüger, *Kritische Weisheit: Studien zur weisheitlichen Traditionskritik im Alten Testament* (ed. Thomas Krüger; Zurich: Pano, 1997) 173–93 (quotation from p. 192).

40. The previously mentioned observations about the book of Ruth and the Torah on this particular issue can be supplemented by calling attention to the references to Exodus 16 (the manna narrative) and, of course, to Leviticus 25 (Braulik, "Book of Ruth," 3). On this issue, see also Fischer, *Rut*, 48.

41. Fishbane, *Biblical Interpretation*, 121 n. 43.

notion of "Israel" to the definition provided by the Law of the Assembly. At the same time, the author shows by means of allusions to the Torah that the deeds of Ruth are in accordance with the Torah. But his reasoning stems first of all from the idea of retribution and not from the idea of conformity to an authoritative Torah. The author of Ruth shows, in this case, an alternative to the Torah in answering current questions about how society should be constructed. In the book of Ruth, society is characterized by the bonds of reciprocity and a commitment to Yнwн as the God of Israel.

III. Historical Conclusions

In this final section, I would like to draw a few very concise historical conclusions from my earlier discussion. As many scholars assume, the Ezra narrative was written in the late Persian or the early Hellenistic period.[42] There is some dispute whether the letter of Artaxerxes in Ezra 7 constitutes an original document, goes back to an original document, or is a complete fiction.[43] I am personally inclined to believe that this document is a fiction from the early Hellenistic period.[44] But this "Hellenistic view" is not overly important for my remarks here. The high esteem that the "law" receives in the letter of Artaxerxes, which in the Hebrew portion of Ezra 7 is identified with the Torah,[45] seems more germane to the discussion here. It is impossible to go into the details of literary criticism in the Ezra narrative in this context, but it seems obvious that the importance of the "law" in the letter of Artaxerxes is consistent with the execution of the measures "according to the Torah" in Ezra 9–10.[46] Here, the Torah authorized in Ezra 7 is applied to a special case of temporal importance,

---

42. The most recent thorough investigation on this subject is by Juha Pakkala (*Ezra the Scribe: The Development of Ezra 7–10 and Nehemiah 8* [BZAW 347; Berlin: de Gruyter, 2004]), who assumes a complex development of the Ezra material. Interestingly, he states that the written Torah was already the raison d'être of the putative oldest stratum, the "Ezra source" (p. 278), which he finds in some verses of Ezra 7–9 and Nehemiah 8 (pp. 227–36).

43. This discussion took place in the late 19th century between Eduard Meyer and Julius Wellhausen. See Reinhard G. Kratz, "Die Entstehung des Judentums: Zur Kontroverse zwischen E. Meyer und J. Wellhausen," *ZTK* 95 (1998) 167–84, reprinted in: idem, *Das Judentum im Zeitalter des Zweiten Tempels* (FAT 42; Tübingen: Mohr Siebeck 2004) 6–22. The discussion was renewed by the contributions of Peter Frei, in which he proposed his imperial-authorization thesis. This influential thesis has been repeated, discussed, and challenged in several volumes by a variety of contributors. See, for example, the studies collected in *ZABR* 1 (1995); and in *Persia and Torah: The Theory of Imperial Authorization of the Pentateuch* (ed. James W. Watts; SBLSymS 17; Atlanta: Society of Biblical Literature, 2001). See also n. 50 below.

44. See my *Edikt des Artaxerxes: Eine Untersuchung zum religionspolitischen und historischen Umfeld von Esra 7,12–26* (BZAW 337; Berlin: de Gruyter, 2004).

45. See n. 8 above.

46. See Grabbe, *Ezra–Nehemiah*, 144–45; Grätz, *Edikt des Artaxerxes*, 53–55.

the problem of mixed marriages.[47] The Torah is clearly the criterion for resolving the issue, and we may assume that the case of the mixed marriages is just one example of the way that one was to deal with comparable problems, by their "homogenization with the Torah."[48] The texts of Qumran with their references to the Torah (and the Prophets) and with their similar methods in appropriating the Torah show us that the hermeneutical method of Ezra lived on. Therefore, we can consider the Ezra narrative a model for interpreting and using the Torah that would later become important for Jewish communities.

However, the book of Ruth shows that late Persian or early Hellenistic Judaism was far from uniform in evaluating and applying the Torah. The Ezra narrative surely was written to assist in the introduction of the Torah as authoritative law in Judea.[49] Within Ezra, the letter of Artarxerxes serves as a means of authorization. But the narrative of Ruth, with its own attitude toward the Torah, proves that either the author was unaware of the document written by the Persian officials, or this document did not exist during the time in which the author wrote. I therefore assume that an official obligation to the Torah issued by the Persian court or by anyone else in late Persian or early Hellenistic times never existed. In this, my view accords with views espoused by other scholars in recent studies.[50] Hence, the authorization of the Torah in Ezra 7 seems to be more virtual than real, as Lester Grabbe states.[51] Moreover, its main concern

---

47. That the measures reported in Ezra 9–10 historically comprised the whole people of Yehud is doubtful, in light of the tendentious character of the Ezra narrative. But it seems clear that a prohibition of these "mixed marriages" was self-evident for those circles, who wrote and handed down the Ezra material.

48. To use the expression of Jacob Milgrom once again. As Milgrom ("Scriptural Foundations," 95) has stated, homogenized laws are products of history. This seems to be true insofar as they reflect historical questions that should be addressed in accordance with the authoritative Torah.

49. See Pakkala, *Ezra the Scribe*, 278.

50. See Udo Rüterswörden ("Die persische Reichsautorisation der Thora: Fact or Fiction?" *ZABR* 1 [1995] 47–61), who assumes that the letter of Artaxerxes in Ezra 7 is a "fiction." In my opinion, the document in Ezra 7:12–26 wholly stems from the early Hellenistic period and imitates royal Hellenistic donation records (Grätz, *Edikt des Artaxerxes*). But this does not mean that no official decree concerning the province of Yehud ever existed. Moreover, the content of Ezra 7:26—the distinction between "matters of YHWH" and "matters of the king"—which in fact is very important for Frei's argumentation, has many parallels in postexilic biblical literature, as Gary N. Knoppers has shown, "An Achaemenid Imperial Authorization of Torah in Yehud?" in *Persia and Torah: The Theory of Imperial Authorization of the Pentateuch* (ed. James W. Watts; SBLSymS 17; Atlanta: Society of Biblical Literature, 2001) 115–34 (esp. 123–29). Being aware of the possibly fictitious character of Ezra 7:26, he concludes: "One does not have to postulate a Persian interest in or a demand for the authorization of an entire law code, much less an imperial interest in the prohibition of mixed marriages, to explain all the actions taken by the community leaders, Ezra, and Nehemiah" (p. 134).

51. Lester L. Grabbe, "The Law of Moses in the Ezra Tradition: More Virtual than Real?" in *Persia and Torah: The Theory of Imperial Authorization of the Pentateuch* (ed. James W. Watts; SBLSymS 17; Atlanta: Society of Biblical Literature, 2001) 91–113.

seems to be comparable to the main concern of the *Letter of Aristeas*.[52] The positions of Ezra and Ruth toward the Torah are therefore apparently two possibilities for dealing with the written Torah by the authors, and probably for the social groups to which these authors belonged.[53] But it is very likely that an official rule for understanding and applying the Torah in those times (either the late Persian or the early Hellenistic Period) never existed. In light of this fact, the book of Ruth does not contradict an official agenda but contradicts a method of dealing with a written corpus that was highly valued by certain circles in early Judaism such as, for instance, by the author of the Ezra narrative.[54] The author of the book of Ruth showed a different attitude toward the Torah when he created his narrative. Certainly, he knew and esteemed the Torah, and he proved this by making several allusions to the Torah. Nevertheless, with respect to the key question posed in his book, he took up primarily the basic idea of retribution, with its widely accepted logic of reciprocity. The Torah was used in this case to provide examples for the deeds of Ruth that conform to what the Torah in its narrative portions associates with amity and obedience to God.

The different hermeneutics of the Torah displayed in Ruth and Ezra are linked to different circles within early Judaism, each of which was trying to answer current questions in a theologically grounded way.[55] The Torah appears in those times to have been highly esteemed by all of these different circles but seems to have been interpreted and assessed in different ways. For the author of Ezra, the Torah was the starting point of his theological reflections on the issue of mixed marriages. For the author of Ruth, the starting point was the simple idea of retribution, which is enacted with deeds according to the Torah. The Torah in this context delivered only the examples, not the case.

In (early) Second Temple times, the legal status of the Torah was therefore far from being uniform.[56] The witness of two biblical books written in the

---

52. See Reinhard G. Kratz, *Die Komposition der erzählenden Bücher des Alten Testaments: Grundwissen der Bibelkritik* (Göttingen: Vandenhoeck & Ruprecht, 2000) 83. On the *Letter of Aristeas* as a "combination of invention, idealization, and attempted verisimilitude," see Oswald Murray, "Aristeas and Ptolemaic Kingship," *JTS* 18 (1967) 337–71 (quotation from p. 339).

53. Fishbane observes that "the new community of Israel was a community of communities, a variety of Judaisms, each one laying claim to the received pre-exilic Torah traditions—*through their separate and separating interpretations of them*" (*Biblical Interpretation*, 123, italics his).

54. See Fischer (*Rut*, 63–64), who claims that the book of Ruth constitutes a literary counterposition (*Gegenposition*) to the position adopted in Ezra 9–10 and Nehemiah 13. It would be interesting to examine all of the material with respect to tracing the *literary* dependencies of these biblical books.

55. This important issue is rightly addressed by Schaper, "Exegesis" 137.

56. The parentheses indicate that this phenomenon lived on, because the Torah's authoritative value was acquired in the first place by *interpretation*, as the well-known examples from early Judaism,

postexilic era show us two different ways of dealing with the Torah. The Torah could be the binding starting point of any theological or social question with a constitutional character, as well as a dignified document without these far-reaching attributes.

---

mainly Qumran, indicate. See, in addition to the above-mentioned article of Milgrom ("Scriptural Foundations"), the contribution of Reinhard G. Kratz, "Innerbiblische Exegese und Redaktions-geschichte im Lichte empirischer Evidenz," in *Das Alte Testament und die Kultur der Moderne: Beiträge des Symposiums "Das Alte Testament und die Kultur der Moderne" anlässlich des 100. Geburtstags Gerhard von Rads (1901–1971), Heidelberg, 18.–21. Oktober 2001* (ed. Manfred Oeming et al.; Altes Testament und Moderne 8; Münster: LIT, 2004) 37–69; reprinted in idem, *Das Judentum*, 126–56.

The Septuagint of the Pentateuch and Ptolemaic Rule

Arie van der Kooij
Leiden University

I. A Return to the Letter of Aristeas

The five books of the Pentateuch were translated into Greek shortly after the Persian period (in the first half of the 3rd century B.C.E.) in Alexandria. I would like to discuss the question of the origins of this translation to see whether—by way of analogy or otherwise—the production of the Greek version of the Pentateuch may shed light on the issue of the promulgation and acceptance of the Torah in the Persan period. Does the translation of the Torah into Greek have a bearing on this issue, and if so, in which respect? The historical question why the Pentateuch was translated into Greek is actually still disputed. If, as in a well-known answer, the Greek version was produced because of religious, synagogal needs, then the promulgation of the Septuagint of the Pentateuch would have no bearing on the Torah in the Persian period. Things become different, however, if the translation was carried out because the Ptolemaic king wanted to have access to the laws by which the Jews were supposed to live, as has been argued recently. It has even been suggested that the Septuagint of the Pentateuch received official sanction through inclusion in the judicial system of the Ptolemaic court. Thus, the crucial matter is whether, analogous to the issue of the Torah in the Persian period, the promulgation of the Torah in Greek was due to a Ptolemaic initiative or encouragement or whether it should be seen as an inner-Jewish phenomenon.

In order to deal with this matter in this section, I will discuss several answers that have been given to the question why the books of the Torah were rendered into Greek, beginning of course with the *Letter of Aristeas* (2nd century B.C.E.), which provides the most ancient answer to this question.[1] I will argue

---

Author's note: I am greatly indebted to the helpful and valuable comments made by the editors. Needless to say, responsibility for any remaining errors is mine.

1. For editions of the *Letter of Aristeas*, see Henry St. John Thackeray, "Appendix: The Letter of Aristeas," in Henry Barclay Swete, *An Introduction to the Old Testament in Greek* (Cambridge:

that the Jewish community in Alexandria was hardly involved in the project to produce a Greek version of the Torah. Rather, it was a matter of the Ptolemaic court, on the one hand, and the Jewish authorities in Jerusalem, on the other. From this perspective, in section II I will explore four hypotheses suggested by other scholars, in an attempt to answer the question which party took the initiative and why.

According to the *Letter of Aristeas*, the translation of the Torah was part of the policy of the Ptolemaic king, Philadelphus (282–246 B.C.E.), to collect if possible all the books of the world. The royal librarian, Demetrius of Phaleron, was commissioned to do this. Demetrius proposed including "the books of the Law of the Jews" (§30), for which a translation would be necessary. The king then sent a letter to the high priest of the Jews, announcing his plan and requesting assistance. Eleazar, the high priest, agreed to help and sent a total of 72 translators, 6 men from each tribe—men of good behavior, expert in Hebrew and in Greek, and learned in the Law—to Alexandria to prepare the translation. The work was done on the island of Pharos under the direction of Demetrius. The new version was read to the leaders of the Jewish community in Alexandria, as well as to the Ptolemaic king. It was received most favorably by both parties.

Because the *Letter* clearly bears the marks of an apologetic document, the question of its historical reliability has been disputed.[2] It has long been recognized as a pseudepigraph. Scholars such as Humphrey Hody (1659–1707) have demonstrated that the author was not an eyewitness but must have been a Jew who lived after the events he narrated. Accordingly, the *Letter*'s historical reliability has since been viewed with great skepticism.[3]

In keeping with this tendency, Henry St. John Thackeray developed the following view about the origins of the Greek Pentateuch. The Pentateuch was the first of the Old Testament books to be translated as a whole, probably by a small company of translators working from Hebrew scrolls that may have been imported from Palestine. The translation was not originally for the sake of the royal library but "for synagogue use."[4] The Jews in Alexandria were in need of

Cambridge University Press, 1914) 531–606; Moses Hadas, ed. and trans., *Aristeas to Philocrates (Letter of Aristeas)* (New York: Harper, for The Dropsie College for Hebrew and Cognate Learning, 1951); André Pelletier, ed., *Lettre d'Aristée à Philocrate: Introduction, texte critique, traduction et notes, index complet des mots grecs* (SC 89; Paris: Cerf, 1962).

2. The *Letter* defends the Greek version of the Pentateuch, made in Alexandria, by arguing that it was made by competent scholars in a most accurate way (see §§310–311).

3. See Sidney Jellicoe, *The Septuagint and Modern Study* (Oxford: Clarendon, 1968) 31; Sylvie Honigman, *The Septuagint and Homeric Scholarship in Alexandria: A Study in the Narrative of the Letter of Aristeas* (London: Routledge, 2003) 3.

4. Henry St. John Thackeray, *The Septuagint and Jewish Worship: A Study in Origins* (The Schweich Lectures 1920; 2nd ed.; London: Oxford University Press, 1923) 9.

a Greek version of the Pentateuch that could be used for reading purposes in their synagogue. This theory has found wide acceptance and remains popular to the present day.[5] A major difficulty, however, is that it presupposes synagogue practices that actually are of a much later date. There is no evidence that the Pentateuch was read continuously in a synagogal setting in the first half of the 3rd century B.C.E. in Egypt.[6] In fact, it is unclear whether the Pentateuch was read in any public places other than the temple of Jerusalem at that time.

Paul Kahle advanced a different view by arguing that the *Letter of Aristeas* does not refer to the original translation of the Pentateuch but to a revised version that was made on the basis of earlier "unofficial" versions that came into existence among Greek-speaking Jewish communities in the early years of the diaspora.[7] This theory, too, makes the problematic assumption that the Torah was used for synagogal reading outside Palestine and that it was translated to meet the needs of the Egyptian Jewish community. More importantly, the hypothesis of a development from unofficial versions to an official (revised) version assumes a Targum model. It is based on the idea that the official Targums were preceded by oral translations, which were secondarily put into writing. Scholars no longer subscribe to this "Greek Targum" theory, however, but have instead accepted the Lagardian hypothesis, according to which the actual manuscripts go back to an *Urtext*.[8]

Alternatively, scholars such as Sebastian Paul Brock and Charles Perrot have suggested that, although the liturgical matter may have been part of the picture, the translation arose out of the "educational" needs of the Jewish community in Alexandria.[9] This view has the advantage that the primary reason for the translation is no longer seen anachronistically in terms of reading practices in the synagogue.

---

5. See, for example, John William Wevers, *Notes on the Greek Text of Genesis* (SBLSCS 35; Atlanta: Scholars Press, 1993) xiii; Siegfried Kreuzer, "Entstehung und Publikation der Septuaginta im Horizont frühptolemäischer Bildungs- und Kulturpolitik," in *Im Brennpunkt: Die Septuaginta— Studien zur Entstehung und Bedeutung der Griechischen Bibel* (ed. Siegfried Kreuzer and Jürgen Peter Lesch; 2 vols; BWANT 161; Stuttgart: Kohlhammer, 2004) 2.73 (he is hesitant); Michael Tilly, *Einführung in die Septuaginta* (Darmstadt: Wissenschaftliche Buchgesellschaft, 2005) 46.

6. See, for example, Elias Bickerman, "The Septuagint as a Translation," in *PAAJR* 28 (1959) 1–39 (repr. in idem, *Studies in Jewish and Christian History: Part 1* [AGJU 9; Leiden: Brill, 1976] 167–200, 172); Sebastian Paul Brock, "The Phenomenon of the Septuagint," in *The Witness of Tradition* (OtSt 17; Leiden: Brill, 1972) 15; Charles Perrot, *La lecture de la Bible dans la synagogue: Les anciennes lectures palestiniennes du shabbat et des fêtes* (Hildesheim: Gerstenberg, 1973) 143 (lectio continua only after 70 C.E.).

7. Paul Kahle, *The Cairo Geniza* (2nd ed.; Oxford: Blackwell, 1959) 209–14.

8. For the hypothesis of Paul de Lagarde, see Jellicoe, *Septuagint*, 61–63.

9. Brock, "Phenomenon," 16; Perrot, *La lecture de la Bible*, 143.

Recent research has seen a resurgence of interest in the perspective of the *Letter of Aristeas*: namely, that the initiative was taken by the Ptolemaic court. This still leaves open the question why the Ptolemaic authorities might have taken an interest in a Greek version of the Pentateuch. According to Bruno Hugo Stricker, Elias Bickerman, Leonhard Rost, and Dominique Barthélemy, the Greek version was needed because the king wanted to have a copy of the books containing the laws and customs according to which the Jewish community in Alexandria was to live.[10] Likewise, Joseph Mélèze-Modrzejewski argues that "royal judges and officials" needed access to the text of the Torah in order to apply it effectively.[11] He goes so far as to suggest that the translation received a kind of official sanction through its inclusion in the judicial system of Ptolemy II Philadelphus (282–246 B.C.E.).

In support of their theory, these scholars point to a particular event dating to the Persian period. They refer to the way Darius I was involved in the codification of Egyptian laws. About 519 B.C.E., Darius ordered Aryandes, the satrap of Egypt, to convene a committee of Egyptian wise men (warriors, priests, and scribes) to record the former laws of Egypt in two languages: Demotic and Aramaic.[12] The project took nearly 15 years. These scholars suggest that Darius I's role in all of this was similar to the role of the Ptolemaic king's role regarding the Torah.[13]

Although this parallel raises some questions (see below), the view that the Greek version of the Pentateuch was initiated by the Ptolemaic court has recently become the prevailing view. Scholars have correctly pointed out that there is good reason to believe that a translation of the Pentateuch from as early as the 3rd century B.C.E. should be seen as the result of an official project, be-

---

10. Bruno Hugo Stricker, *De brief van Aristeas: De hellenistische codificaties der praehelleense gods-diensten* (Verhandelingen KNAW, afd. Letterkunde, Nieuwe Reeks 62/4; Amsterdam: Noord-Hollandsche Uitgeverij Maatschappij, 1956); Bickerman, "Septuagint," 171–75; Leonhard Rost, "Vermutungen über den Anlass zur griechischen Ubersetzung der Tora," in *Wort, Gebot, Glaube: Beiträge zur Theologie des Alten Testaments, Walther Eichrodt zum 80. Geburtstag* (ed. Hans Joachim Stoebe; ATANT 59; Zurich: Zwingli, 1970) 39–44; Dominique Barthélemy, "Pourquoi la Torah a-t-elle été traduite en Grec?" in *On Language, Culture, and Religion: In Honor of Eugene A. Nida* (ed. Matthew Black and William Allen Smalley; Approaches to Semiotics 6; The Hague: Mouton, 1974) 23–41 (repr. in idem, *Études d'histoire du texte de l'Ancien Testament* [OBO 21; Fribourg: Éditions Universitaires / Göttingen: Vandenhoeck & Ruprecht, 1978] 322–40).

11. Joseph Mélèze-Modrzejewski, *The Jews of Egypt: From Rameses II to Emperor Hadrian* (trans. Robert Corman; Princeton: Princeton University Press, 1997) 104–11.

12. See Albert Ten Eyck Olmstead, *History of the Persian Empire: Achaemenid Period* (Chicago: University of Chicago Press, 1948) 142.

13. In addition to this parallel, Mélèze-Modrzejewski (*Jews of Egypt*, 106) has drawn attention to a papyrus from Oxyrhynchus (XLVI 3285), which contains part of a Greek version of ancient local law in Demotic.

cause private translations are not known before the 2nd century B.C.E.[14] Hence the Ptolemaic court was involved in one way or another. But who else?

It is a commonly held view that the Jewish community in Alexandria was the actual party for whom, or by whom, the Torah was translated. However, all arguments based on this assumption have neglected the question whether the Jewish (priestly) authorities in Jerusalem might have been involved in one way or another. It is surprising that this question has not been dealt with so far because, particularly in the case of an official translation of the Jewish Torah, it is most likely that the authorities in Jerusalem played an important role in the project.[15] In this regard, the *Letter of Aristeas* presents a reliable picture in specifying that the Ptolemaic court asked the high priest in Jerusalem to supervise the translation. This is more plausible because, first, Jerusalem and Judea were part of the Ptolemaic Empire and, second, the books of the Torah as well as the expertise to read and interpret them were found in Jerusalem, particularly in temple circles.[16]

But then, what about the Jews in Alexandria and in Egypt? The Jewish community at that time, in the first decades of the 3rd century B.C.E., in Alexandria as well as in settlements elsewhere in Egypt, consisted mainly of soldiers, slaves (prisoners of war), mercenaries, and peasants.[17] The Jewish community in Alexandria was probably not yet very large and not yet organized in a separate (semiautonomous) community, although it would be in the 2nd century B.C.E.[18] Furthermore, the books of the Torah and the Prophets were primarily

---

14. See Marguerite Harl, Gilles Dorival, and Olivier Munnich, *La Bible grecque des Septante: Du Judaïsme hellénistique au Christianisme ancien* (Paris: Cerf, 1987) 78: "Il faut l'initiative officielle" (Dorival). See also Natalio Fernández Marcos, *The Septuagint in Context: Introduction to the Greek Version of the Bible* (trans. Wilfred G. E. Watson; Leiden: Brill, 2000) 63; Gilles Dorival, "Introduction," in *La Bible des Septante: Le Pentateuque d'Alexandrie—Texte grec et traduction* (ed. Cécile Dogniez and Marguerite Harl; Paris: Cerf, 2001) 40; Nina L. Collins, *The Library in Alexandria and the Bible in Greek* (VTSup 82; Leiden: Brill, 2000); Wolfgang Orth, "Ptolemaios II und die Septuaginta-Übersetzung," in *Im Brennpunkt: Die Septuaginta—Studien zur Entstehung und Bedeutung der Griechischen Bibel* (ed. Heinz-Josef Fabry and Ulrich Offerhaus; BWANT 153; Stuttgart: Kohlhammer, 2001) 97–114.

15. See Harald Hegermann, "The Diaspora in the Hellenistic Age," in *The Cambridge History of Judaism*, vol. 2: *The Hellenistic Age* (ed. William David Davies and Louis Finkelstein; Cambridge: Cambridge University Press, 1989) 134.

16. See Emanuel Tov, "Approaches towards Scripture Embraced by the Ancient Greek Translators," in *Der Mensch vor Gott: Forschungen zum Menschenbild in Bibel, antikem Judentum und Koran: Festschrift für Hermann Lichtenberger zum 60. Geburtstag* (ed. Ulrike Mittmann-Richert, Friedrich Avemarie, and Gerbern S. Oegema; Neukirchen-Vluyn: Neukirchener Verlag, 2004) 226.

17. See *Corpus Papyrorum Judaicarum* (ed. Victor A. Tcherikover, with Alexander Fuks; 3 vols.; Cambridge: Harvard University Press, 1957) 1.19; John M. G. Barclay, *Jews in the Mediterranean Diaspora: From Alexander to Trajan (323 BCE–117 CE)* (Edinburgh: T. & T. Clark, 1996) 20–22.

18. See Peter M. Fraser, *Ptolemaic Alexandria I: Text* (Oxford: Clarendon, 1972) 55. On the issue of *politeuma*, see most recently Honigman, *Septuagint and Homeric Scholarship*, 99–100.

kept in the temple of Jerusalem. They were only read and studied by priests and scribes, who were the scholars of the time in the temple state of Judea, just as the priests were in the Egyptian temples.[19]

Moreover, synagogues already existed in Alexandria in the first half of the 3rd century B.C.E.[20] Presumably they were places of "prayer" (προσευχή, pl. προσευχαι), teaching, and perhaps judicial resolution.[21] It is far from certain, however, that at that time these were also places where the Torah was read in public, as usually is assumed.[22] Indeed, this suggestion would not be in line with the Torah itself.[23] So the προσευχαί were not sites that would have requested a translation into Greek. In addition, one should not forget that the idea of producing a written translation of ancient books in Hebrew, which were regarded as making up the literary heritage of the Jewish nation, was quite new—it had never been done before in ancient Judaism.[24] Thus, contrary to what usually is taken for granted on the basis of practices in later periods, the production of a translation of the Torah in the first half of the 3rd century B.C.E. is far from self-evident.

In my view, therefore, the Jewish community in Alexandria was hardly likely to decide on or to have been involved in the project to produce a Greek version of the Pentateuch in terms of an official translation. Rather, it was mainly a matter of the "official" parties: the Ptolemaic court on the one hand, and the (priestly) authorities in Jerusalem on the other. So the question arises which party might have taken the initiative. This question is, of course, related to the question why might the Greek version have been produced at all.

---

19. See, for example, Manetho (ca. 280 B.C.E.), "high-priest and scribe of the sacred shrines of Egypt." See Fraser, *Ptolemaic Alexandria I*, 505–11, 506.

20. Regarding the earliest Greek documentation of *proseuchai* in Egypt (second half, 3rd century B.C.E.), see William Horbury and David Noy, *Jewish Inscriptions of Graeco-Roman Egypt: With an Index of the Jewish Inscriptions of Egypt and Cyrenaica* (Cambridge: Cambridge University Press, 1992) 35–37 (inscription no. 22); 201–3 (no. 117).

21. See John Gwyn Griffiths, "Egypt and the Rise of the Synagogue," *JTS* 28 (1987) 11–12.

22. See, for example, Donald D. Binder, *Into the Temple Courts: The Place of the Synagogues in the Second Temple Period* (SBLDS 169; Atlanta: Society of Biblical Literature, 1999) 402.

23. As is stipulated in Deut 31:11, the (deuteronomic) Torah should only be read in public "at the place that he (God) will choose" (Jerusalem; see Neh 8:1–8). This does not mean that the Torah did not play any role; it may well be that its text, in Hebrew, was consulted by specialists (compare Neh 8:14, 1 Macc 3:48).

24. It has been suggested that passages from the Torah read in Hebrew may have been rendered in Greek *orally* (see Bickerman, "Septuagint," 172). However, this idea does not apply if the Torah was not read in public in the synagogues in Egypt (see preceding note).

II. The "Trigger" for the Translation of the Torah into Greek: Four Hypotheses

In this section, I will deal with the question formulated above by exploring four possible answers (hypotheses) that are based on suggestions made by scholars.

Hypothesis 1: Jerusalem Takes the
Initiative with Alexandria's Approval

It seems reasonable to assume that the Pentateuch was rendered into Greek to promote a way of life according to its teachings. Jerusalem and Judea at that time were part of the Ptolemaic Empire, and one can imagine that the leaders of Jerusalem were interested in a Greek version that would encourage the Jews in Egypt to live according to the Torah. Seen from their perspective, a translation of the Torah then would serve for teaching purposes, in a way similar to the statement by the grandson of Ben Sira in his Prologue to the Greek version of his grandfather's Wisdom, where he says that he made the translation "for the benefit of those living abroad who . . . are disposed to live their lives according to the standards of the Law" (lines 34–36).[25]

This would mean that the initiative was taken by the leaders in Jerusalem. The Ptolemaic court, as one can imagine, would then have approved the translation project because it was in line with its policy toward the Jews—to let them live according to their ancestral laws. Moreover, it could be helpful for reasons of administration and jurisdiction to have a copy of these laws in a Greek version.

At first glance, this hypothesis that the initiative was taken by Jerusalem with the approval of Alexandria is attractive. It is not convincing, however. Why would the authorities in Jerusalem of that time want to have the Torah translated for their countrymen in Egypt but not for Jews in other parts of the diaspora, such as Mesopotamia? Furthermore, religious specialists such as priests and Levites who had a thorough knowledge of religious practices and customs could easily have taught the members of the Jewish community in Alexandria. An interesting passage in this regard is found in Chronicles: "They [officers, priests, and Levites] taught in Judah, having the book of the Law of the LORD with them; they went about through all the cities of Judah and taught among the people" (2 Chr 17:9).[26] It is not known whether this passage about particular

---

25. See Brock, "Phenomenon," 16; Perrot, *La lecture de la Bible*, 143. See also Martin Rösel, *Übersetzung als Vollendung der Auslegung: Studien zur Genesis-Septuaginta* (BZAW 223; Berlin: de Gruyter, 1994) 258.

26. On this passage, see Gary N. Knoppers, "Jehoshaphat's Judiciary and 'the Scroll of YHWH's Torah,'" *JBL* 113 (1994) 59–80, 64.

initiatives taken by Jehoshaphat, according to the author of Chronicles, reflects
a practice in late Persian Judea (but see Neh 8:15), or whether it only testifies to
what was considered an ideal situation. Be this as it may, from the perspective of
this passage, it seems plausible that the authorities in Jerusalem would think
along similar lines—namely, that the priests were the men who should teach the
Torah in Jewish communities outside Jerusalem on the basis of a copy of the Torah that was available to them and that they were able to read in Hebrew (pri-
vately, for study purposes).[27]

Hypothesis 2: The Ptolemaic Court Takes the Initiative for the Translation

One could argue that it was the Ptolemaic court, not the authorities in Jerusalem, who took the initiative and requested that the high priest of Jerusalem
carry out the translation. The translation would presumably give the court access to the laws of the Jewish population of Alexandria and facilitate Ptolemaic
jurisdiction over them. This alternative is very close to the view of scholars such
as Bickerman and Barthélemy, the difference being the role ascribed to the authorities in Jerusalem. According to these scholars, the translation of the Pentateuch should be seen as part of a broader policy of translation of local law codes,
in a way similar to the Persian legal project. However, this hypothesis raises
questions too. Admittedly, the Persian legal project may well be a nice parallel
to the mission of Ezra, the priest, but one wonders whether it provides an appropriate parallel to a translation of the Torah into Greek as ordered by the
Ptolemaic king.[28] Unlike the case of the Egyptian laws and the law of Ezra,
which were laws of a particular nation and country, in the case of the Jews in
Alexandria and Egypt, one is dealing with communities of immigrants. As
Brock has argued, "the Jewish community in Egypt is not sufficiently large to
warrant such an official translation."[29]

There is another reason that it is not plausible that the Ptolemaic court
would have been interested in a Greek version of the Torah for reasons of jurisdiction. The Jews in the Ptolemaic Empire were granted permission to live according to their own laws and customs, just as were the Egyptians. As Fraser

---

27. If, however, the authorities of Jerusalem were not interested in having specialists teaching
among their fellow Jews in Egypt, it is conceivable that Jewish scholars in Egypt provided the
communities with the necessary information as far as laws and customs were concerned, perhaps
even without having access to a copy of the Torah (from Jerusalem), as seems to have been the
case in Elephantine.

28. As suggested by Richard C. Steiner, "The *mbqr* at Qumran, the *episkopos* in the Athenian
Empire, and the Meaning of *lbqr'* in Ezra 7:14: On the Relation of Ezra's Mission to the Persian
Legal Project," *JBL* 120 (2001) 636.

29. Brock, "Phenomenon," 13 n. 4.

states, "Basically, native Egyptian law, administered by Egyptian judges, continued as before, and it was to this law that the great bulk of the population was naturally subject."[30] Distinct from this category of law was the law of the Ptolemaic ruler, the king's law, which was expressed in general edicts and laws on special topics.[31] This law was superior to both Egyptian law and Jewish. In view of this situation, it does not seem likely that the Ptolemaic court was strongly interested in a Greek version of the Torah of the Jews. It makes it even more unlikely that this version was included in the judicial system of the Ptolemies, as has been suggested by Mélèze-Modrzejewski.[32]

Hypothesis 3: Priests in Jerusalem Solicit the Translation to Gain Prestige

Alternatively, the leading priests in Jerusalem might have been interested in a Greek version of the Pentateuch because of the cultural policy of the Ptolemaic rulers in Alexandria.[33] The translation, then, was made for reasons of prestige, comparable to the works in Greek by scholars such as the Egyptian "high priest and scribe of the sacred shrines of Egypt," Manetho (ca. 280 B.C.E.); and his Babylonian "colleague," Berossus.[34] Both priest-scholars dedicated their work to their respective Greek kings, Ptolemy II, and Antiochus I. However, it is far from certain that these works should be seen as an appropriate parallel to the translation of the Torah. The books of the Pentateuch are different in nature from the historiographical works of Manetho and Berossus.[35]

In the past few years, Sylvie Honigman has advanced the theory that, because the *Letter of Aristeas* testifies to an acquaintance with the work of Alexandrian scholars (such as Aristarchus) who were dealing with a critical edition of the text of Homer, the early history of the Septuagint of the Pentateuch is best understood against the background of the history of editorial work on the Homeric texts. "Needless to say," writes Honigman, "the assumption implied by such a working premise is that the LXX was primarily translated not for pragmatic needs, but for the sake of prestige."[36] In Honigman's theory, the Jews in Alexandria were the ones who took the initiative, stimulated by "the royal

---

30. Fraser, *Ptolemaic Alexandria I*, 107.

31. See Fraser, ibid.

32. For criticism of this view, see also Dorival, *La Bible grecque des Septante*, 73–75; Fernández Marcos, *Septuagint in Context*, 63–64; Honigman, *Septuagint and Homeric Scholarship*, 108–13.

33. By "cultural policy," I mean the Ptolemaic patronage, which greatly stimulated scholarship in literature and science in Alexandria. This policy included the founding of the two great institutions of learning in the city, the Mouseion and the Library.

34. See Bickerman, "Septuagint," 174–75.

35. See Robert Hanhart, "Fragen um die Entstehung der LXX," *VT* 12 (1962) 155–58.

36. Honigman, *Septuagint and Homeric Scholarship*, 120.

propaganda that promoted the ideology linked to the editorial activity that was being carried out in the library."[37] It may be that the author of the *Letter* belonged to Jewish intellectual circles late in the 2nd century B.C.E. who were familiar with Alexandrian textual scholarship of the time, but it does not seem likely that this was also the case with Jews in Alexandria in the beginning of the 3rd century B.C.E. Moreover, as I have argued above, the assumption that Jews in Alexandria took the initiative to translate the Torah is not plausible either. It cannot be denied that the cultural policy did play a role and that the translation could have been produced under the patronage of the Ptolemaic court, but the question remains: what might have been the specific reason for the translation project?

Hypothesis 4: The Role Played by Demetrius of Phaleron

According to the *Letter of Aristeas*, it was Demetrius of Phaleron who proposed having a Greek copy of the Torah added to the collection of books in the royal library at Alexandria. The *Letter* is not the only early source that points to Demetrius. This view is also found in one of the preserved fragments of the Jewish exegete and philosopher Aristobulus, which dates to the first half of the 2nd century B.C.E.: "But the entire translation of all [the books of] the Law was made in the time of the king called Philadelphus, your ancestor, who displayed a great munificence, while Demetrius of Phaleron directed the undertaking."[38] I agree with scholars such as Collins and Orth that the tradition about Demetrius should be taken seriously.[39] The fact that Aristobulus is apparently independent of the *Letter of Aristeas* increases the likelihood of this hypothesis.

Demetrius of Phaleron was tyrant of Athens from 317 to 307 B.C.E.[40] After his expulsion from Athens, he fled to Egypt and advised Ptolemy I Soter (306/4–283/2 B.C.E.) on more than one matter, likely including the civil code of Alexandria and the foundation of the library. It is not considered plausible, however, that he held the office of "royal librarian," a title given him by the *Letter of Aristeas*.[41] Furthermore, it is not certain whether he continued this position under Ptolemy II Philadelphus (282–246 B.C.E.), as both the *Letter of Aristeas* and Aristobulus assume. Ancient sources seem to imply that he was in conflict with Ptolemy II and was banished by him.[42]

---

37. Ibid., 138.

38. For this passage, see Matthew Black and Albert-Marie Denis, eds., *Apocalypsis Henochi Graece: Fragmenta Pseudepigraphorum quae supersunt Graeca* (PVTG 3; Leiden: Brill, 1970) 222.

39. See Collins, *Library*, 58–114; Orth, "Ptolemaios II," 108–10.

40. See Fraser, *Ptolemaic Alexandria I*, 114, 314–15; Collins, *Library*, 88.

41. Fraser, *Ptolemaic Alexandria I*, 321, 690.

42. For another view, see Collins, *Library*, 73–74.

Demetrius was a Peripatetic philosopher. He was the most outstanding pupil of Theophrastus, who was the successor of Aristotle and tutor of Alexander the Great. Interestingly, the Peripatetic philosophers, such as Theophrastus and Demetrius, were greatly interested in a comparative study of laws and codes as documents pertaining to the constitution of a given people, both Greeks and non-Greeks.[43] Ptolemy I shared this interest. It therefore is likely that scholars of the time who were motivated by the Ptolemaic patronage prompted the translation of the books of the Pentateuch.[44]

According to the *Letter of Aristeas*, Demetrius advised the king to add the Torah to the collection of books in the library. Although it is unlikely that Demetrius was the "royal librarian," as the *Letter* claims, the proposal made by Demetrius makes perfect sense if indeed the Torah was translated for the purposes of reading and study. Together with the Mouseion, the library was founded to foster Alexandrian scholarship. It thus was only natural to make the Greek version of the Torah available in the library.

All this means that the Greek version of the Pentateuch was produced on the initiative of the Ptolemaic court for reasons of scholarly interest in the laws and constitutions of various peoples. This also helps explain why the translation focused on the Torah.[45]

III. Conclusion

The Septuagint of the Pentateuch was not produced for religious or liturgical (synagogal) use or for the benefit of the Ptolemaic administration or for reasons of prestige. Instead, the driving force was presumably scholarly interests within the framework of the cultural policy of the time in Alexandria. Hence, the Ptolemaic court initiated the translation project. The authorities in Jerusalem were the other party involved, not the Jews in Egypt, so it stands to reason that the translators came from Jerusalem. These translators belonged to circles in which the books of the Torah were read and studied—that is, priests and scribes. Hence, specific elements of interpretation in the Septuagint of the Pentateuch

---

43. See Orth, "Ptolemaios II," 108–10. For Demetrius, see also *Der Neue Pauly: Enzykopädie der Antike* (16 vols.; Stuttgart: Metzler, 1996–2003) 3.429–30. For preserved fragments of his works, see Fritz Wehrli, *Die Schule des Aristoteles: Texte und Kommentar*, vol. 4: *Demetrios von Phaleron* (2nd ed.; Basel: Schwabe, 1968).

44. See Orth, "Ptolemaios II," 110.

45. According to the *Letter of Aristeas*, as well as Aristobulus and Josephus, the second of the Ptolemies was the king at the time of the translation of the Law. As stated above, Demetrius of Phaleron played an important role under Ptolemy I, not his successor. This discrepancy can be dismissed, because it may well be that the translation project started under Ptolemy I but was completed under Ptolemy II, the result being that the latter became the king known for the Greek Pentateuch.

may reflect the reading and understanding of the Torah from Jerusalem temple circles.

What does this mean for the question posed at the beginning of this essay? The promulgation of the Septuagint of the Pentateuch was due to the initiative of the Ptolemaic court but not in terms of a *Reichsautorisation* of the Jewish Torah. The interest of the court in the Torah was not motivated by the wish to facilitate Ptolemaic jurisdiction over the Jews in Alexandria and Egypt, as scholars have argued. Rather, it concerned the Torah as a document containing the constitution and the laws of the Jews in Palestine that needed to be made accessible in Greek for study purposes; hence, to be made available in the library.

Note that there is other evidence of this type of interest, as far as the Torah of the Jews is concerned. A Greek scholar of the time, Hecataeus of Abdera (ca. 300 B.C.E.), devotes a long passage in his *Aegyptiaca* to the Jews and Judea. Its focus is mainly on the laws and customs of the Jewish people. The reader is told that Moses, "outstanding both for his wisdom and for his courage," took possession of the land (Judea) and founded cities, such as Jerusalem. Hecataeus then states: "In addition, he established the temple that they hold in chief veneration, instituted their forms of worship and ritual, drew up their laws, and ordered their political institutions."[46] In this statement, the laws of Moses are clearly related to the issue of the polity (*politeia*) of the Jewish nation.[47]

Thus, if indeed the promulgation of the Torah in Greek arose from a strong scholarly interest in Alexandria at the time (first half, 3rd century B.C.E.), it does not help us understand the promulgation in the Persian period because the interest in laws and constitutions that was typical of scholars in Alexandria, such as Demetrius, was not part of the cultural situation in the Persian period.[48] This is not to say that research on the Greek Pentateuch would not have any bearing on the status of the Torah in the late Persian period. It would be important, in my view, to investigate whether the Greek version might reflect a particular interest in the matter of polity by the Jewish authorities in Jerusalem, and if so, to which Jewish polity or constitution it might point.[49]

46. See Menahem Stern, ed., *Greek and Latin Authors on Jews and Judaism*, vol. 1: *From Herodotus to Plutarch* (Jerusalem: Israel Academy of Sciences and Humanities, 1974) 28.

47. See also Josephus, *Ant.* 1.10: "I found then that the second of the Ptolemies, that king who was so deeply interested in learning and such a collector of books, was particularly anxious to have our Law and the order of the constitution based thereon translated into Greek" (*Jewish Antiquities, Books I–IV* (trans. Henry St. John Thackeray; LCL 242; London: Heinemann / Cambridge: Harvard University Press, 1967) 7.

48. One can imagine that the scholarly setting in which the Greek Pentateuch arose stimulated its study by Jewish scholars in Egypt such as Aristobulus and Philo.

49. An interesting passage, in my view, is LXX Exod 19:6. See my "Kingdom of Priests: Comment on Exodus 19:6," in *The Interpretation of Exodus: Studies in Honour of Cornelis Houtman* (ed. Riemer Roukema et al.; CBET 44; Leuven: Peeters, 2006) 173–75.

The Use of the Pentateuch in the Temple Scroll and the Damascus Document in the Second Century B.C.E.

SIDNIE WHITE CRAWFORD

University of Nebraska–Lincoln

The history of the Pentateuch in the period after its promulgation and acceptance as Torah (Eng. Law) in the 5th and 4th centuries B.C.E. was relatively
unknown until the discovery of the Judean Desert manuscripts (i.e., the Dead
Sea Scrolls) in the latter half of the last century.[1] The discovery of these manuscripts, in particular those from the 11 caves surrounding Khirbet Qumran, has
illumined the practices of scriptural exegesis within one Jewish movement in
the 3rd and 2nd centuries B.C.E. This essay will examine the exegesis of the
Pentateuch by two texts dated to the 2nd century B.C.E.: the *Temple Scroll* and
the *Damascus Document*. While these two documents differ dramatically in their
exegetical *method*, they reach very similar exegetical *conclusions*. I hope to demonstrate that the similarity of these conclusions is evidence for a particular line
of scriptural interpretation that is found within the Jewish movement now
known as Essene.[2] This line of scriptural interpretation begins with the understanding and acceptance of the Pentateuch as divinely revealed Law, binding on

---

1. I would like to thank Bernard M. Levinson, Gary N. Knoppers, Frank Moore Cross, and
the members of the Biblical Colloquium, whose comments and criticisms made this a better paper.
All mistakes remain my own. In this study, "Law" with a capital L refers to the teachings of Moses,
gathered together in the five books of Moses or "Pentateuch" (Genesis, Exodus, Leviticus, Numbers, and Deuteronomy). The Law was considered binding on all Jews for all time, although different interpretations of the Law competed for adherents in the late Second Temple period, as shall be
demonstrated below. As a caveat to this definition, it is well to bear in mind the caution of Johann
Meier: "it may not be appropriate always to think of Law and Pentateuch as synonyms during the
late Second Temple period" (as quoted in George Brooke, "Biblical Interpretation at Qumran," in
The Bible and the Dead Sea Scrolls: The Second Princeton Symposium on Judaism and Christian Origins
[ed. James H. Charlesworth; 3 vols.; Waco, TX: Baylor University Press, 2006] 1.287–319; quotation from p. 296).

2. I will use Josephus, Philo, and Pliny's name "Essene" for this movement as a convenient
label, although the group called itself by a variety of names, and the word "Essene" (or its equivalent) does not appear in the Qumran scrolls.

all Jews for all time. However, to the Essenes, the Pentateuch as Torah did not stand alone; it needed to be interpreted according to the techniques embraced by their movement. This exegetical method yielded certain emphases and conclusions congenial to the Essene movement. Thus, a particular line of Essene scriptural interpretation can be isolated among the texts of the late Second Temple period, as will be demonstrated with respect to the *Temple Scroll* and the *Damascus Document*.

By the second half of the Second Temple period, approximately 200 B.C.E. to 70 C.E., the Torah was accepted by all Jews, both in Palestine and the diaspora, as the divinely revealed basis for communal life and ritual practice. Passages from two 2nd-century B.C.E. works, the Wisdom of Jesus ben Sirach and 4QMiqṣat Maʿaśê ha-Torah, name the Law as the first part of the authoritative Scripture of Israel (Ben Sirach Prologue; 4QMMT C 10).[3] The sheer number of manuscripts of the five books of the Pentateuch found in the various Judean Desert sites discovered in the second half of the 20th century also illustrates the importance of the Torah in Jewish life and thought. Beginning at the largest site, Khirbet Qumran, in the 11 caves there were found 19 or 20 manuscripts of Genesis; 18 manuscripts of Exodus, including one Greek manuscript; 16 manuscripts of Leviticus, including 2 Greek copies and one Aramaic copy; 8 manuscripts of Numbers, one of them Greek; and 31 or 32 copies of Deuteronomy, including one Greek manuscript.[4] The 5 manuscripts of 4QReworked Pentateuch should also be mentioned in this count, although their status as authoritative Torah remains in doubt.[5] Altogether, 44 percent of the so-called biblical

---

3. Elisha Qimron and John Strugnell, *Qumran Cave 4, V: Miqṣat Maʿaśê Ha-Torah* (DJD 10; Oxford: Clarendon, 1994) 58–59.

4. See Emanuel Tov, "A Categorized List of all the 'Biblical Texts' Found in the Judaean Desert," *DSD* 8 (2001) 67–84, esp. 70–80.

5. The five manuscripts grouped under the rubric "4QReworked Pentateuch" are 4Q158, 4Q364, 4Q365, 4Q366, and 4Q367. See John M. Allegro, *Qumran Cave 4 (4Q158–4Q186)* (DJD 5; Oxford: Clarendon, 1968) 1–6; and Emanuel Tov and Sidnie A. White, "Reworked Pentateuch," in *Qumran Cave 4, VIII: Parabiblical Texts, Part 1* (ed. Harold Attridge et al.; DJD 13; Oxford: Clarendon, 1994) 187–351. These manuscripts are characterized as containing a running scriptural text reworked by scribal intervention. This reworking consists of exegetical additions to the received text and the rearrangement of certain pericopes, usually to gather together passages pertaining to a particular topic. While the original extent of 4Q158, 4Q366, and 4Q367, being short and fragmentary, is unknown, 4Q364 and 4Q365 were almost certainly originally complete manuscripts of the Pentateuch. Their base text was a pre-Samaritan text type that also evidences scribal intervention that goes beyond the harmonizations of the pre-Samaritan textual family and includes the addition of new material into the received text. See my "Reworked Pentateuch," in *Encyclopedia of the Dead Sea Scrolls* (ed. Lawrence H. Schiffman and James C. VanderKam; 3 vols.; New York: Oxford University Press, 2000) 2.775–77. Whether or not these texts were accepted by the Qumran community as authoritative Torah scrolls is a matter of debate. I hold the position that their status as authoritative Scripture is indeterminate, and therefore a final judgment should

manuscripts found at Qumran are copies of the books of the Pentateuch.[6]

The other find sites, while yielding smaller numbers, also testify to the importance of the Torah in Jewish life in this period, because all of these sites contain the remains of refugee groups, and it is probable that they carried into hiding the documents that they considered most important or sacred. These sites (Wadi Murrabaʿat, Naḥal Ḥever, Masada, Wadi Sdeir, and Wadi Seiyal) yielded 4 Genesis manuscripts, one Exodus manuscript, 2 Leviticus manuscripts, 4 Numbers manuscripts, and 3 Deuteronomy manuscripts.[7] Thus it can be stated with confidence that the five books of the Pentateuch were held in reverence and copied extensively during this period and that attempts were made to preserve them during the cataclysmic events of the late first and early 2nd centuries C.E.

The Qumran finds, in addition to the Pentateuch manuscripts listed above, give further evidence of the sacred and authoritative status of the Pentateuch for the Jewish community that maintained the communal compound at Qumran for at least 150 years, from approximately 135–100 B.C.E. to 68 C.E., and that stored its manuscripts in the surrounding caves.[8] My assumption in this essay is that the Jewish group at Qumran was part of the wider Essene movement in the late Second Temple period. Thus, much of the literature discovered at Qumran reflects the theology and hermeneutics of the Essenes.[9] What becomes clear on examination of the Qumran literature is that Scripture, and especially the Torah, has a "pervasive presence" in the literature and that the

---

be withheld. See my *Rewriting Scripture in Second Temple Times* (Studies in the Dead Sea Scrolls and Related Literature; Grand Rapids, MI: Eerdmans, in press). Other scholars believe that the manuscripts 4Q364 and 4Q365 of 4QReworked Pentateuch are simply Torah scrolls and should be categorized as Torah scrolls. See Michael Segal, "4QReworked Pentateuch or 4QPentateuch?" in *The Dead Sea Scrolls Fifty Years after Their Discovery* (ed. Lawrence H. Schiffman, Emanuel Tov, and James C. VanderKam; Jerusalem: Israel Exploration Society, 2000) 391–99; and Eugene C. Ulrich, "The Qumran Scrolls and the Biblical Text," in ibid., 51–59; and now also Emanuel Tov, "Three Strange Books of the LXX: 1 Kings, Esther, and Daniel Compared with Similar Rewritten Compositions from Qumran and Elsewhere" (presentation at the Wüppertal Septuagint Meeting, forthcoming). I would like to thank Professor Tov for sharing this paper with me prior to publication.

6. Tov, "A Categorized List," 70.

7. Ibid., 80–81.

8. Roland de Vaux, the original excavator of Khirbet Qumran, places the date of the earliest Hellenistic settlement at ca. 135 B.C.E. (Roland de Vaux, *Archaeology and the Dead Sea Scrolls* [London: The British Academy / Oxford University, 1973] 5). Jodi Magness, in a reexamination of the archaeological evidence, argues for a settlement date no earlier than 100 B.C.E. (*The Archaeology of Qumran and the Dead Sea Scrolls* [Studies in the Dead Sea Scrolls and Related Literature; Grand Rapids, MI: Eerdmans, 2002] 66–69).

9. For a convenient discussion of the Qumran–Essene hypothesis and its defense, see James C. VanderKam and Peter Flint, *The Meaning of the Dead Sea Scrolls* (New York: HarperCollins, 2002) 239–50.

words of the Pentateuch permeate the language of the scrolls, whether by direct quotation, allusion, or imitation.[10]

However, the picture is complicated by two related phenomena. First, in the late Second Temple period, as is now almost universally acknowledged, the text of the individual books of the Pentateuch was not fixed. Variants abounded. Some were the result of simple scribal error that was repeated in subsequent copies, but others were true variants preserved in different strands of the scribal tradition. In two of the books of the Pentateuch, Exodus and Numbers, the number of true variants is large enough and the differences between versions systematic enough to yield two distinct editions. These editions are the proto-Rabbinic version (from which the Masoretic Text descends) and the pre-Samaritan version (an extensively harmonized text).[11]

What does it mean to speak of the pre-Samaritan edition of the Torah as a heavily harmonized text? It may be useful to discuss this matter, however briefly, because scholars operate with some divergent understandings of what the process of harmonization entails. The ancient scribal practice of harmonization was meant to smooth out perceived differences between two parallel scriptural texts. The motivating force behind the act of harmonization was the notion that the text of Scripture is perfect and must be perfectly harmonious.[12] In one kind of harmonization, a scribe would notice a detail missing in Text A and import it into Text A from Text B. An example of this is found in Genesis 30–31. In the MT, Jacob reports to his wives that God has directed him in a dream to return to the land of Canaan. However, Jacob is never seen actually having the dream. Thus, in the Samaritan Pentateuch (a descendant of the pre-Samaritan textual family) an account of Jacob's dream is added after Gen 30:36. Another type of harmonization involves "command and fulfillment" passages. In these passages, a command is given and then matched by an account of its

10. Moshe J. Bernstein, "Scripture: Quotation and Use," in *Encyclopedia of the Dead Sea Scrolls* (ed. Lawrence H. Schiffman and James C. VanderKam; 3 vols.; New York: Oxford University Press, 2000) 2.839–42 (quotation from p. 839).

11. There are several examples of the pre-Samaritan text-type preserved in the manuscripts from Qumran. These include 4QpaleoExod[m], 4QNum[b], and the base text of 4Q364. See Patrick W. Skehan, Eugene C. Ulrich, and Judith Sanderson, "4QpaleoExodus[m]," in *Qumran Cave 4, IV: Palaeo-Hebrew and Greek Biblical Manuscripts* (DJD 9; Oxford: Clarendon, 1992) 53–130; Nathan Jastram, "4QNum[b]," in *Qumran Cave 4, VII: Genesis to Numbers* (ed. Eugene Ulrich and Frank Moore Cross; DJD 12; Oxford: Clarendon, 1994) 205–67; and Emanuel Tov and Sidnie Ann White, "364. 4QReworked Pentateuch[b]," in *Qumran Cave 4, VIII: Parabiblical Texts, Part 1* (ed. Harold Attridge et al.; DJD 13; Oxford: Clarendon, 1994) 197–254.

12. James H. Kugel, "Ancient Biblical Interpretation and the Biblical Sage," in *Studies in Ancient Midrash* (ed. James Kugel; Cambridge: Harvard University Press, 2001) 1–26. See further Emanuel Tov, "The Nature and Background of Harmonizations in Biblical Manuscripts," *JSOT* 31 (1983) 3–29; Jeffrey H. Tigay, "Conflation as a Redactional Technique," in *Empirical Models for Biblical Criticism* (ed. Jeffrey Tigay; Philadelphia: University of Pennsylvania Press, 1985) 53–96.

fulfillment, usually in very similar language. However, in cases where command and fulfillment do not match, the harmonizing text will add the necessary details to make sure they do match. This type of harmonization occurs, for instance, in the pre-Samaritan version of the plague and Passover narratives.

In any event, there is no evidence that one or the other of the two different editions (the proto-Rabbinic version and the pre-Samaritan version) was more highly esteemed at Qumran. One manuscript of the pre-Samaritan tradition eventually became the canonical text of the Samaritans, while a descendant of the proto-Rabbinic text became the canonical text of the Jews. But the Qumran finds predate the fixing of the canonical text.

Second, there was no Jewish "canon" in our sense of the term as a normative list of sacred writings of a particular religious tradition in the late Second Temple period. While it is very clear from the evidence at Qumran that the five books of the Pentateuch form the core of their authoritative books, other works closely related to the Pentateuch were also authoritative and were used to provide scriptural backing for the Qumran community's interpretive tradition and theology in the same way the books of the Pentateuch were used. These books include four of the five sections of *1 Enoch*, *Aramaic Levi*, and *Jubilees*.[13] Their use of these "noncanonical" books as authoritative is reflected in their ritual practices and theology, most obviously in their embrace of the solar calendar against the lunar calendar observed by other Jews.[14] Thus, the Essenes had a wider group of books considered authoritative than other Jewish groups of the time (that is, the Pharisees and the Saduccees), who did not reckon these works as authoritative.

---

13. Parts of *1 Enoch* date to at least the 3rd century B.C.E. The antiquity of *1 Enoch* is confirmed by the presence of 11 manuscripts of portions of *1 Enoch* in the original Aramaic at Qumran. For texts and translation, see Michael A. Knibb, *The Ethiopic Book of Enoch: A New Edition in the Light of the Aramaic Dead Sea Fragments* (2 vols.; Oxford: Clarendon, 1978); and George W. E. Nickelsburg and James C. VanderKam, *1 Enoch: A New Translation* (Minneapolis: Fortress, 2004). *Aramaic Levi*, a work unknown before the discoveries at Qumran, dates to the late 3rd to early 2nd century B.C.E. For text and translation, see Jonas C. Greenfield, Michael E. Stone, and Esther Eshel, *The Aramaic Levi Document: Edition, Translation, Commentary* (SVTP 19; Leiden: Brill, 2004). The book of *Jubilees*, a retelling of Genesis 1–Exodus 19, set as a revelation to Moses on Mount Sinai by an "angel of the presence," dates to the mid-2nd century B.C.E. For text and translation, see James C. VanderKam, *The Book of Jubilees: A Critical Text* (2 vols.; CSCO 510–11; Scriptores Aethiopici 87–88; Leuven: Peeters, 1989); O. Wintermute, "Jubilees," in *The Old Testament Pseudepigrapha* (ed. James H. Charlesworth; 2 vols.; Garden City, NY: Doubleday, 1983) 2.35–142.

14. Shemaryahu Talmon, "Calendars and Mishmarot," in *Encyclopedia of the Dead Sea Scrolls* (ed. Lawrence H. Schiffman and James C. VanderKam; 3 vols.; New York: Oxford University Press, 2000) 1.108–17; and James C. VanderKam, *Calendars in the Dead Sea Scrolls* (New York: Routledge, 1994). Aside from the use of the solar calendar, other evidence for the authoritative status of these works will be given below, in the discussions of the *Temple Scroll* and the *Damascus Document*.

The Beginning of the Essene Movement

The Essene movement's origins are shadowy, but most scholars agree that the movement's roots are in a Priestly-Levitical milieu that in the 3rd century B.C.E. produced two of the books of *Enoch* and *Aramaic Levi*.[15] Both these works are loosely related to the book of Genesis. The *Enoch* literature draws on the antediluvian patriarch Enoch (Gen 5:18–24), who, in the books that bear his name, becomes the recipient of special revelation concerning the divine realm (including the solar calendar) and a model of righteousness. *Aramaic Levi*, as its name suggests, concerns Levi the son of Jacob and his assumption of the priesthood. According to *Aramaic Levi*, the role of the priests includes maintaining the purity of the cult and teaching the correct understanding of the Law (passed down from Noah through the patriarchs to Levi).[16] In these two works two themes already appear that dominate Essene thought: special revelation or knowledge from God and the importance of the priests as the guardians of the Law and the cult.

The two books of *Enoch* and *Aramaic Levi* also contain close readings of the texts of the Pentateuch and manifest a desire to "close the gaps" in the Torah, that is, to harmonize it. In the case of *Enoch*, the puzzle of what happened to Enoch in Gen 5:24 ("Enoch walked with God; then he was no more, because God took him") is answered extensively in the visions and revelations found in his books. The question of how Levi, one of the perpetrators of the massacre of the Shechemites (Gen 34:25–31) and roundly condemned by Jacob (Gen 49:5–7), could have been the divinely chosen ancestor of the priestly line is answered in *Aramaic Levi* by a rehabilitation of Levi's character. Thus, it is evident that the interpretation of the Pentateuch is one of the foundations of the Essene movement.

By the 2nd century B.C.E. this Priestly-Levitical movement appears to have solidified and may now be referred to as Essene. Its adherents began to produce more literature, literature that illustrates the three principles mentioned above: (1) special revelation, (2) the importance of priests as guardians of Law and cult, and (3) a close reading of Scripture with an eye to explaining perceived difficulties in the text. I will investigate two examples of Essene compositions from the

---

15. Theories of the origin of the Qumran community abound in the scholarly literature. As examples, see Gabriele Boccaccini, *Beyond the Essene Hypothesis: The Parting of the Ways between Qumran and Enochic Judaism* (Grand Rapids, MI: Eerdmans, 1998); Florentino García Martínez and Adam van der Woude, "A 'Groningen' Hypothesis of Qumran Origins and Early History," *RevQ* 14 (1990) 521–41; Lawrence H. Schiffman, *Reclaiming the Dead Sea Scrolls: The History of Judaism, the Background of Christianity, the Lost Library of Qumran* (Philadelphia: Jewish Publication Society, 1994) 83–95; VanderKam and Flint, *The Meaning of the Dead Sea Scrolls*, 289–92.

16. Michael Stone, "Levi, Aramaic," in *Encyclopedia of the Dead Sea Scrolls* (ed. Lawrence H. Schiffman and James C. VanderKam; 3 vols.; New York: Oxford University Press, 2000) 1.486–88.

2nd century B.C.E., the *Temple Scroll* and the slightly later *Damascus Document*, with special attention to their use of the Torah and their exegetical results. What will emerge is a recognizable body of Essene exegesis, which concentrates on certain themes and concerns, and forms a distinct body of literature.[17]

The Temple Scroll

The *Temple Scroll* was produced in the early to mid-2nd century B.C.E., although it is composed of earlier sources.[18] In its final form, which fortunately exists in the almost complete copy 11QTemple[a], it is an example of the category Rewritten Scripture. A Rewritten Scripture text is defined by a close adherence to a recognizable and already authoritative base text (narrative or legal) and a recognizable degree of scribal intervention into this base text for the purpose of exegesis. A Rewritten Scripture text will often make a claim to the authority of revealed Scripture, the same authority as its base text.[19] The *Temple Scroll* fits well into this category.

The *Temple Scroll* follows, in its broad outline, the order of the Pentateuch, beginning in its first extant column at Exodus 34 and ending with Deuteronomy 23. Within this broad outline, the composer/redactor uses various exegetical techniques to rework the text of the Torah to serve his group's agenda concerning the interpretation of the Law. For the composer/redactor, the Torah is clearly the authoritative base text with which he is working, but the base text must be interpreted in order to reveal its true meaning. The interpretation is incorporated into the text itself, thus creating a new work that makes a bid for authority equal to the original text.[20] Because the Torah's authority stems

---

17. As George Brooke rightly notes, there is little that is distinctive about Essene exegetical *methods* (italics mine). See Brooke, "Qumran Biblical Interpretation," 294. However, because Essene exegesis is driven by a distinctive set of beliefs, the *results* are unique.

18. For the *editio princeps*: Yigael Yadin, *The Temple Scroll* (3 vols. and supplement; rev. Eng. ed.; Jerusalem: Israel Exploration Society, 1983). For other manuscripts of the *Temple Scroll*, see Florentino García Martínez, E. J. C. Tigchelaar, and Adam S. van der Woude, "11QTemple[b]," in *Qumran Cave 11, II: 11Q2–18, 11Q20–31* (DJD 23; Oxford: Clarendon, 1998) 357–410; Émile Puech, "4QRouleau du Temple," in *Qumrân Grotte 4, XVIII: Textes Hébreux (4Q521–4Q528, 4Q576–4Q579)* (DJD 25; Oxford: Clarendon, 1998) 85–114. See also the new edition of the *Temple Scroll* by Elisha Qimron, *The Temple Scroll: A Critical Edition with Extensive Reconstructions* (Beer Sheva: Ben-Gurion University of the Negev Press / Jerusalem: Israel Exploration Society, 1996). For further discussion, see my *Temple Scroll and Related Texts* (Companion to the Qumran Scrolls 2; Sheffield: Sheffield Academic Press, 2000) 22–26.

19. For a fuller discussion of this definition, see my *Rewriting Scripture*.

20. On the technique of voicing used by the authors of the *Temple Scroll* as a bid for authority, see Bernard M. Levinson and Molly M. Zahn, "Revelation Regained: The Hermeneutics of כי and אם in the Temple Scroll," *DSD* 9 (2002) 295–346; Crawford, *Rewriting Scripture*. Whether this bid for authority was accepted by the community to whom it was made is an unresolved question. See my *Rewriting Scripture*, and the bibliography there.

from its supposed revelation to Moses on Mt. Sinai, the *Temple Scroll* presents itself as revealed to Moses on Sinai as well. In fact, it presents itself this way with audacity, by having God speak directly to Moses, in the first person:

> that I may turn from the fierceness of my anger, and show you mercy, and have compassion on you, and multiply you, as I swore to your fathers, if you obey my voice, keeping all my commandments which I command you this day, and doing what is right and good in the sight of the LORD your God. (11QTemple[a] 55:11–14)

The base text for this passage is Deut 13:18b–19, couched in the third person:

> in order that the LORD your God may turn from his anger and show you mercy and have compassion on you and multiply you, as he swore to your fathers: if you obey the voice of the LORD your God, obeying all his commandments, which I [Moses] am commanding you today, doing what is right in the sight of the LORD your God.[21]

This use of the theonymous first person, placing the revelation directly in the mouth of God, if accepted, makes the *Temple Scroll*'s authority uncontestable.[22] Here the principle of special revelation is visible.

The *Temple Scroll*'s exegetical interests are not all-encompassing. The composer/redactor does not attempt to interpret the entire Torah from Exodus 34 to Deuteronomy 23, beginning to end.[23] Rather, he concentrates on matters of cult, especially the physical temple and its furnishings, the proper sacrifices, the role of the priests and the Levites, the festival calendar, and issues of purity and impurity. He is concerned to protect the holiness of the temple and its cult and to make sure that life in the land surrounding the temple adheres to the proper observance of purity and holiness.[24] One example from the purity regulations will suffice as an illustration.

---

21. See further, Yadin, *Temple Scroll*, 1.71–72; 2.248–49.

22. For a discussion of the *Temple Scroll*'s strategy for claiming divine authority in the context of earlier rewritings of Mosaic legislation, see Bernard Levinson, "The Manumission of Hermeneutics: The Slave Laws of the Pentateuch as a Challenge to Contemporary Pentateuchal Theory," in *Congress Volume: Leiden, 2004* (ed. André Lemaire; VTSup 109; Leiden: Brill, 2006) 322–23.

23. The use of the term *composer/redactor* rather than *composer* or *author* acknowledges the fact that behind the *Temple Scroll* lie several sources that have been edited together, along with original material, to produce this unique composition. See further Andrew Wilson and Lawrence Wills, "Literary Sources of the Temple Scroll," *HTR* 75 (1982) 275–88; Michael Wise, *A Critical Study of the Temple Scroll from Qumran Cave 11* (SAOC 49; Chicago: Oriental Institute of the University of Chicago, 1990); and my *Temple Scroll*, 22–24.

24. As Jacob Milgrom first observed, the *Temple Scroll* thus embraces the principle of the Holiness Code (H), that the land itself is holy and thus all who inhabit it must avoid impurity ("The Qumran Cult: Its Exegetical Principles," in *Temple Scroll Studies* [ed. George Brooke; JSPSup 7; Sheffield: JSOT Press, 1989] 165–80, 167).

And if a man has a nocturnal emission, he shall not enter into any part of the temple until he will complete three days. And he shall wash his clothes and bathe on the first day, and on the third day he shall wash his clothes and bathe, and when the sun is down, he may come within the temple. And they shall not come into my temple in their *niddāh*-like uncleanness and defile it. And if a man lies with his wife and has an emission of semen, he shall not come into any part of *the city of the sanctuary* [עיר המקדש; translation and italics of this Hebrew phrase are mine], where I will settle my name, for three days. (11QTempleᵃ 45:7–10)[25]

The Pentateuch texts specifically concerned with the emission of semen are Lev 15:16–18 and Deut 23:10–12. In these texts, the impurity lasts only for a day and requires just a single immersion; the man is allowed back into the camp (the holy precinct surrounding the sanctuary) after sunset. In the *Temple Scroll*, an emission of semen renders a man impure for three days and requires two immersions and two launderings before the man is allowed to return to the city of the sanctuary.[26] The three-day period of purification is based on Exod 19:10–15, where Moses forbids sexual intercourse for three days before the encounter with God at Sinai. The application of this passage to the problem of the emission of semen within the temple or its surrounding city yields the slightly different treatments of seminal emission found in this regulation. The first instance is caused by nocturnal emission but the second by sexual intercourse. Because nocturnal emission is accidental, the man who suffers it must leave the holy precincts immediately and undergo the three-day purification period. However, sexual intercourse is a deliberate act, so it is simply banned (by implication) within the holy precincts, as Moses did before Sinai, and the man must follow the three-day prescription before entering the temple city.[27] In this example, it is apparent that the exegetical thrust of the *Temple Scroll* moves in the direction of maximum holiness: both for the temple and its cult and for the land and its inhabitants.[28] The perspective is the perspective of

---

25. Donald W. Parry and Emanuel Tov, eds., *Parabiblical Texts: The Dead Sea Scrolls Reader, Part 3* (Leiden: Brill, 2005) 181. All quotations of the *Temple Scroll* are taken from Parry and Tov, unless otherwise noted. *Niddāh* refers to impurity caused by menstrual blood and thus is appropriate as a term for any impurity that is the result of sexual function.

26. Jacob Milgrom, "Deviations from Scripture in the Purity Laws of the Temple Scroll," in *Jewish Civilization in the Hellenistic-Roman Period* (ed. Shermayahu Talmon; Philadelphia: Trinity Press International, 1991) 159–67. The *Temple Scroll* does not distinguish in matters of purity between the temple compound itself and its surrounding city; both are held to the same high degree of ritual purity. For further discussion, see my "Meaning of the Phrase עיר המקדש in the Temple Scroll," *DSD* 8 (2001) 1–13.

27. I discuss the implications of this command for the temple city and married life in "The Meaning of the Phrase עיר המקדש in the Temple Scroll."

28. Hannah Harrington observes that "over 80% of the laws extant in the [Qumran] Scrolls concern matters of holiness, i.e., the temple cult and ritual purity" ("Holiness and Law in the Dead Sea Scrolls," *DSD* 8 [2001] 124–35, quotation from p. 127).

the priestly caste; everything exists to serve the temple and its cult. Thus the *Temple Scroll* illustrates the second principle I pointed out regarding the earliest works of the Essene movement: the importance of the priests as guardians of Law and cult.

Finally, the *Temple Scroll*, by its very act of reworking the text of the Pentateuch, illustrates the third principle: a close reading of Scripture with a special concern for perceived difficulties in the text. Let me give one example as illustration. At the very end of 11QTemple[a] 66:11–17, the prohibitions against incest appear:[29]

> A man shall not take his father's wife, nor shall he uncover his father's skirt. A man shall not take his brother's wife, nor shall he uncover his brother's skirt, be it his father's son or his mother's son, for this is impurity. A man shall not take his sister, his father's daughter or his mother's daughter, for this is an abomination. A man shall not take his father's sister or his mother's sister, for it is wickedness. A man shall not take his brother's daughter or his sister's daughter, for it is an abomination. A [man] shall not take. . . .

The base text for this passage is Deut 23:1 ("a man shall not marry his father's wife, and he shall not uncover his father's skirt"), but the composer/redactor then exercises the exegetical technique of gathering together scriptural passages concerning incest: the brother's wife (Lev 18:16, 20:21), the sister (Lev 20:17 and Deut 27:22), and the aunt (Lev 18:12–14). So far all of these prohibitions are scriptural; however, the last prohibition, against marrying one's niece, is not.[30] The prohibition does answer a question that could be raised by a close reading of the text: if it is wrong to marry one's aunt, is it equally wrong to marry one's niece? The *Temple Scroll*'s answer is affirmative. Although, as the discussion of the *Damascus Document* will show, sound exegetical reasoning lies behind the prohibition, that reasoning is not presented here. The prohibition is apodictic; it simply stands as a pronouncement from the mouth of God.[31]

Note that incest is variously described as "impurity" (נדה), "abomination" (תועבה), or "wickedness" (זמה). While the composer/redactor is obviously echoing biblical language (for example, Lev 18:17 and 20:21 in the incest prohibitions themselves), the repetition of the opprobrious terms highlights the

---

29. In 4Q524, the oldest extant manuscript of the *Temple Scroll*, the text continues past the end of 11QTemple[a] with more regulations for interdicted and permitted marriages. See Puech, "4QRouleau du Temple," 103–8; my *Temple Scroll*, 14, 61–62.

30. Because the *Temple Scroll* is written from a male perspective to a male audience, the prohibition is written in terms of masculine familial relationships.

31. For further discussion of the apodictic nature of this pronouncement, see Bernard M. Levinson, "Textual Criticism, Assyriology, and the History of Interpretation: Deuteronomy 13:7a as a Test Case in Method," *JBL* 120 (2001) 211–43, esp. 231–33.

composer/redactor's concern for the holiness and purity of the land, the land of which the center is the temple.

The *Temple Scroll* illustrates a type of exegesis from the late Second Temple period in which the exegesis of the sacred base text (in this case the Pentateuch) is incorporated into the base text without a marker and presented as equally valid revelation. If a reader accepts the pseudepigraphic fiction of the *Temple Scroll*, that this revelation was given by God to Moses on Mt. Sinai, then there is no need for the composer/redactor to justify what with hindsight might be called "derived" laws. They are just laws. That this is the composer/redactor's intention is underscored by the first preserved column of 11QTemple[a], which begins in Exodus 34, beginning in the extant portion of the column with verse 10. Unfortunately the opening column of the *Temple Scroll* has not survived, but the setting can be presumed from the base text: Moses goes up Mt. Sinai for the second time, after the episode of the golden calf (Exodus 32), when God makes the covenant once again. It is this (second) covenant that remains valid. By using this setting for the opening of the *Temple Scroll*, the composer/redactor makes his position clear: this *sēper tôrâ*, "book of the law," has the same authority as the universally acknowledged Pentateuch. Although much of the *Temple Scroll*'s law stems from exegesis or interpretation of its pentateuchal base text, this exegesis is hidden in the guise of revelation. Also, the composer/redactor hides behind his pseudonymous persona; although Moses is never mentioned by name, he is the one who presumably is writing down God's words (note the reference in col. 44:5 to "Aaron, your brother"). There is therefore no need for the composer/redactor either to identify himself or the tradition within which he works. The claim to direct divine revelation is enough.

This position differs from that of the *Damascus Document*, which makes the claim of revealed truth, but also clearly differentiates itself from Scripture and makes its exegesis obvious. Further, it mentions the titles of several figures responsible for this exegesis, with the Teacher of Righteousness prominent among them. The *Temple Scroll*'s position also differs from that of the later rabbis, who, while making the claim that their Oral Torah comes from Moses and Sinai like the written Torah, differentiate between the two, make their exegesis explicit, and call upon a long chain of tradition to validate their rulings.

The *Temple Scroll* is one example of a category of works, Rewritten Scripture, that appears to have flourished in the 2nd century B.C.E. but had begun to fall from favor already in the 1st century B.C.E. and disappeared completely by the 2nd century C.E.[32] The type of exegesis favored by the *Damascus Document*,

---

32. Our latest extant example of literature falling into this category is Pseudo-Philo's *Liber Antiquitatum Biblicarum*, dated to the late 1st century C.E. George W. E. Nickelsburg, *Jewish Literature between the Bible and the Mishnah* (2nd ed.; Minneapolis: Fortress, 2005) 165–70.

in which the scriptural text is differentiated from its interpretation by clear markers that identify the exegesis leading to the interpretation, gained ascendancy throughout this period.

The Damascus Document

The *Damascus Document* (D) was originally discovered at the end of the 19th century in the Cairo Genizah.[33] It was published by Solomon Schechter in 1910.[34] Until copies were found in the Qumran caves, opinions varied as to its age and its origin, but the discovery of ten copies at Qumran gives solid boundaries for its date and its community of origin. The oldest copy, 4Q267, is radiocarbon-dated to the 2nd century B.C.E., and 4Q266 is given the oldest paleographical date of the *Damascus Document* manuscripts, the first half of the 1st century B.C.E.[35] Because 4Q267 and 4Q266, though fragmentary, seem to have contained the text of the *Damascus Document* in its substantially final form, D must have been redacted or composed in the mid- to late 2nd century B.C.E., around the same time as or slightly later than the *Temple Scroll*.[36] This is either before or possibly at the time of the founding of the Qumran community, according to the archaeological evidence cited above. Thus the *Damascus Document*, like the *Temple Scroll*, was brought into the Qumran community and was a product of its wider parent movement, the Essenes.

Also like the *Temple Scroll*, the *Damascus Document* is composite, and its composer/redactor drew on previously existing sources.[37] The *Damascus Document* (D) consists of two main sections, the Admonition (CD cols. 1–8 [19–20]) and the Laws (CD cols. 15–16, 9–14), with the Laws making up at least two-thirds of the complete text. As Joseph Baumgarten states, "The essential character of the *Damascus Document* which is now emerging is that of an elaboration of laws

---

33. The abbreviation "D" stands for the entire manuscript tradition of the *Damascus Document*, both the Qumran cave manuscripts and the manuscripts from the Cairo Genizah. The abbreviation "CD" refers only to the Cairo Genizah manuscripts, from which the conventional column and line numbering is adopted. The reader is referred to Geza Vermes, *The Complete Dead Sea Scrolls in English* (rev. ed.; London: Penguin, 2004) 147. All quotations from the *Damascus Document* are taken from the work of Vermes, unless otherwise noted.

34. Solomon Schechter, *Fragments of a Zadokite Work* (Cambridge: Cambridge University Press, 1910).

35. Charlotte Hempel, *The Damascus Texts* (Companion to the Qumran Scrolls 1; Sheffield: Sheffield Academic Press, 2000) 55.

36. Cecilia Wassen, *Women in the Damascus Document* (Academia Biblica 21; Atlanta: Society of Biblical Literature, 2005) 40.

37. There is a wide literature concerning possible sources for the *Damascus Document*. For a helpful recent discussion, see Maxine Grossman, *Reading for History in the Damascus Document: A Methodological Study* (STDJ 45; Leiden: Brill, 2002).

. . . with a hortatory preface and conclusion."[38] The Laws can be further divided into two categories: legal rulings based on exegesis of scriptural laws meant for all Israel; and regulations governing life in a specific community, presumably the Essene settlements or camps.[39] This differs from the *Temple Scroll*, which presents itself as a *sēper tôrâ* ("book of the law") valid for all Israel, and does not contain any specific communal or sectarian language.[40]

The *Damascus Document* differs from the *Temple Scroll* in its manner of self-presentation. Although the *Damascus Document* makes several claims to special revelation or knowledge, it does not present itself as divinely authorized Scripture, given by God to Moses at the same time as the Torah. Rather, its authority stems from its divinely inspired *exegesis* of Scripture; Scripture is a separate entity, but it needs interpretation to ensure its continuing correct observation.[41] This is the role of the divinely inspired exegetes, those to whom God's special knowledge is revealed. As the opening of D states: "[And now listen] to me and I will let you know the awesome des[igns of God] and His marvelous [mighty deeds]. I will recount to you [all that is concealed] from man [all the d]ays of his life" (4Q266, 1a–b, 5–7), and "[He (God) revealed hidden things to their eyes, and] opened their ears so that they might hear deep [secrets] and understand" (4Q266, 2, 1, 5). Likewise, its last extant line reads, "Behold, it is all in accordance with the final interpretation of the Law" (4Q266 11, 18–21). Thus it is clear that the interpretation of the Law contained in the *Damascus Document* is the result of divine inspiration.

In between its opening and closing, D quotes, alludes to, and uses for its own exegetical purposes passages from all five books of the Pentateuch. Unlike the *Temple Scroll*, D indicates clearly that it is interpreting a separate sacred text by the use of formulas that mark a scriptural citation, such as אשר אמר ("which he said"), כי כן כתוב ("for thus it is written"), or ועל X אשר אמר ("and concerning X, which he said").[42] These formulas indicate that these scriptural citations are

---

38. Joseph M. Baumgarten, *Qumran Cave 4, XIII: The Damascus Document (4Q266–273)* (DJD 18; Oxford: Clarendon, 1996) 7.

39. For further discussion, see Charlotte Hempel, *The Laws of the Damascus Document: Sources, Tradition and Redaction* (STDJ 29; Leiden: Brill, 1998); Wassen, *Women in the Damascus Document*, 33–44.

40. The best discussion concerning how to identify sectarian language in the Dead Sea Scrolls remains that of Carol Newsom, " 'Sectually Explicit' Literature from Qumran," in *The Hebrew Bible and Its Interpreters* (ed. William Propp, Baruch Halpern, and David Noel Freedman; Biblical and Judaic Studies from UCSD 1; Winona Lake, IN: Eisenbrauns, 1990) 167–87.

41. See George W. E. Nickelsburg, "Revelation," in *The Encyclopedia of the Dead Sea Scrolls* (ed. Lawrence H. Schiffman and James C. VanderKam; 3 vols.; New York: Oxford University Press, 2000) 2.770–72.

42. Baumgarten, *The Damascus Document*, 11. See also C. Elledge, "Exegetical Styles at Qumran: A Cumulative Index and Commentary," *RevQ* 21 (2003) 165–208.

being used as proof texts, to buttress the legal ruling being given.[43] Thus the *Da-mascus Document* differs markedly from the *Temple Scroll* by its self-presentation; it is not meant to be accepted as Scripture but as a divinely authorized interpre-tation of Scripture.

It is apparent that the *Damascus Document* stems from the same circle of ori-gin as the *Temple Scroll*, a Priestly-Levitical circle, which formed at least as early as the 3rd century B.C.E., coalesced into the Essene movement in the 2nd cen-tury, and survived until the destruction of the temple in 70 C.E. The two works have several things in common, besides their reliance on Torah: their claims to special revelation, an emphasis upon the importance of priests and purity and impurity in matters of Law and cult (which leads to a thrust to more severity in their legal interpretations), a close reading of Scripture, and a familiarity with the early works of this priestly movement, portions of *Enoch*, and, in the case of D, *Aramaic Levi* and *Jubilees*.[44] Further, the two share what Baumgarten and Daniel Schwartz term "salient congruities" in legal rulings, including bans on polygamy, uncle-niece marriage, intercourse within the temple city, and the scraping of oils and liquids from walls.[45] I will use two of these congruities in the following discussion of the exegetical strategies of D.

In my discussion of the prohibitions against incest found in 11QTemple[a] column 66, I noted that the prohibition against sexual intercourse with one's aunt is extended to include intercourse with one's niece. Given the self-presen-tation of the *Temple Scroll* as divinely revealed Scripture, the prohibition is made apodictically, without justification. In the *Damascus Document*, the same prohi-bition is found, this time with the exegetical justification laid out: "And each man marries the daughter of his brother or sister, whereas Moses said, 'You shall not approach your mother's sister; she is your mother's *near kin* [שאר; ital-ics mine].' But, although the precept against incest is written for men, it also applies to women. When, therefore, a brother's daughter uncovers the naked-ness of her father's brother, she is *near kin* [שאר]" (CD 5:7–11).[46] This prohi-bition gives the citation formula ומשה אמר ("and Moses said"), followed by a quotation of Lev 18:13. The exegetical reason for the prohibition follows: the precept is written for males, but it applies equally to females. Jacob Milgrom

43. Bernstein, "Scripture: Quotation and Use," 841.

44. The *Damascus Document* mentions the ancient title of *Jubilees* in CD 16:2–4, and refers to *Jubilees* in CD 10:7–10. It alludes to *Aramaic Levi* at CD 4:12. The periodization of history found in *1 Enoch* 90 and 93 is similar to that found in CD 1.

45. Joseph M. Baumgarten and Daniel R. Schwartz, "*Damascus Document*," in *The Dead Sea Scrolls: Hebrew, Aramaic, and Greek Texts with English Translations; Damascus Document, War Scroll and Related Documents* (ed. James H. Charlesworth; Tübingen: Mohr Siebeck / Louisville, KY: West-minster John Knox, 1995) 5.

46. On these issues, see further Levinson, "Textual Criticism," 231–33.

terms this exegetical reasoning "equalization or homogenization," where the law is extended to apply equally to other members of the same species.[47] The introduction to the legal ruling, an accusation of uncle-niece marriage against some unspecified "they," should also be noted. It is well known that the Pharisees allowed, even encouraged uncle-niece marriage, and that prominent families practiced it.[48] The *Damascus Document*, a product of the Essene movement, places itself in no uncertain terms on the opposite side of the question and gives its exegetical reason for doing so. Further, it lays out in the lines above the consequences of uncle-niece marriage: profanation (using the root טמא) of the temple (CD 5:6).

The equation of incest and profanation of the temple may seem surprising, until one recalls the emphasis placed on the holiness of the temple and the land in the Priestly-Levitical, Essene line of interpretation for which I am arguing. This emphasis originates in the Holiness Code found in Leviticus, in which the land itself is holy and immoral acts pollute the land, and, as discussed above, is also found in the *Temple Scroll*.[49]

The tone of the prohibition found here in the *Damascus Document* is polemical, unlike the tone of the *Temple Scroll*, which is neutral if not irenic. This ruling does occur in the Admonition, the section of D that is by its very nature polemical. However, the very fact of the existence of this polemical introduction to D's law collections indicates that by the mid- to late 2nd century B.C.E. the legal battle lines between the various groups were being much more sharply drawn.

The second example I wish to discuss comes from the Laws section, from the first category of Laws, legal rulings meant to apply to all Israel. This example also concerns the profanation of the temple: "No man shall lie with a woman in the city of the sanctuary (עיר המקדש), to defile the city of the sanctuary with their uncleanness (בנדתם)" (CD 12:1–2). This prohibition was implied in the *Temple Scroll*, which ordered a man who had had intercourse not to enter the עיר המקדש ("the city of the sanctuary") for three days. The reasoning behind the prohibition was laid out above. The ruling in the *Temple Scroll* implies that, if you cannot enter the city of the sanctuary after sexual intercourse, intercourse within the temple city is certainly forbidden. The law in D makes that implication explicit. The law is apodictic; no justification is given. This indicates that

47. Milgrom, "The Qumran Cult," 171. He notes that this reasoning is equivalent to the rabbinic principle of *binyan ab*.

48. Tal Ilan, *Jewish Women in Greco-Roman Palestine* (Peabody, MA: Hendrickson, 1995) 75–79.

49. The consequences of the pollution of incest are made explicit in Lev 18:24–29, where the land "vomits out" the former inhabitants. In Num 19:13, 20, those who do not undertake the proper purity rituals after touching a dead body are accused of defiling the tabernacle. I am grateful to Bernard Levinson and Baruch Levine for bringing these examples to my attention.

the ruling was familiar to the audience of D; no justification was needed because the exegetical reasoning was already well known. However, the tone of the law is sharp; the word used for "uncleanness" (root נדה) is the same word used in the *Temple Scroll* passage on the subject, which uses the word to describe the impurity of any seminal emission. The use of this sharp tone leads to the conclusion that the text is polemical, aimed at the contemporary residents of Jerusalem who are indulging in sexual intercourse. This prohibition may strike the contemporary reader as unrealistic, but it is important to remember that the goal of Essene scriptural interpretation and practice was to achieve maximum purity in the holy land, especially in the temple and its cult. This leads to a stringent interpretive bias, especially in the laws of sexual conduct.[50]

The first example of scriptural exegesis taken from D illustrates the same close reading of Scripture and a concern to "close the gaps" that were found in the *Temple Scroll* and the earlier 3rd-century literature, as well as a concern for the purity of the temple. The second example illustrates more directly the concern for the holiness and purity of the temple, stemming from the priestly focus of this literature. When these examples are combined with the claim to special revelation illustrated above, it can be said with assurance that the *Damascus Document* is part of an assemblage of Jewish literature that shares the same concerns and exegetical principles, an assemblage I have labeled Essene.

Conclusion

This assemblage of Jewish literature, collected, revered, and expanded by the Essene movement, as illustrated by its subset at Qumran, originated in Priestly-Levitical circles in the mid–Second Temple period. The exact provenance of this circle is unknown, but it must have formed within the priestly and scribal elites located in Jerusalem in the late Persian and early Hellenistic periods (4th century B.C.E.). It is possible that this Priestly-Levitical circle or movement housed the scribal tradition that produced the pre-Samaritan version of the Pentateuch, which originated in Palestine.[51] As discussed above, the pre-Samaritan text-type is a *harmonizing* text-type; therefore it fits into the exegetical concern found again and again in all the works discussed in this essay, a concern to make the sacred text consistent by bringing one authoritative text into harmony with another.[52] If the pre-Samaritan text-type did come into existence within this Priestly-Levitical circle, then the origin of this circle can be traced back even as

---

50. Harrington, "Holiness and Law," 126–27.

51. Frank Moore Cross, *The Ancient Library of Qumran* (3rd ed.; Sheffield: Sheffield Academic Press, 1995) 142.

52. So also Brooke, "Biblical Interpretation at Qumran," 315.

far as the 4th century B.C.E. This Priestly-Levitical circle began to produce its own literature by the 3rd century B.C.E., including parts of *1 Enoch* and *Aramaic Levi*, which demonstrated their particular exegetical concerns: (1) special revelation, (2) the importance of priests as guardians of Law and cult, and (3) a close reading of Scripture with an eye to explaining perceived difficulties in the text. By the 2nd century B.C.E. this Priestly-Levitical circle produced the Essene movement. The Essenes composed their own literature, including the *Temple Scroll* and the *Damascus Document*, manifesting those same exegetical concerns.

If this line of reasoning is accepted, then it is possible to trace a continuous line of Torah interpretation with this particular set of exegetical concerns from the beginning to the end of the Second Temple period. The process began with the promulgation and acceptance of the Torah as Scripture in the 5th century B.C.E. and continued in the 4th century B.C.E. with the scribal activity that produced the harmonizing pre-Samaritan text-type. By the 3rd century B.C.E., this line of interpretation appeared in new works, related to but separate from the Torah. In the 2nd century B.C.E., specifically Essene compositions with those exegetical concerns emerged. The Qumran collection, whose latest manuscripts date to the mid-1st century C.E., demonstrates that a subset of the Essene movement, still with the same exegetical concerns enumerated above, existed until the end of the Second Temple period. Thus, the discovery of all these texts together in the caves at Qumran shines a brighter light than was previously thought possible on the history of the Pentateuch and its interpretation in the Second Temple period.

The Torah as the Rhetoric of Priesthood

JAMES W. WATTS

Syracuse University

In the Second Temple period, the Torah gained canonical authority through its association with the priesthoods of the Jerusalem and Samaritan temples. The Torah, in turn, legitimized these priests' control over both the temples and, for much of the period, over the territory of Judah as well. An original function of the Pentateuch then was to legitimize the religious and, by extension, the political claims of priestly dynasties. This point has rarely been discussed and never been emphasized by biblical scholars, however, which makes the subject of the Torah's relationship to the Second Temple Aaronide priesthood as much about the ideologies of academic culture as about ancient religious history.

Fear of theocracy is once again a prominent feature of Western political culture. With so-called fundamentalists of various religious traditions bidding for political power and Western military deployments defined frequently in terms of a struggle between liberal democracy and militant religious fanaticism, many public statements voice concern about the growing influence of religion and of religious leaders on political affairs. Concerns of this sort are a very old and persistent theme in Western culture. They date from late antiquity and the Middle Ages and have played prominent roles in the political and religious revolutions that have repeatedly changed the course of European history.

Suspicion of theocracies has influenced biblical studies as well. Scholars know well and warn their students of its distorting effect on 19th-century descriptions of ancient Israel's religious history. Newer ideologies, however, have not been any more sympathetic to the rhetoric of priestly hierocracy. For example, proponents of neither Marxism nor of liberal capitalism look favorably upon aristocratic oligarchies, which in economic terms is what the Jewish priesthood became in the Second Temple period. Nor can feminist critics be expected to celebrate the priests' patriarchal hierarchy that systematically excluded women from Israel's institutionalized religious leadership.

As a result of this political history, modern scholarship has been prone to celebrate Israel's prophets and to be fascinated with its kings, but not with its priests. Though ideological critics are no doubt correct that the Bible has usually been read much too sympathetically, this has not been the case with the Priestly literature of the Torah, especially with its rhetoric of priestly privilege. Priestly rhetoric has routinely been criticized and dismissed, or defended only by turning it into something that it originally was not. Our biases, however, place stumbling blocks in the path of studies of the origins and nature of Priestly rhetoric in its original historical situation, that is, as used by priests to influence their listening and reading audiences in ancient Israel and Judah. Interpreters with historical interests cannot avoid bringing our own culture and ideological commitments into our work, but we can become conscious of the effects of such biases and begin to imagine other interpretive possibilities. Reading, just like theater, requires a conscious suspension of disbelief, not just in order to accept (momentarily) the imaginative worlds that books can present but also to accept (momentarily) the ideologies that they reflect and project. What is needed to advance our understanding of the origins of Priestly literature (henceforth P) are new, imaginative construals of the *values* in Priestly rhetoric, construals that consciously try to avoid the biases inherited from later religious and political commitments.

Leviticus justifies control of Israel's priesthood by Aaron's descendents and their monopoly over most of its duties, privileges, and sources of income. As many interpreters over the last two centuries have noted, Leviticus's portrayal of the preeminence of the high priest and the Aaronides' monopoly over the priesthood corresponds historically to the situation of Jewish and Samaritan priests in the Persian and Hellenistic periods. A hierocracy even developed in Second Temple Judaism. It was strongest under the Hasmoneans in the second and first centuries B.C.E. but they built on foundations of priestly authority and political influence that had grown steadily over the previous three centuries.[1] It was in the Second Temple period that the Pentateuch, with the Priestly rhetoric of Aaronide legitimacy at its center, began to function as authoritative Scripture for Jews and Samaritans. It is therefore to this period and this hierocracy that P's rhetoric applies, either by preceding the hierocracy and laying the ideological basis for it (if P dates to the Exilic Period or earlier) or by reflecting and legitimizing an existing institution as it began to accumulate religious and civil authority (if P dates from the early Second Temple period).[2]

---

1. For one recent reconstruction of the historical situation behind the hierocracy, see Reinhard Achenbach, *Die Vollendung der Tora: Studien zur Redaktionsgeschichte des Numeribuches im Kontext von Hexateuch und Pentateuch* (Beihefte zur Zeitschrift für altorientalische und biblische Rechtsgeschichte 3; Wiesbaden: Harrassowitz, 2002) 130–40.

2. Critical scholarship has usually dated P to the Exile or later (e.g., classically, Julius Wellhausen, *Prolegomena to the History of Israel* [trans. J. S. Black and A. Menzies; repr., Gloucester, MA: Peter Smith, 1973; German 1st ed., 1878] 165–67), a position that continues to be maintained by a large number of contemporary commentators. A significant minority, however, advocate a date

The preserved Priestly rhetoric does not speak in its own voice, which makes the rhetorical situation in the Second Temple period hard to assess. Exodus, Leviticus, and Numbers use the voice of God and the actions of Moses to legitimize the role and authority of the Aaronide priests. The priests thus disguised their role in the arguments of their times by hiding behind God and Moses and casting their speeches in the distant past. As a result, it may appear that much of the preserved Second Temple rhetoric tilts against the high priestly family and criticizes their practices (Ezra, Nehemiah, Malachi, 1 and 2 Maccabees, 4QMMT).[3] That view can only be maintained, however, if one categorizes the Torah as "preexilic" and so ignores its rhetorical impact in the Second Temple period.[4] Whatever their date of composition, the Pentateuch's Priestly texts functioned with far greater rhetorical power in the Persian and Hellenistic periods than they ever had previously, because they functioned increasingly as scripture. The reason for their growing authority was precisely the fact that the Torah did express the voice of the Aaronide priests who controlled both the Jerusalem and Samaritan temples and sponsored the scriptures that authorized these temples' rituals.

The early stages of the canonization of Scripture depended upon the books' association with the Samaritan and Jewish priesthoods. It seems to me that this point is incontrovertible regardless of which particular explanation for the Torah's growing authority one accepts. Whether the Pentateuch became authoritative because of Persian imperial authorization, as Peter Frei maintained, or because of the influence of the temple library, as Jean-Louis Ska argues, or because of its erudite deployment by temple scribes to support theocracy, as Eckart Otto maintains, or because of its use to enculturate a Judean elite against Hellenistic influences, as David Carr proposes, or because of its use as the textual

---

in the 8th century B.C.E. or earlier (most prominently Jacob Milgrom, *Leviticus 1–16* [AB 3; New York: Doubleday, 1991] 23–35). Some readers may be surprised that I do not engage such issues here. It has become a reflex for many biblical scholars to mentally categorize all approaches to the Pentateuch on the basis of the literary dating and compositional issues they propose. Much can be said about the literature and rhetoric of the Pentateuch, however, that does not depend on speculative reconstructions of its history. The subject of this essay is a case in point. Only a compositional theory that dated Leviticus 1–16 in the Hasmonean period or later (a difficult position to maintain, because the earliest fragments of Leviticus among the Dead Sea Scrolls have been dated on paleographic grounds to the mid–3rd century B.C.E.) could contradict the point I am making here and therefore make compositional issues relevant to this topic.

3. Chronicles presents a more complicated evaluation of priests and Levites; see Gary N. Knoppers, "Hierodules, Priests, or Janitors? The Levites in Chronicles and the History of the Israelite Priesthood," *JBL* 118 (1999) 49–72.

4. This trend is corrected by the essays of Eckart Otto (pp. 171–184) and Sebastian Grätz (pp. 273–287) in this volume that explore aspects of the interaction between the evolving Torah and other Second Temple period literature.

authority for temple rituals as I have suggested, the Torah's influence grew in tandem with the influence of the dynasty of the first postexilic high priest, Joshua, who claimed descent from Aaron.[5] As the temple law book, the Torah shared the prestige of the Jewish and Samaritan temples and in turn validated the monopolistic claims of the temples and, especially, their priesthoods over the offerings of Israel.

Scholarship usually links the Torah with the temple, rather than with the priesthood, but I think that the emphasis should be shifted to the priests. A single family of Aaronide priests led not one but two religious and ethnic communities of increasing size and influence in the last five centuries B.C.E.[6] According to Josephus, a Samaritan leader gained permission from Alexander to

---

5. Peter Frei, "Zentralgewalt und Lokalautonomie im Achämenidenreich," in *Reichsidee und Reichsautorisation im Perserreich* (ed. Peter Frei and Klaus Koch; OBO 55; Fribourg: Universitätsverlag, 1984 [2nd ed. 1996]) 8–131; idem, "Die persische Reichsautorisation: Ein Überblick," *ZABR* 1 (1995) 1–35; translated as "Persian Imperial Authorization: A Summary," in *Persia and Torah: The Theory of Imperial Authorization of the Pentateuch* (ed. and trans. James W. Watts; SBLSymS 17; Atlanta: Society of Biblical Literature, 2001) 5–40; Jean-Louis Ska, "'Persian Imperial Authorization': Some Question Marks," in *Persia and Torah: The Theory of Imperial Authorization of the Pentateuch* (ed. James W. Watts; SBLSymS 17; Atlanta: Society of Biblical Literature, 2001) 161–82; Eckart Otto, *Das Deuteronomium im Pentateuch und Hexateuch* (FAT 30; Tübingen: Mohr Siebeck, 2000) 248–62; David M. Carr, *Writing on the Tablet of the Heart: Origins of Scripture and Literature* (New York: Oxford University Press, 2005) 201–85; James W. Watts, "Ritual Legitimacy and Scriptural Authority," *JBL* 124 (2005) 401–17, republished in *Ritual and Rhetoric in Leviticus* (Cambridge: Cambridge University Press, 2007) chap. 9.

6. The history of the Persian period high priesthood has been the subject of intensive historical investigation and debate as to the exact succession of high priests. A list of the high priests preserved in Nehemiah 12 names six generations: Joshua/Jeshua, who oversaw the building of the second temple, and his descendents Joiakim, Eliashib, Joiada, Jonathan/Johanan, and Jaddua. This list is supported by Josephus and, to some extent, by the Elephantine papyri. Josephus attests that the same family controlled the high priesthood for another century: Jaddua was the ancestor of high priests Onias I, Simon I, Manasseh, Eleazar, Onias II, Simon II, Onias III, and his brother Jason. Frank Moore Cross and others have argued that the six names of Nehemiah's list are too few for a period of two hundred years. Cross suggested that the practice of papponymy, naming a son for his grandfather, led to the omission of several generations from the list (Frank Moore Cross Jr., "A Reconstruction of the Judean Restoration," *JBL* 94 [1975] 4–18; see also Roland de Vaux, *Ancient Israel* [trans. John McHugh; New York: McGraw-Hill, 1961] 401–3; Geo Widengren, "The Persian Period," in *Israelite and Judaean History* [ed. John H. Hayes and J. M. Miller; OTL; Philadelphia: Westminster, 1977] 506–9; Hugh G. M. Williamson, "The Historical Value of Josephus' *Jewish Antiquities*," *JTS* 28 [1977] 49–67; Lester L. Grabbe, "Josephus and the Reconstruction of the Judean Restoration," *JBL* 106 [1987] 231–46). James VanderKam has defended Nehemiah's list as accurate ("Jewish High Priests of the Persian Period: Is the List Complete?" in *Priesthood and Cult in Ancient Israel* [ed. Gary A. Anderson and Saul M. Olyan; JSOTSup 125; Sheffield: JSOT Press, 1991] 67–91; idem, *From Joshua to Caiaphas: High Priests after the Exile* [Minneapolis: Augsburg Fortress, 2004] 97–99). This debate does not, however, significantly undermine the testimony of ancient sources that a single family seems to have controlled the high priesthood in Jerusalem from ca. 535 until 175 B.C.E.

build a temple on Mt. Gerizim for his son-in-law, the son of a Jerusalem high priest, to serve as high priest himself.[7] Intermarriage between Samaritan leadership and the Jewish high priestly dynasty had previously stirred controversy in the Persian period (Ezra 10:18–23, Neh 13:28). The fact that Samaritans and Jews shared both the Torah and a common priesthood can hardly have been a coincidence. Aaronide priests of Joshua's family also founded and directed a Jewish temple in Leontopolis, Egypt.[8] It seems that the Aaronide priests, or some of them at any rate, were far less committed to Deuteronomy's doctrine of the geographic centralization of cultic worship in Jerusalem than they were to P's doctrine of the Aaronides' monopoly over the conduct of all cultic worship, wherever it might take place.

The Aaronide high priests claimed special authority to wield the voices of the Torah (Lev 10:10–11) and, probably, of the prophets as well. It may be that at some times other factions, within and outside the priesthood, were able to deploy the authority of the Torah against Joshua's dynasty, as seems to have been done by Ezra, an Aaronide himself from a slightly different branch of the family.[9] The descendents of Joshua seem to have retained their hold on the high priesthood until the 2nd century, however, and on the legitimizing rhetoric of the Torah as well. In light of the priesthood's practices, it is therefore not

---

7. On the family relationship between Samaritan and Jewish high priests, see Josephus, *Ant.* 11.302–3, 321–24.

8. Josephus's somewhat contradictory accounts of this temple can be found in *Ant.* 12.397, 13.62–73 and *J.W.* 7.426–32.

9. 1 Esd 9:39, 40, 49 actually grants Ezra the title *archiereus* "chief priest," but no similar title appears in Ezra or Nehemiah either for Ezra or for anyone else. Ezra 7:1 traces his genealogy through the high priestly line back to Aaron, but it does not link up with the postexilic high priests listed in Neh 12:10–11; see also 12:26. Interpreters are divided over whether he held the post or not; see n. 5 for reconstructions of a single family's monopoly over the high priesthood, excluding Ezra. For summaries of the debate, see Klaus Koch ("Ezra and Meremoth: Remarks on the History of the High Priesthood," in *"Sha'arei Talmon": Studies in the Bible, Qumran, and the Ancient Near East Presented to Shemaryahu Talmon* [ed. Michael Fishbane, Emanuel Tov, and Weston W. Fields; Winona Lake, IN: Eisenbrauns, 1992] 105–10) and Ulrike Dahm (*Opferkult und Priestertum in Alt-Israel: Ein kultur- und religionswissenschaftlicher Beitrag* [BZAW 327; Berlin: de Gruyter, 2003] 83–84), both of whom concluded that Ezra was, in fact, high priest. Gary N. Knoppers has pointed out that the title "the priest" with which Ezra is designated appears also in Chronicles as a common designation for high priests ("The Relationship of the Priestly Genealogies to the History of the High Priesthood in Jerusalem," in *Judah and the Judeans in the Neo-Babylonian Period* [ed. Oded Lipschits and Joseph Blenkinsopp; Winona Lake, IN: Eisenbrauns, 2003] 109–33). The rhetoric of Ezra–Nehemiah, however, weighs against the conclusion that it intends to describe Ezra as high priest; see VanderKam, *From Joshua to Caiaphas,* 45–48. Not only do the books not explicitly distinguish Ezra in that role, but his reforms do not deal with how priests do their business in the temple, which was the high priest's primary responsibility, but rather with their marriages and other relations with foreigners. Contrast this with the contents of 4QMMT, the letter from Qumran, which in the 2nd century B.C.E. questioned the Jerusalem priests' conduct of the offerings precisely in order to challenge their legitimacy, especially that of their high priest.

accidental that the Torah contains no general prohibition on intermarriage, as
the authors of the books of Ezra and Nehemiah think it should. The Aaronide
rhetoric of Leviticus at the heart of the newly canonized Torah occupied the
most powerful position from which to influence these debates.

Ancient and modern interpreters have routinely criticized and dismissed
Priestly rhetoric, or defended it by turning it into something that it originally
was not, through allegory, moral analogy, and theological spiritualization.[10] If
we can momentarily bracket some of our negative value judgments about ancient priests with which medieval and modern history and tradition have indoc-
trinated us and try to evaluate the ancient Jewish priesthood in its own
religious, political, and historical context, this would make possible a more sympathetic evaluation of the ancient Jewish hierocracy. This seems to be what the
Priestly writers hoped would result from their legitimation and celebration of
the Aaronide priesthood. There is solid evidence in Second Temple period literature that the Torah achieved this, and more. The Priestly work extends the
priests' authority beyond ritual procedures only to matters of teaching Israel the
distinction between clean and unclean and holy and common (Lev 10:9–11),
and Deuteronomy extends their authority only a little further to the extent of
staffing a high court of appeal (Deut 17:8–13) and teaching the Torah as a
whole (31:9–13). Nevertheless, P's elaborate descriptions of the investiture and
anointing of Aaron and his sons (Leviticus 8–9; also Exodus 28, 39) distinguishes the priesthood as the most celebrated office of leadership in the Torah.[11]

---

10. See Watts, *Ritual and Rhetoric in Leviticus*, chap. 1.

11. Much of the scholarly discussions of the offices of Israel have focused on Deuteronomy's descriptions of prophets, priests, and kings. In comparison with P's elaborate celebration of the
Aaronides, however, Deuteronomy's treatment of these offices is very utilitarian and limited. The
king, famously, has no duties but to copy and read the Torah (Deut 17:14–20). Prophets receive a
more positive commission, but the text's chief concern has to do with the validity of the prophet's
message, which must be determined by its accuracy (18:15–22) and its accord with the henotheistic
teachings of Deuteronomy itself (13:2–6[1–5]). Bernard M. Levinson has recently described Deuteronomy's program as a utopian constitution that designates separate spheres of judicial, cultic, and
monarchic authority under the governance of a legal text, which is Deuteronomy itself ("The First
Constitution: Rethinking the Origins of Rule of Law and Separation of Powers in Light of Deuteronomy," *Cardozo Law Review* 27 [2006] 1853–88). Ancient Israelite society never actually operated
in such a fashion, as Levinson is the first to admit. One should note, however, that Deuteronomy's
program of cultic centralization in the Jerusalem temple did not produce a balance of power, even
in theory, so much as a tilt in power toward the temple's hierarchy: "levitical priests" must supervise
the king's copying of the scroll of law (17:18) and rule on judicial cases "too difficult" for local
courts (17:8–13), and it is they, of course, who control the reading and teaching of the Torah itself
(31:9–13). So, despite their many differences from one another, Deuteronomy supports P's privileging of priests. Deuteronomy's focus on Levites rather than P's Aaronides would hardly have im-
peded the Torah's pro-priestly function in the Second Temple period, when priestly genealogies
harmonized both groups into one family. On this point, see Otto, *Das Deuteronomium im Pentateuch*

It is not surprising then that the Torah's unparalleled celebration of the priests gave them increasing political influence as the Second Temple period progressed. The Wisdom of Jesus Ben Sira (3rd century B.C.E.) shows clearly the influence of P's rhetoric on Jewish political ideals. In his "praise of famous men" (44:1), Ben Sira gives Aaron (45:6–22) greater space than Moses (44:23–45:5), lingering over the high priest's vestments (cf. Exodus 28). He then concludes his book with a peon of praise for the high priest Simon son of Onias. He first celebrates Simon's construction projects and political achievements as if he were a king (50:1–4) before lavishing much greater attention on his appearance "when he put on his glorious robe and clothed himself in perfect splendor" (vv. 5–11) and officiated over the temple offerings (vv. 12–21). It is no wonder that later Roman governors insisted on controlling the use of such politically potent clothing.[12] The ability to imagine such sympathetic receptions for P's rhetoric of priesthood is therefore a precondition for understanding its intended function, as biblical scholars are increasingly coming to recognize.[13]

The Priestly Code's rhetoric of the divine right of priests to control Israel's offerings will, however, not carry much weight with modern audiences for whom rituals of this sort are little more than historical curiosities or religious symbols. More plausible will be a reevaluation of the ancient hierocracy on the basis of its historical effects, rather than on its supposedly divine origins. Its value needs to be judged against the achievements of the priestly dynasty whose rule it legitimated. It is against the background of priestly history in the Second Temple period, therefore, that the rhetoric of Leviticus should, in the first instance, be judged.

---

und Hexateuch, 248–62, esp. 260, who argues for Priestly, specifically Zadokite, interests behind both Deuteronomy separately and the hexateuchal and pentateuchal redactions that combined it with the other books.

12. Josephus, *Ant.* 15.402–8, 19.93, 20.6–16. The *Letter of Aristeas* (96–99), Philo (*Mos.* 2.109–35; *Spec.* 1.82–97), and Josephus (*Ant.* 3.151–78; *J.W.* 5.227–36) also give extensive descriptions of the priestly garments that echo through rabbinic literature and that attest not only to the fascination they aroused but also to the rhetorical function of literary descriptions in furthering the priesthood's mystique and power; see Michael D. Swartz, "The Semiotics of the Priestly Vestments in Ancient Judaism," in *Sacrifice in Religious Experience* (ed. Albert I. Baumgarten; SHR 93; Leiden: Brill, 2002) 57–80.

13. This point has been emphasized over the last forty years through the detailed explication of priestly rituals by, especially, Jacob Milgrom and Baruch Levine in their monographs and commentaries. They have defended the rationality and realism of priestly rituals against the old and widespread tendency to disparage them as primitive and superstitious. This trend has not yet, however, led to reevaluations of the religious achievements of the Second Temple priesthood itself, though the methodological case for interpretive sympathy when reading about priests has recently been argued by Antony Cothey ("Ethics and Holiness in the Theology of Leviticus," *JSOT* 30 [2005] 131–51 [135]) and by Jonathan Klawans (*Purity, Sacrifice, and the Temple: Symbolism and Supersessionism in the Study of Ancient Judaism* [Oxford: Oxford University Press, 2006] 248).

By what standards should we judge the priests' effectiveness? There are many possibilities, running the gamut of our contemporary religious and political opinions. I suggest starting with two criteria that balance ancient and modern sensibilities. The first should consist of the religious standards set forth by the Hebrew Bible itself, because they represent the values to which the priests themselves subscribed and the values that their contemporaries expected them to epitomize. Furthermore, these standards remain potent religious ideals in the modern world. Though the contents of the Hebrew Bible are diverse and express multiple opinions on various issues, for the most part they nevertheless subscribe to a common ideal of how Israel's religion should be expressed. Included in this ideal is loyalty to YHWH, the god of Israel, expressed in some texts as pure monotheism, and also expressed by a commitment to fulfilling the ethical and religious stipulations of the Torah, conceived either as oral divine instruction in earlier texts or as the written laws of the Pentateuch in later texts. Evaluating the priests' leadership against these standards typical of biblical literature can help us avoid complete anachronism. Our judgments will employ values to which the ancient priests themselves most likely subscribed, because they wrote a significant part of the Hebrew Bible and championed the written Torah's authority.

How well does the Aaronides' record stack up against broad biblical ideals? The Aaronide priests oversaw the establishment of cultic worship in Judah at Jerusalem, in Samaria on Mt. Gerizim, and in Egypt at Leontopolis on the basis of the Torah's ritual instructions.[14] Furthermore, it was in the Second Temple period that the Torah as a written text began to function normatively for temple practice in both Jerusalem and on Mt. Gerizim, and probably in Leontopolis as well. The Torah was officially recognized as Jewish temple law by the Persians (according to Ezra 7) and was sufficiently respected by the Ptolemaic rulers of Egypt for them to sponsor an official Greek translation of it (according

---

14. The orthodoxy of the Samaritan's practice was contested by ancient Jews who derided it as idolatrous (see 2 Kgs 17:24–41; Josephus, *Ant.* 13.3), but it is difficult to take this criticism seriously. Samaritans, like Jews, revere the Torah and its laws. Though interpretive and textual differences, as well as ethnic rivalries, separated the two communities, and though there is evidence of vast variations in the nature and degree of religious observance within both communities in the Second Temple period, aspersions against the Samaritan cult reflect polemics, rather than historical practices; see Pieter W. van der Horst, "Anti-Samaritan Propaganda in Early Judaism," in *Persuasion and Dissuasion in Early Christianity, Ancient Judaism, and Hellenism* (ed. Pieter W. van der Horst et al.; Leuven: Peeters, 2003) 25–44. On the cultural similarities between the two communities, see Gary N. Knoppers, "Revisiting the Samarian Question in the Persian Period," in *Judah and the Judeans in the Persian Period* (ed. M. Oeming and O Lipschits; Winona Lake, IN: Eisenbrauns, 2006) 265–89. With respect to the close connections between the Judean and Samaritan Pentateuchs and the relatively late separation between the Samaritans and the Jews, see the essay by Reinhard Pummer in this volume (pp. 237–269).

to the *Letter of Aristeas*.[15] Whether or not these official recognitions were really as significant as these Jewish texts make them appear, it is clear that as the Second Temple period progressed the Torah was increasingly recognized as a symbol of Samaritan and Jewish religious distinctiveness. Accompanying the Torah's elevation to iconic status was the establishment and growing recognition of monotheism as normative for Jews and Samaritans. Though in the late 5th century the existence of a polytheistic Jewish temple in Elephantine, Egypt, passed without negative comment in the correspondence of that community with authorities in Judea and Samaria, such a situation is unlikely to have been so easily tolerated in the 2nd century and later.[16]

In other words, as the dynasty of Joshua gained preeminence and power in the Second Temple period, increasing numbers of Jews and Samaritans seem to have conformed to the Bible's most basic notions of proper religious practices and beliefs.[17] This was the case to a much greater extent than at any previous time, according to the account in the books of Kings of the religious standards of the monarchic period and according to most modern historical accounts of that period as well. It can safely be said, then, that on the basis of the Bible's own standards, the priestly hierocracy of the Second Temple period produced markedly better religious results than did the monarchs of the preexilic period, most of whose religious policies are repudiated by biblical writers as rejections of God's covenant with Israel.

It is, of course, hardly surprising that the priests led Jews and Samaritans to live in basic accord with the Torah's teachings: they wrote and edited much of it, and probably played a decisive role in canonizing it. The surprise comes rather from the failure of modern commentators to point out the correspondence between biblical ideals and the achievements of the Aaronides' hierocracy.[18] The

---

15. On the Septuagint and the *Letter of Aristeas*, see the essay by Arie van der Kooij in this volume (pp. 289–300).

16. See Reinhard Kratz's helpful contrast between the Jewish communities at 5th-century Elephantine and 2nd-century Qumran in this volume (pp. 77–103). I do not, however, think that the Pentateuch was originally in some tension with the interests of the Jerusalem priesthood, as Kratz suggests. It is notable that out of all the positions of authority in Second Temple Jewish society, only the institution of the priesthood receives explicit and extensive rhetorical support from the Torah. It depicts the high priesthood as the most important office in Israel.

17. My blithe reference to "the Bible" in this paragraph is, of course, anachronistic since there was no canon at the beginning of the Second Temple period, the Torah became increasingly authoritative through the middle of the period, and the full Tanakh gained recognition only late in the period, if then. I use the term here intentionally, however, to emphasize the convergence between priestly influence and the ideals of the emerging scriptures.

18. Even studies of priestly roles and the history of Israelite/Judean priesthoods tend to focus primarily on the preexilic and immediately postexilic priesthoods and limit the priests' influence to the "theological" ideas contained in P, giving little or no attention to their influence on the later political and religious development of Second Temple Judaism; see, for example, Joseph Blenkinsopp, *Sage,*

heritage of later religious and political struggles against theocratic institutions continues to weigh heavily on how the religion of the Second Temple period is portrayed in scholarship, especially in broader treatments of biblical theology or religion.[19]

I turn therefore to a different, more secular standard for evaluating the priests' effectiveness, namely the practical effects of their rule. What were its consequences for the people of ancient Israel, Judea, and Samaria? This evaluation imaginatively poses a question common in modern political campaigns: were Samaritans and Jews better off due to priestly leadership and rule, or not? Though political expediency is no virtue according to many biblical texts, political success garners respect from most ancient and modern historians. From the long perspective of two millennia, it is easier to reach a consensus on what counts as "successful" leadership than it is for more contemporary events. The Judean kings who revolted against Babylon in the early 6th century B.C.E. and the Jewish rebels who fought against Rome in 66–70 C.E. were obvious failures by this standard, as the disastrous effects of their policies for the people of Judea make clear.

How effective was the Aaronide hierocracy in promoting the survival and welfare of Jewish and Samaritan peoples? To answer this question is to judge the leadership of the Aaronides on the basis of political pragmatism, or on "the artfulness of cultural persistence" to use Steven Weitzman's more attractive

Priest, Prophet: Religious and Intellectual Leadership in Ancient Israel (Louisville, KY: Westminster John Knox, 1995) 113–14, despite his astute description of the effects of anti-priestly biases in scholarship (66–68); also Lester L. Grabbe, *Priests, Prophets, Diviners, Sages: A Socio-Historical Study of Religious Specialists in Ancient Israel* (Valley Forge, PA: Trinity Press International, 1995). One significant effort to rectify this imbalance was Richard D. Nelson's *Raising Up a Faithful Priest: Community and Priesthood in Biblical Theology* (Louisville, KY: Westminster John Knox, 1993). He chronicled the bias in biblical scholarship against priests, which he blamed primarily on Protestant thought, and wrote positive theological reflections on the priesthood (101–5). Though Nelson recounted the glorification of the high priest in Second Temple literature, however, his own evaluation of Joshua's Second Temple dynasty remained muted. His final list of priestly heroes ("Ezekiel, the Priestly Writer, Ezra, and the Maccabees" [105]) omits the high priestly line entirely, except insofar as it is represented by P.

19. Take only one prominent example of this nearly universal tendency in modern biblical studies: Walter Brueggemann's *Theology of the Old Testament: Testimony, Dispute, Advocacy* (Minneapolis: Fortress, 1997) categorized the Hebrew Bible's means for mediating the divine presence as "Torah," "King," "Prophet," and "Sage," but where one would naturally expect to see "Priest," he listed "Cult" instead (567–704). His discussion under that heading marked a major advance over most other theologies that give ritual worship much shorter shrift. He highlighted the theological stereotyping that has bedeviled Christian biblical theologies and worked hard to avoid it by devoting 30 pages to the cult's theological implications. Nevertheless, discussion of the priesthood receives only 1 page of that (664–65). Like much of the rest of the field, Brueggemann hid the political implications of the Pentateuch's Aaronide claims by focusing on rituals and shrines rather than on priestly personnel.

phrase.[20] The political tendencies of the Aaronide hierocracy led by Joshua's dynasty are fairly clear and relatively consistent, as attested by a variety of sources over six centuries. The high priests in Jerusalem maintained accommodationist policies towards imperial overlords (Persia, Alexander, the Ptolemies) resulting in three centuries of largely peaceful relations with them.[21] They oversaw the reconstruction or, at least, the reorganization of the Jewish community in Jerusalem and Judea and its gradual growth in population and wealth. The same period of time witnessed the growth in wealth and political influence of Jewish communities in Babylon and especially in Egypt, where Jewish priest/generals leading Jewish armies sometimes played major roles in Ptolemaic politics. Though the extent of Aaronide influence in Babylon is unknown, priests and Levites made up the bulk of returning exiles from Babylon in the 6th and 5th centuries. Later, Aaronides founded and maintained a Jewish temple in Egypt for almost three centuries. The Samaritans also recovered from the catastrophes of the Assyrian wars and, like the Jews, solidified their religious and ethnic identity at least partly under the religious leadership of Aaronide priests.

One might well ask whether the various governors of Judea and Samaria in the Persian and Ptolemaic periods should get some of the credit for these political and religious accomplishments. It is, of course, the job of governors to accommodate imperial interests, so such policies no doubt reflect their influence. With the sole exception of Nehemiah, however, no governor of these territories gets significant recognition in the surviving rhetoric from the period (except in the Elephantine papyri). By the Ptolemaic period, if not before, the office itself seems to have been dispensed with in Judah as the temple's high priests took over greater political functions, eventually culminating in the hierocracy of the

---

20. Steven Weitzman, *Surviving Sacrilege: Cultural Persistence in Jewish Antiquity* (Cambridge: Harvard University Press, 2005), who presents a series of vignettes into strategies for cultural survival and persistence in order to revalue more positively a history that has often suffered from historians' neglect and disdain. Weitzman's focus on literary evidence leads him to ignore the history of the rise of the Aaronide hierocracy (6th to 2nd centuries B.C.E.) for the very good reason that there are few literary sources for this period. My own less subtle analysis of broad political trends uses other means to make a similar case for reconsidering the values that guide historical depictions of this period.

21. The fact that one 4th-century Judean governor and, perhaps, high priest minted coins with inscriptions in Paleo-Hebrew script led William Schniedewind to see their origin in "a nationalist Jewish movement led by the priests" (*How the Bible Became a Book* [Cambridge: Cambridge University Press, 2004] 174). That is possible, but the coins still bear the title "governor," which hardly suggests outright rejection of the empire. A more likely setting for this development has been suggested by David Carr. He described the increasing valuation of the Hebrew language in the Second Temple period as an act of cultural resistance against Hellenistic influences (*Writing*, 253–62). Hellenism was already making inroads in the area of Judea in the mid-4th century and the date of this coin may show that using the Hebrew language as a strategy of cultural resistance originated before the Hasmonean period.

Hasmoneans. Even Nehemiah's text (together with Ezra's) was relegated to the canonical backwater of the *Ketubim*, while P's celebration of the Aaronide priesthood took pride of place at the center of the Torah. Later Second Temple literature allows one to estimate their literary influence: Nehemiah (person and book) does not appear in 1 Esdras or among the Dead Sea Scrolls; the latter include one fragmentary manuscript of Ezra. Ezra the scribe, however, does not appear in Ben Sira's review of "famous men," while Nehemiah does (49:13). By contrast, the Qumran library contained at least fifteen manuscripts of Leviticus in three different languages (Hebrew, Greek, Aramaic) and countless references and allusions to its contents in other works. Many Second Temple period books include the celebration of the priesthood as a major theme (e.g., Ben Sira, *Jubilees*, *Testament of Levi*, *Aramaic Levi*, etc.).[22] Though the books of Ezra and Nehemiah rightly play a decisive role in modern historical reconstructions of Persian-period Judea, their value as historical sources should not obscure the fact that, as texts, they seem to have had relatively little rhetorical influence in the Second Temple period itself. Most of the rhetoric preserved from the period does not celebrate the roles of governors and other imperial officials.

Aaronide priests led Samaritans and Jews from catastrophe and devastation in the 7th or 6th centuries B.C.E. to become populous, increasingly wealthy and influential temple communities by the late 3rd and 2nd centuries. The Seleucids and Romans would find Jews and Samaritans to be militarily troublesome, which is itself testimony to their power and how far Aaronide leadership had brought these communities in the preceding period. This record of accommodationist policies is in marked contrast to the nationalistic policies of Israel's and Judah's kings, and of the later Hasmonean rulers who took the high priesthood and, eventually, the royal title as well in their pursuit of independence. Though successful in the short term, their policy would fail to preserve Judea's independence and their dynasty in the 1st century B.C.E. In the following century, it led to national catastrophe. Contrary to modern presuppositions about the typical tendencies of theocracies, many powerful Aaronides showed considerable tolerance for foreigners and foreign ways, as exemplified by intermarriage between members of the Samaritan and Jewish priesthoods and by the priests' interest in Hellenistic culture.[23] These policies came under withering criticism from those advocating more exclusive perspectives.

---

22. See James Kugel, "Levi's Elevation to the Priesthood in Second Temple Writings," *HTR* 86 (1993) 1–63.

23. It was not just Jewish and Samaritan priests that consolidated their grasp on their offices and incomes by accommodating imperial overlords politically. A single Egyptian family controlled the high priesthood of Ptah in Memphis throughout the Ptolemaic period—a span of 13 high priests over 10 generations. By its loyal support of the Ptolemaic monarchs, this family capitalized on its strategic position near Alexandria in an ancient capital of Egypt to monopolize this supreme office

Of course, some of the high priests were complicit in more nationalistic ventures as well, and the more exclusive policies of leaders like Ezra and Nehemiah did not preclude their close cooperation with the Persian overlords. So the distinction I am drawing is not hard and fast. It is nevertheless notable that the priests' pursuit of a *modus vivendi* with imperial powers and/or ethnic neighbors earned them sharp criticism from those, like Ezra, Nehemiah, the Maccabees, the Qumran community and the Zealots, who claimed a divine mandate for policies of separation and exclusion. In the long run, however, the priests' pragmatism produced better results for the material and political welfare of Jews and Samaritans than did more confrontational policies, the military successes of the Hasmoneans not withstanding. Though one looks in vain for an explicit defense of such accommodationist policies toward imperial powers in the Pentateuch or other Second Temple literature before Josephus, the Aaronide policies are probably responsible for the prominent preservation in the biblical canon of anti-nationalistic oracles by preexilic prophets like Isaiah, Jeremiah and Ezekiel.[24] They almost certainly account for the absence of royal institutions and rhetoric from the Torah itself.

Obviously, I do not advance these reevaluations of the Aaronide record in hopes of reviving an outdated and discredited model of religious and political leadership. I share the critical perspectives of many modern ideologies on the dangers of theocracy. These critiques become anachronistic hindrances, however, when they subconsciously color historical evaluations of the Second Temple period. The Aaronides' record of promoting "biblical" religious standards and of using relatively tolerant policies to improve the well-being of their communities compares favorably with all of ancient Israel's alternative leadership models and experiences up to the end of the Second Temple period. Histories of the period need to reflect this record in order to produce more balanced interpretations of Aaronide rhetoric and its significance for religious history.[25]

---

and its incomes. See Dorothy J. Thompson, "The High Priests of Memphis under Ptolemaic Rule," in *Pagan Priests: Religion and Power in the Ancient World* (ed. Mary Beard and John North; Ithaca, NY: Cornell University Press, 1990) 95–116.

24. Klawans noted, however, that Second Temple priests maintained a more inclusive cult than the cult advocated by Ezekiel and that this played a role in the relative importance of the latter's texts in this period: "We can safely assume that early Second Temple priests played some role in the canonization—and centralization—of Leviticus and Numbers and the relative ostracizing of Ezekiel 40–48." Contrary to the prevailing assumptions of biblical interpreters, he argued correctly: "Here we find anonymous priests defending what would strike us as just and good—openness and inclusion—against the vision of an exclusivist prophet" (*Purity, Sacrifice, and the Temple*, 74).

25. This paper is an abbreviated and revised version of an argument that appears in my *Ritual and Rhetoric in Leviticus: From Sacrifice to Scripture* (Cambridge: Cambridge University Press, 2007), chap. 7. It is reproduced here by permission of Cambridge University Press.

Index of Authors

Index of Scripture

New Testament

Apocrypha

Index of Other Ancient Sources